Introduction to Retailing

Seventh Edition

Robert F. Lusch
University of Arizona

Patrick M. Dunne
Texas Tech University

James R. Carver
Aubum University

SOUTH-WESTERN
CENGAGE Learning™

Australia • Brazil • Japan • Korea • Mexico • Singapore • Spain • United Kingdom • United States

SOUTH-WESTERN
CENGAGE Learning™

**Introduction to Retailing,
Seventh Edition**
Robert F. Lusch, Patrick M. Dunne,
James R. Carver

Vice President, Editorial Director:
Jack W. Calhoun

Editor-in-Chief: Melissa Acuna

Executive Editor: Mike Roche

Developmental Editor: Elizabeth Lowry

Vice President of Marketing: Bill Hendee

Senior MarComm Manager: Sarah Greber

Marketing Coordinator: Shanna Shelton

Content Project Manager: Kelly Hillerich

Media Editor: John Rich

Print Buyer, Manufacturing:
Miranda Klapper

Production Service: MPS Limited

Sr. Art Director: Stacy Shirley

Cover Designer: LouAnn Thesing

Cover Image: Shutterstock

Photography Manager: John Hill

For product information and technology assistance, contact us at
Cengage Learning Customer & Sales Support, 1-800-354-9706

For permission to use material from this text or product,
submit all requests online at **www.cengage.com/permissions**
Further permissions questions can be emailed to
permissionrequest@cengage.com

Library of Congress Control Number: 2009932374

International Student Edition ISBN-13: 978-0-538-75507-8
International Student Edition ISBN-10: 0-538-75507-5

Cengage Learning International Offices

Asia
cengageasia.com
tel: (65) 6410 1200

Australia/New Zealand
cengage.com.au
tel: (61) 3 9685 4111

Brazil
cengage.com.br
tel: (011) 3665 9900

India
cengage.co.in
tel: (91) 11 30484837/38

Latin America
cengage.com.mx
tel: +52 (55) 1500 6000

UK/Europe/Middle East/Africa
cengage.co.uk
tel: (44) 207 067 2500

Represented in Canada by Nelson Education, Ltd.
nelson.com
tel: (416) 752 9100 / (800) 668 0671

For product information: **www.cengage.com/international**
Visit your local office: **www.cengage.com/global**
Visit our corporate website: **www.cengage.com**

Printed in China by China Translation & Printing Services Limited
1 2 3 4 5 6 7 13 12 11 10 09

To my co-author of 25 years, Patrick Dunne, who has been an exceptional collaborative co-creator of this textbook from the first edition through this seventh edition. Thank you for being a great teacher.

ROBERT F. LUSCH

To my nephew, Brian Dunne, who is carrying on the family tradition of running a retail operation.

PATRICK M. DUNNE

To my younger brother and best friend, John C. Carver, who continues to push me even after his early passing.

JAMES R. CARVER

Foreword

The retail industry has faced many challenges, but one thing is certain: The industry is resilient and will come out on top. Retailers are innovative and dynamic, and the retail landscape is competitive. The many changes in the world of retailing also offer exciting times for retailers and consumers alike.

This seventh edition of *Introduction to Retailing* gives the reader an insight into all aspects of retailing in a well thought out and methodical approach that is sensitive not only to the industry's current environment but also to its future changes. Professors Dunne, Lusch, and Carver have conducted the highest level of research to stay current with the industry. This enables the reader to engage in a well-rounded dialog about the retail industry. To gain the best possible understanding about the industry, this latest edition covers all major disciplines for retailing including human resources, operations, marketing, merchandising, multichannel retailing, finance, supply-chain management, and more. The conversational writing style presented in the book makes even the most critical issues easy to understand.

The National Retail Federation co-brands this seventh edition of *Introduction to Retailing* by Dunne, Lusch, and Carver to encourage people who may be considering careers in retailing and others who may be beginning their journey into understanding retailing.

The National Retail Federation is the world's largest retail trade association. NRF represents an industry with more than 1.6 million U.S. retail establishments, more than 24 million employees—about one in five American workers—and 2008 sales of $4.6 trillion.

It is our hope that your study of the retail industry reveals diverse challenges and opportunities for a fulfilling career that can last a lifetime.

Daniel Butler
VP Merchandising and Retail Operations
National Retail Federation

National Retail Federation®

This edition brings some new blood to *Introduction to Retailing*. James Carver, who joined the author team, has already had a considerable impact on the material presented as the authors continue to seek to offer an *Introduction to Retailing* text that describes the exciting challenges that a career in retailing offered college students. This is especially important given the changes that have occurred in the world's economic environment since the previous edition was published. At the same time, the authors wanted a textbook that students would enjoy reading. Today, as we introduce our seventh edition of the highly accepted text, we believe we have accomplished our goals.

This edition of *Introduction to Retailing*, like retailing itself, has undergone major revisions from prior editions. Fifty-nine of the book's 70 story boxes ("Global Retailing," "Service Retailing," "Retailing: The Inside Story," and "What's New?") and cases are new or updated to better reflect retailing's changing environment. As noted above, a major contributor of the new ideas in this edition is Dr. James Carver of Auburn University. Dr. Carver was a student of Dr. Dunne and Dr. Lusch; as a result, his thoughts and views fit into the popular flow of the book. Therefore, despite these new and exciting additions, we sought to maintain the conversational writing style that past adopters have come to appreciate.

Given the influence of the Internet, the continuing growth of the service industry, and the ever-changing global market, we also felt that there has never been a more exciting time to study and pursue a career in retailing. Thus, we tried to capture this excitement with the story boxes and text content. Each chapter of this edition updates retailing changes now occurring as well as a behind-the-screen story relating to the chapter's topic. We have continued to offer the in-depth coverage of the topics that readers have come to expect. As a result, we believe that students and instructors will like this edition even more than they did the highly successful first six editions.

With retail providing 15 percent of the jobs in today's economy, we have a strong belief that retailing offers one the best career opportunities for today's students. Thus, *Introduction to Retailing* was written to convey that message, not by using boring descriptions of retailers and the various routine tasks they perform, but by making the subject matter come alive by focusing on the excitement that retailing offers its participants in an easy-to-read conversational style filled with pictures and exhibits. This text demonstrates to the student that retailing as a career choice can be fun, exciting, challenging, and rewarding. This excitement arises from selecting a merchandise assortment at market, determining how to present the merchandise in the store, developing a promotional program for the new assortment, and planning next season's sales in an ever-changing economic environment. And the reward comes from doing this better than the competition. While other texts may make retailing a series of independent processes, this edition, like the first six editions of *Introduction to Retailing*, highlights the excitement, richness, and importance of retailing as a career choice. *Introduction to Retailing* provides the student with an understanding of the interrelationship of the various activities that retailers face daily. To do this, we attempted to show how retailers must use both creativity and analytical skills in order solve the problems and pursue the opportunities of today's fast-paced environment.

In keeping with our goal of maintaining student interest, *Introduction to Retailing* focuses on the material that someone entering the retailing field would need to know. We were more interested in telling the student what should happen, and what is happening, than in explaining the academic "whys" of these actions. Thus, when knowledge of a particular theory was needed, we generally ignored the reasoning behind the theory for a simple explanation and an example or two of the use of the theory. In presenting these examples, we drew from a rich array of literature sources, as well as from our combined 80 years of work in retailing.

Students and teachers have responded favorably to the "personality" of *Introduction to Retailing* because the numerous contemporary and relevant examples, both in the text itself and in each chapter's various story boxes, provide realistic insights into retailing. One student wrote to say "thanks" for writing a book that was "so interesting and not too long." A faculty member noted she was "so pleased with the writing style because it was easier to understand, and the examples used were very appropriate and helped to present the material in a meaningful and easy-to-grasp manner for students." Still another liked *Introduction to Retailing* because the writing style was "conversational," thus lending itself to very easy reading, so that she felt confident that her students would read the chapters. "The content coverage was excellent. Terms were explained in easy-to-understand language. And, although most of the topics of an advanced retailing text were presented, the extent and presentation of the material was very appropriate to an introductory course." Another reviewer was especially pleased that we were able to incorporate so many current examples.

Text Organization

Introduction to Retailing, which features an attractive, full-color format throughout the entire text, is divided into five parts that are, in turn, divided into 14 chapters that can easily be covered over the course of the term. Part 1 serves as an introduction to the study of retailing and provides an overview into what is involved in retail planning. Part 2 examines the environmental factors that influence retailing today: the behavior of customers, competitors, channels, as well as our legal and ethical behavior. Part 3 examines the role that location plays in a retailer's success.

Part 4 deals with the operations of a retail store. This section begins with a chapter on managing the retailer's finances. Special attention in this section is given to merchandise buying and handling, pricing, promotion and advertising, personal selling, and store layout and design. The book concludes with Part 5 and managing people—both customers and employees.

Chapter Organization

Each chapter begins with an "Overview" that highlights the key topic areas to be discussed. In addition, a set of "Learning Objectives" provides a description of what the student should learn after reading the chapter. To further aid student learning, the text material is integrated with the learning objectives listed at the beginning of the chapters and the summaries at the end. In addition, the text features a prominent placement of key term definitions in the margin to make it easier for students to check their understanding of these key terms. If they need a fuller explanation of any term, then the discussion is right there—next to the definition.

The body of text has photos, exhibits, tables, and graphs that present the information and relationships in a visually appealing manner. Each chapter has four retailing box features that cover the inside story of a particular retailing event or decision ("Retailing: The Inside Story"); what is happening in the international retail market ("Global Retailing"); the impact of technology, especially the Internet, on retailers ("What's New?"); and retailers who provide services ("Service Retailing") that have addressed the issues presented in that chapter. These boxes are typically lengthier real-world examples than can be incorporated in the regular flow of text material. Some of these box features are humorous, while others present a unique way to solve problems retailers faced in their everyday operations.

Each chapter ends with a student study guide.

The first feature of this section to the text is a chapter "Summary" by learning objectives followed by "Terms to Remember." These are followed by the traditional "Review and Discussion Questions," which are also tied into the learning objectives for the chapter, which are meant to test recall and understanding of the chapter material, and provide students with an opportunity to integrate and apply the text material. Another feature is a "Sample Test Questions" with multiple-choice questions that cover each chapter's learning objectives. The answers to these questions are at the end of the book.

The second half of the study guide is the applications section, which opens with a "Writing and Speaking Exercise" that attempts to aid the instructor in improving the students' oral and written communication skills as well as their teamwork skills. Here the student, or group of students, is asked to make a one-page written report or oral presentation to the class incorporating the knowledge gained by reading the chapters. Some instructors may prefer to view these as "minicases."

A "Retail Project" has the student either visiting a library or a website or finding an answer to a current retail question.

The next feature of each chapter's study guide is a "Case." The cases are located at the end of the text after Chapter 14. Most of these are drawn from actual retail situations. The authors believe that the ability to understand the need for better management in retailing requires an explanation of retailing through the use of case studies. These cases will cover the entire spectrum of retail operations and involve department stores, specialty shops, direct retailing, hardware stores, grocery stores, apparel shops, discount stores, and convenience stores.

Since many of the students taking this class will one day open their own retail businesses, the next section is for them. "Planning Your Own Retail Business" presents a very specific problem, based on the chapter's material, that a small business manager/owner will face in his or her day-to-day operations. Importantly, the student, by working the problems, can witness the financial impact of retail decisions.

Finally, key terms and concepts are presented in boldface type in each chapter, and their definitions are presented in the margins.

Supplementary Material

The Supplementary material includes an overview of the chapter, several detailed teaching tips for presenting the material, a detailed outline, the answers to questions for review and discussion, suggestions for handling the writing and speaking exercises, retail projects, cases, and planning your own business.

■ The test bank contains more than 2,000 questions. These questions are true–false and multiple choice. The test bank is available in Word as well as ExamView—Computerized Testing Software. This software is provided free to instructors who adopt the text.

- PowerPoint slides includes a chapter overview, key terms and definitions, charts, tables, and other visual aids by learning objectives.

- A retail spreadsheet project called *The House* is a spreadsheet analysis of the financial performance of a family clothing store in a small college town. As you read and work with the material in this electronic text, you can answer the problems and, if necessary, print out your answers. The software used is Microsoft Office, which integrates word processing (Word) and spreadsheet analysis (Excel). You will be able to work the problems as they are presented since the spreadsheet worksheets are linked to the electronic text.

- The Instructor's Manual includes an overview, learning objectives, an outline, answers to the end-of-chapter material, and a "Teaching in Action" section.

The book's companion Website at www.cengage.com/international contains a section on choosing a retailing career and 12 to 20 online questions (true–false and multiple-choice) for each chapter.

A DVD supplement offers a professionally written and produced video case package that provides intriguing, relevant, and current real-world insight into the modern marketplace. Each video is supported with application questions located on the website.

ACKNOWLEDGMENTS

Many people contributed to the development of this text over seven editions and 25 years. For their helpful suggestions as reviewers of the various editions of this text, we are especially grateful to the following individuals:

Charles S. Areni
University of Sydney

Phyllis Ashinger
Wayne State University

Chad W. Autry
Oklahoma City University

Steve Barnett
Stetson University

Barbara Bart
Savannah State College

Holly E. Bastow-Stoop
North Dakota State University

Pelin Bicen
Texas Tech University

Jeffrey G. Blodgett
University of Illinois at Springfield

Jerry E. Boles
Western Kentucky University

Elten D. Briggs
University of Texas at Arlington

Doreen Burdalski
Albright College

Melinda Burke
University of Arizona

David Burns
Xavier University

Doze Yolaine Butler
Southern University

Louis D. Canale
Genesee Community College

Jason M. Carpenter
University of South Carolina

John Clark
California State University—Sacramento

Victor Cook
Tulane University

Christy A. Crutsinger
University of North Texas

Ron Daigle
Sam Houston State University

John A. Dawson
University of Stirling

Dennis Degeneffe
University of Minnesota

Roger Dickinson
University of Texas at Arlington

Farrell Doss
Radford University

Janice Driggers
Orlando College

Mary Ann Eastlick
University of Arizona

Joanne Eckstein
Macomb Community College

Jonathan Elimimian
Johnson C. Smith University

Sevo Eroglu
Georgia State University

Kenneth R. Evans
University of Oklahoma

Ann E. Fairhurst
University of Tennessee—Knoxville

John Fernie
Heriot-Watt University

Robert C. Ferrentino
Lansing Community College

Judy Zaccagnini Flynn
Framingham State College

Sandra Forsythe
Auburn University

Sally L. Fortenbery
Texas Christian University

Bill Fuller
Missouri Valley College

D. Elizabeth Goins
University of Illinois at Springfield

Linda K. Good
Michigan State University

Donald H. Granbois
Indiana University

William Green
Sul Ross State University

Blaine S. Greenfield
Bucks County Community College

Sejin Ha
Purdue University

Carol Hall
University of South Carolina

Jared Hansen
University of North Carolina at Charlotte

Norman E. Hansen
Northeastern University

Jack Hartog
Hanze University

Shelley S. Harp
Texas Tech University

Joseph C. Hecht
Montclair State University

Patricia Huddleston
Michigan State University

Charles A. Ingene
University of Mississippi

Narayan Janakiraman
University of Arizona

Marian H. Jernigan
Texas Woman's University

Julie Johnson-Hillery
Northern Illinois University

Laura Jolly
University of Georgia

Mary Joyce
Bryant College

Maria Kalamas
Kennesaw State University

Jikyeong Kang
University of Manchester

William Keep
Quinnipiac College

J. Patrick Kelly
Wayne State University

Karen W. Ketch
University of Kentucky

Jiyoung Kim
The Ohio State University

Tammy Lamb Kinley
University of North Texas

Gail H. Kirby
Santa Clara University

Bruce Klemz
Winona State University

Dee K. Knight
University of North Texas

Jim Kress
Central Oregon Community College

Grace Kunz
Iowa State University

Frederick Langrehr
Valparaiso University

Marilyn Lavin
University of Wisconsin—Whitewater

Marilyn Lebahn
Northwest Technical College

Dong Lee
Fairmont State College

Melody L. Lehew
Kansas State University

Deborah Hawkins Lester
Kennesaw State University

Michael Levin
Texas Tech University

Michael A. Levin
Otterbein College

Michael W. Little
Virginia Commonwealth University

John W. Lloyd
Monroe Community College

Dolly D. Loyd
University of Southern Mississippi

Paul MacKay
East Central College

Shawna L. Mahaffey
Delta College

Louise Majorey
Cazenovia College

Elizabeth L. Mariotz
Philadelphia University

Raymond Marquardt
Arizona State University

Michael McGinnis
University of Southern Alabama

Paul McGurr
Fort Lewis College

Ron McNeil
Iowa State University

Bob Miller
University of Central Michigan

Nancy J. Miller
Iowa State University

Diane Minger
Cedar Valley College

Linda Minikowske
North Dakota State University

Marguerite Moore
University of South Carolina

Michelle A. Morganosky
University of Illinois—Urbana

Mark Mulder
Grand Rapids Junior College

David W. Murphy
Madisonville Community College

Lewis J. Neisner
University of Maryland

Pamela S. Norum
University of Missouri

Elaine M. Notarantonio
Bryant College

Katherine A. Olson
Northern Virginia Community College

Jan P. Owens
Carthage College

Shiretta Ownbey
Oklahoma State University

Charles R. Patton
University of Texas at Brownsville

V. Ann Paulins
Ohio University

John Porter
West Virginia University

Dawn Pysarchik
Michigan State University

Denise Reimer
Iowa Lakes Community College at Emmetsburg

Glenn Richey
University of Alabama

Lynne Ricker
University of Calgary

Jacqueline Robeck
University of Wisconsin—Stout

Robert A. Robicheaux
University of Alabama at Birmingham

Rod Runyan
University of Wisconsin—Stevens Point

Nancy K. Ryan
St. Edwards University

Ben Sackmary
*New York State University—Buffalo
College*

Kare Sandivek
Buskerud University College

Robin Schallie
Fox Valley Technical College

Duane Schecter
Muskegon Community College

Jean Shaneyfelt
Edison Community College

Ian Sinapuelas
San Francisco State University

Donna Smith
Ryerson University

Leigh Sparks
University of Stirling

Cynthia L. J. Spencer
University of Hawaii

Samuel A. Spralls III
University of Central Michigan

Robert Stassen
University of Arkansas

Brenda Sternquist
Michigan State University

Leslie D. Stoel
Ohio State University

Pauline M. Sullivan
Texas State University

Patrick Swarthout
Central Lakes College

Harriet P. Swedlund
South Dakota State University

William R. Swinyard
Brigham Young University

Paul Thistlewaite
Western Illinois University

Jane Boyd Thomas
Winthrop University

Jeff W. Totten
McNeese State University

James A. Veregge
Cerritos Community College

Irena Vida
University of Tennessee

Mary Walker
Xavier University

Mary Margaret Weber
Emporia State University

Scarlett C. Wesley
University of Kentucky

Deborah Whitten
University of Houston

Mike Wittmann
University of North Texas

Allen Young
Bessemer State Tech College

Deborah D. Young
Texas Woman's University

We would be remiss if we failed to thank all those in the retailing industry for their input in the text. We particularly want to thank Sue Busch Nehring, Best Buy; Ellen Spiess, Savers, Inc.; Doral Chenoweth and Marvin J. Rothenberg, both retired consultants; Mike Kehoe, Bain & Company, Inc; Susan Pistilli, International Council of Shopping Centers; Kevin Coupe, morningnewsbeat.com; Jim Duddleston, Schick-Wilkinson; Wally Switzer, 4 R's of Retailing, Inc.; Jim Maurer, Pierce's Northside Market; William R. Davidson and Katherine Clarke, TNS Retail Forward; Jim Lukens, D.W. Green; Terry Lundgren, Macy's; Teddy Tenenbaum, Mr. Handyman of Los Angeles; Mickey Reali, Orville's; Chris Gorley, Starbucks; and Wayne Copeland, Jr., entrepreneur extraordinary. We also want to acknowledge our gratitude for permission to use boxes or cases from Claes Fornell, University of Michigan; Stephen Bell, ShangBy Inc.; Steve Seabury, Pitney Bowes MapInfo; Jay Townley, The Gluskin Townley Group; James Moore, Moore's Bicycle Shop, Inc.; Anne Alenskis, Idaho Power Company; Carol J. Greenhut, Schonfeld & Associates, Inc.; Bill Kirk, Weather Trends International; Marijayne Manley, Leeton School District; Mark Fallon, Jeffrey R. Anderson Real Estate; Simon Hay, dunnhumby; Alison M. Chestovich, breast cancer survivor; Stuart Morris, itravel2000.com; and Jan Owens, Carthage College. In addition, we want to acknowledge the many contributions of Lynne Ricker, University of Calgary. Lynne not only is the author of this text's Canadian edition but also was a source of several "Global Retailing" boxes. Finally, the authors are grateful that Jared Hansen, University of North Carolina at Charlotte, shared his vast experience as a retail buyer in preparing Chapter 9 for this edition.

A very special thanks goes to the below-mentioned for their significant contributions to this seventh edition. These individuals offered timely suggestions to early drafts of many of these chapters. For their insight and encouragement we are especially grateful. Thanks again to David Overton, JCPenney's; Dan Butler, National Retailing Federation; Paul Adams, Paul Adams and Associates, and Katherine R. Clarke, TNS Retail Forward. We also want to thank Paul McGurr for updating *The House*.

To the team at Cengage, we can only say we're glad you let us be a part of the team. These individuals include Mike Roche, Executive Editor and current Project Fixer-Upper; Elizabeth Lowry, who served a second shift as our Development Editor; Kimberly Kanakes, Marketing Manager; Jana Lewis and Kelly Hillerich, our Content Project Managers; and Kelly Franz, the Photo Editor.

Finally, we want to take this opportunity to thank our wives for their love and understanding, especially as seemingly endless deadlines approached. Thanks, Judy and Virginia. (James is still available.)

Patrick M. Dunne	Lubbock, Texas
Robert F. Lusch	Tucson, Arizona
James R. Carver	Auburn, Alabama

Robert F. Lusch

Robert F. Lusch received his PhD in business administration from the University of Wisconsin and his MBA and BS from the University of Arizona. He holds the Jim and Pamela Muzzy Chair in Entrepreneurship at the Eller School of Management, University of Arizona.

His expertise is in the area of retailing, entrepreneurship, marketing strategy, and distribution systems. Professor Lusch has served as the editor of the *Journal of Marketing*. He is the author of more than 150 academic and professional publications, including 18 books. The Academy of Marketing Science awarded him its Distinguished Marketing Educator Award, the American Marketing Association awarded him the IOSIG Lifetime Achievement Award, and the American Marketing Association has twice presented him the Harold Maynard Award.

Professor Lusch has served as President of the Southwestern Marketing Association, Vice President of Education and Vice President Finance of the American Marketing Association, chairperson of the American Marketing Association, and trustee of the American Marketing Association. He has also actively consulted with many retail organizations and was instrumental in the development and guidance of three enterprises that became Inc. 500 firms.

Patrick M. Dunne

Patrick M. Dunne, who recently retired from the Rawls School of Business at Texas Tech University, received his PhD in marketing from Michigan State University and his BS from Xavier University.

In more than 40 years of university teaching, Dr. Dunne has taught a wide variety of marketing and distribution courses at both the undergraduate and graduate levels. His research has been published in many of the leading marketing and retailing journals. In addition, he has authored more than 20 books, many with Dr. Lusch. These books have been printed in seven languages. Dr. Dunne has also been honored with several university teaching awards.

Dr. Dunne has also taught at Michigan State University, Drake University, and the University of Oklahoma. In addition, he served as Vice President of both the Publications and Association Developmental Divisions of the American Marketing Association. Professor Dunne also was an active consultant to a variety of retailers ranging from supermarkets to shopping malls.

James R. Carver

James R. Carver, an Assistant Professor at the Lowder College of Business, Auburn University, received his PhD in marketing from the University of Arizona and his MBA and BBA from Texas Tech University.

Dr. Carver has taught retailing at both Texas Tech and Arizona. Prior to being added as a coauthor for the seventh edition of *Retailing*, he assisted the two lead authors in the fifth and sixth editions. His research interests include retailer pricing policies, supply-chain management, and the role of chief marketing officers within the retail firm.

Brief Contents

Contents

part

1

Perspectives on Retailing

OVERVIEW:

In this chapter, we acquaint you with the nature and scope of retailing. We present retailing as a major economic force in the United States and as a significant area for career opportunities. Finally, we introduce the approach to be used throughout this text as you study and learn about the operation of retail firms.

LEARNING OBJECTIVES:

After reading this chapter, you should be able to:

1. Explain what retailing is and why it is undergoing so much change today.
2. Describe the five methods used to categorize retailers.
3. Understand what is involved in a retail career and be able to list the prerequisites necessary for success in retailing.
4. Explain the different methods for the study and practice of retailing.

LO 1

What Is Retailing, and Why Is It Undergoing So Much Change Today?

What is retailing, and why is it undergoing so much change today?

It is easy to take for granted the impact retailing has on our economy and lifestyle. The full importance of this statement was recently pointed out to one of the authors when his niece, after working in New York City and Atlanta, made a career move to a town of 15,000 in the upper Midwest. While the town had a regular Walmart (not a Supercenter), she was now 41 miles from a Target and Walmart Supercenter and almost three hours from a major department store. While she now spent less time in stores, she was frustrated by the lack of selections. As a result, her overall spending declined. This situation illustrates the impact retailing has on the economic prosperity of any nation as well as the lifestyle of individuals. History has shown that the nations that have benefited from the greatest economic and social progress have been those with a strong retail sector.[1] After all, it is retailing that is responsible for matching the individual demands of the consumer with vast quantities of supplies produced by a huge range of manufacturers and service providers.

Retailing's contribution to a nation's economic growth can be further pointed out by these two examples. First, in 2006, the Nobel Peace Prize was given to Bangladesh economist Muhammad Yunus and the Grameen Bank, a microretail bank which he founded decades earlier. The prize committee recognized the importance of financing the business aspirations of "millions of small people" with loans as little as $20 to help some of the world's most impoverished people start businesses so that they could work to bring about their own development by establishing small retail outlets that helped build the retailing sector of the economy.

The second example can be found by looking at the impact of the world's largest retailer, Walmart, on the U.S. economy. One business writer suggested tongue in cheek that Walmart, which was founded in Arkansas fewer than 50 years ago, deserved the Nobel Peace Prize. Since the award is given to an individual and not an organization and since Sam Walton is deceased, the company will never be considered for such an award. Nonetheless, consider the retailer's many contributions to society, which include the following.[2]

- Walmart provides employment to more than 2 million people. The best defense against poverty is a job.

- The company pays hundreds of millions of dollars each year in dividends that help fund the retirement of millions of people.

- Walmart sells food, clothing, and other necessities at prices that are 15 percent to 25 percent below what other supermarkets charge. This not only helps millions of low-income families stretch their dollars but also provides shopping alternatives for many people in small-town markets.

- The company helps push down the inflation rate and keep interest rates low. This is particularly beneficial for millions of families when making payments on their homes, household appliances, or autos. (In fact, one study concluded that Walmart has raised consumer discretionary income by almost 1 percent per year because of its low prices.[3]) Even Warren Buffett, the famous investor, noted that the retailer has "contributed more to the financial well-being of the American public than any other institution I can think of." His own back-of-the-envelope calculation of this contribution: $10 billion a year.[4]

- Walmart has developed an emergency-relief standard to get supplies to areas devastated by hurricanes, fires, and tornados that has resulted in better coordination between private companies and the Federal Emergency Management Agency.[5]

- Walmart has distributed $415 million in cash and in-kind merchandise annually to 100,000 charitable organizations around the world.

- The company enhances the business of other nearby stores because the retailer increases the area from which to attract customers.

- Walmart has been pursuing environmental sustainability from windmills to recycling to other energy-saving measures.[6]

- Walmart has more organic produce than most of its competitors.

Still, not everyone likes and admires Walmart. For example, in *Fortune* magazine's annual poll of 1,000 chief executive officers (CEOs), Walmart has gone from being the nation's most admired company (in both 2003 and 2004) to fourth in 2005, 12th in 2006, 19th in 2007, and off the top 20 list entirely in 2008.[7] However, most retail analysts attribute this dropoff to growing criticism of this nonunion company by two labor union–funded groups (Walmart Watch and Wake-Up Walmart),[8] the settlement of 63 lawsuits about shortchanging employees on overtime wages,[9] and a slumping stock price since 2000. However, the northwest Arkansas retailer has since returned to its core retail strategies and worked closely with activists to improve its labor, health care, and environmental practices.[10] In fact, during the recent recession, Walmart and McDonald's were the only major retailers to see both their sales and stock prices increase. This increase in popularity with consumers and investors resulted in the company being ranked 11th in 2009.[11]

Another criticism of Walmart is the popular belief that Walmart has a significant negative effect on the mom-and-pop business sector. Academic research, however, has found that such beliefs are statistically unfounded. The research concluded that "after examining a plethora of different measures of small business activity and growth...it can be firmly concluded that [Walmart] has had no significant impact on the overall size and growth of U.S. small business activity."[12] Thus, while Walmart may cause some poorly managed mom-and-pop businesses in outlying towns to fail, those failures actually pave the way for the entry of other new small businesses that increase overall consumer satisfaction and productivity.

What about those countries without an efficient and effective retailing system? History has clearly shown that nations that have failed to develop a productive and customer-focused retailing system will ultimately have to devise one in order to improve their populations' well-being. One reason Eastern European countries experienced such low rates of economic growth when they were under Communist control was their lack of a retail structure. Consumers were forced to shop in stores that offered outdated merchandise and were barely the size of a large room. Interestingly, when American and Western European retailers opened for business in these countries, they became instant successes. The joy and excitement these new forms of retailing provided the citizens was amazing and illustrated the value people of all cultures place on a retailing system that is responsive to their needs and wants. Even Albania, a nation of 3 million and one of Europe's most depressed countries due to its long-standing communist rule, had its first modern mall open in 2009. This 150-store center, which includes a hypermarket, is located between Tirana and Durres. The mall has generated great excitement as consumers, especially young people, can now save time and do all their shopping at one place.[13] Therefore, the rest of this text will be dedicated to showing how a retail system works and how it can always be improved.

retailing
Consists of the final activities and steps needed to place merchandise made elsewhere into the hands of the consumer or to provide services to the consumer.

Retailing, as we use the term in this text, consists of the final activities and steps needed either to place a product in the hands of the consumer or to provide a service to the consumer. In fact, retailing is actually the last step in a supply chain that may stretch from Europe or Asia to your hometown. Therefore, any firm that sells a product or provides a service to the final consumer is performing the retailing function. Regardless of whether the firm sells to the consumer in a store, through the mail, over the telephone, through the Internet, door to door, or through a vending machine, the firm is involved in retailing.

The Nature of Change in Retailing

Many observers of the American business scene believe that retailing is the most "staid and stable" sector of business. While this observation may have been true in the past, quite the contrary is occurring today. Retailing includes every living individual as a customer and accounts for 20 percent of the worldwide labor force, and consumer spending represents nearly a third of America's total economy. As the largest single industry in most nations, retailing, or spending by consumers, is necessary for businesses to "grow and hire again." This was especially evident when the government directed its 2009 stimulus packages toward increasing the consumers' spending power.[14]

Today, retailing is undergoing many exciting changes, only a few of which will be covered in this chapter. However, each chapter of this text has a "What's New?"

Retailing: The Inside Story

Airlines: Being Lucky Is Better than Planning Well

In the mid-1990s, as a way of improving their profits, without increasing their cost structure, air carriers began to sell their tickets over the Internet in order to eliminate the travel agents with their 10-percent to 15-percent commission. The idea worked so well that within a few years nearly half of all available seats on U.S. airlines were sold on the Internet.

However, by posting their prices online, the carriers created a marketplace in which every consumer had easy access to every airline's lowest fares. In addition, the explosive growth of discount airlines in the unregulated industry forced the major carriers to reduce the price on even more seats. The consumer now had all the information (prices, departure and arrival times, available seats, and past performance records) readily available. Over the next decade, airline profits continued to slide, despite the absence of commissions paid to travel agents, as the web surfers' ability to find bargain fares caused average revenue per mile to drop. Even worse, powerful new third-party travel websites—Priceline.com, Expedia.com, Orbitz.com, and Travelocity.com—were soon offering even better deals on flights that further reduced the carriers' profits.

The airlines were a mess. Then fate dealt them a benefit disguised as a bombshell. The price of oil—the biggest expense in operating an airline flight—jumped from less than $50 a barrel in 2007 to nearly $150 in the summer of 2008.

Soon the airlines cut back on their flights and instituted a "fuel surcharge" on checked bags. A few airlines even went so far as to institute a fee on frequent-flyer reward tickets. Since oil was so high, consumers, while not liking them, accepted these "new" fees. Within months, though, oil was back to its 2007 levels or below. However, most of these airline fees remained. Why?

Well, airlines had finally found a way to extract more revenue out of customers than just fares. The 2008 fuel crisis enabled them to finally charge for different services—like using an à lá carte menu at the restaurant. The baggage fees, charges to purchase sandwiches on board, and the charges to use telephone reservationists have significantly improved the profitability of the entire industry. Some airlines even began to charge for those once-free soft drinks and packages of trail mix besides doubling the price of beer and wine. In addition, in 2009, the airlines, always desperate for new sources of revenue, started offering access to the Internet. Here, however, despite the high markup on the service, passengers welcomed the new service as an end to web withdrawal.[15] After all, in Europe Ireland's Ryanair had been using such a pricing system for the prior three years and had seen its profits soar.[16] However, in 2009, it had to beat a hasty retreat after introducing the idea of charging for use of the on-flight restroom.

As a result, every extra service now requires a fee. The concept of charging for what people use or don't use is something that is here to stay in the airline industry. Gone are the days of free hot meals in coach. Now, unless one airline determines it can capture its competitors' customers by dropping one or more of these fees, fliers will pay for everything from pillows to bottled water. After all, if the other airlines match the lone competitor, all the airlines will suffer a drop in profits.

Actually, the reality of oil at $150 per barrel, instead of destroying the industry, gave the airlines the courage to pursue a strategy they wanted to pursue for years—being able to increase revenue without having to make expensive upgrades to the system.

Thus, was it good planning that achieved this or the ever-changing environment that did it? That sudden shock to the U.S. economy in the summer of 2008 actually may have saved the air carriers. In addition, it also paved the way for a new set of websites, such as TripAdvisor.com, whose fee estimator adds baggage charges into fares and shows on-board costs like meals and headsets.[17] Who said you can't make lemonade out of lemons?

box just to discuss in greater detail some of the other changes taking place that will impact the future of retailing. These boxes will address the new practices, skills, and strategies that retailers are using to stay ahead of the competition. Remember that during the recent recession, the number one reason most CEOs were replaced was for mismanaging change, such as failing to anticipate how the credit crisis would impact their business. Sometimes the new approaches implemented by retailers don't work as planned. This is illustrated in this chapter's "Retailing: The Inside

International travelers not only face additional costs of travel as explained in the Inside Retailing story but also the increased level of security and custom inspections add psychic costs and make travel less appealing.

Story" box detailing how, as a result of attempting to improve profits by eliminating the travel agent's commission; airlines saw their revenues decline only to be rescued by a major increase in oil prices.

According to the U.S. Census Bureau, currently there are slightly more than 1.1 million retail establishments selling physical or tangible products in the United States with total annual sales approaching $3.7 trillion, or nearly $12,500 per capita.[18] There are 10 retail establishments for every 1,000 households. This equates to average annual sales of roughly $3.3 million per store.[19] Most retailers, however, are smaller, and many have annual sales of less than $750,000 annually. On the other hand, a single retail store can easily have sales in excess of $50 million annually, which is common for a Walmart Supercenter or a Ford or Toyota new car dealership selling 1,500 new cars annually.

These figures don't reflect the changes that have occurred behind these dollar amounts. The number of new retail enterprises that were developed in the last quarter-century is truly amazing. Most of these new businesses have actually been new institutional forms such as Internet retailing, warehouse retailing, supercenters, and home delivery of fast foods. Change is truly the driving force behind retailing. Let's explore some of the trends that are affecting retailing today.

E-Tailing

Interestingly, embedded in the word *retail* is one of the most important trends in the retail industry, and that is e-tailing (just remove the "r" from retailing and you have e-tailing).

The great unknown for retail managers is what the ultimate role of the Internet will be. Contrary to the fears of many retailers a decade ago, the Internet hasn't destroyed **Bricks-and-Mortar retailers**, or those operating in a physical building. But the Internet, which accounts for less than 5 percent of retail sales, has changed consumer behavior. Today bricks-and-mortar retailers have to adapt to changing customers. These customers, especially the younger ones, are accustomed not only to the speed and convenience of purchasing online but also to the control it gives them. E-tailing, after all, enables consumers to shop when they like and from where they like. In addition, it provides access to vast amounts of information, ranging from a product's attributes to who has the lowest price. No real-world store can match that.

With the growth of the web 2.0, the Internet has become much more interactive and social in nature. This has important implications for retailers. For instance, with some Internet websites, individuals can band together for group buying; the group is able to negotiate with a retailer or manufacturer for a large transaction size represented by dozens or even hundreds of potential customers. Also, many e-tailers offer personalized help online. For instance, K-Swiss allows visitors to its website to chat with a customer service representative seven days a week, 24 hours a day.

bricks-and-mortar retailers
Retailers that operate out of a physical building.

To combat e-tailing, bricks-and-mortar retailers must give their customers more control over the shopping experience, even if it means bringing web-style technology into the store in an attempt to replicate the best things about online shopping but in a more personal way. Retailers should not fight this trend because the customer is already bringing the web into the store. For instance, young shoppers with cell phones send photos of a potential purchase to their friends and then friends text message back, which allows the young shopper to get input on the potential purchase. Consequently, the retailer needs to get on the web technology trend. In-store kiosks, for example, are particularly useful to show the final product before a special, customized order is placed. They allow a shopper to see the finished product before purchasing and provide an online experience in the store. Other retailers have set up their own websites, while others have begun to use nontraditional methods to reach out to the consumer. However, the sad truth is that as consumers flock to social-networking sites and virtual worlds, retailers aren't always there for them. This chapter's "What's New?" box describes the way retailers can use YouTube to reach their target markets.

However, the most important thing for physical store retailers to grasp is the shift in power between retailers and consumers. Traditionally, the retailers' control over pricing information provided them the upper hand in most transactions. Today the information dissemination capabilities of the Internet have made consumers better informed. This has increased their power when transacting and negotiating with retailers. The web has provided consumers with detailed pricing information about products ranging from bikes to office supplies to digital televisions, thus enabling them to negotiate better deals. Some bricks-and-mortar retailers may have to discontinue some product categories as consumers engage in an activity called *outshopping*. Outshopping, which will be discussed in greater detail in Chapters 4 and 7, occurs when the customer gets needed information (such as proper size or how to assemble a product) in the store and then orders it online for a lower price and to avoid paying state sales tax.

Retailers must keep experimenting with various strategies, both in-store and online because the next generation of technology will change the consumers' expectations of what they demand from their retailers. That is why stores like Walmart, Gap Inc., Target Corp., Sears Holdings Corp., and Amazon.com Inc. are pushing new mobile programs. They hope these efforts make it easier for customers to shop online with their cell phones. Even if the prices touted digitally are basically the same as those offered in the store, retailers say customers can get news of sales earlier than with other methods, such as commercials or circulars. After all, failure to keep up with the Internet will spell failure for the retailer.

Price Competition

Some people claim that America's fixation with low prices began after World War II when fair-trade laws, which allowed the manufacturer to set a price that no retailer was allowed to sell below, paved the way for America's first discounter, E. J. Corvett. Actually, this revolution more than likely began with the birth of Walmart in Rogers, Arkansas, in 1962. At the time, there were 41 publicly held discount stores and another two dozen privately owned chains already in business.[20] What Sam Walton did that forever changed the face of retailing was to realize, before everybody else, that most of any product's cost gets added after the item is produced. As a result, Walton began enlisting suppliers to help him reduce these costs and increase the efficiency of the product's movement from production to placement on store shelves. Also, Walton, who had never operated a computer in his life,

What's New?

YouTube: Retailing's Inexpensive Way to Reach Consumers

In the early 1990s, as the Internet emerged it was seldom used by retailers. At best, it was similar to an electronic newspaper or Yellow Pages where retailers could post pop-up advertisements; in short, it was primarily one way retailers pushed information to potential customers. However, with the emergence of the web 2.0, the Internet has become more collaborative. In fact, there is more traffic that involves individual customers talking to and sharing information with each other than the retailer sharing information or having conversations with consumers. Nonetheless, retailers can benefit from this more conversational and interactive web by understanding how their customers are using the Internet to communicate.

Now social networks, ranging from MySpace to Facebook to LinkedIn to YouTube, are what drive Internet usage and traffic. Social-network systems use online technologies and practices enabling consumers to communicate among themselves by sharing content, opinions, insights, experiences, perspectives, and media. In fact, one of the worst things you can do to somebody is to delist him or her as friend on a social network.

However, more importantly with social networking today, the customer is becoming both a producer and a consumer. This is especially true with YouTube, where individuals produce videos or short films and then post them for others to view. Not surprisingly, the videos can be a form of positive praise for the retailer but also negative such as when disgruntled employees or customers decide to tell the world about their experiences. For instance, in April 2009 two Domino's Pizza employees produced and posted a video on YouTube that showed one of them preparing sandwiches after putting the cheese up his nose. This was a clear violation of health standards and disgusting for people to watch. Worse yet, it was a public relations nightmare for Domino's Pizza.

YouTube went online in 2005, and in 2006 was purchased by Google for $1.65 billion. Today YouTube has 100 million video views per day and ranks only behind Yahoo and Google as the most visited site on the Internet.

An average YouTube viewer is 32 years old. In terms of consumer behavior, 40 percent of YouTube viewers regularly advise others about products or services, 29 percent purchase online regularly, and 63 percent occasionally buy online.

Although the customer can be the source of the video this does not prevent the retailer from producing its own videos. In fact, YouTube is becoming an important medium for informing consumers about products and services, influencing consumption, and managing brand image. For example, Blendtec, a blender manufacturer, developed a campaign video series on YouTube. Various household objects such as rake handles and iPods, were run through its blender in the extreme blending series "Will It Blend." Blendtec created a companion microsite, WillItBlend.com, to go with its YouTube videos. Employees were e-mailed and asked to pass on information about the videos and the website. Customers also were involved in this social network system when they received e-mails asking for suggestions of things to blend. Their combination of videos on YouTube and the website and consumer involvement was developed on a limited budget, but the campaign received media attention. Blendtec spokespeople appeared on a *Today Show* segment and iVillage Live, and they were interviewed by *Newsweek*, *Playboy*, and the *New York Times*. Company sales of commercial and at-home blenders increased significantly because of this campaign. Blendtec's marketing focus on something fun and worth watching encouraged consumers to pass on information. YouTube helped Blendtec establish its brand and demonstrate its product. The targeted "Will It Blend?" series helped web revenue increase four times over the previous top month of sales.

YouTube is an excellent way for small and large businesses alike to market their products and attract new customers. Businesses benefit from the inexpensive cost of advertising on YouTube. One expert has recommended eight reasons for a firm to promote its business on YouTube:[21] (1) increase brand awareness, (2) advertise products, (3) create retail promotions, (4) generate direct sales, (5) support products, (6) educate consumers on product use, (7) communicate with employees, and (8) recruit new personnel. This expert further suggests that in order for a video to attract the viewer's eye and have value it must be entertaining, educational, or informational. Best of all, the outcome for many businesses using YouTube for retail marketing is a large return on a small investment.

Source: *This box was prepared by Pauline Sullivan and Katherine Shaw, both from Florida State University.*

made a major commitment to computerizing Walmart as a means to reduce these expenses. As a result of the introduction of the computer to retail management, Walmart's selling, general, and administrative costs as a percentage of sales reached a low of only 16 percent by the early 1990s. Since that time they have risen a bit to around 18 percent to 19 percent, and this has been due to global expansion efforts and a variety of other factors. Importantly, both in the 1990s and today, all of its competitors' operating expenses are 3 percent to 5 percent higher, which continues to put Walmart at a relative competitive advantage. Simply put, Walmart became the world's largest retailer by relentlessly cutting unnecessary costs and demanding that its suppliers do the same. Those who claim that Walmart is obsessed with its bottom line (profits) miss the point: Walmart is obsessed with its top line (sales), which it grows by focusing on the consumer's bottom line. Costco is another retailer that seeks to boost store traffic by getting shoppers to come in for a "super, low price" on key products. Consider gasoline. The chain uses gas as a *loss leader* (selling a product at or below its cost) to generate traffic and increase its inside-of-the-store-sales. The success of this strategy is shown by the fact that during the recent recession, almost a third of the U.S. population used an alternative gasoline retailer, such as warehouse clubs and supercenters, to get gas. This was up 50 percent from three years earlier.[22] In addition, Costco's 29 million member households need a membership card, which costs $50 to $100 a year and goes straight to the firm's bottom line (net profit on an income statement).[23]

Demographic Shifts

Other significant changes in retailing over the past decade have resulted from changing demographic factors such as (1) the fluctuating birthrate, (2) the growing

Najlah Feanny/Corbis

When fuel prices soar quickly as they did in the summer of 2008, many households direct more of their gasoline purchases to Costco or Walmart. Often these large retailers sell gasoline at 7 cents to 10 cents a gallon less than nearby competitors. The price of gasoline is important to all retailers because for every extra dollar spent on gasoline, the consumer has that much less to spend on other merchandise.

importance of the 70 million Generation Y consumers (those born between 1978 and 1994), (3) the move of Generation X into middle age, (4) the beginning movement of the baby boomer generation into retirement, and (5) the increasing number of immigrants. Many people simply failed to realize how these factors, which had profound effects on our society, could also impact retailing. For example, a decade ago how many people realized the advent of the three-generation household, where not only the kids return after college but also the grandparents move in instead of entering an assisted living quarters. Some experts believe that "ParentCare Centers" will soon replace today's KinderCare Centers. In addition, consider how America's recent immigrants have made once-exotic foods like sushi and burritos everyday options. Also, quick meals of all sorts can now be found in supermarkets, convenience stores, even vending machines. Even supermarkets, which were long thought to be the only retailer capable of catering to all markets, must be aware of the effect of these demographic changes on their business.

Successful retailers must become more service oriented, offering better value in price and quality, as well as more convenient store hours; more promotion oriented to include more effective and useful in-store signage; and better attuned to their customers' needs. For example, one of the reasons that Lowe's is threatening Home Depot's dominance in the do-it-yourself market is due to Lowe's awareness of its core customer: the female, who is directly responsible for 80 percent of home-improvement sales.

With population growth slowing, retailers are no longer able to sustain their long-term profit projections simply by building new stores to gain additional sales as they did in the past. Profit growth must come by either increasing same-store sales at the expense of the competition's market share or reducing expenses without reducing services to the point of losing customers. (**Same-store sales** is a retailing term that compares an individual store's sales to its sales for the same month in the previous year. **Market share** refers to a retailer's sales as a percentage of total market sales for the merchandise line or service category under consideration.) As a result, today's retail firms are run by professionals who are able to look at the changing environment and see opportunities, exert enormous buying power over manufacturers, and anticipate future changes before they impact the market rather than just react to these changes after they occur. After all, whereas in the past retailers drove the market, in today's economy and the economy of the future, it will clearly be driven by the consumer. However, not even the best of these professionals can always agree about what the consumer will want in the future.

Store Size

Prior to the recession of 2008, the emphasis for many retailers was to increase store size because of the old axiom that said "The more merchandise customers see, the more they will buy." This idea can best be seen by looking at the country's two largest drugstore chains: Walgreens and CVS. Drug stores, in addition to selling over-the-counter remedies and prescriptions at the back of the store, now have clinics that millions of Americans can use instead of going to emergency rooms for common ailments.[24] In addition, they use the front end of these stores to sell general merchandise. In fact, the majority of their sales come from many different unrelated nondrug items, such as food, apparel, photo supplies, greeting cards, seasonal items such as school supplies, gardening supplies and Christmas decorations. This phenomenon is referred to as **scrambled merchandising**. Scrambled merchandising is the result of the pressure being placed on many retailers to increase profits by carrying additional merchandise or services (with higher profit

---

same-store sales
Compares an individual store's sales to its sales for the same month in the previous year.

market share
Is the retailer's total sales divided by total market sales.

scrambled merchandising
Exists when a retailer handles many different and unrelated items.

margins) that will also increase store traffic. As a result, nearly half of the consumers entering a drugstore are not there to have a prescription filled (low-margin business) but to purchase substantially higher margin items from the front end. Another example of scrambled merchandising is the convenience store that sells low-margin gasoline but makes its money selling higher-margin bread, milk, beer, cigarettes, magazines, lottery tickets, and fast food.

However, the recent economic downturn and the resulting slowdown in consumer purchasing has caused some retailers to reevaluate their strategies. These retailers realized that having supersized stores increased several major costs:

1. rent—which is usually paid on the square feet of space used;

2. inventory costs—if spending is down, retailers may reduce their various selections offered within the product categories; and

3. labor costs—the larger the store, the greater the staffing needs.

Furthermore, retailers have found out that some consumers actually prefer smaller stores, since these stores provide the convenience of being able to get in and out more quickly. Therefore, retailers have recently begun reducing their store size. If they were locked into a lease or owned their building, they expanded their scrambled merchandising policy. For example, drugstores have recently added medical clinics, and supermarkets have added banks and dry cleaners inside their stores. One supermarket in England has even introduced a dental clinic.[25] This scrambling of merchandise also applies to services, such as ATMs, phone cards, and car wash services. Today this practice has gone so far that consumers can now pick up gift cards for home improvement retailers (Home Depot and Lowe's), restaurants (Outback and Olive Garden), and even prepaid debit cards next to the greeting cards in supermarkets, drugstores, and convenience stores.

Probably the best example of scrambled merchandising is the supercenter, which is a combination of the more traditional general merchandise store with a

Spencer Platt/Getty Images News/Getty Images

RediClinic is just one of the numerous low-cost medical clinics found in supermarkets, drugstores, and large retail stores such as Walmart beginning to proliferate throughout the United States.

supermarket and an automotive service center. Earlier in this chapter, it was pointed out that Walmart was the only general merchandise retailer to experience an increase in sales and stock price during the past recession. This was a direct result of the chain's emphasis on supercenters. The customer could save money by only traveling to one location to buy everything from gasoline to food to prescription drugs. In fact, even before the economic slowdown and oil crisis of 2008, Americans made fewer shopping trips per week.[26] It is expected that this trend will continue for the foreseeable future regardless of economic conditions.

Two retail formats that have recently seen not only a significant decrease in average store size but also a decrease in number of stores are department stores and category killers. Department stores are closing their downtown locations, which often were their largest stores, because the downtown areas of many cities have become "ghost towns." Also, what initially made the department stores successful—having a large selection of different merchandise categories under one roof—was superseded by the mall. Sears Holdings, which is a combination of the Sears and Kmart chains, attempted to overcome this demise of the department store with a new format: Sears Grand. Its plan was to compete with the new breed of smaller strip shopping centers, anchored by stores like Best Buy, Home Depot, and Target. Sears stores, after all, were losing prized customers to the smaller centers. But by converting old Kmart stores, which were near the smaller centers, into Sears Grands, the company hoped to lure shoppers back to buy Kenmore washers, Craftsman tools, and Diehard car batteries. The project flopped despite the fact that Sears later renamed the stores Essentials, but not because Kmart shoppers rejected Sears products. It failed because the experiment seemed to consist only of tossing Kenmore stoves and Craftsman hammers into an old Kmart store, rather than creating a vibrant new shopping experience.[27] In addition, several other department store chains have either gone out of business or merged with another chain negating the need for the merged chain to continue to operate two stores at a given location—be it downtown or in the small mall.

category killer

Is a retailer that carries such a large amount of merchandise in a single category at such good prices that it makes it impossible for customers to walk out without purchasing what they need, thus killing the competition.

The term **category killer** derives from its marketing strategy: Carry a large amount of merchandise in a single category at such low prices that it makes it impossible for customers to walk out without purchasing what they need, thus "killing" the competition.

Toys "R" Us, which began operations in 1948 and became publicly traded in 1978, was the first category killer.[28] Sadly, the company also has the unfortunate distinction of being the largest category killer to fail. In 2005, the entire company, in an attempt to avoid bankruptcy, was sold to a group of investors as it and other independent toy retailers suffered from highly competitive toy merchandising efforts of Walmart and Target. These two discounters introduced brutal low prices year-round on a limited selection of toys, but during the all-important holiday shopping season, when busy parents were already in the discount stores they found a triple- or quadruple-sized toy section. The changing tastes of children also contributed to the woes of toy retailers. Today's kids are migrating to electronic and computer games at an earlier age. Today, the future looks a little brighter for Toys "R" Us, which in 2008 after closing almost 100 stores the previous two years, started replacing its older stores with larger superstores combined with Babies "R" Us outlets.[29]

Other well-known category killers include Best Buy, Home Depot, Office Depot, BuyBuy Baby, PetSmart, and Bed Bath & Beyond. In addition, category killers have diverted business away from traditional wholesale supply houses. For example, Home Depot appeals to the professional contractor and Office Depot to the business owner who traditionally purchased supplies from hardware wholesalers and office-supply and office-equipment wholesalers. However, in recent years, several other "killers"—Circuit City, FAO Schwarz, and CompUSA—have fallen on bad times.

Many new students to retailing believe that what happens in the United States occurs around the world. This isn't the case. One former student, who sold grocery products in both the United Kingdom and Latin America, described the differences between these markets. In the United Kingdom, one of his customers (Boots Chemist) accounted for 60 percent of his business. Contrast that with Latin America (excluding Chile), which has a highly fragmented trade structure. In these countries, more than three-quarters of the consumers buy their wares from mom-and-pop stores, some no bigger than a closet. These outlets are crammed with food and other household items and serve as the pantries of the world's poorest consumers for whom both money and space are tight. In Latin America, instead of having one major account, he distributed the same product to more than 6,000 stores. His largest customer was chain with 70 stores, and the next largest had only 25 stores.

Many analysts initially believed that when Walmart and the United Kingdom's Tesco, which has 4,000 stores across 14 countries, entered these developing markets, the mom-and-pop shops would disappear. Actually, the opposite happened. As these countries' economies grew, more tiny shops opened to serve the market. The ex-student also noted that

> besides the economic differences, there is a vast social/cultural difference between the Latin American and North American markets. Latin American cities are much more like Europe (or New York/San Francisco) than Dallas or Houston. Families have one car (or no car), so they typically walk to purchase their things. After all, who wants to walk home carrying four or five bags of groceries, even if you could afford it? Thus, even though Mexico is one of [Walmart's] most successful markets, high-frequency stores are still regularly visited by two-thirds of the population.[30]

This chapter's "Global Retailing" box illustrates that the opportunities for success in retailing are available both in the United States and globally for those who create exciting and engaging shopping experiences coupled with more customized offerings.

Success in retailing depends on a retail manager's ability to properly interpret what societal changes are occurring and what these changes mean to the store's customers, and then build a strategy to respond to these changes. Therein lies the excitement and challenge of retailing as a career. After all, 50 years ago, the Walmart strategy of building a major enterprise in small town America and offering "everyday low prices" was probably considered foolhardy. This was at a time when retailers thought growth could be achieved only by competing in the big cities where large population bases were located. Yet someone who purchased 100 shares of Walmart when it went public on October 1, 1970, for $16.50 a share and reinvested the dividends would, by 2010, be holding more than 200,000 shares worth more than $9 million. This is the reason that the Walton family members are always near the top of Forbes's list of the richest people in the world—Sam Walton had invested virtually everything he had in his firm and refused for many years to allow the company to pay dividends but felt the Walton family and shareholders were better off by reinvesting earnings in the firm. Unlike other entrepreneurs who achieved wealth and "cashed out," he did not sell any of his stock. He felt this would send the wrong message to Walmart associates and also the investment community. Anyone else

Global Retailing

It Is Not All about Mass Merchandising

A variety of social commentators proclaim that retailing around the globe is being taken over by large mass merchandisers such as Walmart, Carrefour, and Aldi. However, a careful study around the world clearly demonstrates that there is a revival of uniqueness and novelty and in many cases centered on creating unique and not mass-produced merchandising and shopping experiences. Consider for example, the Museum of Contemporary Art in Los Angeles, which recently created a merchandising event especially for Japanese artist Takashi Murakami by offering Louis Vuitton handbags as well as other luxury merchandise. The Louis Vuitton handbags featured designs by Murakami. Shoe companies are moving toward more mass customization, and this not only includes Nike but also Steve Madden, who offers customized heels designed by customers. Schedoni, an Italian leather crafter, has teamed up with PUMA to produce a line of customer footwear.

Another trend is also occurring in the renovation of shopping malls to transform them into more exciting experience platforms. Consider Tokyo Midtown, which is part of a multiuse development that has been upgraded to appeal to upscale shoppers. Even more extreme is when a shopping center can be built from the ground up. For instance, VivoCity in Singapore not only has 300 retailers under one roof but also an outdoor amphitheatre, a 300-meter harbor front promenade, and a 20,000-square-foot open plaza. Shopping in VivoCity one finds constant surprise and nonstandardized offerings. For instance, Eu Yan Sang is a major health-care brand in Asia, and it has created a Chinese medicine clinic that includes a yoga studio, spa, and health food café. In the store, it sells traditional Chinese medicine products to complement the services offered by the Chinese medicine clinic.

In São Paulo, Brazil, where Carrefour entered the retail market more than 30 years ago and Walmart in the last decade, there still remains creative merchants who cater to niche markets and provide highly differentiated offerings. For instance, an independently owned and operated nonchain bookstore in São Paulo has an in-house movie theater (which

This wine shop in a grocery store in Sao Paolo, Brazil, carries wines that sell for up to the equivalent of $3,000 U.S. dollars.

Global Retailing (*continued*)

helps to build store traffic) and a large children's section in which a dragon more than 30 feet tall (as shown in the photograph) captures the attention and builds the imagination of children. Another local merchant in São Paulo is a family owned grocery store that has been operating for more than 75 years and is able to position itself to avoid direct mass market and merchandising competition with Carrefour and Walmart by serving a local niche market of high-income households. From the accompanying photo you can guess that having a wine selection with prices as high as $6,600 real

(about $3,000 U.S.) means that their target market are the wealthy and well-to-do citizens of São Paulo.

Undoubtedly, Walmart and Carrefour will continue to build hypermarkets or superstores with nearly 100,000 stockkeeping units (SKUs) in more than 140,000 square feet of space. Nonetheless, as these mass merchandisers continue their global expansion and as markets become more overstored, the global trend and opportunity is to create exciting and engaging shopping experiences coupled with more customized offerings.

This bookstore in Sao Paulo with dragon aims to capture the imagination of children.

who invested a similar amount of money in Walmart stock in 1970 and continued to hold the stock would be equally wealthy today.

Of course, the future can never be predicted with certainty. This text attempts to provide you with the tools to meet these upcoming challenges and be a success in retailing. The answer to what the future will bring lies in the disquieting fact that retailers do not operate in a static, closed environment; they operate in a continuously changing and competitive one. These changes are discussed in greater detail in Chapters 3 through 6. For now, we will concentrate on the following environmental elements: the behavior of consumers, the behavior of competition, and the behavior of supply-chain members (the manufacturers and wholesalers that the

Exhibit 1.1
External Environmental
Forces Confronting Retail
Firms

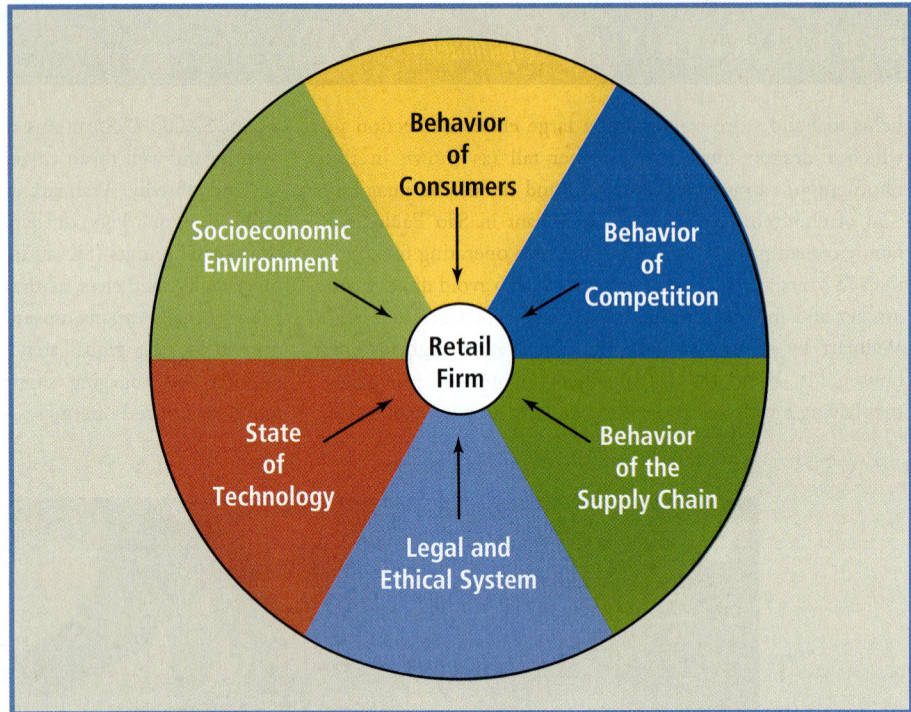

retailer buys from), the legal system, the state of technology, and the socioeconomic nature of society. Exhibit 1.1 depicts these elements.

A final comment about the changing face of retailing: Remember, business entrepreneurs are not obliged to conform to old norms and social standards. They are free to forge new retail approaches that capitalize on emerging market opportunities. In retailing, this is all the more evident when we consider fashion trends; what in the past would have lasted for years now may last only a few months.

LO 2   Categorizing Retailers

Describe the five
methods used to
categorize retailers.

Categorizing retailers can help the reader understand competition and the changes that occur in retailing. There is no single acceptable method of classifying retail competitors, although many classification schemes have been proposed. The five most popular schemes used today are described in Exhibit 1.2.

Exhibit 1.2
The Five Methods Used to
Categorize Retailers

Census Bureau	Number of Outlets	Margin/Turnover	Location	Size
3-digit NAICS code	Single unit	Low margin/low turns	Traditional	By sales volume
4-digit NAICS code	2–10 units	Low margin/high turns	Central shopping districts	
5-digit NAICS code	11+ units	High margin/low turns	Shopping centers	By number of employees
		High margin/high turns	Free-standing nontraditional	

Census Bureau

The U.S. Bureau of the Census, for purposes of conducting the Census of Retail Trade, classifies all retailers using three-digit North American Industry Classification System (NAICS) codes. The website for locating these codes is www.census.gov/epcd. Some examples of these NAICS codes are shown in Exhibit 1.3.

As a rule, these three-digit NAICS codes are too broad to be of much use to the retail analyst. Four-digit NAICS codes provide much more information on the structure of retail competition and are easier to work with. For example, NAICS 454 is nonstore retailing, which consists of approximately 50,000 retailers. Within this are NAICS 4541, which consists of 16,000 electronic shopping and mail-order houses, L.L. Bean (www.LLBean.com) and Harry and David (www.harryanddavid.com), for example; NAICS 4543, consisting of 28,000 direct-selling establishments, and so on.[31]

In almost all instances, the NAICS code reflects the type of merchandise the retailer sells. The major portion of a retailer's competition comes from other retailers in its NAICS category. General merchandise stores (NAICS 452) are the exception to this rule. General merchandise stores, due to the variety of general merchandise carried, compete with retailers in most other NAICS categories. For example, department stores compete for clothing sales with specialty apparel stores, such as Gap and The Limited; mail-order retailers, such as L.L. Bean; or off-priced stores, such as T.J. Maxx or Ross Dress for Less. In fact, most retailers must compete to a considerable extent with general merchandise stores because these larger stores usually handle many of the same types of merchandise that smaller,

Exhibit 1.3
Using NAICS Codes

Code	Type of Business	Number of Establishments (thousands)	Percent of Total	Sales (billions)	Percent of Total	Number of Employees (thousands)	Percent of Total
44-45	Retail Trade	1,123	100%	3,688	100%	15,339	100%
441	Motor Vehicle & Parts Dealers	129	11%	886	24%	1,948	13%
442	Furniture & Home Furnishings Stores	66	6%	112	3%	576	4%
443	Electronics & Appliance Stores	50	4%	102	3%	469	3%
444	Building Material & Garden Equipment and Supplies Dealers	87	8%	327	9%	1,263	8%
445	Food & Beverage Stores	153	14%	515	14%	2,938	19%
446	Health & Personal Care Stores	85	8%	209	6%	1,037	7%
447	Gasoline Stations	117	10%	374	10%	909	6%
448	Clothing & Clothing Accessories Stores	151	13%	202	5%	1,556	10%
451	Sporting Goods, Hobby, Book, & Music Stores	61	5%	82	2%	631	4%
452	General Merchandise Retailers	46	4%	525	14%	2,671	17%
453	Miscellaneous Store Retailers	128	11%	108	3%	820	5%
454	Nonstore Retailers	50	4%	247	7%	521	3%

more limited retailers sell. In a very broad sense, all retailers compete with each other since they all compete for the same limited consumer dollars.

A second cautionary note about using this Census Bureau data is that comparisons between years may not be accurate. In a note on its website, the Census Bureau cautions that sales made to a customer in a foreign country through a U.S. website are included in the bureau's estimates. Thus, when the dollar is strong, many foreign customers may purchase from an American e-tailer and vice versa when the dollar is weak, Americans may purchase on overseas websites. For example, Blue Nile, the Seattle-based online jewelry retailer, recently reported a sales increase of 3.8 percent over the previous year. However, the company said that all of that gain came from Internet sales to customers outside the United States due to a weak dollar. Thus, while the sales increase was good for the company, it actually doesn't indicate strength in overall U.S. retail spending.[32]

Another shortcoming of using the NAICS codes is that they do not reflect all retail activity. The Census Bureau's definition equates retailing only with the sale of "tangible" goods or merchandise. However, by our definition, selling of services to the final consumer is also retailing. This suggests that retailing is also conducted by businesses such as barber and beauty shops, health clubs, dry cleaners, banks, insurance agencies, funeral homes, movie theaters, amusement parks, maid services, medical and dental clinics, one-hour photo labs, and so on. For instance, NAICS 772, which is not classified under retail trade, consists of almost 490,000 eating and drinking establishments. Remember, any time the consumer spends money, whether on tangibles (merchandise) or intangibles (services), retailing has occurred.

Number of Outlets

Another method of classifying retailers is by the number of outlets each firm operates. Generally, retailers with several units are a stronger competitive threat because they can spread many fixed costs, such as advertising and top management salaries, over a larger number of stores and can achieve economies in purchasing. However, single-unit retailers, such as your neighborhood IGA grocery store, do have several advantages. They are generally owner- and family-operated and tend to have harder-working, more motivated employees. Also, they can focus all their efforts on one trade area and tailor their merchandise to that area while gaining buying efficiencies by being a member of the IGA group. In the past such stores were usually able to spot emerging customer desires sooner and respond to them faster than the larger multiunit operations.

Any retail organization that operates more than one unit is technically a chain, but this is really not a very practical definition. Therefore this text will only consider a retail operation to be a chain if it has 10 or more stores. Various trade associations estimate that chain stores account for 43 percent of all retail sales (including 99 percent of all department store sales and 66 percent of all grocery store sales). Though chain operations account for 60 percent of nondurable goods sales, they account for only about 23 percent of durable goods sales. After all, most auto dealerships and furniture stores are still independent or have fewer than 10 units.[33]

Not all chain operations enjoy the same advantages. Small chains are local and may enjoy some economies in buying and in having the merchandise tailored to their market needs. Large chains are generally regional or national and can take full advantage of the economies of scale that centralized buying, accounting, training, advertising, and information systems, and a **standard stock list** can achieve. A standard stock list requires that all stores in a retail chain stock the same

standard stock list
Is a merchandising method in which all stores in a retail chain stock the same merchandise.

merchandise. Other national chains such as Walmart, recognizing the variations of regional tastes, use the **optional stock list approach**, which gives each store the flexibility to adjust its merchandise mix to local tastes and demands. This point is driven home by the name of a retail consulting firm composed of former Walmart employees—4 R's of Retailing, Inc. (right merchandise, right quantity, right place, and right time.) After all, as one JCPenney executive told the authors, stores in the Rio Grande Valley of Texas sell primarily smalls and mediums in men's shirts, while in Minnesota the chain sells a preponderance of larger sizes.

Both types of stock lists provide scale advantages in other retailing activities. For example, promotional savings occur when more than one store operates in an area and can share advertising, even while tailoring specific merchandise to specific stores.

Finally, chain stores have long been aware of the benefits of taking a leadership role in the marketing supply chain. When a chain store retailer is able to achieve critical mass in purchases, it can get other supply-chain members—wholesalers, brokers, and manufacturers—to engage in activities they might not otherwise engage in, and it is then referred to as the **channel advisor** or **channel captain**. For example, the chain store retailer might get other supply-chain members to include direct-to-store deliveries, increased promotional allowances, extended payment terms, or special package sizes, all of which help the retailer operate more efficiently.

In recent years, chains (as will be discussed in greater detail in Chapter 4) have relied on their high level of consumer recognition to engage in **private-label branding**. Private-label branding may be *store branding*, when a retailer develops its own brand name and contracts with a manufacturer to produce the product with the retailer's brand, or *designer lines*, where a known designer develops a line exclusively for the retailer. Thus, instead of competing with another retailer selling the same brand, here the retailer is the only one selling the product. Today, the whole concept of private labels has taken on a new dimension as retailers have nationally promoted these items. These private labels are advertised in the newspaper as brands and are heavily promoted in stores.

In the past, private labels were inexpensive knockoffs of popular items. Today, though, some of the best retailers have significantly increased the quality and style of their private merchandise to promote it front and center. Retailers target these private labels, which have their own distinct personality, to specific markets and advertise them in their own promotional pieces. Consider, for example, the American Living brand, JCPenney's comprehensive lifestyle brand created by a division of Polo Ralph Lauren. It includes a full range of apparel for women, men, and children, along with footwear, accessories, home furnishings, and textiles offering an updated classic style with impeccable quality at a smart price. Just as many consumers believe Arizona Jeans to be a national brand, Penney's hopes to do the same with its American Living brand. In addition, Walmart recently expanded its private-label line of food and household cleaners to take advantage of recession-pinched consumers' increasing desire to buy cheaper store brands rather than more expensive brand-name products.[34]

Another reason why private labels are so popular with retailers is that by designing and manufacturing their own labels, retailers can cut out the designer and the middleman. Doing so can translate into profit margins that can be at least 20 percent better than a manufacturer's name-brand label. Some chains, such as Save-A-Lot, a unit of Supervalu, have dropped national brands like Fritos, Dr. Pepper, Pampers, and Coca-Cola and replaced them with their own brands: Corntitos, Dr. Pop, Waddles, and Bubba Cola. Small retailers, because of their lack of economies of scale, can't use private labels unless they are part of a buying group.

optional stock list
Is a merchandising method in which each store in a retail chain is given the flexibility to adjust its merchandise mix to local tastes and demands.

channel advisor or channel captain
Is the institution (manufacturer, wholesaler, broker, or retailer) in the marketing channel that is able to plan for and get other channel institutions to engage in activities they might not otherwise engage in. Large store retailers are often able to perform the role of channel captain.

private label branding
May be store branding, when a retailer develops its own brand name and contracts with a manufacturer to produce the product with the retailer's brand, or designer lines, where a known designer develops a line exclusively for the retailer.

Courtesy of JC Penney

JC Penney "American Living" private label logo. In addition to American Living, Penney's has introduced the following exclusive designer lines: I Heart Ronson, Nicole by Nicole Miller, Allen B, Bisou Bisou, and Le Tigre in recent years.

gross-margin percentage
A measure of profitability derived by dividing gross margin by net sales.

gross margin
Is the difference between net sales and cost of goods sold.

operating expenses
Are those expenses that a retailer incurs in running the business other than the cost of the merchandise.

inventory turnover
Refers to the number of times per year, on average, that a retailer sells its inventory.

high-performance retailers
Are those retailers that produce financial results substantially superior to the industry average.

low-margin/low-turnover retailer
Is one that operates on a low gross margin percentage and a low rate of inventory turnover.

The major shortcoming of using the number-of-outlets scheme for classifying retailers is that it addresses only traditional bricks-and-mortar retailers. This scheme thus ignores many nontraditional retailers such as catalog-only sellers and e-tailers. How many outlets does Amazon.com have? One could argue that each new online computer is a potential retail outlet for the e-tailing giant.

Margins versus Turnover

Retailers can also be classified in regard to their gross-margin percent and rate of inventory turnover. The **gross-margin percentage** shows how much **gross margin** (net sales minus the cost of goods sold) the retailer makes as a percentage of sales; this is also referred to as the *gross-margin return on sales*. A 40-percent gross margin indicates that on each dollar of sales the retailer generates 40 cents in gross-margin dollars. This gross margin will be used to pay the retailer's **operating expenses** (the expenses the retailer incurs in running the business other than the cost of the merchandise—e.g., rent, wages, utilities, depreciation, insurance). **Inventory turnover** refers to the number of times per year, on average, that a retailer sells its inventory. Thus, an inventory turnover of 12 times indicates that, on average, the retailer turns over or sells its average inventory once a month. Likewise, an average inventory of $40,000 (retail) and annual sales of $240,000 means the retailer has turned over its inventory six times in one year ($240,000 divided by $40,000), or every two months.

High-performance retailers, those that produce financial results substantially superior to the industry average, have long recognized the relationship between gross-margin percent, inventory turnover, and profit. One can classify retailers into four basic types by using the concepts of margin and turnover: (1) low margin, low turnover; (2) high margin, low turnover; (3) low margin, high turnover; and (4) high margin, and high turnover.

Typically, the **low-margin, low-turnover retailer** will not be able to generate sufficient profits to remain competitive and survive. Thus, there are no good

The Kindle is an electronic book reader which allows customers to download an entire book. Consequently it reduces the inventory of books for Amazon.com and thus increases inventory turnover. Some "experts" predict that within a decade all textbooks will come this way.

examples of successful retailers using this approach. **High-margin, low-turnover retailers** (bricks and mortar) are quite common in the United States. Furniture stores, high-end women's specialty stores and furriers, jewelry stores, gift shops, funeral homes, and most of the mom-and-pop stores located in small towns across the country are generally good examples of high-margin, low-turnover operations. Some **clicks-and-mortar retailers** sell both online and in physical stores; examples include Coach and Tiffany's.

On the other hand, the **low-margin, high-turnover retailer** only really developed after World War II with the advent of the discount store. Sam Walton ran a Ben Franklin five-and-dime store and was among the first to see that selling one item a week for 99 cents with a 50-cent margin wasn't as good as selling six of those items a week at 69 cents and making 20 cents on each. Bernie Marcus and Arthur Blank revolutionized the hardware business by starting Home Depot with its low-margin, high-turnover strategy and replacing smaller hardware stores using a high–low approach. Amazon.com is probably the best-known example of a low-margin, high-turnover e-tailer.

Finally, some retailers find it possible to operate as **high-margin, high-turnover retailers**. As you might expect, this strategy can be very profitable. Probably the most popular examples are convenience food stores such as 7-Eleven, Circle K, and Quick Mart; and the concessions and sports apparel businesses at major athletic events. However, because in the early stages of Internet commerce most e-tailers are trying to achieve a high turnover rate, there are no examples of e-tailers using this strategy.

As noted above, the low-margin, low-turnover retailer is the least able of the four to withstand a competitive attack because this retailer is usually unprofitable or barely profitable; when competition increases, profits are driven even lower. On the

high-margin/low-turnover retailer
Is one that operates on a high gross margin percentage and a low rate of inventory turnover.

clicks-and-mortar retailers
Retailers that sell both online and in physical stores.

low-margin/high-turnover retailer
Is one that operates on a low gross margin percentage and a high rate of inventory turnover.

high-margin/high-turnover retailer
Is one that operates on a high gross margin percentage and a high rate of inventory turnover.

other hand, the high-margin, high-turnover retailer is in an excellent position to withstand and counter competitive threats because profit margins enable it to finance competitive price wars.

While the margin and turnover scheme provides an encompassing classification, it fails to capture the complete array of retailers operating in today's marketplace. For example, service retailers and even some e-tailers such as Priceline.com carry no inventory. Thus, while this scheme provides a good way of analyzing retail competition, it neglects an important type of retailing: service retailers. Keep in mind, however, that with a bit of imagination the concept may still apply. Often in a service-retailing business such as a restaurant or barber or beauty shop what the retailer needs to turn is not inventory but people. If you have worked in a restaurant then you probably know the concept called "turning the tables," which is the practice of getting customers in and serving them quickly and efficiently and getting them out so the table can be used to serve other guests. In a fine-dining establishment, a dinner can take three hours and thus the turnover of tables or customers is low but the gross margin on the food and beverages is quite high. On the other hand, with a cafeteria the visitors go through the serving line and are seated and depart in 30 minutes. Margins are lower but turnover of tables or customers is higher. Think of how this concept could apply to a beauty shop.

Location

Retailers have long been classified according to their location within a metropolitan area, be it the central business district, a regional shopping center, or a neighborhood shopping center or as a freestanding unit. These traditional locations will be discussed in greater detail in Chapter 7. However, the last decade saw a major change in the locations that retailers selected. Retailers are now aware that opportunities to improve financial performance can result not only from improving the sales per square foot of traditional sites but also from operating in new and nontraditional retail areas.

In the past, rather than expand into untested territories, many retailers simply renovated their existing stores. Not today. Now retailers are reaching out for alternative retail sites. American retailers today are testing all types of nontraditional locations to expand their businesses. For example, to get more people to eat pizza when they rent videotapes, Pizza Hut introduced kiosks in video rental stores with direct phone lines to the local Pizza Hut. McDonald's has locations in service stations along interstate highways, airports and even in some Walmart stores. Loblaw, a Canadian grocer, has a women's health club in its store near Toronto, E*Trade, the online brokerage firm, is expanding its non-Internet presence with financial service centers in Target stores. Even the bricks-and-mortar banks now realize that their locations are now less of a vehicle for transactions and much more a vehicle for selling financial products: mutual funds, mortgages, trusts, and investment services. As a result, they are putting in pharmacies, little post offices, and even Starbucks in their buildings as a means of increasing traffic.[35]

Also, given the high income levels of many airline travelers and the increasing amount of layover time between flights and the absence of food on many flights, many retailers have opened stores in airports, an idea that originated with and has long been used by European and Asian retailers. Airport retailers have been able to succeed by offering fast service, convenience, pleasant and clean environments, product variety and quality, entertainment, and competitive prices. For example, one of New York City's toniest retail venues today—where shoppers can browse in

EMILE WAMSTEKER/Bloomberg News/Landov Media

Walmart operates large discount stores around the world, however, most locations they select require the availability of large parking lots because most customers transport their purchases back home in their automobiles.

boutiques featuring merchandise from DKNY, adventure sports outfitter ExOfficio, Japanese housewares retailer Muji, Ron Jon Surf Shop, H. Stern Jewelers, and Danish designer Sand—isn't on Fifth or Madison avenues. It's The Shops at John F. Kennedy International Airport. In addition, a wide selection of food and a spa and pharmacy with an on-site nurse are available there, too. Travelers can also find Brooks Brothers in Pittsburgh's airport and Coach and Body Shop in San Francisco's. So popular have these stores become with passengers that retail rents now account for more than 50 percent of airport revenues.[36] Probably the most significant of the new nontraditional shopping locations today is the combination of culture with entertainment and shopping, something that was unheard of a decade ago. Today such locations, such as Bass Pro hunting and fishing superstores, have proven that the edges are blurring between shopping and entertainment for the masses.

Retailers do not want to miss out on urban or inner-city neighborhoods, which frequently have large minority populations. By 2015, it is projected that the spending power of Latinos and African Americans will reach $1.4 trillion and $1.1 trillion, respectively. Dollar Tree, Dollar General, Jewel-Osco, and Pathmark are leaders in opening stores in urban locations.

Before ending our discussion of location, it is important to point out that this is an area of retailing that may undergo significant changes in the next decade. The Internet suggests that future locations may be as close as a consumer's computer or BlackBerry. Some retailers today are now able to operate out of an office in the home or car equipped with an iPod.

Size

Many retail trade associations classify retailers by sales volume or number of employees. The reason for classifying by size is that the operating performance of retailers tends to vary according to size; that is, larger firms generally have lower operating costs per sales dollar than smaller firms do. For example, based on the recently available information from various trade associations, the authors concluded that operating expenses were 39 percent for firms with sales between $5 million and $45 million and 35 percent for larger operations. These retail trade associations provide confidential information to their members showing similar breakdowns on gross margins, net profits, net markups, sales per square foot of selling space, and so forth. Retailers will find this information meaningful when comparing their results against others of a similar size within their product category.

While size has been useful in the past, it is unclear whether the changes brought about by technology will make this classification obsolete. For example, imagine a fully automated retailer where, as a consumer places an order online, an automated stock-picking warehouse packages the selected merchandise and forwards it to the shipping area to be sent by UPS to the customer. Is Blockbuster comparable to Netflix or Target to Overstock.com in terms of the number of employees needed?

LO 3 A Retailing Career

What is involved in a retailing career?

Retail is the largest industry in the nation. That means there are many different kinds of retail entities that fuel our nation's economy. Someone once said that "managing a retail store is an easy job. All you have to do is get consumers to visit your store (traffic) and then get these consumers to buy something (convert the traffic into customers) while operating at a lower cost than your competition (financial management)." Assuming that this simplistic statement is correct and forgetting what is involved in each of these tasks, what type of person is needed to manage a retail store?

an economist	Yes _____	No _____
a fashion expert	Yes _____	No _____
a marketer	Yes _____	No _____
a financial analyst	Yes _____	No _____
a personnel manager	Yes _____	No _____
a logistics manager	Yes _____	No _____
an information systems analyst	Yes _____	No _____
an accountant	Yes _____	No _____

In reality, the answer is "yes" to all of these roles. A retail store manager needs to be knowledgeable in all these areas. As we have pointed out, few industries offer a more fast-paced, ever-changing environment where results are quickly seen on the bottom line than retailing. Few job opportunities will train you to become an expert not in just one field but in all business disciplines. Retailing offers you the economist's job of forecasting future sales, the fashion expert's job of predicting consumer behavior and how it will affect future fashion trends, and the marketing manager's job of determining how to promote, price, and display your merchandise. Further, it offers the financial analyst's job of seeking ways to reduce various expenses; the personnel manager's job of hiring the right people, training them to perform their duties in an efficient manner, and developing their work schedules; the logistics manager's job of arranging delivery of a "hot item"; the information systems analyst's job of analyzing sales and other data to determine opportunities for improved management practices; and the accountant's job of arriving at a profitable bottom line.

In summary, a retailer is like a master chef. Anyone can buy the ingredients, but only a master chef can make a masterpiece. Over the course of a career, you will have to deal with many issues. Among them are:

1. what product(s) or service(s) to offer,
2. what group of customers to target,
3. where to locate the store,
4. how to train and motivate your employees,
5. what price level to use,
6. what levels of customer service (store hours, credit, staffing, parking, etc.) to offer your customers,
7. how to lay out the store,
8. how to control store operating expenses and police employees and customers to cut down on shoplifting and employee theft of merchandise, and
9. how to leverage the Internet to support your mission.

Exhibit 1.4 illustrates the career paths available to the college graduate at a typical retailer. Note that there are two major paths: store management and buyer. (For a more detailed discussion of the various careers available today in retailing, including jobs in accounting, finance, advertising, information technology, logistics, and store design, see the excellent discussion of retailing careers at www. macyscollege.com/college/careers/careerpaths. In addition, CareerBuliders.com provides information on all aspects of the job search. This site offers tips on resume writing, distributing the resume, interviewing, and even career assessment.)

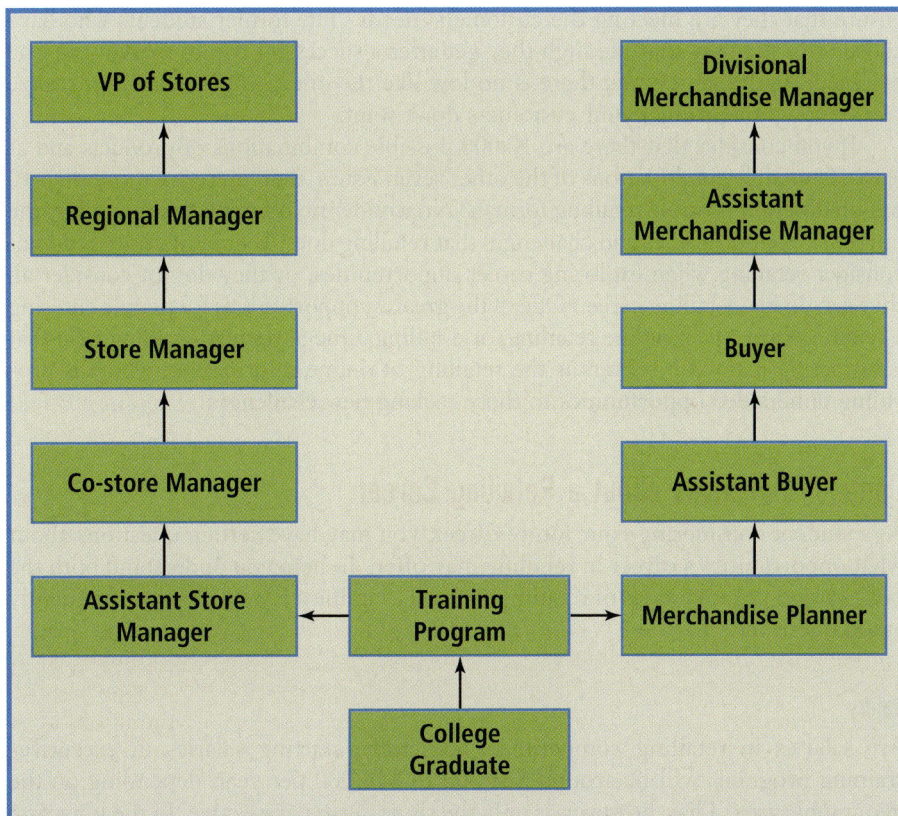

Exhibit 1.4
Retailing's Two Career Paths

Boxes and arrows: VP of Stores ← Regional Manager ← Store Manager ← Co-store Manager ← Assistant Store Manager ← Training Program ← College Graduate. Training Program → Merchandise Planner → Assistant Buyer → Buyer → Assistant Merchandise Manager → Divisional Merchandise Manager.

store management
The retailing career path that involves responsibility for selecting, training, and evaluating personnel, as well as in-store promotions, displays, customer service, building maintenance, and security.

If you elect the **store-management** path, you will have many decisions to make that affect the store's profitability. Selecting, training, evaluation, and all other aspects of personnel management are your responsibility. This path is very people skill oriented as you will be responsible for in-store promotions, displays, customer service, building maintenance, and store security. In addition, there is a need to coordinate your efforts with buyers and department managers in order to meet customers' needs, thus maximizing store sales. This career path does require frequent moves as you increase your responsibilities. In addition, this path involves working weekends and evenings. In fact, former students who have chosen this career path say they loved being a manager. Every day is different from the previous one, but most of all, they loved teaching, mentoring, and coaching the young people who are in their first job. What the ex-students disliked most about being a manager was dealing with "poor work ethic" employees and shoplifters. Still, this path offers a very rewarding pay package as you advance to store manager and beyond. Several of the ex-students, while still in their 30s, were making substantial six-figure incomes.

buying
The retailing career path whereby one uses quantitative tools to develop appropriate buying plans for the store's merchandise lines.

If your inclination is toward **buying**, you can follow that career path. After spending some time as an assistant buyer, you will be promoted to buyer, which is the equivalent of the CEO of a small business unit. Buyers will use quantitative tools such as the merchandise budget and *open to buy* in their work. Buyers, who usually work out of the retailer's main office but do spend a great amount of time traveling have to develop appropriate buying plans for their merchandise lines. Also, buyers are not only responsible for selecting the merchandise but also must select the vendors and negotiate terms with them. In fact, as a buyer you could also serve on a team with the retailer's product development staff as it works with a supplier to design a private-label offering for your store. Finally, buyers must coordinate with store managers to ensure that they are meeting the customers' needs. The former students who have chosen this path say that the high they get after a successful trip to market can't be matched. At the same time, there is no low like the one you get when you realize you've bought a product your customers don't want.

If you consider that there are 10,000 possible combinations of products and at least 10 possible combinations of the other seven issues, then there are more than 10 billion different possible retailing formats. No wonder no other occupation offers the immediate opportunities and challenges that retailing does. Yet many students do not consider retailing when exploring career opportunities, or they do not consider all they can do in a retailing career. One of the greatest opportunities for people entering a retailing career is in online retailing, or e-tailing. One particular e-tailing field that is attracting many job seekers is the retailing of online information, which is providing unheralded opportunities to those seeking new challenges.

Common Questions about a Retailing Career

As a student considering your future career, you may have certain questions about what opportunities a career in retailing may offer. To help you understand both the positive and negative sides of retailing, we will examine a few of the most frequently asked questions.

Salary

Are salaries in retailing competitive? Generally, starting salaries in executive-training programs will be around $42,000 to $56,000 per year, depending on the geographic area. That, however, is only the short-term perspective. In the long run, the retail manager or buyer is directly rewarded on individual performance. Entry-level retail managers or buyers who do exceptionally well can double or triple their incomes in three to five years and often within seven to 10 years can have incomes twice those of classmates who chose other career fields. As mentioned earlier, it is not uncommon for a college graduate with five to eight years of experience to earn a six-figure income. In fact, Macy's Chairman and CEO Terry Lundgren was president of Federated Department Stores at age 35.

Career Progression

Can one advance rapidly in retailing? Yes. Obviously, this answer depends on both the retail organization and the individual. A person capable of handling increasing amounts of responsibility can move up quickly. There is no standard career progression chart; http://retailindustry.about.com/od/retailjobscareers/Retail_Jobs_ Career_Advancement.htm shows career opportunities available with many of the country's leading retailers by geographic area as well as other fine companies seeking college graduates. Keep in mind that franchising (discussed in Chapter 5) is also a potential career option at some point in your retailing career. Even when he sold his retail chain (Mervyns) to Dayton-Hudson more than 25 years ago, Mervyn Morris decided he wanted to become a Cadillac dealer and thus became the operator of a franchise business.

Geographic Mobility

Does a retailing career allow one to live in the area of the country where one desires? Yes and no. Retailing exists in all geographic areas of the United States with sufficient population density. In the largest 300 cities in the United States, there will be sufficient employment and advancement opportunities in retailing. In order to progress rapidly, a person must often be willing and able to make several moves, even if the changes may not be attractive in terms of an individual's lifestyle. Rapidly growing chain stores usually find it necessary to transfer individuals, especially those in the store-management career path, in order to open stores in new geographic areas. Fortunately, these transfers are generally coupled with promotions and salary adjustments. Finally, a person may stay in one geographic area if he or she desires. However, this may cost that person some opportunities for advancement and salary increases.

Societal Perspective

Professional merchants are considered respected and desirable members of their communities, state, and nation. Leading retail executives are well-rounded individuals with a high social consciousness. Many of them serve on the boards of nonprofit organizations, as regents or trustees of universities, as active members of the local chambers of commerce, on school boards, and in other service-related activities. Retailers serve society not only outside their retailing career but also within it as well. For example, civic events such as holiday parades are often sponsored by local merchants. In addition, many retail firms support local groups and charities with cash, food, and other goods and services as a means to "reinvest" some of their profits in the communities they serve.

Unfortunately, there are also unscrupulous, deceiving merchants that society can do without. This is true in all professions. There are unscrupulous lawyers, bankers, doctors, and police officers who give their professions a negative image at times. On the other hand, there are professional and ethical lawyers, bankers, doctors, and police officers who are good for their professions and for society as a whole. It is not the profession that dictates one's contribution to society but the soundness of one's ethical principles. Early in your career (preferably as a student), you need to develop a firm set of ethical principles to help guide you throughout your managerial career.

Prerequisites for Success

What's required for success as a retail manager? Let's look at several factors that influence a retailer's success.

Hard Work

Most successful retailers, like successful individuals, will respond to the preceding question with a simple "hard work." Beginning retailers have long known that they earn their salary 9 to 5, Monday through Friday, but earn their advancement after 5 o'clock. Still, one can have a balanced and happy life coupled with a retailing career by using good time-management and planning skills.

Analytical Skills

The retail manager must be able to solve problems through numerical analysis of facts and data in order to plan, manage, and control. The retail manager is a problem solver on a day-to-day basis. An understanding of the past and current performance of the store, merchandise lines, and departments is necessary. It is the analysis of these performance data that forms the basis of future actions in the retailing environment. Today's retailer must be able to analyze all the financial data that are available before going to market. For example, Costco has had vendors redesign product packages to fit more items on a pallet, the wooden platforms it uses to ship, and display its goods. In one case, the retailer had the manufacturer put cashews into square containers instead of round ones, which enabled the retailer to decrease the number of pallets shipped by 24,000 a year, cutting the number of trucks needed by 600. Likewise, by having other manufacturers reshape everything from laundry detergent buckets to milk jugs; Costco was able to reduce the number of pallets per year by 200,000.[37]

In addition, quantitative and qualitative analysis of customers, competitors, suppliers, and other constituencies often help to identify emerging trends and innovations. Combined with current performance results and market knowledge, continual monitoring of these constituencies provides insight into past performance and alerts the retailer to new directions. Many retailers also get information from reading trade journals, such as *Stores, Women's Wear Daily, Progressive Grocer*, and *Chain Store Age*; discuss current happenings with their buying office; visit markets; and even talk to their competitors as a means to keep up. One successful retailer told the author to not just analyze the merchandise, customers, competitors, and suppliers, but to do the same with its employees. Do they understand the retailer's philosophy, its values, preferred behavior, and code of conduct? It is amazing that Walmart always invokes the image of Sam Walton and what he stood for, but very few current employees were working for the retailer when Mr. Sam , as he was known by everyone in the chain, died.

Creativity

The ability to generate and recognize novel ideas and solutions is known as *creativity*. A retail manager cannot operate a store totally by a set of preprogrammed

Service Retailing

Using Creativity to Take on Walmart

Moore's Bicycle Shop is located in a southern college town of 50,000 and is surrounded by three Walmart Supercenters. A couple of years ago, its owner, James Moore, became frustrated when he noticed customers walking out of his shop without making a purchase when he was unable to offer them a $125 bicycle. His previous source of these "inexpensive" bikes was Mongoose. However, Mongoose had earlier discontinued selling to independent bicycle retailers, such as Moore, in favor of having an exclusive contract with the much larger Walmart.

Recently, Moore began to notice customers bringing in some Walmart bikes for repair. These bikes, which were sold as "clearance specials" consisted of defects or returns that Walmart would put on the sidewalk and sold "as is." Unfortunately for the customers, the cost of the work needed to make their bikes safe and functional often exceeded what they originally paid, and the customers often left without getting the necessary repairs.

Using his creativity, Moore wrote the three Walmart managers, offering to purchase sight unseen all of their returned bicycles on the condition that he get *all* the returns and not just the worst of the batch. He offered a simple rate structure of $10 for kid's bikes and $15 for adult bikes. He also addressed the issue that the practice of selling defective merchandise was not good from a liability standpoint. In addition, he suggested that their customers might feel cheated with their bargains when they learned the "clearance bikes" were not cost-effective to fix. In short, Moore noted that Walmart might be selling potentially dangerous products to disappointed customers.

At first, Walmart offered him 68 bicycles at an average price less than $12. A few bikes only needed a flat repaired, most needed a minimal degree of time and parts, while a few were only usable for parts. James took the best six bikes and within two hours had them repaired and sold for enough to pay for all 68 used bikes.

Today Moore prices most of these repaired bikes either at Walmart's regular price or even higher after explaining the higher price included the shop's six-month comprehensive warranty and the fact that the bikes had already gone through the critical break-in period (where most adjustments are needed) and had been serviced by "expert" mechanics.

Over the past couple of years, Moore has purchased several hundred more Walmart returns, resulting in a win–win situation for all three parties.

Walmart wins because it no longer has lines of defective merchandise greeting customers at the front door, and the managers are able to clear their storage clutter with one phone call.

The customer wins as they are no longer being sold bikes that are unsafe to ride and too costly to repair. More often than not, the victims of these sidewalk "specials" were the customers least able to afford making a buying mistake by purchasing a faulty or unusable product.

Moore won for two reasons. First, he was now able to provide an identical product to the price-conscious shopper at the same price as Walmart. Second, in the future many of his "new" customers would often trade that "inexpensive" bike in for a better-quality bike. The shop also wins because its labor productivity is now maximized as it always has a backlog of Walmart returns to repair during its otherwise slower periods. Consequently, the shop mechanics now work year-round.

However, nothing excites Moore more than the thought that, with a little creativity, he is now able to take a product that costs less than $12 and, after investing about 15 minutes of employee time and $5 in parts, he can sell it for $125.

Source: *This box is based on information supplied by James Moore, Moore's Bicycle Shop, Hattiesburg, Mississippi, and used with his written permission.*

equations and formulas. Because the competitive environment is constantly changing, there is no standard recipe for retailing. Therefore, retail executives need to be idea people as well as analysts. After all, success in retailing is the result of sensitive, perceptive decisions that require imaginative and innovative techniques.

For example, as the American economy continued in its slowdown a few years ago, many retailers were afraid to embrace new ideas. Instead of using their creative power to increase their competitive advantage, these retailers either just continued doing things as they always had done them, cut costs without thinking about the impact on customer satisfaction, or copied what their competitors were doing.

James Moore

Creativity is one of the easiest ways for small retailers to compete with the discounters. Witness the action of Moore's Bicycle Shop in its dealings with Walmart.

None of these actions enabled the retailer to actually differentiate itself from the competition. In fact, many students mistakenly assume that price is the only way for retailers to compete and that the arrival of a discount chain always spells disaster for small-town retailers. After all, the small local stores cannot match the discounters' purchasing volume. This is not the case if the retailer is able to use creativity to differentiate itself from the competition. The chapter's "Service Retailing" box illustrates one of the most creative ways a small bike sales and repair retailer took on the big discounters. Moore's Bicycle Shop simply did it by using the discounter as a supply source.

Decisiveness

The ability to make rapid decisions, and to render judgments, take action, and commit oneself to a course of action until completion is termed *decisiveness*. A retail manager must be an action person. Better decisions could probably be made if more time were taken to make them. However, more time is frequently unavailable because variables such as fashion trends and consumer desires change quickly. Thus, a manager must make decisions quickly, confidently, and correctly in order to be successful even if perfect information is not always available. For example, buyers often make purchase decisions six months to a year before the merchandise arrives at the store.

Flexibility

The ability to adjust to the ever-changing needs of the situation calls for flexibility. The retail manager must have the willingness and enthusiasm to do whatever is necessary (although not necessarily planned) to get the job completed. Because plans must be altered quickly to accommodate changes in trends, styles, and attitudes, successful retail managers must be flexible. For example, changes in e-tailing occur continuously as retailers adjust prices and product offerings to changing consumer tastes and the competitive actions of other retailers.

Initiative

Retail managers are doers. They must have the ability to originate action rather than wait to be told what to do. This ability is called *initiative*. To be a success, the modern retail manager must monitor the numbers of the business (sales volumes, profits, inventory levels) and seize opportunities for action.

Leadership

Working in retailing is really working on a team. The ability to inspire the team members to trust and respect your judgment and the ability to delegate, guide, and persuade this team calls for *leadership*. Successfully conducting a retail operation means depending on the team to get the work done; in any large-scale retailing enterprise, one person cannot do it all. A manager succeeds when his or her subordinates do their jobs. In fact, the concept of the team approach is one of the most important hiring criteria for many retailers.

Organization

Another important quality is the ability to establish priorities and plans and follow through to achieve these results. This prerequisite is *organization*. Retail managers are often forced to deal with many issues, functions, and projects at the same time. To achieve goals, the successful retailer must be a good time manager and set priorities when organizing personnel and resources.

Risk Taking

Retail managers should be willing to take calculated risks based on thorough analysis and sound judgment; they should also be willing to accept responsibility for the results. Success in retailing often comes from taking calculated risks and having the confidence to try something new before someone else does. For example, no one can say that Jeff Bezos's decision to start Amazon.com and Sam Walton's decision to start Walmart were not without risk. All successful buyers have at one time or another purchased merchandise that could be labeled as losers. After all, if buyers never made errors, that would mean they were afraid to take "risks" and probably passed up many winners. However, they must have the ability to recognize when they make a mistake.

Stress Tolerance

As the other prerequisites to retailing success suggest, retailing is a fast-paced and demanding career in a changing environment. The retailing leaders of the 21st century must be able to perform consistently under pressure and to thrive on constant change and challenge.

Perseverance

Because of the difficult challenges that a retail career presents, it is important to have *perseverance*. All too often, retailers may become frustrated due to the many things they can't control. For example, a blizzard may occur just before Christmas and wipe out the most important shopping days of the year. Others may become exasperated with fellow employees, the long hours (especially the weekends), or the inability to satisfy some customers. The person who has the ability to persevere and take all of this in stride will find an increasing number of career-advancement opportunities.

Enthusiasm

Successful retailers must have a strong feeling of warmth for their job; otherwise they will convey the wrong image to their customers and department associates. Retailers today are training their sales forces to smile even when talking to customers on the telephone "because it shows through in your voice."[38] Without *enthusiasm*, success in any field will elude you.

LO 4	The Study and Practice of Retailing

What are the different methods for the study and practice of retailing?

As we have seen, two of the prerequisites to success as a retail manager are analytical skills and creativity. These attributes also represent two methods for the study and practice of retailing.

Analytical Method

The analytical retail manager is a finder and investigator of facts. These facts are summarized and synthesized so a manager can make decisions systematically. In doing so, the manager uses models and theories of retail phenomena that enable him or her to structure all dimensions of retailing. An analytical perspective can result in a standardized set of procedures, success formulas, and guidelines.

Consider, for example, a manager operating a Starbucks shop where everything is preprogrammed, including the menu, decor, location, hours of operation, cleanliness standards, customer-service policies, and advertising. This store manager needs only to gather and analyze facts to determine if the preestablished guidelines are being met and to take appropriate corrective action if necessary.

We mentioned earlier in this chapter how Walmart has made use of the sophistication of its computer system when hurricanes, tornados, or other emergencies occur. For example, when a hurricane is approaching a coast, the area's stores are stocked up with bottled water, flashlights, generators, and tarps. The retailer also will have chain saws, mops, and Pop-Tarts (which stay preserved until opened, taste good, and can be eaten by the whole family) in reserve for after the storm. This is the result of analyzing the data from previous storms.

One thing for a small retailer to consider is watching the Russell 2000 Index. This index, which measures the performance of the small-cap segment of the U.S. equity universe, is a great forecasting tool for future business conditions. Thus, even if they don't trade stocks, small retailers should keep their eye on this stock market index. And since most small retailers operate in one or a few cities, they should be aware of the major employers in the area and how they are faring. Although the Russell 2000 Index captures small-cap firms, it is possible that if a large Fortune 1000 firm in your local community fails or has a downturn and closes a local manufacturing plant, distribution center, or administrative office, then that will impact what members of the local community can spend at your store.

Creative Method

Conversely, the creative retail manager is an idea person. This retail manager tends to be a conceptualizer and has a very imaginative and fertile mind capable of creating a highly successful retail chain. In addition to the discussion earlier of James Moore and his creativity, Costco's CEO James D. Sinegal is another creative genius. Because he insists on capping margins at 14 percent of sales, he once even considered taking the unusual step of having Costco grow its own pumpkins in order to continue to offer customers a pumpkin pie for its long-standing price of

$5.99. After all, the retailer sells more than a million of the store-baked pies in the three days before Thanksgiving.[39]

A Two-Pronged Approach

As shown through the examples of our Starbucks manager and Costco's James Sinegal, retailing can indeed be practiced from both perspectives. The retailer that employs both approaches is most successful in the long run. Aren't stores like Starbucks successful using only the analytical method? No. The Starbucks manager can operate analytically quite successfully. However, behind the franchisee is a franchisor that is creative as well as analytical. On the creative side was the development of the company name and logo. On the analytical side was the development of standardized layouts, fixtures, equipment, and employee training. It is the combination of the creative with the analytical that has made Starbucks what it is today.

The synthesis of creativity and analysis is necessary in all fields of retailing. One retail expert noted that "many successful merchandisers are fast duplicators rather than originators."[40] To decide who or what to duplicate requires not only creativity but also an analysis of the strategies that retailers are pursuing. This is an exercise in weighing potential returns against risks. Thus, according to this expert, "creativity in retailing is for the sake of increasing the sales and profits of the firm."[41] If creativity is tied to sales and profits, then one cannot avoid analysis; profit and sales statistics require analysis.

Retailers can't do without either creativity or analytical skills. We will attempt to develop your skills in both of these areas. At the outset, however, you should note that the analytical and creative methods for studying retailing are not that different. Whether you use creativity or analytical skills, they will be directed at solving problems.

A Proposed Orientation

The approach to the study and practice of retailing that is reflected in this book is an outgrowth of the previous discussion. This approach has four major orientations: (1) environmental, (2) management planning, (3) profit, and (4) decision making.

Retailers should have an environmental orientation that will allow them to anticipate and adapt continuously to external forces in the environment. Retailing is not static. With social, legal, technological, economic, and other external forces always in flux, the modern retailer finds it necessary both to assess these changes from an analytical perspective and to respond with creative actions.

Retailers should have a planning orientation that will help them to adapt systematically to a changing environment. A retailer that wants to have the competitive edge must plan today for the future. Exhibit 1.5 illustrates the problems facing a retailer that is reactive rather than proactive in planning. Exhibit 1.5a shows the standard performance for a retailer's plan: The plan is introduced, sales peak as competitors react to the plan, and finally the plan becomes obsolete. Exhibit 1.5b shows the old method of reacting to a competitor's attack: The retailer tries to extend the sales peak by matching the competitor's plan until another competitor makes both of their plans obsolete. Exhibit 1.5c shows why this text places special emphasis on the development of creative retail strategies. Here the retailer is proactive and already has another plan ready before either the market changes or the competition attacks its original plan.

Retailers also need a profit orientation, since all retail decisions will have an effect on the firm's financial performance. The profit orientation will therefore

Exhibit 1.5
The Importance of Proactive Planning

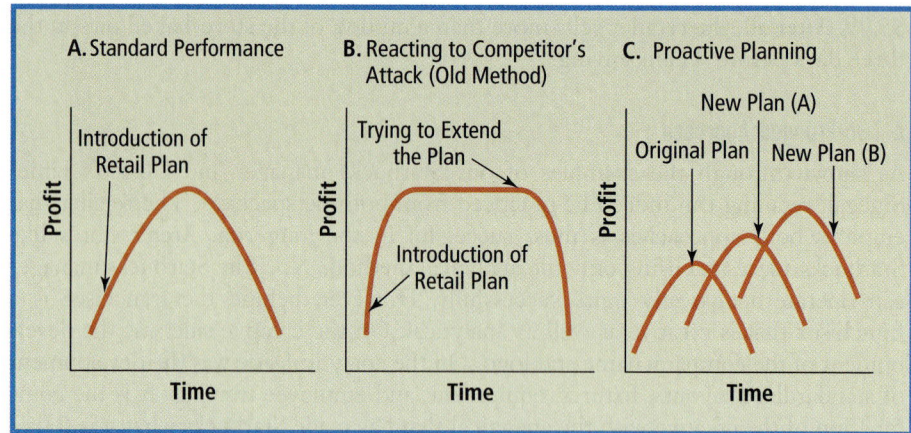

focus on the fundamental management of assets, revenues, and expenses. Management tools that show how to evaluate the profit impact of retail decisions will be discussed.

Retailers should have a decision-making orientation that will allow them to focus on the need to collect and analyze data for making intelligent retail decisions. To aid in this process, executives need a retail information system to help program their operations for desired results.

The Book Outline

This book is composed of 14 chapters, each with its own study guide and application section. The chapters are intended to reinforce each other. The end-of-chapter materials provide a way to bring the real world into your studies by launching you into the kinds of situations you might face as a retail manager. Through careful analysis of this material and discussion with fellow students, you will discover retailing concepts that can be vividly retained because of the concrete context. Furthermore, this material will require you to think of yourself as a retail decision maker who must sometimes make decisions with less-than-perfect information.

Introduction to Retailing

This book is divided into four parts. The first part, "Introduction to Retailing," has two chapters. In Chapter 2, "Retail Strategic Planning and Operations Management," you will be exposed to the basic concepts of strategy, administration, and operations planning and management in retailing that will be used in the remaining chapters.

The Retailing Environment

The second part, "The Retailing Environment," will focus on the external factors that the retailer faces in making everyday business decisions. The four chapters examine, in detail, the factors shown in Exhibit 1.1. Chapter 3, "Retail Customers," will look at the behavior of the retail consumer and the socioeconomic environment. Chapter 4, "Evaluating the Competition in Retailing," examines the behavior of competitors as well as the technological advances taking place in the market. Chapter 5, "Managing the Supply Chain," focuses on the behavior of the various members of the supply chain and their effect on the retailer. Chapter 6,

"Legal and Ethical Behavior," analyzes the effect of the legal and ethical constraints on today's retailer.

Market Selection and Location Analysis

It has often been said that the three keys to success in retailing are: location, location, and location. In Chapter 7, "Market Selection and Retail Location Analysis," we discuss the various elements to consider in determining the feasibility of targeting a given market segment and entering a given retail market, and then we look at site selection.

Managing Retail Operations

In the fourth part, "Managing Retail Operations," we discuss the merchandising operations of a retail firm. This part deals with the day-to-day decisions facing retailers. Chapter 8, "Managing a Retailer's Finances," discusses various financial statements, the key methods of valuing inventory, and the development of merchandise planning budgets by retailers. Chapter 9, "Merchandise Buying and Handling," looks at how a retailer determines what to buy for its market and how these purchases are made. The appendix following Chapter 9 discusses the merchandising of apparel goods. Chapter 10, "Retail Pricing," discusses the importance to the retailer of setting the correct price. In addition to the various markup methods used by retailers, the chapter also looks at markdowns. Chapter 11, "Advertising and Promotion," provides a complete discussion (with the exception of personal selling, which is covered along with services offered by retailers in Chapter 12, "Customer Services and Retail Selling") of how a retailer can and should promote itself. Chapter 13, "Store Layout and Design," discusses the impact of proper layout and design on retail performance. Chapter 14, "Managing People," examines the role of the two most important people (customers and employees) in the success of a retail firm.

The text concludes with a glossary of all major terms used in this text, as well as an index of the retailers mentioned.

SUMMARY

This chapter seeks to acquaint the reader with the nature and scope of retailing by discussing its impact on the economy, the types of retailers, and its prerequisites for success.

What is retailing, and why is it undergoing so much change today?

LO 1

Retailing consists of the final activities and steps needed to place a product in the hands of the ultimate consumer or to provide a service to the consumer. Retailing is not staid and stable; rather, it is an exciting business sector that effectively combines an individual's skills to make a profit in an ever-changing market environment. That is why some retailers are successful and others, which are either unwilling or unable to adapt to this changing environment, fail.

What are the five various methods used to categorize retailers?

LO 2

Retailers can be classified in a variety of ways. Five of the more popular schemes are NAICS code, number of outlets, margins versus turnover, location, and size. None, however, sheds adequate light on competition in retailing.

STUDENT STUDY GUIDE

LO 3 What is involved in a retailing career?

In the long run, a retailing career can offer salary comparable to other careers, definite career advancement, and geographic mobility. In addition, a career in retailing incorporates the knowledge and use of all the business activities or disciplines (accounting, marketing, finance, personnel, economics, and even fashion). In retailing, no two days are alike; each offers its own set of opportunities and problems. The prerequisites for success in retailing besides hard work include analytical skills, creativity, decisiveness, flexibility, initiative, leadership, organization, risk taking, stress tolerance, perseverance, and enthusiasm. These are all important, but it is especially vital for the retail manager to develop an attitude of openness to new ideas and a willingness to learn. After all, the market is always changing.

LO 4 What are the different methods for the study and practice of retailing?

To be successful in retailing, an individual must use both analytical and creative methods of operation. The four orientations to the study and practice of retailing proposed in this text are an *environmental orientation*, which allows the retailer to focus on the continuously changing external forces affecting retailing; a *planning orientation*, which helps the retailer to adapt systematically to this changing environment; a *profit orientation*, which enables the retailer to examine the profit implications of any decision; and a *decision-making orientation*, which allows the retailer to focus on the need to collect and analyze data for making intelligent creative retail decisions.

TERMS TO REMEMBER

retailing	gross margin
bricks-and-mortar retailers	operating expenses
same-store sales	inventory turnover
market share	high-performance retailers
scrambled merchandising	low-margin, low-turnover retailer
category killer	high-margin, low-turnover retailers
standard stock list	clicks-and-mortar retailers
optional stock list approach	low-margin, high-turnover retailer
channel advisor	high-margin, high-turnover retailers
private-label branding	store-management
gross-margin percentage	buying

REVIEW AND DISCUSSION QUESTIONS

LO 1 What is retailing, and why is it undergoing so much change today?

1. Wouldn't a country be better off with fewer retail outlets? After all, with fewer stores, consumers would not waste money making impulsive purchases, and they would save more.
2. Is scrambled merchandising really a good idea? Does it make sense that if you are good in one area of merchandising that you will be good in all areas? Talbots, after all, is excellent in merchandising fashionable women's clothing but failed in selling men's and kids' clothing.
3. What factors are contributing to the recent trend of decreasing store size?
4. Currently, there is a great deal of debate about the future impact of the Internet on retailing. Which of the following items—a vacation package for

spring break, a wedding gift for a friend, a pair of jeans for yourself, or an end table for your apartment—would you be least likely to purchase online? Why?

Describe the five methods used to categorize retailers. `LO 2`

5. How can a retailer operate with a high-margin, high-turnover strategy? Won't customers avoid this type of store and shop at a low-margin store?
6. Isn't it better for a retail chain to always use a standard stock list? After all, it would confuse a customer if a JCPenney's in Chicago is different than one in Miami.

What is involved in a retailing career? `LO 3`

7. What concepts or techniques from economics, fashion, accounting, or information systems do you believe would be most useful in retail decision making?
8. What kind of leadership skills does it take to be successful in retailing? Isn't leadership the most important prerequisite for success in retailing?

Explain the different methods for the study and practice of retailing. `LO 4`

9. To be successful in retailing, which skill is most important: being creative or being analytical? Why?
10. Visit a local retailer that you would describe as creative and seek to determine which analytical skills that retailer also possesses.

SAMPLE TEST QUESTIONS

Retailing `LO 1`

a. may be defined as any cash purchase for merchandise.
b. is the same the world over.
c. is the final move in the flow of merchandise from producer to consumer.
d. is the sale of an item by the manufacturer to a wholesaler.
e. is not necessary to produce economic growth.

Which of the following is not one of the ways by which retailers are categorized? `LO 2`

a. number of outlets
b. size
c. margin versus turnover
d. location
e. gender of the manager

Due to increased corporate responsibilities, the manager of a bike shop has asked the assistant manager to take responsibility for screening and hiring new sales associates. The manager is allowing the assistant to make the decisions independently but has scheduled weekly meetings for the two to discuss any issues of concern and to provide any needed insight. The manager is demonstrating which desirable retailing attribute? `LO 3`

a. prioritizing
b. leadership
c. creativity
d. laziness
e. enthusiasm

LO 4

In attempting to determine whether a branch of a sandwich shop should be opened in a small town outside the original trading area, a retailer gathered information on demographics, competitors' sales, and available real estate in that area. The retailer was employing the _____ method of retail decision making.

a. tactical
b. strategic
c. analytical
d. creative
e. intuitive

WRITING AND SPEAKING EXERCISE

Halfway between your apartment and the campus is a small convenience store where you regularly purchase a cup of coffee to get you ready for those early morning classes. Over the last two years, you have become friends with the owner. Late last night when you filled up your gas tank, you noticed that he was still there working on his books. While visiting with you, he states that the store has been profitable, but he feels it could do better if he could lower the high rate of employee turnover. He asks you for advice on this problem.

Prepare a short presentation for the owner listing what you think he should look for in hiring part-time employees. Also, list what employee traits he should seek to avoid.

RETAIL PROJECT

How would you use the Internet to purchase your next car? Using the search engine on your computer, select two or three different auto websites. List their web addresses, such as www.autobytel.com, and make a report describing what they have on their websites. Which one do you like best? Why? Can you purchase online from each website? What is the buying process? Can competitors gain anything from looking at these websites? Finally, what is missing from these websites that you feel should be on them?

PLANNING YOUR OWN RETAIL BUSINESS

If you think you might want to be a retail entrepreneur, you can use the "Planning Your Own Retail Business" computer exercises at the end of each chapter to assist you in this process. In addition, this text's website (www.cengage.com/international) has an exercise called "The House: Understanding A Retail Enterprise Using Spreadsheet Analysis" that can be used to help you understand the dollars and cents of retailing.

This first exercise is intended to acquaint you with how sensitive your retail business will be to changes in sales volume. Let's assume that you plan that your retail business will generate $350,000 per year in annual sales and that it will operate at a gross-margin percentage of 40 percent. If your fixed operating expenses are $80,000 annually and variable operating costs are 10 percent of sales, then how much profit will you make?

(*Hint:* Sales $\times$ gross-margin percentage $=$ gross margin; gross margin $-$ fixed operating expenses $-$ sales $\times$ variable operating expenses as % of sales $=$ net profit.) Use a spreadsheet program on your computer to compute your firm's net profits; next, analyze what happens (1) if sales drop 10 percent and (2) if sales rise 10 percent. Why are bottom line results (net profits) so sensitive to changes in sales volume?

Retail Strategic Planning and Operations Management

OVERVIEW:

In this chapter, we will explain the importance of planning in successful retail organizations. To facilitate the discussion, we introduce a retail planning and management model that will serve as a frame of reference for the remainder of the text. This simple model illustrates the importance of strategic planning and operations management. These two activities, if properly conducted, will enable a retail firm to achieve results exceeding those of the competition.

LEARNING OBJECTIVES:

After reading this chapter, you should be able to:

1. Explain why strategic planning is so important and be able to describe the components of strategic planning: statement of mission; goals and objectives; an analysis of strengths, weaknesses, opportunities, and threats; and strategy.
2. Describe the retail strategic planning and operations management model, which explains the two tasks that a retailer must perform and how they lead to high profit.

| LO 1 | Components of Strategic Planning |

Explain why strategic planning is so important and describe its components.

In most endeavors, a well-defined plan of action can mean the difference between success and failure. For example, a driver does not go from Fargo to Kansas City without a well-defined plan of which highways to use. Political candidates and their advisors develop a campaign plan long before the election. Successful college students plan their assignments so that they are not forced to pull an all-nighter just before an assignment is due. Similarly, a clearly defined plan of action is an essential ingredient in all forms of business management. This is especially true in the highly competitive field of retailing, where the number of stores has expanded faster over the past decade than consumer demand.

Planning is the anticipation and organization of what needs to be done to reach an objective. This sounds simple enough, but as any retail buyer will tell you, it is difficult to know in advance of each upcoming season what styles, quantities, colors, and sizes the customers will want. Superior planning by retailers enables them to offset some of the advantages their competition may have such as a good location.

People not familiar with retailing often wonder how retailers can anticipate what consumers are going to want next season. In reality, success for all retailers, large and small, is generally a matter of good planning and then implementing that plan. For example, years ago the management of Lowe's made the key decision that has defined the retailer ever since. After arguing for months about what direction to take the home-improvement chain, management decided to become the "customers' first choice for home improvement in each and every market we serve." Lowe's shifted from opening small stores in small markets to building mega-outlets with brighter lights and wider aisles. In addition, the company targeted female customers, which is important because women make 80 percent of home-improvement purchase decisions.[1]

Failure to develop good plans can spell disaster for a retailer. Remember all those easy-to-get "no income, no job, no problem" loans that led to the recent housing crisis? Consider also what proved to be a major planning error by Gap Inc. A few years back, the retailer suffered a downturn in sales due in part to having the wrong merchandise mix in its stores and an overlap between its three main divisions—Gap, Old Navy, and Banana Republic. Without a clear definition of what each store should be, customers headed for the low price: Old Navy. Today, Old Navy is clearly focused on 20-something women, though its customers have included men, teens, and children as well. In addition, the retailer now pushes wardrobe collections, rather than an à lá carte approach to fashion, and has introduced business-casual clothing, a departure from Old Navy's past offerings of jeans, T-shirts, socks, and the like. It also uses advertising that is more urbane than its past campy TV spots.[2]

Consider, also, what proved to be a different type of planning error by Barnes & Noble and its website: www.barnesandnoble.com. Initially, the chain made the decision not to integrate the website with its stores. Thus, at one of the company's typical bricks-and-mortar stores, there was very little mention of the chain's online alternative. Bricks-and-click integration (using both physical stores and online sales operations) comes at a cost: potentially cannibalizing one's established businesses with the introduction of an e-tailing operation. Barnes & Noble may have had five or six million customers online, but it had tens of millions walking through its stores. Why promote a website that offered heavy discounts—and at a point in time when no sales tax was charged—to consumers who were willing to pay full price? What Barnes & Noble failed to realize was that if they didn't promote the site, many of its customers would eventually switch to Amazon's website.

Conversely, just before its recent financial problems forced it to liquidate all its stores, Circuit City began promoting that it had the same prices both in-store and online in an attempt to generate revenue. The chain's intent was to bring customers into its stores with the "lowest" price guarantee offer so that it could sell the customers additional impulse items rather than have them go to Best Buy. In addition, by offering both the same price in-store and online as well as the ability to return online purchases to the physical store, the company sought to minimize the number of lost customers to its Internet rivals (namely, pricegrabbers.com and roboshopper.com). Consequently, while the chain believed that a portion of its in-store customers might shift some purchases to its online locations, the chain felt the overall number of purchases was likely to increase. Little wonder that many existing bricks-and-mortar retailers such as Target and Walmart are constantly developing plans that seek to translate their brand strength to their online venture by vigorously cross-promoting the two ventures, even if that means cannibalizing existing in-store sales. These retailers have realized that if they don't plan for the future, they risk becoming "forgotten retailers of another era." This is just an example of why planning is so important in retailing today.

Due to Circuit City's poor assumptions in developing its strategic plans, it had to declare bankruptcy in early 2009.

strategic planning
Involves adapting the resources of the firm to the opportunities and threats of an ever-changing retail environment.

mission statement
Is a basic description of the fundamental nature, rationale, and direction of the firm.

Strategic planning involves adapting the resources of the firm to the opportunities and threats of an ever-changing retail environment. Through the proper use of strategic planning, retailers hope to achieve and maintain a balance between resources available and opportunities ahead. All retailers want to be among the minority of firms that are able to change the rules of the game being played or, if they can't change the rules, to have a strategy to win the game as it is currently being played. That strategy should consist of a specific objective, an area of operation, and the understanding of what makes you better than your competitors. Let's take a closer look at the components of the strategic planning process.

Strategic planning consists of four components:

1. development of a mission (or purpose) statement for the firm;

2. definition of specific goals and objectives for the firm;

3. identification and analysis of the retailer's strengths, weaknesses, opportunities, and threats—referred to as *SWOT analysis*; and

4. development of basic strategies that will enable the firm to reach its objectives and fulfill its mission.

Mission Statement

The beginning of a retailer's strategic planning process is the formulation of a mission statement. The **mission statement** is a basic description of the fundamental nature, rationale, and direction of the firm. It provides the employees and customers with an understanding of where future growth for the firm will come from. Yet not every retailer has a mission statement. In fact, less than 60 percent of all businesses have written mission statements. Consequently, because so many businesses don't know where they want to go and how to get there, they end up as failures. However, the lack of a written statement is not a cause by itself for success or failure if the firm has a clearly understood, even if unwritten, plan of action. For example, Walmart doesn't have a written mission statement. Walmart does, however, have a clearly defined sense of direction, which as described by Sam Walton based on Marshall Field's directive is to "give the lady what she wants"?[3]

While mission statements vary from retailer to retailer, good ones usually include three elements:

1. how the retailer uses or intends to use its resources,

2. how it expects to relate to the ever-changing environment, and

3. the kinds of values it intends to provide in order to serve the needs and wants of the consumer.

A mission statement can be short or long, as long as it provides direction for the future of the firm. Consider Starbucks' mission statement: "To inspire and nurture the human spirit—one person, one cup, and one neighborhood at a time."[4] You don't have to be a regular latte drinker to understand the coffee retailer's sense of purpose.

James Moore, discussed earlier in Chapter 1, has this mission statement for his bike shop:

> Moore's Bicycle Shop is dedicated to bringing the non-cyclists into the sport by matching their recreational needs with the most economical bicycle that will meet or exceed their anticipated cycling demands. While we are capable of serving the professional both in terms of product and services, the entry level cyclists and family cyclists are our focuses. We prefer to downplay the competitive aspect of cycling and promote cycling as an escape from the competitive pressures of life. Our reputation has been built one customer at a time and we realize that it must be maintained in that manner.

Such a statement describes how Moore and another bike shop in town are able to survive. The other shop targets high-end merchandise for sophisticated experienced riders.[5]

As the above examples point out, a mission statement really answers the question, "What business should the retailer be in?" A critical issue in defining a retail business is to do so at the most meaningful level of generalization. This is why most mission statements should be general yet still provide direction as well as be motivational. Starbucks is in the coffee business, and its earlier failed attempts to enter the food market illustrate this. Borders book company, for example, viewed its mission as

> to be the best-loved provider of books, music, video, and other entertainment and informational products and services. To be the world leader in selection, service, innovation, ambiance, community involvement, and shareholder value. We recognize people to be the cornerstone of the Borders experience by building internal and external relationships, one person at a time.[6]

As its mission statement implied, Borders did not see itself selling books over the Internet. Therefore, rather than build a separate dot-com business that sapped profits, Borders took a more modest approach. That's because Borders believed that online book sales would not capture more than 10 percent of the book market worldwide.[7] Convinced that the opportunities were better in the bricks-and-mortar world, Borders sought to develop its flagship chain by positioning its website as a way to enhance the retail experience and build brand loyalty by offering access to borders.com within its superstores. Borders' own research showed that 80 percent of its customers were already buying online, so management figured it would be wasteful to spend money going after the already established separate online businesses. This decision proved to be ill-fated. In early 2009, after finding no buyers, the company decided to put itself up for sale and started to aggressively sell assets.

Although the company blamed a tight credit market and competition from discount chains and other online operations, Borders' failure was the result of ignoring the power of e-tailing. Borders did not have an exclusive online presence, and its homepage was a drab catchall for store locations, gift cards, and company information. In addition, the coupons that it e-mailed to its Borders Rewards members were good for in-store purchases only. In fact, it wasn't until May 2008 with the relaunch of Borders.com that the Ann Arbor–based retailer had a competitive online site.[8] By ignoring the ways in which online shopping has permeated the lives of untold millions of customers, Borders made one of the biggest business mistakes of the past decade.

As a further example of what makes a good mission statement and what doesn't, consider how a poor mission statement can be improved. The Avon Theater, which was located in downstate Illinois near one of the author's hometown, claimed it was "in the movie business and would show only PG-13 movies at the lowest prices in our trading area." Maybe if it had used a better statement such as "We are in the entertainment business and we shall seek to show the movies that customers want at prices that reflect the market's price sensitivity," the theater might still be in business.

As the above examples show, just having a mission statement is not enough in today's business climate. The retailer must adhere to its mission and not change with every new fad. During the recent recession, Starbucks' CEO Howard Schultz said that the key to the company's survival was a commitment not to abandon its core values and become a discount-driven brand. After all, "if we are a premium brand, it doesn't mean we can't provide value," Starbucks CEO Howard Schultz remarked.[9] As such, the retailer found ways to compensate for the economic downturn while remaining true to its core values.[10]

However, at times a mission statement must be changed. After trying unsuccessfully to operate on a national scale with an inefficient distribution system, The Great Atlantic & Pacific Tea Co. (A&P) reversed its fortunes by redefining its mission. Once the biggest food retailer in the United States, A&P transformed itself from a fatigued giant into an efficient regional operator. Today it operates in the Northeast under the A&P, Pathmark, Food Emporium, and Waldbaum's banners.[11]

Statement of Goals and Objectives

The second step in the strategic planning process is to define specific goals and objectives. These goals and objectives should be derived from and give precision and direction to the retailer's mission statement. Goals and objectives should identify the performance results that the retailer intends to bring about through the execution of its major strategies.

Goals and objectives serve two purposes. First, they provide specific direction and guidance to the firm in the formulation of its strategy. Second, they provide a control mechanism by establishing a standard against which the firm can measure and evaluate its performance. If the results are less than expected, then it signals that corrective actions need to be taken.

While goals and objectives can be expressed in many different ways, retailers will usually divide them into two dimensions: (1) market performance, which compares a firm's actions to its competitor's; and (2) financial performance, which analyzes the firm's ability to provide a profit level adequate to continue in business. In addition to the market performance and financial performance objectives, some retailers may also establish (3) societal objectives, which are phrased in terms of helping society fulfill some of its needs; and (4) personal objectives, which relate to helping people employed in retailing to fulfill some of their needs.

Let us examine each type of these goals and objectives in more detail.

Market Performance Objectives

market share
Is the retailer's total sales divided by total market sales.

Market performance objectives establish the amount of dominance the retailer seeks in the marketplace. The most popular measures of market performance in retailing are sales volume and **market share** (retailer's total sales divided by total market sales or the proportion of total sales in a particular geographic or product market that the retailer has been able to capture).

Research has shown that profitability is clearly and positively related to market share.[12] Thus, market performance objectives are not pursued for their own sake but because they are a key profit path.

Financial Objectives

Retailers can establish many financial objectives, but they can all be conveniently fit into categories of profitability and productivity.

Profitability Objectives   **Profit-based objectives** deal directly with the monetary return a retailer desires from its business. When retailers speak of "making a profit," the definition of profit is often unclear. The most common way to define profit is the aggregate total of net profit after taxes—that is, *the bottom line of the income statement*. Another common retail method of expressing profit is as a percentage of net sales. However, most retail owners feel the best way to define profit is in terms of *return on investment* (ROI).[13]

This method of reporting profits as a percentage of investments is complicated by the fact that there are two different ways to define the term *investment*. *Return on assets* (ROA) reflects all the capital used in the business, whether provided by the owners or by creditors. *Return on investment* (ROI), also referred to as *return on net worth* (RONW), reflects only the amount of capital that the owners have actually invested in the business.

The most frequently encountered profit objectives for a retailer are shown in Exhibit 2.1: the strategic profit model (SPM). The elements of the SPM start at the far left and move right. These five elements include net profit margin, asset turnover, return on assets, financial leverage, and return on net worth.

1. **Net profit margin** is the ratio of net profit (after taxes) to net sales. It shows how much profit a retailer makes on each dollar of sales after all expenses and taxes have been met. For example, if a retailer is operating on a net profit margin of 2 percent, then it is making two cents on each dollar of sales. In general, retailers operate on lower net profit margins than manufacturers. The net profit margin ratio is derived exclusively from income or operating statement data and does not include any measures from the retailer's balance sheet. Thus, it does not show how effectively a retailer is using the capital at its disposal.

2. **Asset turnover** is computed by taking the retailer's annual net sales and dividing by total assets. This ratio tells the retail analyst how productively the firm's assets are being used. Put another way, it shows how many dollars of sales a retailer can generate on an annual basis for each dollar invested in assets. Thus, if a retailer's asset turnover rate is 3.0, it is generating $3 in sales for each $1 in assets annually. The asset turnover ratio incorporates key measures from the income statement (sales) and the balance sheet (assets). As such, it shows how well the retailer is using its capital to generate sales. In general, retailers experience higher rates of asset turnover but lower net profit margins than do manufacturers.

3. **Return on assets (ROA)**, which is annual net profit divided by total assets, depicts the net profit return the retailer achieved on all assets invested regardless of whether the assets were financed by creditors or by the firm's owners. As shown in Exhibit 2.1, ROA is the result of multiplying the net profit

net profit margin
Is the ratio of net profit (after taxes) to total sales and shows how much profit a retailer makes on each dollar of sales after all expenses and taxes have been met.

asset turnover
Is total sales divided by total assets and shows how many dollars of sales a retailer can generate on an annual basis with each dollar invested in assets.

return on assets (ROA)
Is net profit (after taxes) divided by total assets.

margin by asset turnover. For example, a retailer with a net profit margin of 2 percent and an asset turnover of 4.0 would have a ROA of 8 percent (2 percent multiplied by 4 equals 8 percent).

financial leverage
Is total assets divided by net worth or owners' equity and shows how aggressive the retailer is in its use of debt.

4. **Financial leverage** is total assets divided by net worth or owners' equity. This ratio shows the extent to which a retailer is using debt in its total capital structure. The low end of this ratio is 1.0 times and depicts a situation in which the retailer is using no debt in its capital structure. As the ratio moves beyond 1.0, the firm is using a heavier mix of debt versus equity. For example, when the ratio is 2.0 times, the firm has two dollars in assets for every dollar in net worth, which is equivalent to a mix of 50-percent debt.

return on net worth (RONW)
Is net profit (after taxes) divided by owners' equity.

5. **Return on net worth (RONW)** is net profit divided by net worth or owner's equity. Return on net worth, shown at the far right of the SPM, is usually used to measure owner's performance. Note that, as shown in Exhibit 2.1, the ROA multiplied by financial leverage yields RONW. Thus, if a retailer has an ROA of 8 percent and a financial leverage of 2.0, then its RONW would be 16 percent (8 percent times 2.0 equals 16 percent).

The important point to remember from this discussion of profitability is that department or specialty stores, which have higher gross margins (net sales minus cost of goods sold) and lower asset turnover rates, compete differently than discounters, which generally have lower gross margins but higher asset turnover. For discounters, this results in less inventory per dollar of sales and a need for fewer capital assets outside of inventory. Discounters expect to gain a higher asset turnover by reducing their gross margins, and specialty and department stores expect a lower asset turnover rate with their higher gross margins.

stockouts
Are products that are out of stock and therefore unavailable to customers when they want them.

Remember that attempts to increase asset turnover by merely reducing inventory levels can have serious consequences for a retailer. These lower inventory levels may produce higher turnover rates, but they can also lead to **stockouts** (where products are not available for customers when they want them), thus creating a dissatisfied customer who may never return.

Exhibit 2.1
Strategic Profit Model

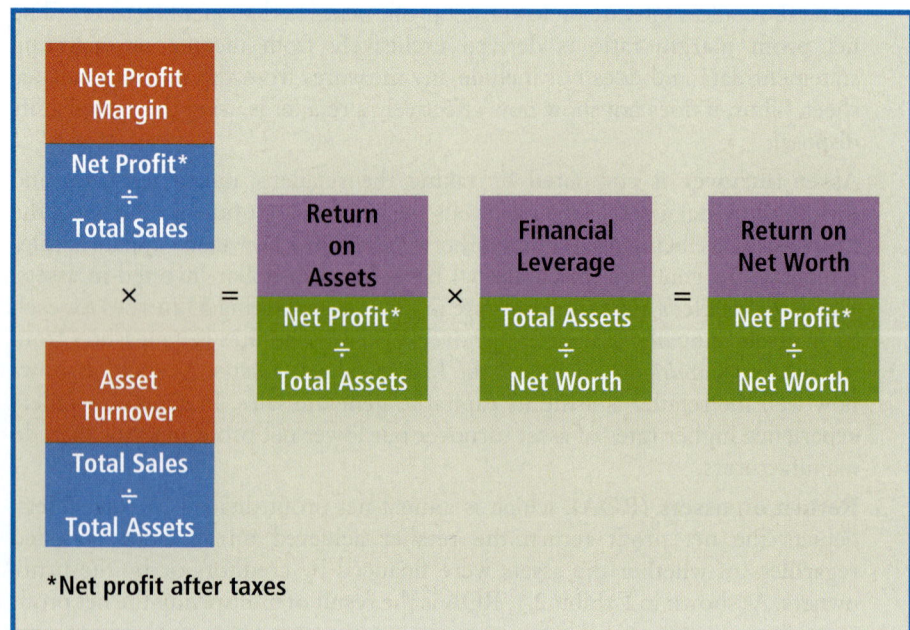

Managers are usually evaluated on return on assets since financial leverage is beyond their control. In addition to the five elements of the SPM, another measure of profitability is the gross margin percentage, which is gross margin divided by net sales.

All retailers establish some form of profit objective. The specific profit objectives developed will play an important role in evaluating potential strategic opportunities.

Productivity Objectives   **Productivity objectives** state how much output the retailer desires for each unit of resource input. The major resources at the retailer's disposal are space, labor, and merchandise; productivity objectives for each may be established.

1. *Space productivity.* Space productivity is defined as net sales divided by the total square feet of retail floor space. (In this discussion, whenever we refer to net sales we are talking about annual net sales.) A space productivity objective states how many dollars in sales the retailer wants to generate for each square foot of store space. As we discussed in Chapter 1, this was one of the major reasons why some retailers are reducing the size of their stores.

    Even retailers selling a service, and not a physical good, have a space utilization problem. This chapter's "Retailing: The Inside Story" describes how service retailers are using yield management tools to improve their space productivity, even if customers and some employees don't like these techniques.

2. *Labor productivity.* Labor productivity is defined as net sales divided by the number of full-time–equivalent employees. A full-time–equivalent employee is one who works 40 hours per week; typically two part-time workers equal one full-time employee. A labor productivity objective reflects how many dollars in sales the retailer desires to generate for each full-time–equivalent employee. Typically, this is measured on an annual basis, but could also reflect weekly or even daily sales per employee such as in retail automobile sales or jewelry store sales.

3. *Merchandise productivity.* Merchandise productivity is net sales divided by the average dollar investment in inventory. This measure is also known as the *sales-to-stock ratio*. Specifically, this objective states the annual dollar sales the retailer desires to generate for each dollar invested in inventory. Sometimes the retailer may state this goal for a merchandising season (such as summer) for an apparel store.

Productivity objectives are vehicles by which a retailer can program its business for high-profit results. For instance, it would be impossible for a supermarket chain to achieve a respectable return on assets while experiencing dismal space (sales per square foot), labor (sales per full-time employee), and merchandise productivity (sales per inventory dollars). In short, productivity is a key determinant of profit in retailing.

Societal Objectives

While generally not as specific or as quantitative as market and financial objectives, **societal objectives** highlight the retailer's concern with broader issues in our society. The five most frequently cited societal objectives are employment objectives, payment of taxes, consumer choice, equity, and being a benefactor.

1. *Employment objectives.* Employment objectives, which were especially significant during the recent recession, relate to the provision of employment

productivity objectives
State the sales objectives that the retailer desires for each unit of resource input: floor space, labor, and inventory investment.

societal objectives
Are those that reflect the retailer's desire to help society fulfill some of its needs.

Retailing: The Inside Story

Is Mickey Mouse Booked in the Seat Next to You?

If you have ever spent time waiting in an airport at a gate for a flight, particularly at a busy time of year like spring break or Thanksgiving, then you have likely seen gate agents calling for volunteers to take vouchers due to an overbooked flight. It is even possible you've seen some passengers sprinting toward the gate at the very last minute only to find out the flight is full and they are denied boarding. This happens because airlines must overbook their flights to make up for no-shows. This overbooking allows airlines to maximize unit revenue or **RASM** (revenue per available seat mile). Using the historical data for each individual flight, airlines try to project the number of no-shows. For example, if a sold-out flight from Chicago to New York carries 112 passengers and the airline determined that four passengers would not show, then the airline would overbook by four passengers to ensure that seats do not go out empty. This is just one of the many tactics that retailers such as airlines employ to maximize revenue. However, as you can imagine, these strategies depend heavily on good data.

However, this system is not foolproof and may even be sabotaged from the inside. Given the negative, and potentially hostile, reactions of consumers who find out they purchased a ticket on an overbooked flight, many gate agents resent this particular tactic. Thus, to provide a cushion, these airline employees might try to enter a fake booking into the reservation system. Thinking that the forecasting system is wrong by overbooking the flight by four, the agents may feel two or three is more appropriate. So they will enter names like "Mickey Mouse" or "Mr. A. Test." Alternately, without intentions related to overbooking at all, a travel agent my try to hold space for "Homer Simpson" or some other fictitious name and forget to cancel the record later. Unfortunately, if these bookings are not caught, they can lead to bad data, which can lead to even more overbooking. The historical rate may have been four, but then with the two other fictitious no-shows, the system will begin to forecast six no-shows for future flights.

As part of the revenue management strategies first introduced in the late 1980s when airlines started using sophisticated software programs to balance supply with demand, **yield management** is the understanding, anticipating, and reacting to changing customer needs in order to maximize the revenue from a fixed capacity of available services. In the airlines' case, this fixed capacity was the number of seats on a plane. In the case of hotels, the number of rooms is fixed; for a golf course, it is available tee times.

Yield management strategy is rather simple. Airlines, for example, use it to maximize their RASM. The key is optimizing the revenue by balancing sales of the expensive seats, rooms, or tee times with the cheap ones. Your college probably uses such a system for its sporting events by trying to find the trade-off between selling discount tickets to fill up the arena and selling expensive tickets at midcourt and only filling up a portion of the arena. At the same time, retailers don't want to unduly offend anyone. Since this process involves understanding target customers and analyzing previous purchases, it can be very challenging, yet exciting.

Yield management works best in markets with five characteristics: (1) low marginal costs, (2) fixed capacity, (3) perishable product, (4) fluctuating demand, and (5) different market segments. These are the same five characteristics facing many service retailers. Let's briefly examine each characteristic and see how it relates to someone selling a service.

1. *Low marginal cost*: Service retailers have a low marginal cost, where the cost of selling one more unit doesn't significantly impact total costs, thus making them want to maximize revenue. Therefore, hotel managers, with a low additional cost of cleaning a room, and airlines, who may burn a little extra fuel to carry the additional passenger, will use yield management to "max out" revenue.

2. *Fixed capacity*: If, for example, hotels could add or remove rooms, then there would be no reason to try to manage capacity. However, since hotels can't add or subtract rooms on a daily basis to meet demand, they can either max out revenue on their existing rooms or lose revenue by pricing a room too inexpensively.

3. *Perishable product*: If a golf course, for example, can't sell all its available tee times one day, the unused inventory can't be stored away for another day. It is lost. Yield management seeks to minimize unused inventory by determining course usage based on history so as to maximize revenue.

4. *Fluctuating demand*: All service retailers have peak seasons and slow seasons that may involve months of the year, days of the week, or hours in a day. Airlines, for example,

increase their revenues by increasing ticket prices over the summer and lowering prices in slow periods and also by the time of day the flight departs and arrives.

5. *Different market segments*: To be effective, yield management must be able to segment the market into different segments that can't cross-sell to each other. Your college, for example, doesn't want students reselling their athletic tickets to nonstudents. Keeping this in mind, service providers seek a trade-off between maximum load factor: highest-paying customers (big donors) versus price-conscious customers (students). One is willing to pay a higher price for seats on the 50-yard line, and the others will settle for cheap end-zone seats. Such a strategy allows colleges to fill seats that would otherwise be empty. Someday soon your college may be using yield management with tuition fees.

---

opportunities for the members of the retailer's community. In good economic times, they may be even more specific and related to hiring the disabled, social minorities, or students.

2. *Payment of taxes*. Paying taxes is the retailer's role in helping finance societal needs that the government deems appropriate, from welfare programs to national parks.

3. *Consumer choice*. A retailer may have an objective of competing in a way that gives consumer a real alternative. A retailer with such an objective desires to be a leader and innovator in merchandising and thus provides the consumer with choices that previously were not available in the trade area. The best example of this choice is Body Shop. The retailer shuns animal testing of its products, purchases ingredients from environmentally friendly producers in the Amazon rain forest, and keeps packaging and promotional material to a minimum. Still, it does carry such controversial offerings as hemp-based oils and soaps.[14]

4. *Equity*. An equity objective reflects the retailer's desire to treat the consumer and suppliers fairly and not endanger their living conditions. In addition, retailers will not engage in price gouging consumers in instances of merchandise shortages. Consumer complaints will be handled quickly, fairly, and equitably. Further, retailers adopting this objective will inform consumers, to the extent possible, of the strengths and weaknesses of its merchandise. Dollar General, for example, was one of the first retailers to install point-of-sale equipment that protected the privacy of shoppers with visual impairments. These devices allowed those of the retailer's customers who had difficulty reading information on a touch screen to privately and independently enter their confidential information. Also, Ethisphere, a leading international think tank dedicated to business ethics, recently honored Gap Inc. as "one of the world's most ethical companies." Gap was cited because it went above and beyond legal minimums to ensure that workers making its merchandise were treated well and received a fair wage for their work.[15]

5. *Being a benefactor*. The retailer may desire to underwrite certain community activities. For example, many department store retailers make meeting rooms available for civic groups to use for meetings. Other retailers help underwrite various performing arts either with cash donations or by hosting social events that in turn help draw customers to their stores. Local supermarkets often sponsor food drives at Thanksgiving and Christmas to aid the needy. Three supermarket chains (Meijer, Publix, and Wegmans) were among the first to

rasm
Is the revenue per available seat mile calculation used by airlines.

yield management
Is the understanding, anticipating, and reacting to changing customer needs in order to maximize the revenue from a fixed capacity of available services.

give away the antibiotics most often taken for childhood ailments such as strep throat. Today many other chains are following their example. Nationally, Target and Walmart each contribute more than $100 million annually to various causes. Even the small $4 billion foundation that was established in 1924 by Sebastian Kresge, the founder of a five-and-dime store bearing his name, continues to offer grants to nonprofit organizations in fields ranging from libraries to food banks and hospitals.[16]

Personal Objectives

personal objectives
Are those that reflect the retailers' desire to help individuals employed in retailing fulfill some of their needs.

The final set of objectives that retailers may establish is personal. **Personal objectives** can relate to the personal goals of any of the employees, managers, or owners of the retail establishment. Generally, retailers tend to pursue three types of personal objectives: self-gratification, status and respect, and power and authority.

1. *Self-gratification.* Self-gratification focuses on the needs and desires of the owners, managers, or employees of the firm and their pursuit of what they truly want out of life. For example, individuals may have opened up a sporting goods store because they enjoy being around athletically oriented people. These individuals may also be avid amateur golfers, and operating a sporting goods store lets them combine work with pleasure. Basically, these individuals are experiencing and living the life they really want.

2. *Status and respect.* All people strive for status and respect. In stating this objective, one recognizes that the owners, managers, and employees need status and respect in their community or within their circle of friends.

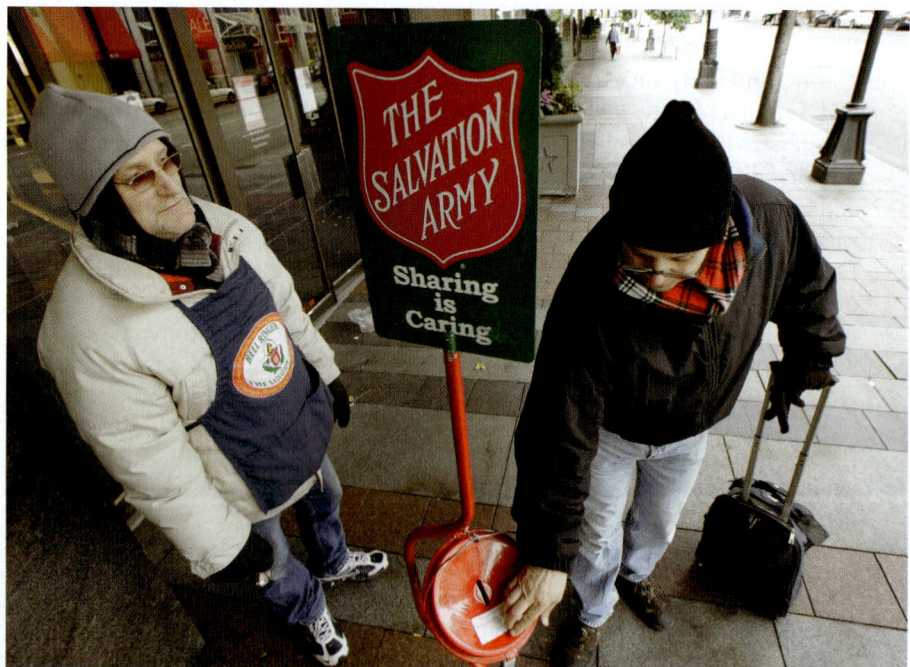

While most retailers desire to help out certain community charities by collecting money outside its doors, doing so may force the retailers to let any and all groups do the same thing on the retailer's property.

Recognizing this need, the retailer may, for example, give annual awards to outstanding employees. For example, not only are Starbucks' employees called "partners," but also the CEO spends hours each week calling store managers to applaud good work.[17]

3. *Power and authority*. Objectives based on power and authority reflect the need of managers and other employees to be in positions of influence. Retailers may establish objectives that give buyers and department managers maximum flexibility to determine their own destiny. They are trusted with the power and authority to allocate scarce resources such as space, dollars, and labor to achieve a profit objective. Many retailers, realizing the importance of keeping customers happy, have empowered their frontline employees with the authority to "make things right" for unhappy customers. Having the power and authority to allocate resources and take care of customers makes employees feel important and gives them a sense of pride when they excel at making things right.

Exhibit 2.2 is a synopsis of the market performance, financial performance, societal, and personal objectives that retailers can establish in the strategic planning process. Clearly revealed in this exhibit is the fact that all retail objectives, of whatever type, must be consistent with and reinforce the retailer's overall mission.

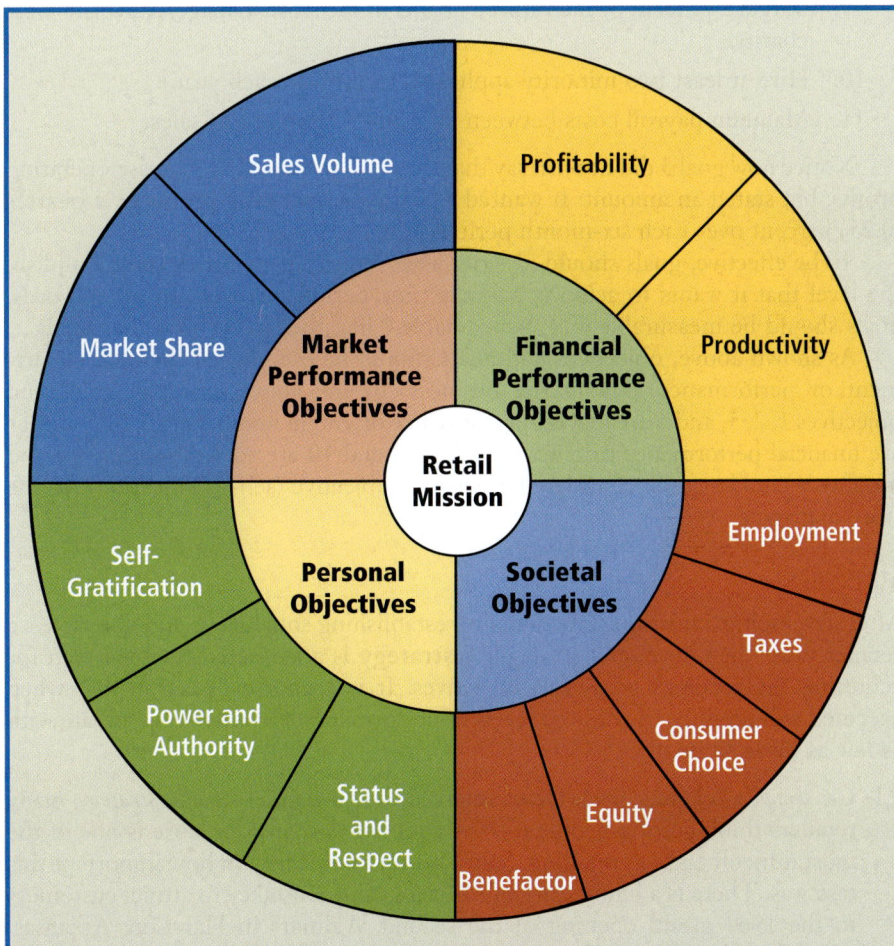

Exhibit 2.2
Retail Objectives

Returning to our earlier discussion, the following are the goals and objectives of another bicycle chain, Bicycle Southwest:

1. Open or acquire one store over the next four years.
2. Remodel one existing store every three years.
3. Increase the operating profit margin in each store by a quarter (0.25) percent for each six-month period.
4. Increase clothing sales in existing stores by 10 percent over the preceding year.
5. Improve the quality of promotion activities, including in-store appearances, publicity, contests, cross-promotions, school promotions, and in-store circulars.
6. Increase awareness and recognition levels of consumers in each new location to equal that of previous existing locations within two years.
7. Improve teamwork among all employees, especially those at similar management levels in order to increase overall labor productivity by 10 percent over the preceding year.
8. Restructure the buying operations so as to coordinate buying activities with other members of the trade association to increase quantity discounts by 20 percent over the next two years.
9. Target 2 percent of each store's profits to the store manager's favorite local charity.
10. Hire at least two minority applicants chainwide each year.
11. Maintain payroll costs between 20.5 and 22 percent of sales.

Notice how goal 3 did not just say that the retailer wanted to increase operating profits, but stated an amount: It wanted to increase operating profits by a quarter (0.25) percent over each six-month period.

To be effective, goals should identify what the company wants to accomplish, the level that it wants to achieve, and the time period involved. In other words, goals should be measurable and "schedulable," like the chain's first four goals.

As shown above, objectives and goals should be established for each department or performance area in the business. In the above example, goals and objectives 1, 2, 5, and 6 are market performance oriented; numbers 3, 4, 6, 7, and 11 are financial performance oriented; numbers 9 and 10 are societal objectives; and number 9 could also be considered a personal objective (self-gratification) for the store managers.

Strategies

After developing a mission statement and establishing some goals and objectives, a retailer must then develop a strategy. A **strategy** is a carefully designed plan for achieving the retailer's goals and objectives. It is a course of action that when executed will produce the desired levels of performance. Retailers can operate with as few as three strategies:

1. *Get shoppers into your store.* Often referred to as a retailer's *traffic strategy*, many retailers think getting people to visit your website or your store is one of the most difficult tasks in retailing. Sam Walton knew early on how important this task was. There is a funny story of Mr. Sam using a donkey to attract customers to the 1964 grand opening of the second Walmart in Harrison, Arkansas.

strategy
Is a carefully designed plan for achieving the retailer's goals and objectives.

Service Retailing

Is Walmart a Service Retailer?

One of the author's closest friends recently retired and bought an RV to travel around the country. In so doing, he soon discovered that the largest and sometimes most crowded campgrounds for RVs weren't KOA Kampgrounds, Good Sam Club Parks (not related to Walmart), or Passport American Parks. Instead, they were one of the nearly 4,000 Walmart and Sam's Club parking lots.

These locations were more appealing than those other "spaces for rent" campgrounds for several reasons. First, staying a night at Walmart saves about $30, thus allowing these RVers to travel longer and farther on a limited budget. Second, the stores' parking lots are well-lit and many times even have security officers and security cameras. Third, all the Walmarts, but not all the Sam's, stores are open all night, and they have RV supplies, souvenirs, food, tools, and medicine. In addition, many even sell gas and diesel. Fourth, most stores are located just off main interstate routes with easy on- and off-ramps, whereas many of the "for rent" spaces are not as conveniently located. And finally, Walmart does not require reservations, so it is an excellent plan B location if other RV parks in the area are full.

So as to not offend either competitors, who are probably big customers for the chain, or local townspeople, Walmart doesn't advertise its open invitation to campers, nor do its free parking spaces provide hookups for water, power, or sewage disposal. It also asks campers not to stay more than a couple of nights. After all, visitors sooner or later are going to have to go to a real rentable campsite to get fresh water and drain their tanks. Still, Walmart caters to RVers in not-so-subtle ways. For example, understanding the value of getting customers into its stores, the retailer from northwest Arkansas customizes the Rand McNally road atlas sold at all its stores to include the address of each store and its map coordinates. Campers, after all, are profitable customers. In some cases, a camper may spend more than $300, but the average is between $50 and $100. As a result, stores in heavily traveled areas stock extensive recreation-vehicle and camping supplies, which have high gross margins.

Data from the Recreation Vehicle Industry Association (RVIA) indicates that 8.5 million households in the United States currently own at least one RV, and the RVIA expects that number to grow as baby boomers retire. These people like to travel, like the comforts of their own home, and, best of all, have money to spend. Thus, it seems that Walmart will continue as a service retailer.

Source: This box is based on information provided by Charles W. Mayers and used with his written permission.

David Glass, who replaced Mr. Walton as head of the chain, talks about this famous first meeting with Walton and the donkey on the Walmart website (http://walmartstores.com/AboutUs/288.aspx). Today, Walmart knows the importance of getting consumers into its stores. In fact, as this chapter's "Service Retailing" box illustrates, the chain has even become a service retailer in its efforts to attract more consumers to its stores.

2. *Convert these shoppers into customers by having them purchase merchandise.* Often referred to as a "retailer's conversion" or "closure" strategy, this means having the right merchandise, using the right layout and display, and having the right sales force. Each year, the average retailer loses 20 percent to 40 percent of its customers because it didn't take care of them after they entered the store.[18] The customers may claim that there was "no special reason" that no purchase was made. However, the truth is probably that the retailer neglected the customer. This is particularly important to remember since it costs five times as much money to get a new customer into a store as it does to make a sale to someone who had already shopped there or to retain a current customer who may be unhappy. While the issue of generating traffic will be covered later in

Global Retailing

International Retailers May Be Better at Getting Them into the Store

The late Stanley Marcus of Neiman Marcus fame always complained about how American retailers lacked creativity in developing strategies to get shoppers to come back to their stores. This was especially bothersome to him because he realized that it costs five times as much money to get a new customer into a store than it did to get someone who was already a customer back inside to shop. Little wonder, then, that the National Retail Federation considers "customer retention" the major issue facing retailers today.[19]

Most American retailers just aren't creative enough when it comes to generating repeat business. However, successful ones, such as some big box stores, have recently opened more checkout lines in order to avoid the dreaded "long line" reputation. Small, but savvy, fast-food restaurants are copying their fine-dining cousins to make their regular customers feel special: selling items that aren't listed on the public menu. Chipotle, for example, serves off-the-menu quesadillas, while smoothie franchise Jamba Juice makes a host of unlisted smoothies, including Peanut Butter & Jelly and Rainbow Gummie.[20] Even Home Depot offers classes on everything from how to cut energy bills to retiling your bathroom. Yet none of these are as creative as the pure genius used by some international retailers.

Several years ago, an author saw people were lined up more than a hundred deep waiting to enter an IKEA furniture store in early December. Now, the author could understand such a line outside an electronic store, but not a furniture store. After all, furniture is not on many consumers' Christmas wish lists.

What IKEA did was to show American retailers how to run a promotion without giving away the store. The Swedish furniture chain found a different way to build store traffic, which meant increased sales. IKEA, which is already perceived as having the lowest prices, built traffic not by lowering prices even more, as many retailers are accustomed to doing, but by renting Christmas trees.

The foreign retailer ran newspaper advertisements proclaiming that "The spirit of Christmas can't be bought, but for $10 you can rent it." The fine print explained that for $20 ($10 for the rental and a $10 deposit), IKEA would rent the customer a beautiful Douglas fir. (The going purchase price for similar trees at that time was $50 and up.) "After the holidays, just return the tree, pick up your deposit and IKEA will mulch the tree for your garden or donate the mulch to the community. You will also receive a coupon for a free four-year-old Blue Spruce sapling to help save the environment. You can pick up your free tree the first week in April."

While other retailers were running price special after price special, IKEA was fighting off the crowds. IKEA made it worthwhile to not just visit the store but also travel through the entire cavernous structure to complete the transaction at the rear of the store three separate times. Without resorting to discounts, IKEA had the customers lined up, while other furniture stores were empty or selling merchandise below cost. No wonder, then, that IKEA was able to generate great fanfare and hordes of customers.

Similarly, Walmart, with its understanding of the value of getting consumers into its stores, has adapted to local customs in foreign markets. Despite not being successful with its German operation, it did learn another method of drawing customers into its stores with "Singles Shopping." The chain's Dortmund, Germany, store started its singles shopping event almost a decade ago at the suggestion of workers who thought it might help an unmarried bakery worker at the store who complained about being too old for discos and too proud for Internet dating. Soon, every Friday night became a "singles night" at the store, and the event was widespread with other German Walmarts.

The night begins with workers greeting consumers at the store's entrance with a glass of sparkling wine and freshly shucked oysters. They take photos of the customers and tack them on a singles bulletin board, along with their age, interests, and the qualities they seek in a prospective partner. Customers are then sent off with a shopping cart outfitted with a bright-red bow denoting their unmarried status. By the way, Walmart told women who arrive in groups that they "should split up because men can be leery of approaching a pack of women."

Walmart did try the German experiment at a couple of U.S. stores, but it didn't catch on. Still, it was a creative attempt at getting consumers to come back in its stores more often.

this text, the current chapter's "Global Retailing" box illustrates two very different approaches aimed at getting consumers back in a retailer's store.

3. *Do this (get shoppers in your store and convert them into customers) at the lowest operating cost possible that is consistent with the level of service that your customers expect.* This is often referred to as a "retailer's cost management" strategy. Remember, as we pointed out in Chapter 1, most of a product's cost gets added after the item is produced and moves from the factory to the retailer's shelf and finally to the consumer. Thus, good strategies that reduce operating costs while providing the appropriate level of service present significant opportunities for retailers. A great example is a story that Sam Walton loved to tell. He claimed that one of the greatest retail lessons he ever learned, and a major contributor to Walmart's amazing growth rate, came when James Cash Penney visited the Des Moines, Iowa, Penney's store where Sam was a trainee. While Mr. Penney was wandering through the store, a customer approached Sam to buy a set of work clothes for her husband.

Mr. Penney watched from a distance while Sam took excellent care of the customer. Sam wrapped the work shirt and pants in a package (using paper off a roll and string to tie it), gave the customer her change, and thanked her for shopping at Penney's. Sam was proud of the way he handled the transaction and thought he might even merit praise from Mr. Penney. Sure enough, Mr. Penney came over to Sam and said, "Young man, I want to show you something."

Mr. Penney proceeded to get a set of work clothes, just like the woman had purchased, and wrapped it with paper from the roll that overlapped by less than an inch. Then using half the string Sam used, he tied the package. After handing the newly wrapped package to Sam to examine, he imparted his wisdom: "Young man, you know we don't make money on the merchandise we sell. We make our profit on the paper and string we save."

That lesson was never lost on Sam Walton, and today Walmart's executives still preach it. Little wonder then that one executive was quoted as telling an investor conference that "the misconception is that we're in the retail business. Actually, we're in the distribution business." Furthermore, the executive added, although it is generally believed that Walmart buys and sells at the lowest price, in fact, Walmart sells at the lowest price because it has the lowest distribution costs.[21]

The question is often asked, why would a retailer ever want to get rid of a customer? The answer is simple: If the customer will never be profitable because of size, location, or other demands, then that customer must be dropped. Years ago, the author consulted with a mail-order retailer. Ten percent of the retailer's customers would never be profitable since their economic circumstances limited their purchases to less than $50 per year. However, just the cost of sending them four large catalogs per year exceeded $35. After subtracting the cost of the merchandise sold, the retailer was guaranteed to lose money. When management was told to drop these customers, one executive asked "What if they go to our competition?" "You should be so lucky" was the reply. After all, now the rival would have these unprofitable customers, and the client could concentrate only on the profitable customers. Also, if a customer drives other more profitable prospective shoppers away, then the retailer should consider dropping that customer as well. This is also why some malls lament the fact that Friday nights are now prime cruising hours for teenagers. These malls regard the teens as too loud, prone to cussing, and having attitude issues. As a result, they drive away profitable adult shoppers. Thus, despite the fact that teens, especially before they became electronically connected, were once a very profitable segment for a mall, they are now unwanted. These malls now pipe in slow soft music and use overhead lights that accent the teens' pimples.

While the preceding strategies may seem too simple to be operational, they actually do summarize the tasks that every retailer must perform. Many retailers go further and develop strategies that enable them to differentiate themselves from the competition as they accomplish these three tasks.

However, one of the greatest failings in retailing today is that too many retailers have concentrated on just one means of differentiation: price. Price promotions usually attract, but rarely hold, customers. Starbucks, for example, has never used a price promotion because it has realized that the customers gained with price promotions are just as apt to switch to another retailer when it cuts its price below yours. As a result of these constant price deals, retailers have taught consumers that if they wait—and, in many cases, this wait is only a matter of days—the desired merchandise will go on sale. Unless a retailer has substantially lower operating costs than its competitors, as Walmart does, then this is a very dangerous strategy since the competition can easily copy it, resulting in reduced profits or even losses. Some better forms of differentiation for a retailer are physical differentiation of the product, the selling process, after-purchase satisfaction, location, and never being out of stock.

1. *Physical differentiation of the product.* Target follows this strategy with its brilliant and innovative merchandising. It keeps adding apparel by new designers from around the world.[22] Another example is Torrid, a retailer offering cool clothes for plus-sized girls and young women (sizes 12 to 26), who can now match the style, excitement, and selection available at standard size fashion retailers. Casual Male XL is the men's equivalent of this retailer. However, the best example of a retailer differentiating itself from the competition may be the supermarkets. They have learned to avoid getting into a price war with local supercenters and warehouse clubs. Instead they focus on less-hectic stores with exotic or difficult-to-match products and greater convenience. In addition, they cut back on drugs and health and beauty products, which are the discounters' strengths, to stress fresh produce, higher-quality meat, and easy-to-prepare foods. Subdued lighting and high-end selections buttress the nondiscounter experience.[23]

2. *The selling process.* For example, Nordstrom's, Neiman Marcus, and many local jewelers connect with their target customers through their excellent customer service. This also includes speeding up the checkout process. After all, if customers have 20 minutes to spend shopping, they don't want to use five to seven of those minutes just trying to pay the bill.

3. *After-purchase satisfaction.* Many high-quality bike repair shops and major retailers, such as L.L. Bean Inc., achieve this with their "satisfaction guaranteed" programs that enable customers to return with their bike or send back the item of clothing, even after years of wear.

4. *Location.* Stores such as Dollar General and Family Dollar excel at this form of differentiation. These stores used to be considered afterthoughts of American retailing, with a marginalized presence in an industry that thrived on larger, more theatrical outlets. Not today. Dollar stores are generating impressive sales increases with a compelling price, value, and convenience model. The growing consumer appeal of these stores is that they are usually located in strip centers en route to a nearby supercenter, capturing shoppers who would rather

pick up their toothpaste and motor oil quickly instead of searching a cavernous building offering tires and tomatoes, shirts and soup, and bananas and car batteries. In addition, the small size of their stores gives these retailers advantages in negotiating leases in an industry with a surplus of stores, thus reducing their operating costs.

5. *Never being out of stock.* This means being in stock with regard to the sizes, colors, and styles that the target market expects the retailer to carry. For example, Nordstrom offers a free shirt if it is out of stock on a basic size.

These means of differentiation will not only get more consumers into your store but also result in their buying more merchandise once they are there. Note also that in all these examples the retailers are able to develop their own unique niches in the minds of consumers and thus avoid price wars.

So how does a retailer develop a strategy to differentiate itself? This starts with an analysis of the retailer's strengths and weaknesses as well as the threats and opportunities that exist in the environment. This process, which is often referred to as *SWOT analysis* (SWOT for *strengths, weaknesses, opportunities,* and *threats*), involves asking the following questions.

Retailers can differentiate their offerings by excellent product assortment and high personalized service. However, such stores usually need to price higher than other retailers.

Strengths

What major competitive advantage(s) do we have? (These could be lower prices, better locations, better store personnel, etc.)

What are we good at? (This might be the ability to anticipate customer demands better than the competition so that the merchandise is there when the customer wants it.)

What do customers perceive as our strong points? (Customers might perceive that we offer the "best value for the dollar.")

Weaknesses

What major competitive advantage(s) do competitors have over us? (Do they have lower prices, better locations, salespeople, etc.?)

What are competitors better at than we are? (Do they do a better job of selecting merchandise, anticipating demand?)

What are our major internal weaknesses? (Do we do a poor job of employee training? Are our stores in need of remodeling?)

Opportunities

What favorable environmental trends may benefit our firm? (Is our market size growing? Are family income levels rising in our market? Is merchandise priced correctly for the target market?)

What is the competition doing in our market? (Are new firms entering or are existing firms leaving? What is the impact on us?)

What areas of business that are closely related to ours are undeveloped? (Is it possible for us to expand into a related field serving the same customers and take advantage of our good name in the marketplace?)

Threats

What unfortunate environmental trends may hurt our future performance? (Has deflation caused consumers to delay purchasing durable goods hoping that next year prices will be significantly lower? As a result, has the consumer become both price and time sensitive? Has this prevented us from raising our prices in order to pass increasing costs on to consumers? How could our competitor's prices, new products, or services hurt us? Could the entrance of new competitors or the loss of suppliers hurt us?)

What technology is on the horizon that may soon have an impact on our firm? (Will some new electronic equipment soon replace our manual way of performing activities?)

Exhibit 2.3 is the SWOT analysis for a TrueValue store. This family-operated and locally owned hardware store dates back more than 100 years. Although many of these small hardware stores have fallen prey to strong national chain competition from the big box giants such as Home Depot and Lowe's, many continue to survive and prosper in their local communities. This has often been attributed to these independents joining a wholesale cooperative or buying group that helps them achieve efficiencies rivaling those of the national chains. During the 1930s, John Cotter founded Cotter & Company as a retailer-owned wholesale buying cooperative. Cotter & Company was able to pool the purchasing power of many independent retailers to obtain significant buying and distribution economies that allowed the small hardware retailer to compete with the rapidly growing chain stores. In 1997, Cotter & Company merged with ServiStar Coast to Coast, another large retailer-owned wholesale buying cooperative. The combined cooperative was

Exhibit 2.3
Exhibit 2.3
SWOT Analysis for TrueValue

SWOT Analysis Shows How TrueValue Hardware Stores Continue to Succeed

Strengths

What are the major competitive advantages a TrueValue hardware store has over the competition?

TrueValue has a catchy name that combines a key brand (itself) with the name of a local owner—for example, Jim Ruhl's TrueValue Hardware Store. Thus, the store has the integrity of a respected national brand combined with the name of a well-known and respected local operator.

TrueValue's commitment comes from management owning the business. The stores are almost all operated by the people who own the stores. This aligns the interest of the day-to-day managers with the customers. Customer service is generally high because if customers are not served well and do not return, then the financial impact will be immediately felt by the owner–manager.

TrueValue is able to be the only retailer selling a widely recognized, high-quality product such as Stihl. In fact, as a result of a cooperative advertising agreement, TrueValue dealers can run ads saying they carried Stihl products—and that these products weren't available at Lowe's or Home Depot.[24]

Because the stores are locally owned and managed, managers have a very good sense of their trade area and the needs of people in that trade area. Also, since buying is not centralized like it is in a big retail chain, the buying for each store is more in tune with local demand patterns. Many owner–managers know what specific households in the trade area might need and thus order merchandise in anticipation of selling to these households on an individual level. Also, these managers know the names of virtually all of their regular customers and personally greet them when they enter the store. In short, they practice micromarketing.

Most TrueValue stores are in lower-rent facilities that are owned and free of mortgages or debt payments. This allows these retailers to have lower break-even points and to better withstand competitive assaults.

Weaknesses

What are the major competitive advantages that big box retailers have over a TrueValue hardware store?

Home Depot and Lowe's have strong promotional orientations. Often these retailers have local and national television advertising coupled with a heavy use of newspaper inserts. Many times they will run 24 to 36 newspaper inserts per year, which means these large national chains do a better job of creating customer awareness.

Home Depot and Lowe's offer more than 60,000 items, or stockkeeping units (or SKUs, the lowest level of identification of merchandise), compared to a TrueValue store, which may have fewer than 15,000 items. A big box store will be more than 100,000 square feet; a TrueValue store will generally be less than 12,000 square feet.

Home Depot and Lowe's are much more aggressive in pricing frequently purchased and highly visible items. On high-turnover items such as garden hoses, popular lumber sizes, small tools, and gardening items, they are low-price-point competitors.

What are some of the major internal weaknesses of a typical TrueValue hardware store?

A typical store is not operated by computer savvy managers. Although some TrueValue operators are capitalizing on information technology, many other owners do not recognize or pursue the potential of a fully computerized inventory management and purchasing system.

Most stores lack depth of management. If the owner is absent from the store for an extended time due to illness, becomes disabled, or dies, there is often not another person in line to take over operations and ownership. Also, since some stores are independently owned, TrueValue stores sometimes present an inconsistent image across the country. Some stores are immaculate and clean and well organized, while other stores may be dusty and cluttered. But there is little that TrueValue can do. After all, it is difficult to enforce standards of operations with independent store owners.

Many stores, because they are operated by the owners, do not have seven day a week, morning to night operating hours. A big box store is open seven days a week and more than 75 hours; a TrueValue store is often open only six days a week and fewer than 60 hours per week.

(continued)

Exhibit 2.3
(continued)

Opportunities

What favorable environmental trends exist that may benefit a TrueValue Hardware store?

Because dual-income families have less time, people want to shop closer to home. Trips to large malls and shopping areas are declining, and trips to neighborhood shopping centers are on the rise. Also, people are finding that big 100,000 square foot stores are often too big when a shopper only needs a few items. Most TrueValue stores are small in size and located in small community or strip malls. It is noteworthy that Home Depot has noticed this opportunity and is building a new chain of small stores called Villager Hardware. The number of homeowners planning do-it-yourself home-improvement projects has been increasing yearly for two decades. Although many homeowners enjoy doing these projects, they often need advice during the project. TrueValue retailers, with their focus on customer service and knowledgeable staff, can provide excellent service to this highly profitable customer segment.

The phenomenal growth of the Internet has many more households shopping online for hardware and home-improvement items. This is an opportunity for TrueValue hardware stores because the co-op has built an e-tailing site that allows local customers to purchase an expanded assortment of products from their local TrueValue retailer. Rather than being restricted in items (SKUs) due to space constraints, TrueValue retailers can now offer their customers more than 100,000 SKUs.

Threats

What unfortunate environmental trends exist that may hurt future performance TrueValue retailers?

Many owners are finding that their children do not want to take over the family hardware business. These children are moving to other geographical areas and pursuing other careers. The government reporting requirements on small, single-unit businesses are often as many as for a multiunit chain store. Consequently, the time required to meet local, county, state, and federal regulations and do all the associated paperwork is becoming increasingly burdensome.

Source: The authors acknowledge the assistance of Professor Leslie D. Stoel, Ohio State University, with this SWOT analysis.

---

renamed TRU*SERV and had annual sales of more than $6 billion. Today, TRU*SERV supplies more than 6,500 members who operate nearly 10,000 stores. Exhibit 2.3 shows how a SWOT analysis might look for a successful family-operated TrueValue hardware store.

Now the retailer is ready to develop strategies to accomplish its objectives. Again, notice the close relationship between a retailer's goals and objectives and its strategies. Objectives indicate what the retailer wants to accomplish, and strategies indicate how the retailer will attempt to accomplish those goals with the resources available.

The retailer must develop a retail marketing strategy with strong financial elements. A fully developed marketing strategy should address the following considerations: the specific target market, location, the specific retail mix that the retailer intends to use, and the retailer's value proposition.

target market
Is the group of customers that the retailer is seeking to serve.

1. The specific **target market** is the group or groups of customers that the retailer is seeking to serve. It is important for retailers to understand that different target markets demand different product offerings. For this reason, successful retailers must determine which customers make them the most money and then segment them carefully, realign their stores, and empower employees to target those favored shoppers with products and services that will encourage them to spend more and come back often.[25] Exhibit 2.4 illustrates Best Buy's targeting process. The left side of the box shows five different target markets that Best Buy is trying to reach. The center shows the offerings or services that Best Buy will feature in the stores catering to those

Exhibit 2.4

Features Offered by Best Buy to Meet the Needs of Its Various Customer Types

Customer Type	Feature Offering by Store	Customer Name
Affluent tech and home theater enthusiast	Magnolia Home Theater, Geek Squad	Barry
Busy suburban mom	Personal shopping assistant, Geek Squad	Jill
Small business owner	Business pros, Geek Squad	Buzz
Young tech gadget enthusiast	Interactive displays, tailored market assortments, Geek Squad	Ray
Family man seeking good value	Geek Squad, special offers	Mr. Storefront

Source: Used with the written permission of Best Buy.

target markets. The far right lists the customer name that the retailer has assigned each target. According to Best Buy, each of its stores will be aimed at one or two of these customer types.

2. A **location**—whether a traditional store in a geographic space, a person's home in relation to a print catalog or television shopping, or a virtual store in cyberspace—should be consistent with the needs and wants of the desired target market.

3. The specific **retail mix** a retailer intends to use to appeal to its target market and thereby meet its financial objectives is the combination of merchandise, price, advertising and promotion, location, customer services and selling, and store layout and design that the retailer uses to satisfy the target market (see Exhibit 2.5). This chapter's "What's New?" box describes how one U.K. retailer, with the help of a research firm analyzing the data gathered from the chain's loyalty card, was able to tailor its retail mix to withstand the arrival of Walmart.

4. The retailer's **value proposition** is a clear statement of the tangible and intangible results a customer receives from using the retailer's products or services. It is the difference between the benefits offered by one retailer versus those of the competition. A good value proposition answers the question of "Why should I buy this product or service from this retailer?" Walmart has a very simple value proposition; "Save Money, Live Better." In brief, if you shop Walmart you will get the same market offering as other retailers at a lower price and you can then use the savings to enhance your lifestyle in other areas. This is an example of a simple yet compelling value proposition.

Consider the remarks by Stanley Marcus in this chapter's "Global Retailing" box: Retailers all too often show a lack of creativity in developing their value proposition. As a result, they usually react to bad economic times and declining sales by cutting back on all expenses and claiming they are going to get back to "basics." No one is really sure what these "basics" are, but shouldn't these retailers have been taking care of the basics all along? Bad economic conditions are not the time to get aggressive on pricing; they are the time to make sure you have a relevant and easy-to-define value that will transcend good and hard times. After all, if everybody is looking to reduce prices and highlight promotions, then a successful retailer must do something else. It is this something else—the products, the services, the unique take on what a shopper's retail experience should be—that spells out the difference between profit and loss.

location
Is the geographic space or cyberspace where the retailer conducts business.

retail mix
Is the combination of merchandise, price, advertising and promotion, location, customer service and selling, and store layout and design.

value proposition
Is a clear statement of the tangible and/or intangible results a customer/or intangible results a customer receives from shopping at and using the retailer's products or services.

Exhibit 2.5
Retail Mix

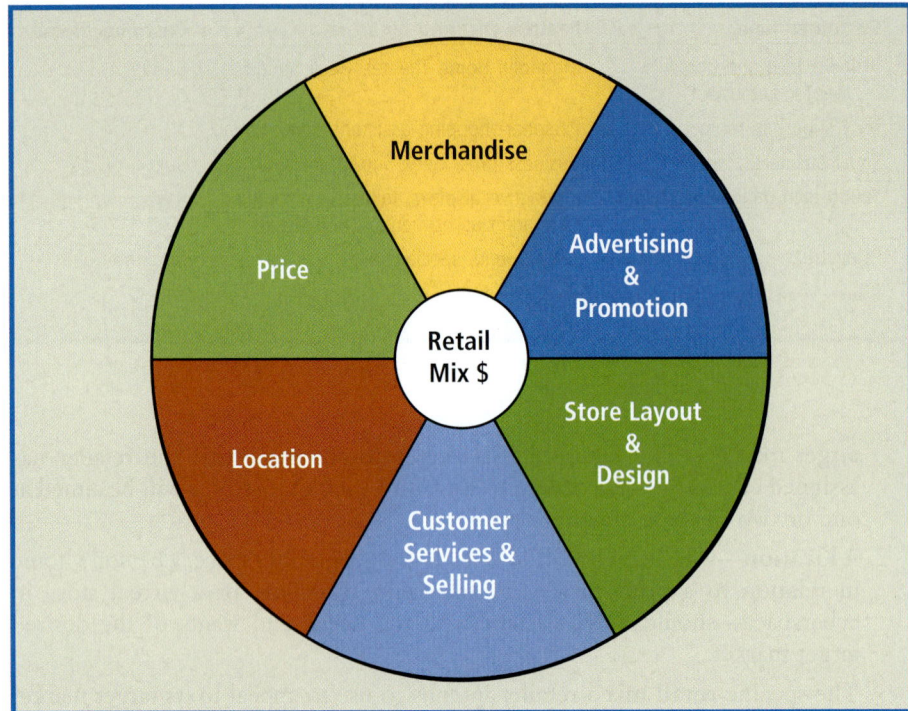

The Retail Strategic Planning and Operations Management Model

Describe the retail strategic planning and operations management model.

Exhibit 2.6, our strategic planning and operations management model, suggests that a retailer must engage in two types of planning and management tasks: strategic planning and operations management. Each task is undertaken to achieve high-profit results. At this point, take a few moments to study this model.

As explained in Chapter 1, this book has an environmental orientation, a management planning orientation, a profit orientation, and a decision-making orientation. You will note that the environmental orientation is represented by the top and bottom bars in Exhibit 2.6, the management planning orientation by the first five vertical sections (strategic planning and operations management), the profit orientation by the high profit box at the far right, and the decision-making orientation by all the decisions that the retailer must make throughout this model.

Strategic Planning

Strategic planning, as we pointed out at the beginning of the chapter, is concerned with how the retailer responds to the environment in an effort to establish a long-term course of action. In principle, the retailer's strategic planning should best reflect the line(s) of trade in which the retailer will operate, the market(s) it will pursue, and the retail mix it will use. Remember, strategic planning requires a long-term commitment of resources by the retailer. An error in strategic planning can result in a decline in profitability, bankruptcy, or a loss of competitive position. On the other hand, effective strategic planning can help protect the retailer against competitive onslaughts.

What's New?

Buy Diapers for the First Time and You Will Get a Coupon for Beer

Twenty years ago, when Walmart entered the United Kingdom by buying the Asda supermarket chain, most Americans assumed that the Bentonville, Arkansas, giant would soon control that country's grocery market as it had done in the United States. However, a local retailer, Tesco, was able to develop a strategy based on using customer information to combat Walmart's core appeal: low prices.

Tesco became the United Kingdom's first supermarket chain to introduce a loyalty program with its Clubcard. On doing so, leading U.K. food chain Sainsbury was quoted as calling Tesco's introduction a gimmick, something akin to "electronic Green Shield stamps." Asda/Walmart didn't think customers wanted to have Tesco track their purchases.

However, Tesco, with the aid of a U.K. marketing research firm, dunnhumby, searched the database generated by its Clubcard, and singled out shoppers who bought the cheapest available item. After all, they would be the most likely to switch over to Asda/Walmart. Tesco identified 300 items that these price-sensitive shoppers regularly bought and lowered the prices of these products. As a result, most shoppers didn't defect to Asda/Walmart. In fact, Tesco's current market share in groceries is 31 percent, which is double that of Asda/Walmart.

The firm dunnhumby, which was founded by a wife and husband team, Edwina Dunn and Clive Humby, doesn't help retailers get new customers. Rather, by crunching data from a retailer's credit-card transactions and its loyalty program, dunnhumby helps make sure they stay customers. By slicing and dicing customer information to the nth degree, the research firm is able to discover hidden and lucrative facts about clients' current customers. Then dunnhumby determines who might respond when a particular item goes on sale, or who will switch to another retailer if a certain product is dropped. Such intelligence enabled dunnhumby to tell Tesco that when shoppers buy diapers for the first time, the retailer should mail those families store coupons for baby wipes and toys—and beer. After all, new fathers tend to buy more beer because they are apt to be home with the baby and can't go to the pub.

Today, Home Depot is using dunnhumby USA to help it gain insight about the "portfolio of professionals"—carpenters, roofers, janitors—who spend far more than the average weekend warrior; and Kroger has entered into a 50–50 joint venture with dunnhumby to manage the grocer's loyalty card program and advise it on how to improve in-store promotions.

Source: Based on *Scoring Points: How Tesco Continues to Win Customer Loyalty*, 2nd ed. (Philadelphia: Kogan Press, 2007) and material supplied by dunnhumby USA, Cincinnati, Ohio, and used with the written permission of dunnhumby USA.

The initial steps in strategic planning are to define the firm's mission, establish goals and objectives, and perform a SWOT analysis. The next steps are to select the target market and appropriate location(s). It is important to note that most retail managers or executives have very little control over location decisions. A newly appointed manager for a chain department store could change promotional strategy, personnel, service levels, credit policies, and even prices but in all likelihood would be constrained by a long-term lease agreement. In fact, only the senior management of most chains is ever involved in location decisions. For the small retailer just starting out, however, or retailers considering expansion, location is an important decision. A full discussion of location and site selection appears in Chapter 7.

After selecting the target market and location, the retailer must develop the firm's retail mix. Retailers can best perform this strategic planning only after assessing the external environment. They should be looking for an opportunity to fulfill the needs of a defined group of consumers (i.e., their target market) in a way that sets them apart from the competition. In other words, retailers should strive to seek a differential advantage over the competition. Retailers will rarely discover a means of gaining a differential advantage by reviewing their own internal

Exhibit 2.6
Retail Strategic Planning
and Operations
Management Model

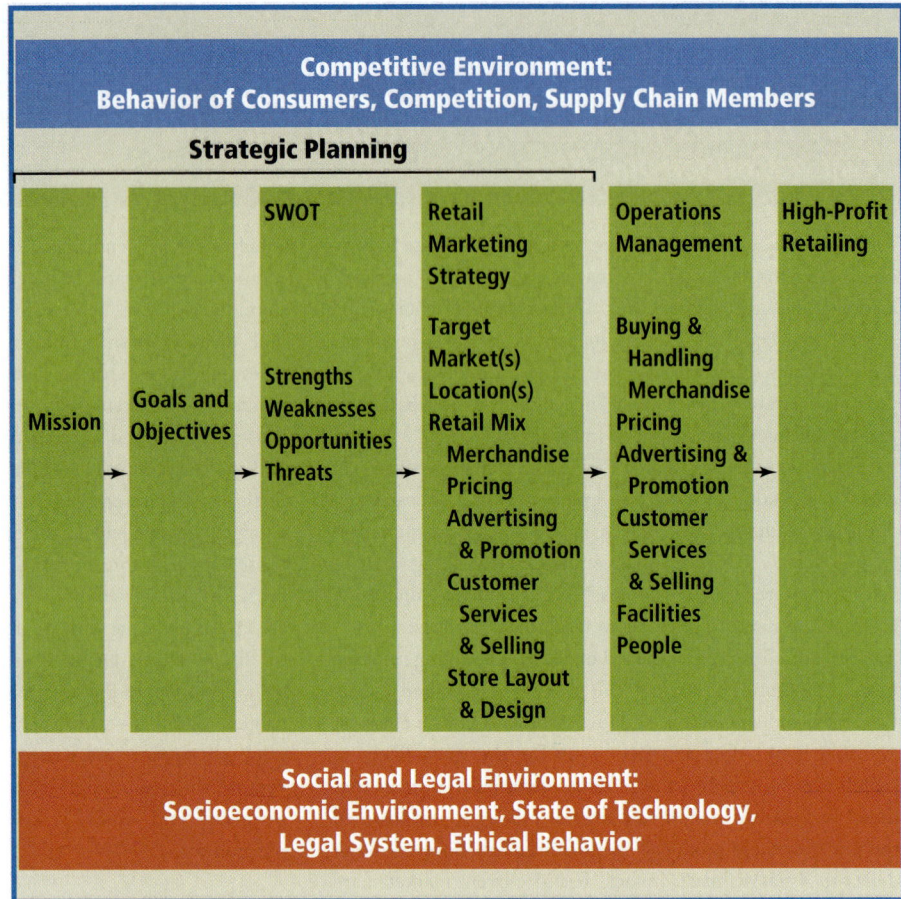

Competitive Environment: Behavior of Consumers, Competition, Supply Chain Members					
Strategic Planning					

Mission	Goals and Objectives	**SWOT**
		 Strengths
		 Weaknesses
		 Opportunities
		 Threats
			Retail Marketing Strategy
			
			 Target Market(s)
			 Location(s)
			 Retail Mix
			  Merchandise
			  Pricing
			  Advertising
			  & Promotion
			  Customer
			  Services
			  & Selling
			  Store Layout
			  & Design
				Operations Management
				
				 Buying & Handling Merchandise
				 Pricing
				 Advertising & Promotion
				 Customer Services & Selling
				 Facilities
				 People
					High-Profit Retailing

Social and Legal Environment: Socioeconomic Environment, State of Technology, Legal System, Ethical Behavior					

operations or by focusing exclusively on the conventional industry structure. Strategic planning opportunities are to be found in the realities of a constantly changing environment. An effective retail strategy can result only from matching environmental forces with a retail marketing program that satisfies the customer better than anybody else. For example, Foot Locker has found success by concentrating on a very narrow segment of the shoe market but offering a very large selection.

Exhibit 2.6 profiles the major environmental forces that should be assessed. Briefly these are consumer behavior, competitor behavior, supply chain behavior, the socioeconomic environment, the technological environment, and the legal and ethical environment.

1. *Consumer behavior.* The behavior of consumers will obviously have a significant impact on the retailer's future. Specifically, the retailer will need to understand the determinants of shopping behavior so that it can identify likely changes in that behavior and develop appropriate strategies. When you think about it, the successful retailers are those that didn't wait for their customers to request something. They are the ones who paid attention, used a little imagination, and solved the need before the customers' requests. Amazon.com is an example of a retailer that has automated this process by the use of software that analyzes what customers purchase and compares this to the purchases of other customers and then anticipates other books and products a customer would

want to purchase. Some auto dealers keep track of how much you drive and then e-mail you or call you to remind you that your auto needs servicing. This is anticipatory marketing, and it is growing considerably in retailing.

2. *Competitor behavior.* How competing retailers behave will have a major impact on the most appropriate strategy. Retailers must develop a competitive strategy that is not easily imitated, which happens all too often with price cuts.

3. *Supply chain behavior.* The behavior of members of the retailer's supply chain can have a significant impact on the retailer's future. For example, are certain supply chain members such as manufacturers or wholesalers always seeking to improve their position in the supply chain by establishing their own Internet sites and thus bypassing the retailer? Remember, back in Chapter 1, we discussed the impact of such a move by the airlines as they tried to bypass the travel agents.

4. *Socioeconomic environment.* The retailer must understand how economic and demographic trends will influence revenues and costs in the future and adapt its strategy according to these changes.

5. *Technological environment.* The technical frontiers of the retail system encompass new and better ways of performing standard retail functions. The retailer must always be aware of opportunities for lowering operating costs.

6. *Legal and ethical environment.* The retailer should be familiar with local, state, and federal regulations of the retail system. It must also understand evolving legal patterns in order to be able to design future retail strategies that are legally defensible. At the same time, the retailer must operate at the highest level of ethical behavior.

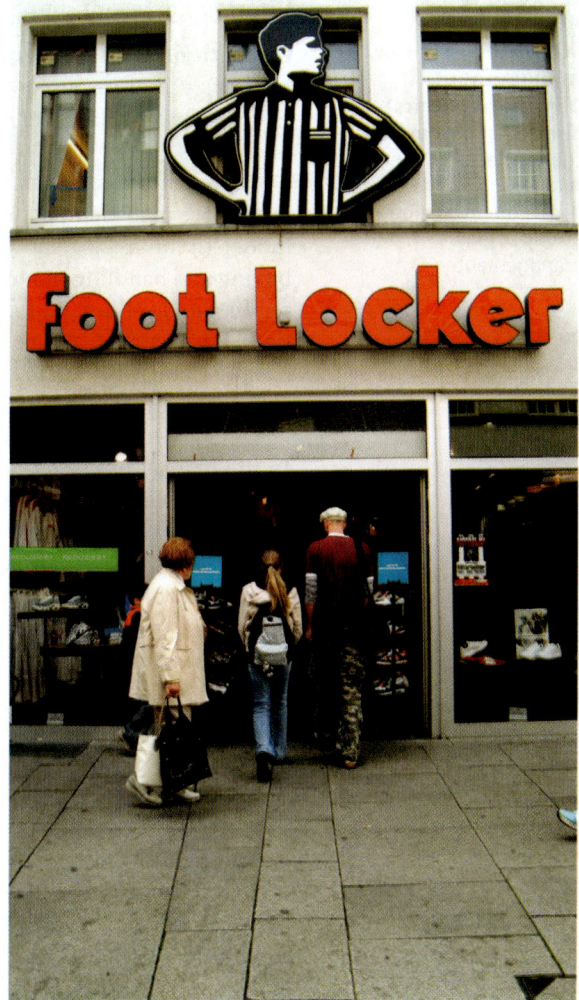

Foot Locker operates in countries outside its home country of the United States and thus needs to understand the environmental forces that face each country. This is a Foot Locker store in Osnabruck, Germany, one of over 500 stores it has in Europe.

Detailed discussions of these environmental forces will be provided in Chapters 3 through 6. For now, realize that although these forces cannot be controlled by a single retailer, the threats emanating from them are often translated into opportunities by successful retailers. For example, Macy's once was an independent operation that catered to the working classes of New York, but due to increasing competition and the ability to spot future environmental changes, it has now become a major national chain operation with 800 stores and nearly $30 billion in sales. (See the case in this chapter for more on Macy's.)

After reviewing its mission, objectives, and environment and developing its retail marketing strategy, the retailer should be able to develop alternative uses of resources in order to obtain the highest performance level. Next the retailer must determine which strategy will yield the best results. Finally, the retailer will concentrate on operations management.

operations management
Deals with activities directed at maximizing the efficiency of the retailer's use of resources. It is frequently referred to as day-to-day management.

Operations Management

Operations management is concerned with maximizing the efficiency of the retailer's use of resources and with how the retailer converts these resources into sales and profits. In other words, its aim is to maximize the performance of current operations.

Most of the retailer's time and energy is devoted to the day-to-day activity of operations management. Our retail strategic planning and operations management model (Exhibit 2.6) shows that operations management involves managing the buying and handling of merchandise, pricing, advertising and promotion, customer services and selling, and facilities. All of these activities require day-to-day attention. For example, the selling floor must be maintained, customers served, merchandise bought and handled, advertisements run, and pricing decisions made each and every day. In other words, operations management is running the store.

In Part 4, we will focus on operations management, the real "guts" of retailing. In the first several years of a retailing career, your primary concern will be almost exclusively with the operations management side of retailing. The strategic planning duties will be handled by the senior executives. However, if you enter retailing via a small or medium-sized firm, you may be making decisions, even strategic ones, immediately. Regardless, when a retailer is able to do a good job at operations management—that is, efficiently using the resources available—then the retailer is said to be operations effective.

High-Performance Results

The far right box of the retail strategic planning and operations management model (Exhibit 2.6) suggests that the cumulative effect of well-designed and executed strategic and operations plans will be the achievement of high profit. Mistakes in either of these two areas will severely hamper the retailer's performance and prevent it from being among the leaders in its industry. For example, McDonald's was once hailed as the most successful innovator in the fast food industry. However, by the early to mid-2000s, Mickey D's, by most measures, was doing terribly. It had endured a deluge of negative publicity thanks to movies such as *Super Size Me* and books like *Fast Food Nation* that criticize the quality of its food and blame it for the nation's obesity epidemic. The retailer had just spent more than $5 billion building new stores without increasing operating income. So it decided to focus on existing restaurants by doing a better job of delivering quality, service, cleanliness, and value on a daily basis.[26] It watched the competition, and where Starbucks failed with its meal offering, Mc Donald's was successful with its premium coffee. Maybe such behavior describes what is meant when retailers say "they are going back to basics." Regardless, McDonald's is again highly successful.

The need to strive for a high profit is tied to the extremely competitive nature of retailing. It is still relatively easy to start a retail business in comparison to starting a business in other industries. New retail entrepreneurs are continually entering the marketplace. As competition increases and more chains use the same format, profit levels naturally deteriorate. Retailers are therefore well advised to set high-profit objectives so that if their planned profits are not reached, they at least have a chance of achieving average profitability. The retailer that aims only for an average profit often finds itself confronting a rather sobering financial performance. Exhibit 2.7 shows how the SPM results of high-performance retailers compare to the median performance for similar retailers. As a general rule of thumb, retailers should strive for the following goals when planning their SPM: net profit margin of 2.5 percent to 3.5 percent, asset turnover of 2.5 to 3.0

		Profit Margin	Asset Turnover	Return on Assets	Financial Leverage	Return on Net Worth
Best Buy	BBY	3.7%	2.8x	10.3%	2.3x	23.5%
Walmart	WMT	3.7%	2.4x	8.9%	2.6x	22.7%
Home Depot	HD	7.2%	2.0x	12.8%	1.8x	23.5%
Office Depot	ODP	1.9%	2.2x	4.6%	2.2x	9.9%
Sears Holding	SHLD	2.5%	2.5x	4.4%	2.1x	9.3%
Target	TGT	4.6%	1.6x	7.5%	2.4x	18.0%
Kohl's	KSS	6.3%	1.6x	10.2%	1.5x	15.7%

Exhibit 2.7
Strategic Profit Model for Some of the Country's Leading Retailers

times, and financial leverage of 2.0 to 3.0 times. Achieving such goals would produce a return on assets of 8 percent to 10 percent and an 18 percent to 25 percent return on net worth.

SUMMARY

This chapter explains the importance and use of planning in retail management. Toward that end, the chapter introduces a model of retail planning.

Explain why strategic planning is so important and describe its components

LO 1

Planning and the financial performance of the retailer are intertwined. High-profit performance does not just happen; it is engineered through careful planning. Not all retailers can be leaders, but the ones that are will be those that did the best job of planning and managing. The components of strategic planning include developing a statement of purpose or mission for the firm; defining its specific goals and objectives; identifying the retailer's strengths, weaknesses, opportunities, and threats; and developing basic strategies that will enable the firm to reach its objectives and fulfill its mission.

Describe the text's retail strategic planning and operations management model

LO 2

Retailers must engage in two types of planning and management tasks: strategic planning and operations management. Strategic planning consists of matching the retailer's mission and goals with available opportunities. The retail marketing strategy that results from this consists of a target market, location(s), retail mix, and value proposition. Operations management consists of planning the efficient use of available resources in order to manage the day-to-day operations of the firm successfully. When retailers succeed at these two levels, they will achieve high-profit results.

TERMS TO REMEMBER

strategic planning
mission statement
market share
net profit margin
asset turnover
return on assets (ROA)
financial leverage

return on net worth (RONW)
stockouts
productivity objectives
societal objectives
personal objectives
strategy
target market

location   operations management
retail mix   yield management
value proposition   revenue per available seat mile (RASM)

REVIEW AND DISCUSSION QUESTIONS

LO 1

Explain why strategic planning is so important and describe its components

1. Why is strategic planning so important in retailing today? Should a retailer, even a small retailer, always have a strategy to change the rules of the game as it is currently being played? Why?

2. How do the retail firm's mission statement and its stated goals and objectives relate to the retailer's development of competitive strategy?

3. Most college students have either strong favorable or unfavorable opinions of their campus nightspots. Suppose you were asked to advise one of the businesses near your campus, what suggestions would you make for it to differentiate itself?

4. Can a mission statement be too narrow in scope? Can it be too broad in scope? Explain your answers.

5. Choose any two supermarkets operating in your college area or hometown. Compare and contrast their retail mix as they seek to satisfy the needs of their target market given their present location. What changes would you suggest to the management of these retailers as they develop their strategic plans for the coming year?

6. An automobile dealer located near your campus visits your class. During her presentation, she notes that her mission statement is "We will provide the best vehicle sales and service experience for our customers. We will do this in a way that will foster the continuous improvement of our people and our company. We will be a top-performing, thoroughly professional, and genuinely caring organization in all that we do." Would you offer any suggestions for changing this mission statement? If so why?

7. Many retailers use their loyalty cards, such as that described in the chapter's "What New?" box, to gather information about customers. Are they invading their customers' privacy? Should this be allowed? After all, how would some of your classmates react if parents found out what movies they viewed on pay-per-view?

LO 2

Describe the retail strategic planning and operations management model

8. What are the major environmental forces that retailers will face over the next five years? Is any one of these more important than the others?

9. Does strategic planning become more or less important as the uncertainty the retailer faces increases?

10. When doing the strategic planning and operations management tasks described in our model, does the retailer use creative thinking or analytical problem solving?

11. A person once said, "A good manager can overcome a bad plan." Agree or disagree with this statement and explain your reasoning. Use current examples, if possible, in your answer. Would your answer be the same if the person said, "A good plan can overcome a poor manager?"

12. Why is it so important for a retailer to seek high-profit performance? Isn't it enough to be above average?

SAMPLE TEST QUESTIONS

When a retailer sets goals based on a comparison of its actions against its competitors, it is establishing _____ goals

LO 1

a. competitive analysis
b. market performance
c. geomarket performance
d. societal performance
e. financial performance

The best way for a retailer to differentiate itself from the competition in the eyes of the consumer is to:

LO 2

a. increase advertising of sale items.
b. offer the lowest prices in town.
c. always be well stocked with the basic items that customers would expect to find in the store.
d. not sell any of the brand names the competition is selling.
e. increase its strategic planning effort.

WRITING AND SPEAKING EXERCISE

Dolph Drake, the owner of Bulldog Books, has three bookstores near the campus of a large state university. In the past, he has run his stores very informally. He likes to claim that he is successful because he doesn't think too much and that he makes most of his decisions by the "seat of his pants." Over the past five years profits at each store have increased between 5 percent and 7 percent each year, despite the fact that the average price of textbooks has doubled. Also, Drake has never given much thought to changing his original plans for his bookstores.

While Drake was the first to open off-campus stores and therefore got the prime locations, competitors are beginning to appear near all three of his stores. In fact, just recently an out-of-town competitor gathered the majority of the end-of-semester textbook buybacks, one of the most profitable activities for a campus bookstore. This out of towner merely set up a drive-through buyback operation at a nearby parking lot so that students could pull up under an awning, hand over their books, and drive off with money within minutes. Even though the competitor left town the next day, Drake expects other book buyers will seek to "hit and run" at the end of the fall semester.

As a result of this recent loss of business, Drake feels that it is time to develop a more structured approach for his business and asks you as part of your summer internship to research the strategic planning process. You are to prepare a memo on the basic steps and tasks that are involved in developing a strategic plan. Be sure to include in your memo a mission statement and a list of objectives that Bulldog Books should seek to achieve.

RETAIL PROJECT

Go to the library and either look at the most recent annual reports for four or five of the top 25 U.S. retailers listed on the inside cover of this text or locate the 10-Ks of those firms on the Internet. (*Note:* All publicly held firms need to file their U.S.

Security and Exchange Commission 10-Ks, a more complete financial analysis of the firm's performance, electronically. To look up this information, go to www.sec.gov/edgarhp.htm.) Use the SPM described in Exhibit 2.1 to calculate your own SPM numbers for these retailers.

Finally, after you have calculated these numbers, which retailer do you believe is the best at achieving financial superiority?

PLANNING YOUR OWN RETAIL BUSINESS

In the "Planning Your Own Retail Business" exercise in Chapter 1, you learned how to estimate the net profits that your business might earn. You saw what would happen if your sales estimate was off by 10 percent. Now it's time to analyze the dollar investment you need in assets to support your business and how you might finance these assets.

Your investment in assets needs to cover inventory, fixtures, equipment, cash, customer credit (i.e., accounts receivable), and perhaps other assets. These assets could be financed with debt or by investments you or perhaps other investors make in the business.

Compute the strategic profit model ratios under the assumption that your first-year sales are $700,000, net profit is $66,000, total investment in assets is $400,000, and the total debt to finance these assets is $250,000. (*Hint:* Net worth is equal to total assets less debt.) What would happen to these ratios if net profit rose to $75,000?

Retail Customers

OVERVIEW:

In this chapter, we examine the effects of the external environment on retailing. We discuss how recent changes in the population and in social and economic trends affect the way consumers behave and the implications of these changes for retailers. We conclude with the development of a consumer shopping and purchasing model that incorporates all of these factors to describe overall shopping and buying practices.

LEARNING OBJECTIVES:

After reading this chapter, you should be able to:

1. Explain the importance of population trends on retail planning.
2. List the social trends that retail managers should regularly monitor and describe their impact on retailing.
3. Describe the changing economic trends and their effects on retailing.
4. Discuss the consumer shopping and purchasing model, including the key stages in the shopping and purchasing process.

Introduction

In Chapter 1 we said that retailing consists of the final activities and steps needed to place a product or service in the hands of the consumer. The previous chapters also stated the point that a retailer, to be a high performer, must be able to differentiate itself from the competition. In doing so, retail managers must realize that, with the possible exception of supermarkets and gas stations, their stores can't serve all possible consumer types. Some consumers will never shop at a nearby Walmart; others will never shop at a Saks Fifth Avenue, Nordstrom, or Neiman Marcus. Therefore, before developing any plans, the successful retailer must first target a specific segment (or segments) of the overall market and study the environmental factors (competition, the behavior of the other supply-chain members, and legal and ethical factors) that affect that segment. Only after determining what segment to target, can the retailer decide on a location, format, and retail mix (the combination of merchandise assortment, price, promotion, customer service, and store layout) that best serves the selected segment.

The easiest way for retailers to differentiate themselves is to satisfy the customer's needs and wants better than the competition. This customer satisfaction, as we will use the term, is different from customer service. **Customer satisfaction** is

customer satisfaction
Occurs when the total shopping experience of the customer has been met or exceeded.

determined by whether or not the total shopping experience has met or exceeded the customer's expectation. If it has, then the customer is said to have had a rewarding shopping experience. Customer satisfaction is important because, as was noted in the previous chapter, it costs the average retailer five times as much money to get a new customer into a store as it does to make a sale to someone who has already shopped there or to retain a current customer who may be unhappy. Not only retailers, but also the nation's economy, depend on the customer having a satisfactory shopping experience. Exhibit 3.1 shows the historically strong relationship between changes in the American Customer Satisfaction Index (ACSI) and future consumer spending growth. The fact that spending and satisfaction generally move together should not be surprising since buyer satisfaction leads to repeat business and increased purchases. After all, a satisfied customer will be encouraged to engage in future spending, while the dissatisfied or unhappy customer will be more hesitant. Little wonder, then, that many economists feel that in the past it was the American consumers' desire to spend that prevented the economy from suffering more severe slowdowns than those that did occur.[1] Perhaps this is why the government first tried to stimulate consumer spending during the most recent recession.

This chapter's "Retailing: The Inside Story" box discusses the ACSI, and how, as seen at the far right of Exhibit 3.1, retailers have seen the satisfaction levels of their customers actually increase as the economy tanked.[2] This pickup in satisfaction actually started during the worst time period of the recent recession—the 2008 Christmas season—when sales declined to record levels despite the presence of major price reductions offered before the holiday. Why then did satisfaction go up? Well, note that in the fall of 2007, before the onset of the recession that December, ACSI began to decline. This is the same pattern as during prior recessions: The ACSI tends to fall before the recession begins and rises as the rebound nears. Hopefully, this will happen again because, as the recent recession deepened, consumer behavior changed much more than in most other economic crises. The year 2008 also saw consumer spending weaken considerably, while household savings rose. Thus, at the early stages of recovery from recessions, it is assumed that there will be less revenue for sellers and more pressure on profit

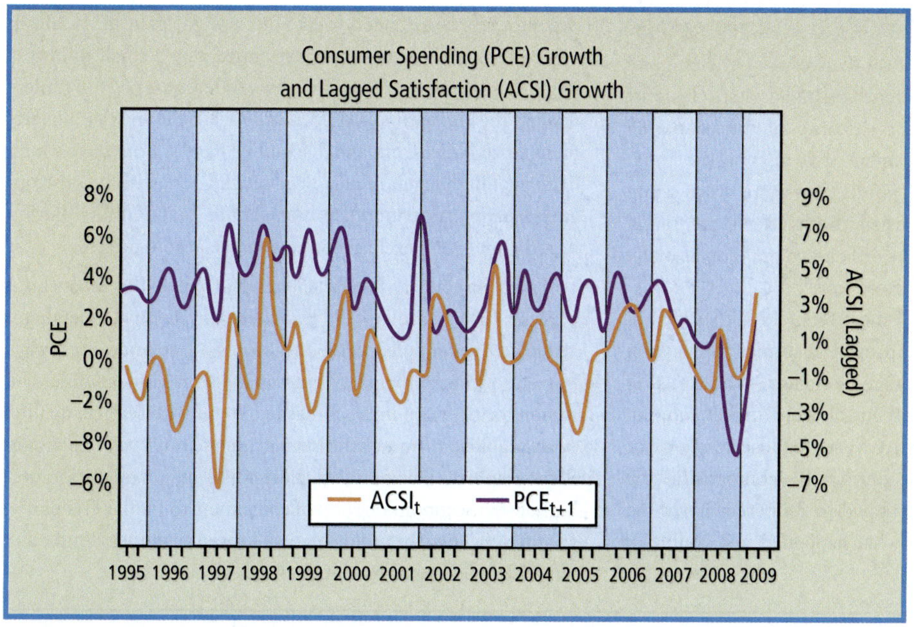

Exhibit 3.1
Personal Consumer Expenditures and Lagged Satisfaction (ACSI)

Retailing: The Inside Story

Are Retailers Satisfying Their Customers?

Overall, retailers have seen only a minor increase in customer satisfaction over the past decade. The retail index has gone from a 74.7 ACSI score in 1998 to 75.2 at the end of 2008. Still that was its highest level since 1994's 75.7 score, and it was 1.5 percentage points higher than at the end of 2007. One contributing factor for this increase was falling gas prices. In fact, the ACSI score jumped 5.7 percent to 74 for service stations. Department and discount stores (+1.4% to 74) and specialty retail stores (+1.3% to 76) also contributed. But even with increasing levels of customer satisfaction, most retailers faced a very difficult time. Sales during the 2008 holiday season plunged. It is important to remember that a good part of the sales decline in late 2008 was due to falling prices. For example, gasoline sales fell by 16 percent in December 2008 alone, but price dropped by more than 50 percent over the year, despite that summer peak of $4 per gallon. Overall retail sales dropped only 0.1 percent in 2008, according to the Commerce Department. When price reductions are factored in, that number is no longer negative. This is not to suggest that things are not bad. They are very bad, but sometimes interpretations of economic data are also a bit exaggerated.

While lower gas prices caused the ACSI increase for service stations, and price reductions in general prevented consumer demand from an even worse free fall, price actually played a somewhat lesser role for customer satisfaction in some of the retail business. Despite heavy discounting during the holiday season, the bulk of the improvement in ACSI was actually due to better customer service. According to Professor Claes Fornell, director of the University of Michigan's National Quality Research Center, "it is likely that sales staff tried harder to please customers because of the economic situation and fear of unemployment. It is also possible that store traffic decreased to the point that there were more personnel per customer than usual. Both effects are rarely sustainable and will be even more difficult to build on as many retailers have since eliminated more jobs."

In fact, while stock prices of most retailers fell sharply in 2008, those companies that improved customer satisfaction were punished less. On average, retailers whose ACSI increased only lost about 30 percent of their market value in 2008, but those with declining ACSI scores lost nearly twice as much (57%) over the same period. By comparison, the Standard & Poors 500 Index dropped by 38 percent over the same time period. Let's review what happened in a couple of the retail industries.

Supermarkets The average ACSI score for supermarkets increased slightly, 75 to 76, from 2008 despite the fact that food and beverage prices increased. Grocery prices rose 6.6 percent in 2008 compared with a 5.7-percent increase in 2007, both the highest single-year increases since 1980. Yet supermarkets appeared to have been able to absorb these increases without suffering any negative effects on customer satisfaction by improving the quality of the shopping experience through redesigned stores, better variety of merchandise, and longer hours. For 2008, a small drop of 1.3 percent in value for money was offset by a 2.6-percent increase in quality, keeping customer satisfaction with the industry stable.

Several supermarkets improved. Safeway went from one of the lowest in 2007 to close to the industry average. The third largest grocery chain in the United States has invested in creating a new store format called the Lifestyle store, featuring more square footage to accommodate expanded selections of perishables, organic foods, and other merchandise. Nearly three-quarters of all Safeway stores were upgraded at the end of 2008, and 90 percent should be converted by the end of 2009. Other chains that made more modest gains include Kroger, Whole Foods, and Winn-Dixie, which were all up 3 percent to 77, 75, and, 73 respectively. Walmart scored the lowest at 68.

Department and Discount Stores Even as retail sales slumped for six straight months to close out 2008, department and discount stores managed to eke out a slight gain in ACSI, up 1.3 percent to 74, caused almost entirely by a small improvement in customer service. Two very different types of retailers topped the list with an ACSI score of 80: the upscale department store Nordstrom and discounter Kohl's. Both have a long history of high levels of customer satisfaction, with Nordstrom emphasizing superior customer service and Kohl's offering brand names and exclusive merchandise at low prices.

Deep discounter Dollar General dropped the most: by 4 percent to a score of 75. Shoppers at Dollar General are attracted to its simple, bare-bones stores where prices are always low but quests for particular merchandise are hit-or-miss. The reason for the drop in ACSI has less to do with service, quality, or availability of merchandise but much to do with changing demographics. During 2008 there was a major migration of a higher socioeconomic group of consumers to Dollar General—another effect of the recession—and these customers tend to be harder to please and have higher expectations.

Retailing: The Inside Story (*continued*)

	ACSI Scores for Selected Retailers 2003 to 2008					
	2003	2004	2005	2006	2007	2008
Supermarkets	74	73	74	75	75	76
Publix	82	81	81	83	83	82
Kroger	71	73	74	76	75	77
Safeway	71	72	71	74	72	75
Whole Foods					73	75
Winn-Dixie	73	72	73	76	71	73
Walmart		70	70	69	71	68
Department & Discount Stores	76	74	75	74	73	74
Nordstrom					80	80
Kohl's	79	79	80	80	79	80
Target		75	78	77	77	77
Dollar General					78	75
Dillards	75	77	76	75	76	75
Walmart	75	73	72	72	78	70
Office Supply Retailers					76	73
Staples					77	76
Office Max					76	77
Office Depot					78	75
Best Buy	72	72	71	76	74	74
Circuit City*	73	72	70	69	71	72
Banks	75	75	75	77	78	75
Wachovia#	76	78	79	80	79	76
Bank of America	74	72	72	72	72	73
JPMorgan Chase		70	70	72	74	73
Wells Fargo	68	70	67	72	69	72
Citigroup				72	69	69
Internet Retailers	84	80	81	83	83	82
Amazon.com	88	84	87	87	88	86
Netflix					84	85
eBay	84	80	81	80	81	78

*Circuit City went bankrupt in 2009
#Wachovia was purchased by Wells Fargo on December 31, 2008
Note: Blank spaces mean the data collected was not meaningful for that year

Office-Supply Retailers The ACSI scores of the office-supply retailers fell. Staples and OfficeMax posted a modest retreat, while Office Depot dropped a sizable 4 percent. Poor customer service and problems with product availability were the most common consumer complaints. Dissatisfied customers have inflicted much punishment on Office Depot. The company will close more than 100 stores over the next few months in an effort to avoid bankruptcy. Investors are not happy either: Stock price declined 79 percent in 2008, twice the size of the market slump.

Banks In the fourth quarter of 2007, customer satisfaction with banking reached an all-time high ACSI score of 78, even as the subprime mortgage crisis was beginning to take a toll on many financial institutions. As ACSI covers satisfaction with checking, savings, and personal loan accounts,

(*continued*)

Retailing: The Inside Story (continued)

mortgages had probably not yet had an impact on the quality of these banking services. A year later, the picture is quite different as banks dropped to a score of 75. Banks' customer services are no longer free of stress as companies have cut costs across their entire range of services in order to offset large financial losses. Branch closings and staff reductions often have adverse effects on customer satisfaction and customer relationships. In addition, mergers and acquisitions have returned—something that often bodes trouble for customer service. The smaller regional banks achieved the highest overall scores, the major banks dropped. Citigroup earned the lowest score: 69.

Source: "Retail Trade: Fourth Quarter Scores" and "Commentary by Professor Claes Fornell," *ACSI* February 17, 2009 Report. Used with the written permission of Professor Claes Fornell.

---

margins and cost cutting. Therefore, jobs lost will reach its limit during this time frame. Thus, the good news at the beginning of 2009, as shown by the increasing ACSI score, was that consumers' expectations about obtaining gratification from future discretionary spending were rising. However, to achieve recovery, it is also necessary that consumers have the means—cash and credit—to spend. At that point in time, this condition was uncertain, and various stimulus packages were debated. Nevertheless, as long as there is a lack of spending power, the ability of ACSI alone to predict consumer spending will be limited. It does not mean, however, that customer satisfaction becomes less important in recessions. On the contrary, it takes on an extra dimension.[3] As you read the chapter's "Retailing: The Inside Story" box, think about whether you agree or disagree with the logic behind this analysis. (Many of you, reading this text in later years, already know the outcome.)

In addition to the tangible product or intangible service offered for sale, another part of the customer's shopping experience is the services provided by the retailer. These **customer services** are the activities performed by the retailer that influence (1) the ease with which a potential customer can shop or learn about the store's offering, (2) the ease with which a transaction can be completed once the customer attempts to make a purchase, and (3) the customer's satisfaction with the product or service after purchase. These three elements correspond to the pretransaction, transaction, and posttransaction components of customer service.

Common services provided by retailers (in addition to having the product that satisfies the customer's needs and wants) include alterations, fitting rooms, delivery, gift registries, check cashing, credit, extended shopping hours, short checkout lines, gift wrapping, parking, layaway, and merchandise-return privileges, as well as the availability of in-home shopping options such as television, print catalogs, and the Internet. It must be remembered that none of these services is actually the merchandise or service being offered for sale; it merely entices the customers that the retailer is targeting.

If a customer is dissatisfied with either the product offered or the services provided, that customer is less likely to choose that retailer in the future, thus decreasing future sales. (Throughout the remainder of this chapter we will use the term *product* to designate either the physical product or service offered for sale and the term *service* to refer to the services the retailer uses to facilitate that sale. However, in the case of a service retailer, the product offered is, in fact, a service.) As illustrated in the previous chapter's "What's New?" box, knowing what products to carry, as well as determining which customer services to offer, is a challenging problem for retailers as they seek ways to improve the shopping experience. Imagine listening to a radio with no tuning or volume knob. The receiver picks up many different signals, some in harmony, some in conflict, so

customer services
Consists of all those activities performed by the retailer that influence (1) the ease with which a potential customer can shop or learn about the store's offering, (2) the ease with which a transaction can be completed once the customer attempts to make a purchase, and (3) the customer's satisfaction with the transaction.

that the result is noise coming through the speaker. You're getting something, but you can't understand it. To make sense of the confusing array of available information, retailers use market-segmentation techniques to tune into segments of the population, hoping to hear a series of clear messages that assist them in providing the correct products and services to their customers. Exhibit 2.4 pointed out how Best Buy used a segmentation strategy to meet the needs of the target market served by a particular store. Here the chain customized 20 percent of its merchandise offerings and trained its salespeople to meet the demands of the store's target market. Many nonretailers are surprised to find out that 80 percent of the merchandise in most chain stores is the same nationwide. It is only the remaining 20 percent that is tailored to each particular store's market.

Understanding different customer segments and their need for convenience might stimulate the retailer to offer additional products through its website, thus providing a critical service component to enhance the customer's experience. As Exhibit 3.2 points out, it is important that the retailer know and understand its customers.

In Exhibit 3.2 we see the three important types of trends—population, social, and economic—that all retailers must monitor because they will affect the way customers undertake the shopping process. As pointed out in Chapter 2, all retailers must perform three basic strategies:

1. get as many of the targeted consumers into the store as possible,

2. convert these consumers into customers by having them purchase merchandise, and

3. perform the first two strategies at the lowest cost possible that is consistent with the level of service customers expect.

If the retailer doesn't understand its customers, it won't be able to accomplish the first two strategies.

Market segmentation is the method retailers use to segment, or break down, heterogeneous consumer populations into smaller, more homogeneous groups based on certain characteristics. Market segmentation helps retailers understand who their customers are, how they think, and what they do. As the chapter's "Service Retailing" box illustrates, using the way hotels are segmented in India as an example, segmentation enables the retailer to build a meaningful strategy based

market segmentation
Is the dividing of a heterogeneous consumer population into smaller, more homogeneous groups based on their characteristics.

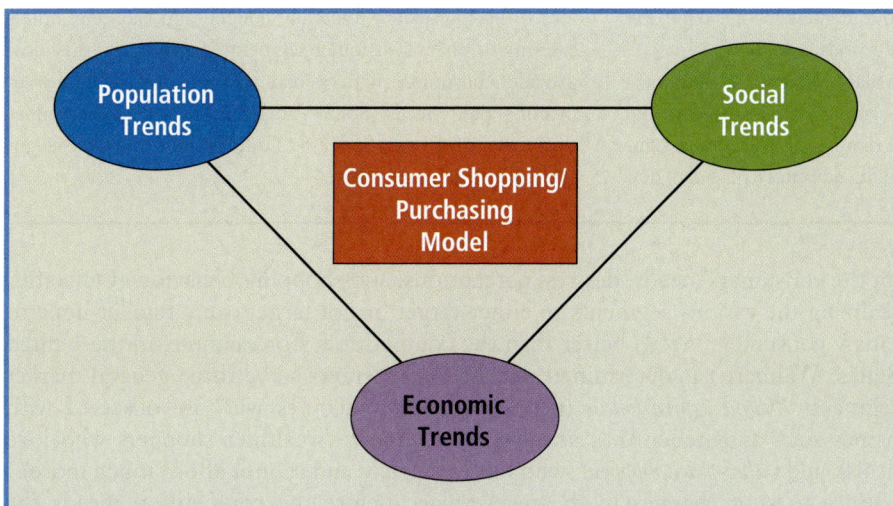

Exhibit 3.2
How Current Trends Affect the Way the Consumer Behaves

Service Retailing

India's Midmarket Hotels[5]

Mention the country India and the term *service retailing* to most folks, and they will immediately think of some type of call center. However, many people do not realize that India has recently become one of the most sought-after tourist destinations. India's amazing diversity offers everything one could ask for. However, comfortable midpriced hotel stays were not always possible in India.

Recently, some friends of one of the authors returned from a trip to India. Although they had traveled there 15 years earlier, much of their discussions concerning their recent three-week excursion focused on one topic: the increase in the choice of hotels. Fifteen years earlier, the couple had been shocked to find that in India—where roughly 20 million people, many of them entry-level business professionals, travel long distances on a daily basis—there were no hotels targeted to serve the mass market of middle-class Indians.

Prior to the turn of the century, there were essentially two types of hotels available: "high-end" hotels charging an average of $400 a night and "low-end" hotels that cost roughly $20 a night. Management at these "high-end" hotels expected perfection. For example, one hotel insisted that the rosebuds in every room be no taller than one-and-a-half times the height of the vase and had senior hotel staff routinely check the softness of the sheets. In fact, one of these high-end hotels went so far as to import toilet paper from Thailand so that it was soft and tender to the skin. This hotel even had its laundries use reflectometers, devices to check the whiteness of towels after they've been washed.

At the other end of the spectrum were the $20-per-night roach dumps. Management at these hotels seemed to care less about perfection. Instead, they offered guests rooms complete with an air conditioner and dirty towels.

With only these two options in place, what was lacking was a midpriced hotel geared for the young data-processing and manufacturing workers who were required to travel on assignments as well as the vacationers taking advantage of India's new

discount airlines. Enter the Tata Group, a hotel chain known for running top-end hotels like the Taj Boston (formerly the Ritz Carlton), The Pierre in New York, and the Campton Place in San Francisco. Following the advice of an India-born professor at the University of Michigan, the Tata Group sought to develop a line of budget hotels that not only were modern, clean, and simple but also came equipped with basic amenities such as Wi-Fi and a gym—all for about $20 a night.

The resulting Taj budget-hotel subsidiary, Roots, was established in December 2003 with a business plan that decreed the hotels would be modern, clean, and economical. Single rooms ($20 a night) would have a single bed, measure 175 square feet, and come equipped with broadband, a flat-screen TV, and a workstation. A 210 square-foot double room would cost about $40.

To offer these amenities at such an affordable price, some of the Tata Group's typical customer services were trimmed or, in some cases, eliminated. For instance, rather than the typical 150 to 200 full-time employees found in each of its high-end hotels, these midrange hotels rely on a staff equivalent to 40 to 50 full-timers. Doing so requires employees to multitask, checking guests in and carrying their luggage to the room. Instead of providing a full-size health club, each Roots Hotel gym offers a few exercise machines, weights, and boxing gear but no pool. Further, the hotel chain substituted large conference rooms for a single meeting room that can seat as many as 10 people and room service for a single restaurant with limited hours of operation.

While in the past India lacked clarity in the differentiation of its hotels, Indian businesspeople have now caught on to the idea of having luxury, midscale, budget, and economy hotels catering to various customer segments. In doing so, they now provide consumers with a real choice when it comes to meeting their needs. Some Americans may even remember that this is the way Super 8, Holiday Inn, and others got started in the United States.

---

on the consumers' needs, desires, perceptions, and shopping behaviors. Only after realizing the various segments to either target or not target can a retailer hope to satisfy consumers' needs better than the competition. For example, in the United States, Walmart has determined that its Supercenters serve three general market segments: *brand aspirationals* (people with low incomes who are obsessed with names such as KitchenAid), *price-sensitive affluents* (wealthier shoppers who love deals), and *value-price shoppers* (who like low prices and cannot afford much more).[4] Failure to spot changes in the marketplace before the competition means the retailer will only be able to react and adapt to what more sensitive retailers have

Keith Brofsky/Getty Images

So as to avoid being considered a follower or "look-alike" retailer, grocery store operators have capitalized on the consumer's interest in organically grown produce as a means to gain a competitive advantage.

already spotted. Thus, while the high-performance retailer may have spotted an emerging trend and made the necessary changes in its retail mix, the average retailer will only be a follower or "look-alike" retailer. Further, what differential advantage does a "me-too" retailer offer the consumer? Copycat practices have led many retailers into financial difficulties.

As in the case of Walmart Supercenters cited in the previous paragraph, most retailers choose to target only a portion of the overall market. Consider, for example, how the three major membership warehouse club operators go after different customer segments. Sam's focuses on small businesses, which are said to spend 50 percent more than individual consumers; Costco, despite carrying a third fewer SKUs, has a reputation for bargain prices and surprise designer goods aimed at meeting the needs of its upscale consumers;[6] and BJ's caters to families by offering larger selections. Each of these merchants has excelled at reaching its target customer, although it probably has excluded other available consumer segments.

Now, let's begin our study of the changing consumer to see how an understanding of population, social, and economic trends can help a retailer select a market segment to target.

population variables
Include population growth trends, age distributions, and geographic trends.

Population Trends

LO 1

Retailers often find it useful to group consumers according to **population variables**, such as population growth trends, age distributions, ethnic makeup, and geographic trends. This is useful for two reasons. First, such data is often linked to marketplace needs. Second, the data is readily available and can be easily applied in analyzing markets.[7]

Explain the importance of population trends on retail planning.

Population Growth

Retailers have long viewed an expanding population base as synonymous with growth in retail markets. Unfortunately, the nation's overall growth rate has declined during each of the past three decades as families have had fewer children. If current average projections are correct, then the U.S. population will increase about 1 percent per year, from 310 million in 2010 to 341 million in 2020. However, it is expected to increase by 42 percent over the next 40 years to 439 million by 2050. The majority of this growth is expected to be the result of immigration.

Implications for Retailers

Any increase in domestic population growth will mean an increased demand for goods and services; however, the growth will be nowhere near the 80-percent increase experienced over the last half-century. Still, even minimal growth in the total population will mean opportunities for retailers. As population growth slows, successful retailers must focus on taking market share away from competitors, managing gross margin by controlling selling price and cost and increasing the productivity of existing stores.

Some retailers will grow by changes in the individual demand for a product. For instance, PetSmart continues to expand its retail operations as the number of pet parents and the number of multiple-pet families increase. In fact, growth in this retail sector is likely to continue given that the pet population has outgrown the overall human population. Another growth opportunity for retailers will be international expansion; however, it is likely that this is a limited-time opportunity. Demographers are predicting a major decline in worldwide fertility rates, which will lead to a global population decline—a radical notion in a world brought up on the idea of overpopulation. While it will take some time, global retailers should be prepared for depopulation.[8]

Age Distribution

The age distribution of the U.S. population is changing. In 1980, the median age was 30, but by 2010 it had risen to nearly 37.[9] The most significant change today is the bulge of early baby boomers moving into their sixties. This group of 78 million Americans born between 1946 and 1964 accounts for more than 25 percent of the population and spends an estimated $2.3 trillion on consumer goods and services annually.[10] However, many experts claim that, for retail planning purposes, this group is much too large and diverse to share a single lifestyle, life stage, or purchasing proclivity. For example, while the first wave of boomers may have already retired and started collecting full Social Security benefits as of January 1, 2012 (after reaching age 66), many others are 15 or so years away from retirement. Therefore, as these older boomers retire, they may not be spending as they did in the past. This is important because baby boomers accounted for about half of all consumer spending in the United States during the 1990s.[11]

Today, many boomers in their late 40s to mid-60s are still spending at levels near their previous pace; however, many have also begun to make a more concerted effort at saving for retirement. This latter group has an increased concern over the long-term viability of Social Security and the likelihood of corporate downsizing, which left many seniors unemployed during the recent recession. In addition, many of these preretirement boomers need to replace the $4 trillion of wealth lost in retirement funds during the recession's stock meltdown as well as the billions lost in the housing crash.

Sadly, the recent recession created immediate financial concerns for more than just the preretirement boomers. Some boomers and members of the Silent Generation (those born between 1900 and 1945) who had already retired, were forced to return to the workforce in order to restore value to their financial holdings. These retirees, who just a few years before "thought they were set for life," make up what is now called the "unretired."[12]

As the ramifications from this recent recession continue to unfold, many boomers are now spending less on apparel, spending more on medicine and recreation, and saving more of their money to pass on to their children. This chapter's "What's New?" box describes the development of a new type of service retailer: consultants, who combine financial planning and law. These individuals are equipped to advise parents and their children on how to manage what will be the largest transfer of wealth in history. Some calculations estimate $41 trillion in wealth—that's $41,000,000,000,000—will be transferred to a younger generation between now and 2052.[13]

As stated previously, seniors should not be viewed as homogeneous. In the past, they were classified as anyone age 60 and older. However, because people now live longer, more useful categories should be utilized. Octogenarians are people ages 80 to 89, nonagenarians are 90 to 99, and centenarians are 100 and above. Today the United States has more than 70,000 centenarians, a number almost 10 times that of four decades ago. In fact, today one in 50 women and one in 200 men will reach that age. Another useful way to categorize seniors is in terms of their health (good or poor) and wealth (inadequate or adequate). Thus there are four types of seniors: good health–adequate wealth, good health–inadequate wealth, poor health–adequate wealth, and poor health–inadequate wealth. Seniors in general have more wealth than several generations ago due to improved Social Security benefits, Medicare, and retirement savings. In addition, seniors are relatively healthier as compared to previous generations. Taking these two factors together, it's not surprising that the population

Retailers must remember that it is doubtful that today's seniors will behave as their parents did a generation before them. A 50 year old in 2015 will not act like a 50 year old in 1995. Successful retailers will be prepared for this.

What's New?

The Great Money Transfer

Baby boomers, whose parents were raised during the Great Depression, were taught to focus on saving money for that "rainy day." However, it appears that today's middle-aged consumers have something different in mind. They are chasing the trillions of dollars that are expected to transfer between generations as baby boomers and members of the Silent Generation sell their businesses and pass away. These middle-aged consumers expect to inherit money from their parents or take control of the 401(k) money their parents accumulated over lengthy careers.

The authors are friends with several couples who, like many other 50-something boomers, live in fancy homes that are mortgaged to the hilt, drive leased luxury cars, and purchase apparel at Saks and Neiman Marcus. These couples represent the newest behavioral trend among boomers—being a "waiter." In other words, they are "waiting for their inheritance." Sadly, many are not just waiting, but have actually become dependent on what economists say will be the largest amount of money, some $41 trillion, ever set aside for transfer between generations.

However, these boomers may be disappointed given that family assets have dwindled in recent years as savings were depleted not only by fluctuations in the stock market and unpredictable housing values but also by the high costs of nursing homes, long-term care, and prescription drugs—increasingly common expenses since Americans are living longer.

Making matters worse, as these family assets dwindled, the "old school" parents avoided any discussion with their children about their finances or what was in their wills. This has led to many a sibling battle over who gets what and when.

As a result, a new type of service retailer has emerged—a combination financial planner and attorney. These professionals seek to avoid family feuds after a parent's death. To do so, they offer services ranging from extensive will planning to counseling on how retirees can communicate inheritance decisions to their children. This communication is important since baby boomers have a significantly different attitude toward money than their parents. Because of their Great Depression experiences, the parents were savers, whereas baby boomers grew up in the prosperity of the 1950s and 1960s never wanting for the basics. Boomers were the spenders who "shopped till they dropped."

Lifestyle changes also increase the need for these service professionals. The higher divorce rates of recent years and the increased number of remarriages have created confusion about the rights of stepchildren and second or third spouses in wills. In addition, wealthy families want someone who not only can help them grow their money but also can guide them through the maze of ever-changing tax laws and other issues that can affect how they hold on to their money until passing it along to the next generation. Today, people don't know how—or don't want to try—to navigate the explosion of investment products or the complexity of tax laws.

Little wonder, then, that these financial planners or lawyers seek to avoid family disputes by placing less emphasis on documenting what a parent wants to say in a will. Instead these counselors spend their time asking detailed questions about the boomer children, such as financial status, living situations, and relationships with siblings. They encourage parents to include their children in estate-planning meetings so that everyone involved will understand who is getting what and why, all in an attempt to avoid an extended battle after the parents' deaths.

One word of warning: More than half of the respondents in a survey of Americans 65 and older stated that they weren't going to divide their assets equally among their children. Instead they plan to give a larger share to the attentive child—the one who provided care, for example.

Source: Based on "Wealth Management Comes to Financial Services Firms," St. Louis Post-Dispatch, October 7, 2007: D1, D3; "Inherit the Windfall: How to Retire on the Money Your Parent Leave Behind," Wall Street Journal, June 7, 2006: D1; "I Inherited My Money the Hard Way: I Earned It," AARP Bulletin, December 2005: 6; "Not Acting Their Age," U.S. News & World Report, June 4, 2001: 54–60; John C. Carver, "Is It Going to Be 'Share the Wealth,'" Texas A&M University, working paper, 1999; "Going Deeper in Debt," AARP Bulletin, March 2003: 22–24; Roger M. Williams, "The New Breed and the Mega-Bucks," Foundation News and Commentary, September–October 2001: 25; and the authors' observations.

segment with largest percentage growth over the past five years is the "active" senior who has both the health and the wealth to enjoy him- or herself.

So-called baby busters or Generation Xers—those born between 1965 and 1977—are another interesting age group. Unlike baby boomers, this age group is a declining percentage of the population. The 47 million Gen Xers are, as a rule, more skeptical, have a more balanced work ethic, and are less impressed by titles, authority, or status than any other group. Xers are especially cynical about things held dear by previous generations, particularly baby boomers. In fact, if the boomers created yuppies (young urban professionals), Gen Xers have given rise to a new kind of elite: yawns (young and wealthy but normal).[14] Some people suggest the behavior of Xers is the result of their growing up during the years leading up to and following the end of the Cold War as well as coming of age during the recession of the early 1990s.

Almost 80 million members of the so-called Generation Y—also called the "Net Generation," "iGeneration," "Google generation," "echo boomers," and "millennium generation"—are those who were born between 1978 and 1994. This group is emerging as a major buying and consuming force in the economy. In addition to being the last generation of Americans wholly born in the 20th century, this group is racially diverse (more than one in three is not Caucasian) and has been pampered, nurtured, and programmed with a slew of activities since they were preschoolers. Since Yers were the first to grow up with the Internet in its developed form—including music downloads, instant messaging, and camera phones—many of them have never wound a watch, purchased a record, used a typewriter, or had a landline phone in their home or apartment. They think nothing of text messaging rather than calling, downloading music off the Internet, or having tongue rings. In many ways, they are the most "optimistic" generation in this country's history. They tend to have higher disposable incomes than their age group in prior generations, are interested in good health, and tend not to rely on others for their success. Research has also found that Gen Y provides a wealth of potential to employers because of their vigor, enthusiasm, talent, early experience, and high expectations.[15] They want a professional career but place a higher priority on family and home. Three out of four have a working mother, and one out of four is in a single-parent household. Emerging evidence also suggests that Gen Yers' values are more conservative than those of their parents as evident by their tendency to live separately before marriage. Exhibit 3.3 illustrates the key differences between these age groups.

	Baby Boomers	Gen X	Gen Y
Also known as	Boomers	Baby busters	Echo boomers Millennium generation Digital generation
Dates of birth	1946–1964	1965–1977	1978–1994
Number in U.S.	78 million	47 million	80 million
Annual spending	Over $2.3 trillion	Over $800 billion	$1 trillion
Experienced	Birth of rock and roll Space exploration Racial divides Sexual revolution	Growing divorce rate Gang violence Pop culture Information explosion	Age of technology Multilayered information Growth in branding Recycling
Respond to	Authority	Creativity	Learning
Perspective on technology	Fearful	Proficient	Indoctrinated
Attitude	Realistic	Pessimistic	Optimistic

Exhibit 3.3
Boomers, Xers, and Yers

Implications for Retailers

The most significant implication of an aging population for retailers, particularly those targeting boomers, is that their customers' big spending years are generally behind them. However, retailers must resist the temptation to overlook these segments. Despite the fact that boomers still spend an estimated $2.3 trillion on consumer goods and services annually, few retailers fully appreciate today's older boomer consumer. Instead, they continue merchandising and marketing to younger and less affluent Xers and Yers.

Retailers who ignore boomers—thinking they're past their spending prime—are limiting their success. After all, boomers will continue to buy cars, travel, and indulge in expensive "toys" for themselves as well as for presents for their kids and grandkids.[16] This point was driven home to one of the authors by the owner of a successful regional department store. He said, "Let Dillard's target the 30- and 40-year-olds. I love having the seniors by myself. I just have to realize that every time a funeral goes by, it was probably one of my customers. Still more and more folks are getting older." Sadly, this chain was taken over by a larger retailer a decade ago and later filed Chapter 11 when the new operator repositioned it to appeal to "hip" 30- to 40-year-olds.

Besides understanding the various needs of each age segment, retailers must also understand what motivates consumers to spend money. Younger adults are by their very nature acquisition oriented. These first-time renters and home buyers need to acquire material objects and usually judge their progress by such possessions; older adults tend to conserve what they have. Therefore, as the population ages, a significant driving force for total economic growth may dry up unless retailers provide consumers with a reason to shop.

This "graying" of America will have enormous consequences for businesses beyond retailing as older consumers tend to be skeptical and less interested in shopping. Retailers must be able to speak the older consumers' language, avoid talking down to or patronizing them, shun "phony friendliness," and understand that, as they age, older consumers need easy-to-navigate store layouts and clearly labeled merchandise.[17]

It is doubtful that all the baby boomers will behave as their parents did a generation before them. Retailers who make this assumption will be mistaken. A 50-year-old in 2015 will not act like a 50-year-old in 1995. In fact, they may even keep some of the habits of a 30-year-old in 1995 (which is what they were) tempered with the wisdom of maturity. Many of these so-called Pepsi Generation types will probably enter the "gray market" kicking and screaming. They will demand that retailers embrace their values, such as youthfulness and invincibility, no matter what the product or service: food, insurance, entertainment, or medicine. Therefore, while some firms seek to meet the increased demand for health care services and travel, restaurants (where the over-60 category accounts for more than 30 percent of the breakfast and dinner trade) will have to consider such items as the design of their tables and seats, and financial service firms will have to reconsider their product offerings to this fixed-income category of consumers. This is especially true for women between 50 and 70 who have the time, money, and motivation to take control of their future but are unlikely to be swayed by flashy ads.

In addition to altering the types of products offered to these aging segments of the population, retailers will also need to shift the types of services provided if they are to gain the consumers' dollar. In general, retailers will have to use bigger print, provide brighter lighting in parking lots, and install fewer displays that block store aisles. They would also be wise to rethink the way they portray and target senior citizens in their advertising. Today's successful retailers will be those who come up with new and ingenious ways to not just attract this audience but also compel them to walk in the door. For instance, many shopping centers are considering the use of valet parking and lounges with concierge services that make not only shopping easier but also the shopper feel pampered. Once these consumers reach the store, the retailer's job is to convince them that there simply isn't another merchant that can cater to their needs and wishes. On a final note, retailers must also remember that a significant percentage of this group is media and technology savvy; younger consumers are not the only ones buying iPods, camera phones, and the like.

Although many retailers have some significant planning to do if they are to maintain their boomers' patronage, retailers must also not forget about the Gen Xers and Gen Yers. These two groups are not only different in age but also significantly different in their buying behavior. They will be difficult for retailers to reach without a well-considered effort. In fact, because many of them grew up during the rapid advancements in technology and connectivity (instant messaging, camera phones, the Internet, and iPods), they are more sophisticated than previous generations when it comes to shopping. The shopping behavior for Gen Yers, for example, is based on different criteria than previous generations. They are concerned with how the product makes them appear and less concerned about the shopping process.[18] Some banks have even lured Gen Yers, not with low interest rates, but with online user friendliness whereby they can drag money from one account to another all on the same screen. Realizing the Yers' interests, many banks are even allowing their customers to set their own rules for transferring funds into savings accounts.[19]

Gen Yers also seem to be turned off by promotions that don't take them seriously. These antifashion and antiestablishment consumers still want entertainment or events when they shop; however, the promotions used must be relevant to them, funny, and say, "We understand." Retailers dealing with this market must also remember that 60 percent of 18- to 25-year-olds today rarely carry cash; instead they purchase with debit or credit cards, enticing some observers to call them "Generation P" (for plastic).[20] Finally, probably the biggest difference between the various generations is that 62 percent of web users under age 30 consider the Internet to be the best place to find good deals, while only 32 percent of users age 65 and older do.[21]

Some retailers have also made a major mistake by overlooking the teenagers and the so-called tweeners (those aged 8 to 14). These younger shoppers spend $40 billion annually and influence another $450 billion in purchases. Retailers of all sorts should target these shoppers in addition to their parents. After all, while their parents might cite price as the primary reason for purchasing a particular item for their children, "child request" was a close second. Teens and tweeners have trained their parents to know what to buy for them. While many companies analyze which products appeal to the older generations, retailers seldom think about marketing specifically to those under 20. Some retailers are using the Internet to reach out to these young consumers since most of them are more often at their computer than they are at the mall.

One company that has realized the power of the under-20 consumer is Aeropostale. After originally targeting teenage males, the retailer shifted its strategy to take advantage of the younger female market. Aeropostale realized that females tend to purchase more clothes, and female fashion offers higher profit margins. Now instead of going head-to-head with Abercrombie & Fitch and American Eagle Outfitters for the high-school and college-age shoppers, the chain carries clothes that are slightly less sexy and revealing to appeal to tweeners and their parents. Aeropostale has also benefited from less competition for the younger age group.

The recent recession has also introduced another trend for these under-20 shoppers: buying secondhand. These retailers not only allow the consumer to save money but also appeal to a growing ecofriendly sentiment among teenagers. Just as their parents discuss "bargain conquests" at parties, these younger consumers talk of the coolness of getting a super deal on those vintage jeans. Today's youth are really aware of what is happening to their economy and to their families.[22]

Ethnic Trends

More than 160 years ago, Ralph Waldo Emerson wrote about America as the utopian product of a culturally and racially mixed "melting pot." Emerson explicitly welcomed the racial intermixing of whites and nonwhites, a highly controversial view during his lifetime. However, it is only in the last half-century that the United States has moved from a predominantly white population to a society rich in racial and ethnic diversity. Today non-Hispanic whites account for only 68 percent of the U.S. population.[23] Further, the ever-growing minority population is comprised of nearly as many Hispanics as blacks, surging numbers of Asians, and a small but growing American Indian population. In fact, the U.S. Census Bureau now projects that by 2042 non-Hispanic whites will no longer make up the majority of the population. Instead, they are now expected to fall to 46 percent of the population by 2050, with the Hispanic population rising from 15 percent today to 30 percent by 2050. In addition, African Americans are expected to grow their current 13 percent to 15 percent and Asian Americans from 5 percent to almost 10 percent in 2050. Consequently, the term "minority" is likely to have a very different meaning in the next few decades.

Implications for Retailers[24]

Given the growth rate projections for the U.S. population overall, retailers must understand Hispanic shoppers and their $1.2 trillion of purchasing power. Today, 65 percent of them are under age 35, and they're an average of 9 years younger than the overall U.S. population (27.3 years to 36.4 years). However, probably the most important statistic to remember is that between now and 2020, the Hispanic American teen population will grow by 62 percent versus a 10-percent rate for all teens. In fact, by 2020 they will be the largest U.S. teen population, with 88 percent of them born in the United States.

One of the two of the most common mistakes that retailers make when targeting Hispanics is assuming that their population in the United States is homogeneous. Most U.S. Hispanics are Mexican, but some are from other Central and South American or Caribbean nations such as Cuba, the Dominican Republic, and Puerto Rico. Hispanics in Miami are culturally different from Hispanics in Houston.

The other common mistake made by retailers is that all Hispanics behave the same in the marketplace. Actually, second-generation Hispanic Americans, who have been immersed in American culture, are very different in their shopping behavior than foreign-born

The proportion of the U.S. population that is Hispanic and African-American is expected to rise. Retailers will need to adjust their merchandising strategies to appeal to these market segments.

Hispanics, who usually view themselves as completely Hispanic and have minimal contact with or interest in mainstream U.S. culture. However, as language skills improve, many choose to join the mainstream. Exhibit 3.4 shows the top- and bottom-ranked lifestyle attributes for a cross-section of Hispanic Americans in

Exhibit 3.4
Top- and Bottom-Ranked
Lifestyle Attributes

Top-Ranked Lifestyle Attributes   tns/RF

Hispanic Rank vs. Total shoppers	Total Hispanics
1 vs. 5	Do most shopping at stores where they can buy everything at one time
2 vs. 2	Usually eat home-cooked meals
3 vs. 22	Know brands of products they are going to buy before they go shopping
4 vs. 4	Do most shopping at stores known for everyday low pricing
5 vs. 20	Cooking is a great source of satisfaction for me
6 vs. 21	Buy more fresh foods than packaged foods
7 vs. 19	Take the time to browse when shopping for groceries
8 vs. 28	Like to take time to browse when shopping for health/beauty products
9 vs. 3	Pay close attention to exact price paid for most grocery items
10 vs. 6	I always try to buy products that are on sale

Source: TNS Shopper360. Used with written permission of TNS Retail Forward

Bottom-Ranked Lifestyle Attributes   tns/RF

Hispanic Rank vs. Total shoppers	Total Hispanics
76 vs. 58	Grocery shopping is an unpleasant necessity
75 vs. 64	I often check a store's Web site for specials or coupons before shopping
74 vs. 26	I redeem a lot of coupons
73 vs. 66	Shopping for non-food household products is an unpleasant necessity
72 vs. 76	I get bored buying the same brands even if they are good
71 vs. 61	I'm always in a hurry when I'm grocery shopping
70 vs. 41	I and /or another member of my household is on a diet
69 vs. 73	I don't have time to make major, stock-up types of shopping trips
68 vs. 67	When I see a new product on the shelf, I often buy it just to see what it is like
67 vs. 53	I often check for information on where a product is made before purchasing it

Source: TNS Shopper360. Used with written permission of TNS Retail Forward

comparison to all shoppers. As one can see, lifestyle attributes offered by retailers, may be valued differently by different consumer groups.

Not to be ignored is the fact that African Americans, with a population of 40 million, currently make up 13 percent of the population with a purchasing power of $1.1 trillion. However, while their population is expected to grow to 60 million by 2050, their percentage of the overall population is likely to change by only a few percentage points. Conversely, the Asian American population, with 15 million consumers, 5 percent of the total population, and a purchasing power of $670 billion, is expected to double by 2050.

Geographic Trends

The location of consumers in relation to the retailer will often affect how they buy. In this section of overall population trends, we take a closer look at how geographic trends affect retail operations.

Shifting Geographic Centers

Retailers should be concerned not only with the number of people, their ages, and their ethnicity but also with where they reside. Consumers, especially as they age, will not travel great distances to make retail purchases. All consumers want convenience and will therefore tend to patronize local retail outlets.

Because the U.S. population for the past 200 years has been moving toward the West and the South, growth opportunities in retailing should be the greatest in these areas. For example, between 2000 and 2007, the eight fastest-growing states were all in the West and South (Nevada, Arizona, Utah, Idaho, Colorado, Georgia, Texas, and Florida). In fact, between now and 2050, the South's and West's populations are expected to grow by 44 percent and 45 percent, respectively, whereas the Midwest is expected to grow only 10 percent and the Northeast 7 percent. As will be pointed out later in this chapter, there are marked overall differences in the behavior of consumers based on the region in which they live.

Implications for Retailers

As consumers continue to shift in geographic location, Northeastern and Midwestern retailers are experiencing slower growth, and national retailers are adding stores and distribution centers (warehouses) in the South and West. As this trend continues, retailers must remember, for example, that when people in the North retire to the South, they generally will change the type and style of clothing they purchase year-round (both online and in stores). If the national chains don't plan for this, it could send shockwaves up the supply chain all the way back to the textile manufacturers. As a result, it is important that retailers understand the purchasing behavior of consumers in each region of the country.

Yet a common mistake made by retailers is to assume that all consumers in a certain geographic area have the same purchasing habits. While households in the Northeast tend to marry later and spend more on education, food, housing, and apparel as a percentage of consumer expenditures, they all don't spend that way. Midwesterners on average spend more on entertainment, tobacco, and smoking supplies. Those in the South spend relatively more on transportation and health care and make more cash contributions. Finally, those in the West spend more on personal insurance and pensions, housing, and entertainment.

Exhibit 3.5 contains another important lesson for retailers. Not only do consumers living in Texas have different consumption patterns than people living in other states, but also, Texas consumers are quite dissimilar from one another based on their location within the state. (Note the amount of lard used in West Texas, home of two of the authors. It is a common ingredient in many ethnic dishes, including Mexican food.) In fact, these same differences have been found to occur in different parts of the same city. As a result, many of the leading retailers have developed "micromarketing" merchandising strategies.

Micromarketing involves tailoring merchandise in each store to match the preferences of its neighborhood. It is made possible with the use of the optional stock list approach, discussed in Chapter 1, and computer software programs that match neighborhood demographics with product demand. For example, two of the biggest Sears stores in the area are nearly the same size and do about the same in annual dollar sales; yet the merchandise makeup of the two is quite different. The urban store, which is close to many gourmet bakeries, doesn't carry bread makers, but bread makers are popular items in the more upscale suburban store 15 miles

micromarketing
Is the tailoring of merchandise in each store to the preferences of its neighborhood.

Exhibit 3.5
Texas Consumers' Percentage of National Average Usage

Product	Dallas/Fort Worth (%)	Houston (%)	San Antonio/ Corpus Christi (%)	West Texas/ New Mexico (%)
Biscuits/Dough	148*	122	103	85
Butter	51	57	39	57
Fresh Eggs	94	112	141	110
Juice/RFG	74	104	76	66
Lard	26	121	**	419
Canned Ham	39	21	22	28
Sausage	134	179	219	73
Baked Beans	82	76	51	60
Cocktail Mixes	118	79	82	112
Pasta	71	80	72	76
Rice/Popcorn Cakes	84	69	58	73
Cosmetics	237	133	329	221
Cold/Sinus Tab/Cough Drops	157	113	125	105
Deodorant	119	118	125	86
Hair Coloring	137	122	238	130
Laxatives	152	116	164	117
Cat Food	88	73	81	67
Diapers	115	135	160	74
Facial Tissue	82	66	64	78
Paper Napkins	71	74	78	68
Motor Oil	112	92	279	114
Shoe Polish & Accessories	147	145	171	147
Tape	163	105	175	149
Hosiery	164	126	156	110

*National average = 100%
**Not measured in this market.
Used with the permission of Information Resources, Inc.

A large urban city is often composed of many smaller markets or neighborhoods such as this Chinese neighborhood in San Francisco. Retailers operating in these neighborhoods need to adjust their merchandise and services to serve the local market.

metropolitan statistical areas (MSAs)
Are freestanding urban areas with populations in excess of 50,000.

away. The same thing occurs with Macy's in Cincinnati, where the downtown Fountain Place Macy's displays luggage more prominently than others. Cincinnati stores because the downtown store attracts more business travelers than other locations, perhaps people attending conventions. Meanwhile, consumers boosted sales of high-end denim at the chain's Kenwood store, a trend that was not as strong with shoppers at other Macy's stores in the region.[25]

Urban Centers

Most of the U.S. population resides in metropolitan areas with populations greater than 50,000, which the U.S. Census Bureau calls **metropolitan statistical areas** (MSAs). The proportion of the population residing in these cities has increased dramatically, from 64 percent in 1950 to 80 percent today. However, the urban or metropolitan population varies considerably by state. For instance, California, Massachusetts, and New Jersey are more than 90 percent urban or metro; whereas Maine, Mississippi, Vermont, and West Virginia are less than 50 percent urban or metro.[26] Further, in the past the migration to MSAs was directed more toward suburban than central city areas, yet some experts feel that a significant increase in gas prices may reverse this trend.

Implications for Retailers

Every shift in consumer population patterns has major implications for retailers, especially when it comes to expenditures made for household products. While these recent shifts have resulted in a slowdown for downtown retail activity, sales increases in freestanding suburban locations have more than offset any decline.

There are also opportunities for retailers in smaller markets. During the past decade, retail activity has grown rapidly in secondary markets, areas with populations less than 50,000. Historically, most chain retailers have ignored these markets. But in addition to their rapid growth, secondary markets are attractive because of the low level of retail competition, lower building costs, cheaper labor, and fewer building and zoning regulations. As MSAs have begun to stabilize, secondary markets have become more attractive.

Mobility

In many countries, people are born, raised, married, widowed, and die in the same city or immediate geographic vicinity. While this was once true in the United States, it certainly is not characteristic of contemporary America. Typically, Americans change residence about a dozen times in a lifetime. This is twice the rate of the British and French and four times as often as the Irish. A major factor for this heightened mobility is the country's divorce rate. Of the 13 percent of the population that moves each year, about 69 percent remain in the same county, about 23 percent move to a new county but stay in the same state, and approximately 15 percent move to a new state. (The "total moves" percentages total more than 100 percent because some Americans moved more than once that year.)[27] Retailers must remember that the farther one moves from a prior residence, the more one needs to establish new retail shopping patterns.

Goodshoot/Jupiter Images

Local farmers are able to serve the customer directly through small local public markets as pictured in this vegetable market in Beijing, China.

Implications for Retailers

A study regarding mobility has found that in almost half of large families, where the children don't go to college, one child will live within five miles of the parent(s) when the parent(s) reaches age 60, and in more than three-quarters of the cases within 50 miles of the parent(s).[28] Thus, with the recent trend toward higher education (discussed in the next learning objective), which results in more job variations; retailers can only expect consumer mobility to increase. This presents a problem because retailers serve local markets and tend to cater to well-defined demographic groups. If the population moves, the retailer may find that its target market no longer resides in its immediate area. Likewise, retailers in areas undergoing rapid population growth will want to be prepared to serve these new consumers quickly as many retail-oriented decisions must be made on the spot. After a move, consumers must locate new sources for food, clothing, household goods, and recreation. This presents an advantage for chain stores, since a consumer moving from Des Moines, Iowa, to Baton Rouge, Louisiana, knows what to expect at a Men's Warehouse, Target, Old Navy, or Macy's.

Social Trends

LO 2

What social trends should be monitored, and what are their impacts on retailing?

In this section, we continue our examination of demographic factors that affect the modern retailer by looking at several social trends: the increasing level of educational attainment, the state of marriage and divorce, the makeup of the American household, and the changing nature of work. To get the most current data regarding these trends, the reader should visit the home page of the Commerce Department's Census Bureau website (http://census.gov). This site provides easy access to the latest census figures.

Education

The education level of the average American is increasing. In 2007, 86 percent of individuals aged 25 years and older had a high school degree and 29 percent had a college degree.[29] The Gen Xers, who were between ages 30 and 42 in 2007, are the most educated generation ever. (However, as soon as the last members of Gen Y reach age 25, they will become the most educated.) One in three has completed four years of college, which is almost as high as the 41 percent of those 25 years and older who had a high school degree in 1960.[30] Currently, more men than women have college degrees, 30 percent to 28 percent.[31] However, figures suggest this trend is rapidly changing given there were 23 percent more women enrolled in college than men in 2006.[32] As a result, it is forecast that in the very near future women—who are increasingly pursuing higher-paying career fields such as business, psychology, biology and life sciences, and engineering—will earn nearly 60 percent of the bachelor's and master's degrees in U.S. colleges and universities.[33]

Implications for Retailers

Educational attainment is the single most reliable indicator of a person's income potential, attitudes, and spending habits. Thus, college-educated consumers differ in their buying behavior from other workers of the same age and income levels. They are more alert to price, quality, and advertised claims. However, when retailers use education to segment the marketplace, they often overlook the 32 million Americans over age 25 who have some college experience but who failed to earn a degree. In many ways, people with some college best define the term "average" American.[34] They have more money than high school graduates but less than college graduates. They also fall between these groups in their propensity to shop in department stores, spend on apparel, buy new cars, travel, read books, watch TV, and invest in stocks and bonds.

Since education levels for the population, in aggregate, are expected to continue to rise, retailers can expect consumers to become increasingly sophisticated, discriminating, and independent in their search for consumer products. They will also demand a staff capable of intelligently dealing with their needs and wants.

Education is also a key determinant of the use of the Internet for shopping. Today's 30- and 40-year-olds grew up with the computer and feel comfortable with it. Given their higher level of education, they are more prone to shop electronically because they don't need the assurances or hand-holding that some retailers provide. This may present problems for many traditional service providers. For example, travel agencies in recent years have been left out of the loop as cybershoppers now "surf the net" to purchase airline tickets, hotel rooms, rental cars, cruises.

State of Marriage

A relatively new social phenomenon has occurred during the past quarter century. In 1970, less than 10 percent of the U.S. male population between ages of 30 and 34 had never married and slightly more than 6 percent of the same female population had never married. In 2007, these percentages had increased to 32 and 24 percent, respectively.[35] Married couples are one of the slowest-growing household types not only in this country but also worldwide. In 1970, males married at a median age of 23 and females at 21; today, the median age for males is about 28 and 26 for females; however, there are marked regional differences in these numbers. Not only are many people postponing marriage but also some are choosing not to marry at all. In the

45- to 54-year-old age bracket, 14 percent of males and 10 percent of females have never been married.[36]

Implications for Retailers

This trend toward single-person households presents many opportunities for the retailer because of the increased need for a larger number of smaller houses complete with home furnishings. This is especially true for the young adult market. As a result, retailers may need to adjust their store hours to accommodate the needs of this market. In addition, with more men living alone, supermarkets will have to direct promotions toward their needs and habits, particularly since men tend to focus on getting specific items and then getting out of the store as quickly as possible.

Divorce

Since 1960, the U.S. divorce rate has increased by 250 percent. While many have offered potential explanations for this trend, few have given as compelling a justification as Professor Gary Becker of the University of Chicago. Professor Becker was awarded the Nobel Prize for theorizing that families, just like businesses, rationally make decisions that maximize benefits. The theory suggests that in the traditional family, working husbands and stay-at-home wives each performed labor that, when combined, provided the greatest payoff for the time involved. However, as women's wages rose, it became more profitable for them to enter the labor force. As a result, spouses became less dependent on each other and divorce rates increased. An interesting statistic is that the average divorce occurs approximately 7.2 years after marriage, confirming the conventional wisdom about the proverbial seven-year itch.

Implications for Retailers

When a divorce occurs, many retail purchases are required. A second household, quite similar to that of the never-married individual, is formed almost immediately. These new households need certain items such as furniture and kitchen appliances, televisions and stereos, and even linens. Divorce may also impact the way people shop once they are settled into their new homes. Retailers must make specific adjustments for divorced, working women with children by adjusting store hours, providing more consumer information, and changing the product assortment.[37]

Makeup of American Households

Because households are the basic consumer unit for most products, household growth and consumer demand go hand-in-hand. Yet, because of the differing sizes and habits of various generations, the change in the makeup of households is notoriously hard to predict. The number of households without children increased 18 percent in the 1980s, 11 percent in the 1990s, and 11 percent between 2000 and 2007. In fact, most people are unaware that 53 percent of all households have no children.[38]

Some interesting trends have also occurred over the last two decades. For example, between 1990 and 2007 the number of people living alone ("home aloners") increased by 35 percent.[39] This trend, which represents nearly one-fourth of all households, is the result of an increased desire for privacy, an increase in young adults delaying marriage, an increase in never marrieds, and a large increase in the number of people who live alone after the death of a spouse. Also, the number of unmarried couples ("mingles") has increased by 167 percent since 1980. This trend, although it represents only 5 percent of all couple households,[40] is significant to the retailer because it represents a purchasing unit that is hard to understand by conventional household or family norms. The retailer, as well as the social scientist, has little knowledge of how much joint decision making occurs in such a household.

boomerang effect
the recent trend of children returning to live with their parents after having already moved out.

Finally, there are two more interesting facts about the changing American household. The first is called the **boomerang effect**—so called because the parents think the children have left for good, but they keep coming back. This was particularly true during the recent recession. The online job site Monster.com reported that nearly half of all 2008 graduates returned home after graduation and that 4 out of 10 from the previous year's class were still living with their parents.[41] Others analysts estimate that, over the next decade, 40 percent of children will return to live with their parents after having previously left. While this projection is extremely sensitive to future economic conditions, several factors will account for the projected 7 million boomerang households: People who marry in their 20s are just as likely to divorce as those who marry as teens, high-school dropouts will not be able to find permanent work, and so on. In addition, when the average college grad owes nearly $20,000 in student loans and has almost $2,900 in credit card debt, living with the folks helps.[42] The second factor to alter the makeup of the American household involves the situation in which parents of the household's head or spouse move in to live with their children. Often these parents are not healthy enough to live full-time by themselves, but their health is not so bad that they need full-time assistance in a nursing home. When this occurs, it is often referred to as a **sandwich generational family** or **trigenerational family** when all three generations (parents, grandparents, and children) live together in the same house or apartment.

sandwich generational family or **trigenerational family**
occurs when three generations (parents, grandparents, and children) live together in the same house.

Implications for Retailers

Today, the combination of so-called home-aloners, mingles, singles, dinks (dual-income, no-kids households), and empty nesters accounts for nearly 75 percent of all U.S. households. This market is not concerned about back-to-school sales and other family-oriented retail activities. Instead, they're more interested in HDTVs, high social image, and gourmet foods. However, it is important that retailers recognize the differences within this market. Younger women normally spend more on clothing, and men spend more on alcohol, cars, and eating out. As they age, women begin to spend more than men on cars and entertainment while men remain the best customers for eating out. The older segment of the single-household market will require special attention from today's retailers. Between now and 2015, the "wild and crazy single guys" of the 1980s and early 1990s will turn into "tired and pudgy older guys" who no longer live like college students, although some may wish they could.

As you can see in our "Global Retailing" box, this changing structure in the makeup of households is not just an American trend, but a worldwide trend.

Changing Nature of Work

In the United States and other industrialized economies, work has become less central to one's life. In the past, work was often the way people identified themselves and obtained meaning in their lives. Perhaps because of deterioration in

Global Retailing

Worldwide Changes in Household Structure

The United States isn't the only country in which nontraditional households are becoming mainstream. Retailers in other developed countries are also facing similar trends. For example, the rise in the number of single parents, unmarried couples, and people living alone is common to most countries in the developed world. The difference is in the pace at which these trends are progressing.

Four main factors have changed the makeup of households and families in the last two decades: Women are having fewer children, more children are being born out of wedlock, populations are aging, and marriage is down while divorce is up.

Consider what is happening today in Japan, where an entire generation of people in their 30s came of age during Japan's so-called lost decade, a stretch of economic stagnation from 1990 to the mid-2000s. Throughout this period, Japanese companies were in a retrenchment mode, and young people faced what came to be known as a "hiring ice age." Many settled for part-time work to make ends meet or chose to withdraw completely from society until conditions improved. While they hoped to eventually find their way into regular career paths, many are now being passed over in favor of new graduates—a serious problem in a country that still values lifetime employment and frowns on midcareer job hopping. As a result, Japan currently has the highest suicide rate and lowest birthrate of all industrialized countries, as well as a rising incidence of untreated depression cases.[43]

European countries are also experiencing significant changes in the structure of households. For instance, Scandinavia sets the pace for out-of-wedlock births and cohabitation. Sweden and Denmark have the largest shares of births to unmarried couples. Interestingly, though, these countries don't have the highest shares of single parents. Instead, unmarried mothers in these countries often live with their partners.

It's not clear which country has the highest share of "mingles" or cohabitating couples because some countries now include them with married couples in official household statistics. One estimate shows that virtually all young Swedes cohabitate before they marry.

Sadly, the United States tops the list for single parents, partly because of high divorce rates, but also because American single parents are more likely to be young, never-married women on their own rather than cohabitaters.

Because of the vast differences in social behavior throughout the world, many people make various faux pas when visiting foreign countries or entertaining guests from other countries. In fact, according to a survey sponsored by Vayama, nearly half (47%) said they did something when traveling outside the United States that they later learned was considered inappropriate behavior. Therefore, before conducting business or any other type of dealings with people from a foreign country, it is suggested that one consults Vayama's website (www.vayama.com/jsp/destination/country Etiquette.jsp). The site has put together a set of social tips that help one not only avoid embarrassment but also fully experience the culture of the other countries.

---

institutional confidence or the overall prosperity of our economy, as Americans we identify less with our employment. At the same time, peoples' hobbies are becoming more work oriented. Many are gardening, investing time and money in learning to cook, and doing projects around the house. At the same time, we continue to see a rise in self-employed and home-based workers. In 2007, the most recent year for which data is available, there were nearly 10.5 million self-employed individuals and an estimated 6.4 million home-based businesses in the United States.[44] However, as a result of the recent recession, these numbers are expected to increase in the coming years.

In addition to working from home or running a home business, many consumers are obtaining meaning from consumption. They have literally become durable goods junkies, collecting RVs, boats, workshops, HDTVs, swimming pools, and so on. To pay for these extras, these people often hold several jobs. In 2007, 7.7 million individuals had multiple jobs.[45] Many of these individuals were starting a small business while holding onto their main job; others were earning money to purchase something special, saving for future consumption, or saving for retirement.

Implications for Retailers

Because people are finding less meaning in their work, they are less loyal to their employers. Nearly 25 percent of all workers have held their job for fewer than 12 months, and the median length of service in a job is 4 years.[46] For entry-level personnel in retailing, turnover approaches 75 percent or more per year. Consequently, retailers need to find ways to enrich job experiences and lower turnover. One study found that turnover in the supermarket industry cost $5.8 billion annually. For instance, a cashier who departs costs the retailer $4,212; a department manager, $9,354; and a store manager, $56,844. These costs of employee turnover include paperwork errors, inventory shrinkage, and improper use of equipment. All of these errors occur due to the lack of experience of new employees. These errors lead to lower levels of customer service and satisfaction, which in turn leads to lost sales and profits.[47] One major opportunity for retailers is employing home-based and disabled workers. Home-based workers can handle telephone inquiries and do clerical work or bookkeeping. Likewise, disabled workers may represent a previously untapped pool of talent for the retailer.

Finally, since many individuals are holding multiple jobs, retailers can tap into this pool of individuals for part-time workers. Retailers have done this in the past, primarily at the clerk level. Today there are opportunities for retailers to employ part-timers in a variety of positions, including accounting, inventory control, merchandising, buying, and store management.

LO 3

Economic Trends

How do the changing American economic trends affect retailing?

In this section, we look at the effects of income growth, the declining rate of personal savings, the increase in the number of working women, and the widespread use of credit on the modern retailer.

Income Growth

In 2006, the median household income was slightly over $58,400, which, after adjusting for inflation, was an increase of less than 4 percent annually since 1990. However, not all consumer groups have equally shared this income increase. African American, Hispanic, and Caucasian family households experienced a 4 percent increase in annual income to $38,200, $40,000, and $61,200, respectively, from 1990 to 2006. Notably, Asian Pacific Islander family households, which were not tracked in 1980, had the highest household family income, which stood at $74,600 in 2006.[48]

As Exhibit 3.6 points out, incomes are continuing to shift among the various classes of Americans. Today, the American upper classes have a higher share of the nation's aggregate income in comparison to 1980. Further, the top fifth accounts for more than 50 percent of the nation's income while the bottom two-fifths, or lowest 40 percent of the population, earn less than one-seventh (14.0 percent) of the nation's income, down from 16.9 percent in 1980. The distribution of wealth is further emphasized by the fact that 1 percent of the population holds 40 percent of all the wealth. Thus, it appears that the rich are getting richer and the poor are

Year	Fifth Lowest	Fifth Second	Fifth Third	Fifth Fourth	Highest Fifth	Top 5%
2006	3.4	8.6	14.5	22.9	50.5	22.3
2000	4.3	9.8	15.4	22.7	47.7	21.1
1990	4.6	10.8	16.6	23.8	44.3	17.4
1980	5.3	11.6	17.5	24.4	41.1	14.6

Source: U.S. Bureau of Census, *Statistical Abstract of the United States: 2009*, Table 675.

Exhibit 3.6
Share of Aggregate Income Received by Each Fifth and the Top 5% of U.S. Households, 1980–2006

getting poorer. However, this data is partially misleading because income mobility in the United States is quite high. A significant proportion of the lowest-income households move up the income scale over a 10-year period while at the same time a significant proportion of the richest households move down the income scale. Consequently, it is quite possible that those that are rich today will be poorer in the future and vice versa.

Implications for Retailers

The imbalance in income growth across households has created an increased demand for value-oriented retailers such as discounters and manufacturers' outlets. In addition, it explains why many of the upscale retailers (such as Macy's, Nordstrom, and Neiman Marcus) before the recent recession had not suffered the economic pressures that many of their lower-scale counterparts faced. Retailers of luxury automobiles, lavish foreign vacations, and executive-style houses in gated communities had also done well. At the same time, the low income level and low income growth among some segments of the population explains the growth of chains, such as Dollar General, as well as recycled merchandise retailers.

Economists tend to view income from two different perspectives: disposable and discretionary. **Disposable income** is simply all personal income minus personal taxes. For most consumers, disposable income is their take-home pay. **Discretionary income** is disposable income minus the money needed for necessities to sustain life, such as minimal housing, minimal food, and minimal clothing. Retailers who sell necessities, such as supermarkets, like to see incomes rise and taxes decrease. These retailers know that while consumers won't spend all their increased disposable income on the retailer's merchandise, they will nevertheless increase spending. Retailers who sell luxury goods want to see discretionary income increase. However, the recent economic slowdown has had a negative effect on both types of incomes as the value of houses and stock market portfolios declined during this slowdown. In addition, many workers lost jobs, and others were forced to take pay cuts. As a result of these factors, the net worth of Americans fell almost 20 percent in 2008. This was the first decline in American household net worth since 2002.[49]

Another, often overlooked, implication for retailers is that many Americans now use the Internet, especially eBay, as a source to sell unwanted or unneeded merchandise and increase their income. This is especially evident during the first quarter of the year when many Americans use eBay to get rid of that unwanted Christmas scarf or that tie from Aunt Bessie. In fact, a whole new industry has developed to assist consumers who don't use eBay regularly. Drop shops, which will handle the entire selling process for a fee, are listed on eBay's website. Others may "regift" the unwanted merchandise to someone else or donate the item to

disposable income
Is personal income less personal taxes.

discretionary income
Is disposable income minus the money needed for necessities to sustain life.

charity. Also, during the recent recession, many pawnshops experienced a significant increase in business. In the past, pawnshop customers had an average household income of about $29,000. However, this increased to more than $50,000 as middle- and upper-middle-class customers faced ravaged stock portfolios, tightened bank credit, and unexpected layoffs and needed quick cash. In areas dogged by high unemployment and foreclosure rates, the pawn business was especially robust.[50] All of these activities are a variation on garage sales: The seller not only gets rid of stuff he or she doesn't need but also, in many cases, raises spending money.

Personal Savings

A major criticism of the U.S. economic system is that it does not reward personal saving. Expressed as a percentage of disposable income, savings have dwindled from a post–World War II high of 8.8 percent in 1981 to 4.6 percent in 1995, to a dismal 0.4 percent in 2007.[51] While this may seem odd, it is important to note that during most of the last decade, the economy, stock market, and especially the housing market experienced exceptionally strong growth. As a result, many people stopped saving and began to invest in the stock market. Some people might consider this a form of saving despite its additional elements of risk.

Regardless, it should also be pointed out that the government's numbers regarding the savings rates fail to address the treatment of capital gains or losses. When the government measures disposable income, it counts wages, interest earned, and dividends; however, it overlooks realized or unrealized capital gains or losses. Consequently, changes in wealth that result from variations in home and equity values are omitted. The government's numbers also count the full cost of purchases made over time—such as cars and appliances. Thus, the government's data tends to undervalue savings because it fails to consider the wealth effect. The *wealth effect* claims that for every $100 of additional wealth generated in an individual's stock market holdings, that individual will spend $4 (4 percent). Such spending lowers the nation's savings rate because, as the stock market rises, spending increases without an increase in wages and salaries. Savings will also be decreased in this example because the government will subtract taxes on the stock market gains from disposable income. While the net wealth of the United States increased by 82 percent between 1992 and 2000, it only increased by 39 percent from 2000 to 2008. Such growth encouraged Americans to spend freely, which in turn furthered the overall economic growth of the country. However, in the last quarter of 2007, net wealth began to fall as stock and housing values slipped. Obviously, these decreases in property values or stock prices will present problems for retailers.[52]

One additional point should also be made. Although the national savings rate in the United States is only a fraction of the rates in Europe, Japan, and China, it must be remembered that each country measures income and savings differently. Thus, comparisons between countries are often unclear.

Implications for Retailers

Retailers have enjoyed continued sales growth over the past decade; however, this growth is not due to significant increases in household income. Instead, retailers have benefited from the spending rather than saving mindset of the consumer. Yet retailers must be prepared for the next decade, when baby boomers and Gen Xers plan for retirement while simultaneously reducing their spending and increasing their savings.

Some economists fear that in another decade retired boomers will begin to remove much of their money from the stock market. If this occurs in great numbers, then the United States could see another declining market that would likely result in a reverse wealth effect. This is because consumers losing money in the stock market tend to save about four cents for every dollar lost (4 percent). Another fear is that because of good health, many boomers may postpone retirement, leading to a surplus in labor supply. As the marketplace becomes saturated with available workers, overall wages fall, which could negatively impact future retail sales.[53]

Women in the Labor Force

Over the past five decades, women have become a dominant factor in the labor force. In 1970, 43 percent of all women over age 16 were in the labor force; today it is just under 60 percent.[54] This trend is true of all age groups, even women ages 25 to 34, who might be expected to be raising families. Seventy-six percent of all women ages 25 to 34 are currently in the labor force; yet this high percentage is not simply due to the postponement of having children. Instead, the percentage of working, married women with preschoolers increased from 30 percent in 1970 to 62 percent in 2007.[55] Further, slightly more than a quarter of all female employees are able to make use of flexible schedules at the workplace.[56] As we discussed earlier, more women are obtaining college degrees, and more than 83 percent of women with college degrees are in the workforce.

This significant rise in the number of working women has protected many households from inflation and recession. In fact, many economists suggest that the working woman has been the nation's secret weapon against economic hardships. For example, the median household income for married households where both spouses are in the workforce rose more than 18 percent (after adjusting for inflation) between 1990 and 2006 to almost $83,000.[57] In addition to the working wife, another reason for the huge increase in household income for dual wage-earner families is that, where once a professional man would marry a secretary, nurse, or school teacher (all admirable occupations, but not the highest paying), today many professional men are marrying professional women. As a result, the household income for these couples is increasing faster than the norm. This is not only another cause of the polarization of income shown in Exhibit 3.6 but also creating a new social phenomenon in America—couples too tired for sex.[58]

Implications for Retailers

The rise in the number of working women has many retail implications. First, as the number of dual wage-earner families increases, many of these families have less time for shopping and are more prone to looking for convenience and additional services from retailers. Working men and women are often unable to shop between the hours of 8 A.M. and 6 P.M. Monday through Saturday. Thus, these individuals prefer that retailers hold sales and special events in the evenings or on weekends. Time-pressed shoppers also find that price is sometimes less important than convenience, availability, and service. Bricks-and-mortar retailers—in addition to making the shopping experience pleasant, if not exciting—must develop strategies that accommodate these customers' needs. They must extend store hours (early mornings, evenings, and weekends) and offer conveniences (express checkouts). Bricks-and-mortar retailers should also provide alternatives to in-store shopping, such as catalogs, online shopping, and even delivery if they want to compete for the time pressed shopper's store loyalty.

Widespread Use of Credit

Retailers, especially department stores and those selling big-ticket items, have long offered their own credit cards to customers. However, today the trend is away from the retailer's store-branded cards and toward third-party cards (Visa, MasterCard, Discover, American Express, etc.). Spurred on in recent years by active promotional campaigns and low interest rates, consumers in 2006 were staggering under an estimated $2.2 trillion in consumer debt.[59] In the United States, more than two-thirds of households now have a credit card, and more than 90 percent of households with annual incomes over $50,000 have at least two credit cards.[60]

Credit card firms are seeking for the trend to continue. They offer promotional incentives such as free airline miles, rebates on new auto purchases, and rebates on future purchases. For the retailer, credit card use has increased sales and profits. Consequently, retailers as varied as supermarkets and the family veterinarian are now forced to accept these third-party cards. Other retailers, such as Kroger, Walmart, Nordstrom, and Toys "R" Us, are now cobranding their names with the national card issuers.

Implications for Retailers

Retailers benefit from credit cards. Research shows that customers spend more when they use a credit card than when they must pay in cash. However, since the growth in credit has been outstripping the growth in personal income, it is evident that households will face a liquidity crisis as income growth slows or becomes negative. After all, 24 percent of households rarely pay off their credit card balance.[61] Such massive debt loads must be paid off, thereby leaving little income for future retail purchases. Finally, as noted earlier, today's college grad owes nearly $20,000 in student loans and has almost $2,900 in credit card debt. No wonder so many young people postpone getting married, having children, and buying a first house.

LO 4   Consumer Behavior Model

What is involved in the shopping and purchasing model, including the key stages in the buying process?

Now that we have examined the population, social, and economic trends of today, we can develop a model that describes and, to some degree, predicts how these factors come together to affect consumer buying patterns. We call this the *consumer shopping and purchasing model*. Consumers are typically confronted with fundamental decisions when it comes to meeting their needs and wants: What products or brands can potentially fulfill their needs, and where should they purchase these products or brands? Our model is sufficiently general to deal with both of these questions.

Examine the consumer shopping and purchasing model in Exhibit 3.7. This model suggests that consumer behavior is a process with a series of stages or steps. The six stages in the model are stimulus, problem recognition, search, evaluation of alternatives, purchase, and post-purchase evaluation.

Stimulus

stimulus
Refers to a cue that is external to the individual or a drive that is internal to the individual.

cue
Refers to any object or phenomenon in the environment that is capable of eliciting a response.

A **stimulus** involves a cue (external to the individual) or drive (internal to the individual). A **cue** is any object or phenomenon in the environment that is capable of eliciting a response. Common examples of retail marketing stimuli are advertisements, point-of-purchase displays, coupons, salespeople, and free samples. All

Problem Solving

| Stimulus | → | Problem Recognition | → | Active Information Gathering (Search) | → | Evaluate Alternatives | → | Purchase | → | Post-Purchase Evaluation |

Exhibit 3.7
Consumer Shopping and Purchasing Model

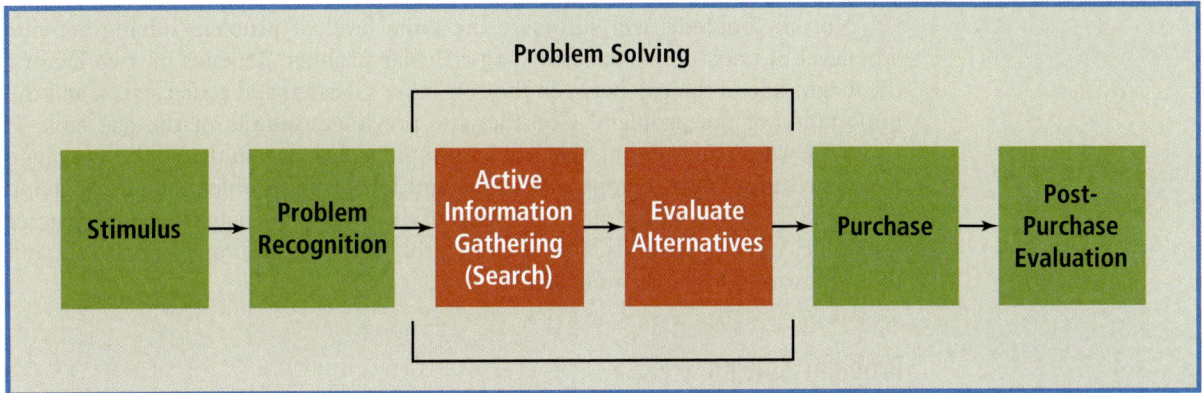

of these examples are cues controlled by the seller or retailer. In addition, there are cues that the retailer does not control. For example, word-of-mouth advertising is common in retailing. Many visits to e-tailing sites are the result of a visitor having a good experience and telling others.

A second type of stimulus is internal to the individual and is referred to as a *drive*. A **drive** is a motivating force that directs behavior. Drives can be physiologically based (hunger and the need to stay warm in the cold) or learned (the desire to spend spring break in Cancun). When drives are strong, they are more likely to prompt purchase behavior. The old adage "never go grocery shopping when you are hungry" illustrates this point.

Individuals can be exposed to both types of stimuli. For instance, one may see an advertisement (cue) for a restaurant at the same time that one is hungry (drive); a person living in Minnesota may be coping with a long, cold winter and browsing the Internet when she sees an advertisement for a vacation on the warm and sunny beaches of Hawaii.

As consumers move through their daily routines in an information economy, they are constantly exposed to hundreds of messages regarding products, services, and where to purchase them. As a result, one of the scarcest resources is human attention. All retailers are competing with virtually all other organizations and individuals for the consumer's attention. Consequently, the individual is always involved in **passive information gathering**, which is the task of receiving and processing information regarding the existence and quality of merchandise, services, stores, shopping convenience, parking, advertising, and any other factor that a consumer might consider in making a decision of where to shop and what to purchase.

Problem Recognition

Stimuli can often lead to problem recognition. **Problem recognition** occurs when the consumer's desired state of affairs departs sufficiently from the consumer's actual state of affairs. When this happens, the consumer is in a state of unrest until he or she finds a way to resolve this difference. Consider a few examples: (1) While driving across town, you notice that your car's gas tank is almost empty; (2) you hear an advertisement for a new Sony CD player and realize that your 10-year-old stereo needs replacing; (3) you will be graduating from college shortly and do not own any suitable clothes for your new career; and (4) you receive your tax refund and realize you now have money to go to Cancun for spring break.

drive
Refers to a motivating force that directs behavior.

passive information gathering
Is the receiving and processing of information regarding the existence and quality of merchandise, services, stores, shopping, convenience, pricing, advertising, and any other factors that a consumer might consider in making a purchase.

problem recognition
Occurs when the consumer's desired state of affairs departs sufficiently from the actual state of affairs, placing the consumer in a state of unrest.

Not all problems will stimulate the same level of problem-solving activity. The level of one's desire to resolve a particular problem depends on two factors: the magnitude of the gap between the consumer's desired and actual states, and the importance of the problem. Consider the previous example of the gas tank. If your tank were a quarter full, the problem would be less urgent than if the gas gauge were on empty. Next, compare your recognition of the problem about replacing your old CD player with your recognition of the problem of acquiring a new career wardrobe. In all probability, one of these problems is more important to you, and thus you would be more motivated to solve it first.

Problem Solving

The next two stages in the consumer shopping and purchasing model—active information gathering (or search) and evaluation of alternatives—will determine the degree of problem solving that occurs. Individuals solve problems by searching for information and then evaluating their options or alternatives. The search for information and careful evaluation of alternatives occurs to reduce risk. If consumers do not select the best product, they can incur financial loss (financial risk), personal harm (safety risk), or the decline of respect from family and friends (social risk).

The amount of problem-solving activity consumers engage in varies considerably, depending on their prior experience and the need to reduce financial, personal, and social risk. Consumers learn quickly, and when they locate the product, brands, and retailers that are good at satisfying their needs at a low or acceptable level of risk, then the degree of problem solving decreases. Exhibit 3.8 illustrates the three levels of problem solving. Note that these levels are determined by whether or not the consumer has a strong preference for a specific brand or retail store.

habitual problem solving
Occurs when the consumer relies on past experiences and learns to convert the problem into a situation requiring less thought. The consumer has a strong preference for the brand to buy and the retailer from which to purchase it.

Habitual Problem Solving

With **habitual problem solving**, the consumer relies on past experience and learning to convert the problem into a situation requiring less thought. Here the consumer has a strong preference for the brand to buy and the retailer from which to purchase it. Some consumers are not only habitual users of products but also heavy users. For instance, in fast-food restaurants, only one in five persons is a heavy user; however, they account for 60 percent of fast-food restaurant visits.[62]

Exhibit 3.8
Degrees of Consumer Problem Solving in Shopping and Purchasing

Brand Preference \ Retailer Preference	Strong	None or Weak
Strong	Habitual Problem Solving	Limited Problem Solving
None or Weak	Limited Problem Solving	Extended Problem Solving

By relying on past experience, the consumer has already arrived at an adequate solution to many of their more routine problems. Frequently purchased products of relatively low cost and low risk (e.g., toothpaste, milk, bread, soda pop) tend to belong in this category; however, products of a higher value may also be in this category. For example, when confronted with the need for a new automobile, some people can be loyal to both a particular brand and a specific retailer. Such individuals may be loyal to Ford and may patronize a favorite Ford dealer in their geographic area.

Limited Problem Solving

Limited problem solving occurs when the consumer has a strong preference for either the brand or the store but not both. The consumer may not have a store choice in mind but may have a strong preference for the brand to purchase. In this instance, since the brand has already been determined, the consumer has, in a sense, restricted the problem-solving process to deciding which retailer to patronize among those that carry the brand. Because the consumer may not be aware of all the retailers that carry the item, some searching may be required. To illustrate further, assume the picture tube on your TV fails and you decide to get a new TV. You know that you want a Sony, but since you are new in town, you do not know where to get the best deal. Also, you recognize that your search does not need to be limited to retailers in your community, and the Internet can help you locate the retailer with the lowest price. You prefer a local retailer who can service your set; however, you have decided that this additional convenience is not worthwhile if the local retailer's price is more than 10 percent higher than an out-of-town retailer's price. Although we refer to this category as *limited* problem solving, deciding which brand or store to select may still be an extensive process. Problem solving should therefore be viewed as a continuum.

limited problem solving
Occurs when the consumer has a strong preference for either the brand or the store, but not both.

Extended Problem Solving

Extended problem solving occurs when the consumer recognizes that a problem exists yet does not have a strong preference for either the brand or the store. For example, a woman in her early 20s has recently received a promotion and a 25-percent raise from the bank that employs her. Over the last year, she has postponed purchasing several major durable goods that she wants—a car, living-room furniture, and a DVD player. With the 25-percent raise, she can afford some, but not all, of these items. She has little prior information and experience regarding alternative brands and retailers that sell these products; therefore, she must engage in extensive problem solving to select the products she should buy, determine which brands are appropriate, and learn which retail outlets carry what she wants. Extensive problem solving typically involves infrequently purchased expensive products of high risk. Here, the consumer desires a lot of new information, which implies a need for extensive problem solving.

extended problem solving
Occurs when the consumer recognizes a problem but has decided on neither the brand nor the store.

Problem-Solving Stages

Once consumers recognize that a problem exists and believe a potential product solution exists within the marketplace, they will engage in problem solving. The first step is **active information gathering**, which is when consumers proactively gather information. Many consumers begin their active information gathering with a search engine such as Google to find out about the desired product or service, its

active information gathering
Occurs when consumers proactively gather information.

price, and where it is available. Consumers are then confronted with the second stage in problem solving—the evaluation of alternatives. The evaluation of alternatives typically involves three stages:

set of attributes
Refers to the characteristics of the store and its products and services.

1. In the first stage, consumers develop a set of attributes on which the purchase decision will be based. The **set of attributes** refers to the characteristics of the store and its products and services. These can include such things as price, product quality, store hours, knowledgeable sales help, convenient parking, after-sale service, and so on. These attributes are often based on general information sources such as preexisting knowledge, advertising, discussions with friends and relatives, and magazines such as *Consumer Reports* as well as the many information sources online.

2. In the second stage, consumers narrow their consideration set to a more manageable number of attributes. Although consumers want to think that they have considered a wide range of options so as not to miss a golden opportunity, they do not want to be confused by myriad options. In this phase, consumers might visit stores or browse online to gather more specific information, such as price ranges, to narrow their list.

3. In the final stage, consumers directly compare the key attributes of the alternatives remaining on their "short list." Here, consumers are very active in their search for specific information and often begin ascertaining actual prices through store visits, browsing the store's website, or preliminary negotiating when appropriate.

One of the most important variables of problem solving is the source of information used by consumers. It is important for retailers to understand what information resources their target market prefers to use and match their communication programs to these resources.

Purchase

Based on information gathered and evaluated in the problem-solving stage, the consumer decides whether to purchase and which product and retailer to choose. Of course, a possible outcome of the problem-solving stage is a decision not to buy or to delay the purchase. A consumer might conclude that an adequate product or service isn't available or that the cost (financial or otherwise) is greater than previously thought. Although a purchase is not made, the information gathered is often mentally recorded and influences future shopping processes.

The purchase stage may include final negotiation, application for credit if necessary, and determination of the terms of purchase (cash, credit card, etc.). Sometimes unexpected, last-minute factors can intervene during the transaction phase and preempt the purchase. For instance, the consumer can become aware of unanticipated costs such as taxes, delivery fees, or other charges and decide not to buy.

The purchase stage is often seen by retailers as an opportunity to use suggestion selling to sell add-on or related purchases such as extended service warranties, batteries for toys, and impulse merchandise. Both online and bricks-and-mortar retailers use this technique. For instance, at Amazon.com once you select books to purchase, the company suggests other titles you might have an interest in buying. If handled properly, consumers view this selling practice as a customer service, as if the retailer were "looking out" for the customer's long-term satisfaction. On the other hand, if handled poorly, the customer can view this as an attempt to gouge them. In extreme cases, the customer may even decide to cancel the initial transaction.

Post-Purchase Evaluation

The consumer shopping and purchase process does not end with the purchase. Ultimately, consumers are buying solutions to their perceived needs, and successful retailers take an active interest in ensuring that their customers feel satisfied over the long term and that their needs have been resolved. The consumer's use and evaluation of a product is therefore a critical, although sometimes overlooked, stage in the consumer behavior process.

One of the most important moments in the use and evaluation stage occurs immediately after the transaction, in the first hours and days in which the consumer uses the product or service. During this critical time, consumers form lasting impressions regarding the soundness of their purchase decision. These impressions will likely influence all future purchase decisions. In the event of a problem, consumer dissatisfaction can lead to **post-purchase resentment**, where the consumer's dissatisfaction results in resentment toward the retailer.

If post-purchase resentment is not identified and rectified quickly by the retailer, it can have a long-term negative effect on the retailer's bottom line. This is because a satisfied customer may tell a few friends, but a dissatisfied customer usually will tell a dozen or more; however, in cases where an online chat room or Internet complaint site is used, it may be millions. Just Google any retailer's name followed by the word *sucks* and you will see the true feelings of many dissatisfied consumers. For instance, "Walmart sucks" turned up 1.23 million results, "Starbucks sucks" turned up 1.18 million results, and "Home Depot sucks" listed 84,900 results.[63]

Fortunately, if the retailer is proactive in its customer-satisfaction program and responds quickly to budding resentment, it can be overcome. The problem is that many unhappy consumers do not report their dissatisfaction, so retailers must be diligent in their monitoring of those "sucks" websites. Retailers also must remember not to get angry with these posters. In fact, the retailer should be thankful for them because they're doing the retailer a great favor; they care enough about these retailers to tell them exactly what went wrong and what needs to be fixed. Other customers may simply head straight to the competition. By listening to their customers' complaints, establishing proactive policies such as full-satisfaction guarantees, and boldly communicating these policies to their target market, retailers are likely to hold on to more of their customers in the event of a mistake.[64]

Beyond this, many retailers have started customer follow-up programs, such as customer-satisfaction reply cards, given out at the time of purchase or mailed to the customer several days later. Electronic cash registers have aided in this process by efficiently gathering the names, addresses, and telephone numbers of customers, recording the merchandise purchased, and automatically mailing the customer satisfaction surveys. It is important that retailers seek to find out why some past customers no longer shop at their stores.

Many large retailers—especially chains where individual stores are not under central control such as franchises and dealerships—have taken this customer-satisfaction process one step further. They have instituted programs that measure customer satisfaction on an ongoing basis and compare customer-service ratings of individual retail locations against preestablished benchmarks or a chainwide average.

post-purchase resentment
Arises after the purchase when the consumer becomes dissatisfied with the product, service, or retailer and thus begins to regret that the purchase was made.

SUMMARY

This chapter focuses on why retailers must continuously monitor those changes in the environment that affect consumer demand. By now it should be clear that the rapid changes occurring in our society require both sensitive management and good retail information systems. Retailers need resourceful managers who not only can provide leadership in handling the challenges of these changes but also can profit from the opportunities they present.

LO 1

Explain the importance of population trends on retail planning.

We began Chapter 3 with a discussion of the major population trends occurring in the United States today and their implications for the future of retailing. These trends include a slowdown in the population growth rate, a change in the age distribution as America gets older, the changing ethnic makeup of America, the geographic shifting of the population to the South and West, the growth of large urban centers, and the increases in consumer mobility.

LO 2

What social trends should be monitored, and what are their impacts on retailing?

Five major social trends and their implications for retailing were discussed. These five trends include the increasing educational levels of consumers, the changing state of marriage (including the expansion of the never-married population), the effect of higher divorce rates, the changing makeup of the American household, and the changes in the nature and importance of an individual's work.

LO 3

How do the changing American economic trends affect retailing?

The chapter considers the effects of the imbalance of income growth among various consumer segments, this country's low level of personal savings, the impact of women in the labor force in averting economic crisis, and the impact of the widespread use of credit on retailing.

LO 4

What is involved in the shopping and purchasing model, including the key stages in the buying process?

Shopping and purchasing can be viewed as a six-stage process. A stimulus (stage 1) triggers problem recognition (stage 2); this leads to problem solving. Problem solving consists of two stages: active information gathering or search (stage 3) and evaluation of alternatives (stage 4). The degree of problem solving can vary from habitual, which occurs when the consumer already has a strong preference for both the brand and the retailer from which to purchase it, to extended problem solving, which occurs when the consumer has not decided on the brand or the store. Evaluation of alternatives can lead to purchase (stage 5), and purchase is followed by post-purchase evaluation (stage 6).

TERMS TO REMEMBER

customer satisfaction
customer services
market segmentation
population variables
micromarketing

metropolitan statistical areas
boomerang effect
sandwich generational family or
    trigenerational family
disposable income

discretionary income
stimulus
cue
drive
passive information gathering
problem recognition

habitual problem solving
limited problem solving
extended problem solving
active information gathering
set of attributes
post-purchase resentment

REVIEW AND DISCUSSION QUESTIONS

Explain the importance of population trends on retail planning. **LO 1**

1. During the recent recession, some so-called retail experts urged retailers to cut expenses to the bone and not to worry about their customer-service levels. Was this a good idea? What is the reasoning behind your answer?
2. Between 2010 and 2050, what type of retailers will be most affected by changes in the ethnic makeup of the population? Will these same retailers be affected by the changing age distribution?
3. It is important for a retailer to understand that as boomers age, they change their shopping behavior. Can you provide one example from current events where a retailer successfully adapted to this changing behavior? Can you provide an example where a retailer hasn't done a good job of adapting to these changes?

What social trends should be monitored, and what are their impacts on retailing? **LO 2**

4. What strategies should retailers develop given the higher level of educational attainment today? Explain your reasoning.
5. Should retailers care about trends such as the delay or even postponement of marriage by modern Americans? After all, how does this affect apparel retailing? restaurant retailing? home furnishing retailers?
6. Which recent trend—parents returning to live with their children or children returning to live with their parents—is going to have the most significant impact on retailers? What can retailers do to take advantage of these trends?

How do the changing American economic trends affect retailing? **LO 3**

7. Why is it more difficult for retailers to manage their businesses when economic turbulence is high?
8. In recent years, the net wealth of the average American has grown at a slower rate, if not declined. Should retailers worry about this? Why?
9. How are retailers affected by the fact that today's college students are graduating with a highest amount of student debt ever? Can you give an example where this will help a retailer? Will this hurt any retailers?

What is involved in the consumer behavior model, including the key stages in the buying process? **LO 4**

10. Why is the consumer shopping and purchasing model presented within the text called a *process* model? Explain how understanding this process could affect a retailer's actions.

11. Does a consumer begin the shopping and purchasing process at the need-recognition stage?
12. Why should a retailer care about a customer after a sale has been made?

SAMPLE TEST QUESTIONS

LO 1

Which of the following statements regarding current U.S. population trends is correct?
   a. The baby boomers are now moving into their 30s and 40s.
   b. Americans change their residences about a dozen times in their lifetime.
   c. Markets with a population of fewer than 50,000 do not present many opportunities for retailers.
   d. The United States population is expected to increase about 15 percent a year over the next decade.
   e. The country's total population is expected to grow at a record rate during the first half of the 21st century.

LO 2

The boomerang effect is a relatively new phenomenon that describes:
   a. the recent trend for firms to seek bankruptcy protection.
   b. the way styles from years ago come back as today's most popular styles.
   c. the recent trend of children returning to live with their parents after having already moved out.
   d. the use of price as the main means to attract new customers.
   e. the recent trend of having most companies report losses for the current quarter.

LO 3

Discretionary income is:
   a. all personal income after taxes and retirement savings.
   b. all personal income after savings.
   c. all personal income minus the money needed for necessities such as food, clothing, housing, and so on.
   d. all personal income after taxes minus the money needed for necessities.
   e. all personal income after taxes.

LO 4

Post-purchase resentment:
   a. usually only has short-term negative consequences for the retailer.
   b. cannot be fixed.
   c. is easily detected.
   d. is often transferred from the product to the retailer where it was purchased.
   e. is not a problem if the retailer measures customer satisfaction at least every other year.

WRITING AND SPEAKING EXERCISE

When retailers fail to deliver adequate customer service, there isn't much customers can do except shop elsewhere—that is, unless they are willing to go the extra mile. As noted earlier in Chapter 2's "Global Retailing" box, some retail experts believe that American retailers may not be very creative. However, after years of being in the classroom, the authors know that retailing students certainly are.

A few years ago, a student of one of the authors began collecting info on the executives of any company that failed to meet his service expectations. The list was rather long and covered a wide range of firms. There was the local newspaper for failing to put in all the previous night's sports scores, an airline who left him stuck on the tarmac while on a spring break vacation, a supercenter whose checkout scanner always seemed to overcharge him on "sale" items, the local cable company for just plain lousy service, and so on. Well, anyway, all of these retailers (yes, all of these fit the definition of retailing from Chapter 1) had websites that listed the top executives from president (or head of local operations) to the manager of customer service. For those that listed e-mail addresses, he just copied those. For others, he just compiled his own list of names where a John Jones became johnjones, jjones, or jonesj at the firm's e-mail address. Then he set up a new Yahoo e-mail account. Finally, on Christmas Eve afternoon, he sent all these names e-mails, wishing them a Merry Christmas. What he got back was an inbox full of out-of-office replies, complete with contact information including direct numbers to reach them. In the past when he tried to reach them, he had problems with voicemail routing systems and never could reach these folks. Now, however, he had a list of correct e-mail addresses and direct phone numbers.

Pity anybody who failed to deliver the service he expected (or demanded) the following year.

Prepare a short memo describing what you think the author should have done when he heard about this behavior. Be sure to include in this memo what you think of the student's behavior. Was the student right or wrong in his actions?

RETAIL PROJECT

By the time you read this chapter, much of the demographic data mentioned in it will be outdated. You can get up-to-date data one of two ways. You can go to the government document section of your local library and use the most current issue of *Statistical Abstract of the United States*. Or you can use your computer to connect with the Census Bureau's website (www.census.gov). A series of easy directions will guide you to the most current available data for any geographic area—from the entire nation to any county or town in any state. Using your mouse you can easily specify what kind of information you want. Also since the census does more than just count people, you can obtain breakdowns on different variables beyond those used in this chapter. For instance, they collect statistics regarding occupations and average pay per occupation (Tables 596 and 628), average home values by state (Table 974), home values by type of unit or household (956), and even the number of U.S. households with central air-conditioning, a fireplace, and so on (Table 929). (*Note*: The tables provided here correspond to those in the U.S. Bureau of Census, *Statistical Abstract of the United States: 2009*. Table numbers may change as new editions of the abstract are published.)

PLANNING YOUR OWN RETAIL BUSINESS

In this chapter, you learned that a major determinant of retail performance is how broadly or narrowly you define your market. In addition, when planning your retail business it will be important that you develop your retail marketing strategy to appeal to this particular market. For example, a women's apparel store could cater to all age groups, professional working women, or teens; it could also target various income groups such as low, moderate, or high income. Further, it could target women of different sizes from petite to full-figured.

For the store you are planning, assume that there are 18,000 households in your community and that these are within a reasonable driving distance. You have determined that if you broadly define your store's market, 65 percent of households in the community would be shoppers at your store and would shop there an average of 3.4 times per year. On the other hand, if you define your market much more selectively by focusing on a well-defined niche, you estimate only 28 percent of households would shop your store; however, they would shop an average of 9.2 times annually.

In this situation, would a broadly or more narrowly defined market create more customer visits to the store? (*Hint:* Total store visitors, also referred to as *traffic*, is equal to the total number of households in the market multiplied by the proportion that would shop your store, multiplied by their average shopping frequency.) What other factors should you consider when deciding how narrowly or broadly to define your market?

Evaluating the Competition in Retailing

OVERVIEW:

The behavior of competitors is an important component of the retail planning and management model. Effective planning and execution in any retail setting cannot be accomplished without the proper analysis of competitors. In this chapter, we begin by reviewing various models of retail competition. The types of competition in retailing are described next. We then discuss the evolution of retail competition. Finally, we examine the upcoming retail revolution in nonstore retailing, developing retail formats, global and technological changes, and the use of private labels as a strategic weapon.

LEARNING OBJECTIVES:

After reading this chapter you should be able to:
1. Explain the various models of retail competition.
2. Distinguish between various types of retail competition.
3. Describe the four theories used to explain the evolution of retail competition.
4. Describe the changes that could affect retail competition.

LO 1

Models of Retail Competition

What are the various models of retail competition?

This chapter examines the effects of competition on a retailer's performance. As noted in Chapter 1, retailing was once a growth industry able to increase profits solely on the basis of an increasing population base. Today, though, population growth rates are slowing. As a result, national and regional retailers can grow only by taking sales away from their competition. However, retail competition at the local level is often more complex.

In many regional communities, the area's population and disposable income have grown even as the nation's economic base contracts. For example, for years Tampa, Phoenix, and Las Vegas were like many Sunbelt communities: vibrant local economies that grew as retirees and second-home owners entered the market. Such locals offered retailers the opportunity to grow without having to take sales away from a competitor. Recently, as a result of the housing crises of 2008–2009, this is no longer true. These cities have seen major declines in housing prices and the tripling of unemployment rates. As a result of the wealth effect, explained in Chapter 3, retail sales in these cities have shrunk.

As the above example illustrates, a retailer must always be on the offensive, studying the changing competitive environment, especially its local competition, and differentiating itself from that competition. Only by creating a differential advantage that is extremely difficult to copy in both time and money can a retailer hope for continued success. Prime examples of such differentiation are category killers, like Home Depot and Lowe's, with their large selections; Walmart, whose distribution system results in significantly lower operating costs than its competitors; Target, with its more fashionable and contemporary merchandise than other mass merchandise discounters; and the Walt Disney Company, which is famous for excellent customer service. Retailers that merely copy the actions of others without a lower cost structure or point of differentiation will experience substandard performance.

The successful retailer will visit retailers of all sizes in its trading area to learn what merchandise and services competitors are and are not offering, which offerings receive aggressive pricing emphasis, and which promotional tactics are successful. These tactics are particularly beneficial for smaller retailers. Often, many people believe that local retailers cannot compete with the large discounters, but this isn't true. For example, the small appliance store owner would benefit by understanding that these chains usually carry only a limited selection within a product category and provide little personalized or specialized service. By knowing which televisions the discounter carries, and how they are priced, the small retailer can match the price on similar units, offer better services, and stock a more complete range of units.

Other chains have created a niche that has worked well against these discounters. Consider, for example, the tactic used by the dollar stores (Dollar General, Family Dollar, and Dollar Tree). These chains successfully operate small stores within the shadow of the large discounters by providing convenience and low prices on a limited product selection. By enabling their customers to get in and out quickly, these stores are able to compete with the larger chains. Yet the niche served by these dollar stores is risky since they tend to target households earning $30,000 a year or less, a segment that offers little in the way of discretionary spending on high-margin items and requires that the dollar stores make few, if any, errors in their merchandise selection.

Small, locally owned retailers may also use a tactic like the one tried by a variety store in Viroqua, Wisconsin. When Walmart located a store nearby, it gave each of its employees $20 to shop Walmart. Because its employees were local and understood the community, they learned that their store would not be price competitive in health and beauty items or housewares—and that Walmart had few offerings for the agricultural community. Further, the addition of a new private school in town increased the number of residents with more sophisticated tastes than those of the typical Walmart customer. By catering to these underserved customer segments, the variety store has thrived.

A small retailer's competition is not just the large discount stores in the area. Smaller retailers would be wise to check the local drugstore, like Walgreens, that stocks similar items; the Internet for competitive pricing information; and category killers that might offer a deeper selection and a better level of service than the discounter. For example, Best Buy lured female customers away from traditional discounters and small specialty electronics stores by providing merchandise selections tailored to each local market area and training its sales associates not to "talk down" to them, as had often happened in other electronics stores.[1]

It is important to remember that no retailer, however clever, can design a strategy that will completely insulate it from competition. This is true even for the retailer that has done an excellent job in developing and following its mission statement, setting its goals and objectives, and conducting its SWOT analysis; customers will always have shopping choices. The rapid growth of discount department stores, convenience stores, and catalog and Internet retailers attests to this fact. Further, as the cost of entry into retailing is relatively low, as compared with other businesses, and merchandising innovations are often unable to be patented, competition will always remain as other retailers seek to copy a profitable strategy.

Competition in retailing, as in any industry, involves the interplay of supply and demand. One cannot appreciate the nature and scope of competition in retailing by studying only the supply factors—that is, the type and number of competing retailers that exist. One must also examine consumer demand factors as highlighted in Chapter 3. Keeping this in mind, let's examine a formal framework for describing and explaining the competitive environment of retailing.

The Competitive Marketplace

One of the most important tasks to perform prior to examining the competitive environment is deciding how you will compete as a retailer. Competition can be waged on many fronts. A retailer must be clear about what advantages it will emphasize and where its resources will have the greatest impact in attracting and satisfying customers.

This framework helps to identify your primary competitors, as well as threats from secondary competitors. For example, a full-line grocery store competes most directly with similar grocery stores; all of them try to attract the same type of customer in terms of price sensitivity, preferences in merchandise selection, and geographic convenience. A discount grocery store such as Rainbow Foods is also after the grocery store's customer, but it appeals particularly to those who put an emphasis on low prices over a wide selection of specialty items. However, any business that may win the customer's food dollar should also be viewed as a competitor.

Over the past decade, almost a third of a household's food dollar was spent on food consumed outside the home—that is, in restaurants, workplace cafeterias, vending machines, and other venues. The percentage is much higher for certain demographic groups such as higher-income households who can better afford to eat out and young men who prefer not to cook at home. The fact that the same consumer can and will purchase the same product category (food) at different retailers, points to the fact that different retailers are more or less competitive to varying degrees, given different consumer buying situations and preferences. Customers may choose to shop at traditional grocery stores or supercenters for most groceries, but many will also choose to patronize specialty grocers such as Whole Foods for organically raised meats or Trader Joe's for a particular brand of muesli cereal, eat in a number of restaurant formats for different reasons throughout the week, and purchase grab-and-go foods from convenience stores.[2]

Retailers compete for target customers on five major fronts or factors:[3]

1. the price for the benefits offered;

2. service level;

3. product selection (merchandise line width and depth);

4. location or access—that is, the overall convenience of shopping the retailer; and

5. customer experience (the customer's positive feelings and behaviors in the purchase process).

In any competitive environment, retailers must clear a minimum acceptable threshold on each of these criteria in order to stay in business. Further, they must distinguish themselves in the marketplace by dominating on one key factor and differentiate themselves on a secondary factor within that primary competitive set. For example, Walmart, Target, and Dollar General compete primarily as general merchandise discounters. However, Walmart emphasizes its excellent prices on a wide selection of top name brands, Target highlights its design-forward private-label goods and store atmosphere, and the dollar stores are more convenient than the larger discounters.

Many retailers compete for customers on a local level and must be aware of their direct and secondary competitors in their shopping area. Customers typically will not travel beyond local markets to purchase routine household goods and prefer to shop in the most convenient way possible. When they do travel beyond local markets, however, it is usually because their city or town is too small to support retailers with the selection of merchandise they desire. Some customers will always want to shop out of town, but most cities with populations of more than 50,000 can provide the consumer with sufficient selection in almost all lines of merchandise. In cities with populations less than 50,000, households generally need to travel to another town or city for large purchases such as a new automobile, television, furniture, or for special items of clothing such as a wedding dress or favored brand name.

Market Structure

Economists use four different economic terms to describe the competitive environment of retailing: pure competition, pure monopoly, monopolistic competition, and oligopolistic competition.

Pure competition occurs when a market has:

1. homogeneous (similar) products;
2. many buyers and sellers, all having perfect knowledge of the market; and
3. ease of entry for both buyers and sellers—that is, new retailers can start up with little difficulty and new consumers can easily come into the market.

In pure competition, each retailer faces a horizontal demand curve and must sell its products at the going "market" or equilibrium price. To sell at a lower price would be foolish, since you could always get the market price. Of course, you could not sell your merchandise at a higher price because customers know they can buy the item for less.

Pure competition is rare in retailing. Often, neither consumers nor retailers know all the prices in the marketplace without investing extensive time and effort to acquire this knowledge. Further, not all customers value an item similarly. Even in a very good example of pure competition, such as two vendors selling bags of peanuts or bottles of water outside a sporting event, customers seldom explore a number of sites before making a choice.

The second type of economic environment also does not occur very often in real life. In a **pure monopoly**, the seller is the only one selling a particular product and will set its selling price accordingly. However, as the retailer seeks to sell more units, it must lower the selling price. This is because consumers who already have one unit will tend to place a lower value on an additional unit. This is called the *law of diminishing returns* or *declining marginal utility*. For example, a hot fudge sundae would taste great right now, but the second, third, or ninth one, purchased and consumed today, would be less desirable. Similarly, not all customers are equally impressed with a product. The monopolist would have to price more aggressively to entice customers who place a lower value on the item than do its target customers. The customer whose favorite color is hot pink might buy a hot pink blazer at full

pure competition
Occurs when a market has homogeneous products and many buyers and sellers, all having perfect knowledge of the market, and ease of entry for both buyers and sellers.

pure monopoly
Occurs when there is only one seller for a product or service.

price, but it is unlikely she will buy another one soon. In addition, the retailer is likely to discount the remaining blazers to customers who are less thrilled with hot pink—that is, hot pink has less "utility" for these customers in the first place.

Even so, situations of near monopoly do exist. The gas station that is many miles from its nearest competitor or the restaurant open late at night on a lonely highway are examples of near monopolies. Similarly, customers can "self-inflict" a monopoly when a brand name is highly valued, and only one (or a few) retailer controls its sale. Harley-Davidson, like many other luxury-brand sellers, realizes its brand-loyal customers place such a high value on their motorcycles that the company limits areas of distribution and allows its retailers to reap the reward.

monopolistic competition
Occurs when the products offered are different, yet viewed as substitutable for each other and the sellers recognize that they compete with sellers of these different products.

Monopolistic competition is a market situation that develops when one of two situations occur:

1. Retailers sell different (heterogeneous) products in the eyes of consumers that are still substitutes for each other. Here, two or more retailers may be selling the same product, but one retailer is able to differentiate itself on another dimension. Thus, consumers perceive the retailers as selling different products, given the total shopping experience.

2. Sellers may be the only ones selling a particular brand but face competition from other retailers selling similar goods and services.

The word *monopolistic* means that each seller is trying to control its own segment of the market. However, the word *competition* means that substitutes for the product are available. For example, a Pepsi-Cola is a substitute for a Coca-Cola. The degree of the seller's control depends on the extent to which customers view the competitor's product as similar. This is why retailers in monopolistic competition attempt to differentiate themselves with the products or services they offer. Some of the common means of achieving this differentiation are offering better customer service, credit, more convenient parking, a larger or more attractive merchandise selection, cleanliness, free setup and delivery, and a more convenient location, as well as the brand or store image created and developed through marketing communications such as advertising or store events.

oligopolistic competition
Occurs when relatively few sellers, or many small firms who follow the lead of a few larger firms, offer essentially homogeneous products and any action by one seller is expected to be noticed and reacted to by the other sellers.

Oligopolistic competition occurs when a market meets the following conditions:

1. Essentially homogeneous products are sold—such as gasoline.

2. There are relatively few sellers or many small firms who always follow the lead of the few large firms.

3. There is an expectation that any action by one party will be noticed and reacted to by the other parties in the market.

As in pure competition, oligopolies are likely to end up selling at a similar price since everybody knows what others are doing. Nonprice competition is extremely difficult since consumers view the products and services as essentially the same. This is why major airlines almost always lower their prices on identical travel routes when a low-cost competitor enters one of their markets. As was the case when Southwest entered the Denver market, American and United both dropped fares to cities served by Southwest.

Retailing is often characterized as monopolistic competition or, in rare cases, oligopolistic competition. The distinction lies in the number of sellers. For an oligopoly to occur, the top four firms need to account for more than 60 percent to 80 percent of the market. Oligopolistic competition rarely occurs on a national level, but consolidation in many industries has left a few large players in some product categories. For example, Home Depot and Lowe's often dominate the home-improvement market, and Macy's and Dillard's have a similar impact on the department store category.

Oligopolistic competition is more common at a local level, especially in smaller communities, among food stores and department or discount department stores. However, if prices become too high, merchandise selection too limited, or services too poor, residents of these communities will travel to larger communities to shop. This is known as **outshopping**. However, even when retailing becomes concentrated at the local level, there are several checks on the retailers' power. One of these checks is nonstore shopping (e.g., the Internet). If prices at furniture and other specialty stores become too high, local shoppers may increase their usage of nonstore shopping alternatives. In fact, existing catalog retailers and bricks-and-mortar stores are proving particularly adept at developing multichannel strategies to attract customers from a wider geographic area. L.L. Bean has seen its catalog businesses boom with the addition of an online site, and stores such as Walmart have fine-tuned their Internet offerings. However, the most likely cause for outshopping in the United States today is lawmakers. In New York City, for example, state and city tobacco taxes have risen so many times that the retail cost can exceed $9 a pack—about double the national average. As a result, the Tax Foundation estimates that there is "a 75% gap between cigarette sales in the city and cigarette consumption." In other words, three out of four cigarettes smoked by residents of New York City were bought elsewhere.[4]

Interestingly, during the recent energy crisis, the high cost of gasoline limited the growth of outshopping. In fact, many rural locations were able to outperform their big city competitors.[5]

The Demand Side of Retailing

As stated previously, most retailers face monopolistic competition, and we assume such a market structure to be the case for the remainder of the text. In a monopolistically competitive market, the retailer will be confronted with a negatively sloping demand curve. In other words, consumers will demand a higher quantity as price is lowered, assuming the retailer has chosen the merchandise that the customer wants, communicates the value of shopping at his or her store, and makes the product available. Thus, the typical retailer faces a demand function like the one shown in Exhibit 4.1.[6]

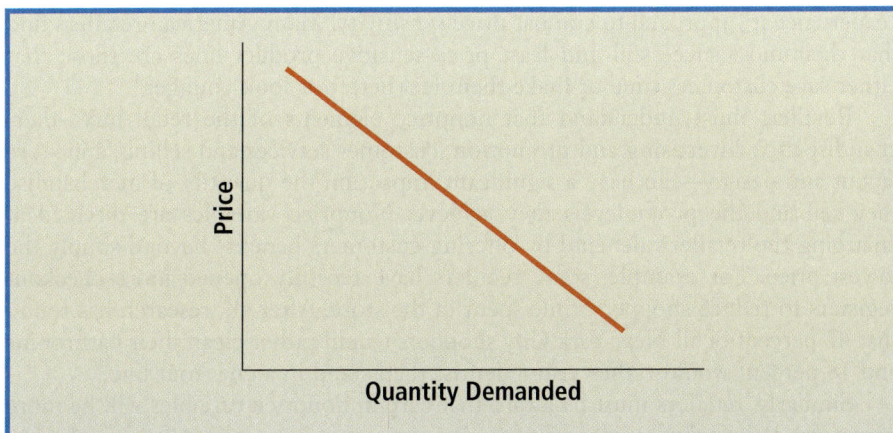

Exhibit 4.1
Demand as a Function of Price

Such customer behavior implies knowledge of the competitive alternatives. Customers who have greater knowledge of available alternatives and the differences in product features will often patronize a wider range of retailers.[7] Interestingly, this is often exacerbated by retailers themselves. As retailers become more proactive in their marketing efforts (using such tactics as selling over the Internet, aggressive advertising, multiple catalogs, and prospecting for new customers), consumers become increasingly aware of a wider range of alternatives, better prices, better service, and better features. This knowledge leads many customers to migrate from local retailers that do not sufficiently measure up to their growing demands.

Thus, in most cases, higher prices will result in less demand for the retailer because households have limited incomes and many purchase alternatives. This reality should suggest that retailers cannot be profitable by setting prices at the highest possible levels. Retailers will find it necessary to set prices somewhere below the maximum possible price but above zero. Extremely low prices will sell large quantities but not generate sufficient sales revenue to cover costs and generate a profit; retailers are simply unable to meet the maximum customer demand at a profit. At the same time, extremely high prices will result in low quantities sold and hence, although the price per unit may be high, the sales revenue would not cover both variable and fixed costs. As a result, retailers must routinely monitor competitors' prices in the trade area, as well as understand the impact of catalogs and the Internet. Retailers also need to recognize when a drop in a competitor's prices is temporary and inconsequential to long-term competition (i.e. the competitor will be out of business if it prices too low) or when the competitor has set a new permanent pricing standard that requires them to adjust their profit expectations.

Nonprice Decisions

Retailers often believe they must always match or be lower than a competitor's price. This is often not the case. Many customers place a high value on attributes other than price when selecting a place to shop. For instance, some consumers choose to pick up a loaf of bread at a convenience store or bakery, even when it is cheaper at a supercenter or supermarket. These customers are willing to pay a higher price because they place a higher value on their time or have a special preference for a certain bakery bread. However, many may be surprised to discover that the special loaf of bread may cost several times the $3.79 price, when one considers travel and related costs to the bakery.

This chapter's "Service Retailing" box describes how some spas have used the "experience it" approach to combat price sensitivity. Many American retailers find that their most successful and least price-sensitive product lines are those that either save customers time or make them feel better or look younger.[8]

Retailers must understand that nonprice elements of the retail mix—merchandise mix, advertising and promotion, customer services and selling, and store layout and design—can have a significant impact on the quantity of merchandise they sell and the profit levels they achieve. Nonprice variables are directed at enlarging the retailer's demand by offering customers benefits beyond simply the lowest price. For example, some retailers have recently opened more checkout registers to reduce shoppers' time spent in the store. After all, research has found that 42 percent of all New York City shoppers would rather clean their bathrooms and 18 percent would rather visit a dentist than stand in a checkout line.[9]

Similarly, retailers must be aware that certain nonprice variables will be more successful than others given the market segments they choose to target. As

Service Retailing

The "Experience It" Approach

Some retail experts argue that consumers are no longer buying only tangible products and traditional service; instead, they're purchasing an experience. Walt Disney is recognized as the pioneer in this "experience it" approach to retailing. Both Disneyland and Epcot Center were built so that consumers could experience the future. Today, this experience-it approach is found in many retail markets, one being the health spa and resort business.

Canyon Ranch, which was founded in 1979 by Mel Zuckerman in Tucson, Arizona, is considered the pioneer in the high-end health spa and resort business. Canyon Ranch was designed to be more than just a fabulous vacation; it was to be an *experience* that would influence the quality of your life from the moment you arrived to long after you returned home. It was a place to explore your potential for a happier, healthier, and more fulfilling life. In all promotional material, Canyon Ranch stressed the word *intention* when talking about the experience. Its website stated, "[W]e are more intent than ever on motivating our guests to translate their healthiest thoughts into positive, ongoing action—and we do whatever it takes to make that happen.... Our mission is not selling vacations; it's creating an environment in which you can make a direct, emotional connection between what you know you should do and what you actually do every day."

Thus, this destination spa company was luring guests for body poundings and weight-loss regimens long before the modern spa proliferation was even a gleam in marketers' eyes. With the simple message question "Has there ever been a time when you could have used an escape to Canyon Ranch more?" the resort sought to highlight consumers' need for escape. In fact, this message was very successful during the stressful times of the recent recession.[10]

Over the years, Canyon Ranch has expanded and now has a woodlands health resort in the lush Berkshires of Lenox, Massachusetts. It also has SpaClubs in the Venetian Resort on the Las Vegas Strip; Gaylord Palms Resort in Kissimmee, Florida; and on board the Queen Mary II ocean liner. Yet, as in all competitive markets, successful innovators are often copied.

A new resort, Miraval Spa, has entered Canyon Ranch's hometown of Tucson. Ranked as the number-one resort and spa by the prestigious Zagat Survey, Miraval has challenged Canyon Ranch and other competitors in providing the best possible "experience." Miraval positions itself as helping people create a life in balance. To accomplish its mission, it offers a variety of workshops such as "Partners, Pleasure, and Passion: A Couples Retreat"; "Power and Passion: Engaging Feminine Sexual Radiance"; and "Partners and Passion: Taking it to the Next Level." In addition, Miraval has recruited well known holistic and integrative medicine expert, Dr. Andrew Weil as director of integrative health and healing. Dr. Weil personally teaches workshops on healthy aging that are targeted to America's fast growing "graying" market segment. Predictably, Canyon Ranch is fighting back with its own new and innovative offerings. Yet even these high-end service providers are not exempt from price competition.

Winter is the prime season in Tucson because temperatures hover in the 60s and 70s (daily summer temperatures regularly exceed 100 degrees). During this peak winter season, price had always been non-negotiable and extremely high. But this changed in 2006 when Miraval offered a special: a weeklong stay for $4,735 (single occupancy) or $3,780 (double occupancy), which was 15 percent off the regular package price.

Retail service innovators have realized that the spa and resort business is not an exclusively high-end market. In fact, one of the fastest-growing areas of service retailing is stand-alone spas. These provide half-day to full-day treatments with no cost of overnight lodging. Not surprisingly, the cost drops dramatically, with many treatments costing less than $75. Unless you happen to live in a small town of 25,000 or less, you are likely to see numerous "day" spas in your local business directory.

Another interesting growth area is medical spas. These spas often focus on dermatology, providing such medical treatments as Botox or Restylane, certain chemical peels, and intense-pulsed-light skin treatments. Increasingly, the entrepreneurs are medical doctors who are leaving their traditional medical practices with low insurance reimbursements for cash-paying spa customers. In 2000, there were only a few dozen medical spas in the United States; today, there are more than 1,500, and the number is growing weekly. These spas are successful because they provide a salon-like setting with quick

(continued)

Service Retailing *(continued)*

service (sometimes even on a walk-in basis), are conveniently located, and offer attractive prices. The spas are also open weekends and evenings, hours not common in traditional medical offices. Importantly, just as the high-end spas faced price competition as the number of competitors increased, so have medical spas. For example, in December 2005, Lumity MedSpa in West Los Angeles was offering a holiday special of

40 percent off all laser hair removal, and Botox was bargain priced at $9 a unit.

Source: "Competition Forces Spas to Offer Big Deals," *Wall Street Journal*, February 28, 2006: , ; Joseph B. Pine II and James H. Gilmore, *The Experience Economy* (Harvard Business School Press Boston, 1999); "Spas in Retail Centers Offer Cosmetic Medical Treatments, *Wall Street Journal*, January 3, 2006: ;www.miravalresort.com, January 11, 2009; and www.canyonranch.com, January 11, 2009.

discussed in Chapter 3, Hispanics are one of the fastest growing segments in the United States today. Yet as Exhibit 4.2 points out, this segment values certain nonprice variables differently as compared to the rest of U.S. shoppers.

Although certain nonprice variables may be more or less advantageous given the retailer's target market, competing on price alone is a no-win situation because price is the easiest variable for competitors to copy. For example, a bricks-and-mortar retailer can simply change the price scanner and the shelf marker; an e-tailer can easily change the price on its website. *Advertising Age*, for example, pointed out that when the six major online drugstores mounted a price battle to gain new customers, they wound up spending $2 on ads for every $1 in revenue; they failed to develop a differential advantage that the competition couldn't easily copy.[11] Similar results were also found when e-tailers offered free shipping. Many e-tailers, including Amazon.com, found that offering free shipping meant an unprofitable sale in the short term and little long-term purchase loyalty. Such promotions were expensive, and customer orders dropped substantially once the free shipping was eliminated. Now many e-tailers require minimum-purchase requirements to qualify for free shipping and other price-oriented benefits.

Exhibit 4.2
Shopping Trip Goals and Store-Selection Reasons

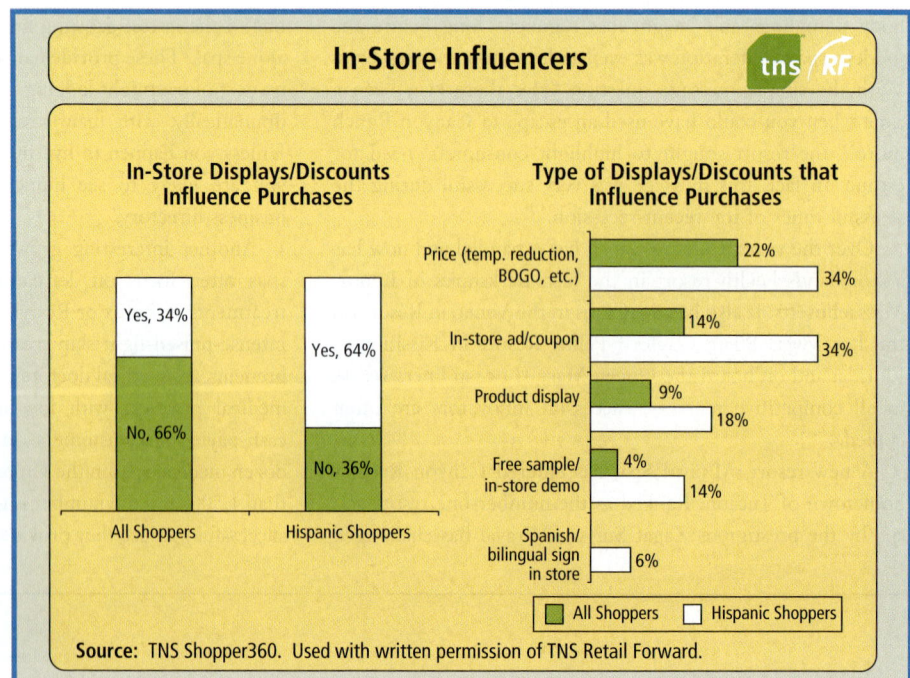

In-Store Influencers   tns RF

In-Store Displays/Discounts Influence Purchases

- All Shoppers: Yes, 34% / No, 66%
- Hispanic Shoppers: Yes, 64% / No, 36%

Type of Displays/Discounts that Influence Purchases

	All Shoppers	Hispanic Shoppers
Price (temp. reduction, BOGO, etc.)	22%	34%
In-store ad/coupon	14%	34%
Product display	9%	18%
Free sample/in-store demo	4%	14%
Spanish/bilingual sign in store		6%

Source: TNS Shopper360. Used with written permission of TNS Retail Forward.

Consider some of the ways a retailer could use nonprice variables to achieve a protected niche:

1. The retailer could position itself as different from the competition by altering its merchandise mix to offer higher-quality goods, greater personal service, special-orders handling, or a better selection of large sizes. (**Store positioning** is the process whereby a retailer distinguishes itself from competitors in specific ways in order to be the preferred provider for certain market segments. It's the act of designing the retailer's merchandise and image so as to occupy a distinct and valued place in the targeted customer's mind.) Such features may increase the maximum price consumers are willing to pay or the distance consumers are willing to travel to shop for these goods, thereby enlarging the retailer's trade area. Neiman Marcus and Nordstrom's have done an excellent job of positioning themselves using this strategy. Exhibit 4.3 details the steps involved in choosing a correct positioning strategy.

2. The retailer can offer private-label merchandise that has unique features or offers better value than do competitors. Exhibit 4.4 lists the private labels for one of this country's major retailers. The strategy of using private-label branding to secure a protected niche is discussed in detail at the end of this chapter.

3. The retailer could provide other benefits for the customer. For example, as gas prices go up, so does the drawing power of retailers who offer cheap fuel. Because shoppers are more likely to consolidate shopping trips as fuel prices increase, many discounters have followed the lead of warehouse clubs and European grocery stores, sacrificing margins on gasoline to increase sales inside their stores.[12]

4. The retailer could master stockkeeping with its basic merchandise assortment. For example, Nordstrom strives to always have men's dress shirts in stock and will give the customer a free shirt if the store is ever out of stock in basic sizes. Compare this policy with a competitor who has a similar item in stock only 95 percent of the time. If you go into this store to pick up just five items, the chances are almost one in four that the store will be out of at least one item ($0.95 \times 0.95 \times 0.95 \times 0.95 \times 0.95 = 0.773$).

store positioning
Is when a retailer identifies a well-defined market segment using demographic or lifestyle variables and appeals to this segment with a clearly differentiated approach.

---

1. Assess how shoppers and even competitors view the retailer by asking them to describe the retailer's stores, merchandise, services, and overall image. Determine what's good and bad about the current position. Determine whether the current positioning must be changed to increase sales.

2. Determine what the best position for the retailer is. Next identify how to market the retailer's products, promotions, and image to convey and reinforce this desired position. What are the meaningful differences between the retailer and its competition?

3. Analyze the retailer's current target customers. Are these the correct ones? Who will benefit most from the retailer's new positioning? Does the retailer's target market really value the anticipated change in positioning?

4. Factor in current environmental trends. What trends are on the way that might benefit or harm the retailer's new position?

5. Implement the new positioning strategy but remember that a retailer's business objective drives its market strategy, which drives its positioning strategy. After all, if the business objective is to have fewer customers who spend more per sale by buying higher quality, the strategy must reflect this in the products or services offered. The retailer's positioning strategy will also determine the messages to communicate to its target customer.

Exhibit 4.3
How to Implement a Store Positioning Program

Exhibit 4.4
Some of JCPenney's
Private Labels

JCPenney Private Brands

Arizona

Worthington

Mixit

a.n.a.

Exclusive Brands

I Heart Ronson

Bisou Bisou

Le Tigre

Flirtitude

Reprinted by permission of JC Penney

   A variation of nonprice competition is to become a "destination" store for certain products. For example, Hanneford's grocery store in York, Maine, guarantees that it will have hot roasted chickens available and ready for takeout every day between 4 P.M. and 7 P.M. or you get a coupon for a free chicken. (Even so, Hanneford's will always have a chicken ready within 30 minutes during this time

Courtesy of JC Penney

JC Penney Arizona private-label clothing is an important part of the JC Penney store positioning strategy.

Bob Pardue/SC/Alamy

Bass Pro Shops Outdoor World differentiates itself with its merchandise and in-store demonstrations and thus has become a destination store for the active sports-person.

period even if it temporarily runs out due to unexpectedly heavy demand.) Another example is Bass Pro Shops, which has become a sportsman's paradise by combining merchandise with in-store demonstrations and experiences, including a trout pond. Its flagship store in Springfield, Missouri, is even located adjacent to the American Fish and Wildlife Museum.

Remember, most retail decision variables, whether price or nonprice, are directed at influencing demand. The profitability of these decisions depends on the marginal cost of the action versus the marginal revenue it generates (see Chapter 10 for a discussion of pricing).

Competitive Actions

We just discussed how most bricks-and-mortar retailers attract customers from a limited geographic area and that this area expands as prices are lowered. But even at a zero price, households can only afford to travel a certain distance to get their goods and services. Therefore, several, if not many, retailers in each line of retail trade are needed to service most cities.

A good measure of competitive activity in a market is the number of retail establishments of a given type per thousand households. When the number of stores per thousand households gets too large, the market is considered **overstored**. These retailers face a major performance imperative because often their return on investment is below their cost of capital. As a result, they will implement both price and nonprice actions in an attempt to increase both sales and profits. This highly competitive situation reduces the average return on investment and lowers the profitability of all retailers. Some will eventually exit the market. One classic case of a retailer overstoring a trade area is Starbucks. At one time, before closing nearly 600 outlets in 2008, this Seattle-based coffee retailer had multiple stores in the same shopping center and even some across the street from each other.[13]

However, if the number of stores per thousand households is small in comparison to other markets, the market is said to be **understored**. With too few

overstored

Is a condition in a community where the number of stores in relation to households is so large that to engage in retailing is usually unprofitable or marginally profitable.

understored

Is a condition in a community where the number of stores in relation to households is relatively low so that engaging in retailing is an attractive economic endeavor.

retailers to adequately service local demand, profits may be high enough to attract new retail competitors, or existing retailers may be enticed to expand. A market is in equilibrium in terms of number of retail establishments if the return on investment is high enough to justify keeping capital invested in retailing, but not so high as to invite more competition.

As just indicated, competition is most intense in overstored markets because many retailers are achieving an inadequate return on investment. It should also be remembered that while e-tailers may not be in close geographic proximity to other e-tailers and retailers, they are easily accessible via a customer's computer. From the customer's perspective, this effectively puts e-tailers in very close proximity because they can all be shopped at the same location. Thus, the early exit of many e-tailers was the result of the Internet being overstored given the demand at the time, as well as many e-tailers' inability to control back-office costs. Similarly, the online purchases of basic airline tickets, which was discussed in Chapter 1's "Retailing: The Inside Story," resulted in the demise of many small travel agencies that relied simply on processing tickets rather than providing value-added services. Travel agencies that served largely as ticket writers and not as revenue generators faced an increasingly overstored retail environment.

Suppliers as Partners and Competitors

A retailer's suppliers should be considered both partners and competitors for the customer's dollar. Suppliers, as will be pointed out in Chapter 5, are critical to the retailer's trade, but they are also in competition for gross margins throughout the supply chain. Every extra dollar charged by the supplier is one less for the retailer when retail prices are stagnant. One remedy for the retailer is to develop a loyal group of patrons that encourages the supplier to accommodate the needs of its retail partner. As more manufacturers evaluate their investments and marketing money for retailers and explore their own direct-to-consumer marketing, retailers must determine how they can be most productive for their suppliers yet still maintain profitability.

When they provide a unique product or promotion, suppliers can be a critical competitive advantage to retailers. Many specialty retailers across categories vie to be the first with the latest products or to stock exclusive merchandise. Saks Fifth Avenue prides itself as the first to carry a new perfume in many retail areas. Further, suppliers can cooperate in improved merchandising and operations, such as developing a package design that is easier to read on the shelf or establishing efficient inventory-management systems. For example, OfficeMax has worked with office-supply manufacturers to use more informative labeling and packaging. This has greatly reduced the number of packages that customers rip open in the store to learn if the products are right for them.

However, suppliers have learned to become cautious in their relationships with large retailers. In off-the-record conversations with the authors, some manufacturers have insisted that Walmart has been known to stock their product to see how it sells—and then come out with its own private label that directly competes with the manufacturer.

LO 2

Types of Competition

What are the various types of retail competition?

It is possible to merge the preceding discussion of competition in retailing with the classification schemes used by the Department of Commerce in conducting the Census of Retail Trade.

Intratype and Intertype Competition

Intratype competition occurs when two or more retailers of the same type, as defined by North American Industry Classification System (NAISC) codes in the Census of Retail Trade, compete directly with each other for the same household dollars. This is the most common type of retail competition: TGI Friday's competes with Chili's, Avon competes with Mary Kay, Saks Fifth Avenue competes with Neiman Marcus, Family Dollar competes with Dollar General, and Amazon.com competes with bn.com (Barnes & Noble online).

Due to the changing nature of retailing, retailers are often forced to alter their strategy as their competition changes. For example, in the early 1990s, Sears wanted to compete head on with low-priced discounters such as Walmart and Kmart. Today, after merging with Kmart in 2005, Sears is trying to reposition itself against middle-of-the-road merchants JCPenney and May Department Stores by appealing to women, emphasizing apparel, and carrying popular Kmart private labels such as Martha Stewart. To generate more up-market store traffic, Sears acquired catalog merchant Lands' End, whose merchandise is now found in most of its stores. Sears has also tried to capitalize on the "nesting" and "cocooning" trend among many consumers by developing the Great Indoors, large freestanding home centers that offer both deeper selections of home furnishings and housewares and the convenience of at-the-door parking. Yet Sears still appears to be trying to find itself: Is it a Kmart or a Sears? After all, its once-dominant household appliance business—with its Kenmore, DieHard, and Craftsman brands—has been chipped away by Best Buy, Home Depot, and Lowe's. Its clothing business has suffered at the hands of JCPenney's and Kohl's, and even its identity as the place for one-stop shopping has been taken over by Walmart.

Every time *different* types of retail outlets (as defined by NAICS codes) sell the same lines of merchandise and compete for the same limited consumer dollars, **intertype competition** occurs. This is increasingly seen as many retailers compete using a scrambled merchandising strategy. As discussed in Chapter 1, scrambled merchandising occurs when a retailer carries many different, unrelated product lines, often outside its traditional product mix, as a means of enhancing one-stop shopping convenience for its customers. Examples of this include the following:

- Discounters now handle cosmetics and fragrances that were traditionally the province of traditional department stores.

- Not only have supermarkets (such as Albertsons, Kroger, and Safeway) taken market share away from fast-food restaurants with their home meal replacements (HMRs) but also travelers returning from trips are bringing HMRs home from the airport. In addition, both discounters and supermarkets with their floral departments, greeting card sections, banks, and pharmacies have changed the competitive landscape for traditional florists, card shops, banks, and drugstores.

- Many auto dealers, needing to create new additional revenue streams due to the recent sluggish economy, are beginning to sell auto insurance. These entrepreneurially driven dealerships have found that the customers like the convenience of having all their needs serviced by one business after a wreck.[14]

- Convenience stores (such as 7-Eleven) sell not only motor oil and related auto care products but also fast food, lottery tickets, and pain relievers.

- Not only are home improvement retailers such as Lowe's and Home Depot and supermarkets such as Kroger and Safeway competing against each other but also they are now engaged in an intertype battle with Walmart, which wants to be the

intratype competition
Occurs when two or more retailers of the same type, as defined by NAICS codes in the Census of Retail Trade, compete directly with each other for the same households.

intertype competition
Occurs when two or more retailers of a different type, as defined by NAICS codes in the Census of Retail Trade, compete directly by attempting to sell the same merchandise lines to the same households.

market-share leader in all the lines it carries. Little wonder then that Home Depot has recently been devoting rack space to home theater systems.

In each of the preceding examples, intertype competition expanded, and gross margins on the respective merchandise lines declined.

Divertive Competition

divertive competition
Occurs when retailers intercept or divert customers from competing retailers.

Another concept that helps to explain the nature of competition in retailing is **divertive competition**. This occurs when retailers intercept or divert customers from competing retailers. For example, a woman in need of a birthday card may plan to purchase one the next time she visits the local shopping mall, which has a well-stocked Hallmark card store. However, while picking up a prescription at the drugstore, she walks by a card stand and decides to purchase the greeting card at the drugstore. In this situation, the drugstore retailer has intercepted this customer from the Hallmark store.

A divertive tactic gaining in popularity today is to operate a gas station on one's property. In doing so, retailers catch customers who have already shopped and do not want to make another stop to get gas. Similarly, consumers who need gas may choose to consolidate shopping trips and shop the retailer's store after purchasing gas. Today, many warehouse clubs, discounters, and supermarkets use this tactic.

break-even point
Is where total revenues equal total expenses and the retailer is making neither a profit nor a loss.

Another category where divertive tactics are seeing an increased use is lingerie, the second fastest-growing apparel category. Retailers like JCPenney, Target, and Kohl's are seeking to cash in on this hot trend by launching lingerie lines or giving old ones a makeover. In an attempt to divert business from Victoria's Secret, these department stores are redecorating their dressing rooms and offering professional fitting services. In addition, other retailers, including Chico's FAS Inc., American Eagle Outfitters Inc., and Lane Bryant, have created stand-alone lingerie stores.[15]

wheel of retailing theory
Describes how new types of retailers enter the market as low-status, low-margin, low-price operators; however, as they meet with success, these new retailers gradually acquire more sophisticated and elaborate facilities, and thus become vulnerable to new types of low-margin retail competitors who progress through the same pattern.

To comprehend the significance of divertive competition, which can be intertype or intratype competition, one needs to recognize that most retailers operate very close to their **breakeven point** (the point where total revenues equal total expenses). For instance, supermarkets, which have extremely low gross margin return on sales, tend to have high breakeven points, ranging from 94 percent to 96 percent of current sales. General merchandise retailers, with a higher gross margin return on sales, face lower breakeven points of 85 percent to 92 percent of their current sales. In either case, a modest drop in sales volume could make these retailers unprofitable. As a result, the use of scrambled merchandising is growing as retailers seek a larger share of the customer's wallet.

LO 3   Evolution of Retail Competition

What are the four theories used to explain the evolution of retail competition?

A discussion of the evolution of retailing not only provides a better understanding of the history of retail formats but also enhances our ability to make predictions about their future. Several theories have developed to explain and describe the evolution of competition in retailing. We will review three historical theories and a new concept that helps to explain why a variety of retail formats have the potential to be profitable.

The Wheel of Retailing

The **wheel of retailing theory**, illustrated in Exhibit 4.5, is one of the oldest descriptions of competition in retailing.[16] This theory states that new types of retailers enter the market as low-status, low-margin, and low-price operators. This

Exhibit 4.5
Wheel of Retailing

entry phase allows retailers to compete effectively and take market share away from the more traditional retailers. However, as they meet with success, these new retailers gradually enter a trading-up phase and acquire more sophisticated and elaborate facilities, often becoming less efficient. This creates both a higher investment and a subsequent rise in operating costs. Today, some academics refer to this stage as the "Big Middle," a market space where the largest numbers of potential customers reside.[17] Predictably, these retailers will eventually enter the vulnerability phase and must raise prices and margins to cover rising costs. In doing so, they become vulnerable to new types of low-margin retail competitors who progress through the same pattern. This appears to be the case today with outlet malls. Once bare-bones warehouses for manufacturers' imperfect or excess merchandise, outlet malls quickly evolved into fancy, almost upscale locations where retailers try to outdo each other's accent lighting, private dressing rooms, and generous return policies. As a result, the cost of operating such locations increased and put them in more direct competition with increasingly competitive department stores.

While the wheel of retailing may explain the evolution of some retail forms, it is less clear about the success of some new niche retailers; retailers that successfully compete on nonprice factors, such as luxury retailers or convenience stores; and the role of cost control in improving customer satisfaction as well as competitiveness, as Walmart and discount clubs have done.

Nina Raingold/Getty Images

Some analysts suggest that gasoline stations are starting to follow the retail accordion theory as they expand assortments which creates an opportunity for a competitor to narrow assortments back to focusing only on gasoline.

The Retail Accordion

Several observers of the history of retailing have noted that retail institutions tend to evolve from outlets that offer wide merchandise assortments to specialized stores that offer narrow assortments and then return to the wide assortment stores, continuing this pattern again and again. This contraction and expansion of merchandise assortment suggests the term **retail accordion**.[18]

Retail historians have observed that retail trade in the United States was dominated by the general store until 1860. The general store carried a broad assortment of merchandise ranging from farm implements to textiles and food. After 1860, due to the growth of cities and roads, retail trade became more

retail accordion
Describes how retail institutions evolve from outlets that offer wide assortments to specialized stores and continue repeatedly through the pattern.

specialized and was concentrated in the central business districts of cities. By 1880 to 1890, department and specialty stores were the dominant competitive force. Both carried more specialized assortments than the general store. In the 1950s, retailing began to move again to wider merchandise lines. Typical was the supermarket, which added produce and dairy products and nonfood items such as kitchen utensils, health and beauty aids, and small household appliances. Today specialization in merchandise categories has once again become a dominant competitive strategy. Witness, for example, the success of Sports Authority stores, Barnes & Noble bookstores, and Abercrombie & Fitch Co. Even Walmart is heeding this trend by building freestanding 40,000-square-foot Neighborhood Market grocery stores in selected cities.

However, the accordion theory is vague about the competitive importance of providing wide assortments for various target customer groups. For example, the customer who wants one-stop-shopping convenience has led to success for Walmart's Superstores and other retailers using scrambled merchandising. Simultaneously, many category killers have been successful by specializing in a deep but narrow selection of merchandise lines, and specialty stores like Forever 21 and high-end "hot" designers like Gucci have succeeded by offering a highly edited point of view for their customer segments. Again, a major criticism of this theory is its implication that there is one "right" direction for successful retailing, when many are possible if well executed.

The Retail Life Cycle

The final framework we will examine is the **retail life cycle**. Some experts argue that retailing institutions pass through an identifiable cycle. This cycle has four distinct stages: It starts with (1) *introduction*, (2) proceeds to *growth* and then (3) *maturity*, and

retail life cycle
Describes four distinct stages that a retail institution progresses through: introduction, growth, maturity, and decline.

Exhibit 4.6
Retail Institutions in Their Various Stages of the Retail Life Cycle

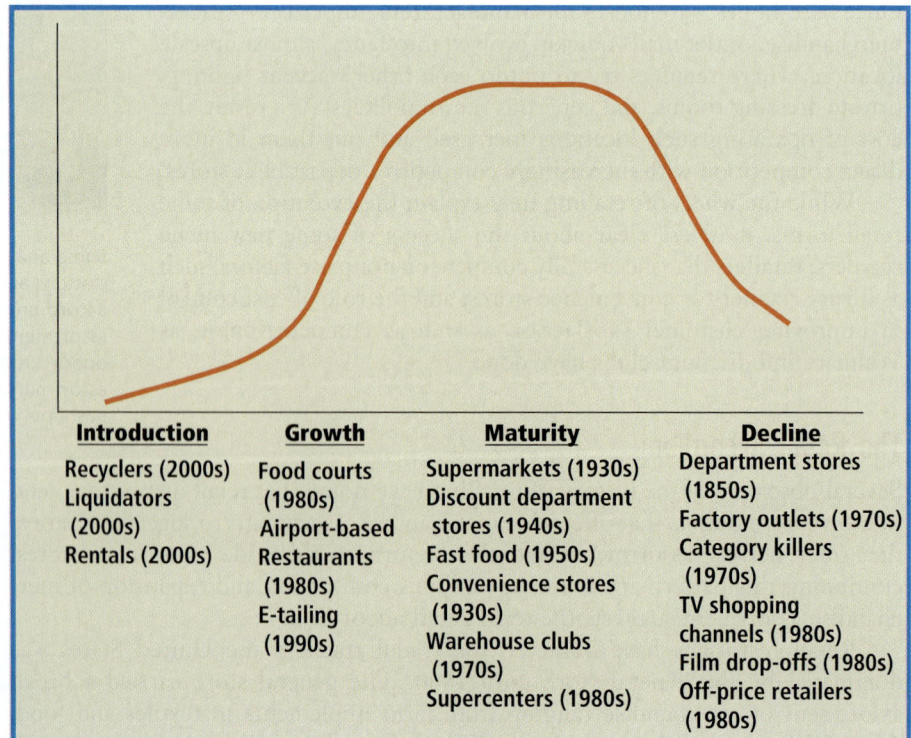

Introduction	Growth	Maturity	Decline
Recyclers (2000s)	Food courts (1980s)	Supermarkets (1930s)	Department stores (1850s)
Liquidators (2000s)	Airport-based Restaurants (1980s)	Discount department stores (1940s)	Factory outlets (1970s)
Rentals (2000s)	E-tailing (1990s)	Fast food (1950s)	Category killers (1970s)
		Convenience stores (1930s)	TV shopping channels (1980s)
		Warehouse clubs (1970s)	Film drop-offs (1980s)
		Supercenters (1980s)	Off-price retailers (1980s)

ends with (4) *decline*. Exhibit 4.6 illustrates the various stages of the retail life cycle for many of our current retail institutions. We discuss each stage briefly.

Introduction

This stage begins with an aggressive, bold entrepreneur who is willing and able to develop a different approach to the retailing of certain products. Most often the approach is oriented toward a simpler method of distribution and passing the savings on to the customer. Other times it could be a different version of an existing product or service centered on a distinctive product assortment, shopping ease, locational convenience, advertising, or promotion. For example, during the recent economic crisis, Americans saw the advent of new forms of rentals. These recent rentals were untraditional in that companies such as Zip Cars rented automobiles by the hour to consumers in large cities or to students on campuses. Other innovative firms offered an alternative to expensive purchases by renting consumers a Coach, Dooney & Bourke, or Dior handbag by the week.[19] Such repacking of traditional products has resulted in many consumers thinking back to the introduction of Starbucks when consumers questioned the need for a $4 cup of coffee. As might be expected, during this stage, profits are low, despite the increasing sales level, due to amortizing developmental costs and not yet achieving sufficient scale economies.

Growth

During the growth stage, sales and usually profits explode. New retailers enter the market and begin to copy the idea. For example, the rapid growth of e-tailers has encouraged others to enter the market and capture a portion of the growing interest of shopping casually from home. Toward the end of the growth stage, cost pressures arise from the need for a larger staff, more complex internal systems, increased management controls, and other requirements of operating large, multiunit organizations. Consequently, late in this stage both market share and profitability tend to reach their maximum level.

Maturity

In maturity, several factors occur that cause market share to stabilize and profits to decline. First, managers have become accustomed to managing a high-growth firm that was simple and small, yet now they must manage a large, complex firm in a nongrowing market. Second, the industry has typically overexpanded. Third, competitive assaults increase as firms with new retailing formats or more-efficient methods enter the industry (entrepreneurs starting a new retail life cycle).

Decline

Although decline is inevitable for some formats (few people get their milk delivered to the door anymore), retail managers will try to postpone it by changing the retail mix. These attempts can postpone the decline stage, but a return to earlier, attractive levels of operating performance is unlikely. Sooner or later, a major loss of market share will occur, profits will fall, and the once-promising idea will no longer be needed in the marketplace.

The retail life cycle is accelerating today. New and more competitive concepts move quickly from introduction to maturity since the leading operators have aggressive growth goals and their investors demand a quick return on equity. Consider, for example, how fast the one-hour photo drop-offs lasted. Today, most consumers have digital cameras. In addition, larger retailers with capital and

Global Retailing

North America's Oldest Retailer

Recently, a television quiz show asked, "What is the oldest retailer in North America?" One contestant answered "A&P" (for the Great Atlantic & Pacific Tea Company), and the other answered "Sears." Both were wrong. A&P was founded in 1859, and Sears, Roebuck and Company started business in 1886. The oldest U.S. retailer is Brooks Brothers, which Henry Sands Brooks opened for business on April 7, 1818, as H. & D. H. Brooks & Co. In 1870, Brooks's four sons inherited the family business and renamed the company "Brooks Brothers." In addition, Lord & Taylor (1826) and Macy's (1858) are both older than A&P. (See the discussion of the current A&P in Chapter 2.)

However, none of these U.S. retailers correctly answers the question. The oldest retailer in North America is Canadian retailer The Hudson's Bay Company, which was chartered by King Charles II on May 2, 1670, to trade fur pelts; it remains one of Canada's major retail players. How "The Bay," as it is known in Canada, survived the changing retail environment is an interesting story that describes how it continues to adjust to the retail life cycle.

Throughout its history, The Bay has operated department stores, discount department stores, big-box chains, a smaller regional chain, and an online shopping site. Currently, the company has more than 600 stores in Canada, a country with a population of about 32 million people.

Understanding the changing nature of competition in the marketplace has helped The Bay remain successful over a long period of time. The backbone of the company is its department store chain known as The Bay. The chain has stores from coast to coast in Canada and occupies top-flight downtown, flagship locations in all major cities. It also has a presence in most of the major suburban malls in Canada. Over the years, The Bay has evolved into a mid- to upper-price-point, full-line department store. It focuses on fashion, cosmetics, and soft goods but still carries electronics and appliances. The stores carry many of the same brands as American retailer Macy's as well as a number of brands exclusive to The Bay. Only one other major, national department store remains in Canada: Sears. Others such as Eaton's have disappeared as the department store concept lost popularity and moved into decline.

With department stores in decline, The Bay has been successful by expanding into other retail endeavors. In 1978, The Bay purchased Zellers, a discount department store offering a mass merchandise concept. Using an everyday low-price policy, Zellers has succeeded. The development of a loyalty program for Zellers also helped it weather the storm of Walmart entering Canada in 1994 by buying 122 Woolco stores. Notably, Kmart Canada did not survive. In 1998, Zellers bought all the remaining Kmart stores and converted them to the Zellers format.

Anticipating the growth of the specialty superstore market, The Bay launched Home Outfitters in 1999. This kitchen, bed, and bath specialty superstore is currently the fastest-growing specialty store chain in Canada and has survived the onslaught of many competitors such as Linens 'n Things, seeking to steal their market share.

In 2000, The Bay launched hbc.com, the company's online store. Hbc.com has been successful for The Bay to date and keeps it moving forward with retail concepts that are in the growth stage.

Throughout this time, The Bay has also hung onto its small value-priced general merchandiser, Fields. Although not very well-known, Fields has continued to be successful. These stores are located only in western Canada and are focused on smaller retail centers, a market somewhat overlooked by larger retailers. Today, many retail analysts are looking forward to watching the evolution of Fields as Walmart expands into smaller centers in Canada.

Jerry Zucker, an American businessman, purchased The Bay in 2006, ending more than 335 years of The Bay as a publicly traded company. In late 2008, NRDC, owner of Lord & Taylor, bought The Hudson's Bay Co. Under this new ownership team, the Bay is looking to continue its successful history as a premier player in Canadian retailing. A portfolio of retail concepts in differing stages of the retail life cycle should ensure continued success.

Source: This box was prepared by D. Lynne Ricker, University of Calgary, and coauthor of this text's Canadian edition.

---

expertise in concept rollout can acquire many entrepreneurs in the early stages of the retail life cycle. This chapter's "Global Retailing" describes how North America's oldest retailer has survived by adjusting to the retail life cycle.

Resource-Advantage Theory

The final theory to describe the evolution of retail competition is **resource-advantage theory**.[20] This theory is based on the idea that all firms seek superior financial performance in an ever-changing environment. Retail demand is dynamic because consumer tastes are always changing, and supply is dynamic because, as firms search for superior performance, they are forced to change the elements of their retail mix to match changing consumer preferences.

Resource-advantage theory illustrates two important lessons for retailers:[21]

- Superior performance at any point in time is the result of achieving a competitive advantage in the marketplace as a result of some tangible or intangible entity (or "resource"). The retailer is able to use this entity, such as an innovation regarding location, procedures or merchandise selection, to offer greater value to the market place or to operate their firms at a lower cost relative to competitors.

- All retailers cannot achieve superior results at the same time. The retailer is able to use this entity, such as innovation regarding location procedures or merchandise selection, to offer greater value to the marketplace or to operate their firms at a lower cost relative to competitors.

Thus, it is important for currently high-performing retailers to maintain their vigilance over the actions of lower-performing competitors so as not to be overtaken.

The result is ongoing market turbulence in which new retail forms and offerings continually appear, and consumers continually shift their buying preferences and retail patronage. As retailers compete with each other through different combinations of resources (merchandise selection, pricing, service, communication, positioning, distribution improvements, and relationship building), each of these multifaceted competitive positions can meet the needs of different customer groups. The resulting fragmentation in the marketplace means that many different retail forms are viable, as long as the customer group is sufficiently substantial (i.e., large enough to generate acceptable profit for the retailer) and the retailer is astute in managing its customer relationships and operations. So long as each retailer meets the needs of its target customers better than competitors, while controlling their own costs of satisfying those customers, the retailer will prosper.

This is one explanation of why dollar stores such as Dollar General can survive in the same markets with larger discounters that offer better prices, wider assortments, and groceries. Many consumers, lacking personal transportation, rely on Dollar General as a quick, convenient place for sundries and grab-and-go foods.

The fact remains that not all customers are equally knowledgeable about retail alternatives, not all retailers are as astute about understanding their customers, not all customers have similar preferences or access to retail alternatives, and not all retailers have the resources to meet the competition for their traditional customers. Amway has recently seen retailers ranging from Walmart to Tractor Supply make inroads into its suburban and rural base and online merchants tap its traditional "shop-at-home" customers. As a result, Amway is seeking to reposition itself. These marketplace discrepancies allow for less-than-optimal retail environments but also reveal opportunities to the retailer who is willing to study its customers and markets and do a better job in managing its operations. Following these actions, it is then imperative that the retailer communicate its superiority to target customers, thus pushing competition to a new and evolved level.

resource-advantage theory
Resource-Advantage Theory argues that firms gain competitive advantage by offering superior value to customers and/or having lower costs of operating.

Future Changes in Retail Competition

What future changes could affect retail competition?

Retailers in today's ever-changing marketplace can expect dynamic changes in competition. Trends shaping the retail landscape include an increase in competition from nonstore retailers, the advent of new retailing formats, heightened global competition, the integration of technology into current operations, and the increasing use of private labels.

Nonstore Retailing

Back in Exhibit 1.3, it was pointed out that nonstore retail sales (NAICS Code 454), including direct sellers, catalog sales, and e-tailing, account for 7 percent of total retail sales. However, most retail analysts predict that, as a result of several key forces at work today, only Internet sales will experience significant growth over the next decade, while the other forms of nonstore retailing, direct selling and catalog sales, will remain steady or decline. Thus, the growth of this form of selling is based on accelerated communication technology and changing consumer lifestyles. Thus, retailers need to continuously monitor developments in nonstore retailing.

E-Tailing

The general belief among retail experts is that electronic, interactive, at-home shopping is definitely the place to be. Every major player in the retail industry, computer industry, telecommunications industry, and the transaction processing industry is committed to this growth. The only prerequisite needed for the Internet's success is having enough consumers with access, whether it is via a personal computer, cell phone, or BlackBerry. Already more than 80 percent of American households are connected either at home or at work, and a rather astonishing fact is that more people now use cell phones and not landline phones as their primary means of phone communication. More important is the fact that today's teens and 20-somethings are the first generation to grow up fully wired and technologically fluent. These consumers, especially college students, use social-networking websites such as MySpace and Facebook as a way to establish their identities; they are also more apt to text message than call a friend.

As pointed out in Chapter 1's "What's New?" box on YouTube, many people believe these social networks have created new forms of social behavior that blur the distinction between online and real-world interactions to the point that today's young adults largely ignore the differences. Most Gen Xers and baby boomers tend to view the Internet as a supplement to their daily lives. They use the Net to gather information, buy items (CDs, books, stocks, gifts, and even fast food), or link up with others who share a passion for their favorite sports team. Yet, for the most part, their social lives remain rooted in the traditional phone call and face-to-face interaction.

Generation Y folks, by contrast, are able to exist in both worlds simultaneously. Increasingly, America's middle- and upper-class youth use social networks as virtual community centers, a place to go and sit for awhile (sometimes hours). While older consumers come and go on the Net for a specific task, Gen Yers are just as likely to socialize online as off. This is partly a function of how much more comfortable young people are on the web: 87 percent of 12- to 17-year-olds use the Internet, versus two-thirds of adults.

As the Internet grows, Americans will make increasing use of it as a shopping method. Many shoppers will opt for its convenience and broad selection. Browsing will be easier and the choices more extensive. (Nevertheless, consumers will still want

Why Is It Important to Be Multi-Channel?

tns RF

■ Online still the fastest-growing retail channel

Annual E-Commerce Retail Sales
(Millions of Dollars and Share)

Compound Annual Growth Rates
1998–2003: 62.6%
2003–2008: 19.9%
2008–2013: 15.0%

Forecast

Millions $
Share of Retail Sales

Share = Right Scale

$27,673 $34,353 $44,842 $56,615 $70,938 $87,397 $106,583 $127,690 $140,112 $153,198 $174,629 $203,270 $238,517 $281,245

2000 2002 2004 2006 2008 2010 2012

Source: Provided by Retail Forward, July 2009

Exhibit 4.7
Retail E-Commerce Retail Sales

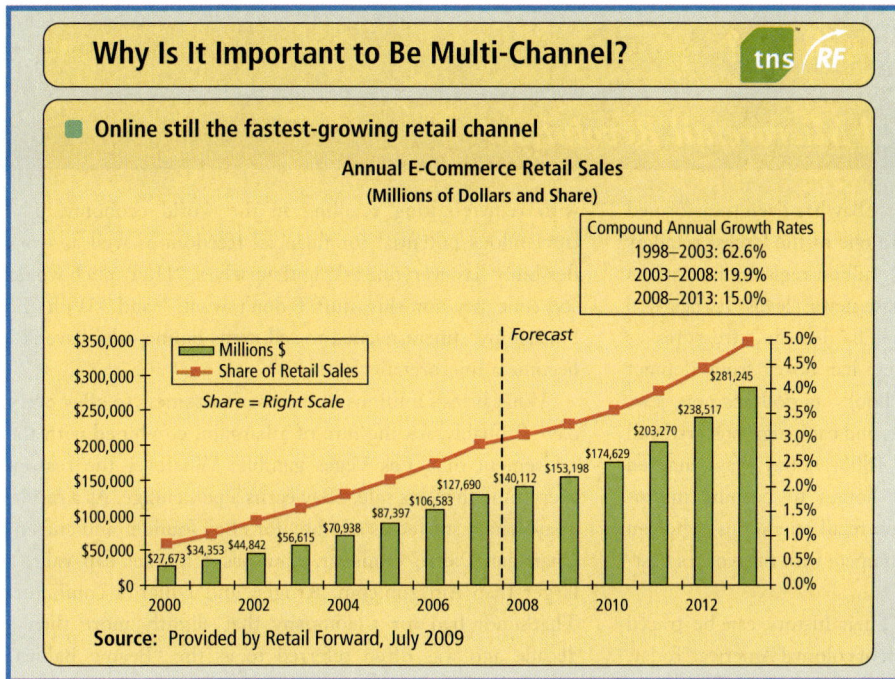

the social experience of shopping outside the home; after all, with so many stores nearby, shopping at a bricks-and-mortar retailer after doing active information gathering on the computer will become even more convenient.) As a result, Internet shopping is expected to increase from its current level of slightly less than 3 percent of retail sales to a little more than 5 percent over the next decade (see Exhibit 4.7).

While some so-called experts had once claimed that Internet sales would reach 50 percent of total retail sales, this prediction will never come to pass for the following six reasons.

1. As shown in Exhibit 1.3, 24 percent of all retail sales involve automobile dealers. The taxes paid by new car dealers to their state governments will ensure that states will continue to ban Internet sales and protect the current system. Likewise, gasoline station sales, which make up 10 percent of all retail sales, are not likely to be made over the Internet.

2. Discounters, who account for a third of all general merchandise sales, will have a particularly difficult problem selling via the Internet. After all, consumers looking for bargains won't want to pay for shipping and handling. The same argument could be made for bulky items such as furniture. An IKEA spokesperson recently admitted that the chain's website (www.ikea.com) was clunky and offered only a narrow selection of products, since many products are simply too large to be shipped cheaply.[22]

3. Half of all food and beverage sales, or more than 7 percent of all retail sales, are sold by on-premise restaurants.

4. As mentioned earlier, because of the recent economic slowdown, the United States is currently overstored. Many consumers, after searching the Internet, opt for the instant satisfaction of purchasing from a nearby bricks-and-mortar retailer instead of waiting for an overnight delivery.

What's New?

eBay: A Microretail Revolution

In the 15 years since its founding, eBay has been transformed from a small dot.com company to one of the largest retailers in the United States. With its 12 million registered members and users, the online auction house never sleeps. Its nearly 6 million daily auctions offer such hard-to-find treasures as flight bags from defunct airlines, hat boxes from defunct department stores, out-of-print books, period costume jewelry, an Art Deco dressing mirror, and campaign posters from presidential elections in the 1800s. eBay has enabled individuals working from their homes to become microretailers (small one- or two-person retail operations) who can reach a global marketplace and compete with the world's best-known retailers.

Microretailers are not new. Their history can be traced back to the door-to-door peddlers of colonial America. Today, for example, microretailers specializing in hot dogs, pretzels, newspapers, and other consumables can be observed operating in the downtown area of any major city. In the past, though, their relatively small trade area (restricted to a few city blocks) and merchandise assortment limited their competitive threat to more traditional retailers. However, the retail world is changing, and eBay—with merchandise covering 4,300 categories—is one of the catalysts.

eBay has clearly revolutionized the opportunities available to microretailers. In that sense, the company can be credited with reinvigorating retailing in the world economy. The tremendous potential for financial freedom as well as work flexibility has everyone asking themselves, "How much would someone pay for this stuff I don't want?" and "With the limited investment needed to sell items online, why haven't I become a microretailer already?"

What brings millions of Internet customers to eBay every day? Probably, it's the lure of a bargain, combined with the excitement of a Las Vegas gamble. Whatever the reason, every time there's a sale, eBay earns a percentage. As a result, eBay, which started as a hobby for eBay founder and current Chairman Pierre Omidyar, now has a market cap value[23] larger than Amazon.com, Kroger, and Dillard's combined. That's not bad for a company that slightly more than a decade ago was often referred to as the "Beanie Babies" website.

Today, eBay has become the largest website for the buying and selling of used cars, motorcycles, auto parts, and collectibles. In fact, more than $1,000 worth of goods are bought and sold every second.

What is most astounding about this eBay revolution is the fact that the company itself holds no inventory and ships no product. Rather, it is an entirely new concept that took advantage of the Internet and has no direct bricks-and-mortar competition.

---

5. Some items, especially fashion clothing, must be tried on or seen in person before buying. As anyone who has ever seen an array of televisions in a store knows, each set has a different tint. The same can be said for a computer monitor.

6. A final factor limiting e-commerce is the "security issue." Many consumers are afraid of identity theft; as a result, only about 40 percent of all Americans purchased even one item on the Internet in 2008.

It is important to remember that the Internet will not increase overall consumer demand. While online sales will definitely cannibalize store and catalog sales, they will not increase the average consumer spending power. Strategies by clicks-and-mortar retailers that integrate a single message and seamless operations will be more powerful than a pure e-tailing strategy. This will be especially true once clicks-and-mortar retailers learn the importance of addressing the total customer experience through any contact point with the customer. A final point to remember is that e-tailers must pay attention to customer service. Most e-tailers do a good job during busy seasons, such as Christmas and Valentine's Day. However, in an effort to reduce operating costs, they reduce their service standards at other times. Customers are demanding such basic services as e-mail confirmation of orders and real-time confirmation of available inventory. Since customer service is a particular vulnerability for traditional retailers, e-tailers should seek their niche here.

However, the most significant contribution of the Internet to retailing is that it has enabled everyone to be a retailer, albeit a microretailer, by using eBay. This tremendous impact on individuals of all ages is best seen by the number of training seminars, community colleges, senior centers, and so on, offering classes on how to buy and sell on eBay. This chapter's "What's New?" box explores the phenomenon of how the eBay revolution has made it possible for anyone to be an e-tailer.

New Retailing Formats

The practice of retailing is continually evolving. New formats are born and old ones die. Innovation in retailing is the result of constant pressure to improve efficiency and effectiveness in a continual effort to better serve the consumer. The pressure to better serve has also resulted in a shortened life cycle for retail formats. However, just as retailers find it extremely difficult to predict what will be the "hot new item" for an upcoming season, especially Christmas, they have the same trouble predicting the success of new retail formats.

For example, in the early 1980s, most retail experts agreed that hypermarkets (which are one and one-half times the size of a supercenter) would be retailing's success story of the 1980s. However, despite their overwhelming success in Europe and their limited success in the United States (Meijer's in Michigan and Kroger's Fred Meyer division in the Northwest), these superlarge stores, which resembled airplane hangars, were instead one of retailing's biggest failures. What happened?

Customers probably felt that any store that had "rest areas" and stockers wearing roller skates was just too big to shop. Also shoppers were unnerved by ceilings and shelves that rose several stories high. In addition, category killers such as Toys "R" Us and Sports Authority offered greater selection, wholesale clubs offered better prices, and supermarkets, discount drug stores, and other discounters offered more convenient locations. Although hypermarkets were a superior competitive offering in Europe, where the traditional alternatives were small, crowded shops with high prices, they did not have a noteworthy competitive advantage in the overstored American retail landscape.

Another retail format that didn't achieve the success predicted was the off-price retailer. **Off-price retailers** were similar to discounters with one important difference. While discounters offer continuity of brands—that is, they carry the same brands day in and day out—off-pricers, which are more opportunistic, carry only brands that they are able to get on special deals from the manufacturer or close-out wholesalers. Thus, the off-price retailers failed because the regular merchants, including discounters, became more competitive on the prices of the brands that the off-pricers were selling. Moreover, the off-price merchandise brands and selection could be wildly unpredictable as manufacturers became better at planning production and inventories.

off-price retailers
Sell products at a discount but do not carry certain brands on a continuous basis. They carry those brands they can buy from manufacturers at closeout or deep one-time discount prices.

The three primary examples of off-price retailers are factory outlets, independent carriers, and warehouse clubs. Factory outlets, which are owned and operated by the manufacturer, stock the manufacturers' surplus, discontinued, or irregular products. Independent off-price retailers such as Loehmann's, Stein Mart, TJ Maxx, and websites such as Overstock.com carry an ever-changing assortment of higher-quality merchandise. Warehouse (or wholesale) clubs such as Costco and Sam's were the most successful of the off-pricers. These mature-stage retailers operate out of enormous, low-cost facilities and charge patrons an annual membership fee. They sell a limited selection of brand-name grocery items, appliances, clothing, and miscellaneous items at a deep discount. Warehouse stores, which have low costs because they buy products at huge quantity discounts and use limited labor, usually have low gross margins (gross margin will be explained in detail in Chapter 8) averaging nearly 10 percent to 12 percent, which is a third of traditional retailers.

supercenter
A cavernous combination of supermarket and discount department store carrying more than 80,000 to 100,000 SKUs that allows for one-stop shopping.

One highly successful and recently introduced format is the **supercenter**—a cavernous combination of supermarket and discount department store carrying more than 80,000 to 100,000 SKUs that range from televisions to peanut butter and DVDs. These stores offer the customer one-stop shopping (and as a result are capable of drawing customers from a 50-mile radius in some rural areas) and lower the customer's total cost in terms of time and miles traveled. They are expected to continue being a profitable format for mass merchants.

The supercenter concept has even branched out into the automobile market. Glitzy, computerized auto superstore chains such as AutoNation, Driver's Mart Worldwide, and CarMax Auto Superstores are giving nightmares to the nation's 22,000 traditional car dealers. Since its introduction in the mid-1980s, this new breed of retailer has streamlined an industry in which more than 15 percent of a car's price consists of retailer expenses and has made shopping easier for the customer. These massive, publicly traded chains sell new and used cars using "cheap" Wall Street money to finance, sell, rent, lease, and repair cars. Just like the supercenters in the grocery industry, these auto superstores are making competition tougher for other auto retailers.

Although the supercenters have achieved their promise while hypermarkets and off-pricers neglected to live up to expectations, three successful formats developed over the last decade are expected to continue: stores that recycle usable merchandise in good condition, liquidators, and rental operations. These three formats have one thing in common: They offer the consumer value in an untraditional manner.

Recycled Merchandise Retailers

recycled merchandise retailers
Are establishments that sell used and reconditioned products.

Due to their very small numbers just a decade ago, recycled merchandisers have experienced the fastest growth rate of any retail format over the past five years. As a result of the recent economic slowdown, **recycled merchandise retailers** selling slightly used children's clothes (Once Upon A Child), teen and adult clothing (Plato's Closet), sporting goods (Play It Again Sports), musical instruments (Music-Go-Round), and even videogames (Gamestop) have experienced significant growth.[24] In addition, **pawn shops**, **thrift shops**, **auction houses**, **consignment shops**, **flea markets**, and even **eBay** are also considered to be recyclers.

The recycle concept was pioneered by the Salvation Army in London in 1865 to provide merchandise to poor households as well as generate funds to feed and house the poor. Historically, most recyclers were found in the poorer sections of cities, sometimes tucked away in dreary brick buildings with dumpsters on the side. Not anymore. Today these establishments have soft lighting and wide aisles, clothing in neat racks that is coordinated by color and size, plenty of changing rooms, and well-trained and polite salespeople.

As a record number of retailers were seeking bankruptcy protection in 2009, these stores saw a growth rate approaching 20 percent. No longer was conspicuous consumption chic. Today, even the baby boomers who live in big fancy homes in the suburbs and invest in stocks and mutual funds find it fashionable to pull into parking lots with big PAWN SHOP, THRIFT STORE, or SECOND HAND signs while driving their BMWs.[25]

Now that many preowned clothes shops are using the same media as traditional retailers to advertise their merchandise, shoppers today may find it difficult to distinguish between recyclers and small specialty shops. Because so much of the merchandise is new, nearly new, or gently used, the tattered appearance of traditional thrift stores is no longer expected. Recyclers have developed to serve specific markets such as pregnant women, people requiring large sizes, and children; or even to offer specific merchandise such as toys, sporting goods, outerwear, or jewelry. The apparel group accounting for the fewest resale and thrift store sales is men's clothing. It seems that men hang on to their clothes longer than women and children, leaving much less merchandise available for resale.

Today, there are more than 25,000 secondhand stores nationwide, according to the National Association of Resale and Thrift Shops in St. Clair Shores, Michigan.[26] This chapter's "Retailing: The Inside Story" discusses the history of the country's largest for-profit thrift chain: Savers, Inc.

Liquidators

Between 2008 and 2009, more than 300,000 retail stores, including such well-known retailers as Circuit City, Mervyn's, Linens 'n Things, and Steve & Barry's, closed as a result of bankruptcy. This provided a new retail growth format (albeit another from a very small starting point): liquidators. Often called retailing's undertakers or vultures, firms like Buxbaum Group, Great American Group, and Hilco Organization purchase the entire inventory of the existing retailer and run its "going-out-of-business" sale. They assume responsibility for a retailer's leases,

Retailing: The Inside Story

Savers: The For-Profit Thrift

One of the authors serves as the treasurer of a not-for-profit organization that runs a thrift shop. The shop serves two purposes: (1) to generate funding for other organizational projects, such as housing, medical, or utility assistance, and (2) to provide the retail setting needed to disperse emergency clothing and furniture to families in need. Such an operation is not cheap because a thrift store incurs all the expenses a normal retailer has—management, a physical location, a truck for picking up merchandise, office supplies, insurance, and so on. Granted some of the labor is volunteered, but the expenses alone for the author's store exceed a quarter million per year.

Now consider what would happen if a not-for-profit charity wasn't large enough to support such a large-scale operation. Without that charity, a lot of clothing would wind up in landfills. Instead, a thrift operation doesn't waste anything. Clothes that are too worn or torn to be sold are baled up and sold by the pound to be recycled as new fabric.

It is because of situations in which not-for-profit charities are too small to operate a thrift store that the nation's only for-profit chain recycler was started. Savers, Inc., headquartered in Bellevue, Washington, is a privately held, for-profit thrift store chain offering the best in secondhand shopping. An international company, Savers has more than 200 locations throughout the United States, Canada, and Australia and receives its merchandise by paying cash to not-for-profit partners for

donated clothing and household items. Under Savers' unique business model, the company partners with local not-for-profits by purchasing and reselling donated items. The charity partners collect and deliver donated goods to Savers, which pays the organization a bulk rate for the items regardless of whether or not they ever make it to the sales floor. Reusable items are displayed for purchase in stores, while unsuitable items are shipped to developing countries and material wholesalers for recycling. Last year, Savers contributed $117 million to its 120 not-for-profit charity partners.

The entrepreneur of leveraging this unique for-profit and not-for-profit business model was the late William Ellison, who conjured a sort of secondhand Sears Roebuck. Mr. Ellison was the son of a Salvation Army thrift store manager in Washington state. After trying to sell advertising, he decided to open a commercial thrift shop in San Francisco's Mission District. With a business plan bankrolled by his father, the Purple Heart Thrift Store was owned by a local charity, and Mr. Ellison split profits in exchange for running it. After incorporating the operation as Salvage Management Corp., Bill Ellison was soon managing thrift shops for other charities. But soon after Ellison's shops were established and successful, the charities tended to back out of their agreements and set up their own stores. So Ellison switched strategies and started signing up charities as collection agents

(continued)

Retailing: The Inside Story (*continued*)

Barbie Hull Photography

Savers, a for-profit thrift store chain offering the best in secondhand shopping, gets its merchandise by paying cash to non-profit partners for donated clothing and household items.

"only," whereby he guaranteed them a certain rate per pound of merchandise.

Ellison's recycling strategy was soon a full-scale operation that was so successful that Savers even added a modern inventory system including bar codes as opposed to the handwritten price tags used by most other recyclers.

Source: This box was prepared with the cooperation of Savers, Inc.

payroll, and other costs and agree either to take a percentage of what they sell or agree in advance to purchase the existing inventory. They are gambling that they will be able to unload the merchandise at prices that will generate a solid profit, which is often the case given they rarely pay more than 30 cents on the dollar for the merchandise. Liquidators do more than $15 billion in sales annually and earn between 3 percent and 7 percent of the sales or they take over the company entirely and take all the risks but make all the profits. Here they will pay a small percent of the cost value of existing inventory.[27]

Some might question why retailers don't do this job themselves, as some manufacturers do with outlet malls. First, the retailers in question usually have problems, or they wouldn't need the liquidator's service in the first place. Second, most liquidators pay cash for the merchandise—a plus for the strapped retailer—and then take all the risks and gain the rewards. In addition, liquidators sometimes augment sales by bringing in new merchandise or by adding leftovers from previous liquidations.[28]

Finally, by having outsiders run the closeouts, management can focus on operating the continuing stores and moving on to (hopefully) more successful merchandising.

Running closeouts requires some very special retailing skills. Liquidators have a talent for pricing merchandise and estimating the expense of everything from ad budgets and payrolls to utility bills. Since most of the employees know they will be out of a job as soon as the liquidation is complete, liquidators have to develop special incentive plans to make it more profitable for store personnel to stay and work rather than quit or walk off with merchandise.

Rentals

The idea of renting and not purchasing an item is not new. Renting has been popular for a limited number of items for decades. Most college students have rented VCRs and DVDs. Other consumers have rented furniture on a rent-to-own basis. Similarly, everyone has probably rented a car on a daily or weekly basis. However, the recent slumping economy has generated a renewed interest in this format for an expanded category of products. This chapter will discuss three versions of these new rental formats that are most apt to be used by college students: cars by the hour, fashion items, and textbooks.

Ever needed a car for an hour or so? This is a common problem for college students who live on campus without a car, consumers who live in large cities with extensive mass transit programs and rental spaces that often meet or exceed the car's monthly payment, and senior-citizen communities where the retired consumers have a rather infrequent need for a car. Today, retailers such as Zipcar and Hertz are meeting this need with a retail strategy of renting cars for short periods of time, often by the hour. Such an operation is attractive to customers who make only occasional use of a vehicle.[29] Today, there are more than 700,000 consumers in more than 100 cities and campuses, who pay an annual membership fee to use one of the 10,000 vehicles currently involved in this program. Many expect this number to continue growing at an annual rate of 20 percent as consumers recognize the ease and convenience the program offers.

Given the current economic climate, many fashion-conscious consumers now have less cash for that pricey new handbag, designer dress or gown, piece of jewelry, or other accessories. Maybe renting, and not buying, offers the solution. Today, after paying a small monthly fee, college students can rent a great looking stylish handbag by the month.[30]

The final area of rental growth effecting college students is textbooks. Consider the benefits of renting textbooks to the student. The typical college student spends slightly more than $500 a term for textbooks and gets around $200 when selling them back at semester's end, according to federal statistics. In addition, price increases have recently been outstripping inflation. But books cost (typically) only a third that much at the 50 or so schools around the country that rent books. These schools typically charge a "usage fee" of about $7 to $8 per credit hour, meaning a student taking 15 credit hours of classes would only pay either $105 or $120 at the beginning of the semester. After final exams, students simply return the books and they avert those end-of-semester "bookstore won't buy back my book" blues. The major drawbacks for a school trying to adopt such a program are faculty commitment and the huge upfront costs that schools would incur when building the initial inventory of textbooks.[31]

Today, more than two dozen e-tailers, including Chegg.com, campusbook-rentals.com, and bookrenter.com, offer students millions of texts to choose from and allow them to rent books for a set period, anywhere from a month to a semester or summer—the rental term determines the cost. Many retail analysts expect this number to grow despite the recent introduction of another alternative: the digital textbook using a Sony reader. However, growth for this format appears to be limited because research by student public interest research groups has found that 75 percent of students surveyed said they'd prefer a printed textbook to a digital one. The biggest complaint given about going digital: students don't want to lug their computers around campus.[32]

Heightened Global Competition

The rate of change in retailing around the world appears to be directly related to the stage and speed of economic development in the countries concerned, but even the least-developed countries are experiencing dramatic changes. Retailing in other countries exhibits greater diversity in its structure than it does in the United States. In some countries, such as Italy, retailing is composed largely of specialty houses carrying narrow lines. Finnish retailers usually carry a more general line of merchandise. The size of the average retailer is also diverse—from the massive Harrod's in London and Mitsukoshi Ltd. in Japan, both of which serve more than 10,000 customers a day, to the small one- or two-person stalls in developing African and Latin American nations.

New types of retailing have emerged from all areas of the world. These changing formats can be attributed to a variety of economic and social factors that are the same worldwide: a widespread concern for health, a steady increase in the number of working women and two-income families, inflation, consumerism, and so forth. These factors, and their effects on consumer lifestyles, encourage high-profit retailers around the world to seek new market segments, make adjustments in their retail mix, alter location patterns, and adopt new multisegment strategies. In the process, many new retail concepts and formats have emerged and spread.

Still, it is amazing that retailers from larger countries often do not have the same success, compared to that of retailers from smaller countries, when entering a new country. Consider, for example, the fact that at the end of fiscal year 2008 Walmart, in addition to its 4,141 stores in the United States, was operating 3,121 units in Argentina, Brazil, Canada, Central America, China, Japan, Mexico, Puerto Rico, and the United Kingdom.[33] However, in that year, the chain sold its operations in both Germany and South Korea when they failed to meet profit expectations.

In Germany, Walmart found the discount retail market too tough for one to crack as homegrown discount retailers already offered very low prices. Walmart also failed to understand the frugal and demanding ways of German shoppers. For similar reasons, Walmart's biggest global competitor, Paris-based Carrefour, which operates more than 15,000 stores in 29 countries yet is second to Walmart in total sales, never entered the market citing German regulations restricting store hours and other retailing basics.[34] Walmart, despite becoming the largest grocery retailer in markets like Brazil, faced similar challenges from Carrefour and others in Britain. Meanwhile, H&M, the Swedish women's apparel chain, and Zara, the vertically integrated apparel chain from Spain, both create excitement and sales in most foreign markets they enter. Yet Kmart, Sears, and JCPenney have all abandoned their foreign-expansion plans. Many successful British merchants such as Conran's Habitat, a housewares chain, and Laura Ashley have not been able to replicate their success in the United States. Still to be seen is how successful a recent entry to the U.S. market will be. Daiso, which means "big creation" in Japanese, is a Japanese dollar store—more precisely, a $1.50 store that is not to be confused with the usual U.S. dollar store. Because Japanese retail is so different, the store is very interesting and has a certain design aesthetic. The chain isn't like a typical U.S.

dollar store, Daiso may have inexpensive merchandise, but it is "cheerful, in the way that Target is; it's about color and fun."[35]

Retail experts attribute this failure by large-country retailers to two factors. Some think it is a lack of understanding of the new country's culture. Even Walmart made major mistakes when it entered international markets. In Canada, its cultural faux pas was distributing English-language circulars in French-speaking Quebec. On entering Mexico, the chain built large parking lots at some of its stores only to realize that most of their customers rode the bus and then had to cross these large, empty parking lots carrying bags full of merchandise. Walmart responded by creating a shuttle bus service. This error was especially embarrassing for Walmart since one of the key factors for its overall success was the fact that the company started and stayed in small rural markets until it completely understood its customers and channel partners. It was this a mistake by Walmart that led Best Buy to buy a 50-percent interest in the United Kingdom's Carphone Warehouse Group. By doing so, the American retailer was able to partner with someone who understood the market environment instead of going alone and stumbling.[36]

The late Michael O'Connor, former president of the Super Market Institute and retail consultant, had another explanation. He felt that the failure of many retailers to succeed in international markets was the result of larger countries having successful economies and retailers becoming accustomed to success. Retailers in smaller countries do not take success for granted and thus tend to take more time and be more careful with key decisions. According to O'Connor, by being a little less sure of themselves, executives from smaller countries sought more counsel and listened to more opinions before developing strategic plans.[37] Along the same lines, smaller country retailers have always had to deal with international issues in order to expand.

One smaller country retailer who has made an impact on international retailing is Ingvar Kamprad, president of IKEA. This firm, which was highlighted in Chapter 2's "Global Retailing" box, was the first to successfully develop a warehouse retailing format that could be followed around the world. The firm's warehouse format, which is based on economies of scale in the areas of marketing, purchasing, and distribution and which utilizes customer participation in the assembly and transportation of the merchandise, generates almost 90 percent of its revenues from global operations—more than any other major worldwide retailer.

Several apparel retailers have also recently entered the American market due to the weak dollar, which reduced the cost of their initial investment, and favorable terms on store leases as landlords looked for new tenants to replace retailers who had gone bankrupt. For example, Sweden's Hennes & Mauritz AB, with nearly 200 U.S. stores, calls the United States its "largest expansion market."[38] Also expanding in the United States are Spain's Zara (owned by Inditex SA) and Mango chains, Germany's luxury sport brand Bogner, Russia's Kira Plastinina, Iceland's Kisan, Japan's Muji, and Britain's Topshop chain and Karen Millen brand.[39]

Opening shop in the United States, of course, isn't a slam dunk. There's no guarantee that the economy—or apparel sales—will recover from the current slump any time soon. What's more, the United States is a low-growth market in which retailers have long had to fight for market share. Nonetheless, the United States remains the world's largest consumer market.

Integration of Technology

One of the most significant trends occurring in retailing is that of technological innovation. Technology is having, and will continue to have, a dramatic influence on retailing. Technological innovations can be grouped under three main areas: supply-chain management, customer management, and customer satisfaction.

The plethora of supply-chain management techniques such as quick response, just-in-time, and efficient consumer response are already being enhanced by new initiatives such as direct store delivery (DSD) and collaborative planning, forecasting, and replenishment (CPFR) systems. DSD systems have the potential to fully automate all retail inventory operations from tracking vendor and item authorization to pricing and order taking. DSD systems provide greater accuracy and increased administrative efficiency, allowing retailers to achieve cost advantages. Advancements in DSD systems will create more efficient operations and stronger partnerships as global competition increases. For example, Giant Food, Inc., eliminated a tremendous amount of paperwork and dramatically increased its administrative efficiency with the implementation of a DSD system.

Many industry experts believe that DSD is the engine that will drive industry profits. However, gross profit numbers alone don't tell the entire story. In fact, gross profit numbers can be somewhat misleading when calculating direct and incremental costs of warehouse-delivered products. Instead, activity-based costing analyses demonstrate that, in categories with mixed distribution, DSD products consistently outperform those just going through the warehouse. Other supply-chain systems—such as CPFR—though still in their infancy, have the potential to move retailers and manufacturers far beyond continuous-replenishment models in terms of reducing excess inventory levels, cutting out of stocks at retail, and efficiently meeting consumer demand. However, technological systems such as DSD and CPFR are but the beginning of the technological revolution occurring within the supply chain. Retailers who continue to use technology in innovative ways within the supply chain will achieve greater efficiency in their operations.

Retailers on the forefront of using technology to understand their consumers will achieve higher levels of effectiveness. For example, retailers might use technology to better target their customers and provide better service to them. Talbot's employs its catalog information to open retail outlets in locations with the greatest opportunity. Talbot's determines new store locations by examining clusters of ZIP codes that have accounted for sales of $150,000 or more annually in the categories of classic women's and children's apparel. Pier One uses similar information to determine where to incorporate direct mail advertising within the first six months of a new store's opening in order to achieve profitability more quickly.

Believe it or not, some of the most sophisticated users of database technology are casinos. In the past, one had to be a high roller to gain any "comps" (free products or services given to customers such as free tickets to shows or a free night's stay). Today, when customers use the casino's gaming facilities (such as gambling at a slot machine), they can insert a card that has been assigned to them and tracks their gaming behavior. Customers then present these cards to the casino to receive individual rewards based on their use of the gaming facilities. Through the use of these cards, a casino not only gains a much better understanding of its customers, enabling it to develop more effective retail strategies, but also rewards gamblers at all levels, thus increasing customer satisfaction.

As technology continues to penetrate the retail marketplace, new advancements in customer service and convenience will be evidenced. For example, what replacements are in store for bar code scanners? One cause of long lines at supermarket checkouts is that each item has to be taken out of a shopper's cart, individually scanned, and then bagged. How might technology change this? Recent testing of radio frequency identifiers (RFIDs) on products might eliminate the item-by-item process completely. The RFID reader generates a low-level radio frequency magnetic field that resonates with the RFID tag's metal coil and capacitor, creating an electrical signal that powers the computer chip, which then transmits its stored data back to the reader. The process works well, but the tags have been expensive—as much as $200 each. However, that cost has recently fallen to less than $1 per tag. Although still too expensive for all but high-priced items, advancements in technology will soon be available, making this system affordable to implement. Imagine bagging your groceries while you shop. Once you have finished, you simply push your cart to the checkout and within a few seconds the cashier scans your entire cart, you pay, and off you go.

These technological advances are but a few of the thousands that will change the nature of retailing. What technological innovations do you see on the horizon for retailers?

Increasing Use of Private Labels

As retailing continues to change, the increased use of private labels has emerged as a key business asset in developing a differential advantage for retailers. Private labels can set the retailer apart from the competition, get customers into their store (or website) and bring them back. Today retailers are shifting their emphasis on the development of private-label brands into high gear by using a variety of strategies to build the image of their brands, expand brand recognition, and raise their brand images in the marketplace. Walmart, despite its success in America, learned first-hand the importance of private labels when competing internationally. As mentioned earlier in the chapter, Walmart failed in Germany; private-label merchandise played a major factor. In the United States, for example, store-brand goods account for just under a quarter of the unit volume of food sales. This percentage is slightly higher in most European markets (about 30%). However, Walmart was unprepared for the fact that its major German competitor, Aldi, generated 95 percent of its sales from private labels. Now the German chain is testing whether the recent economic slowdown will cause Americans to shift to in-store labels.[40] After all, private-label brands often have lower wholesale and marketing costs, resulting in higher levels of profit compared to manufacturers' brands. Retailers must remember, however, that research has shown that most department store shoppers value a product's style more than the product's brand name.[41]

In the past, retailers believed that national brands drew customers into their stores, set the standard, and lent credibility to the retailers. At the same time, retailers felt private-label brands could help retailers differentiate their offerings, reach customers seeking lower prices, and boost margins due to the lower costs of private-label merchandise. However, over the past decade, this thinking has changed. Many retailers are focused on developing strong, proprietary private-label brands as their leading brand and supporting them with major advertising and promotional programs. Private brands, such as the JCPenney's labels shown in Exhibit 4.4, are now effectively serving as destination draws in their own right while still providing many of the same benefits of traditional private-label programs. Today, it is not uncommon for major retail chains to generate a third or more of their sales from private labels.

The following are some of the private-label branding strategies currently being used by retailers.

1. *Develop a partnership with well-known celebrities, noted experts, and institutional authorities.* Celebrity partnerships—or the use of people as private-label brands— allow retailers to align with an individual whose personal reputation creates

immediate brand recognition, image, or credibility. Macy's, for example, has the Martha Stewart Collection, and Kohl's features Simply Vera by Vera Wang.

2. *Develop a partnership with traditionally higher-end suppliers to bring an exclusive variation on their highly regarded brand name to market.* Target has a furniture line by Michael Graves and has recently introduced an eco-apparel line by designer Rojan Gregory, which was carried by Barneys, New York, in an attempt to give "new meaning to the phrase mass meets class."[42]

These partnerships offer both parties a win–win situation. The retailer gets an exclusive private label and the opportunity to expand customer appeal, ratchet up price points, and raise margins. The manufacturer builds volume and gains access to a broad new market spectrum.

3. *Reintroduce products that have strong name recognition but that have fallen from the retail scene.* Old brand names do not die. They get recycled. Retailers can add cachet to their store image by resurrecting former up-market brands that have been discontinued but have not lost their image. Recycled brands can help a retailer achieve differentiation through exclusivity and attract consumers unwilling to risk buying an unknown brand name. By reviving a well-known brand with pedigree, the retailer is able to leverage the brand's equity while still having a proprietary line.

Walmart, for example, has purchased the rights from Procter & Gamble to its discontinued White Cloud label on diapers and toilet tissues, and Kohl's has recently reintroduced the Hang Ten brand, a label that was popular in the early 1990s.

4. *Brand an entire department or business; not just a product line.* In an approach designed to differentiate its supercenter food offerings from others, Target has taken its private-label branding strategy one step further by branding its entire supermarket section with the Archer Farms name. Not only does the Archer

Kirkland Signature is Costco's private label and its name was derived from the fact that Costco's corporate headquarters were once located in Kirkland, Washington.

ROBERT SULLIVAN/AFP/Getty Images

Farm name readily draw an association with the Target brand (the archer's target or bulls-eye) but also it enables Target to separate the two sections of the store. In fact, many consumers believe it to be a different company entirely. This may be a plus for Target, whose customers might not otherwise shop for groceries in a discount store.

The Archer Farms market-positioning strategy leads the consumer to believe that this is an upscale grocer that places more emphasis on quality and freshness than price. Such a strategy reinforces Target's protected niche image as the "discounter for consumers who don't want to be seen in a discount store." A "fresh from the farm" tagline underscores the market positioning message. Store design features such as green neon perimeter lighting, graphics depicting farm scenes, colorful illustrations of major food categories, and product descriptions and use suggestions all help create a differentiated grocery-shopping environment. The Archer Farms name was also carried into a private-label program featuring approximately 100 stockkeeping units.

SUMMARY

The behavior of competitors is an important component of the strategic retail planning and operations management model. Effective planning and operations management in any retail setting cannot be accomplished without properly analyzing competitors.

What are the various models of retail competition?

LO 1

Competition in retailing, as in any other industry, involves the interplay of supply and demand. Various models of retail competition were described to illustrate certain principles of retail competition. These models suggested that retail competition is typically local but vulnerable to nonstore retailers that provide better selection and convenience; the retail industry is monopolistically competitive and not a pure monopoly, pure competition, or oligopoly. Retailers today are in a struggle to develop strategies that allow them to protect themselves from competitive threats by achieving some type of differential advantage over their competition. As a result of this goal, retailers are developing price and nonprice strategies that look at the supply as well as the demand side of retailing. This opening learning objective concluded by looking at how competitive activity can make a market attractive or unattractive.

What are the various types of retail competition?

LO 2

Competition is most intense in retailing, and various classification schemes were used to describe this intensity. *Intratype* and *intertype competition* describe retailers who compete against each other in the same line of retail trade or in different lines of retail trade, respectively, but still compete for the same customer with similar merchandise lines. *Divertive competition* describes retailers who seek to intercept customers planning to visit another retailer.

What are the four theories used to explain the evolution of retail competition?

LO 3

Retail competition is both revolutionary and evolutionary. Four theories of viewing changing competitive patterns in retailing were discussed. The *wheel of retailing* proposes that new types of retailers enter the market as low-margin, low-price, and less-efficient operators. As they succeed, they become more complex, increasing their margins and prices and becoming vulnerable to new types of low-margin competitors, who, in turn, follow the same pattern. The *retail accordion theory* suggests that retail institutions evolve from outlets offering wide assortments to stores with specialized, narrow assortments and then return to wide assortments to repeat the pattern. The *retail life cycle theory* views retail institutions, like the products they distribute, as passing through an identifiable cycle during which the basics of strategy and competition change. Finally, *resource advantage theory* was discussed. This theory is based on the idea that all firms seek superior financial performance in an ever-changing environment. Retail demand is dynamic because consumer tastes are always changing and supply is dynamic because firms searching for a superior performance are forced to change the elements of their retail mix to match changing consumer preferences. Thus, retail evolution is characterized by a variety of viable retail formats, ever-changing opportunities, and customer demands.

LO 4   ### What future changes could affect retail competition?

We concluded this chapter with a discussion of changes that could affect retail competition. Industry analysts contend that nonstore retailing will be a major competitive force in the future. This was followed by a discussion of why two recently introduced formats—hypermarkets and off-pricers—failed while the supercenter format was highly successful. Next we looked at three examples of possible new retailing formats that have recently evolved: recycled merchandise retailers, liquidators, and rentals.

Just as the introduction of new retailing formats in one part of the United States will impact retailers in other parts of the country, so it is for international retailing. Retailing in other countries exhibits even greater diversity in its structure than retailing in the United States. The rate of change in retailing appears to be directly related to the stage and speed of economic development in the countries concerned, but today even the least-developed countries are experiencing dramatic changes in retailing, thereby heightening global retail competition. The global analysis section ended with a discussion of why retailers from smaller countries tend to perform better in international competition.

Other changes in retail formats will result from the significant development of technological advances for use in retailing. The chapter concluded with an in-depth discussion of private-label branding and the various strategies for its use today.

TERMS TO REMEMBER

pure competition	intratype competition
pure monopoly	intertype competition
monopolistic competition	divertive competition
oligopolistic competition	breakeven point
outshopping	wheel of retailing theory
store positioning	retail accordion
overstored	retail life cycle
understored	resource-advantage theory

off-price retailers
supercenter
recycled merchandise retailers
pawn shops
thrift shops

auction houses
consignment shops
resource-advantage theory
ebay

REVIEW AND DISCUSSION QUESTIONS

What are the various models of retail competition? `LO 1`

1. Can a retailer ever operate in a pure monopoly situation? If you believe that this is possible, provide an example and explain what dangers this retailer faces. If you believe this is not possible, explain why not.
2. Why is it so important for a retailer to develop a protected niche?

What are the various types of retail competition? `LO 2`

3. Provide an example of intratype competition that was not mentioned in the text. Provide an example of intertype competition that was not mentioned in the text. Can a retailer face both intratype and intertype competition at the same time? Explain your response.
4. Can divertive competition occur only in intertype competition—that is, where two different types of retailers with a similar product compete with each other?
5. Someone once said that "the supercenter format will kill the grocery retailers." However, this hasn't happen. Can you think of an explanation as to why this hasn't occurred?

What four theories are used to explain the evolution of retail competition? `LO 3`

6. Describe the wheel of retailing theory. What are the theory's major strengths and weakness? Does this theory do a good job of explaining what has happened to American retailers today?
7. Describe the retail accordion theory of competition. What are this theory's major strengths and weakness?
8. Would strategies for retailers differ in the four stages of the retail life cycle? What strategies should be emphasized at each of the four stages?
9. If a retail format enters the decline stage of the retail life cycle, does that mean that this format will be gone within the next decade? Or can it linger in the decline stage for years? Can a format ever reposition itself and return to either the growth or maturity stage? Can you think of any current format that could reinvigorate itself?

What future changes could affect retail competition? `LO 4`

10. Will the Internet ever completely replace traditional bricks-and-mortar retailing? Provide a rationale for your response.
11. If a new retail format is a hit in one country, it generally will be successful in all countries. Agree or disagree?
12. What do you think about the projected growth of the rental format? Would you rent your textbooks if an outlet was available on your campus? If your best friend was getting married, would you consider renting a gown, handbag, or jewelry to wear for the rehearsal dinner?
13. Several possible explanations were given as to why retailers from smaller countries tend to do better when entering foreign markets then those from

larger countries. Do you agree or disagree with these explanations? Explain your reasoning.

14. Is it better for a retailer to develop a new private-label brand or to try to revive a once-prestigious brand that has been discontinued? Explain your reasoning.

SAMPLE TEST QUESTIONS

LO 1

What type of competitive structure are most retail firms involved in?

a. horizontal competition
b. monopolistic competition
c. vertical competition
d. pure competition
e. oligopolistic competition

LO 2

When Walmart competes with Kroger, Albertsons, and Safeway by adding groceries to its general merchandise products in its new supercenters, what type of competition is this?

a. extended niche
b. intratype
c. scrambled
d. intertype
e. category killer

LO 3

Walking back to the dorm after class, your roommate complains that she wishes there was a plain old-fashioned hamburger joint, she could go for a simple hamburger, not a fancy triple-decker or one with 17 secret sauces, and not a fast-food restaurant with a playground for 50 kids. Her dilemma describes what theory of retail evolution?

a. retail violin
b. retail life cycle
c. bigger-n-better
d. wheel of retailing
e. compound growth

LO 4

With regard to international trends in retailing, which of the following statements is true?

a. Because of its sheer size, retailing in the United States is more diverse in its structure than any other country.
b. Success with a retailing format in one country usually guarantees success in all countries.
c. The size of the individual stores do not tend to vary.
d. U.S. retailers haven't been as successful in international expansion as some of their competitors from smaller countries.
e. No new successful retailing format has been developed outside of the United States in the last half-century.

WRITING AND SPEAKING EXERCISE

Over the past year and half you worked at your church's not-for-profit resale shop. Over this period, while the economic downturn has hurt sales at the nearby shopping center, it has really benefited your shop. In fact, sales have soared as cash-strapped consumers sought out bargains and donors wanted tax deductions. For example, shop prices for blouses and shirts range from $1 to $15 and designer jeans sold for $5 to $25 a pair compared with regular retail prices that were at least triple those amounts. Actually, the shop attracted a wide range of customers ranging from white collar workers who needed work clothes to bargain shoppers who enjoyed the thrill of the hunt. As a matter of fact, the shop's consumers had a wide range in income and age, except for the students at the nearby college.

As you prepared to return to school to graduate, your boss asked you to prepare a report with your ideas on how to attract college students to the shop. As she sees the problem, students only come to the shop in mid- to late-October seeking polyester suits and wide ties to wear to Halloween parties. They fail to realize what good merchandise the shop is actually selling. What can be done to get them to purchase home furnishings from the shop when they decorate their apartments and dorms in the fall and to seek out clothing that is only gently used instead of going to the shopping center? After all, she added, "We have labels like Old Navy, the Gap, Arizona Jeans, and Ann Taylor. It doesn't make any sense to me why students on a limited budget would want to buy anything brand new if the clothes we sell are well taken care of."

RETAIL PROJECT

You are thinking about buying a Ford Explorer after you graduate this semester. Use the Internet to see if you can get a better deal than the traditional auto retailers offer. All you will have to do is make three online connections, all free.

Start by using DealerNet (www.dealernet.com), created by Reynolds & Reynolds, which provides computer services to dealers. You can see a picture of the Explorer and find out how it compares with competitors like the Jeep Grand Cherokee in such key areas as trunk space, fuel economy, and price.

Suppose you settle on a four-door, four-wheel-drive XLT model. Key over to the prices posted by Edmund Publications (http://www.edmunds.com), a longtime compiler of such information. There you discover what the current sticker price is for the XLT as well as what the dealer pays. You also learn a little-known fact: The XLT carries a 3-percent holdback—essentially a rebate for each Explorer that Ford pays to the dealer at the end of the year. This may help you in evaluating the price your dealer quotes.

When you're ready to order, type in "http://www.autobytel.com." There are several buying services on the web, but AutoByTel is free. From here you can buy the car using AutoByTel directly or placing your order, and you'll get a call from a nearby dealer. The dealer will charge you a fixed amount over the invoice and deliver the car. Now you've saved enough to buy a copy of this valuable text for all your friends.

PLANNING YOUR OWN RETAIL BUSINESS

As a knowledgeable retail entrepreneur, you recognize how harmful new retail competitors entering the market can be to your business. You opened your bookstore only 18 months ago and already have experienced healthy sales. In the year just ended, sales reached almost $782,000. You have estimated that of the 41,000 households in your market, 38 percent visit your store an average of 4.1 times a year. Due to your excellent merchandising and retail displays, 90 percent of visitors to your store make a purchase (referred to as *closure*) for an average transaction size of $13.59. Unfortunately, last week you learned that Borders (a category killer bookstore that also sells music tapes and CDs and serves coffee, refreshments, and pastries) has signed a lease to be part of a new shopping mall in a city of 405,000 located 20 miles north of your store. In this mall there will also be a Lowe's and an Office Depot.

Predictably, you are quite concerned that Borders will take customers from your store. It is hard for you to predict the impact of this new competition; at least they are 20 miles away. Nonetheless, you believe that the percentage of households in your market that will shop your store will decline from 38 percent to 34 percent, and average shopping frequency will decline from 4.1 times per year to 3.9 times per year. You believe you can maintain your excellent closure rate and average transaction size. What is the estimated sales impact of gaining Borders as a competitor? (*Hint:* Annual sales can be obtained by multiplying the number of households in the market by the percentage that patronize your store multiplied by their average shopping frequency or number of visits per year. Then multiply this figure by the closure rate and multiply the result by the average transaction size.)

Managing the Supply Chain

OVERVIEW:

At the outset of this text, we pointed out that retailing is the final movement in the progression of merchandise from producer to consumer. Many other movements occur through time and geographical space, and all of them need to be executed properly for the retailer to achieve optimum performance. Therefore, in this chapter, we will examine the retailer's need to analyze and understand the supply chain in which it operates. After looking at the activities performed within a supply chain, the chapter then reviews the various types of supply chains and the benefits each one offers the retailer. The chapter concludes with some practical suggestions to improve supply-chain relationships, especially the use of a category manager.

LEARNING OBJECTIVES:

After reading this chapter, you should be able to:

1. Discuss the retailer's role as one of the institutions involved in the supply chain.
2. Describe the types of supply chains by length, width, and control.
3. Explain the terms *dependency*, *power*, and *conflict* and their impact on supply-chain relations.
4. Understand the importance of a collaborative supply-chain relationship.

LO 1

The Supply Chain

What is the retailer's role as a member of the larger supply chain?

Consider the following example. The final movement of a retail item occurred on March 6 at 10:47 A.M. when a customer brought home a garden hose that she had just purchased at a Walmart Supercenter in Amarillo, Texas. Thirteen months earlier, a sample of that hose had been in a Hong Kong showroom where a Walmart buyer ordered 200,000 hoses for the next year's selling season from the showroom's vendor. The buyer then hired a Chinese agent to represent Walmart after the buyer returned to Arkansas. This agent was to make sure that the factories met Walmart's regulations regarding working conditions and that the hoses and parts met the retailer's quality standards. Over the next nine months, the hoses were assembled in mainland China using nozzles made in Thailand. The hoses were then transported to a warehouse in El Paso's free-trade zone. In late January, three truckloads of these hoses were shipped from El Paso to the Walmart distribution center in Plainview, Texas, for immediate shipment to the Amarillo Supercenter.

In this example, manufacturing occurred in both China and Thailand, a Mexican warehouse stored the products for several months, and a Mexican motor carrier was used to transport the hoses by truck to the United States, where, after going through customs, the hoses were shipped to the free-trade zone. From there, either a U.S. or a Mexican trucking company took the hoses to Walmart's Plainview distribution center. Within an hour of being received at the distribution center, Walmart's own trucks were taking the hoses to Amarillo. Thus, before the final retail transaction could take place, several physical movements were needed that involved many firms other than the retailer. As the above example illustrates, retailers cannot properly perform their roles without the assistance of other firms. Retailers are *part* of a supply chain—a valuable component, but not the only one.

In contrast to Walmart's rather slow-moving supply chain, this chapter's "Global Retailing" box describes how one Spanish apparel chain, Zara, has revolutionized the fashion world and become the world's second-largest clothing retailer (in sales) by keeping a tight grip on every link in its supply chain.

It is important to understand the retailer's role in the larger supply chain. Retailers have used the term **supply chain** interchangeably with the term **channel**. Traditionally, this consisted of a set of institutions that moves goods from the point of production to the point of consumption. However, with increased concern about the physical environment or ecosystem, many retailers are beginning to view the supply chain as "dirt to dirt." This broadened view traces all of the materials that go into manufacturing and then the institutions that bring the product to the retailer but then also includes what the consumer does to dispose of or recycle the product. Over the last decade, retailers became more aware of the need to expand their view of the supply chain due to harmful ingredients found in products such as lead used in paint for children's toys or foreign substances used in pet food.

Using the more traditional view, the supply chain or channel might include manufacturers, wholesalers, and retailers. For example, the manufacturer could sell directly to an individual for household usage, sell to a retailer for sale to the individual, or sell to a wholesaler for sale to the retailer, who then sells to the individual. Thus, supply chains consist of all the institutions and all the marketing activities (storage, financing, purchasing, transporting, etc.) that are spread over time and geographical space throughout the marketing process. If the retailer is a member of the supply chain that collectively does the best job, that retailer will have an advantage over other retailers.

Why should the retailer view itself as part of a larger channel or supply chain? Why can't it simply seek out the best assortment of goods for its customers, sell the goods, make a profit, go to the bank, and forget about the supply chain? In reality, the world of retailing is not that easy. Profits sufficient for survival and growth would be difficult, if not impossible, to achieve if the retailer ignored the supply chain. This does not mean that a channel should never be altered. *Innovative retailers are always seeking to find a new method to change the existing supply chain and replace it with a better one.* For example, discounters changed their relationships with vendors when they began to buy directly from manufacturers in large quantities, warehouse the merchandise in efficiently run distribution centers, and ship to their own stores as a means of obtaining lower prices. Prior to this change, discounters purchased smaller quantities from wholesalers only when the merchandise was needed. Similarly, as described in Chapter 1's "Retailing: The Inside Story," airlines restructured their supply chains to circumvent the need for travel agents by having customers purchase their own tickets directly from the airlines using the Internet.

supply chain
Is a set of institutions that move goods from the point of production to the point of consumption.

channel
Used interchangeably with supply chain.

Global Retailing

Fast Fashion: It's "Z-Day"

Each year, millions of Americans follow the happenings of February's Fashion Week, hoping to get a glimpse at what will be available in July from designers like Marc Jacobs, Ralph Lauren, and Dolce and Gabbana. However, customers in cities such as Dallas, Atlanta, New York, Miami, and Los Angeles no longer need to wait; in fact, they better not. Fashion has a short shelf life, and at Zara (www.zara.com), it's only a few weeks.

Zara, a clothing company based in La Coruña, Spain, has revolutionized fast turn in fashion. On average, it takes less than two weeks for Zara to spot, design, and ship one of the 300,000 new stockkeeping units (SKUs) it sells in stores each year. Thus, it routinely beats the high-fashion houses to market with nearly identical products that are made with less-expensive fabric and at much lower prices. For example, Zara recently sold a long, pink boucle jacket resembling one of Chanel's current spring and summer offerings for $129 and a pair of black stretch pants similar to a Prada design for $33. The cost of the originals: $7,326 and $350, respectively.

How does Zara do it? Creativity in supply-chain design! First, Zara is part of a corporate-owned, vertical marketing channel, Inditex, which owns and operates retail stores, distribution centers, a design and manufacturing headquarters, and textile-manufacturing facilities.

Second, by controlling all steps in the supply chain, Zara is able to run each step (manufacturing, design, etc.) below full capacity. This is in stark contrast to most competitors who seek large runs to gain economies of scale and the resulting lower costs.

Finally, they produce limited runs of each style; they overlook the possibility of being stocked out on any item. In fact, Zara's business model thrives on these stock outs as they create instant demand.

In addition, Zara has introduced the Z-day concept to its target customers. Z-day, as the Zara faithful know, is the two days a week when new shipments of styles arrive in retail stores. On these days, Zara is packed with 20- and 30-somethings seeking to get their hands on the newest clothes before they're gone. Zara shoppers know that if they find a style they like, they better purchase it immediately or it'll be gone.

Zara's supply chain was designed to create this feeding frenzy. By limiting the number of any one style, customers gain fashion exclusivity while Zara limits the number of discounts taken due to poor-performing lines. In an industry riddled with seasonal discounts, Zara rarely has any because Zara headquarters is in constant communication with its retail stores.

Twice a week (Tuesday and Friday), store managers phone in their orders to market specialists dedicated to each store. During these phone conversations, problems are discussed and new styles are conceived. In addition, customized handheld computers (PDAs) augment these calls and communicate such hard data as orders and sales trends and soft data such as customer reactions, customer requests, and the "buzz" around a new style. Zara's headquarters knows, in real time, what is working and what is not.

By controlling every detail from the dying of fabric and stitching of designs to the delivery and display of fashion within its stores, Zara is able to alter, discontinue, or modify current styles to arrive the following Z-day. To facilitate speed, its headquarters is designed primarily around three halls. Each hall has its own design, planning, manufacturing, and market specialist staff broken down by clothing line: men's, women's, and children's.

The three parallel lines, although expensive, allow information to flow quickly and unencumbered. Using a just-in-time (JIT) model, all aspects of Zara are linked by computer. Designers and market specialists gather data in real time. A small prototype shop is also set up in the corner of each hall to encourage everyone to comment on the new garments as they progress. Once line teams have reviewed the prototypes (often within hours), designers refine them using computer-aided systems and transmit the specs directly to the cutting machines. Bar codes then track the cut pieces of fabric through the various stages of production. Once developed, garments are transferred to a central warehouse where shipments are prepared for every store (usually overnight). Price tags are then placed on the clothes, and necessary items are hung on hangers prior to leaving the warehouse. Clothes shipped to the United States are then loaded on commercial airlines using established schedules, like a bus schedule, and are delivered to each store at the same time every delivery day. Because all clothes have been pre-priced and hung, managers are able to immediately display them the moment they are delivered. Once performed, the entire process starts again the following order day.

Interestingly, it is this last step (hanging) that has really fueled the immediate turnover of fashion. Customers have realized that clothes are shipped on plastic hangers prior to managers switching them to wooden hangers in the store. As all clothes are immediately displayed on arrival, many customers scan for the telltale sign of a gray, plastic hanger on entering Zara.

Source: Based on "Zara Thrives by Breaking All the Rules," *BusinessWeek*, October 20, 2008: 66; "The Mark of Zara," *BusinessWeek*, May 29, 2000: 98; "Rapid Fire Fulfillment," *Harvard Business Review*, November 2004: 104–110; "Style & Substance: Making Fashion Faster as Knockoffs Beat Originals to Market, Designers Speed the Trip from Sketch to Store," *Wall Street Journal*, February 24, 2004: B1; and "Pace-Setting Zara Seeks More Speed to Fight Its Rising Cheap-Chic Rivals," *Wall Street Journal*, February 20, 2008: B1.

Prior to making changes in the overall channel structure, supply-chain members must understand that all channels are affected by five external forces: (1) consumer behavior, (2) competitor behavior, (3) the socioeconomic environment, (4) the technological environment, and (5) the legal and ethical environment. These external forces cannot be completely controlled by the retailer or any other institution in the supply chain, but they need to be taken into account when retailers make decisions. For example, a change in the minimum-wage law will usually increase the retailer's cost of doing business. Similarly, a rapid rise or fall in fuel prices will result in a shift between using rail and motor carriers to deliver product. The retail strategic planning and operations management model (Exhibit 2.6) dramatizes the importance of these external forces in retail decision making.

Supply-chain or channel structure also depends on the number of tasks or functions each member is willing to perform. Eight marketing functions must be performed by any supply chain or channel: buying, selling, storing, transporting, sorting, financing, information gathering, and risk taking. Most of these functions are self-explanatory; however, the concept of "sorting" requires some explanation. Sorting involves breaking down heterogeneous materials or product into more homogenous groups such as sorting oranges into those that are good for eating versus good for juice or other products. It also involves building up assortments of products that shoppers like to find together in a store—for example, orange juice with muffins, eggs, cereal, or bacon.

Whether the economic system is capitalistic, socialistic, or somewhere in between, every supply chain must perform these eight marketing functions. They cannot be eliminated. They can, however, be shifted or divided in differing ways among the different institutions and the consumer in the supply chain.

All forms of retailing were created by rearranging the marketing functions among institutions and consumers. For example, department stores were created specifically to build a larger assortment of goods. They capitalized on the opportunity to perform one or more functions better than the current competition. No longer was it necessary to travel to one store for a shirt and pants, another for shoes, and yet another for cookware; the necessary assortment was available in a single store. Supermarkets increased consumer participation by shifting more of the information gathering, buying, financing, and transporting functions to customers. Before supermarkets, consumers could have the corner grocer select items and deliver them and have them placed on a store credit account for payment every two weeks when the household received income, but with the introduction of supermarkets came self-service and cash and carry. Consumers had to locate goods within the store, select them from an array of available products, pay for the goods, and transport them home. The airlines have now shifted the purchasing of tickets and the printing of boarding passes to the customer. By performing these marketing functions, the consumer is compensated with lower prices.

It is important to note that a marketing function does not have to be shifted in its entirety to another institution or to the consumer; instead, it can be divided among several entities. For example, manufacturers that don't want to perform the entire selling function could have the retailer perform part of the job through in-store promotions, local advertising, or promotions on the retailer's website. At the same time, the manufacturer could assume some of the tasks using national advertising and by developing its own website to provide product information such as installation, cleaning directions, and the manufacturer's warranty.

No member of the channel would want or be able to perform all eight marketing functions entirely. For this reason, the retailer must view itself as being dependent on other supply-chain members.

The institutions involved in performing the eight marketing functions are usually broken into two categories: primary and facilitating. **Primary marketing institutions** are supply-chain members that take title to the goods. **Facilitating marketing institutions** are those that do not actually take title but assist in the marketing process by specializing in the performance of certain functions. Exhibit 5.1 classifies the major institutions participating in the supply chain.

Primary Marketing Institutions

There are three types of primary marketing institutions: manufacturers, wholesalers, and retailers.

Because manufacturers produce goods, we don't often think of them as marketing institutions. But manufacturers cannot exist by only producing goods; they must also sell the goods produced. To produce those goods, the nation's 400,000 manufacturers must purchase many raw materials, semifinished goods, and components. In addition, manufacturers often need the assistance of other institutions in performing the eight marketing functions.

A second type of primary marketing institution is the wholesaler. Wholesalers generally buy merchandise from manufacturers and resell to retailers, other merchants, industrial institutions, and commercial users. An example of a wholesaler is Houston-based Sysco Corporation. Through its subsidiaries, Sysco engages in the distribution and marketing of food and related products primarily to the food-

primary marketing institutions
Are those channel members that take title to the goods as they move through the marketing channel. They include manufacturers, wholesalers, and retailers.

facilitating marketing institutions
Are those that do not actually take title but assist in the marketing process by specializing in the performance of certain marketing functions.

Exhibit 5.1
Institutions Participating in the Supply Chain

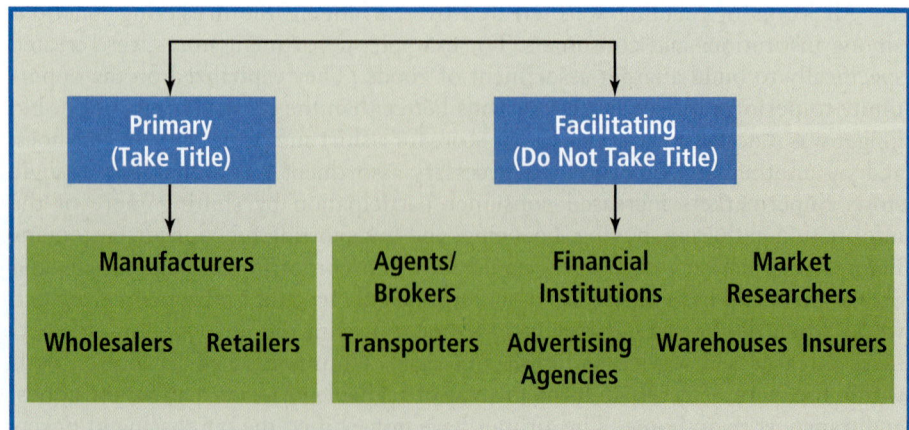

Primary (Take Title)		Facilitating (Do Not Take Title)		
Manufacturers		Agents/Brokers	Financial Institutions	Market Researchers
Wholesalers	Retailers	Transporters	Advertising Agencies	Warehouses Insurers

service industry in the United States and Canada. It distributes frozen foods, fully prepared entrees, fruits, vegetables, and desserts, as well as various nonfood items, including disposable napkins, plates, and cups; tableware; cleaning supplies; and restaurant and kitchen equipment to restaurants, hospitals, nursing homes, schools and colleges, hotels and motels. There are 430,000 wholesalers in the United States, each performing some of the eight marketing functions.[1] Just as it is important for retailers to continuously evaluate their own strategies, it is equally important for them to consider the strategies of the wholesalers in their supply chain.

The third type of primary institution is the retailer. Today there are 1.1 million retail stores or institutions and more than 1.8 million service establishments in the United States.[2] Retailers can perform portions of all eight marketing functions.

It is possible that some firms, such as the membership warehouse clubs (Sam's and Costco) can act as both a wholesaler selling to small businesses and a retailer selling to households. However, for statistical purposes, the Census Bureau considers all membership warehouse clubs to be wholesalers since the majority of their business involves wholesale transactions.

Facilitating Marketing Institutions

Many institutions facilitate the performance of the marketing functions. Most specialize in one or two functions; yet *none of them takes title to the goods*. Institutions that facilitate the buying and selling functions in the supply chain or channel include agents and brokers, who are independent businesspeople who receive a commission or fee when they are able to bring a buyer and seller together to negotiate a transaction. Seldom do agents or brokers take physical possession of the merchandise.

One of the new breed of e-tailing brokers is Priceline.com, Inc. It pioneered the e-commerce pricing channel known as a *demand collection channel*, which allows it to act without holding any inventory. Priceline's channel enables consumers to use the Internet to make bids on a wide range of products and services while enabling sellers to generate incremental revenue. Using its "Name Your Own Price" or "Negotiation" proposition, Priceline collects consumer demand in the form of individual customer offers, guaranteed by a credit card, for a particular product or service at a price set by the customer. Priceline then either communicates that demand directly to participating sellers or accesses participating sellers' private databases to determine whether Priceline can fulfill the customer's offer and earn its brokerage commission. Priceline's business model can be applied to a broad range of products and services and is already being copied.

Marketing communications agencies, or advertising agencies, also facilitate the selling process by designing effective advertisements and advising management on where and when to place these advertisements.

Institutions that facilitate the transportation function are motor, rail, and air carriers and pipeline and shipping companies. Transporters can have a significant effect on how efficiently goods move through the supply chain. These firms offer differing advantages in terms of delivery, service, and cost. Generally, the quicker the delivery, the more costly it is. However, there is usually a trade-off because faster delivery enables the supply chain to have lower warehousing costs.

The major facilitating institution involved in storage is the **public warehouse**, which stores goods for safekeeping in return for a fee. Fees are usually based on cubic feet used per time period (month or day). Frequently, retailers take advantage of special promotional buys from manufacturers but have no space for the goods in their stores or storage facilities. As a result, they find it necessary to use public warehouses.

public warehouse
Is a facility that stores goods for safekeeping for any owner in return for a fee, usually based on space occupied.

Photo courtesy of Vicki Beaver

Priceline.com is a facilitating marketing institutions since it does not take title to its offerings but serves as a broker bringing buyers and sellers together by assisting in the price negotiation process.

A variety of facilitating institutions also help provide information throughout the supply chain. For example, the role of computer specialists, referred to as *channel integrators*, in setting up computer channels for transmitting information is evident throughout the business world. Retailers can now order many types of merchandise online. In fact, many retail analysts believe that Walmart's leap into the number-one spot in worldwide retail sales stems directly from Retail Link, a sophisticated electronics system used to manage its huge supply and distribution network. Retail Link (described in this chapter's "What's New?") enables the suppliers to work in tandem with Walmart as the retail environment shifts.

Due to the success of Retail Link, most of today's major retailers require that all their vendors be linked electronically to their computers, thereby permitting the vendors to automatically ship replacements without purchase orders and receive payment electronically. By saving on distribution costs, these retailers have been able to hold their selling prices constant despite a slight increase in merchandise costs.

Other facilitating institutions aid in financing, such as commercial banks, merchant banks, factors, stock and commodity exchanges, and venture-capital firms. These institutions can provide, or help the retailer obtain, funds to finance marketing functions. For example, retailers frequently use factors for short-term loans to fund working-capital requirements (e.g., to finance the increased level of inventory needed for the Christmas selling season) while relying on banks for long-term loans to continue growth and expansion (adding new stores or remodeling). Venture-capital firms are primarily used by retailers starting a new operation or format.

Finally, insurance firms can assume some of the risks in the channel, insuring inventories, buildings, trucks, equipment and fixtures, and other assets for the retailer and other primary marketing institutions. They can also insure against a

What's New?

Walmart's Not So Secret Weapon: Retail Link

As noted in Chapter 2, Walmart sells at the lowest price because it has the lowest distribution costs. (Remember that operating at the lowest cost is the third of the three tasks that a successful retailer must perform.) A key contributor that enabled Walmart to achieve this goal was the two-way communication system set up between the vendors and Walmart called Retail Link.

Offered at the retailer's expense, Retail Link allows vendors to manage their own lines inside each Walmart store and make informed inventory decisions that are mutually beneficial to the vendor and Walmart. With its constant enhancements, Retail Link is vital to the success of every supplier since it allows it to discover opportunities to grow its business to the benefit of both companies.

Today Walmart's Retail Link ensures that a supplier has instant access to such vital information as:

- percentage of stores currently in stock (vendors that fail to meet Walmart's in-stock target are in danger of being replaced),
- the location of any store with low or no stock on hand,
- the sales performance by store for all the vendor's SKUs,
- a list of other items purchased when one of the supplier's SKUs is purchased,
- sales data for all the vendors' SKUs for the past several years,
- the current number of weeks of inventory on hand at each store based on each store's sell-through rate,
- the effect of promotional activities on sales,
- sales by time of day and day of week, and
- current financial projections.

The key to success when developing a system like Retail Link is providing only that information which suppliers deem necessary; too much information is just as bad as too little. To provide such needed information, reports are built from scratch, and suppliers must indicate what level of detail to include in each report. For instance, is the vendor interested in sales units or sales dollars, shipments to the warehouse, or shipments to the stores? What about markdowns, current inventory on hand, or gross margin? In addition, suppliers must also indicate which stores to include. Are they interested in all 3,700 stores or only a particular region, district, or store? Do they want this information for the current year to date, the current or last month only, just yesterday, last year, or the last 10 years? Further, do they want the information reported (aggregated) by the hour, the day, the week, the month, or the year?

As these questions and others demonstrate, there is almost an infinite number of available reports—too much information for anyone to handle. Thus, the most important, and sometimes the hardest, thing for a supplier to do is decide what information is necessary for the business decision at hand.

Using such data, the category manager and the supplier might see, for example, that a key SKU's sales may taper off late on Sunday afternoons for several weeks in a row only to pick up on Monday afternoons. Such observations might indicate that the current inventory plan isn't adequate. Perhaps sales dropped off on Sunday due to low stock levels and picked up on Monday after the inventory was replenished.

Retail Link is Walmart's internal information system used by the retailer's buyers and replenishment teams to manage the merchandise. Therefore, whether the Retail Link user is a small, locally owned manufacturer; a global consumer package goods company; or a Walmart employee, each member of the supply chain sees exactly the same screens and reporting options. This consistency allows Walmart associates to "compare notes" with every manufacturer and ensure that business goals are being met. This usually occurs weekly, if not more often, since most users of Retail Link run several reports every day.

variety of events such as employee and customer injuries, changes in interest rates, and the impact of terrorist activity.

Having reviewed the various functions and institutions in the supply chain, we are now ready to examine how the primary marketing institutions are arranged into a supply chain.

LO 2   Types of Supply Chains

A large part of the supply chain consists of the primary marketing institutions that perform one or more of the eight marketing functions. But how are these functions and institutions arranged into a supply chain? Exhibit 5.2 shows that there are actually three strategy decisions to be made when designing an efficient and competitive supply chain: supply-chain length, width, and control.

Supply-Chain Length

direct supply chain
Is the channel that results when a manufacturer sells its goods directly to the final consumer or end user.

As shown in Exhibit 5.3, supply chains can be either direct or indirect; classification is determined by the number of primary institutions involved. A **direct supply chain** or channel occurs when manufacturers sell their goods directly to the final consumer or end user. In these rare cases, the lack of involvement by other middlemen pushes the manufacturer to perform *most* of the marketing functions (e.g., transporting is often performed by facilitating institutions or even the consumer). An example of such a supply chain is Firestone, which sells some of its tires through company-owned retail outlets to the consumer. The supply chain becomes indirect once independent members (or retailers. retailers) are added between the manufacturer and the consumer. **Indirect supply chains**, as shown in Exhibit 5.3, may include just a retailer or both a retailer and a wholesaler. Consider, for example, your neighborhood Avon or Mary Kay representative. This representative is an independent retailer who purchases cosmetic products from Avon or Mary Kay and then sells them to a consumer. This channel is described as being indirect because it goes from manufacturer to retailer to consumer. Similarly, when a local independent grocer purchases some Hunt's ketchup from SuperValu, a large food wholesaler that had already purchased the ketchup from its manufacturer, Con-Agra, the channel is also indirect, going from manufacturer to wholesaler to retailer to consumer.

indirect supply chain
Is the channel that occurs when a manufacturer sells its goods through wholesalers and/or retailers.

Sometimes the length of a supply chain is hard to determine. For example, when a consumer purchases cosmetics from a manufacturer's website and that manufacturer mails the merchandise directly to the consumer, the chain is said to be a direct manufacturer-to-consumer channel. However, if the consumer makes a purchase from a different manufacturer's website, such as Avon, and an Avon sales

Exhibit 5.2
Strategic Decisions in Supply-Chain Design

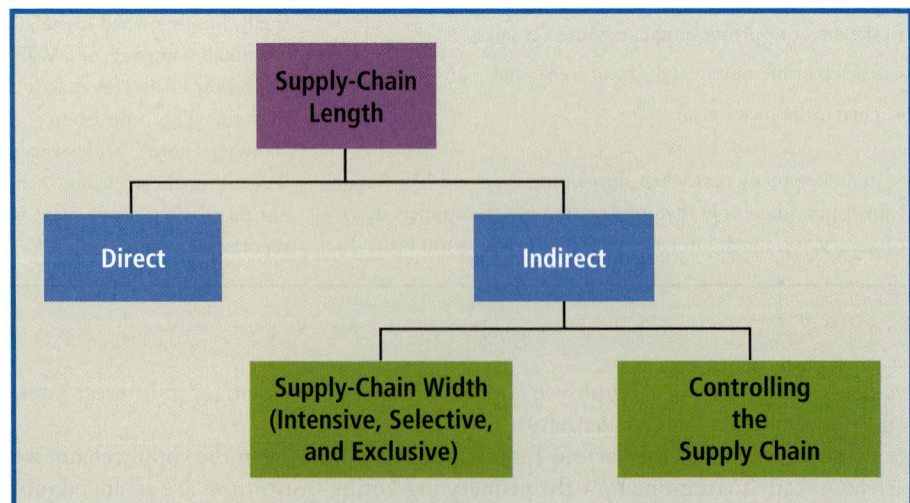

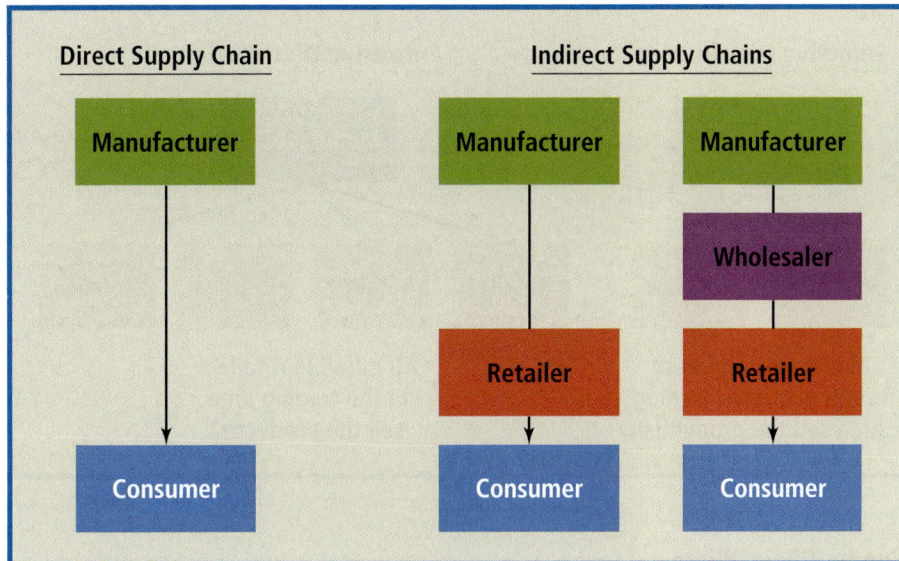

Exhibit 5.3
Direct and Indirect
Supply Chains

Direct Supply Chain

Manufacturer

↓

Consumer

Indirect Supply Chains

Manufacturer

↓

Retailer

↓

Consumer

Manufacturer

↓

Wholesaler

↓

Retailer

↓

Consumer

representative delivers the merchandise to the consumer from her own inventory, then the channel would actually be indirect—manufacturer to retailer (remember that the Avon lady is an independent businessperson) to consumer.

The desired length is determined by many customer-based factors such as the size of the customer base, geographical dispersion, behavior patterns like purchase frequency and average purchase size, and the particular needs of customers. For example, if the consumer was concerned *only* about the price paid for merchandise, then he or she would probably drive to a farmer's roadside stand to purchase a dozen eggs. However, as we pointed out in Chapter 4, factors other than price influence demand. In this case, the consumer might be willing to pay 20 percent to 30 percent more for the convenience of purchasing the eggs at the neighborhood grocer—saving the time and the cost of gas for an hour's drive into the country. Therefore, it is important to remember that, in many cases, indirect channels are actually cheaper in terms of total costs involved.

In addition, the nature of the product—such as its bulk and weight, perishability, value, and technical complexity—is important in determining supply-chain length. For example, expensive, highly technological items such as home entertainment systems will generally use short channels because of the high degree of technical support and liaison needed, which may only be available directly from the manufacturer. Length can also be affected by the size of the manufacturer, its financial capacity, and its desire for control. In general, larger and better-financed manufacturers have a greater capability to bypass intermediaries and use shorter channels. Manufacturers desiring to exercise a high degree of control over the distribution of their products are also more likely to use a shorter chain (e.g., Zara from this chapter's "Global Retailing" box).

Retailers, on the other hand, do not always have a lot of control over their channel length. For example, retailers entering Japan will find that their channel's long length is to a great extent predetermined. Japan's channel structure (often referred to as a *multitier distribution channel*) was formed in feudal times and is the accepted method of doing business in that country. Sometimes the retailer must learn to operate as efficiently as possible within an inefficient channel.

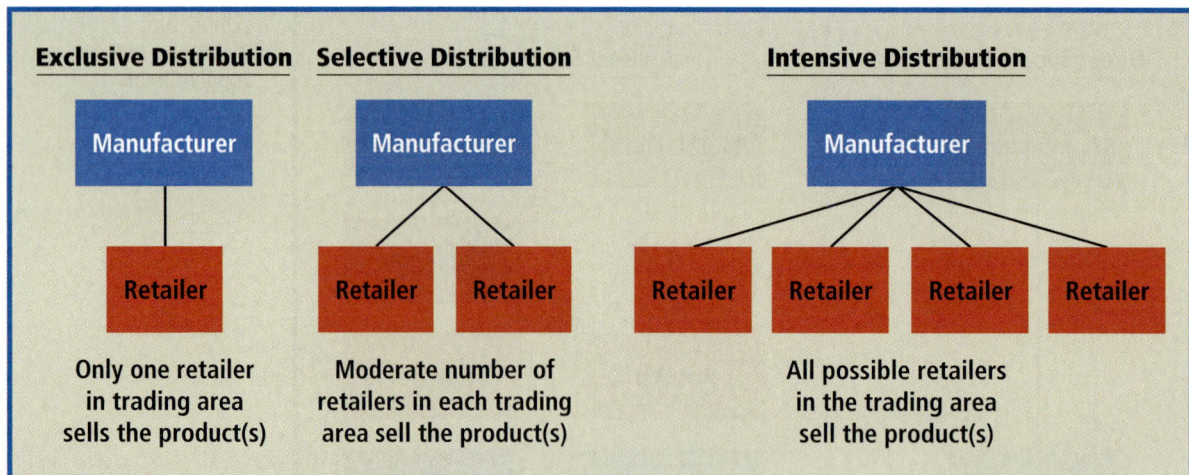

Exclusive Distribution

Manufacturer

Retailer

Only one retailer
in trading area
sells the product(s)

Selective Distribution

Manufacturer

Retailer   Retailer

Moderate number of
retailers in each trading
area sell the product(s)

Intensive Distribution

Manufacturer

Retailer   Retailer   Retailer   Retailer

All possible retailers
in the trading area
sell the product(s)

Exhibit 5.4
Width of Supply-Chain
Structure

**intensive
distribution**
Means that all possible
retailers are used in a
trade area.

selective distribution
Means that a moderate
number of retailers are
used in a trade area

**exclusive
distribution**
Means only one retailer is
used to cover a trading
area.

Supply-Chain Width

Supply-chain width or channel width, shown in Exhibit 5.4, is usually described in terms of intensive distribution, selective distribution, or exclusive distribution. **Intensive distribution** means that all possible retailers are used to reach the target market. **Selective distribution** means that a smaller number of retailers are used, while **exclusive distribution** means only one retailer is used in the trading area.

Although there are many exceptions, as a rule, intensive distribution is associated with the distribution of convenience goods, which are products that are frequently purchased; those for which the consumer is not willing to expend a great deal of effort to purchase. Selective distribution is associated with shopping goods, items for which the consumer will make a price or value comparison before purchasing. Exclusive distribution is identified with specialty goods—usually high-prestige branded products that the consumer expressly seeks out. Thus, soft drinks, milk, and greeting cards (convenience goods) tend to be carried by a very large number of retailers; home appliances and apparel (shopping goods) are handled by relatively fewer retailers; and specialty goods, such as Rolex watches, are featured by only one dealer in a trading area. Some of these specialty goods are so exclusive, Rolls-Royce automobiles for example, that many trade areas may not have a retailer handling them.

Control of the Supply Chain

The previous discussion was concerned with the length and width of a supply chain. However, a more pressing issue is who should control the supply chain. Many chains consist of independent business firms who, without the proper leadership, may look out solely for themselves, to the detriment of the other members. For this reason, experts agree that *no supply chain will ever operate at a 100-percent efficiency level*. Supply-chain members must have as their goal "to minimize the sub-optimization" of the supply chain.

Supply chains follow one of two basic patterns: the conventional marketing channel and the vertical marketing channel. Exhibit 5.5 provides an illustration of these major channel patterns.

Conventional Marketing Channel

**conventional
marketing channel**
Is one in which each
channel member is
loosely aligned with the
others and takes a short-
term orientation.

A **conventional marketing channel** is one in which each member of the supply chain is loosely aligned with the others and takes a short-term orientation.

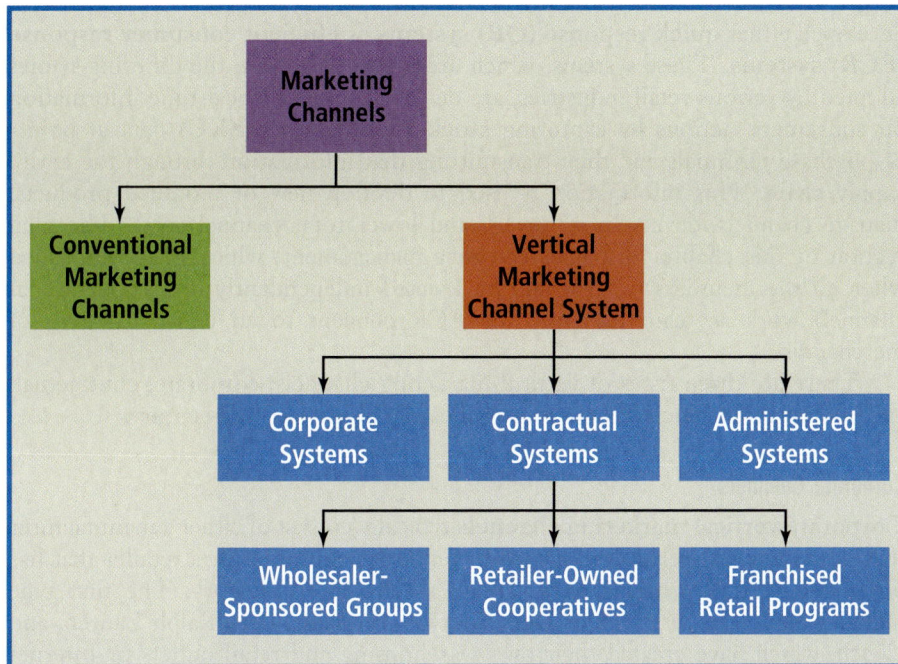

Exhibit 5.5
Marketing Channel
Patterns

Predictably, each member's orientation is toward the subsequent institution in the channel. The prevailing attitude is "what is happening today" as opposed to "what will happen in the future." The manufacturer interacts with and focuses efforts on the wholesaler, the wholesaler is primarily concerned with the retailer, and the retailer focuses efforts on the final consumer. In short, all of the members focus on their immediate desire to close the sale or create a transaction. Thus, the conventional marketing channel consists of a series of pairs in which the members of each pair recognize each other but not necessarily the other components of the supply chain.

The conventional marketing channel, which is historically predominant in the United States, is a sloppy and inefficient method of conducting business. It fosters intense negotiations within each pair of institutions in the supply chain. In addition, members are unable to see the possibility of shifting or dividing the marketing functions among all the participants. Obviously, it is an unproductive method for marketing goods and has been on the decline in the United States since the early 1950s.

Vertical Marketing Channels

Vertical marketing channels are capital-intensive networks of several levels that are professionally managed and rely on centrally programmed systems to realize the technological, managerial, and promotional economies of long-term relationships. The basic premise of working as a system is to operate as close as possible to that elusive 100-percent efficiency level. This is achieved by eliminating the sub-optimization that exists in conventional channels and improving the channel's performance by working together.[3]

Formerly adversarial relationships between retailers and their suppliers are now giving way to new vertical channel partnerships that minimize such inefficiencies.[4] Because vertical channel members realize that it is impossible to offer consumers value without being a low-cost, high-efficiency supply chain, they have

vertical marketing channels
Are capital-intensive networks of several levels that are professionally managed and centrally programmed to realize the technological, managerial, and promotional economies of a long-term relationship orientation.

quick response (QR) systems
Also known as **efficient consumer response (ECR) systems**, are integrated information, production, and logistical systems that obtain real-time information on consumer actions by capturing sales data at point-of-purchase terminals and then transmitting this information back through the entire channel to enable efficient production and distribution scheduling.

stock-keeping units (SKU)
Are the lowest level of identification of merchandise.

corporate vertical marketing channels
Exist where one channel institution owns multiple levels of distribution and typically consists of either a manufacturer that has integrated vertically forward to reach the consumer or a retailer that has integrated vertically backward to create a self-supply network.

contractual vertical marketing channels
Use a contract to govern the working relationship between channel members and include wholesaler-sponsored voluntary groups, retailer-owned cooperatives, and franchised retail programs.

wholesaler-sponsored voluntary groups
Involve a wholesaler that brings together a group of independently owned retailers and offers them a coordinated merchandising and buying program that will provide them with economies like those their chain store rivals are able to obtain.

developed either **quick response (QR) systems** or **efficient consumer response (ECR) systems**. These systems, which are identical despite the differing names adopted by various retail industries, are designed to obtain real-time information on consumers' actions by capturing **stock-keeping unit (SKU)** data at point-of-purchase terminals and then transmitting that information through the entire supply chain. This information is used to develop new or modified products, manage channelwide inventory levels, and lower total channel costs. The final section of this chapter discusses category management, which is accomplished when all the members (who would have acted independently in a conventional channel) work as team to apply the ECR concept to an entire category of merchandise.

There are three types of vertical marketing channels: corporate, contractual, and administered. Each has grown significantly in the last half-century.

Corporate Channels

Corporate vertical marketing channels typically consist of either a manufacturer that has integrated vertically forward to reach the consumer or a retailer that has integrated vertically backward to create a self-supply network. The first type includes manufacturers such as Dell, Sherwin Williams, Polo Ralph Lauren, and Coach, which have created their own warehousing and retail outlets or Internet selling sites. An example of the second type includes Holiday Inns, which for years was vertically integrated to control a carpet mill, furniture manufacturer, and numerous other suppliers needed to build and operate its motels. To illustrate this point, consider that Holiday Inn had to conduct extensive research to overcome manufacturing problems encountered with the production of cinnamon rolls, the trademark of its Holiday Inn Express units.

In corporate channels, it is not difficult to program the channel for productivity and profit goals since a well-established authority structure already exists. Independent retailers that have aligned themselves in a conventional marketing channel are at a significant disadvantage when competing against a corporate vertical marketing channel.

Contractual Channels

Contractual vertical marketing channels, which include wholesaler-sponsored voluntary groups, retailer-owned cooperatives, and franchised retail programs, are supply chains that use a contract to govern the working relationship between the members. Each of these variations allows for a more coordinated, systemwide perspective than conventional marketing channels. However, they are more difficult to manage than corporate vertical marketing channels because the authority and power structures are not as well defined. Supply-chain members must give up some autonomy to gain economies of scale and greater market impact.

Wholesaler-Sponsored Voluntary Groups. **Wholesaler-sponsored voluntary groups** are created when a wholesaler brings together a group of independently owned retailers (*independent retailers* is a term embracing anything from a single mom-and-pop store to a small local chain)—grocers, for example—and offers them a coordinated merchandising program (store design and layout, store site and location analysis, inventory management channels, accounting and bookkeeping channels, insurance services, pension plans, trade area studies, advertising and promotion assistance, employee-training programs) as well as a buying program that will provide these smaller retailers with economies similar to those obtained by their chain store rivals. In return, the independent retailers agree to concentrate their purchases with that wholesaler. It is a voluntary relationship; that is, there are no membership or franchise fees. The independent retailer may terminate the relationship whenever it desires, so it is to the wholesaler's advantage to build competitive merchandise assortments and offer services that will keep the voluntary group satisfied.

In the past, local food wholesalers got practically all of their business from independent grocers. Recently, however, as transportation costs have risen, major chains operating over a wide geographic area have also started using local or regional wholesalers. While welcoming this new business, wholesalers have attempted to keep their independents happy (since they still account for more than 40 percent of their business) by offering them additional services.

Wholesaler-sponsored voluntary groups have been a major force in marketing channels since the mid-1960s. They are now prevalent in many lines of trade. Independent Grocers' Alliance (IGA) and National Auto Parts Association (NAPA) are both examples of wholesaler-sponsored voluntary groups.

Retailer-Owned Cooperatives. Another common type of contractual vertical marketing channel is **retailer-owned cooperatives**, which are wholesale operations organized and owned by retailers; these are most common in hardware retailing. They include such familiar names as TrueValue (which was highlighted in Exhibit 2.3), Ace, and Handy Hardware, and they offer scale economies and services to member retailers, allowing their members to compete with larger chain-buying organizations.

It should be pointed out that, in theory, wholesale-sponsored groups should be easier to manage since they have only one leader, the wholesaler, versus the many owners of the retailer-owned group. One would assume that in retailer-owned cooperatives, individual members would desire to keep their autonomy and be less dependent on their supplier partner for support and direction. In reality, however, just the opposite has been true. A possible explanation is that retailers belonging to a wholesale co-op may make greater transaction-specific investments in the form of stock ownership, vested supplier-based store identity, and end-of-year rebates on purchases that combine to erect significant exit barriers from the cooperative.[5]

retailer-owned cooperatives
Are wholesale institutions, organized and owned by member retailers, that offer scale economies and services to member retailers, which allows them to compete with larger chain buying organizations.

Tom Gannam/AP Photo

Ace Hardware decor specialist Joanne Mendicino points at some new drop bins, part of the new store decor, to Ace retailers Jim and Marylin Berschauer, at a newly remodeled Ace store.

Franchises. The third type of contractual vertical marketing channel is the franchise. A **franchise** is a form of licensing by which the owner of a trademark, service mark, trade name, advertising symbol, or method (the franchisor) obtains distribution through affiliated dealers (franchisees). Each franchisee is authorized by the franchisor to sell its goods or services in either a retail space or a designated geographical area. The franchise governs the method of conducting business between the two parties. Generally, a franchisee sells goods or services supplied by the franchisor or that meet the

franchise
Is a form of licensing by which the owner of a product, service, or business method (the franchisor) obtains distribution through affiliated dealers (franchisees).

franchisor's quality standards. This relationship is regulated by Federal Trade Commission laws. In many cases, the franchise operation resembles a large chain store. It operates with standardized logos, uniforms, signage, equipment, storefronts, services, products, and practices—all as outlined in the franchise agreement. The consumer might never know that each location is independently owned.

Franchising is a convenient and economic means of fulfilling an individual's desire for independence with a minimum amount of risk and investment but maximum opportunities for success. This is possible through the utilization of a proven product or service and marketing method. Consider that one of the benefits of franchising is that it permits a franchisee to select a location in a somewhat sophisticated manner based on the various professional forecasting models that use data from earlier units. Another advantage is in the purchasing of key items. Holiday Inn, for example, knows more about how to buy mattresses and furniture than most of its franchisees. However, a franchisee–franchisor relationship requires an ongoing commitment, with each party expected to uphold its end of the contract though active communication, solidarity, and mutual trust. In those cases where a franchisee–franchisor relationship does not work, it is usually the result of a franchisee misunderstanding the franchising model and the franchisor failing to set expectations or the franchisee not understanding them at the outset. Remember that a franchisee gives up some freedom in business decisions that the owner of a nonfranchised business would retain. The most common franchise mistakes result from a franchisee's incorrect perception of him- or herself as a traditional entrepreneur. In order to maintain uniformity of service and to ensure that the operations of each outlet will reflect favorably on the organization as a whole, the franchisor must exercise some degree of control over the operations of franchisees, requiring them to meet stipulated standards of product and service quality and operating procedures. Exhibit 5.6 lists some of the major advantages and disadvantages of franchising for both parties.

Exhibit 5.6
Advantages and Disadvantages of Franchising

ADVANTAGES TO FRANCHISEE	ADVANTAGES TO FRANCHISOR
1. Access to a well-known brand name, trademark, or product	1. Since franchisee is the owner, more motivated managers on site
2. Assistance in location decisions	2. Local identification of the owner
3. Assistance in buying decisions	3. Economics of scale
4. Being part of a successful format	4. Franchisee must make royalty payments regardless of profitability
5. Acquiring rights to well-defined trade area	5. The rapid rollout of a successful concept requires less capital
6. Lower risk of failure	
7. Standardized marketing and operational procedures	
8. By borrowing from the franchisor, the franchisee has access to a lower cost of capital	
DISADVANTAGES TO FRANCHISEE	**DISADVANTAGES TO FRANCHISOR**
1. Higher costs because of fees due franchisor	1. Loss of some profits
2. Must give up some control of the business	2. Loss of some control
3. Franchisor may not fulfill all promises	3. Franchisee may not fulfill all parts of the agreement
4. Can be terminated or not renewed	

There are some 1,200 franchisors in the United States today, and they can be found at any position in the marketing channel; about 60 percent of them have startup costs of less than $300,000. The franchisor could be a manufacturer such as Chevrolet or Midas Mufflers; a service specialist such as Sylvan Learning, Stanley Steemer, AAMCO Transmissions, H&R Block, Lawn Doctor, Merry Maids, Mr. Handyman, Supercuts, or Century 21 Real Estate; a retailer such as Gingiss Formalwear; or a fast-food retailer such as McDonald's, Dunkin' Donuts, Subway, Domino's Pizza, or KFC. It should be noted that franchising isn't all about food anymore. Consumer service providers such as fitness centers, lawn-care specialists, dance studios, and pet hotels have not opened the most outlets recently, but they have been the best performing.[6] A more complete list can be found at the International Franchise Association website (www.franchise.org).[7]

Another advantage of being a franchisee was illustrated during the recent economic crisis when many financial institutions cut or reduced their loans to the franchisees. Such actions, for example, made it harder for fast-food franchisees to remodel existing locations and buy or open new restaurants.[8] However, while most franchisors normally don't provide financial assistance to existing franchisees, they made an exception during the recent recession. This was because the franchisors were able to get the financing partly because of their historically low default rate on previous loans as well as their current balance sheets. By securing these loans, a franchisor provided capital to be used by the franchisee for expansions, acquisitions, debt consolidation, and refinancing for new and current obligations.[9]

Finally, although only a third of U.S. franchisors are currently operating in foreign countries, another third are looking to expand internationally within the next five years. After all, why compete in overcrowded U.S. markets when many foreign markets are available? Although franchising is seen as an economic-development tool for poor countries, the most widely considered foreign markets are the most prosperous markets of Canada, Japan, Mexico, Germany, the United Kingdom, and, more recently, Southeast Asia—Philippines, Thailand, Taiwan, Singapore, and Indonesia.

McDonald's has been able to successfully introduce and operate its franchise fast food restaurants around the world including, as shown here, in lianjin, China.

Administered Channels

The final type of vertical marketing channel is the administered channel. **Administered vertical marketing channels** are similar to conventional marketing channels, yet one of the members takes the initiative to lead the channel by applying the principles of effective interorganizational management, which is the management of relationships between the various organizations in the supply chain. Administered channels, although not new in concept, have grown substantially in recent years. Frequently, administered channels are initiated by manufacturers because channel members have historically relied on manufacturers' administrative expertise to coordinate the retailers' marketing efforts. Suppliers with dominant brands have predictably experienced the least difficulty in securing strong support from retailers and wholesalers. However, many manufacturers with "fringe" items have been able to elicit such cooperation only through the use of liberal distribution

administered vertical marketing channels Exist when one of the channel members takes the initiative to lead the channel by applying the principles of effective interorganizational management.

policies that take the form of attractive discounts (or discount substitutes), financial assistance, and various types of concessions that protect resellers from one or more of the risks of doing business.[10]

Some of the concessions manufacturers offer retailers are liberal return policies, display materials for in-store use, advertising allowances, extra time for merchandise payment, employee-training programs, assistance with store layout and design, inventory maintenance, computer support, and even free merchandise.

Manufacturers that use their administrative powers to lead channels include Coca-Cola, Sealy (with its Posturepedic line of mattresses), Villager (with its dresses and sportswear lines), Scott (with its lawn-care products), Norwalk (with its upholstered furniture), Keepsake (with diamonds), and Stanley (with hand tools).

Retailers can also dominate the channel relationship. For example, Walmart, besides using its Retail Link, was one of the earliest adopters of ECR systems and today administers the relationship with almost all of its suppliers by asking that all money designated for advertising allowances, end-display fees, and so forth be taken off the price of goods instead. By doing this, the giant retailer believes that its supply chains are managed in the most efficient and effective way possible.

LO 3   Managing Retailer–Supplier Relations

How do dependency, power, and conflict influence supply-chain relations?

Retailers that are not part of a contractual channel or corporate channel will probably participate in different channels since they will need to acquire merchandise from many suppliers. Predictably, these channels will be either conventional or administered. If retailers want to improve their performance in these channels, then they must understand the principal concepts of interorganizational management. In this case, retailers must strategically manage their relations with or retailers. manufacturers.

What are the basic concepts of interorganizational management that a retailer needs to understand? They are dependency, power, and conflict.

Dependency

dependency

Dependency occurs when a retailer needs another supply chain member or vice versa to perform certain marketing functions. When two members of the supply chain are dependent on each other they are referred to as interdependent.

As we mentioned earlier, every supply chain needs to perform eight marketing functions. None of the respective institutions can isolate itself; each depends on the others to do an effective job in order for the channel to be successful.

Retailer A is **dependency** on suppliers X, Y, and Z to make sure that goods are delivered on time and in the right quantities. Conversely, suppliers X, Y, and Z depend on retailer A to put a strong selling effort behind their goods, displaying them properly, and maybe even helping to finance consumer purchases. If retailer A does a poor job, then each supplier can be adversely affected; if even one supplier does a poor job, then retailer A can be adversely affected. In all these alignments, each party depends on the others to do a good job. This concept was recently illustrated when several giant retailers worked with detergent manufactures to develop a concentrated product that would shrink the package size in half. In return, the retailers would help convince the consumer to pay the same price for a package that was half the size because it provided the same cleaning power. This was a win–win (collaboration) situation for both parties because retailers were able to use less shelf space and manufacturers saved on production costs. However, each party was dependent on the other to achieve these goals.

When each party is dependent on the others, we say that they are *interdependent*. While this interdependency is at the root of the collaboration found in today's supply chains, it is also the major cause of the conflict found in supply chains. To better comprehend this interdependency, an understanding of power is necessary.

Power

We can use the concept of dependency to explain power, but first we must define power. **Power** is the ability of one member to influence the behavior of the other supply-chain members. The more dependent the supplier is on the retailer, the more power the retailer has over the supplier and vice versa. For example, a small manufacturer of grocery products would be very dependent on a large supermarket chain if it wanted to reach the most consumers. In this instance, the supermarket has power over the small manufacturer. Likewise, many suppliers are very dependent on Walmart because it is their biggest customer. For example, today Walmart accounts for 15 percent of Procter & Gamble's (P&G's) total revenue, more than the total of many foreign countries.[11] Yet this dependence is not specific to domestic manufacturers. In fact, the *Wall Street Journal* recently ran the following headline across the top of its Marketplace section: "Walmart Sneezes, China Catches Cold" to illustrate the significant dependence so many have on Walmart.[12] Thus, the power one member has over another supply-chain member is a function of how dependent the second member is on the first member to achieve its own goals.

There are six types of power:

1. **Reward power** is based on the ability of A to provide rewards to B. For instance, a retailer may offer a manufacturer a prominent endcap display in exchange for additional advertising monies and promotional support. Yet liquidity problems due to the recent economic slowdown resulted in the use of a different form of reward power: merchandise. Because of the sharp falloff in consumer spending, manufacturers were forced to unload excess inventory to anyone with the means to pay. This resulted in off-price retailers such as T.J. Maxx, Stein Mart, Ross Stores, and Overstock.com receiving some of the best selections of apparel, accessories, and electronic goods, items they would normally not get, at great prices.[13]

2. **Expertise power** is based on B's perception that A has some special knowledge or superior ability. For example, Midas Muffler (a franchisor) has developed an excellent training program for store managers. As a result, franchisees view Midas as an expert in training effective store managers. Seeking the best managers possible, franchisees give up some of their control in order to gain access to this training program.

3. **Referent power** is based on B's desire to be identified or associated with A. Examples of this are auto dealers that want to handle BMWs or Mercedes because of the cars' status, or a manufacturer that wants to have its product sold in Neiman Marcus because of the image that retailer projects. Yet referent power is not always positive. In 2007, tainted pet food led to the deaths of more than a dozen dogs and cats and the illnesses of a thousand more. The food was produced by one manufacturer and sold using 101 different brand names. As a result, the differences in the selling price between the various brands were reflective of the company associated with the brand name used.[14]

4. **Coercive power** is based on B's belief that A has the capacity to punish or harm B if B does not do what A wants. For example, franchisors like Burger King have the right to cancel a franchisee's contract if it fails to maintain franchise standards such as restaurant cleanliness, food menu, hours of operation, and employee dress or uniforms.

power
Is the ability of one channel member to influence the decisions of the other channel members.

reward power
Is based on B's perception that A has the ability to provide rewards for B.

expertise power
Is based on B's perception that A has some special knowledge.

referent power
Is based on the identification of B with A.

coercive power
Is based on B's belief that A has the capability to punish or harm B if B doesn't do what A wants.

legitimate power
Is based on A's right to influence B, or B's belief that B should accept A's influence.

5. **Legitimate power** is based on A's right to influence B or on B's belief that B should accept A's influence. The presence of legitimate power is most easily seen in contractual marketing channels. A manufacturer may, for example, threaten to cut off a retailer's supply if the retailer fails to meet certain standards. For example, Deere & Company recently terminated some if its smaller dealerships after years of selling the company's equipment. Deere and Co. stated that many of these smaller dealers simply neglected to run their businesses as needed by the manufacturer; they neglected to develop new revenue streams (customers) while failing to assist the manufacturer in managing inventory costs. Now the company says that dealers must meet established profit and customer-loyalty targets or fear being merged with other dealers.[15] This chapter's "Service Retailing" box describes a similar fate for the retailers that sell and service America's automobiles.

Also, if the retailer accepts co-op advertising dollars, the manufacturer may control the minimum retail price, since this subject is usually covered in the agreement. Absent such an agreement, the retailer is free to set the selling price. To do otherwise would be a violation of certain federal antitrust laws, which we discuss in the next chapter.

informational power
Is based on A's ability to provide B with factual data.

6. **Informational power** is based on A's ability to provide B with factual data. Not to be confused with expertise power, informational power occurs when the factual data is provided independently of the relationship between A and B. An example of this power would be a small retail store sharing scanner data with a vendor.

Retailers and suppliers that use reward, expertise, referent, and informational power can foster a healthy working relationship. On the other hand, the use of coercive and legitimate power tends to elicit conflict and destroy cooperation in the supply chain.

Conflict

Conflict is inevitable in every supply-chain relationship because retailers and suppliers are interdependent. In other words, every channel member is dependent on every other member to perform some specific task. Interdependency has been identified as the root cause of all conflict in marketing channels. There are three major sources of conflict between retailers and their suppliers: perceptual incongruity, goal incompatibility, and domain disagreement.

perceptual incongruity
Occurs when the retailer and supplier have different perceptions of reality.

Perceptual incongruity occurs when the retailer and supplier have different perceptions of reality. A retailer may perceive that the economy isn't coming out of recession and therefore may want to continue to keep a low level of inventory investments, while the supplier may believe that the economy is recovering and, therefore, that inventory investments should be maintained or possibly increased. Other areas where the retailer and supplier might perceive things differently include the quality of the supplier's merchandise, the potential demand for the supplier's merchandise, the consumer appeal of the supplier's advertising, and the best shelf position for the supplier's merchandise.

goal incompatibility
Occurs when achieving the goals of either the supplier or the retailer would hamper the performance of the other.

A second source of conflict is **goal incompatibility**, a situation in which achieving the goals of either the supplier or the retailer would hamper the performance of the other. For example, Nike and Foot Locker have fought over the retailer's goal of gaining sales with its liberal use of "BOGOs"—industry jargon for "buy one, get one at half-off" sales. Such sales encourage consumers to buy two pairs on a single shopping trip, thereby reducing the chance the consumer would

Service Retailing

The Three-Decade Decline of New Car Dealerships: What Is the Service Impact?

As the data clearly reveals, the United States is facing a three-decade decline in the number of new car dealership franchises. In 1980, the number of dealerships was nearly 28,000. Twenty years later, the number stood at slightly more than 22,000. By 2010, the number of dealerships was projected to be close to 18,000.

Much of this decline is credited to the recessions and increasing costs of energy and gasoline in the 1970s, 1990s, and late 2000s, particularly 2008 and 2009. In addition, the bankruptcies of Chrysler and General Motors in the spring of 2009 further reduced the number of new car dealers. Although this long-term decline in dealerships is likely to affect the economy in several ways, one of the more significant impacts concerns dealerships' service offerings. Dealerships provide services not only to customers but also to auto manufacturers and, on a broader scale, the local communities in which they operate.

New car franchises provide their local communities with a variety of services. First, they offer an assortment of automobiles that can be viewed, test driven, and immediately delivered. It is not uncommon for an individual to enter an automobile dealership at 9 A.M. and leave two hours later in a new car. Yet all too often customers need to get rid of their old car prior to purchasing a new one. Dealers also provide community members with trade-in services; they no longer need to worry about selling their used car to a private party. In this way, dealerships offer one-stop shopping: A customer can purchase and finance a new car, payoff his or her used car, and process the application for title. Dealerships also provide services such as warranty and maintenance work on site rather than requiring customers to ship the product off to the factory to be repaired, as is often the case with most durable goods. Consequently, one could view the reduction in the number of dealerships as a positive. The presence of fewer dealerships in an area often coincides with larger dealers; many offering multiple product lines (e.g., selling Ford, Lincoln, and Mercury at the same dealership). As dealerships grow, it is necessary for them to increase the number of available services in order to maintain the different product lines. Thus, the customer benefits from greater product assortment and more available services.

However, a new car dealership is more than a retail distribution point for providing service to car shoppers; it also exists to service the community. Car dealers often support local clubs and organizations. In fact, the typical dealership provides between $50,000 and $100,000 of annual sponsorship funds for local groups. Most are between $100 and $500 for groups like Rotary, Little League, soccer clubs, rodeo events, charitable golf tournaments, scouting, art museums, K–12 educational events, and so on. Perhaps this is why the local Chevrolet or Ford dealer is often a well-recognized and respected member of the community.

When a local dealer closes and is not replaced with a new operator, the negative impact on the community becomes quite evident. Dealers are a major source of retail sales tax collections and often in a small community can represent 10 percent to 20 percent of the total retail sales tax base. Yet the situation is even more severe in large communities (i.e., metroplexes with more than 1 million people) where the loss of a dealer could equate to a loss of millions in annual sales tax collections. Not only are the 50 to 75 employees at the dealership without a job but also the local government often ends up needing to cut another 50-plus employees due to lower tax revenues. These cuts are often seen in community services from policemen to fire protection and even library staff.

Where does the service impact end? That is difficult to answer. More than 50 years ago, a noted authority said what's good for General Motors is good for the United States. The sharp recession that began in 2008 triggered a large drop in auto sales, which in early 2009 were roughly 30 percent to 50 percent of the prior year (depending on brand and dealerships). This drop-off resulted in more closures of dealerships and ripples as far-reaching as production plants and the auto supply chain.

Although this chapter focuses primarily on the supply chain once a finished product leaves the manufacturer, one must also remember that supply chains feed into each manufacturer. If Chevrolet is selling 40 percent fewer cars, then suppliers of Chevrolet are impacted. Take, for instance, the interior of an automobile that is mostly outsourced. Not only are these subcontractors to Chevrolet impacted but also

(continued)

Service Retailing (*continued*)

the companies that supply these subcontractors with metal, foam, trim, textiles, and so on are affected. In brief, these firms also cut jobs, tax revenues decline, and then government-provided services decline further.

Stated differently, when General Motors—or, in this case, Chevrolet—is damaged, so too is the United States.

Source: H. O. Helmers, Charles N. Davisson, and Herbert F. Taggart. *Two Studies in Automobile Franchising* (University of Michigan, Division of Research, Graduate School of Business AdministrationAnn Arbor, 1974);

Stewart Macaulay, *Law and the Balance of Power* (Russell Sage Foundation New York, 1966); "Local Auto-Linked Suppliers Optimistic," *The Macomb Daily*, November 16, 2008; "Sebastopol's Pellini Chevrolet Closing," *The Press Democrat*, December 24, 2008; "California Auto Dealers Hit Hard by Bad Economy" *Mercury News*, December 19, 2008; "Dealer Closes, Town Feels Pain," *Las Vegas Sun*, December 2, 2008; "Death of a Car Dealership," *Toronto Star*, November 22, 2008; "Chrysler Dealers Feel They Got Bum's Rush," *St. Louis Post-Dispatch*, (June 7, 2009); and authors' research, experience, and consulting in auto industry.

---

dual distribution
Occurs when a manufacturer sells to independent retailers and also through its own retail outlets.

buy the second pair elsewhere.[16] Similarly, some manufacturers don't want their products sold at big-box stores or discounters for fear of cheapening the brand image. That is why Stihl advertises that its power tools "are not sold at Lowe's or Home Depot."

Another example of incompatibility between retailer and supplier goals is a situation known as **dual distribution**. Dual distribution occurs when a manufacturer sells to independent retailers while simultaneously selling directly to the final consumer through its own retail outlets or through an Internet site. (This chapter's "Retailing: The Inside Story" points out some of the problems that a manufacturer must consider when setting up an Internet site.) Thus, the manufacturer manages a corporately owned, vertical marketing channel that competes directly with independent retailers that it supplies through a conventional, administered, or contractual marketing channel.

Retailers tend to become upset about dual distribution when the two channels compete at the retail level in the same geographic area. Remember the case at the end of Chapter 4 where it was pointed out that Trek Bicycles not only sold its bikes through a local independent retailer, but also through its own stores nearby? However, as consolidation continues among department stores, some manufacturers, such as Liz Claiborne, have opened stores selling their "power brands"—Juicy Couture, Lucky, Sigrid Olsen, and Mexx. This practice has angered traditional retailers that buy from these manufacturers and can have an adverse effect on manufacturer–retailer relationships. Other manufacturers, such as Oakley and Tommy Bahama, believe that their stores help build brand awareness and thereby sales for the traditional establishments. The fear of upsetting current sales reps caused Tupperware to pull its products out of Target's 1,200 stores. The attempt at dual distribution was meant to reach shoppers too busy to attend sales parties or deal with door-to-door salespeople. However, the easy availability of Tupperware products in the giant retailer's stores had a "detrimental effect" on Tupperware parties.[17]

When Walmart sold its McLane's wholesaling subsidiary to Warren Buffett's Berkshire Hathaway Inc., many retailing experts felt that this action would ultimately enable Walmart to expand into the convenience store market. If the giant retailer had entered the convenience store market without selling McLane's, the nation's largest wholesaler serving convenience stores, it would have established a dual-distribution network whereby Walmart would operate its own retail outlets in competition with its McLane's division wholesale customers. In such a case, the

Retailing: The Inside Story

A Manufacturer's Internet Site: Friend or Foe to the Retailer

The role of retailers in facilitating the transfer of a manufacturer's product to their customers is critical to a manufacturer's success. Manufacturers realize the value that retailers provide and that strong channel relationships can create a competitive advantage in the marketplace. As such, over the past few decades, manufacturers have invested heavily in developing strong relationships with their retailers.

However, the world of retailing has undergone tremendous changes with the introduction of the Internet. The Internet provided new opportunities for manufacturers to sell more aggressively to consumers online, which could counteract the attempts by retailers to replace national brands with private labels as a means to increase the retailer's gross margins. These Internet sales would strengthen the manufacturers' financial positions and allow them to interact with consumers more effectively. However, the Web can also be a hazardous place for manufacturers. After all, while consumers expect them to sell their products directly online, retailers, especially in slow economic times, don't want additional competition.

Therefore, while having an Internet site is important for manufacturers, they first must answer the following three questions:

1. What is the real cost of a manufacturer becoming an e-tailer?
2. What does such a move do to the existing channel relationships?
3. What can a manufacturer do in advance to avoid having a current supply-chain partner object?

Today, despite the current economic situation, retailers haven't reacted too negatively to manufacturers setting up dual-distribution systems because Web sales are only a small percentage of total sales. In fact, most retailers currently believe that a manufacturer's Web site offers positive benefits. After all, there is an old retail adage that manufacturers promote the product's uses and benefits or superiority while retailers promote the product's availability and price. Therefore, the answer to the first two questions is, for the most part, the dollar cost of setting up a Web site and the additional expenses incurred by handling smaller quantity orders.

The answer to the third question requires some creativity. Consider how two manufacturers—Callaway Golf and PeaceWorks—set up Internet sites so as to not offend their partners.

Callaway Golf created Shop.CallawayGolf.com, where consumers could order golf clubs. However, the customer must pick up the clubs from a local Callaway retailer. The company's technology identified the retailer closest to the customer and awarded the sale accordingly. The benefits are obvious: The sales go to the retailers, and Callaway escapes the task of shipping sets of clubs to consumers. It's a very creative approach designed to avoid any conflict.

Another example of planning ahead to avoid problems was done by PeaceWorks, a New York–based maker of specialty foods. The company wanted to avoid competing with its retailers and it didn't want to get involved with selling to one consumer at a time because it was used to selling container loads of product. Therefore, it decided to allow consumers using its Web site (http://www.peaceworks.com) to purchase only by the case — 48 bars at $2 apiece, one flavor, no discount. In short, it made it quite difficult for the individual consumer to buy online.[18]

---

convenience store operators likely would have dropped McLane. Why would they want to financially support a competitor?

The problem of goal incompatibility is not necessarily one of profit versus image goals. Even if the retailer and supplier both have a return on investment (ROI) goal, they can still be incompatible, because what is good for the retailer's ROI may not be good for the supplier's ROI. Consider the price element in the transaction between the supplier and the retailer. If the supplier obtains a higher price, then its ROI will be higher but the ROI of the retailer will be lower. Similarly, other key elements in the transaction between the retailer and supplier, such as advertising allowances, cash discounts, order quantity, and freight charges, can result in conflict.

A third source of conflict is **domain disagreements**. *Domain* refers to the decision variables that each member of the marketing channel feels it should be able

domain disagreements
Occur when there is disagreement about which member of the marketing channel should make decisions.

to control. When the members of the marketing channel agree on who should make which decisions, domain consensus exists. When there is disagreement about who should make decisions, domain disagreement exists.

Consider the situation mentioned earlier where manufacturers were reluctantly forced to sell their upscale wares to off-price retailers. Many of the major department store chains that initially helped the manufacturer *position* those items as high-image brand names in the mind of the consumer felt betrayed.

diverter
Is an unauthorized member of a channel who buys and sells excess merchandise to and from authorized channel members.

Another controversial domain disagreement practice in today's retail marketing channels occurs when retailers sell merchandise purchased from the vendor to discounters that the manufacturer does not want selling its products. A **diverter** is an unauthorized member of a channel that buys and sells excess merchandise to and from authorized channel members. For instance, suppose a retailer could buy a name-brand appliance intended to retail for $389 at $185 if it purchases 100 units. However, if the retailer orders 200 units it can purchase the item at $158. What does the retailer do? Some retailers will purchase 200 units even though they need only 100. They in turn sell the 100 extra units at a slight loss, say $155, to a discount store that may retail the item for $219. The net result is the retailer loses $3 a unit on 100 units or $300; however, it bought the remaining 100 units at $27 a unit less, for a savings of $2,700. As a result of this price arbitrage, the retailer is $2,400 ahead on the transaction. However, the manufacturer is likely to be upset because the appliance has been diverted into a retail channel it did not intend and over which it has no direct control. Several manufacturers claim it is because of diverting that Target has been able to offer high-end beauty products from such labels as Kiehl's, Origins, and Bare Escentuals in its stores.[19]

gray marketing
Is when branded merchandise flows across national boundaries and through unauthorized channels.

Similar to diverting is a practice known as **gray marketing**, whereby genuinely branded merchandise flows through unauthorized channels that *cross national boundaries*. Gray market channels develop when global conditions are conducive to profits. For example, consider the retailing of prescription drugs. Since Americans pay 67 percent more on average than Canadians for these drugs, the gray market, especially from Canada, has increased substantially.

free-riding
Is when a consumer seeks product information, usage instructions, and sometimes even warranty work from a full-service store but then, armed with the brand's model number, purchases the product from a limited-service discounter or over the Internet.

Diverting and gray marketing can lead to another supply-chain problem: free riding. **Free riding** occurs when consumers seek product information and usage instructions about products, ranging from computers to home appliances, from a full-service specialty store. Then, armed with the brand's model number, consumers purchase the product from a limited-service discounter or over the Internet.

Not all conflict in a channel is bad. Low levels of conflict will probably not affect any channel member's behavior and may not even be noticed. A moderate level of conflict might even cause the members to improve their efficiency, much the same as happens with some of your classmates when you are working on a team project. However, high levels of conflict will probably be dysfunctional to the channel and lead to inefficiencies and channel restructuring.

LO 4 — Collaboration In The Channel

Why is collaboration so important in supply chains today?

Although all supply chains experience some degree of conflict, the dominant behavior in successful supply chains is collaboration. Collaboration, where both parties seek to solve all problems with a win–win attitude, is necessary and beneficial because of the interdependency of retailers and suppliers. Retailers and suppliers must develop a partnership if they want to deal with each other on a long-term and continuing basis. As a result, many supply-chain members have begun to follow a set of best practices as listed in Exhibit 5.7. This vendor partnership is

Exhibit 5.7
Supply-Chain
Management Best
Practices

1. All supply-chain members must remember that satisfying the retail consumer is the only way anyone can be successful.

2. Successful partners work together in good times and bad.

3. Never abandon a supply-chain partner at the first sign of trouble.

4. Work together with your partners to offer products at appropriate prices. No one will win if either partner is dishonest or unfair with the other or with the retail customer.

5. Never abuse power in negotiations. Rather, understand your partner's needs prior to negotiations and work to satisfy those needs.

6. Share profits fairly among partners.

7. Limit the number of partners for each merchandise line. By doing so you can signal greater commitment and trust to your partners, thus building stronger relationships.

8. Set high ethical standards in your business transactions.

9. Successful partners plan together to help the supply chain operate efficiently and effectively.

10. Treat your partner as you would wish to be treated.

often a critical factor for the retailer who does not want to confuse the final consumer with constant adjustments in product offerings resulting from constant changes in suppliers.

Facilitating Supply-Chain Collaboration

Collaboration in channel, or supply-chain, relations is facilitated by three important types of behavior and attitude. These are mutual trust, two-way communication, and solidarity.

Mutual Trust

Mutual trust occurs when the retailer trusts the supplier, and the supplier trusts the retailer. In continuing relations between retailers and suppliers, mutual trust, which is built on past and present performance between members, is critical. This trust allows short-term inequities to exist. If mutual trust is present, both parties will tolerate inequities because they know in the long term they will be fairly treated.[20] For example, a vendor suggests that a retailer purchase a certain product. The retailer does not believe that the product will be successful in its market. However, the vendor insists that many buyers in other markets are purchasing that particular item and even agrees to "make it good" if the product does not sell. In this instance, the buyer will probably buy the merchandise knowing that the supplier can be trusted to make an appropriate adjustment on the invoice amount, provide markdown money, or make up this inequity in some other way in the future if the product does not sell.

Without mutual trust, retail supply chains would disintegrate. On the other hand, when trust exists, it is contagious and allows the channel to grow and prosper. This occurs because of reciprocity. If a retailer trusts a supplier to do the right thing and the supplier treats the retailer fairly, then the retailer develops more trust and the process of mutual trust continues to build. In fact, during the past recession, many smaller or retailers. retailers were able to cut costs by renegotiating contract terms with manufacturers to match deals that the high-volume chains obtained. Here the manufacturers and smaller operators knew that they would need each other, further enhancing the trust between parties and allowing economic recovery to take place.

mutual trust
Occurs when both the retailer and its supplier have faith that each will be truthful and fair in their dealings with the other.

Two-Way Communication

two-way communication
Occurs when both retailer and supplier communicate openly their ideas, concerns, and plans.

As noted earlier, conflict is inevitable in retail supply chains. Consequently, two-way communication becomes the pathway for resolving disputes and allowing the channel relationship to continue. **Two-way communication** occurs when both parties openly communicate their ideas, concerns, and plans. Because of the interdependency of the retailer and supplier, two-way communication is necessary to coordinate actions. For example, when Jockey decides to run a national promotion on its underwear, it needs to coordinate this promotion with its retail supply chains so that when customers enter stores to shop for the nationally advertised items, they will find them displayed and in stock. Two-way communication is critical to accomplishing this coordination.

Communication is not independent of trust. Disputes can be resolved by good two-way communication, and this improves trust. Furthermore, trust facilitates open two-way communication. The process is circular and builds over time. For example, Walmart is not only phasing in energy-efficiency requirements with its suppliers but also pushing gold miners to adopt strict environmental and social standards, verified by independent third parties. With allies Tiffany's and Richline Group, the world's biggest manufacturer of gold jewelry, the retail giant is upsetting miners. However, since mining enough gold to make a typical 18-carat wedding ring leaves behind 20 tons of waste, it appears that two-way communication will demonstrate the benefits of such standards to all parties.[21]

Solidarity

solidarity
Exists when a high value is placed on the relationship between a supplier and retailer.

Solidarity exists when a high value is placed on the relationship between a supplier and a retailer.[22] Solidarity is an attitude and thus is hard to explicitly create. Essentially, as trust and two-way communication increase, a higher degree of solidarity develops. Solidarity results in flexible dealings where adaptations are made as circumstances change. When solidarity exists, each party will come to the rescue of the other in times of trouble. For example, several years ago, Walmart had a problem with shoplifting. It discovered that several Procter & Gamble products were easy to steal. Because of the relationship that existed between the retailer and supplier, P&G soon altered the packaging of the vulnerable products. Among the changes it made were enlarging and adding an extra layer of plastic to the Crest Whitestrips package and using a clamshell, a flat piece of cardboard covered with plastic, on its Oil of Olay products.[23] Another example of supply-chain partners working together to the benefit of each other recently occurred in the book-publishing industry. Here an industry practice dating from the 1930s allowed retailers to return unsold titles, which amounted to more than a third of all titles shipped, to publishers for full credit and without incurring shipping costs. Later these books were sent back to the same bookstore chains, where they are sold for a substantial discount on the list price. The idea of taking back inventory and then returning it wasn't a good idea for anybody. Meanwhile, as mentioned in Chapter 2, Borders Books was facing financial issues. Thus, as a sign of the industry's solidarity, the retailer agreed to accept books on a nonreturnable basis in return for a lower price. Experts were quoted as saying that the economic downturn has made publishers and booksellers more open to departing from tradition and willing to experiment with models that might decrease waste and increase profits for all parties.[24]

Nowhere is this collaboration in today's channels exhibited more clearly than in the shift toward category management.

Category Management[25]

Category management involves the simultaneous management of price, shelf-space, merchandising strategy, promotional efforts, and other elements of the retail mix within the merchandise category based on the firm's goals, the changing environment, and consumer behavior. The task of category management is accomplished by members of a supply chain working as a team, not acting independently, to apply the ECR concept to an entire category of merchandise such as all hand tools, and not just a particular brand such as Stanley. The manager's goal is to enable the retailer to meet specific business goals such as profitability, sales volume, or inventory levels.

Retailers designate a **category manager** from among their employees for each category sold. The retailer begins the process by defining specific business goals for each category. The category manager then leverages detailed knowledge of the consumer and consumer trends, detailed point-of-sale (POS) information, and specific analysis provided by each supplier to the category. With this information, the category manager creates specific modulars that may have different facings for different stores as the retailer tailors its offerings to the specific needs of each market. In addition, category managers work with suppliers to plan promotions throughout the year to achieve the designated business goals for the category.

In cases where the solidarity of the channel partners is high, a supplier may serve as the retailer's category manager. In this case, the chosen supplier takes on the designation of *category advisor*. Walmart, for example, uses this strategy wherein the category advisor works closely with the Walmart buyer to ensure that the category achieves peak performance in all stores. Normally, a supplier is chosen to become a category advisor because it is a trend leader in the specific category and can contribute merchandising and market analysis. Often, but not always, this supplier is also the dominant provider within the specific category. As each buyer has responsibility for several related product categories, each category may have a separate category advisor, depending on need. Further, while a supplier may be recognized as a trend leader in one category, a different supplier may be recognized as the trend leader in another.

At one point, category advisers were called *category captains*. While the responsibilities have not changed, retailers have adopted the new terminology (category advisors) to avoid speculation and confusion about who is responsible for making decisions. Also, to ensure fairness, the individual fulfilling the category advisor position is not supposed to have any sales relationships with Walmart. In fact, this person is not supposed to report to anyone with selling responsibility for Walmart. The category advisor receives access to the sales information for all items and suppliers in the designated category. To keep business confidentiality, advisors do not receive access to data on profitability. Also, they are not allowed to share the information with anyone in their company. Given these boundaries, the question arises, why would a vendor want to pay for the category advisor? Most companies would agree that the ability to better understand the retailer's merchandise direction (or thinking and strategy) is enough of a benefit to justify the cost. If you consider, for example, that Walmart purchases $200 million in greeting cards annually from Hallmark, you quickly see the economic logic of investing in a category advisor.

The category captain or category advisor, working closely with the retail buyer, must make sure that the retailer has the best assortment for each store in order to achieve the greatest sales possible. This includes carrying the competition's merchandise. As a result, the supplier's role as the category captain or category advisor

category management (CM)
Is a process of managing all SKUs within a product category and involves the simultaneous management of price, shelf-space, merchandising strategy, promotional efforts, and other elements of the retail mix within the category based on the firm's

category manager
the individual who uses detailed knowledge of the consumer and consumer trends, detailed point-of-sale (POS) information, and specific analysis provided by each supplier to the category to create various store displays based on local market conditions.

has changed greatly in recent years. Whereas in the past the supplier sought to get as many of its items into the retailer's store as possible, today that supplier has to understand how its products help the retailer achieve its objectives, even if this means selecting a competitor's product over its own. For retailers using a single advisor, a yearly review and possible reassignment of the advisor's role to another supplier helps to keep the category advisor's recommendations objective.

To survive strong competition from other retailers, advising suppliers must stay ahead of consumer trends and meet the ever-changing tastes of the consumer. To aid the supplier who serves as a category advisor, the retailer provides the same POS information (except the competition's prices) that it would give its own employee serving as the category manager.

Category managers must be ready to constantly adjust the space given to each item so that the right merchandise is in the right stores, at the right time, and in the right amount. Over the last decade, category management has enabled retailers to do a better job of staying in stock on the best-selling items and avoid being overstocked on merchandise with a lower turnover rate. The category manager must be able to recognize what critical items need to remain in stock at all times to make the assortment complete. In addition, as will be explained in Chapter 13, the category manager tries to create a shelf layout based on how the consumer shops.

Retailers, however, are far from passive when it comes to accepting a supplier's recommendation. They usually run the supplier's category plan by a second supplier known as the *validator*. Thus, Unilever, for example, could run a reality check for supermarkets using Procter & Gamble as their category advisor or captain. Even more important, retailers must insist that category advisors adhere to the retailer's strategy with regard to pricing, promotions, and so on.

Category management is now standard practice at nearly every U.S. supermarket, convenience store, mass merchant, and drug chain. Its use is growing because the results of this collaboration benefit both retailer and supplier. Retailers using category management report an increase in sales for both parties, a decrease in markdowns, better in-stock percentages on key items for the retailer, an increase in turnover rates and a decrease in average inventory for both retailers and wholesalers, and an increase in both members' ROI and profit.

However, when all retailers begin to use the same category management approach to optimize each store's layout and maximize the gross margin dollars produced per unit of space, many times stores end up looking just like their competitors. This is why Walmart replaced the "captain" with "advisors" so that they could gain the benefits of different approaches.

SUMMARY

LO 1

What is the retailer's role as a member of the larger supply chain?

In reality, it is the retailer's supply chain, rather than its outlet, that competes against other retailers. If the retailer ignores the supply chain in order to maximize short-run profits, then in the long run the chain will work against the retailer. If the supply chain overlooks the retailer, then profits sufficient for survival and growth will vanish. In learning to work within the supply chain, the retailer needs to recognize the eight marketing functions necessary in all marketing channels: buying, selling, storing, transporting, sorting, financing, information gathering, and risk taking. The retailer can seldom perform all eight functions and therefore must rely on other primary and facilitating institutions in the supply chain. Although marketing functions occur throughout the supply chain, they can be shifted or divided in different ways among the institutions in the marketing supply chain.

What are the different types of retail supply chains?

LO 2

Supply chains can be arranged by length, width, and control. Length is concerned with the number of primary marketing institutions in the chain. The supply chain or channel is said to be direct if it involves only the manufacturer and the consumer. An indirect channel adds either a retailer or a wholesaler or both to the supply chain. The channel's width measures the number of retailers handling the product in a given trading area.

Control looks at the two primary marketing channel patterns—conventional and vertical. A conventional marketing channel is one in which each member of the supply chain is loosely aligned with the others, each member recognizing only those it directly interacts with and ignoring all others. Conventional marketing channels are on the decline in the United States, while vertical marketing channels are becoming dominant. In the vertical marketing channel, all parties to the supply chain recognize each other, and one member programs the supply chain to achieve technological, managerial, and promotional economies. The three types of vertical marketing channels are corporate, contractual, and administered.

How do dependency, power, and conflict influence supply-chain relations?

LO 3

In order to operate efficiently and effectively in any marketing supply chain, the retailer must depend on other channel members for assistance. When a retailer becomes highly dependent on other channel members, the other channel members gain power over the retailer. However, other channel members (manufacturers and wholesalers) also depend on the retailer, resulting in interdependency and a sharing of power. Although power and interdependency can lead to conflict, they are more likely to create a high desire for cooperative relationships.

Why is collaboration so important in supply chains today?

LO 4

Because all supply chains experience some degree of conflict, most supply chains today seek to resolve it by using some form of collaboration. Collaboration is necessary and beneficial because of the interdependency of the members and because most retailers and suppliers must nurture a partnership if they want to deal with each other on a long-term basis. This is the only way to perform the marketing functions effectively and efficiently for the benefit of the consumer.

Category management is one of the ways collaboration is used in supply chains today. Category management, where an entire category is managed as a unit, involves the simultaneous management of price, shelf-space merchandising strategy, promotional efforts, and other elements of the retail mix within the category based on the firm's goals, the changing environment, and consumer behavior.

TERMS TO REMEMBER

supply chain
channel
primary marketing institutions
facilitating marketing institutions

public warehouse
direct supply chain
indirect supply chains
intensive distribution

selective distribution	referent power
exclusive distribution	coercive power
conventional marketing channel	legitimate power
vertical marketing channels	informational power
quick response (QR) systems	perceptual incongruity
stock-keeping unit (SKU)	goal incompatibility
corporate vertical marketing channels	dual distribution
contractual vertical marketing channels	domain disagreements
wholesaler-sponsored voluntary groups	diverter
retailer-owned cooperatives	gray marketing
franchise	free riding
administered vertical marketing channels	mutual trust
dependency	two-way communication
power	solidarity
reward power	category management
expertise power	category manager

REVIEW AND DISCUSSION QUESTIONS

LO 1 **What is the retailer's role as a member of the larger supply chain?**

1. Why must a retailer view itself as a member of a larger marketing system? Can't JCPenney's, Costco, or Best Buy be successful on its own?
2. Must a retailer be involved in performing all the marketing functions? If it can rely on other members of the channel, what functions can they perform and which members can perform them?
3. Facilitating marketing institutions, since they don't take title to the goods, add no value to a supply chain. Agree or disagree with this statement and explain your reasoning.

LO 2 **What are the different types of retail supply chains?**

4. For years, Dell was known for selling its computers directly to the consumer. Then it started selling them at Walmart and Best Buy. A classmate contends, "Selling through a middleman is only going to squeeze margins as the retailers demand lower prices. Besides the retailers have to make a profit for themselves." Isn't this clear evidence that a direct supply chain is always the best way to reach a consumer? Agree or disagree and explain your reasoning.
5. Your roommate says he can save money by eliminating the middleman—in this case, the retailer—and purchasing his potato chips at Costco in 8-pound boxes. He says you pay too much by purchasing chips at the nearby 7-Eleven in 4-ounce bags. According to your roommate, the more direct the channel is, the cheaper the item. Who is correct?
6. What is a vertical marketing channel? What is the primary difference between a conventional marketing channel and a vertical marketing channel?

LO 3 **How do dependency, power, and conflict influence supply-chain relations?**

7. You are a manufacturer of a popular consumer product that is sold through independent retailers and some department store chains. Today a large big-box chain approaches you and wants to carry your line. What should you do? How will this affect your relationship with your current retailers?

8. Agree or disagree with the following statement and support your answer. "Retailers should always oppose attempts by the manufacturer to sell its products directly to the consumer from the manufacturer's Web site."

9. Should it be legal for a manufacturer to prevent a discount retailer from purchasing the manufacturer's name-brand products from a diverter and selling these in the discounter's store?

10. Why are retailers so dependent on other supply-chain members? Couldn't they simply perform all eight marketing functions themselves?

Why is collaboration so important in supply chains today?   LO 4

11. Why is trust so important in a supply chain? Can't the largest and most powerful member of the supply chain simply tell the others what to do?

12. With the advent of category management, how has the role of the supplier changed?

SAMPLE TEST QUESTIONS

Facilitating institutions may best be described as specialists that: LO 1

a. take title but not possession of the merchandise.
b. take title to the merchandise in order to facilitate the transaction.
c. manage the supply chain so as to increase overall efficiency above 100 percent.
d. facilitate the transaction by performing all eight marketing functions.
e. perform certain marketing functions in which they have an expertise for the other supply-chain members.

A supply chain in which each member is loosely aligned with the others is a: LO 2

a. highly efficient supply chain.
b. contractual channel.
c. supply chain capable of achieving 100-percent efficiency.
d. supply chain based on the ideals of cooperation and partnership.
e. conventional marketing channel.

The basic root of all conflict in a supply chain is: LO 3

a. each member wants all the power.
b. each member is dependent on the other members of the supply chain.
c. each member is fully capable of performing all eight marketing functions.
d. partnership agreements tend to expire after a year.
e. everybody wants to work independently of the other members.

The key to efficient supply-chain management and the minimization of conflict is: LO 4

a. considering all members as part of the same team and collaborating with each other.
b. letting the retailer run the supply chain.
c. never using coercive power.
d. allowing all members to make at least a 10-percent profit.
e. allowing the manufacturer to make all the decisions.

WRITING AND SPEAKING EXERCISE

Diva's is a 55-store upscale women's shoe chain targeting businesswomen and college students. Most of its stores are located in regional malls in the Southeast and Southwest. The chain has enjoyed rapid growth over the last decade, and its annual sales volume last year was $167 million. Profitability has kept pace with the rapid rise in sales volume.

Diva's prices most of its shoes between $39.95 and $109.95. The top-selling shoes are sold using the chain's private label, Avalanche. A primary reason for the success of Diva's has been its vertical marketing channel. The chain has eliminated most suppliers and relies almost entirely on its own production capabilities. Diva's staff designs most of the shoes and has them made to specification by manufacturers in Mexico.

As a result, the chain's shoes are priced approximately 20 percent lower than competitors' shoes of a similar quality. In addition, the chain has a higher markup than stores that buy from manufacturers and wholesalers. Besides these advantages, vertical integration minimizes potential sources of conflict.

This strategy does have its weaknesses, though. Diva's needs a large amount of capital. Money is needed to purchase raw materials and to defray other costs incurred during manufacture. In addition, since orders are placed approximately nine months to a year in advance of shoe sales, predicting sales is difficult. If orders are placed with manufacturers and business slows down, orders cannot be reduced or canceled. Because they control production, orders cannot be changed. Finally, slow-moving merchandise cannot be returned to vendors. If something does not sell, it has to be marked down in hopes that it will.

Using this strategy, how would the retailer's need for capital affect its ROI during an economic slowdown? (The student might want to refer to the strategic profit model discussed in Chapter 2.) In view of your answer, should the chain change its merchandise mix by adding more well-known national brands?

RETAIL PROJECT

In Chapter 4, we discussed divertive competition and introduced the topic of the breakeven point (BEP), or the point where total revenues equal total expenses. Let's see how this topic will help us determine whether to join a franchise or stay independent.

Assume that you own a sandwich shop. In looking over last year's income statement, you see that the annual sales were $250,000 with a gross margin of 50 percent, or $125,000. The fixed operating expenses were $50,000; the variable operating expenses were 20 percent of sales, or $50,000; and your profit was $25,000, or 10 percent of sales.

In discussions with your spouse, you wonder if joining a franchise operation such as Subway or Blimpie would improve your results. Your research has determined that Subway requires a $10,000 licensing fee in addition to an 8-percent royalty on sales and a 2.5-percent advertising fee on sales. Blimpie, while requiring an $18,000 licensing fee, charges only a 6-percent royalty and a 3-percent advertising fee.

Assuming that you wanted to break even, what amount of sales would you have to generate with each channel during the first year, since both your fixed and variable expenses would increase?

Remember, the BEP is where gross margin equals total operating expenses; in equation form, this is:

Gross Margin = Fixed Operating Expenses + Variable Operating Expenses

Thus, with Subway, your fixed expenses would increase from $50,000 to $60,000, and your variable expenses would increase from 20 percent of sales to 30.5 percent (20% + 8% + 2.5%). Blimpie's would increase fixed expenses by $18,000 and variable expenses by 9 percent. Using the equation, we can calculate the BEP for both.

Subway's BEP:

$$50\% \text{ (net sales)} = \$60,000 + 30.5\% \text{ (net sales)}$$
$$\text{Net sales} = \$307,692$$

Blimpie's BEP:

$$50\% \text{ (net sales)} = \$68,000 + 29\% \text{ (net sales)}$$
$$\text{Net sales} = \$323,809$$

As a result of the increased franchisee expenses, you would have to increase sales more than 20 percent just to break even. To make the same profit you are already making, you would have to add that profit figure to the equation:

Gross Margin = Fixed Operating Expenses + Variable Operating Expenses + Profit

Subway's BEP with a $25,000 profit:

$$50\% \text{ (net sales)} = \$60,000 + 30.5\% \text{ (net sales)} + \$25,000$$
$$\text{Net sales} = \$435,897$$

Blimpie's BEP with a $25,000 profit:

$$50\% \text{ (net sales)} = \$68,000 + 29\% \text{ (net sales)} + \$25,000$$
$$\text{Net sales} = \$442,857$$

Thus, to keep the same profit that you currently make, a franchise would have to help you increase sales by more than 75 percent. There is no doubt the image of the franchise will draw additional customers, and its management may even help cut some of your other expenses. However, as these numbers point out, joining a franchise channel is not always a surefire guarantee of success.

Now, by using either a franchise directory in the library (e.g., the International Franchise Association at www.franchise.org) or a franchisor's home page on the Internet, look up two competing franchise channels in the same line of retail trade. After locating the information about these franchises, do the same cost analysis we just did and determine if, based on these figures, joining a franchise is a good investment.

PLANNING YOUR OWN BUSINESS

Upon graduation, you decide that you wish to get in on the ground floor of the e-tailing revolution and develop your own online business. You decide that a large opportunity exists in providing private-label apparel to a niche segment of Generation Y consumers. In the process of planning your business, your preliminary sales forecasts lead you to believe that your first year's sales will be $500,000. You have identified two major manufacturers that can make the merchandise you want to sell online. One manufacturer is in a distant city and is able to promise seven-day delivery on orders of more than $5,000. The second manufacturer is located only 80 miles away and provides next-day delivery on orders of more than $500 placed by 1 P.M. Unfortunately, the nearby manufacturer has slightly higher prices. Consequently, you estimate that by purchasing through this source your gross margin would be 41 percent versus 43 percent by purchasing from the more distant manufacturer. However, because the nearby manufacturer is able to provide more frequent and smaller deliveries, you estimate that your average inventory would be $25,000 versus $30,000 if you used the more distant manufacturer as a supply source. Each manufacturer sells on terms of 2 percent/10 net 30. This means that if the invoice is paid within 10 days, a 2-percent discount can be taken; if not, the net invoice is due within 30 days. Which supply source should you select? (*Hint:* Compute the gross margin return on inventory investment, which is defined as the gross margin dollars divided by average inventory investment.)

Legal and Ethical Behavior

OVERVIEW:

In this chapter, we discuss how the legal and ethical environment influences retailers' decision making. The discussion covers the legal aspects of decisions made on pricing, promotion (including the use of credit), products or merchandise, and marketing supply chains. The chapter concludes with a discussion of the major ethical decisions facing the retailer today.

LEARNING OBJECTIVES:

After reading this chapter, you should be able to:

1. Explain how legislation constrains a retailer's pricing policies.
2. Differentiate between legal and illegal promotional activities.
3. Explain the retailer's responsibilities regarding the products sold.
4. Discuss the impact of government regulation on a retailer's behavior with other supply-chain members.
5. Describe how various state and local laws, in addition to federal regulations, must be considered in developing retail policies.
6. Explain how a retailer's code of ethics will influence its behavior.

In addition to studying the changing consumer (Chapter 3), competition (Chapter 4), and the supply-chain environment (Chapter 5), retailers must also monitor the legal environment. Many large retailers operate in several states, where local laws and regulations often differ from state to state. As a result, most large retailers maintain legal departments and lobbyists to keep abreast of, interpret, and even influence government regulations. The same can be said for retailers who operate in more than one country. Such activities, though, are usually beyond the resources of small businesses. Yet governments and the business media do a reasonably good job of keeping all retailers informed of pending and new legislation. In addition, retailer associations such as the National Retail Federation (NRF) operate in every state in the United States, as well as most major countries, and work to keep retailers informed of proposed changes in state laws while seeking to protect retailers' interests. Interested readers might want to visit the Federal Trade Commission's (FTC's) website (www.ftc.gov) to review some basic primers on various activities related to the United States that will be discussed in this chapter.

We will now explore the final set of external constraints that affect retail decision making: the legal and ethical environment. These forces are shown in

Exhibit 6.1. After reviewing Exhibit 6.1, consider how retailers were affected with the passage of each of the following new regulations:

■ The U.S. Food and Drug Administration, seeking to cut down on underage smoking, required a photo ID from any person appearing to be younger than 18 years of age and wanting to buy cigarettes or smokeless tobacco.

■ Passage of various state and local laws that prevent smoking in public places, especially restaurants and bars.

■ Regulations in most states concerning the sale of over-the-counter cold medicines containing pseudoephedrine, an ingredient used in the illegal manufacture of methamphetamine, or crystal meth.

■ Cities that have "sign ordinances" regulating retailers' use of billboards and even the signage on retailers' buildings.

■ Restrictions involving retailers' use of product samples.

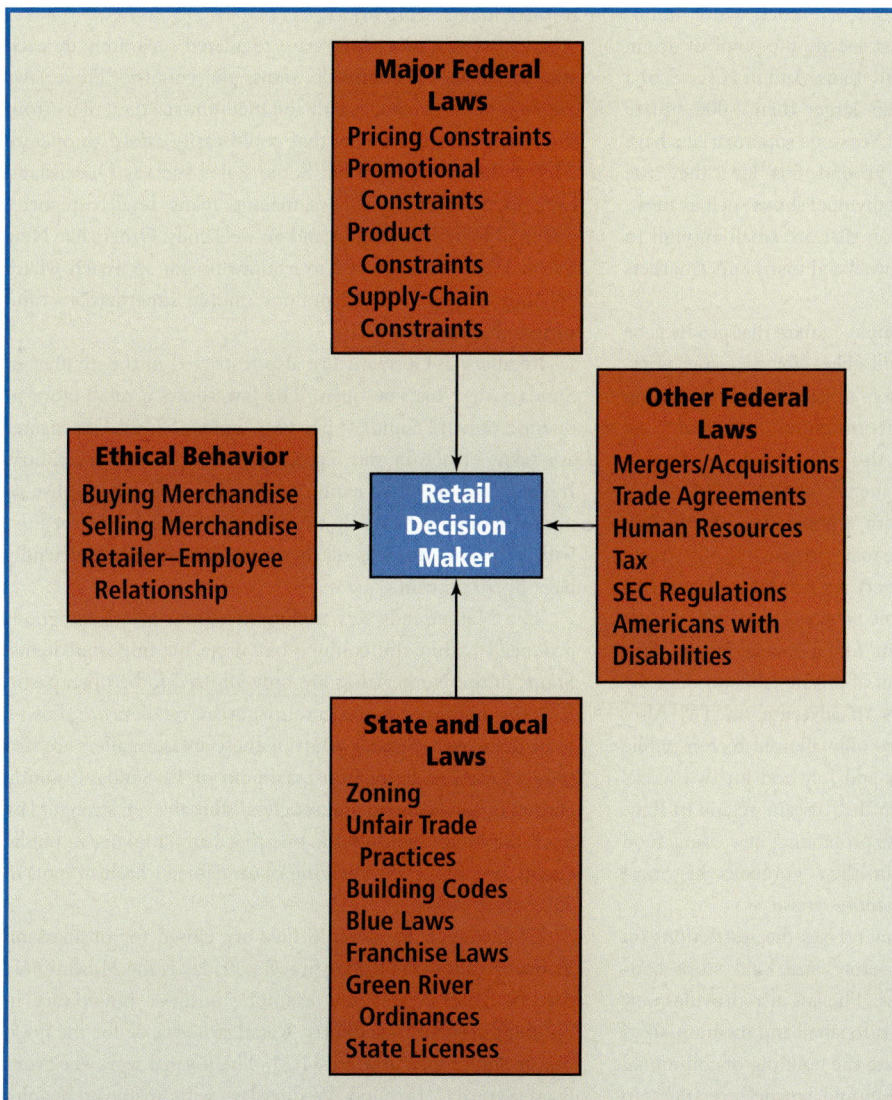

Exhibit 6.1
Ethical and Legal Constraints Influencing Retailers

Global Retailing

For Americans, International Laws Can Be Strange

Each nation's legal system reflects and reinforces its brand of capitalism—predatory in the United States, paternal in Germany, and protected in Japan—and its social values. As a result of these different philosophies, government regulations in foreign nations can sometimes be confusing for retailers. In fact, regulations can even be different in various regions of the same country. For example, Scotland, although part of the United Kingdom, has been more liberal when regulating retailers on issues such as Sunday openings.

Consider some of the laws currently enforced in Canada. Quebec, a province that is 80 percent French-speaking, only allows English on commercial signs if French words dominate. Textiles sold in Canada must specify the point of origin and the contents, or makeup, of all items. And in Nova Scotia there are laws preventing retailers larger than 4,000 square feet from being open on Sundays. Yet some supermarkets have come up with a creative way around this law; they use temporary barriers to split into individual shops such as meat, health, and beauty aids, and so on that are small enough to operate on Sundays. Thus, each weekend many supermarkets turn into minimalls.

Regulations in France, for example, require that products be sold to all retailers—big and small alike—for the same price, thus making it tough for discounters to get any kind of pricing advantage. Discounters have circumvented these rules by offering private-label products. Also, the size of a store in France is limited to 1,000 square meters (almost 11,000 square feet) when operating in a city with a population of less than 40,000. If the city is larger, the size may increase to 1,500 square meters (just over 16,000 square feet). French law also protects manufacturers of major brand-name products in several ways. It permits a three-year prison term for shoppers buying fake products and limits the penetration of private-label products by not allowing French distributors to advertise on TV. Also, under French law, retail stores are only allowed to run public sales for several weeks in January and July and for two weeks sometime during the year. Over in the Tuscany region of Italy, some city councils have passed laws prohibiting new ethnic food restaurants from opening within their gorgeous historical centers. So much for fast food in those cities.

A recently enacted Korean law relaxes the restrictions on store-registration qualifications, store size, and store construction for large discount stores. The law also provides new financial or administrative support to small and medium-sized distribution businesses to stimulate the building of communal logistic centers. Also, both Korean and Japanese retailers, in an attempt to protect the environment from imprudent business developments, must conduct an environmental impact report when building within a city's green zones.

A Norwegian law allows only small food stores (less than 100 square meters) to be open nights and weekends. It also permits gas stations and video stores to offer grocery items. As a result, many larger stores close down most of their store area after 9 P.M. and only keep a 100-square-meter area open. The justification for this regulation is twofold: (1) It allows mom-and-pop shops to survive, and (2) it limits the cost of operation for larger food stores that would probably be forced to offer longer store hours.

In Australia, store hours are regulated separately by each state, resulting in confusion across the country. These laws are designed to protect small and medium-sized retailers from the larger category killers that could easily afford to operate 24/7 if the laws permitted. Some states such as Queensland have highly restrictive laws making many retail categories unavailable in the evenings and on weekends. Others like New South Wales have moved to a more liberal approach where 24-hour shopping is common among supermarkets and variety discount stores.

Retailers in Germany are also restricted in the number of Sundays they may be open. The law allows a retail store to operate only 12 Sundays per year, unless World Cup games are taking place in the region. Another European country, Ireland, was the first nation to impose a tax on the use of plastic shopping bags. By the way, this 2002 law is credited with reducing the use of these environmentally unfriendly bags by 90 percent.

The Netherlands sets minimum selling prices for goods produced within the country but none for imported items. Shops in the Netherlands are only allowed to be open past 6 P.M. one night per week. In tourist areas, retailers are allowed to be open every Sunday. Outside these areas, retailers are also only allowed to be open a maximum of 12 Sundays (jointly chosen by government and retailers). But an even stranger law from the Netherlands is the one that bans smoking in public venues but allows the smoking of cannabis or hashish (pot) in 730 coffee shops.

Countries in the Middle East are closed for business on Fridays to allow for Friday prayers. Friday is the Muslim holy day. In Saudi Arabia, for example, business hours vary in different parts of the country. Retail stores close for the noon prayer and reopen around 4 P.M. The normal workweek runs from Saturday through Wednesday, with many companies

Global Retailing (continued)

required to take a half or full day off on Thursdays. The sale of alcohol is banned in Saudi Arabia, and any kind of advertising that doesn't show women conservatively dressed is also prohibited.

A final country to consider is India, where only 4 percent of its 15 million retail establishments (a number 15 times greater than in the United States) are more than 500 square feet in size. Only recently has India relaxed some of its laws aimed at protecting these small retailers because the government is afraid that removing its ban on foreign direct investment would enable Walmart and its British and French counterparts, Tesco and Carrefour, to open efficient large operations and close millions of the small retail shops.

Clearly, while it is probably more difficult to open and operate retail outlets in these other countries than in the United States, it is still easier to open a branch bank in most countries than in all but a few states in the United States. However, this is rapidly changing as more and more banks are merging, thus forcing branch banking. In addition, an international retailer seeking to open a store in the United States must be prepared for some of our own unusual local laws. For example, a law in Kansas City allows the sale of shotguns, but not cap guns, to children.

Source: This is based on current information supplied by Jack Hartog, Hanze University; John Fernie, Heriot-Watt University; Sigurd Troye, Norwegian School of Economics and Business Administration; Charles Areni, University of Sydney; Sejin Ha, Purdue University; Lynne Ricker, University of Calgary; and "A Walled City in Tuscany Clings to Its Ancient Menu," *New York Times*, March 13, 2009: A6; "Paris Goes on Sale," *New York Times*, January 4, 2009: TR 4; "Seattle Takes Aim at Plastic Bags," *Shopping Centers Today*, September 2008: 11, 13; "What Are the Dutch Smoking?" *BusinessWeek*, June 30, 2008: 18; "Prying Open European Pharmacies," *New York Times*, September 25, 2007: C1, C9; "Special Report: Retailing in India," *The Economist*, April 15, 2006: 69 71; "Europe Still Divided by Sunday Shopping Conundrum," *Shopping Centers Today*, April 2006: 60 62; and "As Luxury Industry Goes Global, Knock-Off Merchants Follow," *Wall Street Journal*, January 31, 2006: A1, A13.

All these laws affect retailers' ability to serve the needs and wants of their target markets. In addition, ethical issues influence retailers' decisions.

To avoid costly blunders, the retailer needs to understand the potential legal and ethical constraints that exist within not only each country but also each city and state in which it operates. Some of the philosophical concepts used in developing laws and regulations in other countries are described in this chapter's "Global Retailing" box. In fact, as the box indicates, the differences in the laws of each nation can drive global retailers crazy. However, they also present some interesting opportunities for the retailer who is alert enough to take advantage of the situation.

Due to the myriad of country-specific laws as illustrated in the "Global Retailing" box, this chapter will deal primarily with various federal constraints that can affect a retailer's decision-making process when it comes to pricing, promotion, products, and supply-chain relationships in the United States. However, due to their sheer number, we will not be able to discuss all of the other federal laws that impact retailers. Also, since state and local laws are quite varied and often more complex, we make only general comments on a few of them. For the most part, we leave it up to you and your classmates to discuss and investigate the impact of state and local laws on retail activities in your state or community.

As Exhibit 6.2 points out, most federal laws affecting retailing seek to "promote competition." These fall into several categories. First, the Sherman Antitrust Act, the Clayton Act, the Federal Trade Commission Act, the Celler-Kefauver Anti-merger Act, and the Hart-Scott-Rodino Act were passed to ensure a "competitive" business climate. Second, the Robinson-Patman Act was designed to regulate pricing practices. Third, the Wheeler-Lea Amendment was created to control false advertising. Although some people may question whether all these regulations are bleeding the economy dry, many others believe that they sometimes boost competitiveness. Other laws have been passed to protect consumers and innocent third parties. A sampling of these consumer protection laws is shown in Exhibit 6.3.

Legislation	Impact on Retailing
Sherman Act, 1890	Bans (1) "monopolies or attempts to monopolize" and (2) "contracts, combinations, or conspiracies in restraint of trade" in interstate and foreign commerce.
Clayton Act, 1914	Adds to the Sherman Act by prohibiting specific practices (e.g., certain types of price discrimination, tying clauses) "whereas the effect . . . may be to substantially lessen competition or tend to create a monopoly in any line of commerce."
Federal Trade Commission Act, 1914	Establishes the Federal Trade Commission, a body of specialists with broad powers to investigate and to issue cease-and-desist orders to enforce Section 5, which declares that "unfair methods of competition in commerce are unlawful."
Robinson-Patman Act, 1936	Amends the Clayton Act, adds the phrase "to injure, destroy, or prevent competition." Defines price discrimination as unlawful (subject to certain defenses) and provides the FTC with the right to establish limits on quantity discounts, to forbid brokerage allowances except to independent brokers, and to ban promotional allowances or the furnishing of services or facilities except when made available to all "on proportionately equal terms."
Wheeler-Lea Amendment to the FTC Act, 1938	Prohibits unfair and deceptive acts and practices regardless of whether competition is injured.
Lanham Act, 1946	Establishes protection for trademarks.
Celler-Kefauver Antimerger Act, 1950	Amends Section 7 of the Clayton Act by broadening the power to prevent corporate acquisitions where the acquisition may have a substantially adverse effect on competition.
Hart-Scott-Rodino Act, 1976	Requires large companies to notify the government of their intent to merge.

Exhibit 6.2
Primary U.S. Laws that
Affect Retailing

Legislative Action	Examples of Laws Designed to Protect Consumers
Mail Fraud Act, 1872	Makes it a federal crime to defraud consumers through use of the mail.
Pure Food & Drug Act, 1906	Regulates interstate commerce in misbranded and adulterated foods, drinks, and drugs.
Flammable Fabrics Act, 1953	Prohibits interstate shipments of flammable apparel or material.
Automobile Information Disclosure Act, 1958	Requires auto manufacturers to post suggested retail prices on new cars.
Fair Packaging and Labeling Act, 1966	Regulates packaging and labeling; establishes uniform sizes.
Child Safety Act, 1966	Prevents the marketing and selling of harmful toys and dangerous products.
Truth in Lending Act, 1968	Requires lenders to state the true costs of a credit transaction; established a National Commission on Consumer Finance.
Fair Credit Report Act, 1970	Regulates the reporting and use of credit information; limits consumer liability for stolen credit cards to $50.
Consumer Product Safety Act, 1972	Created the Consumer Product Safety Commission.
Magnuson-Moss Warranty/ FTC Improvement Act, 1975	Empowers the FTC to determine rules concerning consumer warranties and provides for consumer access to means of redress, such as the "class action" suit; expands FTC regulatory powers over unfair or deceptive acts or practices.
Equal Credit Opportunity Act, 1975	Prohibits discrimination in credit transactions because of gender, marital status, race, national origin, religion, age, or receipt of public assistance.

Exhibit 6.3
Examples of Laws
Designed to Protect
Consumers

Note that all aspects of retailing—price, promotion, product, and supply chains—are regulated. We will begin our discussion by looking at pricing regulations.

Pricing Constraints

Retailers continuously establish prices for the many items they sell. Pricing laws also influence retailers in determining what price they should pay for a product. In making these decisions retailers have considerable, but not total, flexibility. The major constraining factors are summarized in Exhibit 6.4.

Horizontal Price Fixing

Horizontal price fixing occurs when a group of competing retailers establishes a fixed price at which to sell certain brands of products. For example, all retail grocers in a particular trade area may agree to sell a specified brand of eggnog at $2.49 a quart during the Christmas season. Regardless of its actual or potential impact on competition or the consumer, this price fixing by the retailers would violate Section 1 of the Sherman Antitrust Act, which states that "every contract, combination in the form of trust or otherwise, or conspiracy, in restraint of trade or commerce among the several states, or with foreign nations is declared to be illegal."[1] It is also illegal for retailers to reach agreements with one another regarding the use of double (or triple) coupons, rebates, or other means of reducing price competition in the marketplace.

Occasionally, retailers have argued that the Sherman Act does not apply to them, since they operate locally and not "among the several states," the definition of interstate commerce. However, because the merchandise that retailers purchase typically originates in another state, the courts view retailers as involved in interstate commerce even if all their customers are local. Also, most states have laws similar to the Sherman Act, prohibiting such restraints of trade as horizontal price fixing on a strictly local level.

horizontal price fixing
Occurs when a group of competing retailers (or other channel members operating at a given level of distribution) establishes a fixed price at which to sell certain brands of products.

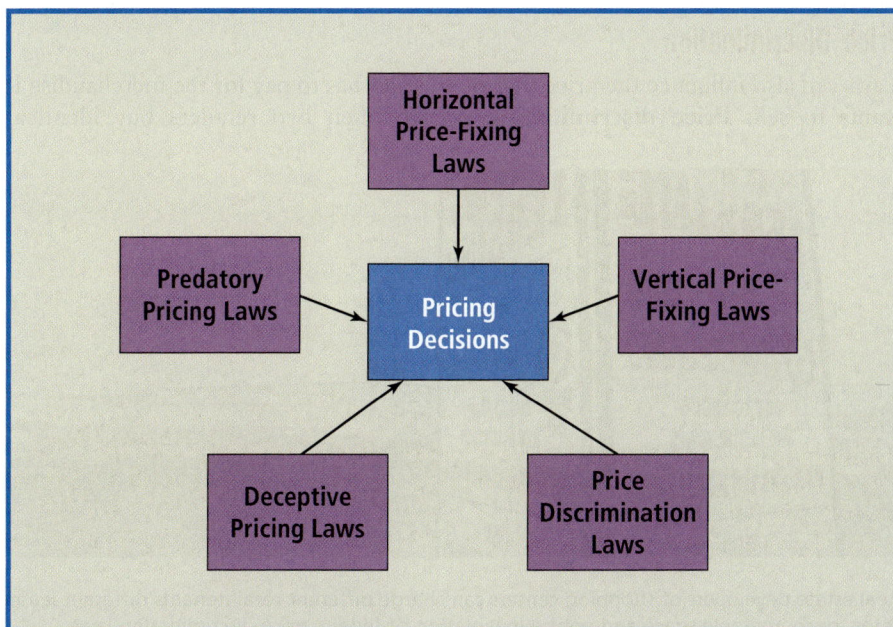

Exhibit 6.4
Pricing Constraints

Vertical Price Fixing

vertical price fixing
Occurs when a retailer collaborates with the manufacturer or wholesaler to resell an item at an agreed upon price.

Vertical price fixing occurs when a retailer collaborates with the manufacturer or wholesaler to resell an item at an agreed-upon price. This is also often referred to as *resale price maintenance* or *fair trade*. Until recently, these agreements were considered illegal and were viewed as a violation of Section 1 of the Sherman Act. However, a 2007 Supreme Court ruling involving handbag sales at a Dallas mom-and-pop store upended that original 1911 precedent, and it potentially could alter the face of U.S. discount retailing. The Court ruled that a "rule of reason" standard should apply to such agreements, weighing their anticompetitive effects against their benefits. The justices felt that allowing manufacturers to require minimum retail prices could lead retailers to offer better customer service such as honoring warranties. Manufacturers also argued that if a small retailer is protected against discount competition, then the retailer has more of an incentive to invest in a highly trained sales force. Without such protection, the store owner would face a free-rider problem, which was discussed in the previous chapter, whereby consumers learn about the great new product at a local store, then go home and buy it over the Internet.

Proponents acknowledge that the lack of resale price maintenance limits intrabrand competition (competition among retailers selling the same brand). However, since the repeal gives retailers incentives to compete on a nonprice basis, these advocates expect that interbrand competition (competition among retailers selling different brands) will increase. After all, they claim that this is what antitrust laws were set up to do.

Thus, if consumers are slaves to fashion, this ruling may deprive them of some discount channels for buying the hottest brands. But the ruling should make it easier for an upstart brand to challenge the entrenched competitors.[2]

It's important to note that the Supreme Court doesn't give a blanket blessing to resale price maintenance. Manufacturers must prove that its use has a procompetition motive and isn't, for example, designed to prop up a certain group of stores or to hinder others such as discounters or Internet retailers.

The chapter's "Retailing: The Inside Story" box describes the history of price fixing.

Price Discrimination

price discrimination
Occurs when two retailers buy an identical amount of "like grade and quality" merchandise from the same supplier but pay different prices.

Laws can also influence the price that the retailer has to pay for the merchandise it wants to sell. **Price discrimination** occurs when two retailers buy identical

J. Pat Carter/AP Photo

Real estate developers of shopping centers can charge different retail tenants different lease rates for comparable space and not be in violation of federal price discrimination laws.

Retailing: The Inside Story

Price Fixing in the United States

Despite the existence of laws against price fixing prior to the Supreme Court's 2007 ruling in *Leegin Creative Leather Products, Inc., v. PSKS, Inc.*, manufacturers could recommend to retailers a price at which they would like to see an item sold, but they could not establish a price at which the retailer must sell the product. However, manufacturers got around this by having retailers sign "co-op" advertising agreements. In such cases, when the manufacturer gives the retailer advertising money, the retailer may be required to sell the item at a specific price. Without a co-op agreement, manufacturers could not legally threaten retailers with supply cutoffs if they did not sell at the recommended price.

According to most retailers, the 2007 case challenged one of antitrust law's oldest and most unreasonable doctrines. This was laid down in 1911 by the *Dr. Miles Medical Co. v. John D. Park & Son* decision, which said that resale price maintenance (RPM) agreements are illegal per se—a blanket condemnation without regard for circumstances. The presumption was that a price floor was simply a means of suppressing competition and gouging consumers. Despite criticism from businesspeople, economists, and lawyers, the rule survived until the Great Depression when Congress passed a law allowing RPMs, which actually made a previously illegal act (the fixing of a price) legal. These agreements were established as a means for small retailers to combat the price advantages of the chain

stores during the depression of the 1930s. These agreements were finally banned in 1976.[3]

Then a dispute occurred between Leegin Creative Leather Products, a California manufacturer of women's fashion accessories, and Kay's Kloset, a Dallas-area boutique. Leegin stopped shipping its products to Kay's Kloset because the store was selling them below a company-mandated price. PSKS, the parent company of Kay's Kloset, filed an antitrust suit against Leegin in 2002, and this was finally resolved in 2007.[4]

Today, most retailers are opposed to the recent Supreme Court's ruling and fear that it could put them out of business because an array of manufacturers are already requiring them to abide by minimum-pricing pacts or risk having their supplies cut off. Jacob Weiss of BabyAge.com, which specializes in maternity and children's gear, reported that nearly 100 of his 465 suppliers within the first year dictated minimum prices, and nearly a dozen others have cut off shipments to him. "If this continues, it's going to put us out of the baby business," he said. As a result, BabyAge is now suing about a half-dozen major baby-gear makers and retailers alleging price collusion.[5]

As a result of this turmoil, a bill has been introduced by Sen. Herb Kohl (D-Wisconsin), a member of the family that founded the Kohl's Department Store chain, which would make retail-price maintenance agreements illegal once again.[6]

---

amounts of "like grade and quality" merchandise from the same supplier but pay different prices. However, these laws do not mean that the retailer cannot sell identical products—for example, a new car—to two different customers at different prices. These laws are meant to protect competition by making sure that the retailers are treated fairly by suppliers.

Not all forms of price discrimination are illegal, however. Federal legislation addressed the legality of price discrimination in the Clayton Act, which made *certain forms* of price discrimination illegal. The Clayton Act was amended and strengthened by the passage of the Robinson-Patman Act. The latter act had two primary objectives: (1) to prevent suppliers from attempting to gain an unfair advantage over their competitors by discrimination among buyers either in price or in providing allowances or services and (2) to prevent buyers from using their economic power to gain discriminatory prices from suppliers so as to gain an advantage over their own competitors.

For price discrimination to be considered illegal, it must meet two conditions. First, the transaction must occur in interstate commerce. Trade between states, which is the definition of interstate commerce, covers all retailers because the items they produce or market generally originate in another state. Second, while competition does not actually have to be lessened, the potential for a substantial lessening of competition must exist. In addition, the act provides that any buyer who knowingly receives the benefit of discrimination is just as guilty as the supplier granting the discrimination.

Considerable attention has been given to the phrase "commodities of like grade and quality." What does this phrase mean? To begin with, commodities are goods and not services. This implies that discriminatory pricing practices in the sale of advertising space or the leasing of real estate are not prohibited by the act. For example, shopping center and mall developers frequently charge varying rates for equivalent square footage, depending on the tenant, the type of merchandise to be sold, and its ability to draw customers to the center.

"Like grade and quality" has been interpreted by the courts to mean identical physical and chemical properties. This implies that different prices cannot be justified merely because the labels on the product are different. Therefore, private labeling of merchandise does not make it different from identical goods carrying the seller's brand. However, if the seller can demonstrate that an actual physical difference in grade and quality exists, then a differential in price can be justified.

The preceding discussion may have led you to believe that the illegality of price discrimination is clear-cut and that retailers no longer have to fear being discriminated against. This is not always the situation. Buyers and sellers use a variety of defenses that enable some types of price discrimination to occur. These defenses include cost justification, changing market conditions, and meeting competition in good faith.

- *Cost Justification Defense.* Such a defense would attempt to show that a differential in price could be accounted for on the basis of differences in cost to the seller in the manufacture, sale, or delivery arising from differences in the method or quantities involved. The burden of such a defense is with the seller.

- *Changing Market Conditions Defense.* This defense would attempt to justify the price differential based on the danger of imminent deterioration of perishable goods or on the obsolescence of seasonal goods.

- *Meeting Competition in Good Faith Defense.* The seller can attempt to show that its lower price to a purchaser was made in good faith in order to meet an equally low price of a competitor, provided that this "matched price" did actually exist and was lawful itself.

Therefore, it is legally possible that one retailer—a large warehouse club purchasing 10,000 cases, for example—might have a lower cost per case than a smaller retailer purchasing only 15 cases. However, the retailer that knowingly receives a discriminatory price from a seller (assuming the goods are of like grade and quality) should be relatively certain that the seller is granting a defensible discrimination based on any of the three preceding criteria. Although the Robinson-Patman Act is mainly concerned with illegal activities of the sellers, if a buyer knowingly misrepresents to the seller a price that another seller is willing to offer and the seller meets that "factious" offer, then the buyer and not the seller is liable.

Sellers are prohibited not only from discrimination in price but also from providing unequal services and payments to different retailers. These services and payments frequently include advertising allowances, displays and banners to promote the goods, in-store demonstrations, and distribution of samples or premiums. The Robinson-Patman Act deals specifically with these practices, and it states that such services and payments or consideration must be made available on proportionately equal terms to all competing customers. Finally, it is important to point out that most of the United States' trading partners do not have laws, such as the Robinson-Patman Act, that ban price discrimination, as well as many of the other regulations to be discussed in this chapter. As a result, many United States retailers have been shocked by what they perceived as an "unfair" playing field when they entered foreign markets. For example, price and quality of product are not always the most important issue when setting up a supply chain in some foreign countries.

Deceptive Pricing

Retailers should avoid using a misleading price to lure customers into the store. Advertising an item at an artificially low price and then adding hidden charges is **deceptive pricing**, which is an unfair method of competition. The Wheeler-Lea Amendment of the Federal Trade Commission Act made illegal all "unfair or deceptive acts in commerce." Not only is the retailer's customer being unfairly treated when the retailer uses deceptive pricing but also the retailer's competitors are being potentially harmed because some of their customers may deceitfully be diverted to that retailer. In addition, FTC Guide 233.1 prohibits the advertisement of an inflated former price to emphasize a price reduction (a clearance or sale). The FTC is also concerned with the comparisons between a retailer's price and supposedly that of a competitor when the comparison price is higher than the competitor's actual price. Another concern of the FTC and state regulators: the misuse of rebates in promoting a price because retailers and manufacturers both know that rebates give the perception of saving money. However, in reality, most of these rebates are never claimed due to simple "consumer inertia" in a system where shoppers treat rebates as a discount in the store but seldom find the motivation to mail in the original cash-register receipt, the Universal Product Code (UPC) from a 12-pack of soda, and a correctly filled out claim form to collect a $1.00 rebate on the 12-pack.

Seeking to avoid any charges of deceptive pricing, some retailers have asked manufacturers not to use the word *free* on special packs of merchandise. These retailers have felt the word *free* to be often misleading after they received customer complaints that merchandise marked "free" really should be free of charge, not just a bigger size at the same price. Recently, these retailers have expanded this policy to also apply to shrink wrapping two products together as in a "two-for-the-price-of-one" package.[7]

deceptive pricing
Occurs when a misleading price is used to lure customers into the store and then hidden charges are added; or the item advertised may be unavailable.

Predatory Pricing

Predatory pricing exists when a retailer charges different prices in selected geographic areas in order to eliminate competition in those areas. This is a violation of the Robinson-Patman Act, which also forbids the sale of goods at lower prices in one area for the purpose of destroying competition or eliminating a competitor, or the sale of goods at unreasonably low prices for such purpose. Generally, predatory pricing charges are difficult to prove in federal court.

predatory pricing
Exists when a retail chain charges different prices in different geographic areas to eliminate competition in selected geographic areas.

Promotion Constraints

LO 2

Is there a difference between legal and illegal promotional activities for a retailer?

The ability of the retailer to make any promotion decision is constrained by two major pieces of federal legislation: the Federal Trade Commission Act and the Wheeler-Lea Amendment of the FTC Act. The retailer should be familiar with three promotional areas that are potentially under the domain of the FTC Act and the

Exhibit 6.5
Promotional Constraints

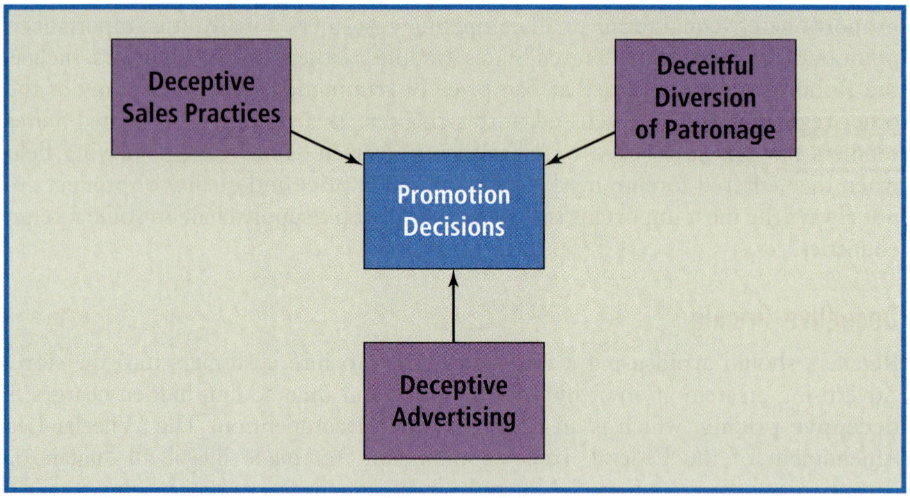

Wheeler-Lea Amendment: deceitful diversion of patronage, deceptive advertising, and deceptive sales practices. Exhibit 6.5 depicts these three areas of constraint.

Deceitful Diversion of Patronage

If a retailer publishes or verbalizes falsehoods about a competitor in an attempt to divert patrons from that competitor, then the retailer is engaging in an unfair trade practice. The competitor would be afforded protection under the FTC Act but also could receive protection by showing that the defamatory statements were libel or slander. In either case, the competitor would have to demonstrate that actual damage had occurred.

palming off
Occurs when a retailer represents that merchandise is made by a firm other than the true manufacturer.

Another form of deceitful diversion of patronage that occurs in retailing is **palming off**. Palming off occurs when a retailer represents merchandise as being made by a firm other than the true manufacturer. For example, an exclusive women's apparel retailer purchases a group of stylish dresses at a bargain price and replaces their labels with those of a top designer. This is deception as to source of origin, and litigation can be brought under the FTC Act and the Wheeler-Lea Amendment. Also, if the designer's dress label were a registered trademark, then protection would also be afforded under the major piece of federal trademark legislation, the Lanham Act (1946).

Although it is difficult to quantify an actual number, the World Customs Organization believes counterfeiting accounts for 5 percent to 7 percent of global merchandise trade, equivalent to lost sales of as much as $600 billion to 650 billion a year.[8] To understand the threat, for example, it's estimated that 37 percent of all copyrighted material exported from North Korea is pirated.[9] As a result, companies are deploying detectives around the globe in search of counterfeits, pressuring foreign governments to crack down, and trying everything from electronic tagging to redesigned products and aggressive pricing to thwart the counterfeiters.[10] However, hundreds of different products, ranging from counterfeit avian flu vaccines to fake bottles of Hennessy cognac have been copied overseas and shipped to the United States for retail sale, sometimes even by the authorized manufacturer of the product. As a result, many liability attorneys are suing not only the foreign manufacturers but also the retailers and even their landlords, who may have unknowingly sold the product.[11] The top categories for counterfeit products are video games and other electronic software, apparel, watches, and golf clubs.

Not all the blame for such actions should be placed on retailers though. After all, a great deal of the merchandise sold in the United States is produced in foreign countries. In many of these foreign countries, trademark law is relatively new and the concept of such protection is not always clear to the workers. When informed of questionable merchandise being sold in their stores, most retailers will discontinue all future purchases and work out some type of agreement with the injured party to sell any remaining stock. After all, the retailers know their reputation is on the line.

Today, however, knockoff artists don't need to operate in parking lots, flea markets, or other retail buildings. They have the Internet. Its anonymity and reach make it perfect for selling knockoffs. However, the question facing the courts today is "if landlords can be held responsible for the actions of their tenants, can eBay be held to the same standard?" Well, in a recent French court decision, Hermès International scored a victory against eBay for selling counterfeit luxury goods. The judge found that eBay, plus the individual seller, had "committed acts of counterfeit" and "prejudice" against it by failing to monitor the authenticity of goods being sold on its website.[12] However, at the same time as the French decision, a federal judge in New York ruled that eBay Inc. fulfilled its legal obligation and took adequate precautions to block the sale of counterfeit Tiffany and Co. jewelry on its site, delivering the first significant victory to the e-commerce company in its running battle with luxury goods companies over fake merchandise.[13]

Not only are product trademarks an issue but also the trademark of a retailer's name may be. The U.S. Supreme Court ruled recently that Victoria's Secret was not damaged by an Elizabethtown, Kentucky, store named "Victor's Little Secret." According to the court, the use of the name neither confused any consumers or potential consumers nor was it likely to do so since the Kentucky store sold adult-themed items in addition to lingerie. While the court unanimously agreed that Victoria's Secret had a valid interest in protecting its name, it resupported the notion that trademark law requires evidence that the competitor actually caused harm to a retailer by using a sound-alike or knockoff name.[14]

Therefore, when choosing a store name, the retailer must make sure that no one else has trademarked the name that it wants. Even names that just resemble trademarks might infringe on the rights of others. After all, trademarks are names and marks that identify the source of a product as a particular company. So, for instance, if your name is Kroger, you won't want to open up a store called "Kroger's" or even "Kroger's Store" because you'd be infringing on the trademark of the well-known supermarket chain. For that reason, the lead author of this text probably wouldn't be allowed to use his last name in Ireland, where the privately owned Dunne's chain is a well-established retail operation.

Another potential problem area for retailers concerns patents. Most retail buyers assume that the wholesaler or manufacturer dealing with them has a valid patent on the merchandise being offered. As a rule, if the patent is ever questioned, a retail buyer should discontinue the product. After all, it is easier and involves less court time to replace the questionable item with a substitute.

Deceptive Advertising

Deceptive advertising occurs when a retailer makes false or misleading advertising claims about the physical makeup of a product, the benefits to be gained by its use, or the appropriate uses for a product. Deceptive advertising is illegal. However, it is often difficult to distinguish between what is false or misleading and what is simply "puffery" or "laudatory language," which retailers can legally use. Puffery occurs when a retailer or its spokesperson states what is considered to be an opinion or a

deceptive advertising
Occurs when a retailer makes false or misleading advertising claims about the physical makeup of a product, the benefits to be gained by its use, or the appropriate uses for the product.

judgment about a product, not a statement of fact. An example is a salesperson saying, "This is an excellent buy, and you cannot afford to pass it up." Probably most important for the retailer to recognize is that the FTC's concern is not the intent of the advertiser but whether the consumer was misled by the advertising. When the FTC challenges any claim contained in advertising or promotional material, several requirements must be met before the commission can find actionable deception: (1) The FTC must prove that the challenged claim is contained in the advertisement, (2) the claim must be deceptive, and (3) the deceptive claim must be material.[15] There is disagreement over whether the above statement was a change in, rather than a summary of, FTC policy toward deception. However, it appears that, for example, an ad for "Danish pastry" would not be considered deceptive because only a few misguided souls believe ... that all 'Danish pastry' is made in Denmark."

The case of Pizza Hut versus Papa John's supports this conclusion. In this instance, Pizza Hut claimed that Papa John's ran a misleading advertisement that denigrated Pizza Hut products. The ad in question was Papa John's use of the advertising slogan "Better ingredients, better pizza." The Fifth Circuit Court of Appeals found that the slogan amounted to nothing more than puffery given that it so exaggerated the company's product. As such, it could not by itself be considered misleading. The court also noted that if Pizza Hut could have proven that consumers were swayed by the ad and as a result lost sales, then the court would have viewed the slogan as misleading and would have ruled against Papa John's.[16]

bait-and-switch advertising
Advertising or promoting a product at an unrealistically low price to serve as "bait" and then trying to "switch" the customer to a higher-priced product.

Bait-and-switch advertising is another type of deceptive advertising. Bait-and-switch advertising is promoting a product at an unrealistically low price to serve as "bait" and then trying to "switch" the customer to a higher-priced product. However, the scope of the FTC's ban on bait-and-switch is much broader than the typical bait-and-switch scenario, and this strictness could, at least theoretically, pose problems for many retailers. For example, federal regulations outlaw all acts or practices by an advertiser that would discourage the purchase of the advertised

Papa John's and Pizza Hut are fierce competitors and have settled some of their disputes over promotional slogans in federal court.

merchandise as part of a bait scheme to sell other merchandise. Among those forbidden acts or practices are:

1. refusing "to show, demonstrate, or sell the product offered";
2. disparaging, by word or deed, the advertised product or the "guarantee, credit terms, availability of service, repairs or parts, or in any other respect, in connection with it";
3. failing to have sufficient quantities of the advertised product to meet "reasonable anticipated demands" at all outlets listed in the advertisement, unless the ad clearly discloses that supply is limited or available only at certain locations;
4. "refusal to take orders for the advertised merchandise to be delivered within a reasonable period of time"; and
5. "use of a sales plan or method of compensation for salesmen … designed to prevent or discourage them from selling the advertised product."[17]

The recent housing crisis has resulted in a new deceptive advertising tactic: pulling a house off the market for a couple of weeks and then presenting it as a new listing, usually with a different agent. While this tactic was used in a few cases before, many agents have claimed it has now become an epidemic.

Deceptive Sales Practices

There are basically two illegal deceptive sales practices: (1) failing to be honest or omitting key facts in either an ad or a sales presentation and (2) using deceptive credit contracts.

Deceptive activities included in the first practice involve not only the failure to tell the customer vital facts during the sales presentation but also repackaging a used product and reselling it as new. All retailers expect customer returns. Rather than ship the product back to the manufacturer, most retailers resell these items as "open." However, to avoid frustrating or deceiving purchasers of these "open items" because parts are missing or there are different processes that come into play for warranties and service plans, retailers must have procedures in place to ensure that open-item products are labeled as such, which includes a list of missing or damaged parts or documentation of what has been repaired.[18]

With regard to deceptive credit, federal laws attempt to "assure a meaningful disclosure of credit terms so that the consumer will be able to compare more readily the various credit terms available to him and avoid the un-informed use of credit."[19] These laws were the result of unscrupulous practices on the part of retailers attempting to hide the true cost of merchandise in unrealistically (and sometimes illegal) high credit terms. For example, the retailer might sell a car at a very low price but then tack on a high (and often hidden) finance charge. Many states have laws limiting these hidden charges.

Product Constraints

LO 3

A retailer's major goal is to sell merchandise. In order to accomplish this goal, the retailer must assure customers that the products they purchase will not be harmful to their well-being and will meet expected performance criteria. Three areas of the law have a major effect on the products a retailer handles: product safety, product liability, and warranties. They are highlighted in Exhibit 6.6.

What responsibilities does a retailer have regarding the products sold?

Exhibit 6.6
Product Constraints

```
┌─────────────────┐                    ┌─────────────────┐
│    Product      │                    │    Product      │
│   Warranties    │                    │    Safety       │
└─────────────────┘                    └─────────────────┘
           ↘                            ↙
               ┌─────────────────┐
               │    Product      │
               │   Decisions     │
               └─────────────────┘
                        ↑
               ┌─────────────────┐
               │    Product      │
               │   Liability     │
               └─────────────────┘
```

Product Safety

Retailers are in a difficult position when it comes to product safety. Most retailers do not produce the goods they sell but purchase them from wholesalers or manufacturers. Retailers have little to say about product quality or safety. Their only weapon is choosing reputable suppliers so as not to carry merchandise they consider unsafe. You might, therefore, conclude that retailers are not responsible for the safety of products they sell; this is definitely not the case.

According to the Consumer Product Safety Act, retailers have always had specific responsibilities to monitor the safety of consumer products.[20] Today, as a result of the Consumer Product Safety Improvements Act that took effect in 2009, retailers face even stronger requirements. This new law was the aftermath of a public outcry over imports of tainted toothpaste and pet food, as well as the infamous importation of lead-laden toys from Asia, especially China. The new regulation applies to all members of the supply chain (retailers, as well as manufacturers, other intermediaries, and importers) and sets new limits for plastic-softening chemicals called *phthalates* in children's products, as well as toughening standards for lead content. However, in many instances, retailers, such as CVS, Toys "R" Us, and Walmart, had already stopped selling baby bottles containing the chemical bisphenol-A because animal studies had linked small doses of the chemical to cancer and other health issues.[21]

Today, retailers worry that they may be held responsible for the safety issues created by products they sold even if they were ignorant of the problems involved. This was especially true in 2009 when peanut products from one manufacturer were found to contain salmonella contamination (see the case at the end of Chapter 5). After all, what is to prevent an injured party from suing all parties involved, especially since the manufacturer in this case filed for bankruptcy when it lacked the financial ability to pay damages? Also, what is to prevent convenience store operators from being sued for illnesses caused by tobacco, alcohol, or food products such as trans-fat–laden potato chips that they sold?[22] Still, the American court system is easier on transgressors than the Chinese government. Zheng Xiaoyu, the former head of China's State Food and Drug Administration, was executed after he was sentenced to death for taking bribes from drug companies and being derelict of duty. His death followed a string of food- and drug-safety lapses—ranging from tainted toothpaste and pet food to suspended anticancer drugs—all things that cast an unflattering light on China's regulatory standards.[23]

Returned jars of Peter Pan Peanut Butter are shown at a super market in February 2007. A salmonella outbreak that grew slowly to nearly 300 cases in 39 states was linked to tainted peanut butter produced in south Georgia. As was illustrated in the case in chapter 5 the cost of a product recall to the retailer, and not only the manufacturer, can be substantial.

Product Liability

Product liability laws invoke the "foreseeability" doctrine, which states that a seller of a product must attempt to foresee how a product may be misused and warn the consumer against the hazards of misuse. The courts have interpreted this doctrine to suggest that retailers must be careful in how they sell their products. This is of particular importance to restaurant, nightclub, and bar owners who fail to consider the consequences of serving a consumer who appears intoxicated. In addition to the federal laws covering product liability, all states have their own regulations.

product liability laws Deal with the seller's responsibility to market safe products. These laws invoke the foreseeability doctrine, which states that a seller of a product must attempt to foresee how a product may be misused and warn the consumer against the hazards of misuse.

Warranties

Retailers are also responsible for product safety and performance under conventional warranty doctrines. Under the current warranty law, the fact that the ultimate consumer may bring suit against the manufacturer in no way relieves the retailer from its responsibility for the fitness and merchantability of the goods. The disheartening fact that confronts the retailer is that the buyer in many states has been permitted to sue both the retailer and the manufacturer in the same legal suit.

Retailers can offer expressed or implied warranties. **Expressed warranties** are the result of the interaction between the retailer and the customer. They may be either written into the contract or verbalized. They can cover all characteristics or attributes of the merchandise or only one attribute. An important point for the retailer (and its salespeople) to recognize is that an expressed warranty can be created without the use of the words *warranty* or *guarantee*. For example, a car salesperson might tell a buyer, "Everybody we've sold this type of car to has gone at

expressed warranties Are either written or verbalized agreements about the performance of a product and can cover all attributes of the merchandise or only one attribute.

least 60,000 miles with no problems whatsoever, and I see no reason why you cannot expect the same. I would not be surprised if you are able to drive 100,000 miles without any mechanical problems." This statement could create an expressed warranty. The court would, however, be concerned with whether this was just sales talk (puffery) or a statement of fact or opinion by the salesperson.

Implied warranties are not expressly made by the retailer but are based on custom, norms, or reasonable expectations. There are two types of implied warranties (which overlap a bit): (1) an implied warranty of merchantability and (2) an implied warranty of fitness for a particular purpose.

implied warranty of merchantability

Is made by every retailer when the retailer sells goods and implies that the merchandise sold is fit for the ordinary purpose for which such goods are typically used.

Every retailer selling goods makes an **implied warranty of merchantability**. By offering the goods for sale, the retailer implies that they are fit for the ordinary purpose for which such goods are typically used. The notion of implied warranty applies to both new and used merchandise. For example, imagine that a sporting-goods retailer located close to a major lake resort sells used inner tubes for swimming and a customer purchases one. The tube bursts while the person is floating on it, and the person subsequently drowns. This retailer may be held liable. Because of the potential legal liability that accompanies an implied warranty, many retailers, especially many online operators, will expressly disclaim at the time of sale any or all implied warranties and seek to mark a product "as is."[24] This is not always legally possible; some retailers will not be able to avoid implied warranties of merchantability.

implied warranty of fitness

Is a warranty that implies that the merchandise is fit for a particular purpose and arises when the customer relies on the retailer to assist or make the selection of goods to serve a particular purpose.

The **implied warranty of fitness** for a particular purpose arises when the customer relies on the retailer to assist or make the selection of goods to serve a particular purpose. Consider a customer who is about to make a cross-country moving trip and plans to tow a 4-foot-by-4-foot, two-wheel trailer behind her SUV. She needs a pair of tires for the rear of the SUV and thus goes to a local tire retailer and asks the salesperson for a pair of tires that will allow her to tow the loaded trailer safely. The customer in this regard is ignorant and is relying on the expertise of the retailer. If the retailer sells the customer a pair of tires not suited for the job, then the retailer is liable for breach of an implied warranty of fitness for a particular purpose. This is true even if the retailer did not have in stock a pair of tires to safely perform the job but instead sold the customer the best tire available.

Consumer product warranties frequently have been confusing, misleading, and frustrating to consumers. As a consequence, the Magnuson-Moss Warranty Act was passed. Although nothing in federal law requires a retailer to warrant a product under this act, anyone who sells a product for more than $15 and gives a written warranty (only written warranties are covered by federal laws, while many types of warranties are subject to state laws) to the consumer is required to provide the consumer with all the details of the warranty.[25]

LO 4   Supply-Chain Constraints

How does government regulation influence a retailer's behavior with other supply-chain members?

Retailers are restricted in the relationships and agreements they may develop with supply-chain or channel partners. These restrictions can be conveniently categorized into four areas as shown in Exhibit 6.7.

Territorial Restrictions

As related to retail trade, **territorial restrictions** can be defined as attempts by a supplier, usually a manufacturer, to limit the geographic area in which a retailer may resell its merchandise. The courts have viewed territorial restrictions as

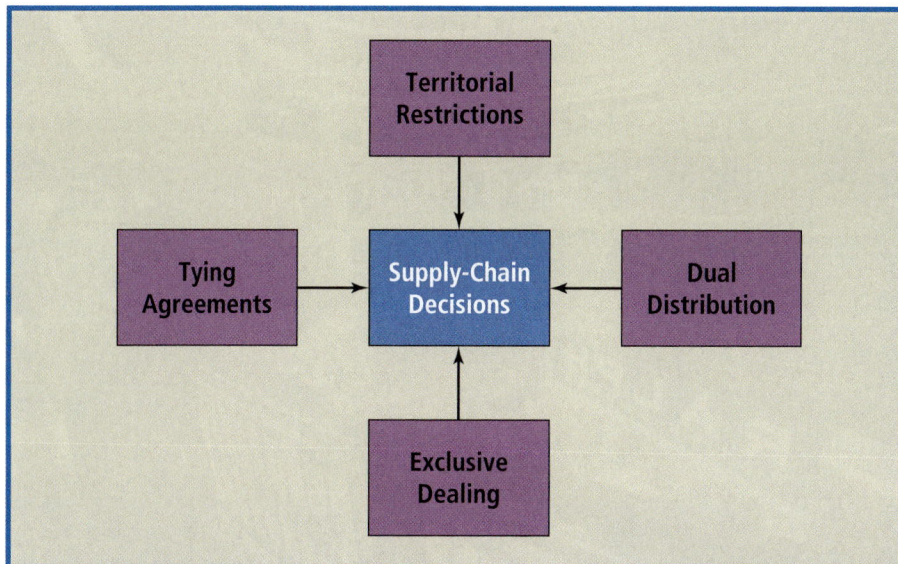

Exhibit 6.7
Supply-Chain Constraints

potential contracts in restraint of trade and in violation of the Sherman Antitrust Act. Thus, even though the retailer and manufacturer may both favor territorial restrictions, the courts will often frown on such arrangements because of the lessening of competition between retailers selling the brand in question. The law does not, however, prevent manufacturers and retailers from establishing territorial limits as long as they do not exclude all other retailers or restrict the sale of the manufacturer's products. Franchise agreements have long had territorial restrictions that provide a protected zone for the franchisee. Because of these zones, the franchisee is able to develop a primary demand for the product without fear of cannibalization by another entry in the protected zone. In cases where the franchisor has permitted another franchisee to invade the "exclusive territory" of another franchisee as outlined in a contract, the original franchisee could sue the parent chain under a breach-of-contract claim. However, a federal appeals court ruling found that when a franchise contract expressly spells out that a franchisee does not have an exclusive territory, the franchisor has the power to place other outlets nearby.[26]

territorial restrictions
Are attempts by the supplier, usually a manufacturer, to limit the geographic area in which a retailer may resell its merchandise.

Dual Distribution

As discussed in the previous chapter, a manufacturer that sells to independent retailers and also through its own retail outlets is engaged in **dual distribution**. Thus, the manufacturer manages a corporately owned vertical marketing system that competes with independent retailers, which it also supplies through a conventional, administered, or contractual marketing channel. Retailers tend to become upset about dual distribution when the two supply chains compete at the retail level in the same geographic area. For example, Ralph Lauren operates wholly owned retail stores and, in addition, uses major independent retailers as outlets. Such supply-chain strategy can have an adverse effect on manufacturer–retailer relationships. Independent retailers will argue that dual distribution is an unfair method of competition and thus is in violation of the Sherman Act. As indicated in Chapter 5, the Internet has created new opportunities for dual distribution, which has increased the levels of channel conflict. Dual distribution also

dual distribution
Occurs when a manufacturer sells to independent retailers and also through its own retail outlets.

Steve Raymer/Corbis

Ralph Lauren uses dual distribution by operating its own retail stores but also by selling through other retailers such as department stores. Here we see a Ralph Lauren store at the Kuala Lumpur City Center shopping mall in Malaysia.

takes place when manufacturers sell similar products under different brand names for distribution through different channels as with private labels.

The courts have not viewed dual-distribution arrangements as antitrust violations. In fact, they have reasoned that dual distribution can actually foster competition. For example, the manufacturer may not be able to find a retailer to represent it in all trade areas, or the manufacturer may find it necessary to operate its own retail outlet to establish market share and remain competitive with other manufacturers. The courts will apply a rule-of-reason criterion. Thus, the independent retailer suing a manufacturer for dual distribution will have to convince the court that it was competed against unfairly and damaged. The retailer's best bet would be to show that the manufacturer-controlled outlets were favored or subsidized (for instance, with excessive advertising allowances or lower prices) to an extent that was detrimental to the independent retailer.

Exclusive Dealing

one-way exclusive-dealing arrangement Occurs when the supplier agrees to give the retailer the exclusive right to sell the supplier's product in a particular trade area.

Retailers and their suppliers occasionally enter into exclusive dealing arrangements. In a **one-way exclusive-dealing arrangement**, the supplier agrees to give the retailer the exclusive right to sell the supplier's product in a particular trade area. The retailer, however, does not agree to do anything in particular for the supplier, hence the term *one-way*. For example, a weak manufacturer often has to offer one-way exclusive-dealing arrangements to get shelf space at the retail level. Truly one-way arrangements are legal.

two-way exclusive-dealing agreement Occurs when the supplier offers the retailer the exclusive distribution of a merchandise line or product in a particular trade area if in return the retailer will agree to do something for the manufacturer, such as heavily promote the supplier's products or not handle competing brands.

A **two-way exclusive-dealing agreement** occurs when the supplier offers the retailer the exclusive distribution of a merchandise line or product if the retailer agrees to do something for the manufacturer in return. For example, the retailer might agree not to handle certain competing brands. Two-way agreements violate the Clayton Act if they substantially lessen competition or tend to create a monopoly. Specifically, the courts have generally viewed exclusive dealing as illegal when it excludes competitive products from a large share of the market and when it represents a large share of the total sales volume for a particular product type.

Tying Agreements

When a seller with a strong product or service forces a buyer (the retailer) to purchase a weak product or service as a condition for buying the strong one, a **tying agreement** exists. For example, a large national manufacturer with several very highly demanded lines of merchandise may try to force the retailer to handle its entire merchandise assortment as a condition for being able to handle the more popular merchandise lines. This is called a *full-line policy*. Alternatively, a strong manufacturer may be introducing a new product and, in order to get shelf space or display space at the retail level, may require retailers to handle some of the new products before they can purchase better-established merchandise lines.

Tying arrangements have been found to be in violation of the Clayton, Sherman, and FTC acts. Tying is not viewed as a violation per se, but it is generally viewed as illegal if a substantial share of commerce is affected. The most serious problems involving tying arrangements are those associated with franchising. Quite often, franchise agreements contain provisions requiring the franchisee to purchase all raw materials and supplies from the franchisor. The courts generally consider tying provisions of a franchise agreement legal as long as there is sufficient proof that these arrangements are necessary to maintain quality control. Otherwise, they are viewed as unwarranted restraints of competition.[27] For instance, franchisees of Wendy's, McDonald's, Taco Bell, and so on cannot be forced to purchase paper goods or food ingredients from the franchisor unless the products are of a quality that the franchisee could not obtain otherwise.

tying agreement
Exists when a seller with a strong product or service requires a buyer (the retailer) to purchase a weak product or service as a condition for buying the strong product or service.

Other Federal, State, and Local Laws

LO 5

What is the impact of various state and local laws, in addition to federal regulations, in developing retail policies?

Several other federal laws also affect retailers, but a detailed discussion of their impact is beyond the scope of this text. However, some limited comments follow. One such set of these laws, which is shown in Exhibit 6.1, is extremely important today because it deals with mergers and acquisitions. As retailers seek to consolidate their operations by selling off unprofitable stores, expand into new markets, or acquire the outlets of other retailers, they must consider the impact on the competitive environment.[28]

Various U.S. trade agreements regulating the amount of importing and exporting American firms can conduct with firms in various countries sometimes limit, if not totally forbid, a retailer's ability to purchase merchandise from certain foreign countries. At one extreme, the United States currently bans all merchandise from Cuba, while at the other extreme our North American Free Trade Agreement membership attempts to reduce all barriers to trade with Mexico and Canada. Such regulations present problems for American retailers operating globally. Consider, for example, Walmart's dilemma. As a U.S. company, the firm can't sell textiles made in Cuba. However, since Canada has no such restrictions against Cuban merchandise, the retailer is not allowed to exclude Cuban-made products due solely to their country of origin. This makes for an interesting problem as to which country's laws are to be followed.

Retailers must also be aware of laws that deal with minimum wages and hiring practices since labor is a retailer's largest operating expense. Chapter 14, "Managing People," will cover the major laws affecting employment and personnel decisions. Chapter 13, "Store Layout and Design," will consider how the Americans with Disabilities Act affects the layout and design of the retailer's store. Finally, Chapter 7, "Market Selection and Retail Location Analysis," will discuss the issue of eminent domain powers used by cities for economic development purposes. Tax laws and Securities and Exchange Commission rules and regulations that deal with the legal form of ownership (sole proprietorship, partnership, or corporation) and shareholder-disclosure requirements are not covered in this text.

In addition to federal laws, many states and municipalities have passed legislation regulating retail activities. Exhibit 6.8 illustrates how state and local laws affect the retailer. Zoning laws, for example, prohibit retailers from operating in certain locations and require building and sign specifications to be met. Many retailers have found these codes to be highly restrictive, especially since some existing firms have been able to influence this type of legislation, thereby protecting their already established local businesses. For example, several states ban the sale of caskets over the Internet. Their laws dictate that coffins can be provided to the public only by licensed funeral directors. And a Louisiana statute prohibits flower selling without a license. These "shut-out" competitors claim these laws are a deliberate attempt by legislators to protect the entrenched businesses that fear competition.[29] In addition, while most states don't allow picketing on a retailer's or a shopping center's property, some states are now allowing such behavior claiming that owners of public retail sales areas have no right to prevent demonstrators from calling for the boycott of a retailer or mall.[30]

Safety practices have become a new rallying point for state and local governing bodies. Today, laws in San Francisco and Boston ban the sale of cigarettes by pharmacies. Over a dozen states ban the shipping of wine directly to a consumer's home by a winery, whether it is located in or out of state.[31] Numerous cities have followed Ireland's lead and have either banned outright the use of plastic shopping bags or imposed a fee on their use. Some states, among them New York and California, have begun banning fast-food places by restricting the use of certain ingredients, regulating menu information, and now dictating whether restaurants are healthy enough to open in their communities. Proponents say these actions are crucial in the fight against obesity, diabetes, and other diseases and health

Exhibit 6.8
State and Local Regulations Affecting Retailers

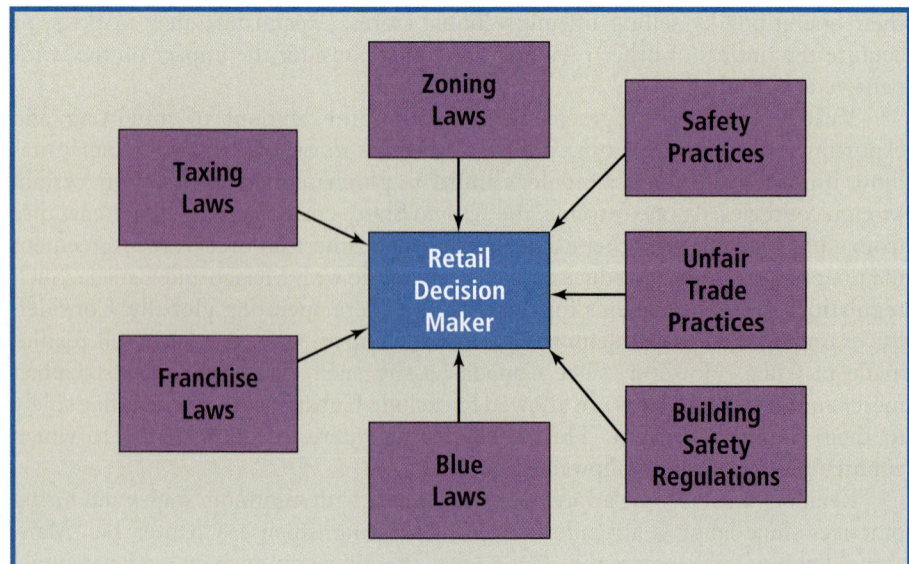

conditions. In fact, by early 2009, 27 states had already imposed small tariffs of 7 percent to 8 percent on vending machine snacks such as candy, soda, and baked goods to combat obesity.[32] Foes say the rules go too far, violating important freedoms.[33] Finally, some cites are opposed to Domino's new ad slogan: "You Got 30 Minutes." While it has been two decades since Domino's last promised to deliver a pizza to someone's door within 30 minutes or it was free, that pledge is still stuck in many customers' heads. These cities fear that the use of this slogan will lead to a rash of accidents as the pizza delivery drivers may drive too fast or run stop lights.[34]

With regard to unfair trade practices, most states have established their own set of laws that prevent one retailer from gaining an unfair advantage over another retailer. As a general rule, *unfair trade practices* laws regulate retailers' competitive behavior (usually relating to pricing, advertising, merchandise stocked, and employment practices). For example, because shoppers are more likely to consolidate their trips when gas prices are high, some retailers that sell general merchandise along with gasoline may seek to sell gas below cost. Thirteen states have laws against such pricing strategies. The specific content of these laws varies, but usually they prohibit the retailer from seeking unfair advantages from vendors or selling merchandise below cost (or at cost plus some fixed percentage markup—6 percent is typical) with the intent of using profits from another geographic area or from cash reserves to destroy or hurt competition.[35] A number of states have also introduced laws preventing both zero-down car leases and zero-percent financing programs because they claim such programs mislead consumers. Also, the franchise laws in many states assume that, unless otherwise spelled out in the franchise agreement, there is an implied agreement not to locate another outlet near a current location without the current franchisee's permission. These state laws are often in conflict with federal regulations. As a result, in many instances, state laws regulating retailers have either been declared unconstitutional or amended to meet federal guidelines.

Many localities have strong building codes that regulate construction materials, fire safety, architectural style, height and size of building, number of entrances, and even elevator usage. Some local ordinances are attempts to aid retailers, such as the attempt by traffic engineers in some cities to reduce downtown traffic to less than 20 miles per hour so that consumers can observe local businesses and their display promotions. Other states enforce *blue laws* that restrict the sale of certain products such as automobiles on Sundays. Many states have passed strong regulations on topics not covered by federal regulations governing the relationship between franchisors and franchisees in order to protect the individual businesspeople of their states. These laws require a full disclosure of all the pertinent facts involved in owning a local franchise. Many experts believe that these state franchise laws protect the current antiquated and inefficient automobile dealerships, which were discussed in Chapter 5, from newer, more efficient forms of competition because the dealers provide 20 percent of state sales tax revenues and are usually the largest advertisers in the local media. Given such a concentration of political clout, most state governments will make it difficult for discounters and Internet sellers to enter the new-car business or for Detroit to control the pricing and promotion of its own products. However, Internet businesses that serve as automotive brokers are emerging. These businesses bring together purchasers and franchised dealers who will sell cars to purchasers at prices negotiated by the Internet brokers. This chapter's "What's New?" box illustrates that many state and local governments, which must operate with balanced budgets, now view Internet purchases as a cash cow. After all, the lost revenue in unpaid sales tax from online transactions could be used to aid the 29 states with shortfalls in state budgets during 2009.

What's New?

Nothing Is More Certain than Death and Taxes

Mark Twain once wrote that only two things are certain in life: death and taxes. After years in which consumers did not have to pay taxes on Internet purchases, developments in 2008 dictate that Mark Twain's view of the world is right once again.

Prior to the recent developments, retailers relied on the 1992 *Quill Corp. v. North Dakota* ruling from the Supreme Court that stated that forcing retailers to learn the ins and outs of every local sales tax was too burdensome. Thus, merchants cannot be required to collect sales tax from a customer in another state unless they have a "physical presence" in the customer's state, usually defined as a store, office, or warehouse. After all, with more than 7,600 state and local sales tax jurisdictions, each with varying rates, lists of taxable items, and definitions of items, the court reasoned that a retailer otherwise couldn't be expected to know how much tax to charge.

As a result of this ruling, state laws in the 45 states that have sales taxes used the "physical presence" clause to collect the tax from e-tailers. (The only states without sales taxes are Alaska, Delaware, Montana, New Hampshire, and Oregon.) This tax was collected on all non–tax-exempt merchandise sold to customers whether through stores, Internet sites, or catalogs. Therefore, many online retailers structured their Internet operations to avoid having facilities or property in most states.

However, this all changed when New York became the first (and so far only) state to require online retailers to collect sales tax even when they have no physical presence in the state, such as a store, a warehouse, or even a sales rep. The state's two main targets were Amazon and rival Overstock.com. Both claimed the law was unconstitutional and filed suit against the state.

The key to this change in the collection status was that New York amended its law to say that having a New York–based affiliate or associate—such as bloggers or other websites that link to an e-tailer and that are paid a percentage of the sale—is tantamount to having a presence in the state. As a result, Amazon collected the tax while awaiting a court decision. However, Overstock took a different route, choosing instead to drop its 3,400 New York affiliates.

Most legal experts don't expect a final decision on this case until 2012. However, several states are already preparing similar legislation. As one legal scholar noted to the author, it is going to take Roto-Rooter to clean up this mess.

Source: This box is based on information supplied to the authors by the National Retail Federation, "Attention, Online Shoppers: Taxes Ahead," *BusinessWeek*, June 16, 2008: 89; and "States Push for Taxation on Internet Sales," *St. Louis Post-Dispatch*, January 13, 2009: C1.

Sometimes states pass laws that don't fit into any of the categories listed in Exhibit 6.8 but which may present problems for retailers. One such issue is what to do with the unused portion of gift cards. Customers often leave a little money on the plastic cards and sometimes lose them altogether. Roughly 10 percent of all cards are unredeemed, allowing many stores and restaurants to keep the spare change, which adds up to an estimated $5 billion a year or more. While most retailers continue to carry the value of the unredeemed cards as a liability on their books, Home Depot and Best Buy recently increased their profits by recording unredeemed but expired cards as income. Since introducing their cards, Best Buy and Home Depot have realized $43 million and $29 million worth of income from such cards.[36]

With budgets to balance and with so much unclaimed money at stake, many states are seeking these funds for their treasuries. Since all states have laws that allow them to take custody of funds abandoned by their residents and hold them until the rightful owner can claim them, it is not surprising that every state regards unredeemed gift cards as unclaimed property. Retailers disagree with these laws, arguing that when the state "escheats" an unused gift card, the retailer is deprived of the profit it expected to earn when the card was redeemed for merchandise. They further point out that retailers actually lose money on the gift card because they have to cover the expense of issuing and accounting for the card, but then turn the value of the card over to the state. Today about half the states claim the full value of gift cards or some portion (such as 60 percent). Some retailers have tried to avoid turning the unredeemed money over to states by imposing conditions on gift cards, such as expiration dates or monthly service fees that whittle away the value of the gift card. That way, the card has no value by the time the state would lay claim to its unredeemed value. However, expiration dates that diminish the value of gift cards are unpopular with consumers. A dozen states now regulate the imposition of an expiration date and/or service fees. For the most current summary of the various state regulations regarding gift cards, visit http://www.consumersunion.org.

In addition, state court systems sometimes make rulings that affect retailers operating across the country. For example, supreme courts of two states are deciding whether or not to hear cases involving injury to a customer when the retailer's employee did not follow a robber's demands as directed by the retailer's rules. Another state court is currently deciding if a retailer discriminated against a female by claiming that only men could be employed as the store's Santas. Also, various cities have passed laws governing retailing, such as Green River Ordinances (named after the town in Wyoming that first passed them), that restrict door-to-door selling. Other communities restrict the excessive use of garage sales, lottery promotions, or sale of obscene materials and dangerous products. In addition, states and cities might require licenses to operate certain retail businesses such as liquor stores and massage parlors.

For further information about these various laws, a retailer should consult the local Better Business Bureau, the National Retail Federation, state and local retail trade associations, or state and local regulatory agencies.

Ethics in Retailing

LO 6

How does a retailer's code of ethics influence its behavior?

Ethics is a set of rules for moral human behavior. These rules or standards of moral responsibility often take the form of dos and don'ts. Some retailers have an **explicit code of ethics**, which is a written policy that states what constitutes ethical and unethical behavior. However, most often an implicit code of ethics exists. An **implicit code of ethics** is an unwritten but well understood set of rules or standards of moral responsibility. This implicit code is learned as employees become socialized into the organization and the corporate culture of the retailer.

Regardless of whether the code of ethics is explicit or implicit, it is an important guideline for making retail decisions. We will shortly review some retail decision areas where ethical considerations are common. However, before doing so, it should be pointed out that legal behavior and ethical behavior are not necessarily the same. Unethical actions may be legal. Laws, after all, represent a formalization of behavioral standards through the political process into rules or laws. Therefore, a retailer needs to behave legally since laws represent a formalized set of ethical rules. In addition, retailers need to look beyond laws and engage in practices that are also ethical. One problem, though, is that reasonable people may disagree as to what is right and wrong behavior. For this reason, retailers should develop explicit codes of ethical behavior for their employees to provide a formal indication of what is right and wrong.

Let's look at three retail decision areas that involve ethical considerations:

1. buying merchandise,
2. selling merchandise, and
3. retailer–employee relationships.

ethics
Is a set of rules for human moral behavior.

explicit code of ethics
Consists of a written policy that states what is ethical and unethical behavior.

implicit code of ethics
Is an unwritten but well understood set of rules or standards of moral responsibility.

In each of these situations, the retailer faces an ethical dilemma and that what is legal may not necessarily represent the best ethical guideline.

Ethical Behavior in Buying Merchandise

When buying merchandise, the retailer can face at least four ethical dilemmas. These relate to product quality, sourcing, slotting fees, and bribery.

Product Quality

Should a retailer inspect merchandise for product quality or leave that to the customer? Although the law does not require such inspections, most retail buyers want to ensure that their merchandise meets the expectations of the store's customers. As a result, some retailers have developed laboratory testing programs to verify that the quality of their private-label products, as well as the manufacturers' own brands, adhere to stricter ethical and environmental standards that go beyond existing government regulations.

Sourcing

Should a retailer inspect the working conditions at all plants producing products sold by the retailer? What about foreign merchandise sources using child labor or that fail to pay fair levels of wages? The only way United States retailers can be sure that they are not buying illegal merchandise is to inspect all suppliers down to the smallest subcontractors. However, some retailers are also having troubles with American suppliers. A program of careful vigilance to overcome such activities can be expensive, and it is doubtful whether American consumers would be willing to bear the cost. Seeking to overcome such complaints, many retailers have begun using private investigators to check out vendors to make sure they are not buying from unsavory characters. Many other major American retailers have agreed to allow independent observers, including human-rights officials, to monitor working conditions in their foreign factories. Consumers can check the websites of the U.S. Department of Labor (www.dol.gov) or CorpWatch (www.corpwatch.org/), a private group dedicated to holding corporations responsible to see if a particular retailer has issues in this area. In an unusual display of corporate candor, Gap Inc. issued a "social responsibility" report acknowledging that many of the overseas workers making the retailer's clothes are mistreated; the company vowed to improve often shoddy factory conditions by cracking down on unrepentant manufacturers. Gap's commitment is particularly significant because thousands of factories were involved.[37] Gap's report can be found at www.gapinc.com/public/SocialResponsibility/socialres.shtml.

Slotting Fees

slotting fees (slotting allowances)
Are fees paid by a vendor for space or a slot on a retailer's shelves, as well as having its UPC number given a slot in the retailer's computer system.

Should retailers demand money from a manufacturer for agreeing to add a new product to their inventory? **Slotting fees** (also called **slotting allowances**) are fees paid by a vendor for space, or a slot, on a retailer's shelves, as well as for having a slot in the retailer's computer system for its UPC number. After all, if an item's UPC code is not in the system, then individual stores cannot stock it. Retailers claim that such fees help defray the extra expenses of adding warehouse space, replacing existing items in the store, and placing the new items in the inventory-control system and provide a form of insurance by guaranteeing at least some profit from carrying the new item. It is estimated that these fees now account for more than 16 percent of new product introduction costs. In the only major academic study to date on the subject, the authors found support for the rationale that slotting allowances enhance market efficiency by optimally allocating scarce retail shelf space to the most successful products. They also concluded that the fees do not thwart competition but helped balance the risk of new product failure between manufacturers and retailers, helped manufacturers signal private information about potential success of new products, and served to widen retail distribution for manufacturers by mitigating retail competition.[38] However, most manufacturers still claim that such fees are only an attempt by retailers to make money buying goods rather than selling goods that meet their customers' needs. Thus, smaller food manufacturers complain that slotting fees limit competition and translate into higher prices for consumers. The competition to get a product into a store is fierce given that a typical grocery store has room for only about 40,000 items and more than 100,000 grocery items are available for consideration. Still the question remains, are slotting fees really necessary?

Bribery

Should a retailer or its employees be allowed to accept a bribe? Bribery occurs when a retail buyer is offered an inducement (which the Internal Revenue Service considers to have a value greater than $25) for purchasing a vendor's products. Such inducements, it should be noted, are legal in many foreign countries. The reader may want to visit the document and publication section at the Transparency International website (www.transparency.org) to see in which countries bribes are still considered part of normal business behavior. However, in the United States, the Foreign Corrupt Practices Act bans bribes as anticompetitive. It is, after all, hard to develop a healthy relationship between a retailer and supplier when bribes are expected.

Walmart, renowned to outsiders for its elbows-out business tactics, is known internally for its bare-knuckled, no-expense-spared investigations of employees who break its ironclad ethics rules. Walmart's employees are not allowed to accept any gifts (including samples) from vendors, not even a cup of coffee or a soft drink when visiting a supplier's showroom. Today, many of the nation's top retailers require not only all their managers and buyers but also their vendors to sign an integrity pledge. Despite such actions, lapses do occur. Home Depot recently fired four merchandise-purchasing employees for allegedly receiving kickbacks to ensure certain flooring products were stocked by the retailer and put in prominent positions.[39]

Since retail buyers are often compensated based on their buying performance, a modern version of bribery occurs when retailers shakedown vendors for markdown money. **Markdown money** is the funds that retailers arbitrarily deduct from vendors' payments when the merchandise doesn't sell briskly enough. This topic will be covered in greater detail in Chapter 10.

markdown money
Markdown money is what retailers charge to suppliers when merchandise does not sell at what the vendor intended.

Ethical Behavior in Selling Merchandise

Ethics can also influence the selling process with regards to the products sold and the various selling practices that salespeople use.

Products Sold

Should a retailer sell any product as long as it is not illegal? For example, should a convenience store operator located near a school carry cigarette paper for those few customers who prefer to roll their own and risk selling the paper to students who might use it for smoking marijuana? Other people have questioned Walmart's decision not to sell adult-themed sex magazines. Long before actions by some

Service Retailing

Privacy and Search Engines

A popular urban legend revolves around the college student who used an Internet search engine to have someone write a term paper for him. After all, the student reasoned, if American companies can go online to outsource their work, why can't students outsource their homework? However, in this case, the term-paper writer, who charged only $100, was the student's professor.

Search engines have become so popular for this type of activity that today it is as easy to buy four pages, complete with bibliography, about the "Ethical Aspects of Walmart's Operation" as it is to download a song.[40] To combat this problem, companies such as Turnitin.com and iThenticate .com help professors in their attempts to stop such plagiarism.

A simpler solution to this problem might be to allow professors to check with the search engines to find out who used their services. Sound far-fetched? After all, wouldn't this be an invasion of privacy and thus illegal? Many people thought so until recently.

However, Internet firms such as Locatecell.com now offer complete searches of phone calls from cell phones. Imagine having someone look up your phone records. Worse yet is the question, how private are the records of your online use of search engines such as Yahoo or Google? Google, for example, uses a cookie that expires in two years but renews itself when a Google service is used. Can someone get them?

Yahoo, for example, was once suspected of supplying information to China's government that led to the jailing of a journalist. His crime was sending an internal Communist Party memo to foreign-based websites. Yahoo said it was only complying with China's laws.

In an even more important case, the United States government asked Google to turn over data on customers' web searches for certain types of porn. Of course, Google resisted. The Justice Department wanted the California-based company to turn over 1 million random Internet protocol (IP) addresses and records of all Google searches from any one-week period. The issue at hand was to see whether online pornography sites were accessible by minors. Google resisted on privacy grounds and said it would "vigorously" oppose any subpoena for web search information.

The government responded by saying it only requested "anonymous data" (the computer's IP address) and that Google's rivals, including Time Warner's AOL, Microsoft's MSN, and Yahoo, had already complied. By the way, the court ruled in Google's favor, recognizing the privacy implications of turning over search terms. However, the refusal by Google—whose guiding philosophy is "Don't be evil"— overlooked an important issue: "Why was a search engine keeping so much information at all?"

Thus, the question remains: Do today's college students want their kids to know in 20 years what Internet sites they searched while they were in school?

---

states and communities, many drug store and general merchandise chains banned the sale of pseudoephedrine, an ingredient found in most popular over-the-counter cold medicines, and lithium batteries because both pseudoephedrine and lithium are used in the production of crystal meth (methamphetamine). Other retailers have chosen not to sell "unrated" movie DVDs, the ones with raunchy humor and explicit sex scenes, despite the fact that they tend to outsell the original versions.[41]

Sometimes not carrying products can add to a retailer's profit. For example, Trader Joe's, the California-based specialty food retailer, performed a sales analysis on all its cigarettes by company and brand and found that only Marlboro merited the space allocated. Therefore, rather than carry just that one brand, the retailer dropped all cigarettes.[42] Today, the topic of what products should be sold has reached the Internet's service providers. This chapter's "Service Retailing" box highlights the issue of what happens to all that information that Internet search engines gather about their users.

Selling Practices

Can a salesperson, while not saying anything false, be allowed to conceal certain facts from a customer? Also, should selling the "wrong" product for the customer's needs be permitted? Many retailers have ethical standards against such practices. However, as long as salespeople are paid on commission, we can expect such behavior to occur. Some highly successful retailers such as Home Depot and Best Buy have sought to overcome this dilemma by never putting their employees at odds with their own code of ethics. Bernie Marcus, the founder of Home Depot, has been quoted as saying, "The day I'm laid out dead with an apple in my mouth is the day we'll pay commissions. If you pay commissions, you imply that the small customer is not worth anything."[43] When Best Buy switched its compensation plan from commissions to salary in 1989, manufacturers such as Toshiba and Hitachi that depended on salespeople to push premium-price items were opposed. However, customers liked the no-pressure atmosphere and sales soon outpaced all rivals.[44] It should be pointed out, however, that paying commissions could be difficult in self-service operations like Home Depot and Best Buy. A rather difficult situation involved the recent switch from analog TV to digital TV. The law required that retailers not sell televisions lacking a digital tuner within two years of the 2009 switch. However, did the retailers have an obligation to inform those customers about the upcoming changeover who may have wanted to purchase an analog set in late 2006 for a Christmas gift?

Ethical Behavior in the Retailer–Employee Relationship

Ethical standards can also influence the retailer–employee relationship in three ways: misuse of company assets, job switching, and employee theft.

Misuse of Company Assets

Most people would agree that the stealing of merchandise is illegal, but what about other types of stealing? What about an employee who surfs the web or trades stock on company time? Also, what about taking an extra break or using the retailer's phone for a personal long-distance call? All of these, while not subject to criminal prosecution, are forms of employee theft and should be considered when an employee develops his or her code of ethics.

Advancements in computer technology and the growth of the Internet have recently challenged one of the most treasured of American rights—the right to privacy. Most retailers have an asset that would have been unheard of a generation ago. In a situation similar to that described above regarding Google, retailers today have databases that contain heretofore private information about nearly every American that most consumers do not even know exists. These databases are constructed in a number of ways, including computer cookies as well as purchased information from state governments (for example, driver's license bureaus or voting records). As a result, current laws provide for consumers to opt out of such databases.

Many e-tailers, for example, know not only what purchases you made from them but also what sections of their website you visited. The majority of e-tailers disclose their privacy policies on their websites. Exhibit 6.9 shows the National Retail Federation's (NRF's) Principles on Customer Data Privacy. In general, most of the major retailers in this country adhere to the NRF's principles. However, the shakeout in e-tailing during the early part of this decade showed just how consumers' rights to privacy could be violated by retailers who had no intention of doing so.

National Retail Federation ®

GENERAL RULE

National Retail Federation Principles on Customer Data Privacy

The privacy of information collected by a retailer about its customers during the course of transactions with those customers should be maintained with the degree of confidentiality that the retailer reasonably anticipates would be expected of it by the typical shopper purchasing that type of merchandise from the retailer. Departures from this standard should be disclosed to customers at or before each time of occurrence, unless previously consented to by the customer or otherwise expressly permitted by law.

PRACTICE PRINCIPLES

Each retailer should adopt a customer privacy policy explaining its practices with respect to the information it collects about its customers.

Policies could either be corporate-wide or divisional depending upon the manner in which the company believes customers view its retail operations.

A retailer should make reasonable efforts to inform its customers of the existence of its customer privacy policies, and make the substance of such policies available, on a regular basis.

At a minimum, a customer privacy policy should allow a customer to elect whether he or she wishes to prevent the marketing of his or her name to other unaffiliated corporations, or to "opt out" of future promotional solicitations from the company(s) to which the policy applies, or both.

Retail companies should develop procedures to reasonably ensure that customer information is not accessible to, or used by, its employees or others in contravention of its policies and customer elections, and that access to personally identifiable data for non-promotional purposes is limited to those individuals with a customer servicing need to know.

Exhibit 6.9
National Retail Federation Principles on Customer Data Privacy

Job-Switching

Do employees have the right to work for whomever they want? Of course, but employees have a responsibility to their previous employers. These firms provided them with training and access to confidential information such as vendor costs, customer lists, and future plans. When an employee leaves one retailer for another, the employee should respect the previous employer's right to retain the confidentiality of this information.

At the same time, the retailer should not seek to replace an employee, usually a manager or executive with a lower-paid, younger person just because the employee reaches the so-called 20-40-80 plateau (20 years or more with the firm, 40 years or older, and making more than $80,000 a year).

Employee Theft

Even as the misuse of company assets is actually a type of theft, outright stealing by employees is an even more serious issue. After all, just as employers have a responsibility to be fair to their employees, so employees have a responsibility to be honest and fair with their employers. However, at a time when retailers attribute almost half of their missing inventory to employee theft, many workers admit to stealing from their employers. Employee theft or *shrinkage* is most prevalent in food stores, restaurants, and bars (the subject of restaurant and bar theft is discussed in greater detail in Exhibit 9.7), department stores, and discount stores. Considering that these types of stores are usually larger in size, sales volume, and number of employees, the lack of close supervision might contribute to this problem. Some retailers, such as Walmart, are trying to address this problem by offering cash bonuses just before Christmas if the store not only makes its profit goal but also keeps shrinkage under a predetermined limit.

The above discussion is not meant to be an all-inclusive list of the ethical dilemmas facing retailing today. It does, however, provide the reader with a big picture of the role of ethics in retailing.

SUMMARY

We began this chapter by describing the multifaceted legal environment that confronts retailers in the United States. We identified constraints on retailers' activities in six broad categories: (1) pricing, (2) promotion, (3) products, (4) supply-chain relations, (5) other federal laws, and (6) state and local regulations. Within each of these broad constraints, we summarized some specific activities that are regulated.

Does legislation constrain a retailer's pricing policies?   LO 1

With regard to pricing—the issue that most frequently confronts retailers—the retailer should first be familiar with two methods of price fixing: with other retailers (horizontal) and with supply-chain members (vertical). In addition, the retailer must consider all the ramifications of price discrimination when purchasing merchandise. In setting retail prices, two other areas of concern are deceptive pricing and predatory pricing.

Is there a difference between legal and illegal promotional activities for a retailer?   LO 2

The retailer should focus on three areas that constitute illegal promotional activities: (1) deceitful diversion of patronage, which includes selling counterfeit or fake products; (2) deceptive advertising, including making false claims about a product and using bait-and-switch tactics; and (3) deceptive sales practices, which include not being completely honest in discussions about merchandise and the use of deceptive credit contracts.

What responsibilities does a retailer have regarding the products sold?   LO 3

With regard to product constraints, the retailer should be aware of legislation dealing with product safety, product liability, and both expressed and implied warranty requirements as they relate to retailing.

How does government regulation influence a retailer's behavior with other supply-chain members?   LO 4

Since all retailers are members of some type of supply chain, it is important to understand supply-chain relationships in terms of the legality of territorial restrictions, dual distribution, exclusive dealing, and tying agreements.

What is the impact of various state and local laws, in addition to federal regulations, in developing retail policies?   LO 5

The retailer must be aware of state and local laws, which include regulations on zoning, safety, unfair trade practices, building safety, blue laws, franchises, and taxes.

How does a retailer's code of ethics influence its behavior?   LO 6

Laws and regulations do not cover every situation a retailer might face in the day-to-day operations of a business. In such cases, codes of ethics for both retailer and employee behavior will provide guidance. A code of ethics is particularly important in buying merchandise, selling merchandise, and managing the retailer–employee relationship.

TERMS TO REMEMBER

horizontal price fixing
vertical price fixing
price discrimination
deceptive pricing
predatory pricing
palming off
deceptive advertising
bait-and-switch advertising
product liability laws
expressed warranties
implied warranty of merchantability

implied warranty of fitness
territorial restrictions
dual distribution
one-way exclusive-dealing arrangement
two-way exclusive-dealing agreement
tying agreement
ethics
explicit code of ethics
implicit code of ethics
slotting fees (slotting allowances)

REVIEW AND DISCUSSION QUESTIONS

LO 1

How does legislation constrain a retailer's pricing policies?

1. A busy corner intersection in Houston has gasoline stations on all four corners. These dealers always seem to have identical prices for their gasoline or, at least, they are within one cent of each other. Is this evidence of horizontal price fixing? Why or why not?
2. Does vertical price fixing help or hurt the small independent retailer? Why?
3. Deceptive pricing harms not only the consumer but also competition. Agree or disagree and explain your reasoning.

LO 2

What is the difference between legal and illegal promotional activities for a retailer?

4. If a student goes to a flea market and buys what he knows to be a fake Polo shirt for $18, is this an example of "deceitful diversion of patronage"? Is anyone hurt by this transaction? Who? Explain your reasoning.
5. Should all types of "puffery" be removed from ads? Explain your reasoning.
6. Do you believe that fake merchandise is sold on eBay? If so, what can eBay do about it, within reason?
7. A New York judge recently ruled that a retailer with the first name of John committed trademark infringement when he renamed one of his existing stores "Trader John's" and redesigned it to look like a nearby Trader Joe's. Was the judge right in his ruling? Why?

LO 3

What responsibilities does a retailer have regarding the products sold?

8. Should a McDonald's franchisee be held liable for selling a Happy Meal to an already overweight child? Why?
9. Should a retailer be held liable for statements made by its sales staff, even if the staff was instructed not to make such statements? Explain your reasoning.

LO 4

How does government regulation influence a retailer's behavior with other supply-chain members?

10. Could a decision by a manufacturer to engage in dual distribution be harmful to the consumer and members of the supply chain? Explain your reasoning.z
11. How could two-way exclusive dealing arrangements be harmful to consumers and competition?

12. Discuss the concept of exclusive dealing. Are exclusive dealing arrangements in the retailer's best interest? Are they in the consumer's best interest?

What is the impact of various state and local laws, in addition to other federal regulations, in developing retail policies? **LO 5**

13. Should a retailer be allowed to sell products below cost in attempt to increase store traffic? Why?

14. In a free-market system such as the one we have in the United States, should cities be allowed to use zoning laws to prevent big-box discounters from entering their markets?

15. Should online retailers be required to collect the sales tax on all their sales for the individual states?

How does a retailer's code of ethics influence its behavior? **LO 6**

16. Retailers should abide by the philosophy that "as long as it is legal, it is ethical." Agree or disagree and explain your reasoning.

17. Because of religious or personal beliefs, a convenience owner may not want to stock a particular product—say, cigarettes or beer—that is normally sold by its category of store. Can government force the retailer to carry a full line of merchandise if that retailer is the only store in a community?

18. Many retailers face the problem of small amounts of unredeemed money that remain on a gift card. Does this "breakage" belong to the retailer as part of its profit, does it belong in the state's treasury, or should it go into the state's unclaimed money fund to the consumer? Explain your reasoning.

SAMPLE TEST QUESTIONS

Ben Cooper's Chevrolet charges two different customers (one a man, the other a woman) two different prices for identical automobiles. This is in all probability a violation of the **LO 1**

   a. Clayton Act.
   b. your state's Unfair Trade Practices Act.
   c. Robinson-Patman Act.
   d. Sherman Act.
   e. This is not illegal since it involved a sale to a final consumer, not just sales between supply-chain or channel members.

An example of deceitful diversion of patronage would be **LO 2**

   a. spreading rumors about a competitor, even if the rumors do not hurt the competitor's business.
   b. telling the truth about a competitor that will hurt the competitor's business.
   c. advertising a product at a very low price and then adding hidden charges.
   d. putting extra large signs in your store's front window offering lower prices than your competitor next door.
   e. illegally using another company's trademark or brand name, which results in the loss of sales for the other company.

When a customer relies on the retailer to assist the customer or to select the right goods to serve a particular purpose, the retailer is establishing: **LO 3**

   a. an implied warranty of fitness.
   b. an implied warranty of merchantability.

    c. a price discrimination defense.

    d. an expressed warranty of fitness.

    e. an expressed warranty of merchantability.

LO 4

D-A Pet Products Company has an extremely popular line of cat food. The company has recently started insisting that retailers who carry its cat food must also carry its rather overpriced cat litter. Due to its price, the litter is not a big seller, and it takes away shelf space from more profitable products. Requiring stores that stock the cat food to also stock the litter is an example of:

    a. a consent agreement.

    b. a tying contract.

    c. unfair advertising.

    d. monopolistic competition.

    e. power marketing.

LO 5

The most stringent laws governing franchises are typically enacted at the _____ level.

    a. federal

    b. state

    c. county

    d. local

    e. international

LO 6

Which of the following is not an ethical dilemma that a retailer faces when buying merchandise?

    a. whether the buyer believes he or she can sell the merchandise

    b. the source of the merchandise

    c. the issue of product quality

    d. whether to demand a slotting fee

    e. whether to ask for a bribe

WRITING AND SPEAKING EXERCISE

As assistant manager for an online flooring retailer, you have been approached by your manager to develop a competition-based pricing policy. Your manager indicates that, since your market is national and pricing of carpets and hardwoods varies by both product and delivery costs, he would like you to develop a pricing strategy based on what online competitors are charging. Your manager believes that your firm could effectively compete on selection and service if only it could establish a pricing policy that would match or beat competitors, thus eliminating their competitive advantage. In other words, he wants you to gather competitive intelligence from your competitors' websites in order to develop a pricing policy that would, in effect, make your flooring cheaper by 2 percent to 3 percent or, at worst, the exact same price (when delivery charges are included) as your competitors. You wonder if this is legal and ethical.

    Prepare a response to the manager outlining your position on the potential legal and ethical implications of the strategy.

RETAIL PROJECT

Having enjoyed the entertainment, as well as the refreshments, at your local drinking establishment during your academic career, you decide to open a bar of your own after graduation. However, based on the material presented in this chapter, you realize that there are quite a few regulations governing these types of retail facilities. Investigate the laws regarding operating a bar and grill. Be sure to consider all local and state regulations about the location of such establishments. Also determine what, if any, laws about security and liability are involved.

In addition, determine the ethical issues involved. For example, do you want to locate near a high school or a rehab center? Do you want to hire people who are less than drinking age to work in the food section?

PLANNING YOUR OWN RETAIL BUSINESS

You are the general manager and partner for a local Ford dealership with a net worth of $1,800,000. At your regular Friday morning meeting with the sales force, you congratulate your staff on being ahead of its sales quota for the year.

Things could not be better, you think to yourself, as you leave the meeting and return to your office. You are going to exceed your $8.5-million sales goal for the year. Your cost of merchandise sold is expected to average 88 percent of sales, and your fixed operating costs are being held to $30,000 a month. With variable costs averaging 5 percent of sales, you are expecting to produce almost a quarter of a million dollars in profit before taxes this year.

Just when things look so great, your partner calls to ask if you read the article in the morning newspaper about last night's city council meeting. It seems that in order to reduce local property taxes and thus keep voters happy, a council member has suggested that the city increase its sales tax by 1 percent. This tax would cover everything sold in the city, including automobiles.

While you hate to see any type of sales tax increase since it raises the price of your automobiles, this one in particular could present your dealership with a major problem. Just last year, several dealers representing most major domestic and foreign car manufacturers moved to a nearby suburban location, creating a sort of "car mall" where shoppers could easily move from one dealership to another and compare the various offerings. One of those car mall dealers was the city's other Ford dealer. This dealer's customers would not have to pay this additional sales tax since the suburb's government planned to keep local sales taxes at the current level and instead reap the benefits of an increase in retail sales as consumers flocked to suburban merchants to get lower prices.

What should you do? Should you absorb the additional tax to keep your prices competitive? What would this do to your profits? Or should you lobby city hall to persuade the council to see the errors of this tax increase?

Market Selection and Location Analysis

Chapter 7
Market Selection and Retail Location Analysis

Market Selection and Retail Location Analysis

OVERVIEW:

In this chapter, we will review how retailers select and reach their target markets through their choice of location. The two broad options for reaching a target market are store-based and nonstore-based locations. The chapter primarily focuses on the decision process for selecting store-based locations. We describe the various demand and supply factors that must be evaluated for each geographic market area under consideration. We conclude with a discussion of alternative locations that retailers consider as they select a specific site.

LEARNING OBJECTIVES:

After reading this chapter, you should be able to:

1. Explain the criteria used in selecting a target market.
2. Identify the different options, both store-based and nonstore-based, for effectively reaching a target market and identify the advantages and disadvantages of business districts, shopping centers, and freestanding units as sites for a retail location.
3. Define geographic information systems (GIS) and discuss their potential uses in a retail enterprise.
4. Describe the various factors to consider when identifying the most attractive geographic market for a new store.
5. Discuss the various attributes to consider when evaluating retail sites within a retail market.
6. Explain how to select the best geographic site for a store.

LO 1

Explain the criteria used in selecting a target market.

Selecting a Target Market

Many retail experts consider the most critical determinants of success in retailing to be (1) selecting a target market and (2) evaluating alternative ways to reach this target market. Traditionally, for retailers desiring to reach a given target market, this has meant selecting the best location for a store. In fact, according to an oft-repeated story, a famous retailer once said that the three major decisions in retailing are location, location, and location. There is truth in that statement because, while the other elements of the retail mix are also important, customers must be able to conveniently reach your store if those elements are to affect shopping behavior. The easier it is to reach the store, the more store traffic a store will have, which leads to higher sales.

Today, however, as retailers are finding alternative ways to reach customers, location refers to more than just a store's physical location. For example, Dell sells computers and peripherals at Best Buy and Walmart, through the mail, over the Internet, and by phone; the University of Phoenix offers an MBA online via a computer in the student's home or place of business, as well as at its own campuses located in major U.S. cities; eBay has established localized websites in more than two dozen countries; and Tupperware continues to sell most of its kitchenware via in-home parties (as was discussed in Chapter 5).

As noted in previous chapters, the Internet is becoming a major force in retailing, with sales expected to reach a little more than 5 percent of total retail sales over the next decade (see Exhibit 4.7). In addition, 2009 was the first time that more than 50 percent of Americans had the capability of making an Internet purchase from their home rather than having to rely on using a computer at work.

The equivalent of a store on the Internet is a retailer's website on the World Wide Web (usually denoted by www). When stopping at an e-tailer's website, visitors first view the firm's **home page**, which is essentially the e-tailer's storefront. From the home page, a person can be linked to other pages that provide more detailed information about merchandise, credit, warranties, terms of trade, and even job information and application forms. The total collection of all the pages of information on the retailer's website is known as its **virtual store**. Whereas a traditional store is located in geographic space, a virtual store is located in cyberspace. One word of caution is that many retailers downplay the significance of the web because it's just 2 percent, 5 percent, or even 15 percent (depending on the retail category) of their sales. While, this might not seem like much, consider how many retailers today are struggling to meet their sales goals. In such cases, 5 percent doesn't seem so small. After all, with total retail growth remaining relatively flat, the

home page
Is the introductory or first material viewers see when they access a retailer's Internet site. It is the equivalent of a retailer's storefront in the physical world.

virtual store
Is the total collection of all the pages of information on the retailer's Internet site.

Gavin Gough / Alamy

Photo courtesy of Vicki Beaver

Macy's has its stores located in every metropolitan area in the U.S. and thus is able to get valuable media exposure when it hosts the Macy's Thanksgiving Day Parade in New York City. Incidentally, the Macy's flagship store in New York City is the world's largest store.

Global Retailing

The Thrill of the Hunt

Every consumer loves hunting for and then finding bargains. Consequently, many are keenly aware that prices for products vary widely, depending on shopping location (e.g., store, city, or even country). One such category where this is particularly true is jewelry. As most jewelry buyers will tell you, the available selection of pearls and other semiprecious stones is often greatest where production takes place.

Since China produces 95 percent of the world's freshwater pearls, the prices for pearl products in China are often 40 percent to 80 percent below those charged in the United States. Unfortunately, for most of us, the closest we will ever get to China is watching the Travel Channel. Enter Stephen Bell, an entrepreneur.

In 2006, while walking though a Shanghai shopping district with his teenage son, Bell came up with the creative idea of selling jewelry online. Jewelry is not only small and easy to ship but also the most popular item purchased by China's tourists. He realized that if the district had Wi-Fi, he could use it to allow consumers in cities ranging from Des Moines to Lexington to experience the joys of shopping in China, and even haggling over price, from their home.

Recognizing American shoppers' desire for deals and the increased fascination with China as the result of the upcoming 2008 Olympics, Bell soon started ShangBy.com, an Internet retailer based in Shanghai and Texas featuring Chinese jewelry. To avoid legal issues, he insisted that the company stay away from cheap Chinese knockoffs; only nonbranded items would be listed on his site. After all, what American consumer could pass on a Tahitian pearl pendant, even if it was unbranded, that retailed for $2,000 at the local jewelry store but was available in China for only $400?

Operating under the slogan "Shop the World," ShangBy lets consumers travel halfway across the globe to make a virtual shopping trip to China for pearls and other jewelry without ever leaving their homes, making the process extremely simple. For example, a consumer in Tucson can log on to the website and let ShangBy's tour guide cruise the jewelry shops of Shanghai with a video crew, broadcasting live on the Internet. The Tucson "ShangBuyer" can even call a toll-free number and ask the guide and the video crew to zoom in on particular items while haggling over the price with store owners. After each ShangBy show, all the items purchased, as well as anything else

Stephen Bell

Global Retailing (*continued*)

the ShangBuyer examined, are listed on the retailer's website for other shoppers to purchase at that same price. This is accomplished by having a ShangBy employee return to the store to buy and ship the item to the customer.

ShangBy.com has become such a whirlwind success that even American talk-show hosts are getting in on the act. On a recent Rachael Ray show, taped live, Shangby.com allowed her and her viewers to visit various vendors in Shanghai where the prices of jewelry were well below those found down the street from her New York City studios. During the show's taping, Rachael purchased two strings of pearls (normally around $300 in the United States) for $62.50 each and had them sent express mail using FedEx.

Today, ShangBy.com is a growing and profitable business that offers as many as three live shopping tours and shows a day during the Christmas season and one or two tours and shows per week during slower shopping periods. According to company management, the most popular time to take a "live" virtual trip around the world to do some pearl shopping is from 9 P.M. to 11 P.M. Eastern Standard Time (8–10 P.M. Central, 6–8 P.M. Pacific). Just think how nice it is for the East Coast shopper to shop China's jewelry markets while sipping a glass of wine and being comfortably attired in robe and slippers.

Source: Based on information supplied by Stephen Bell, founder and CEO of ShangBy, and used with his written permission.

---

web may be a major source of growth for many retailers. The economic value of a retailer's e-tailing website was illustrated during spring 2009 when Circuit City went bankrupt and closed all of its stores. Shortly thereafter, Systemax Inc. purchased the Circuit City brand, the CircuitCity.com website, and Circuit City's customer lists and e-mail addresses. Systemax Inc was established in 1949 and is a multichannel retailer of computers, electronics, and industrial products in North America and Europe.

The chapter's "Global Retailing" box illustrates one of the exciting ways the web has changed retailing. Today, it is possible for a shopper in North America to not only view merchandise but also barter on price in real time with a merchant halfway across the world.

The cyberspace counterpart to a convenient location is the **ease of access** a consumer has to the site. Ease of access refers to the consumer's ability to easily and quickly find a website in cyberspace. To gain access to a site, a consumer can use a retailer's name (for example, http://www.target.com) or a search engine such as Google or Yahoo. Exhibit 7.1 illustrates that the importance of easy access also increases as the number of websites increases. For this reason, retailers use website

ease of access
Refers to the consumer's ability to easily and quickly find a retailer's Web site in cyberspace.

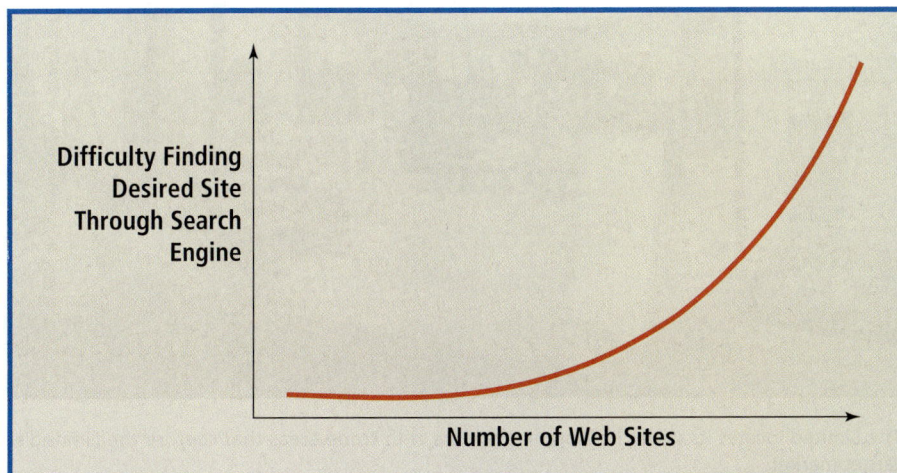

Exhibit 7.1
Ease of Access

Difficulty Finding Desired Site Through Search Engine

Number of Web Sites

optimization services to help move their stores up on the list when a potential customer searches for a particular merchandise category the retailer handles. This is similar to the practice in the not-too-distant past in which many small local retailers would place advertisements in the telephone yellow pages (which were organized alphabetically) and refer to their business as ABC Automotive Repair, or ABC Landscaping, and so on to gain the advantage of being listed first.

Regardless of whether a retailer is planning a traditional store in geographic space, a virtual store in cyberspace, or both, its first step is to develop a cost-effective way to reach the household or individual consumer that the retailer has identified as its target market. It is important to realize that failure to clearly identify one's target market will result in a significant waste of marketing expenditures.

Market Segmentation

target market

Is the group of customers that the retailer is seeking to serve.

In Chapter 3, market segmentation was defined as the method retailers use to segment, or break down, heterogeneous consumer populations into smaller, more homogeneous groups based on their characteristics. Since any single retailer cannot serve all potential customers, it is important that it segment the market and select a target market. A **target market** is that segment of the market that the retailer decides to pursue through its marketing efforts. Retailers in the same line of retail trade often pursue different target markets. For example, Ann Taylor appeals to a more upscale female, The Limited appeals to the moderate-income female, and Ross Dress for Less targets the budget-conscious shopper. Other women's clothiers have segmented customers based on characteristics such as age, size, education, ethnic group, and geographic location. For example, Charming Shoppes, Inc., with its three distinct brands—Lane Bryant (young, 25–35), Fashion Bug (young,

Paul Sakuma/AP Photo

The Limited locates its stores in shopping centers with trade areas that capture the Limited's target market.

20–49), and Catherines (baby boomers, 40-65) has the ability to serve every plus-size woman in the country.

Sometimes it is not easy to reach every target market. Generation Y types are poised to reshape the cultural landscape. However, since they have different priorities than previous generations did at the same age, they are more difficult to pinpoint. It has also been determined that Canadians are difficult for e-tailers to reach because they are more reluctant to shop online.

The topics of target-market selection and location analysis are combined here because a retailer must identify its target market before it decides how to best reach that market. Reaching the target market can be achieved through a store-based location in which the consumer travels to the store or through a nonstore retailing format in which products and services are offered to the consumer at a more convenient or accessible location. These are related topics because individuals of different characteristics are not randomly spread over geographic space. In fact, it has been repeatedly demonstrated that people of similar backgrounds live near each other and have similar media habits, consumption habits, activities, interests, and opinions. Because of this, retailers such as Nordstrom know where to geographically locate their stores, and merchants such as Williams Sonoma (which has a very successful mail-order catalog for high-quality kitchenware) know which ZIP codes, geographic areas, and specific households should receive their catalogs.

Identifying a Target Market

To reach a target market successfully, three criteria should be met. First, the retailer should seek a measurable market segment. This requires the retailer to rely on objective measures for which there is data available (e.g., age, gender, income, education, ethnic group, and religion). Subjective measures, like personality, are too problematic. For example, how would a retailer reasonably or cost-effectively measure the number of compulsive shoppers who like red as their favorite color in the United States? Therefore, retailers most often rely on objective demographic data, which the U.S. Census Bureau provides to businesses at no cost or for a small fee. A number of data integration firms such as National Planning Data Corporation can get this publicly available data into a more usable format for the retailer's intended purpose.

A second criterion is accessibility, or the degree to which the retailer can target its promotional or distribution efforts to a particular market segment. Do individuals in the target market watch certain television programs, listen to particular radio programs or podcasts, frequently visit the same websites (i.e., cluster in cyberspace) or cluster together in neighborhoods? Increasingly, individuals are becoming members of web-based communities or what are referred to as *tribes*. For instance, if you go to www.tribe.net you will see many of the tribes that are being formed and quickly note how relevant they are for many lines of retail trade. As we will see in this chapter, the location decision is largely determined by identifying the most effective way to reach a target market.

Finally, successful target marketing requires that the segment be substantial or large enough to be profitable for the retailer. Consider, for example, Joe Albertson's actions before he opened the first Albertson's grocery store in 1939. He drove through neighborhoods looking for diapers on clotheslines and tricycles in driveways. He knew that these were the signs of families with many mouths to feed and neighborhoods that promised profitability for his grocery stores.[1]

Clearly, a retailer can develop a store to appeal to any market segment regardless of size, such as a store for fans of the Green Bay Packers. However, the

store-based retailers
Operate from a fixed store location that requires customers to travel to the store to view and select merchandise or services.

retailer would have to ask whether enough Packer fans live within its trade area to make the store profitable. While there are surely enough Packer fans in Wisconsin to support such a retailer, a nonstore location such as a website on the Internet would be a more effective way to market to Packers fans worldwide.

Reaching Your Target Market

Identify the different options, both store-based and nonstore-based, for effectively reaching the retailer's target market and identify the advantages and disadvantages of business districts, shopping centers, and freestanding units as sites for retail locations.

As noted above, once a retailer identifies its target market, it must identify the most effective way to reach this market. Exhibit 7.2 illustrates the two basic retail formats that can be used to reach target markets: store-based and nonstore-based retailing. **Store-based retailers** operate from a fixed store location that requires customers to travel to the store to view and purchase merchandise and or services. Essentially, the retailer requires that the consumer perform part of the transportation function, which is one of the eight marketing functions discussed in Chapter 5. However some retailers are beginning to recognize that they can create a virtual store in Second Life or in similar virtual worlds. For instance, in promoting its Scion vehicle, Toyota created Scion City in Second Life. Scion City was a futuristic urban island that had a Toyota dealership. In addition, Scion City had a racetrack where avatars in Second Life could take a virtual test drive.

nonstore-based retailers
Intercept customers at home, at work, or at a place other than a store where they might be susceptible to purchasing.

Nonstore-based retailers reach customers at home, at work, or at places other than a store where they might be open to purchasing. As mentioned earlier, many retailers now reach customers on the Internet. Or, more accurately, the customer chooses to access the retailer on the Internet.

Location of Store-Based Retailers

As shown in Exhibit 7.2, there are four basic types of store-based retail locations: business districts, shopping centers and malls, freestanding units, and nontraditional

Exhibit 7.2
Retail Formats for Accessing Your Target Market

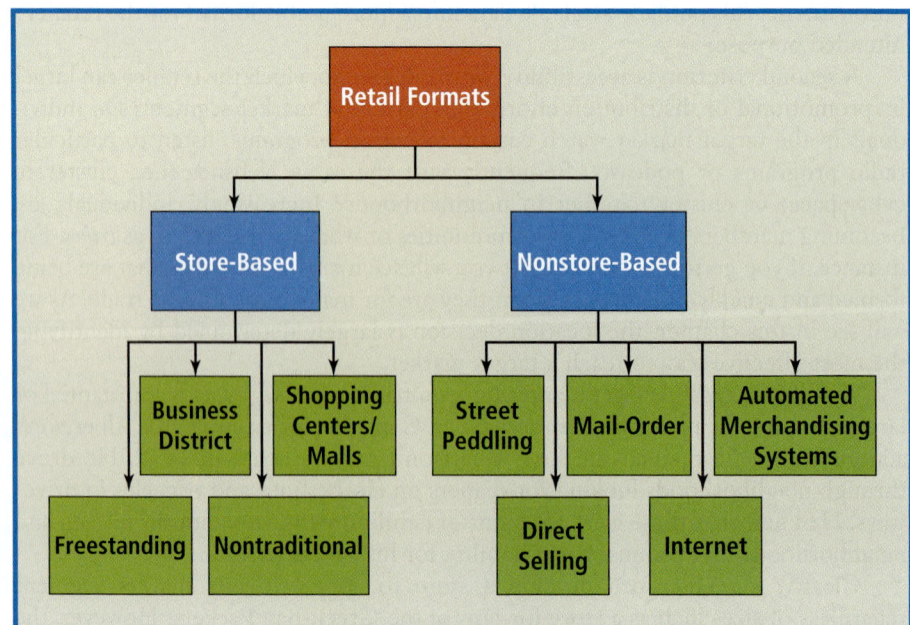

locations. No one type of location is inherently better than the others. Many retailers such as McDonald's, Pizza Hut, and Taco Bell have been successful in all four location types. Each type of location has its own characteristics relating to the composition of competing stores, parking facilities, affinities with nonretail businesses (e.g., office buildings, hospitals, universities), and other factors.

Business Districts

Historically, many retailers were located in a central business district (CBD), usually an unplanned shopping area around the geographic point where all public transportation systems converge. Many traditional department stores are located in the CBD along with a good selection of specialty shops. The makeup or mix of retailers in a CBD, however, is generally not the result of any advance planning and instead largely depends on history, retail trends, and luck. Recently, these department stores have been challenged—on the one side by mass merchants such as Target, Kohl's, and Walmart and on the other side by focused specialty retailers such as Chico's, Smarter Image, and Nike Town. As a result, their market attraction has declined, which has caused some to close and others to merge with competitors. In many instances, these merged chains were located in the same CBD and resulted in one of the stores closing. This, in turn, has hurt the rest of the CBD. Some communities have tried to reinvigorate their city centers by enhancing the shopping experience or using other nonshopping attractions such as river walks, art fairs, music festivals, and entertainment and sports districts. To date, however, the success of these efforts has been mixed.

In addition, several U.S. cities have seen a resurgence of "antichain" sentiment, which makes it difficult for some retailers to expand.[2] These rules, which are particularly restrictive toward chain retailers—usually those with more than 11 stores—are, in reality, attempts by local merchants to keep the Walmarts and Home Depots out of their localities.[3] For example, as of August 2008, 385 cities were

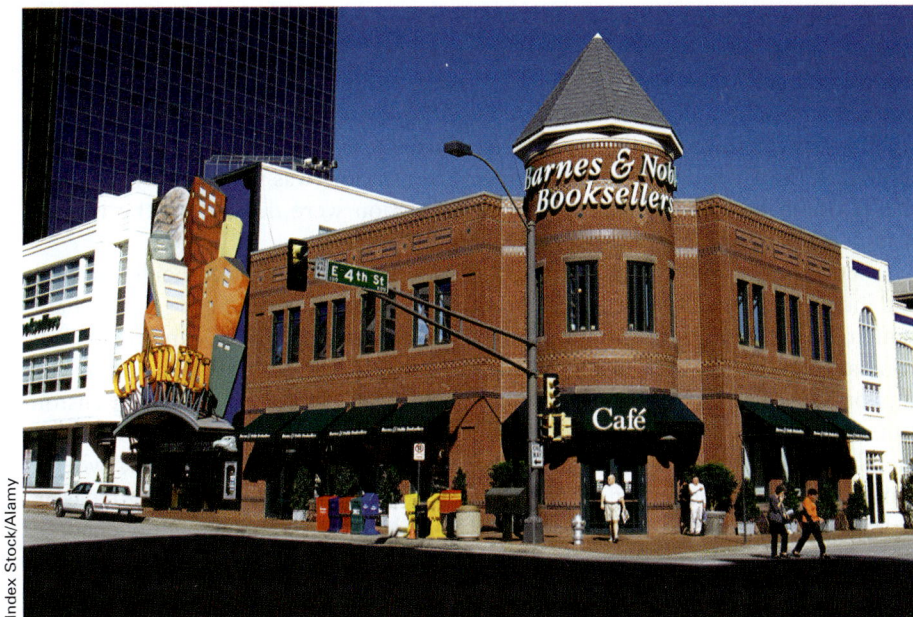

Index Stock/Alamy

Barnes & Noble is not only located in the suburbs, but also in central business districts such as the one shown here in Fort Worth, Texas.

Retailing: The Inside Story

Sam Walton's Own Thoughts

One of the most interesting facets of Walmart's expansion strategy can be seen in a letter Sam Walton wrote to Bob Kahn, a member of the Walmart board of directors and a retail consultant, on May 4, 1988. It read:

Dear Bob,

I am replying to your letter of the 19th concerning the Walmart monopoly of communities. I have realized for some time and, I suspect, many folks have in the company, as well, how fortunate we are to have very little competition in some of the larger communities in the country. That hasn't always been the case, as you well know. The history of our company has been that we have had more competition early on than almost any regional discounter in the United States. However, one by one, our competitors weakened, were mismanaged, and have fallen out in many of the cities that we practically now have to ourselves. That has been the case generally with Howard's, TG&Y, Gibson, Kuhn's, Magic Mart, and certainly some of the variety chains which were once active in this area. These competitors, plus Alco, Pamida, and the group in Indiana, are on the ropes now and I don't choose to believe those companies disappeared because of our effectiveness. Rather, I choose to believe, for the most part, they were mismanaged and, had they been managed well, there could and would have been enough business in their areas for them and for us. That hasn't been the case, as the evidence is now in, **and certainly, we now have a heavy responsibility of taking care of our customers in the best possible way without having the direct competition from a competing discounter in some very sizable markets.**

As the letter indicates, Sam Walton realized the importance of ensuring that the lack of competition would not cause Walmart to lose sight of its objective of being the best it could be. At the same time, Walton wanted to give the consumer fair and honest choices and not have Walmart take advantage of its power.

Today, with Walmart's annual sales equating to half a trillion dollars and its number of employed "associates" approaching 2 million, some experts contend the chain has grown too big. Others, however, call it the savior of the economy, as described in Chapter 1.

Source: Letter from Sam Walton to Robert Kahn, May 4, 1988. Used with the permission of the Kahn family.

---

listed on the www.sprawl-busters.com website as victories. This meant that they had some sort of antichain regulations in place.[4] The supporters of these laws believe that the introduction of big-box stores will destroy their quaint, close-knit downtown business districts that feature coffee shops, boutiques, clothing stores, and maybe even small locally owned department stores. This action, however, is not limited to the United States. When one of the authors was visiting New Zealand, the editorial page and letters to the editor section were devoted to the issue of stopping a Mitre 10 Mega Store in Dunedin.[5]

Such antichain action may actually have a negative impact on neighborhoods and independent retailers in the long run. Areas that vigorously fight against chains stand to lose the reinvestment ability that only a large corporation can provide.[6] To combat these regulations, chains across the country are mustering up community support, especially in times of economic slowdown, as well as producing custom storefront designs and interior schemes that blend with the aesthetics of the other merchants. Walmart, for example, recently tried to overcome these laws when it took advantage of the recent economic problems to expand in the Chicago market. It stressed the promise of new jobs and added sales-tax dollars.[7] This chapter's "Retailing: The Inside Story" box illustrates that Sam Walton recognized that Walmart would not be welcome in every city it desired to enter, but it had a responsibility to treat its customers fairly once it established a store.

The CBD has several strengths and weaknesses. Among its strengths are easy access to public transportation; wide product assortment; variety in images, prices, and services; and proximity to commercial activities. Some weaknesses to consider are inadequate (and usually expensive) parking, older stores, high rents and taxes, traffic and delivery congestion, potentially a high crime rate, and the often-decaying conditions of many inner cities. However, despite these disadvantages, JCPenney recently joined Target, Best Buy, Home Depot, Walmart, Burlington Coat Factory, Staples, and The Container Store by deviating from their historical suburban location policies and adapting their formulas to the most urban of urban environments—New York City.[8] Despite the high costs and other disadvantages of such locations, the chain felt that the high traffic and more than double its national average in sales per square foot of space made these locations economically viable.

Often, the weaknesses of CBDs have resulted in a retail situation known as inner-city retailing. This occurs when only the poorest citizens are left in an urban area. Despite the fact that such areas annually contribute 2 percent to 3 percent of all retail spending, product and service offerings in these areas have decreased while prices have held steady or even increased. Although many consumers are aware that basketball great Magic Johnson has found success opening movie theaters in Harlem as well as in the inner cities of Los Angeles, Cleveland, and Houston, they may not be knowledgeable about the success of other retailers in these urban areas. Retailers such as Dollar General, Vons, Stop & Shop, Supermarkets General, Jewel-Osco, Kroger, First National Supermarkets, A&P, American Stores, Pathmark, and even service retailers such as Sterling Optical, Sprint, and Verizon have used good merchandise selection and heavy public relations to find success in previously underserved inner-city areas. One of the key reasons for their success in these markets is that they have tailored their inventories to the special needs and tastes of inner-city residents. In addition, these retailers have leveraged an underutilized workforce with high retention in an overall tight labor market.

In larger cities, secondary and neighborhood business districts have developed. A **secondary business district (SBD)** is a shopping area that is smaller than the CBD, revolves around at least one department or variety store, and is located at a major street intersection. In fact, Carrefour, the highly successful French hypermarket, selected its name because it communicates the cross-roads where it typically located its huge stores. A **neighborhood business district (NBD)** is a shopping area that evolves to satisfy the convenience-oriented shopping needs of a neighborhood. The NBD generally contains several small stores, with the major retailer being either a supermarket or a variety store, and is located on a major artery of a residential area. An increasing number of national retail chains are finding the neighborhood business district an attractive location for new stores. These chains include retailers such as Ann Taylor, the Body Shop, Starbucks, Crate & Barrel, Williams Sonoma, Wolf Camera, Radio Shack, and Pottery Barn.

The single factor that distinguishes these business districts from a shopping center or mall is that they are usually unplanned. Like CBDs, the store mixture of SBDs and NBDs evolves partly by planning, partly by luck, and partly by accident. No one plans, for example, that there will be two department stores, four jewelry stores, two camera shops, three shoe shops, twelve apparel shops, and one theater in a SBD.

Shopping Centers and Malls

America has had a love affair with shopping centers. These "temples of consumption" experienced their first major growth wave just after World War II. A **shopping center**, which actually traces its history back to Kansas City almost a hundred years ago, is a centrally owned or managed shopping district that is

secondary business district (SBD)
Is a shopping area that is smaller than the CBD and that revolves around at least one department or variety store at a major street intersection.

neighborhood business district (NBD)
Is a shopping area that evolves to satisfy the convenience-oriented shopping needs of a neighborhood, generally contains several small stores (with the major retailer being a supermarket or a variety store), and is located on a major artery of a residential area.

shopping center (or mall)
Is a centrally owned or managed shopping district that is planned, has balanced tenancy (the stores complement each other in merchandise offerings), and is surrounded by parking facilities.

anchor stores
Are the stores in a shopping center that are the most dominant and are expected to draw customers to the shopping center.

planned, has balanced tenancy (the stores complement each other in merchandise offerings), and is surrounded by parking facilities. A shopping center has one or more **anchor stores** (dominant large-scale stores that are expected to draw customers to the center) and a variety of smaller stores. In the past, these anchors were department stores. However, the recent consolidation of department store companies has reduced the number of stores, either chain or independent, that are available to serve as magnets to draw consumers to the center. Today, as a result, many centers are now anchored by a single department store, along with a Cheesecake Factory, Barnes & Noble, Michael's, PetSmart, Office Depot, and maybe a Home Depot or a multiscreened movie theater.

To ensure that these smaller stores complement each other, the shopping center often specifies the proportion of total space that can be occupied by each type of retailer. Similarly, the center's management places limits on the merchandise lines that each retailer may carry. For example, several years ago, Old Navy's now-defunct Torpedo Factory, which sold coffee and submarine sandwiches, wanted to locate in a center with a Starbucks. However, Starbucks had a coffee exclusive arrangement that prevented Torpedo Factory's entry.[9] In addition, a unified, cooperative advertising and promotional strategy is followed by all the retailers in the center. Because of the many advantages shopping centers and malls can offer the retailer, they are a fixture of American life and account for 55 percent of all retail sales in the United States. Some of the advantages a shopping center offers over a CBD location are:

1. heavy traffic resulting from the wide range of product offerings,
2. cooperative planning and sharing of common costs,
3. access to highways and available parking,
4. a lower crime rate, and
5. a clean and neat environment.

Despite these favorable reasons for locating in a shopping center, the retailer operating in a mall does face several disadvantages:

1. inflexible store hours (the retailer must stay open during mall hours and cannot be open at other times),
2. high rents,
3. restrictions as to what merchandise or services the retailer may sell,
4. inflexible operations and required membership in the center's merchant organization,
5. potentially too much competition and the fact that much of the traffic is not interested in a particular product offering, and
6. an anchor tenant's dominance of the smaller stores.

Shopping-center image, preferences, and personality all attract various subsets of consumers, giving retailers located at the center a competitive advantage over other retailers. Therefore, it is extremely important that a retailer considering a shopping-center location be aware of the makeup, image, preferences, and personality of the center under question. For example, the open-air Rookwood Center in Cincinnati developed a whole new trade area for retailers. Prior to its development in the economic depressed area of Norwood, retailers had to locate either in downtown Cincinnati or in the more distant suburbs.

Mark Fallon

Rockwood Center, in Cincinnati, although near an economically depressed area, allowed national chain store retailers to more conveniently serve customers.

As Exhibit 7.3 shows, according to the International Council of Shopping Centers, there are eight different types of shopping centers and malls, each with a distinctive function.

Shopping centers and malls now account for one-half of all retail sales, excluding automotive, in the United States. However, as was recently demonstrated, this love affair can cause a problem for the malls. After all, since personal consumption amounts to some 70 percent of the American economy, if Americans don't spend, then the economy is in trouble. Fiscal health isn't possible until money is again rushing into the cash registers of every retailer. However, during the recent recession, shopping centers and malls struggled with slowing consumer spending and store closings by retailers. They now face another problem that may persist long after the economy bounces back: a decade of overbuilding. The problem is twofold:

1. What do you do with those old stores? After all, who wants a football-field–sized former Mervyn's? What do you do with an old Home Depot or Kmart, boxes so big you can measure its floor space in acres? (For more information about these empty shopping centers and stores, check out http://deadmalls.com.)

2. What about those malls that were just being built as the slowdown began? Consider a six-mile stretch of highway north of Dallas, where three developers are currently racing to finish four huge shopping centers with a combined 3 million square feet of space. Not only will they compete with each other but also three malls already existed within a 10-mile radius.

In short, it may take a decade for America to overcome the current surplus of retail space. (In the country's largest retail markets, retail selling space is now 38 square feet for every person versus 29 square feet 25 years ago.)[10] Consider that the

Exhibit 7.3
ICSC Shopping Center Definitions—U.S.

Type of Shopping Center	Concept	Square Feet (Including Anchors)	Acreage	Typical Anchor(S)		Anchor Ratio*	Primary Trade Area**
				Number	Type		
MALLS							
Regional Center	General merchandise; fashion (mall, typically enclosed)	400,000–800,000	40–100	2 or more	Full-line department store; jr. department store; mass merchant; discount department store; fashion apparel	50–70%	5–15 miles
Superregional Center	Similar to regional center but has more variety and assortment	800,000+	60–120	3 or more	Full-line department store; jr. department store; mass merchant; fashion apparel	50–70%	5–25 miles
OPEN-AIR CENTERS							
Neighborhood Center	Convenience	30,000–150,000	3–15	1 or more	Supermarket	30–50%	3 miles
Community Center	General merchandise; convenience	100,000–350,000	10–40	2 or more	Discount department store; supermarket; drug; home improvement; large specialty/discount apparel	40–60%	3–6 miles
Lifestyle Center	Upscale national chain specialty stores; dining and entertainment in outdoor setting.	Typically 150,000–500,000, but can be smaller or larger.	10–40	0–2	Not usually anchored in the traditional sense but may include book store; other large-format specialty retailers; multiplex cinema; small department store.	0–50%	8–12 miles
Power Center	Category-dominant anchors; few small tenants	250,000–600,000	25–80	3 or more	Category killer; home improvement; discount department store; warehouse club; off-price	75–90%	5–10 miles
Theme/Festival Center	Leisure; tourist-oriented; retail and service	80,000–250,000	5–20	N/A	Restaurants; entertainment	N/A	N/A
Outlet Center	Manufacturers' outlet stores	50,000–400,000	10–50	N/A	Manufacturers' outlet stores	N/A	25–75 miles

*The share of a center's total square footage that is attributable to its anchors;

**The area from which 60–80% of the center's sales originate.

Used with the written permission of the International Council of Shopping Centers.

amount of inventory investment per square foot of retail space is often $50 and beyond. Thus, if you multiply 38 square feet of retail space for every person by $50, you get $1,900 in inventory waiting for each person. This is essentially a pantry that all of us have but for which we do not need to pay the storage cost or invest in the inventory. Due to this oversupply of space, retailers may get lower rents over the next couple of years, but they too will face another economic problem. Once Americans start earning again and thus spending again, they are also likely to save more and thus not overshop and overconsume. After all, they each have this additional pantry of merchandise available when they need it! This suggests that the oversupply of retail space will not disappear anytime soon.

Nevertheless, despite their problems, the country's 1,500 shopping centers and malls are still a part of our lifestyle. Some seniors engage in their daily exercise here, families find malls a good source of low-cost entertainment, and teens use them as social outlets. In many cases, the loyalties of shoppers toward a specific center or mall have over time become equal to or greater than their loyalties to a particular retailer.

Freestanding Location

Another location option is to be freestanding. A **freestanding retailer** generally locates along major traffic arteries without any adjacent retailers selling competing products to share traffic. Freestanding retailing offers several advantages:

1. lack of direct competition,
2. generally lower rents,
3. freedom in operations and hours,
4. facilities that can be adapted to individual needs, and
5. inexpensive parking.

Freestanding retailing does have some limitations:

1. lack of drawing power from complementary stores,
2. difficulties in attracting customers for the initial visit,
3. higher advertising and promotional costs,
4. operating costs that cannot be shared with others,
5. stores that may have to be built rather than rented, and
6. zoning laws that may restrict some activities.

The difficulties of drawing and then holding customers to an isolated or freestanding store is the reason that only large, well-known retailers such as the category killers discussed in Chapter 1 should attempt it. Small retailers may be unable to develop a loyal customer base since customers are often unwilling to travel to a freestanding store that does not have a wide assortment of products and a local or national reputation. Discounters and wholesale clubs, with their large selections, are most often thought of when discussing this location strategy. When these large national chains acquire land for a freestanding store, they are seeking to acquire land in areas in which they expect the community will grow in the future. As a result, they often acquire more than they need and then "out-parcel" (i.e., sell) the remaining land to smaller retailers. Some astute local retailers and small regional chains have found it quite attractive to buy this excess land and build stores, even at a premium price, because of the traffic a large discounter like Walmart generates. Many home-improvement centers and traditional hardware stores such as Ace Hardware and TrueValue hardware, due to the nature of their product offerings, have been able to use the freestanding location strategy successfully in the past.

freestanding retailer
Generally locates along major traffic arteries and does not have any adjacent retailers to share traffic.

The University of North Carolina hosts a Victoria's Secret PINK My Pad contest, which awards college students the chance to turn their dorm room into the ultimate "Pink Pad" with a vast assortment of PINK clothes, accessories, and bedding.

Nontraditional Locations

Increasingly, retailers are identifying nontraditional locations that offer greater convenience. Recognizing, for example, that a significant number of travelers spend several hours in airports and could use this time to purchase merchandise they might otherwise purchase in their local communities, today many airport concourses now look like real regional malls, complete with national brands, casual dining, service kiosks and entertainment and infotainment venues. Consider what travelers using Terminal 5 at Kennedy International Airport will see on the way to and from their flights: more restaurants than ever before. After all, the increased security means that people are arriving earlier for their flights, leaving them with more time to shop. Also, cutbacks in the food service offered on many flights have caused more people to seek sustenance in the airport.[11]

College campuses are also experiencing an influx of nontraditional locations. Not only are the number of food courts in student unions and cosmetic counters in campus bookstores increasing but also they are now allowing temporary "pop-up" stores on major walking paths throughout campuses. For example, Victoria's Secret's Pink, a young women's clothing brand of Limited Brands Inc., opens these campus pop-up stores for a day or two, selling merchandise, handing out promotional items, and collecting used clothing for charity. In addition, cell-phone retailers such as AT&T, Sprint, and Verizon and credit-card providers such as MasterCard and Visa are often seen on campus malls selling to students. After all, nearly 20 million students are enrolled in U.S. postsecondary institutions, and the discretionary spending of 18- to 30-year-old students far exceeds $53 billion a year.[12] Truck and travel stops along interstate highways are also incorporating food courts. Some franchises such as Taco Bell, Arby's, and Dunkin' Donuts are putting small food-service units in convenience stores, university libraries, and classroom buildings. Embassy Suites, a Hilton Hotels chain, saw an opportunity to offer guests additional entertainment, dining, and shopping amenities and built new units next to shopping centers. Hospitals are building emergency-care clinics near where people live in the suburbs and away from the hospitals, lawyers are opening storefront offices wherever there is high pedestrian traffic, and dry cleaners and copying services as well as Yoga studios are locating in major office buildings. Today, some Wells Fargo banks have mini-marketplaces featuring Starbucks coffee bars, dry cleaners, delis, and postal centers. Other banks have opened branch offices in retirement centers.

Some service retailers are an exception, however, since their products are delivered to consumers at home. For example, plumbers, house painters, repair services, maid services, carpet cleaners, and lawn-care firms may not be concerned with their location. Enterprise Rent-A-Car will even deliver your rental car or truck to you. Incidentally, Home Depot recognized that many customers do not have a motor vehicle of sufficient size to transport their purchases, so the company will rent customers a suitable truck by the hour.

Nonstore-Based Retailers

There is a great diversity and variety of nonstore-based retailers. Perhaps the oldest form is the street peddler who sells merchandise from a pushcart or temporary stall set up on a street. Street peddling is still common in some parts of the world such as Mexico, Turkey, Pakistan, India, and many parts of Africa and South America. But it is also seen in this country in such places as New York City and San Francisco, where street-corner vendors sell T-shirts, watches, books, magazines, tobacco, candy, hot dogs, and other products. Peddlers also operate in many other United States cities, oftentimes using family members to operate kiosks and carts in heavily traveled areas such as malls and the parking lots at sporting events.[13]

Chapter 4, "Evaluating the Competition in Retailing," discussed several popular forms of nonstore retailing which are depicted in Exhibit 7.2 (direct sellers, catalog sales, and e-tailing). Yet because retailing in the United States will continue to be predominantly store-based for the foreseeable future, we focus our attention on location analysis for these retailers. However, it should be noted that some innovative retailers are using multiple retail formats to reach their target markets. For example, JCPenney's not only continues to build and remodel traditional stores but also has extensive mail and online operations where different catalogs are developed to target specific customer segments. In fact, most experts predict that over the next few years virtually every traditional store-based retailer will have developed multiple retail formats to reach its target markets.

Interestingly, while catalog sales have dropped slightly for these retailers, online sales have shown tremendous growth. Experts feel that this is the natural outgrowth of consumers searching for merchandise in stores and in catalogs but ordering online and picking up the merchandise at their convenience. Sears, for example, recently opened a warehouse-style concept store in Joliet, Illinois, called MyGofer that allows shoppers to order online and pick up their purchases in the store or at a drive-through portal.[14]

Geographic Information Systems

LO 3

Define geographic information systems (GIS) and discuss their potential uses in a retail enterprise.

One recent technological innovation in retailing is the use of geographic information systems. A **geographic information system (GIS)** is a computerized system that combines physical geography with cultural geography. Physical geography is the latitude (north–south) and longitude (east–west) of a specific point in physical space and its related physical characteristics (water, land, temperature,

geographic information system (GIS)
Is a computerized system that combines physical geography with cultural geography.

culture
Is the buffer that people have created between themselves and the raw physical environment and includes the characteristics of the population, man-made objects, and mobile physical structures.

annual rainfall, etc.). Cultural geography consists of the things that people have put in place in that space. To understand this, one needs to appreciate that **culture** is the buffer that humankind has created between itself and the raw physical environment. It includes characteristics of the population such as age, gender, and income, as well as human-made objects placed in that space like fixed physical structures (factories, stores, apartment building, schools, churches, houses, highways, railroads, airports, etc.) and mobile physical structures (e.g., cars and trucks). In reality, culture includes anything that humans can put onto a physical space, which then becomes an attribute of the physical space. For example, Scottsdale, Arizona, has become known for its very high density of golf courses, but these golf courses were put there by people, not by nature. Other areas are known as high-crime areas, but nature did not put crime there, people did.

Recent advancements in GIS have allowed the retail analyst to also describe the lifestyle (activities, interests, opinions) of the residents of geographic areas. This can be quite helpful in selecting locations for stores that are highly lifestyle sensitive such as Pittsburgh-based Dick's Sporting Goods, Inc. Dick's is a category killer in sporting goods and operates more than 255 stores in 34 states. In fact, executives speaking at a research conference held by the International Council of Shopping Centers noted that with the increased user-friendliness of GIS mapping technology, they have become more research-driven in locating stores. They no longer have to rely on information supplied by real estate brokers that may not be relevant to their business such as "the supermarket across the street is doing $30 million in sales annually."[15] Exhibit 7.4 shows the key components of geographic information systems.

Exhibit 7.4
GIS Components

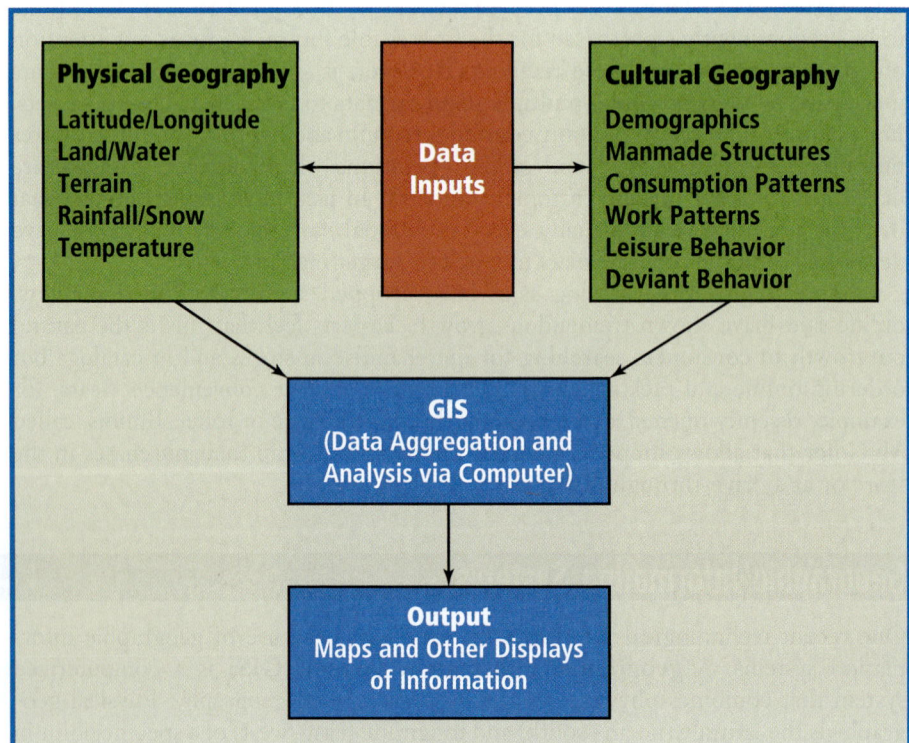

Physical Geography	Data Inputs	Cultural Geography
Latitude/Longitude Land/Water Terrain Rainfall/Snow Temperature		Demographics Manmade Structures Consumption Patterns Work Patterns Leisure Behavior Deviant Behavior

GIS
(Data Aggregation and Analysis via Computer)

Output
Maps and Other Displays of Information

Thematic Maps

Historically, it was not unusual for a retailer to push pins into a map of a city where it was located. Each pin represented where a customer lived. An even more sophisticated retailer might have colored the map to represent different areas of the city in terms of income levels or ethnic composition. This was an early form of thematic mapping. **Thematic maps** are area maps that use visual techniques such as colors, shading, lines, and so on to display cultural characteristics of the physical space. Thematic maps can be very useful management tools for retailers. They can help the retailer visualize a tremendous amount of information in an easy-to-understand format. Today, thematic maps are an important feature of geographic information systems and are fully computerized, making them easy for retailers to develop. Google Earth displays satellite images of varying resolution of Earth's surface, allowing users to visually see things like cities, houses, buildings, or vacant lots. The degree of resolution available is based somewhat on the points of interest and popularity of the site being considered. Today, retailers, especially the smaller ones, are beginning to use Yahoo or Google maps as an inexpensive means of selecting or reviewing possible retail expansion ideas. Google Earth even has the capability to show buildings and structures, such as major highways and bridges, and the service recently added a feature that allows users to monitor traffic speeds at loops located every 200 yards in real time. Finally with the use of other search engines, the retailer can enter the address of neighbors and determine their business and various other information factors about them—a far cry from the way Sam Walton selected his early sites a half-century ago. He would select a town or city and then fly over it in his private plane during the rush hour to determine traffic patterns and scout out possible locations.

thematic maps
Use visual techniques such as colors, shading, and lines to display cultural characteristics of the physical space.

Uses of GIS

As a management technology, GIS has a variety of important uses in retailing. Some of the more popular uses are identified as follows.

1. Market Selection. A retailer with a set of criteria in mind, such as the demographics of its target market and the level of over- or understoring in a market, can have the GIS identify and rank the most attractive cities, counties, or other geographic areas to consider for expansion.

2. Site Analysis. If a retailer has a particular community in mind, a GIS can identify the best possible site or evaluate alternative sites for their expected profitability.

3. Trade Area Definition. If the retailer develops a database of where its customers reside, a GIS can automatically develop a trade area map and update this daily, weekly, monthly, or annually.

4. New Store Cannibalization. A GIS can help the retailer evaluate how the addition of another store in a community might cannibalize sales from any of its existing stores.

5. Advertising Management. A GIS can help the retailer allocate its advertising budget to different stores based on the market potential in their respective trade areas. Similarly, a GIS can help the retailer develop a more effective direct-mail campaign to prospective customers.

6. Merchandise Management. A GIS can help the retailer develop an optimal mix of merchandise based on the characteristics of households and individuals within its trade area.

7. Evaluation of Store Managers. A GIS can provide an important human resource function. It can help assess how well a store manager is performing based on one's trade area characteristics. Consider that two stores of the same size could be performing quite differently because of the demographics and competitive conditions in the two trade areas. Thus, it would be inappropriate to either reward or punish a manager for things over which the manager has no control.

Although most large retailers are using a combination of mapping and demographics during the site-selection process, many small to medium-sized retailers are not using GIS technology to its full potential. This may be due to a lack of technical expertise in using complicated software; if a program isn't easy to use, many firms won't use it. Visualization of these maps is improving, but it isn't possible to make a perfect model of the world. A mall, for example, has to have anchors that draw traffic for the other stores. As soon as an anchor leaves, the economics of the GIS model are changed. This is happening with more frequency today as the consolidation of department store chains and mall saturation has caused malls to seek a new type of anchor. Not only are Home Depots and Best Buys now anchoring some regional malls, as discussed earlier in this chapter, but so are Bass Pro Shops. Other centers are trying different approaches to fill the voids created by these departing stores. Some are trying to recruit midpriced restaurants and theater chains to draw evening visitors and encourage shoppers to convert a quick stop into a day-long excursion. Others are avoiding the addition of new stores and instead adding entertainment or amusement operations such as Legoland Discovery Centres (LDCs). These LDCs are smaller versions of the famous Legoland theme parks, measuring roughly 40,000 square feet and containing a smaller selection of the offerings at the larger parks. They feature rides, 4-D movies (special effects constitute the fourth dimension), miniature replicas of their host cities built from Legos, a children's play area, and a boutique.[16]

LO 4   Market Identification

What are the various factors that should be considered in identifying the most attractive retail market?

The location decision for store-based retailers involves three sequential steps. First, the retailer must identify the most attractive market or **trading area**—the geographic area from which a retailer, group of retailers, or community draws its customers—in which to operate. For some like Carrefour, Home Depot, Walmart, and IKEA, this includes geographic expansion into foreign countries.

One such location is China. Over the last decade, most American and European retailers have identified China as an attractive market for expansion. They contend that China is the most lucrative market for the early to mid-21st century because it has the world's largest population. Acknowledging that its economy has suffered since the end of the 2008 Olympics, many retailers still believe it represents great opportunity due to its outstanding technological infrastructure, and many American and European retailers are continuing to make aggressive expansion plans for China.

trading area
Is the geographic area from which a retailer, group of retailers, or community draws its customers.

On the contrary many retailers such as Kohl's and Kroger, as well as most smaller merchants, concentrate on the United States, and when considering new locations they evaluate only the attractiveness of domestic markets. Further, some retailers chose to concentrate on a small region of the United States, possibly a single state or city.

The second step in the retail location process is to evaluate the density of demand and supply within each market and identify the most attractive sites

Dongang Department Store, Beijing City, Beijing China. The contemporary retail infrastructure in China is on par with the best in the world.

The China National Olympic Stadium known as the Bird's Nest. The 2008 Olympics brought even more worldwide attention to China as a growing retail market which will continue to attract foreign investment by well known retailers.

available within each market. Essentially, this means identifying sites most consistent with the retailer's target market while simultaneously accounting for those markets that may be under- or overstored.

The third step involves selecting the best site (or sites) available. This stage involves estimating the revenue and expenses of a new store at various locations and then identifying the most profitable ones. These three steps are illustrated in Exhibit 7.5.

Retail Location Theories

The most attractive retail markets are not necessarily the largest. A variety of other factors need to be considered in identifying attractive markets (e.g., the level of competition, zoning laws, average wages, and real estate costs). But to start, three theories are especially useful for identifying the best markets.

Retail Gravity Theory

Retail gravity theory suggests that there are underlying consistencies in shopping behavior that allow for mathematical analysis and prediction based on the notion or concept of gravity. **Reilly's law of retail gravitation,**[17] named after its developer, William Reilly, deals with how large urbanized areas attract customers from smaller communities. In effect, it states that two cities attract trade from an intermediate location approximately in direct proportion to the population of the two cities and in inverse proportion to the square of the distance from these two cities to the intermediate place. In other words, people will tend to shop in the larger city if travel distance is equal or even somewhat farther because they believe that the larger city has a better product selection and will be worth the extra travel.

Two decades later, Reilly's original law was revised in order to determine the boundaries of a city's trading area or to establish a point of indifference between two cities.[18] This **point of indifference** is the breaking point at which customers

retail gravity theory
Suggests that there are underlying consistencies in shopping behavior that yield to mathematical analysis and prediction based on the notion or concept of gravity.

reilly's law of retail gravitation
Based on Newtonian gravitational principles, explains how large urbanized areas attract customers from smaller rural communities.

point of indifference
Is the breaking point between two cities where customers are indifferent to shopping in either city.

Exhibit 7.5
Selecting a Retail Location

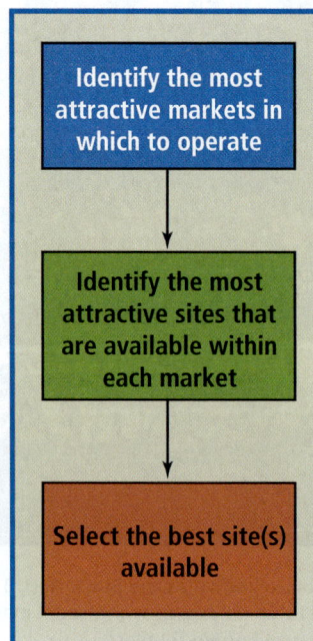

Identify the most attractive markets in which to operate

↓

Identify the most attractive sites that are available within each market

↓

Select the best site(s) available

would be indifferent to shopping at either city. The new formulation of Reilly's law can be expressed algebraically as:

$$D_{ab} = \frac{d}{1 + \sqrt{\frac{P_b}{P_a}}}$$

where D_{ab} is the breaking point from A, measured in miles along the road to B;
d is the distance between A and B along the major highway;
P_a is the population of A; and
P_b is the population of B.

For example, if Levelland and Norwood are 65 miles apart and Levelland's population is 100,000 and Norwood's is 200,000, then the breaking point of indifference between Levelland and Norwood would be 26.9 miles from Levelland and 38.1 miles from Norwood. This means that if you lived 25 miles from Levelland and 40 miles from Norwood, you probably would choose to shop in Levelland since it is within your zone of indifference for Levelland and is beyond your zone of indifference for Norwood. (Readers may want to calculate this for themselves, using Norwood as A and Levelland as B.)

Exhibit 7.6 shows how Reilly's law can be used to determine a community's trading area. As shown in Exhibit 7.6, A has a population of 240,000. City B, with a population of 14,000, is 18 miles north of A, and its breaking point is 14.5 miles north of city A (point X on Exhibit 7.6). City C, with a population of 21,000, is 14 miles southwest of A, and its breaking point is 10.8 miles southwest of A (point Z).

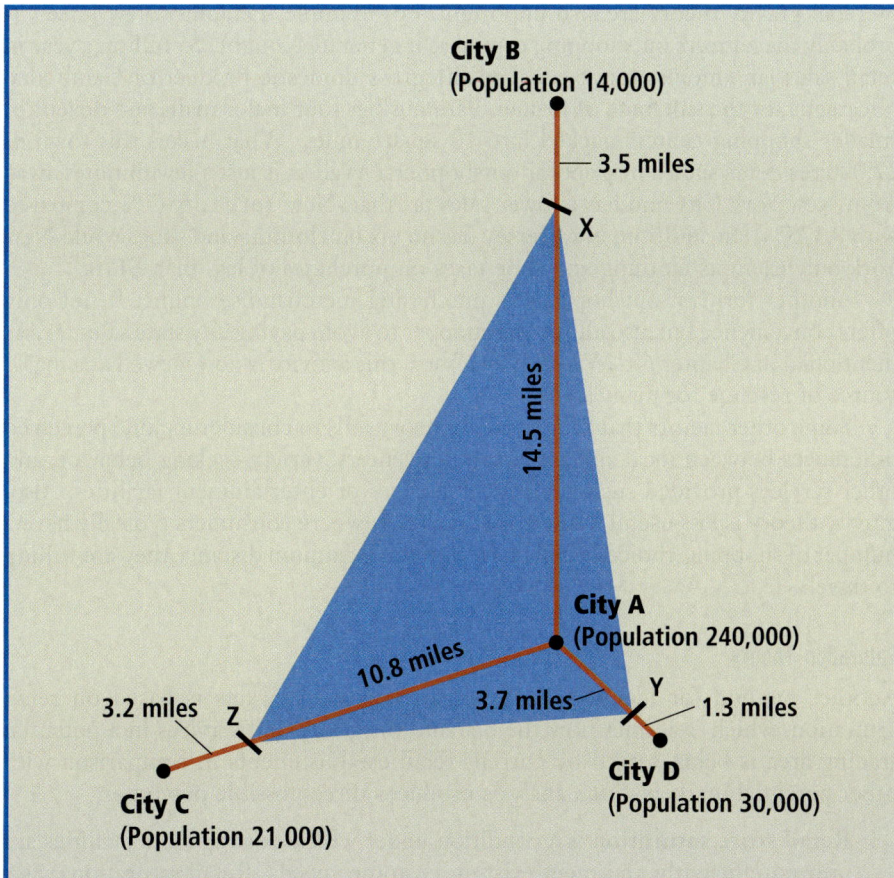

Exhibit 7.6
Trading Area for City A

Finally, D, with a population of 30,000, is 5 miles southeast of A, and its breaking point is 3.7 miles southeast of city A (point Y on the diagram).

Retail gravity theory rests on two assumptions: (1) the two competing cities are equally accessible from the major road, and (2) population is a good indicator of the differences in the goods and services available in different cities. Consumers are attracted to the larger population center not because of the city's size, but because of the larger number of stores and wider product assortment available, thereby making the increased travel time worthwhile. This is why in large cities around the world such as Paris, London, Istanbul, Mexico City, São Paulo, and Tokyo, you can find virtually any merchandise or service that is known to humankind.

However, in its simplicity, retail gravity theory does have several limitations. First, city population does not always reflect the available shopping facilities. For example, two neighboring cities, each with a population of 20,000 and similar demographics, would not be reflected equally if one of the cities had a shopping center with Target as the anchor store and the other did not. Second, distance is measured in miles, not the time involved for the consumer to travel that distance or the consumer's perception of that distance or time involved. Given our current highway system, this limitation is extremely important. Traveling 20 miles on an interstate highway to a mall located at an exit may be easier than the stop-and-start travel involved in going six miles through downtown traffic. Therefore, some retailers will substitute travel time for mileage. Finally, while the theory works reasonably well in rural areas, where distance is a major decision factor, it is not flawless.

Research on outshopping by residents of rural areas—that is, leaving your community to shop elsewhere—suggests that factors other than those considered by retail gravity theory are also important. For example, Paramus, New Jersey, is probably the nation's outshopping capital as it generates roughly $5 billion a year in retail sales, an amount about equal to the gross domestic product of Cambodia, Nicaragua, or the sultanate of Brunei. Paramus has four major malls and dozens of smaller shopping centers packed into 10 square miles. What makes this town of 27,000 residents such a magnet for outshoppers? Well, it is just a few minutes away from New York City and has a lower sales tax than New York City (7% compared with 8.375%). In addition, New Jersey has no tax on clothing and shoes while New York only exempts clothing and shoe taxes on purchases of less than $110.[19]

Another form of outshopping is purchasing merchandise online. It not only offers convenience but also allows the shopper to avoid paying any state sales tax. As mentioned in Chapter 6's "What's New?" box, this activity is now viewed as a major source of revenue for many states.

Some other factors that retail gravity theory fails to consider include perceived differences between local and other trading centers, variety-seeking behavior, and other services provided such as medical services or entertainment facilities. Also, gravity theory is less useful in metropolitan areas where consumers typically have a number of shopping choices available within the maximum distance they are willing to travel.

retail store saturation

Is a condition where there are just enough store facilities for a given type of store to efficiently and satisfactorily serve the population and yield a fair profit to the owners.

Saturation Theory

Another method for identifying attractive potential markets is based on retail saturation, which examines how the demand for goods and services in a potential trading area is being served by current retail establishments in comparison with other potential markets. Such analysis produces three possible outcomes:

1. **Retail store saturation** is a condition under which existing store facilities are utilized efficiently and meet existing customer needs. Retail saturation exists

when a market has just enough store facilities for a given type of store to serve the population of the market satisfactorily and yield a fair profit to the owners.

2. When a market has too few stores to satisfactorily meet the needs of the customer, it is **understored**. In this setting, average store profitability is quite high.

3. When a market has too many stores to yield a fair return on investment, it is **overstored**. Overstored markets are quite costly in terms of lost profit opportunities or, in many cases, losses due to the intense competition.

Saturation theory, therefore, implies a balance between the number of existing retail store facilities (supply) and their use (demand). As indicated in Chapter 4, one typically measures saturation, overstoring, and understoring in terms of the number of stores per thousand households. The consensus among retail location experts is that the United States is currently highly saturated or overstored with retail establishments, and thus retailers are taking a second look at some long-ignored markets such as older downtown areas and also nontraditional locations.

A possible indicator of understored versus overstored markets is the **index of retail saturation (IRS)**.[20] The IRS is the ratio of demand for a product or service divided by available supply and can be measured as follows:

$$IRS = (H \times RE)/RF$$

where IRS is the index of retail saturation for an area, H is the number of households in the area, RE is the annual retail expenditures for a particular line of trade per household in the area, and RF is the square footage of retail facilities of a particular line of trade in the area (including square footage of the proposed store). If you multiply the two terms in the numerator together (households and retail expenditures per household), you obtain dollar sales. Recalling that the denominator is square footage of retail space, it is easy to see that the IRS is essentially the sales per square foot of retail space in the marketplace for a particular line of retail trade.

When the IRS takes on a high value in comparison with the line of trade in other cities, it indicates that the market is understored and thus a potentially attractive opportunity. When the IRS takes on a low value, it indicates an over-stored market, which precludes the potential for significant profits. Home Depot, for example, monitors its sales per square foot for a store because it recognizes that if this ratio is too high, customers may not be well served and competition may be invited into the market. In fact, if sales per square foot are more than $400, it believes it is advantageous to close a thriving store and open two smaller stores. Although this cannibalizes the existing store, it better serves customers and dis-courages competition from entering the market.[21]

Until recently, retail scholars believed that it took at least two competitors to saturate a trade area. However, Starbucks has managed to achieve that status all by itself. This achievement was hinted at in 2007 when the *Wall Street Journal* ran a story titled "Why Did Starbucks Cross the Road?" with the subtitle "To Get to the Customers on the Other Side."[22] The story included an interview with a Starbuck's executive lamenting the fact that the chain only had outlets on three of the four corners at Mission and Fourth in San Francisco. He went on to explain that Starbucks' growth had to come from new stores, and as a result the company planned to open more than 10,000 new stores within four years, which would have increased the chain's total to more than 23,000. After all, "if you're over there, you are not likely to cross the street." And Starbucks' growth came from selling that incremental cup of latte, macchiato, or Frappuccino.[23] Little wonder that a year later, when the nation's economy tanked, the coffee king's first action was to announce closings of 600 to 700 of its 11,000 U.S. locations.

understored

Is a condition in a community where the number of stores in relation to households is relatively low so that engaging in retailing is an attractive economic endeavor.

overstored

Is a condition in a community where the number of stores in relation to households is so large that to engage in retailing is usually unprofitable or margin-ally profitable.

index of retail saturation (IRS)

Is the ratio of demand for a product (households in the geographic area mul-tiplied by annual retail expenditures for a partic-ular line of trade per household) divided by available supply (the square footage of retail facilities of a particular line of trade in the geographic area).

As an example of how the index of retail saturation is used, consider an individual planning to open a DVD-rental operation in either city A or B. This individual has the following information. Residents of both cities spend $12.56 per month on DVD rentals. The total number of households in both cities is also the same—17,000. City A, however, has 2,000 square feet of rental facilities, and city B has 2,500 square feet; and our proposed square footage is 500 square feet. Given this information and using our formula for IRS, we can find the IRS for each city:

$$\text{IRS (city A)} = (17{,}000 \times 12.56)/(2{,}000 + 500) = 85.41$$
$$\text{IRS (city B)} = (17{,}000 \times 12.56)/(2{,}500 + 500) = 71.17$$

Thus, based solely on these two factors of demand (number of households and average expenditure for products by each household) and one factor of supply (the square footage of retail space serving this demand), the individual would choose to locate in A, since its value of $85.41 is higher than B's $71.17.

As nonstore-based retailing continues to grow, retailers need to recognize that the index of retail saturation may become less useful. This is because it incorporates only store-based retailing in the supply component of the index. Nonstore-based retailing companies such as Net Flix are now cutting into the DVD rentals, as are cable and satellite pay-for-view options. Also the trend toward non-store retailing may be a problem for apparel retailers and computer retailers because many households may now make their purchases over the Internet.

Buying Power Index

Sales & Marketing Management magazine annually publishes a survey of buying power. This survey reports on current data for metropolitan areas, cities, and states. It provides some data that are not readily available from other sources such as the Census Bureau. These data include retail sales by specific merchandise categories, effective buying income, and total retail sales by area and population.

The population, retail sales, and buying income data provide the retail manager with an overview of the potential of various trading areas. By comparing one trading area to another, the retailer can develop a relative measure of each market's potential. For each area, the retailer can develop a **buying power index (BPI)**, which is a single weighted measure combining effective buying income (personal income, including all nontax payments such as Social Security, minus all taxes), retail sales, and population size into an overall indicator of a market's potential. Generally, business firms use a formula for BPI that was developed by *Sales & Marketing Management*. The BPI is weighted in the following manner:

buying power index (BPI)
Is an indicator of a market's overall retail potential and is composed of weighted measures of effective buying income (personal income, including all nontax payments such as social security, minus all taxes), retail sales, and population size.

$$\text{BPI} = 0.5(\text{the area's percentage of U.S. effective buying income})$$
$$+ \ 0.3(\text{the area's percentage of U.S. retail sales})$$
$$+ \ 0.2(\text{the area's percentage of U.S. population})$$

It is obvious that effective buying income is the most important factor, followed by retail sales and population. This formula can be further refined by breaking down these general figures into more specific figures geared toward the consumers of the retailer's products.

For example, XYZ Corporation, a retail chain specializing in general merchandise goods, is considering expansion into one of two different trading areas. The proposed trading areas are the markets of Alton–Granite City, Illinois, or Hamilton–Middletown, Ohio. XYZ aims its general merchandise at the 25- to 34-year-old market with incomes above \$35,000. Therefore, this age group will substitute for population, the general merchandise sales will substitute for total retail sales, and households with incomes above \$35,000 will replace effective buying income.

Using data that can be easily obtained from *Sales & Marketing Management*, XYZ can develop the BPI for each city:

$$\text{BPI (Alton–Granite City)} = 0.5\,(.000386) + 0.3\,(.00083) + 0.2\,(.00012)$$
$$= .000466$$
$$\text{BPI (Hamilton–Middletown)} = 0.5\,(.000717) + 0.3\,(.00063) + 0.2\,(.000112)$$
$$= .000570$$

As you can see, the BPI of Hamilton–Middletown is almost 25 percent greater than that of Alton–Granite City even though the cities are nearly equal in size. Therefore, XYZ would probably choose to expand its Ohio market rather than its Illinois market.

Remember that the BPI is broad in nature and reflects only the demand levels for the two proposed trading areas and not the supply level. Therefore, it does not reflect the saturation levels of these two markets. This can be easily taken care of by dividing the BPI for each area by the area's percentage of U.S. retail selling space for general merchandise (the supply factors) to determine each area's attractiveness:

$$\text{BPI (Alton–Granite City)} = .000466/.000452 = 1.03$$
$$\text{BPI (Hamilton–Middletown)} = .000570/.000483 = 1.18$$

In this case, the Ohio trading area is again chosen. This BPI formula does not reflect the availability of competing products or stores in nearby larger cities: Cincinnati, in the case of Hamilton–Middletown; and St. Louis, Missouri, in the case of Alton–Granite City.

Other Demand and Supply Factors

In addition to using retail gravity theory, the index of retail saturation, and the buying power index in evaluating various potential markets, the successful retailer will also look at some other demand and supply factors for each market.

Market Demand Potential

In analyzing the market potential, retailers identify certain criteria that are specific to the product line or services they are selling. The criteria chosen by one retailer might not be of use to a retailer selling a different product line. The major components of market demand potential are as follows.

1. Population Characteristics. Population characteristics are the criteria most often used to segment markets. Although total population figures and their growth rates are of primary importance to a retailer in examining potential markets, the successful retailer can obtain a more detailed profile of a market by examining school enrollment, education, age, sex, occupation, race, and nationality. Retailers should seek to match a market's population characteristics to the population characteristics of people who desire their goods and services.

2. Buyer Behavior Characteristics. Another useful criterion for analyzing potential markets is the behavioral characteristics of buyers in the market. Such characteristics include store loyalty, consumer lifestyles, store patronage motives, geographic and climatic conditions, and product benefits sought. This data, however, is not as easily obtainable as population data.

3. Household Income. The average household income and the distribution of household incomes can significantly influence demand for retail facilities. Further insight into the demand for retail facilities is provided by Engel's laws, which imply that spending increases for all categories of products as a result of an income increase but that the percentage of spending in some categories increases more than for others. Thus, as average household income rises, the community will exhibit a greater demand for luxury goods and a more sophisticated demand for necessity goods.

4. Household Age Profile. The age composition of households can be an important determinant of demand for retail facilities. In communities where households tend to be young, the preferences for stores may be different from communities where the average household is relatively old. For example, consumers 55 and older spend almost four times as much at drugstores as do 30-year-olds.

5. Household Composition. If we hold income and age constant and change the composition of the household, we will be able to identify another determinant of the demand for retail facilities. After all, households with children have different spending habits than childless households with similar incomes.

6. Community Life Cycle. Communities tend to exhibit growth patterns over time. Growth patterns of communities may be of four major types: rapid growth, continuous growth, relatively stable growth, and finally decline. The retailer should try to identify the communities that are in a rapid or continuous growth pattern since they will represent the best long-run opportunities.

7. Population Density. The population density of a community equals the number of persons per square mile. Research suggests that the higher the population density, the larger the average store should be in terms of square feet, and thus the fewer the number of stores that will be needed to serve a population of a given size.

8. Mobility. The easier it is for people to travel, the more mobile they will be.[24] When people are mobile, they are willing to travel greater distances to shop. Therefore, there will be fewer but larger stores in the community. In other words, in a community where mobility is high, there will be a need for fewer retailers than in a community where mobility is low.

The most attractive market areas are those in which the preceding criteria are configured in such a way that they represent maximum market potential for a particular retailer. This will vary by the type of retailer and the product lines it handles. In assessing different market areas, a retailer should first establish the market demand potential criteria that characterize the target market it would like to attract. Exhibit 7.7 illustrates this concept with a fast-food drive-in chain that sells

Exhibit 7.7
Identifying Communities with High Demand Potential for a Fast-Food Drive-In Restaurant

Demographic Characteristic	Desired Target Market	Community A	Community B
Population per square mile	over 400	375	423
Median family income	over $31,000	$28,024	$32,418
% population 14–54	over 60%	48%	63%
% white collar	over 50%	38%	54%
% people living in 1–3 person units	over 70%	61%	72%
% workforce traveling 0–14 minutes to work	over 75%	49%	74%
Average annual household expenditure on eating out	over $600	$521	$619

hamburgers, hot dogs, and drinks. This fast-food chain, with more than 3,000 units from coast to coast, is a 1950s-style drive-in where people usually order burgers and drinks in their autos with carhops providing service.

Exhibit 7.7 shows that the chain has determined that there are seven demographic factors that have a positive impact on fast-food restaurant sales. One of these factors may need explanation. Through research, the chain has determined that its restaurants do better when at least 75 percent of the workforce travels to work in less than 14 minutes. When people have to travel longer to work, they get tired and frustrated about being in their cars and thus are not likely to be interested in eating in their autos at a drive-in restaurant. You might examine the other six demographic factors and develop an explanation for why they would be related to the success of a fast-food drive-in restaurant. The information in Exhibit 7.7 shows the desired target market and data on the seven demographic factors for two possible communities. From analyzing this data, you should conclude that community B is the most attractive market to enter from a demand potential basis.

Market Supply Factors

In deciding to enter a new market, the successful retailer will also spend time analyzing the competition. The retailer should consider square feet per store and square feet per employee, store growth, and the quality of competition.

1. Square Feet per Store. It is helpful to obtain data on the (average) square feet per store in the communities that are being analyzed. This data will indicate whether the community tends to have large- or small-scale retailing. In addition, this is important in terms of assessing the extent to which the retailer's standard type of store would blend with the existing structure of retail trade in the community.

2. Square Feet per Employee. A measure that combines two major supply factors in retailing, store space and labor, is square feet of space per employee. A high number for this statistic in a community indicates that each employee is able to handle more space; this could be due to either a high level of retail technology in the community or more self-service retailing. Since retail technology is fairly constant across communities, any difference in square feet per employee is most often due to the level of service being provided. In communities currently characterized by retailers as offering a high level of service, there may be a significant opportunity for new retailers that are oriented toward self-service (and vice versa).

3. Growth in Stores. The retailer should look at the rate of growth in the number of stores for the last one to five years. When growth is rapid, the community is likely to have better-located stores with more contemporary atmospheres. More recently located stores will coincide better with the existing demographics of the community. Their atmosphere will also better suit the tastes of the marketplace, and they will tend to incorporate the latest in retail technology. All of these factors hint that the strength of retail competition will be greater when the community has recently experienced rapid growth in the number of stores. Retailers, as well as entrepreneurs, can obtain the information needed for computing the square feet per store, square feet per employee, and growth in stores from the Urban Land Institute's *Dollars and Cents of Shopping Centers*, the National Mall Monitor's *Retail Tenant Directory*, and Lebhar-Friedman's *Chain Store Guide*.

4. Quality of Competition. The three preceding supply factors reflect the quantity of competition. Retailers also need to look at the strength or quality of competition. They should attempt to identify the major retail chains and local retailers in each market and evaluate the strengths of each. Answers to questions such as the following would be insightful: What is their market share or profitability? How promotional- and price-oriented are they? Are they customer-oriented? Are they community-oriented and do they financially sponsor many civic and community activities? Do they tend to react to new market entrants by cutting price, increasing advertising, or improving customer service? A retailer should think twice before competing with Walmart on price, Saks Fifth Avenue on fashion, and Nordstrom's on service or shoe selection.

Quite often when a discounter enters a small community and adds 80,000 to 100,000 square feet of retail space, existing small-town retailers feel they cannot compete and must close down. This is undoubtedly true for the already poor-performing retailers; however, despite the discounter's enormous buying advantages, small-town retailers can compete head on with the out-of-towners by providing better customer service, adjusting prices on products carried by the discounters, knowing their customers on a personal basis, and remaining open Sundays and evenings. Customers will appreciate the increased standard of living that the discounter's prices make possible; as a result, the trading area will increase. The apparel retailer, for example, should cut down on basic stock items like socks and underwear but increase its inventory of specialty or novelty items. The sales lost on basic items will be overcome with these newer items and the larger trading area the discounter provides. Another hidden benefit of having a discounter such as Walmart enter a community is that the discounter's $40 million in retail sales results in households in the community saving from 5 percent to 10 percent or more on its sales. This translates into an additional $5 million in purchasing power left over for the local community's retailers. How they spend their savings will be largely determined by what the astute small retailer has to offer that does not replicate the discounter's offerings.

Unfortunately, sometimes there are cases when a small community can no longer support retail establishments. This is especially true when a shopping magnet such as a discounter or supercenter arrives in a nearby town. The magnet store may actually benefit other retailers in its town, provided they make the adjustments discussed above. However, the retailers in the nearby smaller communities are the ones most likely to suffer. The chapter's "What's New?" box describes such a situation that recently occurred in Missouri. Here a group of local high-school students may have saved the community, a reversal of the standard "community saves high school" story.

site analysis
Is an evaluation of the density of demand and supply within each market with the goal of identifying the best retail site(s).

LO 5

Site Analysis

What attributes should be considered in evaluating retail sites within a retail market?

Once a retailer has identified the best potential market, the next step is to perform a more detailed analysis of the market. Only after careful analysis of the market can the retailer choose the best site (or sites) available. **Site analysis** consists of an evaluation of the density of demand and supply within each market. It should be augmented by an identification of the most attractive sites that are currently available within each market. The third and final step, site selection, is the selection of the best possible site.

What's New?

High School Students Start a Grocery Store

Almost a century ago, a retailing expert introduced the idea that communities must have certain types of retail activity if they are to survive. These were, in order, a gasoline service station, a grocery store, and a restaurant.[25] Only then could the community attract other types of retail establishments. Years ago, two of the authors would watch six-man football games in West Texas, where an entire school district (K–12) would have enrollments of fewer than 200 students. What struck the authors was that most of these schools were located in communities without grocery stores or restaurants, and some even lacked gas stations. In fact, the authors did a little research and determined that the average distance to the nearest discounter from these schools was more than 20 miles. As a result of the lack of retail selection, these communities were slowly dying, and enrollments at some of these schools are now down 20 percent to 40 percent.

Recently, Leeton, Missouri, a community of 600 located 16 miles south of Warrensburg (population 16,000) and 30 miles southwest from Sedalia (population 20,000), has experience similar problems. Since the last grocery closed more than a decade ago, the town has had to rely on a convenience store, Casey's, to meet its shopping needs. As a result, the citizens of Leeton were forced to travel 40 to 50 miles round-trip if they wanted to purchase groceries, shop for apparel, get home-improvement items, visit a restaurant, or even spend a night at the movies. Then, during the summer of 2008, gas hit $4 a gallon. The town had a major crisis; it had to do something or die a slow death as was seen in West Texas.

Enter the superintendent of the local school district. He couldn't do anything to bring jobs to Leeton, but he thought that his students could start up a grocery store. It was a win–win situation: The community would get the much needed grocery store, and his students would be offered not only a unique learning opportunity but also a paying job without having to travel great distances.

The grocery run by high school students, thought to be the only one of its kind in the United States, isn't the standard prototype with 35,000 square feet and 15,000 SKUs. Rather, it's in an old bank building that's no bigger than a two-car garage. However, it offers a wider selection of grocery products than that offered by the convenience store and with lower prices. It's a start, and now the two

Maryjane Manley

The grand opening of the Bulldog Express.

(continued)

instructors who were so instrumental in the development of this project, agriculture teacher Bonnie Seymour and business teacher Marijayne Manley, are working with students on stage two of the store's development. They have already decided to stay open during the summer. In addition, they are now trying to determine how to offer greater selection without incurring waste or losing money. For example, while they currently carry frozen meats, something not found at Casey's, they would like to add fresh meat and produce. However, with the store only open four days a week—Monday, Tuesday, Thursday, and Friday—the costs of

adding fresh products may be too great. (By the way, the store is closed on Saturday because that is the day most folks in Leeton travel to the larger cities to complete their main shopping activities.)

Regardless of what they ultimately decide, everybody is a winner. The students were exposed to the discipline, determination, and skills needed to run a retail operation, and the community had their grocery store back.

Source: Based on information supplied by Bonnie Seymour and Marijayne Manley and used with the written permission of Dr. William Nicely, Superintendent, Leeton (MO) School District.

Site analysis begins by evaluating the density of demand and supply in various areas within the chosen market. To do so, retailers commonly use census tract data, ZIP-code areas, or some other meaningful geographic factor to identify the most attractive sites, given the retailer's requirements, that are available for new stores. One of the advantages of using census tract data is that it's readily available from the Census Bureau.

Census tracts are relatively small statistical subdivisions that vary in population from about 2,500 to 8,000 yet are designed to include fairly homogeneous populations. They are most often found in cities and counties of metropolitan areas—that is, the more densely populated areas of the nation. On an even smaller scale, the retailer can use Yahoo or Google, as described earlier in the GIS section of this chapter, to study the site.

Size of Trading Areas

Earlier we discussed the general trading area of a community. Our attention will now shift to how to determine and evaluate the trading area of specific sites within markets. In other words, we will attempt to estimate the geographic area from which a store located at a particular site will be able to attract customers.

At the same time that Reilly was developing retail gravity theory to determine the trading area for communities, William Applebaum designed a technique specifically for determining and evaluating trading areas for an individual store. Applebaum's technique was based on customer spottings. For each $100 in weekly store sales, a customer was randomly selected or spotted for an interview. Incidentally, Applebaum developed this technique more than 50 years ago, and thus we now recommend that for each $500 (vs. the original $100) in weekly sales, a customer is randomly selected for spotting. These spottings usually did not require much time since the interviewer requested only demographic information, shopping habits, and some pertinent consumer attitudes toward the store and its competitors. After the home addresses of the shoppers were plotted on a map, the analyst could make some inferences about trading area size and the competition.[26] Exhibit 7.8 is an example of a map generated using customer spottings.

Thus, it is relatively easy to define the trading area of an existing store. All that is necessary is to interview current customers of the store to determine where they reside. For a new store, however, the task is not so easy. There is a fair amount of

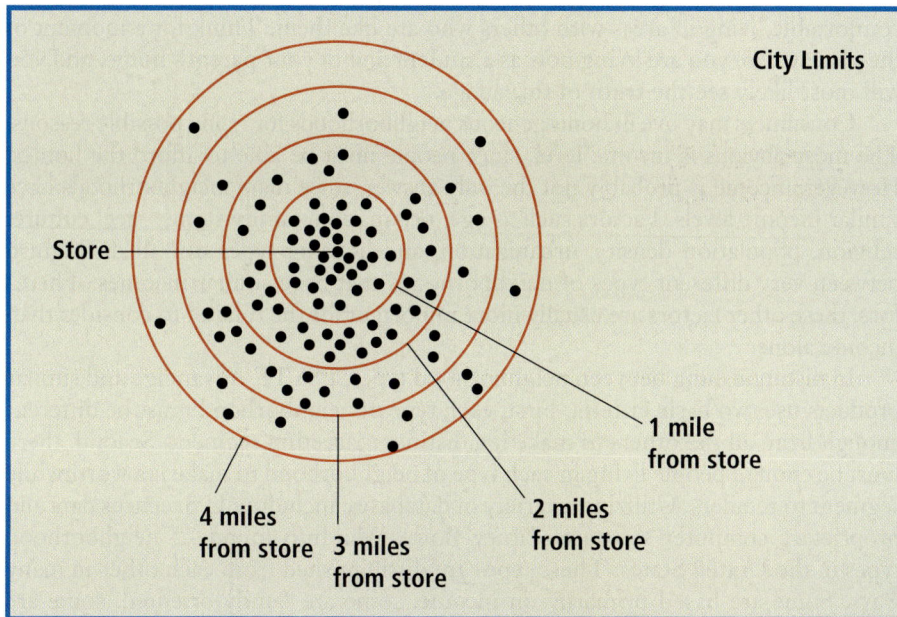

Exhibit 7.8
Customer Spotting Map
for a Supermarket

conventional wisdom that has withstood the test of time about the correlation of trading area size, which can be summarized as follows

1. Stores that sell products the consumer wants to purchase in the most convenient manner will have a smaller trading area than so-called specialty stores.

2. As consumer mobility increases, the size of the store's trading area increases.

3. As the size of the store increases, its trading area increases because it can stock a broader and deeper assortment of merchandise, which will then attract customers from greater distances.

4. As the distance between competing stores increases, their trading areas will increase.

5. Natural and human-made obstacles such as rivers, mountains, railroads, and freeways can abruptly limit the boundaries of a trading area.

Description of Trading Area

Retailers can access, at relatively low cost, information concerning the trading area for various retail locations and the buyer behavior of the trading area. If you use your search engine to locate the Web sites of any of the firms providing geographical information services, you will see how readily available this information is to the typical retailer. For example, consider the work of Pitney Bowes MapInfo (www.pbbusinessinsight.com).

Pitney Bowes MapInfo is a global software company that integrates software, data, and services to help retailers make more insightful location decisions. As a market-research firm specializing in developing psychographic, demographic, or lifestyle analyses of geographic areas, it produces solutions that are available in 20 languages in 65 countries. MapInfo's PSYTE Advantage segmentation system, which breaks down all neighborhoods in the United States into 72 different clusters, is based on the old adage that birds of a feather flock together. In other words, even though the total makeup of the American marketplace is very complex and diverse, neighborhoods tend to be just the opposite: People tend to feel most comfortable living in areas with others who are like them. Think for a moment of the place where you are living now as a student and of your parent's home, and you will most likely see the truth of this adage.

Consumers may live in homogeneous neighborhoods for many possible reasons. The most obvious is income level, since people must be able to afford the homes. However, income is probably not the only answer, since many neighborhoods have similar income levels. Factors such as age, occupation, family status, race, culture, religion, population density, urbanization, and housing types can all distinguish between very different types of neighborhoods that have similar incomes. Therefore, these other factors are usually more important for the retailer to consider than income alone.

In distinguishing between neighborhood types, PSYTE Advantage and similar products use two basic criteria. First, each type of neighborhood must be different enough from all the others to make it a distinct marketing segment. Second, there must be enough people living in each type of neighborhood to make it a worthwhile segment to retailers. Utilizing a variety of databases, including U.S. census data and proprietary computer software, Pitney Bowes MapInfo found 72 neighborhood types in the United States. These types are distinguished from each other in many ways. Some are based primarily on income, some are family-oriented, some are race-oriented, some are urban, some suburban, and some rural. Most combine two or more distinguishing demographic characteristics. The reason Pitney Bowes MapInfo settled on 72, and not some other number of clusters, was that in "solution after solution this number afforded the maximum amount of discrimination with the fewest number of clusters."[27] Exhibit 7.9 identifies these 72 neighborhood types or clusters.

The neighborhood names attempt to capture the essence of the neighborhood and provide an easy way of remembering distinctions. Also associated with the neighborhoods are demographics, lifestyles, retail opportunities, and financial and media habits. Still, in some cases the information about a cluster may be confusing. Consider, for example, cluster 68, which is "College Towns." This segment's behavior cannot be based solely on household income because nearly 40 percent of the cluster's population lives in group quarters such as college dorms. This neighborhood type, which is typical of neighborhoods surrounding college campuses across the country, can be characterized by the fact that more than one-third of its population is between the ages of 18 and 24. Without considering the fact that mom and dad are supporting the kids, the makeup of cars owned and amount of travel would seem contradictory to the cluster's income level.

Demand Density

demand density

Is the extent to which the potential demand for the retailer's goods and services is concentrated in certain census tracts, ZIP code areas, or parts of the community.

The extent to which potential demand for the retailer's goods and services is concentrated in certain census tracts, ZIP-code areas, or parts of the community is called **demand density**. To determine the extent of demand density, retailers need to identify what they believe to be the major variables influencing their potential demand. One such method of identifying these variables is to examine the types of customers who already shop in the retailer's present stores. The variables identified should be standard demographic variables such as age, income, and education since this data will be readily available. Let's construct an example.

A retailer is evaluating the possibility of locating in a community that has geographic boundaries as shown in Exhibit 7.10. It comprises 23 census tracts. The community is bordered on the west by a mountain range, on the north and south by major highways, and on the east by railroad tracks. The retailer has decided that

Exhibit 7.9
PSYTE US ADVANTAGE Cluster Demographics

Cluster	Cluster Name	Population	Households	Mean Hhld Income	Average Hhld Size	Owner Occupied Dwellings	Renter Occupied Dwellings	Median Yr Structure Built	Median Home Value	Family Hhlds	Married Couple Family Hhlds	Bachelor s degree	Managerial and Professional Occ
1	Tuxedo Trails	2,346,218	798,935	$206,840	2.92	93.0%	7.0%	1970	$604,704	84.6%	77.4%	34.6%	62.1%
2	Executive Domain	6,811,130	2,301,069	$155,901	2.91	94.1%	5.9%	1974	$359,016	85.8%	78.9%	35.4%	61.4%
3	Nouveau Manors	2,605,221	860,385	$108,265	3.05	91.3%	8.7%	1993	$220,505	84.9%	77.0%	36.4%	55.3%
4	Parchment Hill	1,240,796	681,790	$181,190	1.97	41.6%	58.4%	1953	$932,092	36.7%	31.6%	37.4%	70.1%
5	Professional Duos	2,583,257	2,583,257	$115,481	2.59	82.0%	18.0%	1954	$378,810	71.2%	59.5%	28.5%	56.5%
6	Balancing Acts	4,780,580	1,562,464	$102,681	3.06	93.4%	6.6%	1981	$205,768	86.5%	77.6%	27.7%	47.3%
7	Equestrian Heights	3,477,347	1,285,906	$100,504	2.69	92.0%	8.0%	1969	$201,777	80.7%	71.9%	27.2%	50.4%
8	Suburban Establishment	2,417,513	1,016,377	$115,613	2.39	67.0%	33.0%	1959	$363,990	59.6%	51.4%	27.9%	57.3%
9	Suburban Wave	6,038,879	2,127,283	$85,833	2.82	85.6%	14.4%	1985	$176,466	79.4%	68.5%	26.3%	44.9%
10	Exurban Tide	5,215,523	1,823,588	$81,251	2.85	90.2%	9.8%	1975	$163,254	81.7%	71.0%	18.1%	37.2%
11	Only in America	7,451,644	2,770,832	$86,247	2.72	72.1%	27.9%	1956	$237,965	71.0%	57.1%	21.3%	43.1%
12	Rural Renaissance	3,391,449	1,186,953	$81,207	2.84	89.7%	10.3%	1973	$166,355	81.5%	71.3%	18.4%	36.7%
13	Sierra Snuggle	7,412,402	2,520,107	$80,178	2.96	82.1%	17.9%	1982	$182,630	79.1%	65.1%	21.2%	39.3%
14	Empty Nest West	2,795,297	1,093,111	$83,877	2.55	83.9%	16.1%	1973	$217,796	74.8%	64.5%	22.4%	44.6%
15	Western Sprawl	1,942,651	661,896	$76,811	3.04	71.8%	28.2%	1976	$244,826	72.0%	57.7%	22.6%	41.6%
16	Frontier Towns	2,638,276	786,164	$71,234	3.35	82.6%	17.4%	1977	$167,145	83.9%	66.9%	13.6%	30.7%
17	Up-Country Environs	2,148,895	815,417	$78,153	2.59	84.9%	15.1%	1976	$156,293	77.3%	66.7%	19.4%	40.5%
18	The Professoriat	1,836,804	818,867	$80,872	2.23	59.3%	40.7%	1959	$234,204	55.0%	44.2%	29.0%	58.2%
19	East Meets East	6,542,899	1,946,981	$68,347	3.41	63.7%	36.3%	1965	$197,506	78.3%	56.7%	14.6%	29.5%
20	Empty Nest East	3,837,941	1,463,478	$67,225	2.61	88.5%	11.5%	1964	$125,850	77.0%	65.8%	14.8%	33.4%
21	Towns in Transition	3,100,265	1,260,106	$68,090	2.45	69.1%	30.9%	1968	$149,311	66.1%	52.3%	21.9%	40.1%
22	Kids, Dogs, Vans	6,538,444	2,296,919	$63,585	2.84	80.5%	19.5%	1981	$125,414	78.7%	63.4%	14.7%	31.0%
23	Life s a Peach	5,549,405	2,377,528	$66,999	2.31	51.8%	48.2%	1980	$163,045	59.0%	44.3%	25.9%	42.6%
24	Urban Villagers	3,569,556	1,946,619	$80,047	1.84	32.1%	67.9%	1951	$334,249	32.1%	24.0%	33.8%	59.4%
25	Cruisin' Couples	3,852,000	1,703,188	$73,553	2.23	78.8%	21.2%	1965	$162,361	64.6%	54.7%	21.2%	44.3%

(continued)

Exhibit 7.9 Continued

Cluster	Cluster Name	Population	Households	Mean Hhld Income	Average Hhld Size	Owner Occupied Dwellings	Renter Occupied Dwellings	Median Yr Structure Built	Median Home Value	Family Hhlds	Married Couple Family Hhlds	Bachelors degree	Managerial and Professional Occ
26	Suburban Melange	3,480,114	1,441,204	$67,547	2.39	49.9%	50.1%	1970	$230,955	57.9%	41.9%	22.7%	40.4%
27	Retirement Horizons	2,541,929	1,077,550	$69,424	2.32	76.1%	23.9%	1963	$143,127	65.7%	53.9%	20.7%	41.5%
28	Quiet Streets	3,832,188	1,397,819	$63,713	2.73	86.4%	13.6%	1964	$117,827	78.4%	68.0%	11.6%	28.6%
29	Family Acres	3,728,309	1,375,025	$62,731	2.70	85.6%	14.4%	1970	$126,122	77.6%	66.0%	11.9%	29.4%
30	Moo's and Modems	4,859,978	1,786,334	$62,483	2.71	86.0%	14.0%	1975	$117,908	79.2%	67.8%	12.3%	29.9%
31	Home to Mama	6,279,909	2,445,660	$60,359	2.56	82.0%	18.0%	1956	$121,654	70.3%	54.5%	12.7%	29.7%
32	Echo Boomtown	1,871,787	951,361	$63,970	1.96	22.5%	77.5%	1973	$197,990	40.0%	28.0%	31.3%	51.1%
33	Live to Work	2,926,580	1,142,731	$60,377	2.49	53.0%	47.0%	1962	$152,576	60.0%	43.7%	17.5%	35.1%
34	Changing Places	6,695,306	3,178,347	$60,699	2.09	54.9%	45.1%	1960	$151,786	51.8%	38.9%	23.3%	42.8%
35	Cultural Exchange	1,201,709	375,759	$59,157	3.22	62.4%	37.6%	1965	$190,666	78.6%	56.4%	10.9%	24.4%
36	Active Seniors	5,168,842	2,587,011	$63,542	1.99	83.3%	16.7%	1978	$176,354	61.8%	54.2%	15.7%	34.6%
37	Outback USA	6,460,640	2,254,249	$52,661	2.88	78.4%	21.6%	1975	$101,617	76.7%	59.1%	8.2%	22.6%
38	New Neighbors	4,163,111	1,620,324	$51,471	2.56	62.5%	37.5%	1954	$108,856	62.9%	43.2%	12.0%	26.6%
39	Duty Calls	2,639,047	912,924	$53,807	2.89	73.7%	26.3%	1952	$89,032	72.7%	37.3%	9.6%	26.6%
40	The Neighborhood	3,591,669	1,284,191	$55,668	2.90	33.2%	66.8%	1947	$209,608	65.3%	43.0%	14.6%	30.6%
41	Old Metro, New Hands	1,641,679	533,845	$52,392	3.05	49.6%	50.4%	1947	$134,006	71.3%	46.6%	8.7%	21.0%
42	Country Roads	3,986,319	1,663,802	$51,168	2.37	68.9%	31.1%	1955	$95,546	64.3%	49.2%	12.1%	27.3%
43	Family Farm Belt	6,302,256	2,457,564	$51,583	2.55	83.8%	16.2%	1962	$83,540	74.7%	63.6%	9.2%	27.0%
44	Middleburgh	3,926,238	1,560,768	$50,364	2.47	66.4%	33.6%	1965	$95,967	67.8%	50.8%	12.4%	27.7%
45	Opportunity Knocks	3,232,502	1,298,000	$49,330	2.45	58.5%	41.5%	1970	$123,940	62.7%	46.1%	14.4%	29.6%
46	Service Corps	3,276,230	1,112,352	$49,188	2.96	63.1%	36.9%	1959	$84,693	73.8%	38.7%	10.0%	24.6%
47	Here to Stay	4,898,779	2,074,688	$53,947	2.32	81.1%	18.9%	1975	$131,886	69.4%	58.6%	12.5%	30.0%
48	Farm and Factory	2,841,983	1,071,635	$48,095	2.63	81.9%	18.1%	1971	$85,424	75.5%	61.3%	6.5%	21.2%
49	Singles Place	4,640,273	2,172,564	$51,147	2.13	27.2%	72.8%	1965	$153,907	44.9%	28.6%	22.2%	37.3%
50	Rust Belt Blues	2,353,937	1,010,483	$48,185	2.31	76.4%	23.6%	1954	$85,702	64.8%	49.5%	10.3%	27.0%
51	Irrigation Nation	1,960,960	737,530	$47,797	2.65	81.5%	18.5%	1975	$82,136	76.1%	61.7%	7.3%	22.7%
52	Military Towns	1,092,769	216,617	$48,026	3.46	3.9%	96.1%	1968	$70,418	94.5%	86.0%	15.1%	31.2%

53	Southern Country	5,836,530	2,197,552	$47,622	2.64	83.0%	17.0%	1978	$79,069	76.6%	62.1%	6.9%	22.4%
54	Home Town Harbor	4,154,531	1,600,780	$47,999	2.42	51.1%	48.9%	1963	$98,356	60.6%	41.3%	11.8%	26.8%
55	Plow and Plateau	4,466,139	1,705,132	$47,983	2.59	77.5%	22.5%	1961	$79,426	71.6%	60.1%	10.4%	29.4%
56	Agrarian Edge	5,707,990	1,937,971	$43,732	2.92	63.1%	36.9%	1969	$91,238	73.4%	51.7%	7.3%	21.3%
57	Backwoods Blues	2,851,388	1,091,764	$42,905	2.58	80.9%	19.1%	1969	$71,758	73.8%	58.4%	5.7%	20.5%
58	Latino Quarter	6,443,375	1,655,701	$45,167	3.99	35.5%	64.5%	1959	$147,683	79.0%	50.5%	6.0%	15.3%
59	Exurban Refuge	4,342,508	1,825,620	$45,029	2.30	70.8%	29.2%	1958	$73,007	64.2%	50.2%	9.8%	26.9%
60	Hispanic Hopes	2,524,486	754,248	$42,487	3.35	30.7%	69.3%	1953	$95,416	71.8%	40.2%	6.6%	15.1%
61	Amer-Indian Corners	4,595,317	1,636,596	$39,787	2.82	52.5%	47.5%	1957	$71,058	66.5%	38.5%	6.4%	18.4%
62	Hip Nation	3,048,802	1,074,755	$34,138	2.81	10.7%	89.3%	1953	$100,281	63.9%	25.7%	6.7%	20.8%
63	Help Wanted	4,917,158	1,928,548	$39,512	2.59	24.0%	76.0%	1969	$111,058	54.6%	32.0%	11.6%	23.2%
64	Extraction Action	4,946,371	1,962,345	$39,943	2.50	81.1%	18.9%	1970	$59,469	72.8%	57.8%	5.4%	21.3%
65	Village Americana	7,930,361	3,266,302	$37,783	2.38	58.6%	41.4%	1955	$65,155	61.7%	40.8%	6.7%	19.8%
66	Border Zone	3,479,233	941,216	$36,447	3.59	64.7%	35.3%	1964	$57,157	82.3%	57.3%	3.4%	14.4%
67	Senior Circles	3,505,446	1,674,143	$35,979	2.01	37.5%	62.5%	1958	$83,381	45.4%	29.5%	9.9%	25.0%
68	College Towns	3,756,878	1,104,492	$40,723	2.23	21.9%	78.1%	1961	$117,974	31.8%	21.4%	24.2%	36.4%
69	Black Memoirs	6,853,884	2,504,727	$35,309	2.69	63.8%	36.2%	1964	$54,609	69.0%	36.8%	5.6%	18.5%
70	Workin' on the Dream	5,820,914	2,168,031	$31,613	2.70	29.1%	70.9%	1957	$67,125	63.9%	24.3%	6.5%	19.1%
71	Project Renewal	2,769,233	552,543	$42,486	2.37	49.6%	50.4%	1962	$80,948	55.7%	38.5%	5.5%	24.7%
72	Urban Stress	1,905,734	627,376	$33,125	3.03	40.6%	59.4%	1947	$58,781	66.4%	22.2%	4.2%	17.7%

Source: PSYTE is a trademark of Pitney Bowes Software Inc. This exhibit is used with the written permission of Pitney Bowes Software Inc., 4200 Parliament Place, Suite 600, Lanham, MD 20706 (http:// www.pbbusinessinsight.com).

Exhibit 7.10
Demand Density Map

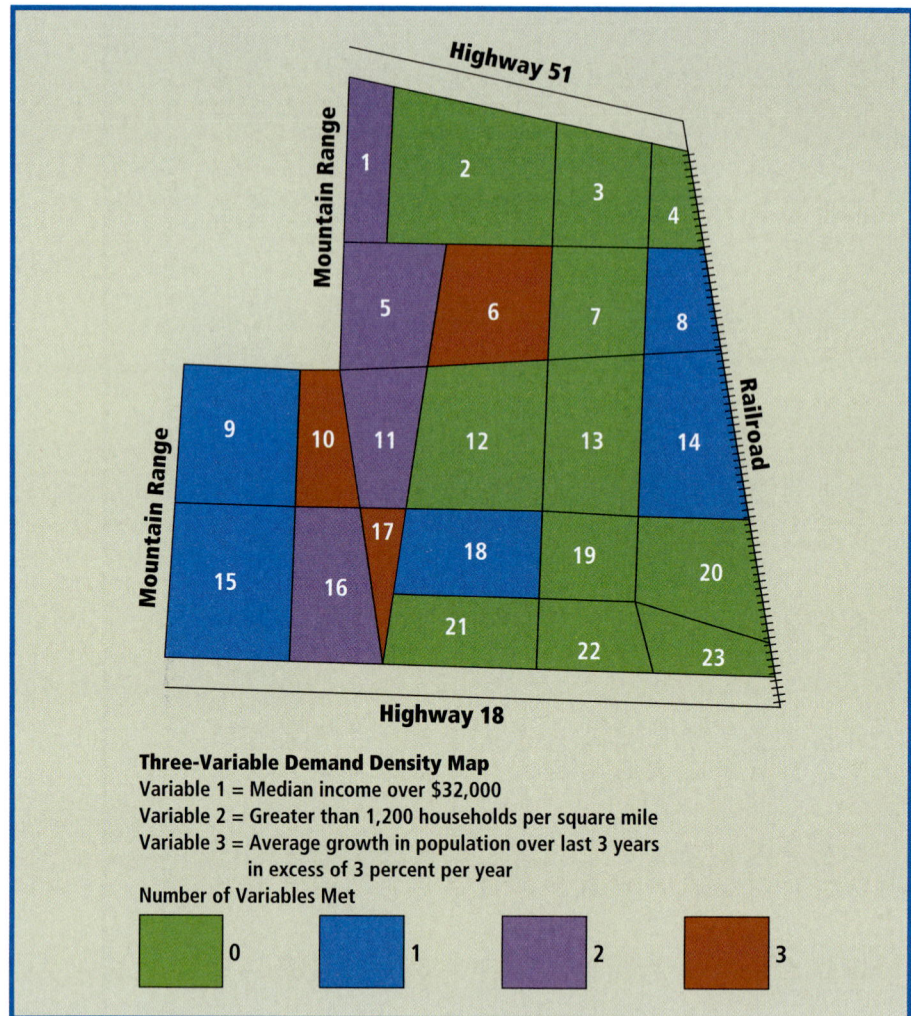

Three-Variable Demand Density Map
Variable 1 = Median income over $32,000
Variable 2 = Greater than 1,200 households per square mile
Variable 3 = Average growth in population over last 3 years
               in excess of 3 percent per year
Number of Variables Met

| 0 | 1 | 2 | 3 |

three variables are especially important in determining the potential demand: median household income above $35,000, households per square mile in excess of 1,200, and average growth in population of at least 3 percent per year over the last three years. In Exhibit 7.10, a thematic map shows the extent to which these three conditions are met for each of the 23 census tracts in the community undergoing evaluation. Thus, you can easily visualize the density of potential demand in each tract. Note that only three tracts (6, 10, and 17) meet all three conditions.

Another method of looking at potential demand for a retailer's product could incorporate the data mentioned earlier when discussing neighborhood types. In this example, suppose a retail computer chain wanted to enter the Atlanta market. The chain would first determine, from its own records, which neighborhood types accounted for the largest sales in comparison to the national average of its product categories. In this case, higher levels of income and education, less than age 45, and percentage of "executive/managers/professional/technical" households were the most important factors. Thus, the neighborhood types "Ivory Towers," "Mortgage Heights," "Night-Lights," and "Team-Mates" may be among the most attractive locations for a computer store (see Exhibit 7.9).

Supply Density

While the demand-density map allows you to identify the area within a community that represents the highest potential demand, the location of existing retail establishments should also be mapped. For example, for nearly three decades, ZIP code 07652 in Paramus, New Jersey, which was discussed earlier in this chapter, has had the largest dollar volume in retail sales of any ZIP code in the United States because it benefits from drawing shoppers from nearby high-taxed New York City. In addition, Paramus is located in Bergen County, which has a population of more than a million and is ranked among the top 20 American counties in terms of household income. Not surprisingly, Paramus has few vacancies and also commands some of the highest rents for retail space in the country. This information about the lack of available space as well as the number of retailers already serving the market is most important because it allows the retailer to examine the density of supply—that is, the extent to which retailers are concentrated in different areas of the market under question.

Exhibit 7.11 shows the density of stores in the community we saw in Exhibit 7.10. Exhibit 7.11 reveals that two census tracts (10 and 17) out of the three most attractive ones have a lack of stores. Also, in the census tracts with fairly attractive demand density (two of the three conditions met), there are currently no retail outlets (see tracts 1 and 5).

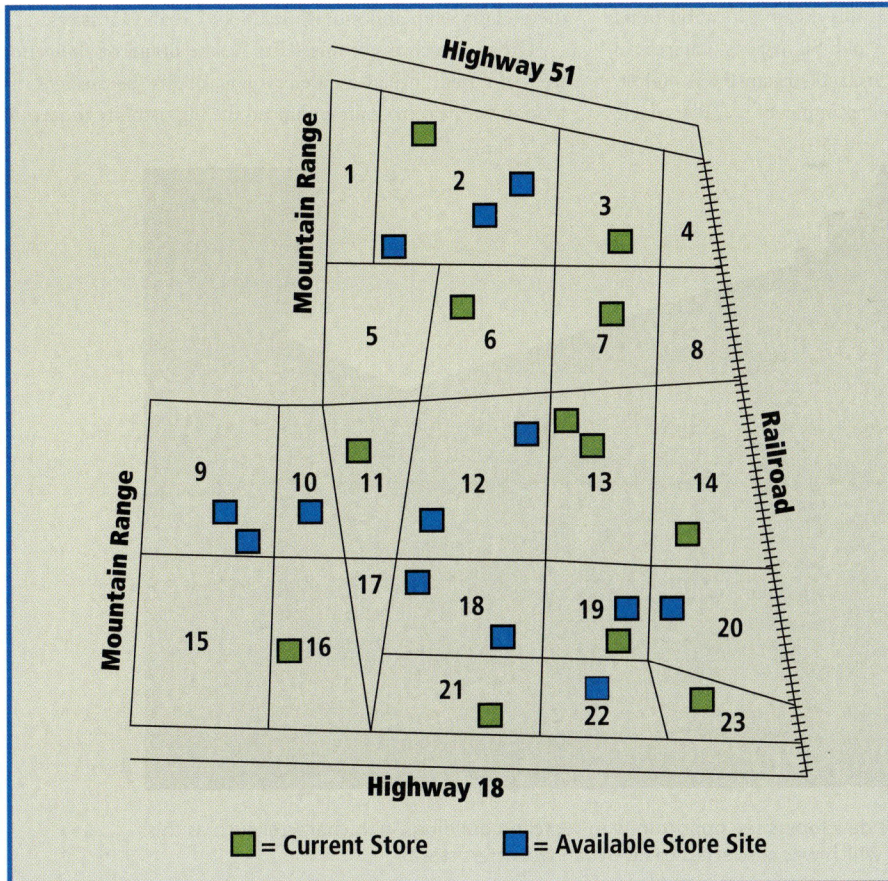

Exhibit 7.11
Store Density and Site Availability Map

Service Retailing

Get Me to That Church!

Banks, medical offices, day spas, nail salons, and real estate offices are among a group of service retailers that has returned to malls and shopping centers as the traditional anchors have either merged with other anchors or gone out of business. This was because the more affordable (i.e., lower) rents and higher traffic counts made these attractive locations. An early example of this trend was the strategy of placing big-box retailers and grocery stores within malls. Today, however, some retailers have found a new and more exciting place for locating outlets: your old neighborhood church.

In past recessions, many times when a retailer closed shop, the landlord was willing to rent to anybody running a legal operation. However, today some retailers are seeking to be creative by differentiating themselves and not just becoming "me-too" types renting unused shopping center space because the price was cheap. These successful retailers realize the importance not only of their location but also of the building's structure in attracting customers.

Some real estate experts trace this creative location trend back to what happened to the old St. Mary's Church in Dublin. This former Church of Ireland structure was built in the early 1700s and is an early example of a gallery-style church. After closing some 50 years ago, it first became an oversized retail outlet. However, it has recently been converted to a most unique establishment—a combination of pubs and restaurants—and is simply called "the Church." Now this restored former church, situated in the heart of Dublin's shopping district, is a major tourist stop as well as a place for locals to gather. (For more information on this internationally known service retailer, see www.thechurch.ie/.)

Recently, on the campus of the University of Cincinnati, a similar trend toward taking advantage of an empty church's structure has taken place. Here a local Cincinnati developer, Mark Fallon, purchased the Third Protestant Memorial Church building and transformed this former place of worship into a place of unabashed retail activity. In additional to having roughly 15,000 square feet on two levels, the church had a much coveted parking lot on a college campus. As a result, the vacant church, which had seen its parishioners move to the suburbs, became the logical destination for one of the country's hip and modish retailers Urban Outfitters.

Urban, which is considered to be the brand of choice for well-educated, urban-minded young adults because of its fashion with a retro flair, embraced the opportunity to retrofit

Mark Fallon

Retail real estate developers see opportunity in recycling buildings with character such as this church building which was converted to an Urban Outfitters store.

the church. After all, the structure was originally built in 1929, and it clearly stood out among the typical campus eclectic mix of bookstores, coffee shops, and fast-food empires. Today the location is the catalyst for a complete redevelopment of the area. It has attracted more than $100 million in both student and general population housing, as well as more than 100,000 square feet of retail and restaurants. In addition, it has also resulted in new garages holding more than 1,400 parking spaces. All of this is attributable to the creative reuse of a church that today stands as the anchor location of the retail corridor at a major university.

Currently, other real estate developers are using this Urban Outfitters store as a model to determine if other urban neighborhoods can be moved from areas of potential blight to an exciting retailing infrastructure with the potential for reinvigorating an area.

Source: This box was prepared with written permission of Mark Fallon, Vice President of Real Estate, Jeffrey R. Anderson Real Estate, Inc., Cincinnati.

Site Availability

Just because demand outstrips supply in certain geographic locations does not immediately imply that stores should be located in those locations. Sites must be available. (*Note:* The case at the end of this chapter goes into great detail on how some developers have made use of **eminent domain law**— the inherent power of the government to seize private property without the owner's consent in order to benefit the community—as a means of securing land to build retail outlets.)

eminent domain law
Is the inherent power of the government to seize private property without the owner's consent in order to benefit the community.

A map should be constructed of available sites in each community being analyzed. We have done this in conjunction with the supply-density map in Exhibit 7.11. The only available site in the top six census tracts (in terms of demand density) is in census tract 10. In tracts 1, 5, and 17, which currently have no retail outlets, no sites are available, which may explain the current lack of stores in these areas. Perhaps these tracts are zoned totally for residential use. Or maybe, while there aren't any traditional retail locations available, there are some available to a creative thinker. As described in this chapter's "Service Retailing" box, many service retailers are not only returning to shopping centers but also moving into some vacant but very unconventional locations.

Although Exhibit 7.11 seems to show only one good potential site, several more may exist. Census tract 9 borders the high-density tract 10, in which there are no present stores and in which only one site is available for a new store. Tract 9, however, has two available sites. Furthermore, tract 12 has an available site that is close to the borders of tracts 11 and 17, which are both attractive but, lack available sites. This same kind of analysis can be done with our high-fashion chain in looking over the Los Angeles market. Some retailers have developed a checklist of all the items they want to consider during the site analysis stage. One such list is shown in Exhibit 7.12.

Site Selection

LO 6

How is the best geographic site selected?

After completing the analysis of each segment in the desired market and identifying the best available sites within each market, retailers are now ready to make the final decision regarding location: selecting the best site (or sites) available. Small to medium-sized retailers without an in-house real estate department are well advised to use the assistance of a real estate professional at this stage. Even if the retailer or its staff has done all the analysis to this point, the assistance of a real estate

Local Demographics	Site Characteristics
Population and/or household base	Number of parking spaces available
Population growth potential	Distance of parking areas
Lifestyles of consumers	Ease of access for delivery
Income potential	Visibility of site from street
Age makeup	History of the site
Educational makeup	Compatibility of neighboring stores
Population of nearby special markets, that is, daytime workers, students, and tourists, if applicable	Size and shape of lot
Occupation mix	Condition of existing building
	Ease of entrance and exit for traffic
Traffic Flow and Accessibility	Ease of access for handicapped customers
Number and type of vehicles passing location	Restrictions on sign usage
Access of vehicles to location	Building safety code restrictions
Number and type of pedestrians passing location	Type of zoning
Availability of mass transit, if applicable	
Accessibility of major highway artery	**Cost Factors**
Quality of access streets	Terms of lease/rent agreement
Level of street congestion	Basic rent payments
Presence of physical barriers that affect trade area shape	Length of lease
	Local taxes
	Operations and maintenance costs
Retail Competition	Restrictive clauses in lease
Number and types of stores in area	Membership in local merchants association required
Analysis of key players in general area	Voluntary regulations by local merchants
Competitiveness of other merchants	
Number and location of direct competitors in area	
Possibility of joint promotions with local merchants	

Exhibit 7.12
Checklist for Site Evaluations

100 percent location
Is when there is no better use for a site than the retail store that is being planned for that site.

professional is important. In fact, more and more large retailers set up separate corporations just to handle their real estate transactions.

In principle, all retailers should attempt to find a **100-percent location** for their stores. A 100-percent location is one where there is no better use for the site than the retail store that is being planned. Retailers should remember that what may be a 100-percent site for one store may not be a 100-percent site for another; the best location for a supermarket may not be the best location for a discount department store.

How is the 100-percent location or site identified? Unfortunately, there is no best answer to this basic question. There is, however, general agreement on the types of things that the retailer should consider in evaluating sites: the nature of the site, traffic characteristics, type of neighbors, and the terms of purchase or lease.

Nature of Site

Is the site currently a vacant store, a vacant parcel of land, or the site of a planned shopping center? Many of the available retail sites will be vacant stores. This is because 10 percent to 15 percent of stores go out of business each year. This does not mean that because a men's apparel store failed in a particular location that a bookstore is doomed to do likewise. However, sometimes a piece of property becomes known as "jinxed" or "snakebit" because of the high number of business failures that have occurred there. Every town usually has one or more such areas. Restaurants, which are one of the toughest businesses to get off the ground, seem to try these locations the most. Even a shopping center can appear to be under an unlucky star. For example, Cincinnati Mills has had six owners in its 20-year history and ended 2008 with a vacancy rate of 44 percent.[28] Therefore, when the retail site that appears to be best suited to the retailer's needs is a vacant parcel of land, the retailer needs to investigate why it is vacant. Why have others passed up the site? Was it previously not for sale or was it priced too high? Or is there some other reason?

Finally, the site may be part of a planned shopping center. In this case, the retailer can usually be assured that it will have the proper mix of neighbors, adequate parking facilities, and good traffic. Sometimes, of course, the center has not been properly planned, and the retailer needs to be aware of these special cases. It is difficult to succeed in a shopping center in which a high percentage of space is not rented.

Traffic Characteristics

The traffic that passes a site, whether it is vehicular or pedestrian, can be an important determinant of the potential sales at that site. However, factors other than traffic flow must be considered. The retailer must determine whether the population and traffic are of the type desired. For example, a retailer of fine furs and leather coats may be considering two alternative sites—one in the central business district and the other in a group of specialty stores in a small shopping center in a very exclusive residential area. The CBD site may generate more total traffic, but the alternative site may generate more of the right type of traffic.

The retailer should evaluate two traffic-related aspects of the site. The first is the availability of sufficient parking, either at the site or nearby. One of the advantages of shopping centers and malls is the availability of adequate parking space. If the site is not a shopping center, then the retailer will need to determine if the parking space will be adequate. It is difficult to give a precise guideline for the space that will be needed. Generally, it is a function of four factors: size of the store, frequency of customer visits, length of customer visits, and availability of public transportation. As a rule of thumb, shopping centers estimate that there should be five spaces for every 1,000 square feet of selling space in medium-sized centers and 10 spaces per 1,000 square feet in large centers.

A second traffic-related aspect the retailer should consider is the direction of traffic relative to the shopping area. Many shoppers prefer not to have to make left-hand turns from a busy roadway into a shopping area. A third consideration is the ease with which consumers can reach the store site. Are the roadways in good shape? Are there traffic barriers—rivers with a limited number of bridges? interstate highways with limited crossings? one-way streets? a high level of street usage resulting in congestion that limits exits to the site? Remember, customers normally avoid heavily congested shopping areas and shop elsewhere in order to minimize driving time and other difficulties.

Type of Neighbors

What neighboring establishments surround the site? There can be good and bad neighbors. What constitutes a good or bad neighbor depends on the type of store being considered at the site. Suppose that you plan to open a children's apparel store and are considering two alternative sites. One site already has a toy store and a gift shop; the other site has a bowling alley and an adult book store. Obviously, in this case, you know who the good and bad neighbors are.

However, determining the good and bad neighbors may not always be that easy, especially for an entrepreneur. A good neighboring business will be one that is compatible with the retailer's line of trade. When two or more businesses are compatible, they can actually help generate additional business for each other. For example, a paint store, hardware store, and auto parts store located next to one another may increase total traffic and thus benefit them all. One of the authors knew a jewelry store with multiple locations that always tried to locate next to an expensive women's apparel store and ideally a furrier. This was because most furriers provided summer storage of furs, which resulted in at least two major visits per year to the furrier as customers picked up furs for the winter and returned them in the summer. Both times were ideal for the neighboring jewelry merchant to intercept customers. In fact, he often had joint promotions with the furrier.

store compatibility
Exists when two similar retail businesses locate next to or nearby each other and they realize a sales volume greater than what they would have achieved if they were located apart from each other.

Research has found that retailers experience a benefit from **store compatibility**. In other words, when two compatible or very similar businesses (e.g., two shoe stores) locate near each other, they will show an increase in sales volume greater than what they would have achieved if they were located separately.[29] For example, when Lowe's opened a store near a Home Depot in Lewisville, Texas, the Home Depot store went from a category B to a category A store. This meant that the addition of a nearby competitor increased Home Depot's sales by 20 percent. Another example is PetSmart, which doesn't mind locating near a PETCO outlet. PetSmart likes to "shove their stores down the competition's throat"—that is, have its stores so close to the competition that customers can easily compare prices and service, However, when PETCO has PetSmart beat on convenience, PetSmart will back away.[30] A final case is Big Lots, a close-out specialist, which likes being near Walmart. In fact, the large discounter is not only a competitor for Big Lots but also its biggest landlord. Today, Big Lots operates 40 stores on sites where Walmart shut down to open a larger unit nearby. An executive for the smaller chain told a real estate conference that many of our customers "like to comparison shop, and if the competition is across the parking lot rather than across town, we feel like we'll win."[31]

retail clusters
Are groups of stores closely located that share similar characteristics such as product category, store format, or customer demographics.

Retail clusters are groups of stores closely located that share similar characteristics such as product category, store format, or customer demographics. Contrary to what some may think, clustering is not another description for Starbucks' saturation location strategy. Rather, the term dates back to the 1950s, when the choicest location for a gas station was believed to be an intersection that already had three other stations. It is seen today with shoe stores in malls, auto dealerships, furniture stores, and restaurants. The major benefit of clustering is twofold for customers. First, once potential customers identify a need for a line of merchandise or service, they don't need to decide on the specific store to visit just the need to decide to travel to the retail cluster. Consider how often a family does this when it decides to go out to dinner and heads in the direction of restaurant row (cluster) and then, when in transit or on arrival at the cluster, selects a specific restaurant for dining. Second, retail clustering allows customers to walk from store to store, comparing prices, products, and service. However, grouping stores doesn't always benefit competitors. Consider membership retailers such as wholesale clubs and fitness centers. After all, if consumers have already paid to use one of the retailers, it is doubtful that they would pay to shop at the other. In such cases, one of three things would happen:

1. The retailers would fight it out to the death, and both would lose.
2. The trade area could expand to become big enough so that both could succeed.
3. One retailer would be forced to completely differentiate itself from the other, and even then they might not both survive.

Terms of Purchase or Lease

Another consideration for the retailer at this point is the lease terms. The retailer should review the length of the lease (it could be too long or too short), the exclusivity clause (whether or not the retailer will be the only one allowed to sell a certain line of merchandise), the guaranteed traffic rate (a reduction in rent should be offered if the shopping center fails to achieve a targeted traffic level), and an anchor clause (which would also allow for a rent reduction if the anchor store in a developing center does not open on time or when the retailer opens). Lease arrangements generally call for either a fixed payment in which the rental charge is usually based on a fixed amount per month or a variable payment in which rent is a specified percentage of sales with a guaranteed minimum rent. It is important for the retailer to choose the one that is best under the circumstances—perhaps a combination of the two methods.

When the retailer decides to locate in a shopping center, it usually has no other choice than to lease. However, in the case of a freestanding location, an outright purchase is often possible. Purchase and lease costs should be factored into the site's expected profitability.

Expected Profitability

The final step in site-selection analysis is construction of a pro forma (expected) return-on-asset model for each possible site. The return-on-asset model comprises three crucial variables: net profit margin, asset turnover, and return on assets.

For purposes of evaluating sites, the potential return on equity is not relevant. This is because the financial leverage ratio (total assets divided by equity) is a top-management decision; it represents how much debt the retail enterprise is willing to assume. Most likely, the question of how to finance new store growth has already been answered or at least contemplated. The retailer should already have determined that it has or can obtain the capital to finance a new store. It is therefore reasonable and appropriate to evaluate sites on their potential return on assets and not return on equity.

If the retailer is to evaluate sites on their potential return on assets, then it will need at least three estimates: total sales, total assets, and net profit. Each of these is likely to vary, depending on the site. Sales estimates will be different for alternative sites because each will have unique trade area characteristics such as the number and nature of households and the level of competition. Estimated total assets could vary because the alternative sites will likely have different prices; the cost of construction could also vary. Finally, estimated profits could vary not only due to varying sales for the different sites but also because of different operating costs. For example, some sites may be in areas where labor expenses, taxes, or insurance rates are higher.

SUMMARY

Selecting a target market and determining which retail format will most effectively reach this market are two of the most important decisions a retailer will make. The retailer can reach potential customers through both store-based retail locations and nonstore retail formats. Geographical information systems can help the retailer gain knowledge of its potential customers and where they reside and how they behave. This can help the retailer better determine how to reach its target market.

STUDENT STUDY GUIDE

Most of the chapter discussed how to select a location for a store-based retailer. The choice of retail location involves three decisions: (1) market identification, or identifying the most attractive markets; (2) site analysis, or evaluating the demand and supply within each market; and (3) site selection, or selecting the best site (or sites) available.

LO 1

Explain the criteria used in selecting a target market.

We began this chapter by stating that an effective target market must be one that is measurable, accessible, and substantial. *Measurability* concerns whether or not objective data exists on the attributes of the target market. *Accessibility* deals with the extent to which marketing efforts can be uniquely targeted at a particular segment of the market. *Substantiality* relates to whether the target market is large enough to be economically worth pursuing.

LO 2

Identify the different options, both store-based and nonstore-based, for effectively reaching the retailer's target market and identify the advantages and disadvantages of business districts, shopping centers, and freestanding units as sites for retail locations.

We next reviewed the four store-based location alternatives available to the retailer: the business district, the shopping center or mall, the freestanding unit, and the nontraditional store location. The central business district is generally an unplanned shopping area around the geographic point where a city originated and grew up. As cities have grown, we have witnessed an expansion of two newer types of business districts: the secondary business district and the neighborhood business district.

A shopping center or mall is a centrally owned or managed shopping district that is planned, has balanced tenancy, and is surrounded by parking facilities. It has one or more anchor stores and a variety of smaller stores. Because of the many advantages shopping centers can offer the retailer, they are a fixture of America and account for 55 percent of all retail sales in the United States.

A freestanding retailer generally locates along major traffic arteries. There are usually no adjacent retailers selling competing products with which the retailer will have to share traffic.

The retailer also has five nonstore-based options: street peddling, mail order, automatic merchandising machines, direct selling, and the Internet.

LO 3

Define geographic information systems (GIS) and discuss their potential uses in a retail enterprise.

Higher-quality market selection and retail location decisions can be made with the use of geographic information systems, which are computerized systems combining physical geography with cultural geography. The GIS technology can be used not only for market selection, site analysis, and trade area definition but also to evaluate new store cannibalization, advertising management, merchandise management, and store-manager performance. With the advent of Yahoo and Google, this technique is available to even the smallest of retailers.

LO 4

What are the various factors that should be considered in identifying the most attractive retail market?

We began our analysis of market selection by looking at a trio of theories that can aid in the location decision. *Retail gravitation theory* assumes that as the population of a community rises relative to nearby communities, it will have relatively more merchandise assortments and availability, which serves as a drawing power for the community to draw customers into its retail shopping district. The *index of retail saturation* reflects the total demand for the product under question and whether the area is overstored or understored, which is the availability of current retailers to service or supply current demand. The *buying power index* enables us to develop an overall indicator of a market's potential. We concluded our discussion on market identification by looking into other factors that could influence a community's supply (square feet per store, square feet per employee, growth in stores, and quality of competition) or demand (market population, buyer behavior, household income, age, and composition, community life cycle, density, and mobility) for goods and services.

What attributes should be considered in evaluating retail sites within a retail market?   LO 5

After reviewing the three location theories, we discussed the second of our three steps in the location process: *site analysis*, which is an evaluation of the density of demand and supply within each possible market. This process begins by determining the size, description, and density of demand and supply of various areas within the chosen market and then identifying the most attractive sites, given the retailer's requirements that are available for new stores within each market.

How is the best geographic site selected?   LO 6

Finally, the retailer should conduct a site-selection analysis of the top-ranking sites in each market. The goal is to select the best site or sites. Retail-site analysts suggest that the following factors should be considered at this stage: nature of the site, traffic characteristics, type of neighbors, terms of lease or purchase, and finally the expected profitability or return on assets.

TERMS TO REMEMBER

home page
virtual store
ease of access
target market
store-based retailers
nonstore-based retailers
secondary business district (SBD)
neighborhood business district (NBD)
shopping center
anchor stores
freestanding retailer
geographic information system (GIS)
culture
thematic maps
trading area

retail gravity theory
reilly's law of retail gravitation
point of indifference
retail store saturation
understored
overstored
index of retail saturation (IRS)
buying power index (BPI)
site analysis
demand density
eminent domain law
100-percent location
store compatibility
retail clusters

REVIEW AND DISCUSSION QUESTIONS

What criteria are used in selecting a target market?   LO 1

1. Why should retailers be concerned about selecting the right target market? How are target market selection and location related?
2. What three criteria should be met to successfully target a market?

LO 2   Identify the different options, both store-based and nonstore-based, for effectively reaching the retailer's target market, and identify the advantages and disadvantages of business districts, shopping centers, and freestanding units as sites for retail location.

3. What types of retailers would be best suited for locating in a lifestyle center?

4. Why are some shopping centers and malls now using big-box stores such as Home Depot, Bass Pro Shops and Kaplan's as anchors? Aren't anchor stores supposed to be department stores?

5. What lines of retail trade do you believe will be most affected by the growth of retailing on the Internet?

6. Why isn't Walmart a good choice to be an anchor at a mall?

LO 3   Define geographic information systems (GIS) and discuss their potential uses in a retail enterprise.

7. How have improvements in the user-friendliness of GIS mapping technology caused retailers to become more research-driven in locating stores?

8. How is it possible for small retailers to use GIS? Isn't it expensive to use GIS?

9. Why do GISs include both physical and cultural geography? Provide some examples of physical and cultural data that should be included in a GIS.

LO 4   What factors should be considered in identifying the most attractive retail market?

10. Someone once said "build a better mousetrap and the world will beat a path to your door." If this is true, why is it important for a retailer to select the correct site within a trading area? Explain your answer.

11. What is the index of retail saturation? How is it used in making a location decision?

12. With the growth of Internet retailing, will the IRS increase or decrease in importance? Why?

13. According to Reilly's law of retail gravitation, cities attract trade from an intermediate place based on what two factors? How are these factors used in making a location decision?

14. Calculate the buyer power indexes for the following three cities:

Junction	0.007	0.005	0.006
Ontario	0.009	0.008	0.009
Edwardsville	0.007	0.006	0.009

15. Compute the index of retail saturation for the following three markets. The data for restaurants is:

Market	A	B	C
Annual retail expenditures per household	$739	$845	$903
Square feet of retail space	610,000	494,000	801,000
Number of households	126,000	109,000	163,000

Based on this data, which market is most attractive? What additional data would you find helpful in determining the attractiveness of the three markets?

What attributes should be considered in evaluating retail sites within a retail market? `LO 5`

16. Identify the factors you would consider most important in locating a fast-food restaurant. Compare these factors with the factors you would use in selecting a site for a supermarket.
17. Explain the concepts of demand density and supply density. Why are they important to retail decision making?

How is the best geographic site selected? `LO 6`

18. Why is it so hard to find that 100-percent retail location?
19. Why do some stores cluster around each other? Doesn't being so close to their competition hurt their profitability?

SAMPLE TEST QUESTIONS

Which of the following is not a criterion used to successfully reach a target market? `LO 1`
   a. The market segment should be measurable.
   b. Promotional efforts can be directed at the market segment.
   c. The market segment should create high sales.
   d. The market segment should be profitable.
   e. Distribution efforts can be directed at the market segment.

Freestanding retailers offer the following advantages: `LO 2`

   a. lack of direct competition.
   b. high drawing power from nearby complementary stores.
   c. higher traffic than shopping malls.
   d. lower advertising costs.
   e. stores must be leased.

Geographic information systems can be used for the following purposes: `LO 3`

   a. site analysis
   b. trade area definition
   c. advertising management
   d. merchandise management
   e. all of the above

The three sequential stages involved in selecting a location for a store-based retailer are: `LO 4`

   a. Identify the most understored markets, identify the most attractive sites that are available within each market, select the best site(s).
   b. Identify the most attractive markets, identify the most attractive sites that are available within each market, select the best site(s).
   c. Identify most attractive markets, identify the vacant parcels of real estate within each market, select the best site(s).
   d. Identify the most understored markets, identify the vacant parcels of real estate within each market, negotiate terms for best site.
   e. Identify the most attractive markets, identify the most attractive sites that are available within each market, negotiate for the lowest priced site.

Site analysis consists of: `LO 5`

   a. analysis of density of demand
   b. consideration of the type of neighbors

c.　analyzing sources of financing for the site (i.e., debt or equity financing)

d.　determining the expected profitability from operating a store at the site

e.　considering the ease with which consumers can reach the site

LO 6　**Which of the following is not an important consideration in selecting the best site for a new retail store?**

a.　nature of the site

b.　traffic characteristics of the site

c.　alternative investments available to the retailer

d.　potential profitability of the site

e.　type of neighbors

WRITING AND SPEAKING EXERCISE

You have a summer job with a small florist shop, Forget-Me-Knot, in Troy, Illinois, a growing area a half-hour east of St. Louis, Missouri. Until recently, Forget-Me-Knot and a smaller flower shop located a mile away in the center of town were able to easily satisfy the demand for flowers and floral arrangements in the area. Kathy Kistenmacher, the owner, believes there is room for another store because of the increasing number of people moving from St. Louis to the small suburban town. In fact, between 2000 and 2010, the city's population increased from 11,000 to 15,500. Kistenmacher sells more than just flowers, which gives her a competitive advantage over other flower shops. She also sells novelty items such as figurines, candles, potpourri, and houseplants. These other items make up 25 percent of Kathy's gross sales.

The shop has been very busy, and sales are growing rapidly. The store is often very crowded between 4:30 P.M. and 6:30 P.M. Therefore, Kistenmacher is contemplating either expanding her current business or opening another store at a new location before someone else sees the opportunity. She does not have the financial capability to do both. The expansion would be less expensive, but another store might attract more customers. Current customer information is given in Exhibit 7.1.

Exhibit 1

1.　Current sales: $452,000
2.　Sales growth rate (annually since 2000): 15 percent annually
3.　Percentage of customers living within three miles: 43 percent
4.　Percentage of customers living within three to six miles: 30 percent
5.　Percentage of customers living more than six miles: 27 percent
6.　Average income of those living within three miles: $32,000
7.　Average income of those living within three to six miles: $61,000

Forget-Me-Knot is currently located at the edge of town two miles from the interstate to St. Louis on the main traffic artery from the interstate. Kistenmacher is considering two possible locations: One is in the middle of town, a half-mile from her current location and only two blocks from her competitor; the other location is next to the Interstate.

The in-town possibility is centrally located, and Kathy feels that this location would attract many people who shop at the renovated downtown shopping area. The highway location, on the other hand, is conveniently located in a small shopping complex. This location would appeal to commuters returning to the town proper from St. Louis. It would also be accessible to other commuters who live in the new subdivisions across the interstate.

Kathy feels that she has to make a change, but she cannot decide which location to choose, or whether she should renovate and expand the existing store. She can choose only one alternative.

Since you have taken a retailing class, Kathy asks for your advice. Therefore, based on the available information, write a memo telling Kathy if she should open another store or just expand her current location. Explain how you determined this strategy. If you recommend an additional store, tell her why you chose that location.

RETAIL PROJECT

Small as well as large retailers can benefit immensely from knowing the trade area of their store. Identify a small local retailer such as a florist, pet store, apparel store, gift store, or restaurant. Contact the store owner or manager and tell him or her that you are a student studying retailing and would like to volunteer to construct a map of the retailer's trade area. To do this, you need to obtain the addresses of all the patrons over a one-week period and plot these on a map. Review the customer-spotting map for a supermarket in Exhibit 7.8 on page 000[sms1]. Develop a method to collect the needed data and construct the map of the trade area. What percentage of customers are within one mile of the store? within three miles? within five miles?

PLANNING YOUR OWN BUSINESS

The retail store you are planning has an estimated circular trade radius of four miles. Within this four-mile radius there is an average of 1,145 households per square mile. In a normal year, you expect that 47 percent of these households would visit your store (referred to as *penetration*) an average of 4.3 times (referred to as *frequency*). Based on those figures, what would you expect to be the traffic (i.e., number of visitors to your store per year)? (*Hint:* Traffic can be viewed as the square miles of the trade area multiplied by the household density multiplied by penetration, which is in turn multiplied by frequency.)

Once you answer this question, do some *sensitivity analysis*, which is an assessment of how sensitive store traffic is to changes in your assumptions about penetration and frequency. What happens if penetration drops to 45 percent or rises to 50 percent? What happens if frequency drops to 4.0 times annually or rises to 4.5 times annually? In this analysis, change only one thing at a time and hold all other assumptions constant.

Managing Retail Operations

Managing a Retailer's Finances

OVERVIEW:

In this chapter, we begin by looking at how a merchandise budget is prepared and how it is used when making plans for an upcoming merchandise season. Next we describe the basic differences among an income statement, a balance sheet, and a statement of cash flow, as well as discuss how a retailer uses these accounting statements in controlling its merchandising activities. Finally, we discuss the accounting inventory systems and pricing methods available to value inventory.

LEARNING OBJECTIVES:

After reading this chapter, you should be able to:

1. Describe the importance of a merchandise budget and know how to prepare a six-month merchandise plan.
2. Explain the differences among and the uses of these three accounting statements: income statement, balance sheet, and statement of cash flow.
3. Explain how the retailer is able to value inventory.

LO 1

The Merchandise Budget

Why is a merchandise budget so important in retail planning, and how is a merchandise budget prepared?

In Chapter 7, we described the role location plays in a retailer's success. Location is important and was discussed prior to the other elements of the retail mix because, for most new retailers, it is the first decision made. Also, once the location decision is made, it is difficult and costly to change.

Another important element of the retail mix is merchandising, which includes pricing. Some experts suggest that all other elements of the retail mix revolve around merchandising, especially when considering chain store operators. After all, most of the merchandise in a JCPenney's store in Grand Rapids, Michigan, is the same as that in Tulsa, Oklahoma; slight variations are most often due to climate. The same may be said about a Carrefour store in Buenos Aires, Argentina, and one in Paris, France. Only after these merchandising decisions are made can retailers concern themselves with the other retail mix elements: promotion, store layout and design, and customer service. However, before we can explain how to make these merchandising decisions, we must first discuss the retailer's means of controlling these activities.

Many people believe that the terms *retailing* and *merchandising* are synonymous; they are not. Retailing includes all the business activities necessary to sell goods and services to the final consumer. **Merchandising** is only one of these activities and is concerned with the planning and control involved in the buying and

merchandising
Is the planning and control of the buying and selling of goods and services to help the retailer realize its objectives.

selling of goods and services to help the retailer realize its objectives. Success in merchandising is the result of total financial planning and control. This chapter is divided into three sections: the merchandise budget, retail accounting statements, and inventory valuation.

Successful retailers must have good financial planning and control of their merchandise. The retailer invests money in merchandise for profitable resale to others. A poor choice of merchandise will result in low profits or maybe even a loss. Therefore, to be successful in retailing, the retailer must have a plan of what is to be accomplished. In retailing, this plan of operation is called the *merchandise budget*. A **merchandise budget** is a plan of projected sales for an upcoming season, when and how much merchandise is to be purchased, and what markups and reductions are likely to occur. The merchandise budget forces the retailer to develop a formal outline of all merchandising activities for the upcoming selling season.

In developing the merchandise budget, the retailer must answer five major merchandising questions:

1. What are the anticipated sales for the department, division, or store?
2. How much stock on hand is needed to achieve this sales plan, given the level of inventory turnover expected?
3. What reductions, if any, from the original retail price are likely to be needed in order to dispose of all merchandise brought into the store?
4. What additional purchases must be made during the season?
5. What **gross margin** (the difference between sales and cost of goods sold) is the department, division, or store likely contribute to the overall profitability of the company, given this merchandising plan?

When preparing the merchandise budget, a retailer must employ the following four rules.

merchandise budget
Is a plan of projected sales for an upcoming season, when and how much merchandise is to be purchased, and what markups and reductions will likely occur.

gross margin
Is the difference between net sales and cost of goods sold.

Music is a merchandise category where it is difficult to budget far in advance because it is virtually impossible to predict the top selling musical artists and new releases. New releases are only known about one month before release. Also because customers can download music direct to their iPods or phones the ability to predict in-store demand for music is more difficult.

First, a merchandise budget should always be prepared in advance of the selling season. This is because buyers for particular departments often prepare their budgets for later approval by a divisional merchandising manager or general merchandising manager. As a result, most retail firms selling apparel or hard-line goods begin the process of developing a merchandise budget three to four months in advance of the budget period. Yet, this is not always the case with some specialty retailers. For example, fine restaurants can easily order special selections like fresh fish on a daily basis. However, most retailers have only two seasons a year: (1) spring–summer, usually February through July; and (2) fall–winter, August through January. (Some small retailers may use a three-month budget where the four seasons begin in February, May, August, and November.) The buyer for a particular department will usually begin to prepare merchandise budgets in early March and September for the upcoming seasons.

Second, since the budget is a plan that management expects to follow during the upcoming merchandise season, the language must be easy to understand. The merchandise budget illustration contained in this chapter has only 11 items; however, the number of items contained in a budget may vary by company due to differences in the particular merchandise and market characteristics. Remember, the budget serves no useful purpose if it cannot be understood by all decision makers.

Third, because the economy is consistently changing, the merchandise budget must be planned for a relatively short period of time. Six months is the norm for most retailers, although some retailers choose to use a three-month, or even shorter, plan. Forecasting future sales is difficult enough without complicating the process by projecting too far into the future. The firm's senior management should be concerned with long-term trends; buyers should focus more on short-term decisions that may influence the merchandise budget.

Fourth, the budget should be flexible enough to permit changes. All merchandise budgets are plans or estimates of predicted future events. As competition and consumers tastes are not always predictable, particularly in regard to fashion preferences, any forecast is subject to error and will need revision.

Keeping in mind this discussion of merchandising decisions and rules, review the blank six-month merchandising budget for the housewares department of a major department store shown in Exhibit 8.1. Do not be alarmed if Exhibit 8.1 is not clear to you at this point. As the chapter continues, we will describe why the budget is set up in this form. In addition, we will explain all the analytical tools necessary to calculate the numbers required when developing a six-month merchandise budget or plan.

Exhibit 8.1 may appear more confusing than it really is because each element is broken into four parts: last year, plan for the upcoming season, revised plan, and actual. This is merely a means of providing the decision maker with complete information. "Last year" refers to last year's sales for the period; "Plan" (plan for the upcoming season) is what the original plan projected; "Revised" shows the results of any revisions made due to changes in market conditions after the original plan was accepted; and "Actual" corresponds to the final, or realized, results.

Exhibit 8.2 presents the same material in a simpler form. Here we will only attempt to show you how and why a retailer develops a six-month merchandising plan. Exhibit 8.3 is a summary of how all the numbers in the merchandise budget are determined. Exhibit 8.2 shows the spring–summer season, February through July, for the Two-Seasons Department Store, Department 353, with projected sales of $500,000, planned retail reductions of $50,000 (10 percent of sales), planned initial markup of 45 percent, and a planned gross margin on purchases of $208,750.

		SIX-MONTH MERCHANDISE BUDGET Housewares Department						
		February	March	April	May	June	July	Total
BOM Stock	Last Year							
	Plan							
	Revised							
	Actual							
Sales	Last Year							
	Plan							
	Revised							
	Actual							
Reductions	Last Year							
	Plan							
	Revised							
	Actual							
EOM STOCK	Last Year							
	Plan							
	Revised							
	Actual							
RETAIL PURCHASES	Last Year							
	Plan							
	Revised							
	Actual							
PURCHASES @ COST	Last Year							
	Plan							
	Revised							
	Actual							
INITIAL MARKUP	Last Year							
	Plan							
	Revised							
	Actual							
GROSS MARGIN DOLLARS	Last Year							
	Plan							
	Revised							
	Actual							
BOM STOCK/SALES RATIO	Last Year							
	Plan							
	Revised							
	Actual							
SALES PERCENTAGE	Last Year							
	Plan							
	Revised							
	Actual							
RETAIL REDUCTION PERCENTAGE	Last Year							
	Plan							
	Revised							
	Actual							

STOCKTURN: Last Year_____   Plan_____   Actual_____
ON ORDER – BEGINNING OF SEASON _____   Plan_____   Actual_____
EOM INVENTORY FOR LAST MONTH _____   Plan_____   Actual_____
REDUCTION PERCENTAGE_____   Plan_____   Actual_____
MARKUP PERCENTAGE _____   Plan_____   Actual_____

Exhibit 8.1
Sample Six-Month
Merchandise Budget

Determining Planned Sales

The initial step in developing a six-month merchandise budget is to estimate planned sales for the entire season as well as for each month. The buyer begins by examining the previous year's recorded sales. Adjustments are then made when

	February	March	April	May	June	July	Total
1. Planned BOM Stock	$225,000	$300,000	$300,000	$250,000	$375,000	$300,000	–
2. Planned Sales	75,000	75,000	100,000	50,000	125,000	75,000	$500,000
3. Planned Retail Reductions	7,500	7,500	5,000	7,500	6,250	16,250	50,000
4. Planned EOM Stock	300,000	300,000	250,000	375,000	300,000	250,000	–
5. Planned Purchases at Retail	157,500	82,500	55,000	182,500	56,250	41,250	575,000
6. Planned Purchases at Cost	86,625	45,375	30,250	100,375	30,937.50	22,687.50	316,250
7. Planned Initial Markup	70,875	37,125	24,750	82,125	25,312.50	18,562.50	258,750
8. Planned Gross Margin	63,375	29,625	19,750	74,625	19,062.50	2,312.50	208,750
9. Planned BOM Stock-to-Sales Ratio	3	4	3	5	3	4	–
10. Planned Sales Percentage	15%	15%	20%	10%	25%	15%	100%
11. Planned Retail Reduction Percentage	10%	10%	5%	15%	5%	21.67%	10%

Planned Total Sales for the Period	$500,000
Planned Total Retail Reduction Percentage for the Period	10%
Planned Initial Markup Percentage	45%
Planned BOM Stock for August	$250,000

Exhibit 8.2
Two-Seasons Department
Store, Dept. 353,
Six-Month Merchandise

Exhibit 8.3
Formulas for the
Six-Month Budget

Determining Planned Sales for the Month

(Planned Sales Percentage for the Month) × (Planned Total Sales)
= (Planned Sales for the Month)

Determining Planned BOM Stock for the Month

(Planned Sales for the Month) × (Planned BOM Stock-to-Sales Ratio for the Month)
= (Planned BOM Stock for the Month)

Determining Planned Retail Reductions for the Month

(Planned Sales for the Month) × (Planned Retail Reduction Percentage for the Month)
= (Planned Retail Reductions for the Month)

Determining Planned EOM Stock for the Month

(Planned BOM Stock for the Next Month) = (Planned EOM Stock for the Current Month)

Determining Planned Purchases at Retail for the Month

(Planned Sales for the Month) + (Planned Retail Reductions for the Month) + (Planned EOM Stock for the Month) − (Planned BOM Stock for the Month) = (Planned Purchases at Retail for the Month)

Determining Planned Purchases at Cost for the Month

(Planned Purchases at Retail for the Month) × (100% − Planned Initial Markup Percentage)
= (Planned Purchases at Cost for the Month)

Determining Planned Initial Markup for the Month

(Planned Purchases at Retail for the Month) × (Planned Initial Markup Percentage)
= (Planned Initial Markup for the Month)

or

(Planned Purchases at Retail for the Month) − (Planned Purchases at Cost for the Month)
= (Planned Initial Markup for the Month)

Determining Planned Gross Margin for the Month

(Planned Initial Markup for the Month) − (Planned Retail Reductions for the Month)
= (Planned Gross Margin for the Month)

planning sales for the upcoming merchandise budget. When comparing this year's sales to last year's sales, retailers do not always compare exact dates (i.e., comparing February 13, 2011, sales to February 13, 2010). This is because dates fall on different days of the week each year. For instance, as shown in Exhibit 8.4, February 13, 2011, was a Sunday, whereas the same date was a Saturday in 2010, a problem for the retailer that is closed on Sundays. Similarly, in 2012, February 13 falls on a Monday, normally a slow day in terms of retail sales. Therefore, retailers use a retail reporting calendar (see Exhibit 8.4), which divides the year into two seasons, each with six months. Thus, January 31, 2011, the first Monday of the 2011 spring season (and the first Monday of February for a retailer using the calendar), would be compared to February 1, 2010, which was the first Monday of the 2010 spring season. In the year 2012, the first Monday of the spring season is January 30.[1] By using this calendar, retailers are better prepared to make direct comparisons to prior years. Yet, many retailers, such as those in fashion or apparel, experience problems once a season, when attempting these comparisons. Complications arise due to the movement of Easter (April 4 in 2010, April 24 in 2011, and April 8 in 2012) and Thanksgiving. For example, in all three years, Easter falls during April;

Exhibit 8.4
Retail Reporting Calendar

SPRING 2010 / FALL 2010

FEB / MAY / AUG / NOV

FEB S	M	T	W	T	F	S		MAY S	M	T	W	T	F	S		AUG S	M	T	W	T	F	S		NOV S	M	T	W	T	F	S
31	1	2	3	4	5	6			2	3	4	5	6	7	8			1	2	3	4	5	6	7		31	1	2	3	4	5	6
7	8	9	10	11	12	13		9	10	11	12	13	14	15		8	9	10	11	12	13	14		7	8	9	10	11	12	13
14	15	16	17	18	19	20		16	17	18	19	20	21	22		15	16	17	18	19	20	21		14	15	16	17	18	19	20
21	22	23	24	25	26	27		23	24	25	26	27	28	29		22	23	24	25	26	27	28		21	22	23	24	**25**	26	27

MARCH / JUNE / SEPT / DEC

MAR S	M	T	W	T	F	S		JUN S	M	T	W	T	F	S		SEP S	M	T	W	T	F	S		DEC S	M	T	W	T	F	S
28	1	2	3	4	5	6		30	31	1	2	3	4	5		29	30	31	1	2	3	4		28	29	30	1	2	3	4
7	8	9	10	11	12	13		6	7	8	9	10	11	12		5	6	7	8	9	10	11		5	6	7	8	9	10	11
14	15	16	17	18	19	20		13	14	15	16	17	18	19		12	13	14	15	16	17	18		12	13	14	15	16	17	18
21	22	23	24	25	26	27		20	21	22	23	24	25	26		19	20	21	22	23	24	25		19	20	21	22	23	24	**25**
28	29	30	31	1	2	3		27	28	29	30	1	2	3		26	27	28	29	30	1	2		26	27	28	29	30	31	1

APRIL / JULY / OCT / JAN

APR S	M	T	W	T	F	S		JUL S	M	T	W	T	F	S		OCT S	M	T	W	T	F	S		JAN S	M	T	W	T	F	S
4	5	6	7	8	9	10		4	5	6	7	8	9	10		3	4	5	6	7	8	9		2	3	4	5	6	7	8
11	12	13	14	15	16	17		11	12	13	14	15	16	17		10	11	12	13	14	15	16		9	10	11	12	13	14	15
18	19	20	21	22	23	24		18	19	20	21	22	23	24		17	18	19	20	21	22	23		16	17	18	19	20	21	22
25	26	27	28	29	30	1		25	26	27	28	29	30	31		24	25	26	27	28	29	30		23	24	25	26	27	28	29

SPRING 2011 / FALL 2011

FEB / MAY / AUG / NOV

FEB S	M	T	W	T	F	S		MAY S	M	T	W	T	F	S		AUG S	M	T	W	T	F	S		NOV S	M	T	W	T	F	S
30	31	1	2	3	4	5		1	2	3	4	5	6	7		31	1	2	3	4	5	6		30	31	1	2	3	4	5
6	7	8	9	10	11	12		8	9	10	11	12	13	14		7	8	9	10	11	12	13		6	7	8	9	10	11	12
13	14	15	16	17	18	19		15	16	17	18	19	20	21		14	15	16	17	18	19	20		13	14	15	16	17	18	19
20	21	22	23	24	25	26		22	23	24	25	26	27	28		21	22	23	24	25	26	27		20	21	22	23	**24**	25	26

MARCH / JUNE / SEPT / DEC

MAR S	M	T	W	T	F	S		JUN S	M	T	W	T	F	S		SEP S	M	T	W	T	F	S		DEC S	M	T	W	T	F	S
27	28	1	2	3	4	5		29	30	31	1	2	3	4		28	29	30	31	1	2	3		27	28	29	30	1	2	3
6	7	8	9	10	11	12		5	6	7	8	9	10	11		4	5	6	7	8	9	10		4	5	6	7	8	9	10
13	14	15	16	17	18	19		12	13	14	15	16	17	18		11	12	13	14	15	16	17		11	12	13	14	15	16	17
20	21	22	23	24	25	26		19	20	21	22	23	24	25		18	19	20	21	22	23	24		18	19	20	21	22	23	24
27	28	29	30	31	1	2		26	27	28	29	30	1	2		25	26	27	28	29	30	1		**25**	26	27	28	29	30	31

APRIL / JULY / OCT / JAN

APR S	M	T	W	T	F	S		JUL S	M	T	W	T	F	S		OCT S	M	T	W	T	F	S		JAN S	M	T	W	T	F	S
3	4	5	6	7	8	9		3	4	5	6	7	8	9		2	3	4	5	6	7	8		1	2	3	4	5	6	7
10	11	12	13	14	15	16		10	11	12	13	14	15	16		9	10	11	12	13	14	15		8	9	10	11	12	13	14
17	18	19	20	21	22	23		17	18	19	20	21	22	23		16	17	18	19	20	21	22		15	16	17	18	19	20	21
24	25	26	27	28	29	30		24	25	26	27	28	29	30		23	24	25	26	27	28	29		22	23	24	25	26	27	28

SPRING 2012 / FALL 2012

FEB / MAY / AUG / NOV

FEB S	M	T	W	T	F	S		MAY S	M	T	W	T	F	S		AUG S	M	T	W	T	F	S		NOV S	M	T	W	T	F	S
29	30	31	1	2	3	4		29	30	1	2	3	4	5		29	30	31	1	2	3	4		28	29	30	31	1	2	3
5	6	7	8	9	10	11		6	7	8	9	10	11	12		5	6	7	8	9	10	11		4	5	6	7	8	9	10
12	13	14	15	16	17	18		13	14	15	16	17	18	19		12	13	14	15	16	17	18		11	12	13	14	15	16	17
19	20	21	22	23	24	25		20	21	22	23	24	25	26		19	20	21	22	23	24	25		18	19	20	21	**22**	23	24

MARCH / JUNE / SEPT / DEC

MAR S	M	T	W	T	F	S		JUN S	M	T	W	T	F	S		SEP S	M	T	W	T	F	S		DEC S	M	T	W	T	F	S
26	27	28	29	1	2	3		27	28	29	30	31	1	2		26	27	28	29	30	31	1		25	26	27	28	29	30	1
4	5	6	7	8	9	10		3	4	5	6	7	8	9		2	3	4	5	6	7	8		2	3	4	5	6	7	8
11	12	13	14	15	16	17		10	11	12	13	14	15	16		9	10	11	12	13	14	15		9	10	11	12	13	14	15
18	19	20	21	22	23	24		17	18	19	20	21	22	23		16	17	18	19	20	21	22		16	17	18	19	20	21	22
25	26	27	28	29	30	31		24	25	26	27	28	29	30		23	24	25	26	27	28	29		23	24	**25**	26	27	28	29

APRIL / JULY / OCT / JAN

APR S	M	T	W	T	F	S		JUL S	M	T	W	T	F	S		OCT S	M	T	W	T	F	S		JAN S	M	T	W	T	F	S
1	2	3	4	5	6	7		1	2	3	4	5	6	7		30	1	2	3	4	5	6		30	31	1	2	3	4	5
8	9	10	11	12	13	14		8	9	10	11	12	13	14		7	8	9	10	11	12	13		6	7	8	9	10	11	12
15	16	17	18	19	20	21		15	16	17	18	19	20	21		14	15	16	17	18	19	20		13	14	15	16	17	18	19
22	23	24	25	26	27	28		22	23	24	25	26	27	28		21	22	23	24	25	26	27		20	21	22	23	24	25	26

however, Easter is the first day of April in the 2010 reporting calendar, the 22nd day of April in the 2011 reporting calendar, and the eighth day of April in 2012. As a result, March's sales will receive all the benefit of the 2010 Easter season, only a majority of the 2012 Easter season, and April sales will significantly improve in 2011 due to Easter in the last full week of April. In addition, Easter sales in 2011 should see an improvement from the warmer weather of late April as many consumers in northern climates don't want to put a coat over a new Easter outfit.

Retail planning is also complicated by the number of "shopping days" between Thanksgiving and Christmas. During the fall season, the period between Thanksgiving and Christmas can vary in length by as much as a week. Since Thanksgiving is the fourth Thursday of November, it can fall between November 22 and 28. As a result, the number of days in the Christmas shopping season will vary from year to year. For example, in 2010 and 2011 there are only four full weekends (Christmas is on a Saturday in 2010 and on a Sunday in 2011) and 29 and 30 shopping days, respectively. However, 2012 will have five full weekends and 32 days between November 22 and Christmas Day, which falls on a Tuesday.

The day of the week on which a holiday falls on can also impact retailers. Consider Valentine's Day. When Valentine's day falls on a Wednesday, many retailers are adversely affected, particularly restaurants. After all, it means an abbreviated romantic evening because most people have to get up early for work the next day. However, for others, like florists, a middle-of-the-week Valentine's day is a plus. Midweek days (Tuesday, Wednesday, and Thursday) routinely translate into more flowers, particularly those pricey long-stemmed roses. After all, many of the recipients won't be taking a three- or four-day weekend and therefore will be getting them at work where fellow workers will see them.

Still even the use of a retail reporting calendar cannot overcome many of the uncontrollable and unexpected variables retailers encounter when forecasting sales. Retailers are just now learning how to deal with the greatest uncontrollable variable they must face—the weather. As the chapter's "Service Retailing" box describes, the consequences of weather can have a major impact on a retailer's planned sales

Peter Pereira/The Standard-Times/AP Photo

The day after Thanksgiving in the United States is a day of big sales and price cutting and thus customers often line up hours before stores open. Many of the toys that Toys "R" Us will have available for this big sales day will have been ordered months earlier.

Service Retailing

How Weather Forecasts Can Improve Retail Performance

Consider the case of auto-service retailers and car battery sales. As anyone who has lived above the Mason-Dixon line knows, finding your car battery dead on a cold morning is one of life's most unpleasant surprises. While all consumers know that frigid weather is the number-one cause of dead batteries, many car owners tend to postpone replacing their battery and are often unprepared when a battery problem occurs.

How can retailers use this information when forecasting sales? To start, it is imperative that they know the most conducive weather for a product's sales—in this case, car batteries—before developing a merchandising budget or planning promotional events.

Figure 1, for example, shows the deviation from average automotive battery sales in Minneapolis, Minnesota, in 5°

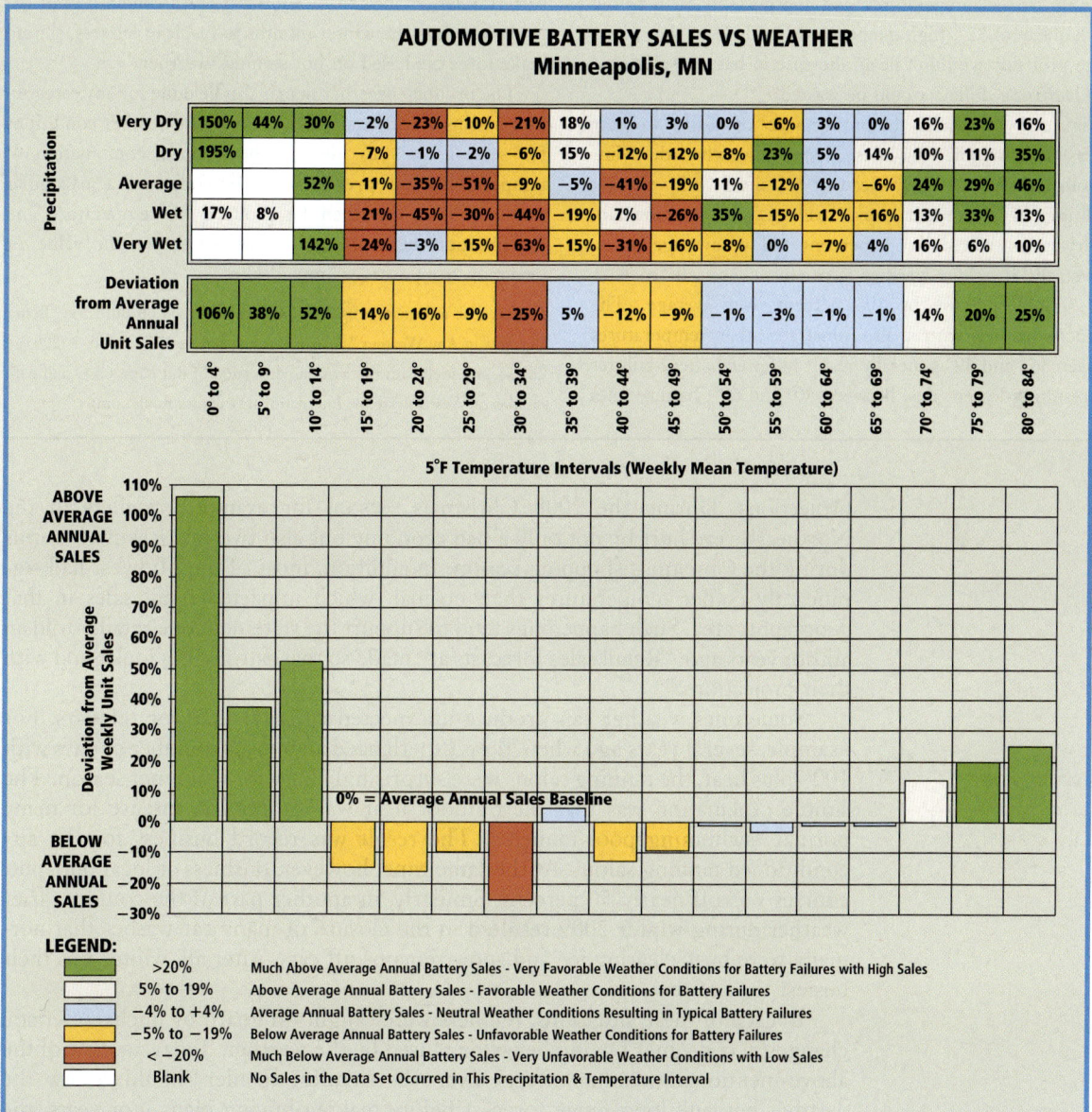

AUTOMOTIVE BATTERY SALES VS WEATHER
Minneapolis, MN

Precipitation	0° to 4°	5° to 9°	10° to 14°	15° to 19°	20° to 24°	25° to 29°	30° to 34°	35° to 39°	40° to 44°	45° to 49°	50° to 54°	55° to 59°	60° to 64°	65° to 69°	70° to 74°	75° to 79°	80° to 84°
Very Dry	150%	44%	30%	−2%	−23%	−10%	−21%	18%	1%	3%	0%	−6%	3%	0%	16%	23%	16%
Dry	195%			−7%	−1%	−2%	−6%	15%	−12%	−12%	−8%	23%	5%	14%	10%	11%	35%
Average			52%	−11%	−35%	−51%	−9%	−5%	−41%	−19%	11%	−12%	4%	−6%	24%	29%	46%
Wet	17%	8%		−21%	−45%	−30%	−44%	−19%	7%	−26%	35%	−15%	−12%	−16%	13%	33%	13%
Very Wet			142%	−24%	−3%	−15%	−63%	−15%	−31%	−16%	−8%	0%	−7%	4%	16%	6%	10%
Deviation from Average Annual Unit Sales	106%	38%	52%	−14%	−16%	−9%	−25%	5%	−12%	−9%	−1%	−3%	−1%	−1%	14%	20%	25%

5°F Temperature Intervals (Weekly Mean Temperature)

0% = Average Annual Sales Baseline

Deviation from Average Weekly Unit Sales

ABOVE AVERAGE ANNUAL SALES

BELOW AVERAGE ANNUAL SALES

LEGEND:

	>20%	Much Above Average Annual Battery Sales - Very Favorable Weather Conditions for Battery Failures with High Sales
	5% to 19%	Above Average Annual Battery Sales - Favorable Weather Conditions for Battery Failures
	−4% to +4%	Average Annual Battery Sales - Neutral Weather Conditions Resulting in Typical Battery Failures
	−5% to −19%	Below Average Annual Battery Sales - Unfavorable Weather Conditions for Battery Failures
	< −20%	Much Below Average Annual Battery Sales - Very Unfavorable Weather Conditions with Low Sales
	Blank	No Sales in the Data Set Occurred in This Precipitation & Temperature Interval

(continued)

Service Retailing (continued)

intervals across five precipitation categories. Temperatures are defined as a weekly mean temperature. Therefore, when it is really cold, with weekly mean temperatures below 14° (implying high temperatures in the middle 20s and low temperatures in the middle single digits), there is a 52 percent increase in battery sales due to weather-driven failures. (Notice that there is a 66 percent swing in sales with just a 5° drop from 19° to 14°.)

Consider the problems a retailer might face if it planned a battery promotion for a particular winter week in Minneapolis only to see temperatures rise unexpectedly to a balmy weekly mean of 32° (high temperatures in the 40s) that week. There probably wouldn't be an increase in battery sales, and the advertising dollars would be wasted!

Figure 1 illustrates the importance of using weather forecasts when projecting sales. Historically, when the Minneapolis area has a weekly mean of 32° along with very wet conditions (200 percent above average rain or snowfall), battery sales will fall 63 percent below average sales. Conversely, if colder weather is predicted—say, 0° to 4°— sales should increase by 106 percent over average. The product–weather matrix also illustrates that temperatures between 15° and 49° generally result in fewer battery failures and resulting lower sales. Between 50° and 69°, battery sales

are near average, with little impact due to weather. However, when temperatures are 70° or higher, failures increase 14 percent to 25 percent above average, and extremely hot weather—above 80° with average precipitation—results in peak summer sales of nearly 50 percent above average. (High temperatures would be in the middle 90s in Minneapolis.) By using a reliable weather forecast to determine the most likely really cold and really hot weeks, Minneapolis retailers are better prepared to strategically plan battery inventory levels and craft effective retailing promotional plans. Conversely, battery retailers located in Southern cities, which do not get cold enough in the winter months to result in failures, should make forecasts based on hot summer weather.

The product–weather matrix can be done for any category by assessing weekly unit sales against past weather conditions for several years to identify the optimal combination of temperature and precipitation for sales of a particular product. Sales can then be grouped by temperature and precipitation intervals and expressed as a unit value or deviation from average annual sales.

Source: The information used in this box was based on Bill Kirk, "Better Business in Any Weather," *ICSC's Research Review*, Vol. 12, no. 2 (2005): 28–34, and used with the written permission of Bill Kirk, CEO and cofounder of Weather Trends International (www.wxtrends.com).

projections. During the 2008 Christmas season, for example, retailers in the Northeast were hurt by not only a bad economy but also two major winter storms during the Christmas shopping season. In addition, most of the Midwest had significantly colder temperatures than normal, which impacted retail sales in that geographic area. Such happenings tend to support the statement one retailer told an author years ago: "Retail sales forecasts are made so that astrologists look good with their projections."

Sometimes weather can produce unexpected consequences for retailers. For example, several years ago when Texas experienced an unusual number of days with 100°-plus heat, the tanning salons were surprisingly busy for a summer season. The simple explanation was that the outdoor heat was simply too intense for many normal "swimming pool tanners." The result was record business for the air-conditioned tanning salons. At the same time, however, business at local putt-putt courses was off nearly 50 percent. Similarly, in another part of the country, drier weather during winter 2009 resulted in the closure of many car washes that normally were busy clearing ice and snow remains off cars. After all, winter was their busiest time of the year.

In each of these situations, retailers were caught off guard by uncharacteristic changes in consumer buying behavior caused by the weather. Today, in view of the above-mentioned weather effects, even the smallest retailer should review the weather bureau's long-range forecast before making buying plans. For years, the late Robert Kahn, a respected retail consultant and long-time member of Walmart's board of directors, tried to convince Sam Walton that the effective use of weather forecasts presented the giant retailer with an opportunity to gain a competitive advantage over its competitors.[2] As a result, most large retailers have now elected to use the sophisticated services of private forecasters such as Weather Trends International (www.wxtrends.com) that have historical data tied to product category sales and tailored to all the locations where the retailer is located. These specific weather projections aid the retailer's sales forecasting so that its gross margins aren't damaged, out of stocks are reduced, and inventory turns are boosted.

Of course, not all sales forecasts are based on weather predictions; many other factors, such as the economy, must also come into consideration. One retailer known for considering a wide variety of factors when estimating future sales is San Francisco--based Williams-Sonoma. Best known for its catalog for cooks, Williams-Sonoma's secret for forecasting sales rests on its highly automated mailing lists. Its database of 5 million customers tracks as many as 150 different pieces of information per customer. With a few keystrokes, the retailer can tell you what you've bought from each of its five annual catalogs (an estimated 60 percent of customers have bought from more than one), what time of the year you tend to buy, how often you buy, what category of merchandise you lean toward, and so forth. Through a complex cross-referencing of the data, Williams-Sonoma's two full-time statisticians are able to project, within 5 percent (on average), each catalog's sales.

Forecasting is most important for service retailers because their services are perishable. Services present unique forecasting problems for retailers because, unlike physical products, they cannot be produced or manufactured, boxed, stored, and shelved. In fact, services theoretically perish the moment they are produced. This perishability is not a problem when demand is steady. However, when demand fluctuates, service retailers have problems. As a result, service retailers often try to balance their demand and supply by continually altering their retail mix in an attempt to better manage sales.

Many restaurant chains now seek to balance their supply and demand with the aid of a computer program that tracks the sales of every menu item on an hourly basis and sets cooking schedules based on the program. After consulting the printout, the restaurant's manager can determine how many baked potatoes to cook and when to put them in the oven so as to meet the expected demand. While it's not completely accurate, the computer bats close to 90 percent, according to one Texas steak-house manager. The same program can also be used to order merchandise and schedule hourly employees. The computer program alone saves the Texas retailer more than 25 hours a week in hand calculations.

Another group of service retailers, for whom proper forecasting can make the difference between realizing a profit or loss, is the travel industry. These retailers need to know how many customers will not show up for each flight. As described in Chapter 2's "Retailing: The Inside Story" box, by accurately estimating who will really be on any given flight, airlines can avoid offending their valued frequent business flyers.

Now let's return to the example in Exhibit 8.2. After reviewing the data available, the buyer for Department 353 forecast that $500,000 was a reasonable total sales figure for the future season. Both June, with a projected 25 percent of the total season's sales, and April, with 20 percent, are expected to be the busiest months. May, with only 10 percent, is expected to be the slowest month. The remaining months will have equal sales. Because April, May, and June account for 55 percent of total sales, then February, March, and July's total must be 45 percent or 15 percent per month so they are equal. The buyer is able to determine planned monthly sales by multiplying the planned monthly sales percentage by planned

Retailing: The Inside Story

Dressing Up Financial Statements

Accounting rules give companies wide discretion in calculating their earnings. By accruing, or allotting, revenues and expenses to specific periods, retailers aim to allocate income to the quarter or year in which it was effectively earned. This *accrual accounting* method is supposed to provide a more accurate picture of what's happening to the business at a given time, and often it does. However, retailers, especially small retailers, have learned that lenders judge the worth and creditability of a business by its financial statements. Thus, today many retailers are using aggressive accounting methods to make their statements look as good as possible. Listed below are several methods retailers have used to window dress their books.

LIFO Liquidation

Retailers using the standard LIFO (last-in, first-out) inventory accounting know that profits look better when the older and less costly goods are sold at inflated prices during periods of inflation. Therefore, earnings can be improved by reducing the basic stock level, the minimum amount of an item to be carried at all times. (Basic stock will be discussed in greater detail in the next chapter.) This will therefore result in some less-expensive older inventory being sold. However, the retailer's future earnings could be hurt when it replaces inventory at higher prices.

Improving the Current Ratio

Since a retailer's **current ratio** (current assets divided by current liabilities) is probably the easiest and most common

way for lenders to analyze a balance sheet, some retailers try to improve their ratios by paying off small portions of their current debt prior to vendor review. For example, suppose a retailer has $20,000 in cash, $30,000 in other current assets, and $30,000 in current liabilities; its current ratio is equal to 1.67:1. Yet lenders prefer to see the current ratio closer to 2:1. In this case, the retailer can use $10,000 of its cash to reduce debt and improve its ratio significantly to 2:1.

Massage Cash

Another simple method for retailers to pump up their cash is to sell some of their receivables to a third party.

Convert Short-Term Loans to Long-Term Loans

A few years ago, some retailers took advantage of another method of improving their financial statements when long-term interest rates declined quickly and closely approached short-term rates. (In normal times, long-term rates are one to two percentage points higher than short-term rates.) With so many willing lenders offering extremely low long-term interest rates, these retailers were able to refinance a portion of their short-term debt for long-term debt.

Extend the Payment Time

Another method troubled retailers have used to improve the appearance of their balance sheet is to have vendors agree to a slower repayment schedule, enabling the retailer to build up its cash balance.

---

current ratio
Current assets divided by current liabilities.

total sales. Since we know February's planned monthly sales are 15 percent of the total planned sales of $500,000, February's planned sales must be $75,000 ($15\% \times \$500,000 = \$75,000$).

It is important to use recent trends when forecasting sales. All too often retailers in nongrowth markets merely use last season's figures for the current season's budget. This method overlooks two major influences on projected sales volume: inflation and competition. If inflation is 10 percent and no other changes have occurred in the retail environment, then the retailer planning on selling the same physical volume as the previous year should expect a 10-percent increase in this season's dollar sales. Similarly, if the exit of a competitor across town is expected to increase the number of customer transactions by 5 percent, this increase should be reflected in the budget. Suppose that last year's sales were $100,000, inflation is 10 percent, and the retailer expects its market share to increase by 8 percent while the total market remains stable. What should the projected sales be? A simple equation used in retail planning is

$$\text{total sales} = \text{average sale} \times \text{total transactions}$$

In the preceding example, the average sale would increase by the 10 percent level of inflation to 1.10 times last year's sales, and total transactions would increase by the 8 percent gain in market share to 1.08 times last year's total transactions, for an increase in total sales of 1.188 times (or 1.10×1.08). This increase will then result in a total sales increase of $18,800 or budgeted total sales of $118,800.

Determining Planned BOM and EOM Inventories

Once the buyer has estimated seasonal and monthly sales for the upcoming season, plans can be made for inventory requirements. In order to achieve projected sales figures, the retailer will generally carry stock or inventory in excess of planned sales for the period, be it a week, month, or season. The extra stock or inventory provides a merchandise assortment deep and broad enough to meet customer needs. A common method of estimating the amount of stock to be carried is the **stock-to-sales ratio**. This ratio depicts the amount of stock to be on hand at the beginning of each month to support the forecasted sales for that month. For example, a ratio of 5:1 would suggest that the retailer have $5 in inventory (at retail price) for every $1 in forecasted sales. Planned average beginning-of-the-month (BOM) stock-to-sales ratios are often either (1) based on industry averages which are available from retail trade associations like the National Retail Federation in the United States (www.nrf.com) and the Australian Retailers Association (www.ar-a.com.au) or (2) calculated directly from a retailer's planned turnover goals.

To calculate a retailer's stock-to-sales ratio based on its desired turnover rate, suppose a retailer wants a target turnover rate of 4.0. By dividing the annual turnover rate into 12 (the number of months in a year), the average BOM stock-to-sales ratio for the year can be computed. In this case, 12 divided by 4.0 equals 3.0. Thus, the average stock-to-sales ratio for this retailer's upcoming season would be 3.

Generally, stock-to-sales ratios will fluctuate month to month because sales tend to fluctuate monthly. Nevertheless, it is important to always review these ratios because, if they are set too high or too low, too much or too little inventory will be on hand to meet the sales target. Remember, it is just as bad to have too much inventory on hand as it is to have too little. Stocking too much inventory could result in inventory-holding costs that outweigh the gross margins to be made on the sale of merchandise.

Returning to our earlier example, based on available data, the buyer for Department 353 in Exhibit 8.2 used a planned stock-to-sales ratio of 3.0 for February, April, and June; a ratio of 4.0 for March and July; and a ratio of 5.0 for May. The buyer was able to determine that $300,000 worth of merchandise was needed beginning March 1 due to a planned stock-to-sales ratio of 4.0 and planned sales of $75,000 (line 1). Two things should be noted. First, stock-to-sales ratios always express inventory levels at retail, not cost. Second, the BOM inventory for one month is equal to the end-of-the month (EOM) inventory for the previous month. This relationship can be easily seen by comparing the BOM figures (line 1) for one month with the EOM figures for the previous month (line 4).

Determining Planned Retail Reductions

All merchandise brought into the store for sale to consumers is not actually sold at the planned initial markup price. Therefore, when preparing the merchandise

stock-to-sales ratio
Depicts the amount of stock to have at the beginning of each month to support the forecasted sales for that month.

budget, the buyer should make allowances for reductions in the dollar level of inventory that results from nonsale events. Generally, these planned retail reductions fall into three types: markdowns, employee discounts, and stock shortages. These reductions must be planned because, as the dollar value of the inventory level is reduced, the BOM stock that is planned to support next month's forecasted sales will be inadequate unless adjustments are made this month. A buyer must remember that reductions are part of the cost of doing business.

A small number of retailers do not include planned reductions in their merchandise budgets. They simply treat them as part of the normal operation of the store and feel they should be controlled without being a separate line item in the budget. This gives management an understated, conservative planned-purchase figure, thereby having the effect of holding back some purchase reserve until the physical inventory reveals the exact amount of reductions. We have chosen to include planned reductions in this text for two reasons: (1) to reflect the additional purchases needed for sufficient inventory to begin the next month and (2) to point out that taking a reduction is not a bad thing. All too often, inexperienced retailers believe that taking a reduction is an admission of error, and therefore they fail to mark down merchandise until it is too late in the season. A buyer must remember that reductions are part of the cost of doing business. Methods available to the retail buyer for minimizing retail reductions caused by retailer mistakes are discussed in Chapter 10.

It should be noted that the reductions in our six-month budget are listed as a percentage of planned sales. The buyer in our example has estimated monthly retail reduction percentages as shown on line 11. To determine planned retail reductions for March (line 3), planned monthly sales are multiplied by the planned monthly retail reduction percentage to yield the planned monthly retail reduction of $7,500 ($75,000 × 10% = $7,500).

Reductions are one of the major items in the merchandise budget subject to constant change. One reason is that the planned reductions may prove inadequate in light of actual conditions encountered by the retailer. If retailers delay too long in taking reductions, especially those resulting from unexpected weather, they may be forced to take even larger price cuts later as the merchandise style depreciates even more in value. Alternatively, consider what happens when the department manager does such an effective merchandising job that not all the reduction money is needed for the period. The solution to both these dilemmas is found in the rules for developing a budget; namely, keeping it flexible so it can be intelligently administered.

Determining Planned Purchases at Retail and Cost

We are now ready to determine whether additional purchases must be made during the merchandising season. The retailer will need inventory for (1) planned sales, (2) planned retail reductions, and (3) planned EOM inventory. Planned BOM inventory represents purchases that have already been made. In the six-month merchandise budget shown in Exhibit 8.2, the March planned purchases at retail for Department 353 are $82,500 (line 5). This figure was derived by (1) adding planned sales, planned retail reductions, and planned EOM inventory and (2) subtracting planned BOM inventory:

$$\$75,000 + \$7,500 + \$300,000 - \$300,000 = \$82,500$$

Once planned purchases at retail are determined, planned purchases at cost can be easily calculated. The retail price always represents a combination of cost plus markup. If the markup percentage is given, then the portion of retail attributed to cost, or the cost complement, can be derived by subtracting the markup percentage from the retail percentage of 100 percent. Given that the markup percentage is 45 percent of retail for Department 353, the cost complement percentage must be 55 percent (100% − 45% = 55%). Planned purchases at cost for March (line 6) must be 55 percent of planned purchases at retail or $45,375 ($82,500 × 55% = $45,375). Planned initial markup for March (line 7) must be 45 percent of planned purchases, or $37,125 ($82,500 × 45% = $37,125).

Determining the Buyer's Planned Gross Margin

The buyer is accountable for the purchases made, the expected selling price of these purchases, the cost of these purchases, and the reductions that are involved in selling merchandise the buyer has previously purchased. Therefore, the last step in developing the merchandise budget is determining the buyer's planned gross margin for the period. As already discussed, in making plans the buyer recognizes that the initial selling price for all the products will probably not be realized and that some reductions will occur. Referring to Exhibit 8.2, the buyer's planned gross margin for February (line 8) is determined by taking planned initial markup (line 7) and subtracting planned reductions (line 3) ($70,875 − $7,500 = $63,375).

Retail Accounting Statements

LO 2

What are the differences among and the uses of these three accounting statements: income statement, balance sheet, and statement of cash flow?

Successful retailing also requires sound accounting practices. The number and types of accounting records needed depend on management's objectives. Large retailers generally require more detailed information, usually based on merchandise lines or departments. Smaller retailers may be able to make firsthand observations of sales and inventory levels and make decisions before financial data are available. For example, a retailer in a developing country owning and operating a 100-square-foot store can easily use observation to obtain a general idea of the store's inventory. Still, the small retailer should consult the accounting records to confirm personal observations.

Properly prepared financial records provide measurements of profitability and retail performance. In addition, they show all transactions occurring within a given time period. However, these financial records must provide the manager not only with a look at the past, but also a preview of the future so as to allow the manager to plan. Financial records not only indicate if a retailer has achieved good results but also demonstrate what growth potential and problems areas lay ahead. Some examples are:

1. Is one merchandise line outperforming or underperforming the rest of the store?
2. Is the inventory level adequate for the current sales level?
3. Is the firm's debt level too high (does the firm owe too much money)?
4. Are reductions, including markdowns, too high a percentage of sales?
5. Is the gross margin adequate for the firm's profit objectives?

These are just a few of the questions that the financial data must answer for the retailer. The authors know of one company where merchandise line "X" was generating an annual profit of $800,000, and merchandise line "Y" was losing money at the rate of $600,000 a year. Management was totally unaware of the situation, just happy to be making $200,000! They were astounded when a little accounting work revealed the true situation.

Global Retailing

International Accounting Rules

The International Accounting Standards Board, formerly the International Accounting Standards Committee (IASC), has been working to achieve uniformity in accounting principles since 1973. Today the organization has representatives from approximately 100 countries and has issued 47 international accounting standards. These standards address a number of topics including goodwill, inventory valuation, and business combinations.

The treatment of goodwill, which is the premium over book value that a retailer pays when it acquires another retail company, varies greatly between different countries. According to international accounting standards, goodwill should be amortized over a period of five to 20 years, although the IASB strongly recommends that companies use the five-year period. Several countries have complied with this standard, including Australia, Mexico, Spain, Japan, and Brazil. However, there is still a great deal of variation among other countries. Switzerland, for example, allows companies to immediately expense goodwill. Hong Kong allows companies to choose whether they want to immediately expense goodwill or amortize it over a period of five to 20 years. The United States does not allow for the amortization of goodwill. Instead, in the United States, goodwill is tested annually for possible impairment. Because of a European mandate, U.K. companies can no longer expense goodwill but must amortize it. China has not yet addressed the treatment of purchased goodwill. The problem with such wide variations in the area of goodwill is that it makes the comparison of financial statements very difficult.

In 1991, the IASC issued exposure draft E32, which would have eliminated LIFO as an alternative method of valuing inventory. The IASC argued that the LIFO method did not assign the most current costs to ending inventories and therefore distorted the balance sheet. It also would have generated higher tax revenues. However, due to public sentiment, the IASC reversed its E32 position and has continued to allow LIFO. This was good news to the United States and other countries that use the LIFO method, since revaluing their inventories with the FIFO or weighted-average method would have resulted in higher ending inventory values and a higher tax liability.

Accounting for business combinations has also been addressed by the IASC. It provides two methods for accounting for mergers and acquisitions. The *purchase method* of accounting for business combinations effectively reports the earnings of two separate businesses as one business through the use of consolidated financial statements. The net assets of the acquired company are carried on these statements at their cost to the acquiring company. The other method of accounting for mergers and acquisitions is the *pooling of interests method*. This method may be used only when the transaction is principally an exchange of voting common shares or if all of the net assets and operations of the two entities are combined into one entity. The pooling of interests method effectively reports the earnings of only one business, and the net assets of the acquired company are carried on the combined entity's financial statements at their premerger value. The reporting requirements of each country essentially result in a difference in the valuation of the acquired companies' net assets. The pooling of interests method will typically result in a lower net asset figure than the purchase method.

Currently, standards issued by the IASB are not mandatory unless a particular country adopts them. This explains the wide variation in reporting requirements. The European Union and Australia mandated the use of international standards for consolidated reporting beginning in 2005. That mandate has gone a long way toward standardizing worldwide practices.

Still, while U.S. retailers may complain about differences between generally accepted accounting principles (GAAP) and IASB rulings as well as IRS regulations, it could be worse. The *Wall Street Journal* reported that a Chinese premier reminded Chinese taxpayers that "tax evasion can result in death by execution."

Source: This box was prepared by Stephen J. Lusch, Ph.D. student, University of Arizona.

---

income statement
Is a financial statement that provides a summary of the sales and expenses for a given time period, usually a month, quarter, season, or year.

Let's look at the three financial statements most commonly used by retailers: the income statement, the balance sheet, and the statement of cash flow.

Income Statement

The most important financial statement a retailer prepares is the income statement (also referred to as the *profit and loss statement*). The **income statement** provides a summary of the sales and expenses for a given time period, usually monthly, quarterly, seasonally, or annually. Comparison of current results with prior results allows the retailer to notice trends or changes in sales, expenses, and profits. However, given the large number of recent accounting scandals, the mere fact that a company reports increased earnings each year and the income statement looks great should not lead one to believe that everything is fine. While new government regulations, as well as changes by the Financial Accounting Standards Board (FASB) and the International Accounting Standards Board (IASB), have been made with the hope of restoring confidence, there still exist some unclear areas regarding the reporting of income and expenses. One such area, which is described in the chapter's "Global Retailing" box, is how retailers around the world should handle goodwill on their financial statements.

Income statements can be broken down by departments, divisions, branches, and so on, enabling the retailer to evaluate each subunit's operating performance for the period. Exhibit 8.5a shows the basic format for an income statement, and Exhibit 8.5b shows the income statement for TMD Furniture.

Gross sales are the retailer's total sales, including sales for cash or for credit. **Returns and allowances** are reductions from gross sales. Here the retailer makes a financial adjustment for customers who became dissatisfied with their purchases and returned the merchandise to the retailer. Since these reductions represent cancellations of previously recorded sales, the gross sales figure must be reduced to reflect these changes.

Net sales, gross sales less returns and allowances, represents the amount of merchandise the retailer actually sold during the given time period. Sometimes it is difficult to determine what figure to report for net sales. As the chapter's "What's New?" box illustrates, retailers often have problems determining how to account for rebates when reporting net sales.

Cost of goods sold is the cost of merchandise that has been sold during the period. While this concept is easy to understand, the exact calculation of the cost of goods sold is somewhat complex. For example, like their own customers, retailers may obtain some return privileges or receive some allowances from vendors, such as a cash discount for prompt payment (which will be discussed in the next chapter). Also, there is the issue of determining how inventory levels will be carried on the company's books. This will be fully discussed in the next section of this chapter.

Gross margin is the difference between net sales and cost of goods sold or the amount available to cover operating expenses and produce a profit.

Operating expenses are those expenses that a retailer incurs while running the business other than the cost of the merchandise sold (e.g., rent, wages, utilities, depreciation, advertising, and insurance).

gross sales
Are the retailer's total sales including sales for cash or for credit.

returns and allowances
Are refunds of the purchase price or downward adjustments in selling prices due to customers returning purchases, or adjustments made in the selling price due to customer dissatisfaction with product or service performance.

net sales
Are gross sales less returns and allowances.

cost of goods sold
Is the cost of merchandise that has been sold during the period.

gross margin
Is the difference between net sales and cost of goods sold.

operating expenses
Are those expenses that a retailer incurs in running the business other than the cost of the merchandise.

Gross Sales	$_____
– Returns and Allowances	$_____
Net Sales	$_____
– Cost of Goods Sold	$_____
Gross Margin	$_____
– Operating Expenses	$_____
Operating Profit	$_____
±Other Income or Expenses	$_____
Net Profit Before Taxes	$_____

Exhibit 8.5A
Retailers' Basic Income Statement Format

Exhibit 8.5B
Sample Income
Statement

TMD Furniture, Inc.
Six-Month Income Statement
July 31

			Percentage
Gross Sales		$393,671.79	
Less: Returns and Allowances		16,300.00	
Net Sales			
Less: Cost of Goods Sold		$377,371.79	100%
Beginning Inventory	$ 98,466.29		
Purchases	218,595.69		
Goods Available for Sales	$317,061.98		
Ending Inventory	103,806.23	213,255.75	56.5%
Gross Margin		$164,116.04	43.5%
Less: Operating Expenses			
Salaries & Wages:			
Managers	$18,480.50		
Selling	17,755.65		
Office	7,580.17		
Warehouse & Delivery	6,685.99	50,502.31	
Advertising	$ 15,236.67		
Administration and Warehouse Charge	800.00		
Credit, Collections, and Bad Debts	1,973.96		
Contributions	312.50		
Delivery	1,434.93		
Depreciation	5,398.56		
Dues	23.50		
Employee Benefits	566.26		
Utilities	3,738.74		
Insurance	3,041.75		
Legal and Auditing	1,000.00		
Merchandise Service & Repair	1,439.16		
Miscellaneous	602.00		
Rent	9,080.00		
Repairs & Maintenance	1,576.99		
Sales Allowances	180.50		
Supplies, Postage	1,135.40		
Taxes:			
City, County, & State	$ 2,000.00		
Payroll	3,902.90	5,902.90	
Telephone	1,520.09		
Travel	404.92		
Warehouse Handling Charges	12,216.86	118,088.00	31.3%
Operating Profit		$ 46,028.04	12.2%
Other Income:			
Carrying Charges	$ 3,377.48		
Profit on Sale of Parking Lot	740.47	4,117.95	1.1%
Net Profit Before Taxes		$ 50,145.99	13.3%

What's New?

How Rebates Affect Net Sales

Rebates are agreements to refund a portion of a purchase price to the consumer. They are offered by both vendors and retailers to encourage sales. During 2009, it was estimated that more than $7 billion of rebates were offered. (This figure doesn't include automobile rebates.)

The financial community has struggled with how to account for such rebates. Should rebates be considered a reduction of sales or a cost of selling the product? Also, should the dollar amount of the rebate be recognized at the time of the sale or when the rebate is actually redeemed?

The Emerging Issues Task Force (EITF) is the part of the Financial Accounting Standards Board that develops consensus concerning newer or unusual types of financial transactions. When the EITF was asked to review the way that retailers account for rebates, it issued a conclusion (EITF 01-09) that required rebates to be recognized as a reduction of sales (rather than a selling expense). In addition, they required that the reduction be recognized at the time the sale was made.

For example, suppose that during a three-month promotion period a retailer sells $1 million of "special" merchandise and offers a 20-percent rebate. Even though the company collects $1 million in sales, they are allowed to recognize sales of only $800,000 and a liability (known as a *liability for rebate claims*) for $200,000. As customers redeem the rebates, the liability is reduced.

However, determining the amount of the liability may be complicated by *breakage* or rebates that are not redeemed because the customer either forgets or does not consider the effort of processing the rebate worthwhile. If the company can estimate the amount of breakage, the company may reduce the liability by the amount of expected breakage. For example, if the company believes that 50 percent of the rebate offers will be redeemed, it will recognize $900,000 in sales and a liability of $100,000.

Collections	$1,000,000
Liability for Rebate Claims	− 200,000
Expected Breakage	+ 100,000
Sales Recognized	$ 900,000

Critics of this accounting method claim that companies can increase or decrease their sales by purposely overestimating or understating the expected breakage. For example, by using a 25-percent breakage in the above example, a privately held retailer can decrease sales recognized by $150,000 in rebates to $850,000. This, in turn, would reduce taxes.

In addition, as was mentioned in Chapter 6, others claim that retailers make redeeming rebates difficult so that while 80 percent of rebates worth over $40 are redeemed, only 5 percent to 10 percent of rebates worth less than $10 are actually redeemed. In fact, industry figures show that 40 percent to 60 percent of all rebates go unredeemed. Some of these rebates are not redeemed because consumers do not bother to send them in; in other cases, even diligent consumers may not get a rebate because they didn't meet all the requirements. Whatever the reason, as a result of these low redemption rates, these critics feel that rebates are deceptive because the customer is really paying something closer to the $7.99 regular price (not the $6.99 "after the $1 rebate" price that was posted above the display).

Source: Prepared by Dr. William Pasewark, Texas Tech University, and used with his permission.

Retailers must consider not only Generally Accepted Accounting Principles (GAAP) regulations when presenting their income statement, but also Internal Revenue Service (IRS) rulings. The IRS provided a tax break for retailers by ruling that they may estimate inventory shrinkage (the loss of merchandise through theft, loss, and damage).[3] This enables retailers to reduce ending inventory and thus taxable earnings. Prior to this change, which resulted from court cases involving Kroger and Target, the IRS did not permit retailers to estimate shrinkage from the last physical inventory to the end of the retailer's tax year, usually the end of January. Since it is not feasible for most retail chains to physically count their entire inventory in a single day in late January, most chains check inventory on a rotating basis throughout the year and can now estimate their losses without being challenged by the IRS.

Operating profit is the difference between gross margin and operating expenses.

operating profit
Is gross margin less operating expenses.

other income or expenses
Includes income or expense items that the firm incurs which are not in the course of its normal retail operations.

Other income or expenses includes income or expense items that the firm incurs outside the course of its normal retail operations. For example, a retailer might have purchased some land to use for expansion and, after careful deliberation, postponed the expansion plans. Now suppose the retailer rents that land. Since renting land is not in the normal course of business for a retailer, the rent received would be considered other income. Likewise, many convenience stores place income from selling money orders under other income, and supermarkets report the rent received from banks and pharmacies operating in their buildings as other income.

It is also on this line of the income statement that most grocery chains report the revenue from their nonselling activities such as slotting fees, promotional allowances, and free goods because this revenue is considered to be earned by buying merchandise rather than selling it.

net profit
Is operating profit plus or minus other income or expenses.

Net profit is operating profit plus or minus other income or expenses. Net profit is the figure on which the retailer pays taxes and thus is usually referred to as net profit before taxes.

Many retailers actually divide the income statement into two sections: the *top half*, those items above the gross margin total, and the *bottom half*, those items below the gross margin total. Sales and cost of goods sold are essentially controllable by the buying functions of the retail organization. In more and more retailing operations today, the buying organization is separate from the store management team, which is primarily concerned with the operating expenses that are shown below gross margin. As a result, store managers often look at gross margin from the bottom up and use this formula:

$$\text{gross margin} = \text{operating expenses} + \text{profit}$$

Sometimes retailers use the terms *top line* (sales), *gross* (gross margin), *line above the bottom* (other income), and *bottom line* (profit) when referring to the key elements of their income statement.

Finally, it is important to point out that, just as they do in the reporting of revenues, GAAP allows for variations in how retailers report certain expenses. Preopening expenses, for example, can be expensed as they occur, during the month the store opens, or capitalized and written off over several years. Advertising can be written off when the ad runs or when payment is made. Store fixtures can be depreciated over five years, 40 years, or some increment in between. Thus, when comparing the financial statements of different retailers, it is important to know how each retailer treated these and other expenses.

Balance Sheet

balance sheet
Is a financial statement that identifies and quantifies all the firm's assets and liabilities. It shows the financial condition of a retailer's

The second accounting statement used in financial reporting is the **balance sheet**. A balance sheet shows the financial condition of a retailer's business at a particular point in time, as opposed to the income statement, which reports on the activities over a period of time. The balance sheet identifies and quantifies all the firm's assets and liabilities. The difference between assets and liabilities is the owner's equity or net worth. Comparing a current balance sheet with one from a previous time period enables a retail analyst to observe changes in the firm's financial condition.

A typical balance sheet format is illustrated in Exhibit 8.6. As Exhibit 8.6a shows, the basic equation for a balance sheet is

$$\text{assets} = \text{liabilities} + \text{net worth}$$

Hence, both sides always must be in balance. Exhibit 8.6b shows the balance sheet for TMD Furniture.

Current Assets		Current Liabilities	
Cash	$____	Accounts Payable	$____
Accounts Receivable	$____	Payroll Payable	$____
Inventory	$____	Current Notes Payable	$____
Prepaid Expenses	$____	Taxes Payable	$____
Total Current Assets	$____	Total Current Liabilities	$____
Noncurrent Assets		Long-term Liabilities	
Building (less depreciation)	$____	Long-term Notes	
Fixtures and Equipment		Payable	$____
(less depreciation)	$____	Mortgage Payable	$____
Total Noncurrent Assets	$____		
Goodwill	$____	Total Long-term Liabilities	$____
		Net Worth	
		Capital Surplus	$____
		Retained Earnings	$____
		Total Net Worth	$____
		Total Liabilities and	
Total Assets	$____	**Net Worth**	$____

Exhibit 8.6A
Retailers' Basic Balance Sheet Format

asset
Is anything of value that is owned by the retail firm.

current assets
Are assets that can be easily converted into cash within a relatively short period of time (usually a year or less).

accounts and/or notes receivable
Are amounts that customers owe the retailer for goods and services.

TMD Furniture, Inc.
Balance Sheet
July 31

Current Assets			Current Liabilities		
Cash	$ 11,589		Accounts Payable	$57,500	
Accounts Receivable	71,517		Payroll Payable	1,451	
Inventory	103,806		Current Notes Payable	14,000	
			Taxes Payable	1,918	
Total Current Assets		$186,912	Total Current Liabilities		$ 74,869
Noncurrent Assets			Long-term Liabilities		
Building (less depreciation)	$ 61,414		Long-term Notes Payable	$52,750	
Fixtures and Equipment			Mortgage Payable	38,500	
(less depreciation)	11,505				
Total Noncurrent Assets		72,919	Total Long-term Liabilities		$ 91,250
Goodwill		100	Net Worth		93,812
			Total Liabilities and		
Total Assets		$259,931	**Net Worth**		$259,931

Exhibit 8.6B
Sample Balance Sheet

An **asset** is anything of value that is owned by the retail firm. Assets are broken down into two categories: current and noncurrent.

Current assets include cash and all other items that the retailer can easily convert into cash within a relatively short period of time (generally, a year). Besides cash, current assets include accounts receivable, notes receivable, prepaid expenses, and inventory. **Accounts receivable** and **notes receivable** are amounts that

Nordstrom has created a high degree of brand equity for the Nordstrom name by focusing on high levels of personalized customer service. Nonetheless, accounting statements in the United States do not allow the brand equity to be recorded on Nordstrom's balance sheet.

prepaid expenses
Are those items for which the retailer has already paid, but the service has not been completed.

retail inventories
Comprise merchandise that the retailer has in the store or in storage and is available for sale.

noncurrent assets
Are those assets that cannot be converted to cash in a short period of time (usually 12 months) in the normal course of business.

goodwill
Is an intangible asset, usually based on customer loyalty, that a retailer pays for when buying an existing business.

total assets
Equal current assets plus noncurrent assets plus goodwill.

liability
Is any legitimate financial claim against the retailer's assets.

current liabilities
Are short-term debts that are payable within a year.

accounts payable
Are amounts owed vendors for goods and services.

customers owe the retailer for goods and services. Frequently, the retailer will reduce the total receivables by a fixed percentage (based on past experience) to take into account those customers who may be unwilling or unable to pay. **Prepaid expenses** are items such as trash collection or insurance for which the retailer has already paid but the service has not been completed. **Retail inventories** make up merchandise that the retailer has in the store or in storage and is available for sale.

Noncurrent assets are those assets that cannot be converted into cash in a short period of time (usually, 12 months) in the normal course of business. These noncurrent or long-term assets include buildings, parking lots, the land under the building and parking lot, fixtures (e.g., display racks), and equipment (e.g., air-conditioning systems). These items, except land, are carried on the books at cost less accumulated depreciation. Depreciation is necessary because most noncurrent assets have a limited useful life; the difference between the asset and depreciation is intended to provide a more realistic picture of the retailer's assets and prevent an overstatement or understatement of these assets' value. However, as every retailer has learned, the value of real estate can fluctuate greatly over time.

Some retailers also include goodwill as an asset. **Goodwill** is an intangible asset, usually based on customer loyalty, that reflects the portion of the book value of a business entity not directly attributable to its assets and liabilities. Goodwill normally occurs only when a retailer purchases an existing business and the dollar value assigned to goodwill is minimal.

Total asset equals current assets plus noncurrent assets plus goodwill.

The other part of the balance sheet reflects the retailer's liabilities and net worth. A **liability** is any legitimate financial claim against the retailer's assets. Liabilities are classified as either current or long-term.

Current liabilities are short-term debts that are payable within a year. Included here are accounts payable, notes payable (which are due within the year), payroll payable, and taxes payable. **Accounts payable** are amounts owed to vendors for goods and services. Payroll payable is money due to employees on past labor. Taxes due the government (federal, state, or local) are also considered a current liability. Some retailers also include interest due within the year on long-term notes or mortgages as a current liability.

Long-term liabilities include notes payable and mortgages not due within the year. **Total liabilities** equal current liabilities plus long-term liabilities.

Net worth, also called **owner's equity**, is the difference between the firm's total assets and total liabilities and represents the owner's equity in the business. The figure reflects the owner's original investment plus any profits reinvested in the business less any losses incurred in the business and any funds that the owner has taken out of the business.

In actuality, the balance sheet does not reflect all the retailer's assets and liabilities. Specifically, such items as store personnel can be an asset or a liability to the business. These items might not appear on the balance sheet but are extremely important to the success of a high-performance retailer. Other items that could be either assets or liabilities, although not in the strict accounting sense, are goodwill, customer loyalty, and even vendor relationships. Each of these items can contribute to the success or failure of a retailer.

Statement of Cash Flow

A third financial statement that retailers can use to help in understanding their business is the **statement of cash flow**. A statement of cash flow lists in detail the source and type of all revenue (cash inflows) and the use and type of all expenditures (cash outflows) for a given time period. When cash inflows exceed cash outflows, the retailer is said to have a *positive* cash flow; when cash outflows exceed cash inflows, the retailer is said to be experiencing a *negative* cash flow. Thus, the purpose of the statement of cash flow is to enable the retailer to project the cash needs of the firm. Based on projections, plans may be made to either seek additional financing if a negative flow is projected, or to make other investments if a positive flow is anticipated. Likewise, a retailer with a positive cash flow for the period might be able to take advantage of "good deals" from vendors.

A statement of cash flow is not the same as an income statement. In a statement of cash flow, the retailer is concerned only with the movement of cash into or out of the firm. An income statement reflects the profitability of the retailer after all revenue and expenses are considered. Often expenses will be incurred in one time period but not paid until the following time period. Thus, the retailer's income statement and statement of cash flow are seldom identical. Consider the example of TMD Furniture for the month of August as shown in Exhibit 8.7a.

August is a slow month for furniture sales because many customers are taking vacations; as a result, TMD is expecting sales of only $40,000 for the month. Of that amount, $15,450 will be for cash, and TMD expects to collect $24,998 on its account receivables. Along with a tax-refund check due from the state for $97, TMD has projected a cash inflow of $40,545 for August. However, because August is the month that several notes and accounts payable are due, TMD Furniture is expecting to have to pay out $48,372 during August. This will result in a negative cash flow for the month of $7,827. TMD has prepared for this by having cash on hand (as reported on the July 31 balance sheet) of $11,589. In reality, many retailers forget about cash and realize the difference between cash flow and profit only after the coffers are empty. In the case of TMD Furniture, paying off the notes and accounts payable had no effect on the income statement. Likewise, the statement of cash flow considered only that part of purchases that were paid for with cash, not those purchased on credit. These credit purchasers had no direct effect on the cash flow. Exhibit 8.7b lists the typical retailer's cash inflow and outflow items. It should be noted that retailers who decide to use major credit cards, instead of handling their own credit operations, are able to convert sales much more quickly into cash

Exhibit 8.7A
Sample Cash Flow Statement

TMD Furniture, Inc. Cash Flow Statement August 31		
Cash Sales	$15,450	
Collection of Accounts Receivable	24,998	
Refund on State Taxes	97	
Total Cash Inflow		$40,545
Cash Outflow		
Rent	$ 1,513	
Purchases at Cash	5,750	
Salaries	8,483	
Utilities	1,450	
Advertising	2,300	
County Taxes	173	
Supplies	921	
Telephone	150	
Paying Off Accounts Payable	20,632	
Paying Off Notes Payable	7,000	
Total Cash Outflow		$48,372
Total Cash Flow		($ 7,827)

Exhibit 8.7B
Typical Cash Inflow and Outflow Categories

Cash Inflows	Cash Outflows
Cash sales	Paying for merchandise
Collecting accounts receivable	Rent expenses
Collecting notes receivable	Utilities expenses
Collecting other debts	Wages and salary expenses
Sale of fixed assets	Advertising expense
Sale of stock	Insurance premiums
	Taxes
	Interest expenses
	Supplies and other expenses
	Purchase of other assets
	Paying off accounts payable
	Paying off notes payable
	Buying back company stocks
	Paying dividends

because they do not need to wait for customers to pay for their purchases—some other party such as a bank assumes this financing function.

The recent economic downturn has resulted in an increasing number of retailers becoming aware of the critical nature of cash flow. In fact, the number one cause of retailing bankruptcies in recent years has been cash flow problems. A retailer can be growing quickly and be profitable yet fail due to inadequate cash flow.

The lack of a sufficient cash flow is not limited to those large troubled chains you hear about on television. Many a small entrepreneur has come up with a brilliant idea for a retail operation only to fall short. In fact, more than a quarter of all retail operations fail during the first two years due to a lack of positive cash flow. The entrepreneur's problems usually start by overestimating revenues and under-estimating costs, resulting in a negative cash flow. By not ensuring they have enough cash on hand to withstand a rocky two-year start-up period, many retailers are assuring themselves of failure. In fact, according to one of the author's mentors, the first thing to look at when examining a retailer's financial records is its accounts payable, particularly government payroll taxes. It seems that when retail firms get into a cash bind, they tend to postpone payments to the government so that they can pay their suppliers and employees. After all, they believe that they can always pay their taxes later. Unfortunately, the government does not always agree with such thinking.[4] As a result, some of these unsuccessful retailers often resort to questionable tactics to improve their financial statements. Besides changing the breakage rate for rebates described earlier in this chapter, some other methods used to inflate retail accounting statements are described in the chapter's "Retailing: The Inside Story" box.

Inventory Valuation

LO 3

How does a retailer value its inventory?

Due to the many different merchandise lines often carried by retailers, inventory valuation is quite complex. A retailer must make two major decisions with regard to valuing inventory: (1) which accounting inventory system to implement and (2) what inventory-pricing method to use.

Accounting Inventory System

Two accounting inventory systems are available for the retailer: (1) the cost method and (2) the retail method. We will describe both methods on the basis of the frequency with which inventory information is received, difficulties encountered in completing a physical inventory and maintaining records, and the extent to which stock shortages can be calculated.

The Cost Method

The **cost method** of inventory valuation provides a book valuation of inventory based solely on the retailer's cost, including freight. It looks only at the cost of each item as it was recorded in the accounting records when purchased. When a physical inventory is taken, all items are counted, the cost of each item is taken from the records or the price tags, and the total inventory value at cost is calculated.

One of the easiest methods of coding the cost of merchandise on the price tag is to use the first 10 letters of the alphabet to represent the price. Here A = 1, B = 2, C = 3, D = 4, E = 5, F = 6, G = 7, H = 8, I = 9, J = 0. A product with the code HEAD has a cost of $85.14. The cost method is useful for those retailers who sell big-ticket items and allow price negotiations by customers. Sales personnel know from the code how much room there is for negotiation while still covering the cost of the merchandise plus operating expenses.

cost method
Is an inventory valuation technique that provides a book valuation of inventory based solely on the retailer's cost of merchandise including freight.

The cost method of inventory valuation does have several limitations:

1. It is difficult to do daily inventories (or even monthly inventories).
2. It is difficult to cost out each sale.
3. It is difficult to allocate freight charges to each item's cost of goods sold.

The cost method is generally used by those retailers with big-ticket items and a limited number of sales per day (e.g., an expensive jewelry store or an antique furniture store), where there are few lines or limited inventory requirements, infrequent price changes, and low turnover rates.

The Retail Method

retail method

Is an inventory valuation technique that values merchandise at current retail prices, which is then converted to cost based on a formula.

The **retail method** of inventory values merchandise at current retail prices. It overcomes the disadvantages of the cost method by keeping detailed records of inventory based on the retail value of the merchandise. However, the fact that the inventory is valued in retail dollars does make it a little more difficult for the retailer to determine the cost of goods sold when computing the gross margin for a time period.

There are three basic steps in computing an ending inventory value using the retail method: calculation of the cost complement, calculation of reductions from retail value, and conversion of the adjusted retail book inventory to cost.

Step 1. Calculation of the Cost Complement.   Inventories, both beginning and ending, and purchases are recorded at both cost and retail levels when using the retail method. Exhibit 8.8 shows an inventory statement for Whitener's Sporting Goods for the fall season.

In Exhibit 8.8, the beginning inventory is shown at both cost and retail. Net purchases, which are the total purchases less merchandise returned to vendors, allowances, and discounts from vendors, are also valued at cost and retail. Additional markups are the total increases in the retail price of merchandise already in stock that were caused by inflation or heavy demand and are shown at retail. Freight-in is the cost to the retailer for transportation of merchandise from the vendor and is shown in the cost column.

Using the information from Exhibit 8.8, the retailer can calculate the average relationship of cost to retail price for all merchandise available for sale during the fall season. This calculation is called the *cost complement*:

$$\text{cost complement} = \text{total cost valuation}/\text{total retail valuation}$$
$$= \$270,000/\$560,000 = 0.482$$

Since the cost complement is 0.482, or 48.2 percent, 48.2 cents of every retail sales dollar is composed of merchandise cost.

Exhibit 8.8
Inventory Available for Whitener's Sporting Goods Sales, Fall Season

	Cost	Retail
Beginning Inventory	$199,000	$401,000
Net Purchases	70,000	154,000
Additional Markups		5,000
Freight-in	1,000	
Total Inventory Available for Sale	$270,000	$560,000

Step 2. Calculation of Reductions from Retail Value. During the course of day-to-day business activities, the retailer must take reductions from inventory. In addition to sales, which lower the retail inventory level, retail reductions can lower retail inventory levels. These reductions include markdowns (sales, reduced prices on end-of-season, discontinued, or damaged merchandise), discounts (employee, senior citizen, student, religious, etc.), and stock shortages (employee and customer theft, breakage). Markdowns and employee discounts can be recorded throughout an accounting period, but a physical inventory is required to calculate stock shortages.

In Exhibit 8.8, it was shown that Whitener's had inventory available for sale at retail of $560,000 for the upcoming fall season. This must be reduced by actual fall season sales of $145,000, markdowns of $12,000, and discounts of $2,000. This results in an ending book value of inventory with a retail level of $401,000. This is shown in Exhibit 8.9.

Once the ending book value of inventory at retail is determined, a comparison can be made to the physical inventory to compute actual stock shortages; if the book value is greater than the physical count, then a stock shortage has occurred. If the book value is lower than the physical count, then a stock overage has occurred. Shortages are due to thefts, breakages, overshipments not billed to customers, and bookkeeping errors (the most common cause). These errors result from a failure to properly record markdowns, returns, discounts, and breakages. Many retailers have greatly reduced their original shortage estimate by reviewing the season's bookkeeping entries. A stock overage, an excess of physical inventory over book inventory, is also usually the result of bookkeeping errors, either miscounting during the physical inventory or improper book entries. Exhibit 8.10 shows the results of Whitener's physical inventory and the resulting adjustment.

Because a physical inventory must be taken in order to determine shortages (overages), and retailers take a physical count only once or twice a year, shortages (overages) are often estimated in merchandise budgets as shown in Exhibits 8.1 and

	Cost	Retail
Inventory Available for Sale at Retail		$560,000
Less Reductions:		
Sales	$145,000	
Markdowns	12,000	
Discounts	2,000	
Total Reductions		159,000
Ending Book Value of Inventory at Retail		$401,000

Exhibit 8.9
Whitener's Sporting Goods Ending Book Value at Retail, Fall Season

	Cost	Retail
Ending Book Value of Inventory at Retail		$401,000
Physical Inventory (at Retail)		398,000
Stock Shortages		3,000
Adjusting Ending Book Value of Inventory at Retail		$398,000

Exhibit 8.10
Whitener's Sporting Goods, Stock Shortage (Overage) Adjustment Entry, End of Fall Season

8.2. As a rule of thumb, retailers may estimate monthly shortages between 0.5 and 3 percent.

Step 3. Conversion of the Adjusted Retail Book Inventory to Cost. The final step to be performed in using the retail method is to convert to cost the adjusted retail book inventory figure in order to determine the closing inventory at cost. The procedure here is to multiply the adjusted retail book inventory ($398,000 in the case of Whitener's) by the cost complement (0.482 in the Whitener's example):

$$\text{Closing inventory (at cost)} = \text{Adjusted retail} \times \text{Cost complement book inventory}$$
$$= \$398,000 \times 0.482 = \$191,836$$

Although this equation does not yield the actual closing inventory at cost, it does provide a close approximation of the cost figure. Remember that the cost complement is an average. Now that ending inventory at cost has been determined, the retailer can determine gross margin as well as net profit before taxes, if operating expenses are known. We will discuss expenses in more detail later. In the Whitener's example, let's use $30,000 for salaries, $1,000 for utilities, $19,000 for rent, and $2,200 for depreciation. These figures are shown in Exhibit 8.11.

The retail method has several advantages over the cost method of inventory valuation:

1. Accounting statements can be drawn up at any time. Inventories need not be taken for preparation of these statements.

2. Physical inventories using retail prices are less subject to error and can be completed in a shorter amount of time.

3. The retail method provides an automatic, conservative valuation of ending inventory as well as inventory levels throughout the season. This is especially useful in cases where the retailer is forced to submit insurance claims for damaged or lost merchandise.

Exhibit 8.11
Whitener's Sporting Goods Income Statements August 1–January 31

	Cost	Retail
Sales		$145,000
Less: Cost of Goods Sold:		
Beginning Inventory (at Cost)	$200,000	
Purchases (at Cost)	70,000	
Goods Available for Sale	$270,000	
Ending Inventory (at Cost)	191,836	
Cost of Goods Sold		78,164
Gross Margin		$ 66,836
Less: Operating Expenses		
Salaries	$ 30,000	
Utilities	1,000	
Rent	19,000	
Depreciation (Fixtures + Equipment)	2,200	
Total Operating Expenses		52,200
Net Profit Before Taxes		$ 14,636

A major complaint against the retail method is that it is a "method of averages." This refers to the fact that closing inventory is valued at the average relationship between cost and retail (the cost complement) and that large retailers offer many different classifications and lines with different relationships. This disadvantage can be overcome by computing cost complements for individual lines or departments.

Another limitation is the heavy burden placed on bookkeeping activities. The true ending book inventory value can be correctly calculated only if there are no errors when recording beginning inventory, purchases, freight-in, markups, markdowns, discounts, returns, transfers between stores, and sales. As noted earlier, many of the retailers' original shortages have later been determined to be book-keeping errors. Most retailers today use the retail method of inventory valuation, which was created in the early 1900s.

Inventory-Pricing Systems

The two methods of pricing inventory are FIFO and LIFO. The **FIFO** (first in, first out) method assumes that the oldest merchandise is sold before the more recently purchased merchandise. However, merchandise on the shelf will reflect the most current replacement price. During inflationary periods, this method allows "inventory profits" (caused by selling the less expensive earlier inventory rather than the more expensive newer inventory) to be included as income.

The **LIFO** (last in, first out) method is designed to cushion the impact of inflationary pressures by matching current costs against current revenues. Costs of goods sold are based on the costs of the most recently purchased inventory, while the older inventory is regarded as the unsold inventory. During inflationary periods, the LIFO method results in the application of a higher unit cost to the merchandise sold and a lower unit cost to inventory still unsold. In times of rapid inflation, most retailers use the LIFO method, resulting in lower profits on the income statement but also lower income taxes. Most retailers also prefer to use LIFO for planning purposes since it accurately reflects replacement costs. The Internal Revenue Service permits a retailer to change its method of accounting only once.

Let's study an example of the effect of the LIFO and FIFO methods of inventory valuation on a firm's financial performance. Suppose you began the year with a total inventory of 15 home-theater packages, which you purchased on the last day of the preceding year for $500 each. Thus, if these home-theater packages were the only merchandise you had in stock, your beginning inventory was $7,500 (15 × $500). Suppose also that during the year you sold 12 packages for $900 each for total sales of $10,800; that in June you purchased eight new home-theater packages (same make and model as your old ones) at $525; and that in November you bought four more at $550. Thus, your purchases would equal $4,200 in June and $2,200 in November for a total of $6,400, and you would still have 15 home-theater packages in stock at year end. Under the LIFO inventory approach, your ending inventory would be the same as it was at the beginning of the year ($7,500) since we would assume that the 12 packages sold were the 12 purchased during the year. However, using the FIFO approach, we would assume that we sold 12 of the original $500 packages and had three left. These three home-theater packages, along with June's and November's purchases, result in an ending inventory of $7,900 [(3 × $500) + (8 × $525) + (4 × $350)]. Now let's see how these approaches can affect our gross margins.

FIFO

Stands for first in, first out and values inventory based on the assumption that the oldest merchandise is sold before the more recently purchased merchandise.

LIFO

Stands for last in, first out and values inventory based on the assumption that the most recently purchased merchandise is sold first and the oldest merchandise is sold last.

	LIFO	FIFO
Net sales	$10,800	$10,800
Less: Cost of goods sold		
Beginning inventory	$ 7,500	$ 7,500
Purchases	6,400	6,400
Goods available	$13,900	$13,900
Ending inventory	7,500	7,900
Cost of goods sold	6,400	6,000
Gross margin	$ 4,400	$ 4,800

The issue of which inventory valuation method (LIFO or FIFO) to use is one of the key issues facing retailers and accountants around the world as they seek to find a common method of reporting financial transactions. For example, under International Accounting Standards, the use of LIFO is disallowed. Therefore, if an American retailer wants to comply with international standards, it must use the FIFO method.

SUMMARY

LO 1

Why is a merchandise budget so important in retail planning, and how is a merchandise budget prepared?

The purpose of this chapter was to introduce you to the major financial statements and their importance in retail planning. We began our discussion with the six-month merchandise budget. This statement projects sales, when and how much new merchandise should be ordered, what markup is to be taken, what reductions are to be planned, and the target or planned gross margin for the season. The establishment of such a budget has several advantages for the retailer:

1. The six-month budget controls the amount of inventory and forces management to control markups and reductions.
2. The budget helps to determine how much merchandise should be purchased so that inventory requirements can be met.
3. The budget can be compared with actual or final results to determine the performance of the firm.

We concluded our discussion of the six-month merchandise budget by showing how each of the figures is determined. We illustrated how to estimate sales, inventory levels, reductions, purchases, and gross margin.

LO 2

What are the differences among and the uses of these three accounting statements: income statement, balance sheet, and statement of cash flow?

The second section of this chapter explained how the retailer uses three important accounting statements: the income statement, the balance sheet, and the statement of cash flow. The income statement gives the retailer a summary of the income and expenses incurred over a given time period. A balance sheet shows the financial condition of the retailer at a particular point in time. The statement of cash flow lists in detail the sources and types of all revenue and expenditures for a given time period.

How does a retailer value its inventory?

LO 3

The final section of this chapter described two decisions a retailer must make with regards to inventory record keeping: which accounting system (cost or retail) to use and whether to use the LIFO or FIFO valuation method.

The cost system is the simplest, but the retail system is the most widely used because of these advantages:

1. Accounting statements can be drawn up at any time.
2. Physical inventories using retail prices are less subject to error and can be completed in a shorter amount of time.
3. The retail method provides an automatic, conservative valuation of ending inventory as well as inventory levels throughout the season.

The FIFO method assumes that the oldest merchandise is sold before the more recently purchased merchandise, so merchandise on the shelf more accurately reflects the replacement cost. During inflationary periods this method allows "inventory profits" to be included as income. The LIFO method is designed to cushion the impact of inflationary pressures by matching current costs against current revenues. Cost of goods sold is based on the costs of the most recently purchased inventory, while the older inventory is regarded as the unsold inventory. In times of rapid inflation most retailers use the LIFO method, resulting in not only lower profits on the income statement, but also lower income taxes. Most retailers also prefer to use LIFO for planning purposes, since it accurately reflects replacement costs.

TERMS TO REMEMBER

merchandising	accounts receivable
merchandise budget	prepaid expenses
gross margin	retail inventories
current ratio	noncurrent assets
stock-to-sales ratio	goodwill
income statement	total asset
gross sales	liability
returns and allowances	current liabilities
net sales	accounts payable
cost of goods sold	long-term liabilities
gross margin	total liabilities
operating expenses	net worth (owner's equity)
operating profit	statement of cash flow
other income or expenses	cost method
net profit	retail method
balance sheet	FIFO
asset	LIFO
current assets	

REVIEW AND DISCUSSION QUESTIONS

Why is a merchandise budget so important in retail planning, and how is a merchandise budget prepared?

LO 1

1. Name a couple of local retailers that can be impacted by unexpected changes in weather patterns. How does weather affect their sales, and what can they do to prevent such fluctuations?

2. It costs money to carry inventory, yet retailers must carry an amount of inventory in excess of planned sales for an upcoming period. Why?

3. Why isn't it a bad thing to take a reduction? After all, aren't reductions an admission of making a mistake?

4. Why should a retailer be allowed to change its merchandise budget after the start of a season? If changes can be made, what would cause such changes?

5. A retailer who last year had sales of $900,000 plans for an inflation rate of 2 percent and a 3-percent increase in market share. What should planned sales for this year be?

6. A retailer believes that since a major competitor has just left the local market, the number of transactions for this year's upcoming season will increase by 4 percent; but because of a slowing rate of inflation, the value of the average sale will increase by only 1 percent. If sales last year were $1,500,000, what will they be this year?

LO 2 **What are the differences among and the uses of these three accounting statements—income statement, balance sheet, and statement of cash flow?**

7. In what ways are the balance sheet and the income statement different? How do retailers use these two financial statements?

8. What accounting statement reports on the retailer's financial performance over a period of time, and which statement reports a retailer's financial condition at a given point in time?

9. What is the difference between a statement of cash flow and an income statement?

10. How would the following activities affect a retailer's balance sheet and income statement for the current year?
    a. The retailer overestimates the amount of year-ending inventory that is obsolete, thus reducing inventory.
    b. The retailer overestimates the breakage on a current rebate program.
    c. The value of your inventory shrinks by a higher than expected amount. You had planned for $46,500 shrinkage, but your July count was $68,200 lower.
    d. The retailer switches from LIFO to FIFO.

11. You are working as a loan officer at a local bank. Earlier today, a former high-school classmate came in to see you about a loan for the family's retail business. After looking over the store's financial statements, you notice that the store is posting a strong net income growth. However, these statements also reveal that the store has had a negative cash flow for the last two years and that account receivables have almost doubled over the same time span. Should this concern you?

12. The Alamo Hardware Store is trying to determine its net profit before taxes. Use the following data to find Alamo's net profit.

Rent	$36,000	Salaries	$94,000
Purchases	$400,000	Sales	$586,000
Ending inventory	$163,000	Utilities	$45,000
Beginning inventory	$148,000	Other income	$5,300

13. A sporting goods store with sales for the year of $400,000 and other income of $32,000 has operating expenses of $123,000. Its cost of goods sold is

$207,000. What are its gross margin, operating profit, and net profit in dollars?

How does a retailer value its inventory?   **LO 3**

14. List the advantages and disadvantages the retail method of inventory valuation has over the cost method.
15. Define FIFO and LIFO and the reasons for using one or the other.
16. Because of the Christmas season, most retailers tend to end their fiscal year at the end of January. Does this make it difficult to determine the value of inventory when preparing financial statements?

SAMPLE TEST QUESTIONS

Which one of the following factors is not found on a six-month merchandise budget?   **LO 1**

a. planned gross margin
b. current liabilities
c. planned sales percentage
d. planned BOM stock
e. planned purchases at retail

The _____ provides the retailer with a picture of the organization's profit and loss situation.   **LO 2**

a. expense report
b. index of inventory valuation
c. statement of cash flow
d. income statement
e. statement of gross margin

The total cost valuation of a retailer's inventory is $120,000, while the total retail valuation of sales was $200,000. Approximately how much of every retail sales dollar is made up of merchandise cost?   **LO 3**

a. 12 cents
b. 40 cents
c. 60 cents
d. $1.20
e. $1.50

WRITING AND SPEAKING EXERCISE

During the economic slowdown of the last few years, the inflation rate has been around 2 percent. However, now the economic forecasters can't seem to agree on the future trend. One group predicts that the inflation rate will double over the next couple of years to 4 percent. The other group seems to believe that there won't be any inflation or maybe even a slight amount of deflation. The cost of goods sold at your family-owned menswear shop mirrors the country's inflation rate, so based on the two forecasts you expect your costs to either remain constant or to increase by 4 percent. Your father asks you to prepare a memo detailing how either of these two forecasts will impact the profitability of the business if it continues to use a FIFO method of valuing inventory.

RETAIL PROJECT

Go to the library and look at the most recent annual reports of some retailers. (If you are using the Internet, go to the retailer's home page or to http://finance.yahoo.com and then enter the retailer's stock symbol and then click "profile."). Using the financial data from these reports, compare the net cash flow to the net income for each of the retailers you chose and explain the reason for the differences.

PLANNING YOUR OWN SMALL BUSINESS

You are unsure what level of sales to forecast for your new drugstore, which you plan to open on New Year's Day. Consequently, you have decided to make some assumptions. You believe that it is reasonable to assume that your trade area will encompass about 25 square miles. The city planning department has told you that within this area the population density is 1,157 people per square mile. You conservatively estimate that 40 percent of these individuals will visit your store an average of 4 times annually and that 85 percent will purchase something on a typical visit. You expect them to purchase an average of $25 per visit. Information from industry sources suggests that drugstores do more business in the fall and winter. In fact, you expect sales during each of the months of November, December, January, and February to be 10 percent of your annual volume. The remaining eight months will share equally the 60 percent of remaining sales. You believe that for your business to be profitable, you need to have a beginning-of-month inventory-to-sales ratio of 3.0 for October through November and 2.5 for the remaining months. You want to plan your beginning-of-month inventory for each of the next 12 months. You also want to begin the first month of your second year of business with $250,000 in inventory at retail prices. Please compute the beginning of the month inventory for each of the next 12 months.

Merchandise Buying and Handling*

OVERVIEW:

In this chapter, we explain the planning that retailers must do regarding their merchandise selection. We also analyze how a retailer controls the merchandise to be inventoried. The selection of and negotiations with vendors are also discussed, as well as the security measures used when handling the merchandise.

LEARNING OBJECTIVES:

After reading this chapter, you should be able to:

1. Describe the major steps in the merchandise buying and handling process.
2. Explain the differences between the four methods of dollar-merchandise planning used to determine the proper inventory stock levels needed to begin a merchandise selling period.
3. Explain how retailers use dollar-merchandise control and describe how open-to-buy is used in the retail buying process.
4. Describe how a retailer determines the makeup of its inventory, including what cross-referencing in the merchandise item file means and how a category-item line review works.
5. Describe how a retailer selects proper merchandise sources.
6. Describe what is involved in the vendor–buyer negotiation process and what vendor contract terms can be negotiated.
7. Discuss the various methods of handling the merchandise once it is received in the store so as to control shrinkage, including vendor collusion, and theft.

LO 1

Major Steps in Merchandise Buying and Handling

What are the major steps in the merchandise buying and handling process?

Retailing involves many important activities, but retailers that experience strong performance are excellent merchants. According to an old retailing adage, "Goods well bought are half sold." Another common adage is "Retail is detail." In this chapter, we will look at the details of merchandise management—the merchandise buying and handling process and its effect on a store's performance.

Merchandise management is the analysis, planning, acquisition, handling, and control of the merchandise investments in a retail operation. *Analysis* is used in

---

*This chapter was written by Professor Jared Hansen, University of North Carolina at Charlotte.

the definition because retailers must be able to correctly identify their customers before they can determine the needs and wants of their consumers. They also have to analyze how the individual items they purchase from suppliers will result in meeting forecasted sales, profits, and markdowns so as to develop their merchandise budgets (discussed in Chapter 8). *Planning* is included because retailers must often purchase their merchandise six to 12 months in advance of the selling season. This requires retailers to predict what the economy, employment, and other trends (e.g., movies, music, clothing styles, and colors) will be in the future. After all, these factors will impact future sales. The term *acquisition* is used because, with the exception of service retailers, merchandise needs to be bought from others, either distributors or manufacturers. Besides, all retailers, even those selling only services, must acquire the equipment and fixtures needed to complete a transaction. Proper *handling* ensures that the merchandise is where it is needed and in the proper shape to be sold. Finally, *control* of the large dollar investment in inventory is important to ensure an adequate financial return on the retailer's merchandise investment.

Whatever career path you decide to take in retailing, you cannot avoid at least some contact with the firm's merchandising activities. This is because merchandising is the day-to-day business of all retailers.

There are many steps involved in merchandising, and it can be confusing trying to see how they all fit together. It can also be confusing trying to connect merchandise management to financial performance (discussed previously in Chapter 8) or pricing and promotions (discussed next in Chapters 10 and 11). However, after reading this chapter, it will be easy to see.

The people involved in each step of the merchandise buying process shown in Exhibit 9.1 will often change, depending on the size of the retailer and who makes the various decisions. For example, the product development team at Target makes most of the product design choices while the buying team focuses on purchasing. In contrast, most of the product design choices are made by the buyers at Walmart, while the product-development team serves as trend consultants by providing buyers with event and holiday style guides. Several fashion-forward firms have been placing more responsibility (i.e., power) in the hands of buyers and decreasing the role of fashion designers.[1] For smaller firms, several of the steps in the buying process may be done by executives rather than buyers. In some retail firms, the buying process is decentralized—department managers in each store place most of the merchandise orders.

merchandise management
Is the analysis, planning, acquisition, handling, and control of the merchandise investments of a retail operation.

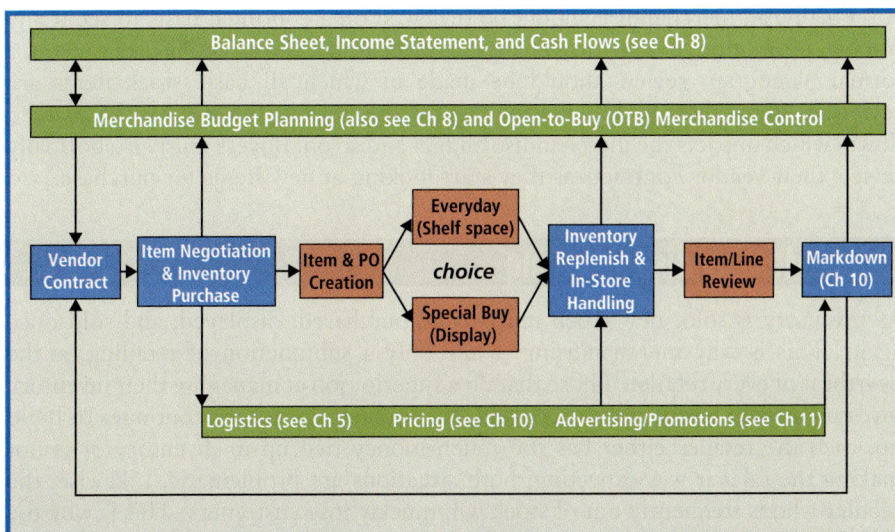

Exhibit 9.1
Major Steps in the Merchandise Management Process

A good buyer will discuss his or her promotional plans for incoming merchandise with the sales team.

Conversely, others, like JCPenney, have moved from a more decentralized to a more centralized buying process where corporate buyers in the company's headquarters perform most of the purchasing. To minimize confusion, the rest of this chapter will assume that the retailer uses a buyer to do all the activities.

As shown in Exhibit 9.1, the process normally starts with dollar-merchandise planning (which is discussed in the next section). Next, the buyer uses an open-to-buy figure to plan the merchandise assortment for the upcoming selling season. The buyer must then determine the source of the different product inventories. Some of the merchandise might be purchased from suppliers that the retailer has done business with in the past; some might be purchased from new suppliers. Regardless of who the retailer purchases from, the buyer must negotiate a vendor contract. Indeed, many retailers try to update the vendor contracts each year.

After agreeing to the terms of the vendor contract, the buyer negotiates and purchases merchandise. In doing so, the buyer must consider how the merchandise will be priced, promoted, shipped, and so on (the green box at the bottom of Exhibit 9.1). The buyer must also account for how both the initial and replenishment purchases will affect the retailer's merchandise budget and open-to-buy (OTB) calculations; both affect the retailer's financial reports.

An important, but often overlooked, step in the buying of merchandise is adding items to the retailer's computer system. Doing so allows the merchandise to be tracked and purchase orders (POs) created. If a buyer forgets to do so or links it incorrectly, customer service and sales problems are bound to occur, and the buyer is likely to be reprimanded or fired.

Buyers must also determine whether each product purchased will be a basic stock item or a special buy. This is important because basic items are included in the retailer's *planogram*. A planogram, discussed in greater detail in Chapter 13, is a schematic that illustrates how and where a retailer's merchandise should be displayed on the shelf in order to increase customer purchases. It is often maintained with the input of vendors.

Finally, all merchandise should be reviewed on a continual basis to see if any pricing, promotion, or logistical changes are necessary. At the end of each season, a formal planogram review should be made in which all basic stock items are reviewed. Items that don't make the cut for the next season need to be marked down, which impacts the merchandise budget and so on. Buyers must also normally review their vendor contracts as they start looking at new items for purchase.

LO 2 — Dollar-Merchandise Planning

What is the difference between the four methods of dollar-merchandise planning used to determine the proper inventory stock levels needed to begin a merchandise selling period?

As inventory is sold, new stock must to be purchased, displayed, and sold once again. This is why merchandising, while only a subfunction of retailing, is the heartbeat of every retailer. Those that do a superior job at managing their inventory investments will be the most successful. If a retailer's inventory continues to build up, then the retailer either has too much money tied up in inventory or is not making the sales it was expecting; both situations are problematic. Likewise, the retailer who is frequently out of stock will quickly lose customers. This is why the business-trade press and retailers take such an interest in inventory levels as different seasons approach. For example, Christmas, which traditionally accounts for 25 percent to 30 percent of annual sales,[2] can be ruined by the lack of inventory to support sales. On the other hand, if the inventory is not sold, the costs involved in carrying excess inventory can force the retailer into taking extra markdowns in addition to having to pay interest on the inventory investment.

Because inventory is the largest investment retailers make, high-performance retailers use a model called **gross margin return on inventory** (GMROI) when analyzing the performance of their inventory. GMROI incorporates how quickly inventory sells and profit into a single measure. It can be computed as follows:

$$(\text{gross margin/net sales}) \times (\text{net sales/average inventory at cost})$$
$$= (\text{gross margin/average inventory at cost})$$

Here the gross-margin percentage (gross margin/net sales) is multiplied by net sales/dollars invested in inventory to get the retailer's gross-margin dollars generated for each dollar invested in inventory. Net sales are typically computed on an annual or 12-month basis. (Note, however, that sales/dollars invested in inventory is not the same as inventory turnover. Inventory turnover measures sales/inventory at retail. In the GMROI equation, we use inventory at cost to reflect the investment in carrying merchandise.) Thus, if a particular item has a gross margin of 45 percent and annual sales per dollar of inventory investment of 4.0, its GMROI would be $1.80 ($0.45 × 4). In other words, for each dollar invested in inventory, on average the retailer obtains $1.80 in gross margin annually. Gross-margin dollars are used to first pay the store's operating expenses (both fixed and variable), with the remainder equaling the retailer's before-tax profit.

In an extreme example of the use of GMROI, the CEO of Sears, Eddie Lampert, declared a few years ago that he would sacrifice some lost sales by reducing inventory levels in Sears and Kmart stores if such action would improve the firm's GMROI.[3] There were several critics of that decision. However, in a 2009 letter to shareholders,[4] Lampert said that stockpiling cash instead of putting funds in inventory helped the company weather the recent recession when many of its competitors announced they were going out of business. Interestingly, the same letter mentioned the closing of a number of underperforming stores and the liquidating of their merchandise. This raises an important question (that could be applied to any retail chain): Were the store closings evidence of the company's continued GMROI focus? Or were they evidence that the strategy didn't work? (After all, how many times will customers return to the same store to buy an item that is out of stock?) Adding another dimension to the story, in 2009 reports surfaced suggesting that many customers were upset several months after having purchased items during a holiday sale (to be shipped to them because the store had no inventory) that they had not yet received. In fact, one customer took Sears to court over it.[5]

Before continuing the discussion of merchandise management, you may want to review a couple of earlier chapters. Because all retailing activities are aimed at serving the customer's needs and wants at a profit, you may want to revisit Chapter 3 on the customer. Likewise, because merchandise management is concerned with the acquisition of inventory from other supply-chain members, you may also want to review Chapter 5 on the behavior of the different supply-chain members.

As pointed out in Chapter 8, successful merchandise management revolves around planning and control. It takes time to buy merchandise, have it delivered, record the delivery in the company records, and properly display the merchandise;

gross margin return on inventory (GMROI)
Is gross margin divided by average inventory at cost; alternatively, it is the gross margin percent multiplied by net sales

Najlah Feanny/Corbis

Merchandise displayed at eye-level is more likely to have a higher GMROI.

therefore, it is essential to plan. Buyers need to decide today what their stock requirements will be weeks, months, or even seasons in advance.

As planning occurs, it is only logical that the retailer exercise control over the merchandise (dollars and units) that it plans to purchase. A good control system is vital. If the retailer carries too much inventory, then the costs of carrying that inventory might outweigh the gross margin to be made on the sale, especially if the retailer is forced to reduce the selling price. At times, a retailer could actually improve GMROI by decreasing the retail price if the sale excites customers to the point that they buy more of the product—at a level where the inventory-turnover increase is more than enough to offset the gross-margin reduction from the reduced sales price. After concluding our discussion on the dollar amount of inventory needed for stock requirements, the remainder of this chapter will look at the other merchandising decisions facing the retailer: calculating the dollar amount available to be spent, managing one's inventory, choosing and evaluating merchandise sources, handling vendor negotiations, handling the merchandise in the store, and evaluating merchandise performance.

Working with upper management, buyers are responsible for the dollar planning of merchandise requirements. In the previous chapter, we described the various factors that must be considered in making the sales forecast, the first step in determining inventory needs. Once planned sales for the period in question have been projected, buyers are then able to use any one of four different methods for planning dollars invested in merchandise: (1) basic stock, (2) percentage variation, (3) weeks' supply, and (4) the stock-to-sales-ratio method.

While our discussion in this chapter will focus on retailers who sell tangible goods, the same basic principles may be applied to service retailers, with one exception. Whereas tangible products are first produced, then sold, and finally consumed, services are first sold but then produced and consumed simultaneously. Thus, service retailers, be they beauty parlors or hospitals, are prevented from stockpiling their inventories, whether it is a hair highlighting process or a heart

Service Retailing

This Hotel Has Gone to the Dogs (and Cats)

It used to be a bad sign when it was said that a hotel "went to the dogs." Not anymore. PetSmart has identified a large group of pet owners that the company refers to as "pet parents," not "pet owners." Pet parents are passionately committed to their pets, and pets are seen as family members by these individuals.

In seeking to address the needs of this group, the retailer focused on providing these customers with a one-stop shopping destination that offered everything needed by these family members in an easy-to-shop, full-service specialty environment. In doing so, PetSmart recognized a unique market segment not being met by the competition—pet boarding. Enter PetSmart's PetsHotel, a boarding and day-care facility for dogs and cats that caters to their every need—even if this includes frequent tender loving care.

Each hotel provides three daily meals prepared just the way their four-legged guests like, free DVDs, and a daily dose of lactose-free ice cream. In addition, PetsHotel offers its guests many amenities not offered by a traditional kennel such as 24-hour supervision, an on-site veterinarian, air-conditioned rooms and suites, daily specialty treats, play time, and the ability to call and talk with your pet through the bone booth. On holidays, the hotel serves a special meal designed especially for pets. On Thanksgiving, for example, dogs feast on turkey and stuffing, followed by a cranberry apple crumb dessert. Felines indulge in turkey and giblets, followed by

kitty milk and cookies. Each dinner is served on special turkey-shaped plates. Of course, dogs (in the Atrium area) and cats (in the Kitty Cottages) are kept in separate areas with separate ventilation systems so they don't smell each other.

However, just as all service retailers must use forecasting tools to adjust their retailing mix and make preparations, especially regarding personnel, to satisfy their customers' wants, this is especially difficult for PetsHotel's management. While regular hotels might experience some fluctuations in demand based on a multitude of factors, they can always count on an occupancy level of between 40 percent and 100 percent. Thus, they will always need someone at the front desk and to work in maintenance and to make repairs overnight. Not so with PetsHotel. Many days, especially during the school year, family travel is limited, and no guests require their services. However, during holidays and summer months, occupancy is likely to reach capacity many days. Even the slightest change in weather can affect occupancy rates as pet parents may decide to leave the four-legged "child" outside while they go on a two-day business trip. Thus, it is very important for service retailers, especially those offering a new type of service, to manage their merchandise mix and personnel needs. However, with careful planning, success is quite possible.

Based on the textbook authors' experiences as pet parents and information found at http://PetsHotel.PetSmart.com, April 20, 2009.

bypass operation, in anticipation of future demand. Given the limited ability to stockpile inventories, service retailers must pay special attention to forecasting demand. This is because even though they do not inventory merchandise, they do inventory or have available personnel to provide services. Thus, a barber shop needs to determine how many barbers to schedule, and a bank needs to decide how many bank tellers to schedule. In a sense, traditional retailers also face this challenge because they need to schedule cashiers or retail clerks in relation to customer traffic flow. In addition, as shown in the "Service Retailing" box on PetsHotel, these service retailers must adjust their retailing mix and make preparations, especially regarding personnel, to satisfy their customers' wants and needs.

Basic Stock Method

The **basic stock method (BSM)** is used when retailers believe that it is necessary to have a given level of inventory available at all times. It requires that the retailer always have a base level of inventory investment regardless of the predicted sales volume. In addition to the base stock level, there will be a variable amount of inventory that will increase or decrease at the beginning of each sales period (one month in the case of

basic stock method (BSM)
Is a technique for planning dollar inventory investments and allows for a base stock level plus a variable amount of inventory that will increase or decrease at the beginning of each sales period in the same dollar amount as the period's expected sales.

our merchandise budget) in the same dollar amount as the period's sales are expected to increase or decrease. The BSM can be calculated as follows:

Average monthly sales for the season	= Total planned sales for the season/ Number of months in the season
Average stock for the season	= Total planned sales for the season/ Estimated inventory – turnover rate for the season
Basic stock	= Average stock for the season – Average monthly sales for the season
Beginning-of-month (BOM) stock at retail	= Basic stock + Planned monthly sales

To illustrate the use of the basic stock method, let's look at the planned sales for Department 353 of the Two-Seasons Department Store shown in Exhibit 8.2. Assume that the inventory-turnover rate for the season is 2.0. (Recall that inventory-turnover rate refers to the number of times that inventory is sold in a season).

Average monthly sales for the season	= Total planned sales for the season/ Number of months
	= \$500,000/6 = \$83,333
Average stock for the season	= Total planned sales for the season/ Inventory turnover
	= \$500,000/2 = \$250,000
Basic stock	= Average stock – Average monthly sales
	= \$250,000 – \$83,333 = \$166,667
BOM @ retail (Feb.)	= Basic stock + Planned monthly sales
	= \$166,667 + \$75,000 = \$241,667
BOM @ retail (Mar.)	= \$166,667 + \$75,000 = \$241,667
BOM @ retail (Apr.)	= \$166,667 + \$100,000 = \$266,667
BOM @ retail (May)	= \$166,667 + \$50,000 = \$216,667
BOM @ retail (Jun.)	= \$166,667 + \$125,000 = \$291,667
BOM @ retail (Jul.)	= \$166,667 + \$75,000 = \$241,667

It is obvious that \$166,667 of basic stock is added to each month's planned sales to arrive at the BOM stock. In those cases where actual sales either exceed or fall short of planned sales for the month, the retailer can easily adjust the amount of overage or shortfall to bring the next month's BOM stock back in line by buying more or less stock. Therefore, the basic stock method works best if a retailer has a low inventory-turnover rate (that is, less than six times a year) or if sales are erratic.

Percentage-Variation Method

percentage variation method (PVM)
Is a technique for planning dollar inventory investments that assumes that the percentage fluctuations in monthly stock from average stock should be half as great as the percentage fluctuations in monthly sales from average sales.

A second commonly used method for determining planned stock levels is the **percentage-variation method (PVM)**. This method is used when the retailer has a high annual inventory-turnover rate—six or more times a year. The percentage variation method assumes that the percentage fluctuations in monthly stock from average stock should be half as great as the percentage fluctuations in monthly sales from average sales.

BOM stock = Average stock for season × 1/2[1 + (Planned sales for the month/Average monthly sales)]

Since the PVM utilizes the same components as the BSM, we can use the data from the previous example.

BOM (Feb.) $= \$250{,}000 \times 1/2[1 + (\$75{,}000/\$83{,}333)] = \$237{,}500$
BOM (Mar.) $= \$250{,}000 \times 1/2[1 + (\$75{,}000/\$83{,}333)] = \$237{,}500$
BOM (Apr.) $= \$250{,}000 \times 1/2[1 + (\$100{,}000/\$83{,}333)] = \$275{,}000$
BOM (May) $= \$250{,}000 \times 1/2[1 + (\$50{,}000/\$83{,}333)] = \$200{,}000$
BOM (Jun.) $= \$250{,}000 \times 1/2[1 + (\$125{,}000/\$83{,}333)] = \$312{,}500$
BOM (Jul.) $= \$250{,}000 \times 1/2[1 + (\$75{,}000/\$83{,}333)] = \$237{,}500$

Weeks' Supply Method

A third method for planning inventory levels is the **weeks' supply method (WSM)**. Generally, the WSM formula is used by retailers such as grocers, whose inventories are planned on a weekly, not monthly, basis and where sales do not fluctuate substantially. It states that the inventory level should be set equal to a predetermined number of weeks' supply. The predetermined number of weeks' supply is directly related to the inventory-turnover rate desired. In the WSM, inventory level in dollars varies proportionally with forecast sales. Thus, if forecast sales triple, then inventory in dollars will also triple.

To illustrate the WSM, let's return to our earlier problem and use the following formulas:

Number of weeks to be stocked = Number of weeks in the period/ Stock turnover rate for the period
Average weekly sales = Estimated total sales for the period/ Number of weeks in the period
BOM stock = Average weekly sales × Number of weeks to be stocked

Thus,

Number of weeks to be stocked $= 26/2 = 13$
Average weekly sales $= \$500{,}000/26 = \$19{,}231$
BOM stock $= \$19{,}231 \times 13 = \$250{,}000$

Having determined the number of weeks' supply to be stocked (13 weeks) and the average weekly sales ($19,231), stock levels can be replenished on a frequent or regular basis to guard against stockouts.

Stock-to-Sales Method

The final method for planning inventory levels, and the one used in Chapter 8, is the **stock-to-sales method (SSM)**. This method is quite easy to use but requires the retailer to have a beginning-of-the-month stock-to-sales ratio. This ratio tells the retailer how much inventory is needed at the beginning of the month to support that month's estimated sales. A ratio of 2.5, for example, would tell the retailer that it should have two and one-half (2½) times that month's expected sales on hand in inventory at the beginning of the month.

Stock-to-sales ratios can be obtained from internal or external sources. Internally, the statistics can be obtained if the retailer has designed a good accounting system and has properly stored historical data so that the figures can be readily retrieved. Externally, the retailer can often rely on retail trade associations (such as the Menswear Retailers Association) or on national groups such as the National Retail Federation (nrf.com) in the United States, the Australian Retailers Association (ara.com.au), the Retail Merchants Association of New Zealand (retail.org.nz), the Retail Council of Canada (retailcouncil.org), the Japan Retail

weeks' supply method (WSM)
Is a technique for planning dollar inventory investments that states that the inventory level should be set equal to a predetermined number of weeks' supply, which is directly related to the desired rate of stock turnover.

stock-to-sales method (SSM)
Is a technique for planning dollar inventory investments where the amount of inventory planned for the beginning of the month is a ratio (obtained from trade associations or the retailer's historical records) of stock-to-sales.

Association (http://www.japan-retail.or.jp/english/index.htm), or the Hong Kong Retail Management Association (hkrma.org). These and other trade associations collect stock-to-sales ratios from participating merchants and then compile, tabulate, and report them in special management reports or trade publications.

However, these ratios should only be used as a guide to determine how much inventory to have on hand at the beginning of each month. Successful chain store retailers have long known that even stores located near each other require not only different merchandise mixes but also different inventory levels per sales dollars. This is a reflection of the store's trading area, layout, and competition. However, inventory turnover remains a key factor in a retailer's financial performance. Planned average BOM stock-to-sales goals can be easily calculated using turnover goals. If you divide the number of months in the season by the desired inventory-turnover rate, then we can compute an average BOM stock-to-sales ratio for the season. For example, if you desired an inventory-turnover rate of 2.0 for the upcoming six-month season (4.0 annually), your average BOM stock-to-sales ratio would be 3.0 (6/2.0 = 3.0).

| LO 3 | Dollar-Merchandise Control |

How does a retailer use dollar-merchandise control and open-to-buy in the retail buying process?

Once the buyer has planned for the dollar merchandise necessary for the beginning of each month (or season), it is essential that the buyer not make commitments for merchandise that would exceed that dollar plan. In short, the dollars planned for merchandise need to be controlled. This control is accomplished through a technique called **open-to-buy (OTB)**.

OTB represents the dollar amount that a buyer can currently spend on merchandise without exceeding the planned dollar stock discussed previously. When planning for any given month (or season), the buyer will not necessarily be able to purchase a dollar amount equal to the planned dollar stock for that month (or season). This is because some merchandise may be already on order but not yet delivered. To illustrate this point more succinctly, let's compute the open-to-buy for an upcoming month.

open-to-buy (OTB)
Refers to the dollar amount that a buyer can currently spend on merchandise without exceeding the planned dollar stocks.

Assume that at the beginning of February the buyer for Department 353 of the Two-Seasons Department Store (Exhibit 8.2) has already ordered, but not yet received, $15,000 worth of merchandise at retail. Keeping planned EOM stock at $300,000 and planned reductions for February at 10 percent of planned sales, the buyer's planned purchases for February will remain $157,500. However, the open-to-buy for February will only be $142,500 at retail since it is necessary to account for the $15,000 of merchandise already ordered but not yet received. The computations would look like this:

1. Planned sales for February	+ $ 75,000
2. Plus planned reductions for February	+ 7,500
3. Plus EOM planned retail stock	+ 300,000
4. Minus BOM stock	− 225,000
5. Equals planned purchases at retail	$157,500
6. Minus commitments at retail for current delivery	− 15,000
7. Equals open-to-buy	$142,500

The OTB figure should not be set in stone because it can be exceeded. Consumer needs are the dominant consideration. If actual sales exceed planned sales, then additional quantities should be ordered above those scheduled for purchase according to the merchandise budget; however, this should not be a common occurrence. If it is, then the sales planning process is flawed. Either the buyers are too conservative in estimating sales or they are buying the wrong merchandise. This chapter's "What's New?" box discusses an innovative way the front line employees at Best Buy aid their buyers in making decisions on new product ideas. In any case, the buyer, along with management, should always determine the causes of OTB adjustments. Some of the most common buying errors include

1. buying merchandise that is priced either too high or too low for the store's target market,

2. buying the wrong type of merchandise (i.e., too many tops and not enough skirts) or buying merchandise that is too trendy,

3. having too much or too little basic stock on hand,

4. buying from too many vendors,

5. failing to identify the season's hot items early enough in the season, and

6. failing to let the vendor assist the buyer by adding new items or new colors to the existing mix. (All too often, the original order is merely repeated, resulting in a limited selection.)

Merchandise planning is a dynamic process subject to many changes. Consider how planning your stock levels might be affected by any or all of the following: (1) Sales for the previous month were lower or higher than planned, (2) reductions are

What's New?

Do Frontline Employees Really Know Best?

One of the more difficult parts of merchandising is forecasting future sales, especially for new products. Managers spend a lot of time doing this. Yet the forecasts often don't match reality. To account for this, Best Buy has come up with a new way to forecast. Instead of using veteran manager forecasting gurus, they turn to their hourly store employees. They call it "TagTrade" because frontline employees trade bets or wagers on certain events that relate to retail sales such as the number of gift certificates that will be purchased during the weekend prior to Father's day or whether the management's forecast for gift certificates sold during this period will be exceeded. The retailer has discovered that the employee's collective answer is usually more accurate than the firm's official forecasts. The reason: Frontline employees are closer to the customer. About 2000 of the 115,000 U.S. employees have chosen to participate in this program so far. They get fake money to wager, and the top trader wins a $200 gift certificate. Such forecasting programs are called prediction markets.

Because the employee predictions have been closer to real performance than management's forecasts, Best Buy executives have had to learn how to use the predictions without humiliating or upsetting their management. When done well, they've opened up more communication between frontline employees and senior managers. Other companies such as Google, GE, Intel, and Microsoft also use prediction markets to tap the thoughts of their frontline employees.

With encouragement from former Best Buy CEO, Mr. Anderson, a few managers have begun using it, but no buyer or executive is required to do so. In fact, the retailer has no plans to require managers to use it because that might ruin it or skew the input gathered from the employees. However, the few buyers who have participated in the program have used it to test new product ideas, see what sales forecasts might look like, or test reactions to price increases or decreases. Thus, even though Best Buy's TagTrade is only "live" a couple of times a year, it does point out the need to be creative and innovative to succeed in retailing today.

TagTrade illustrates the fact that successful retailers such as Best Buy are not afraid to test new ideas. Perhaps a similar employee-feedback program might have helped Circuit City and others retailers in bankruptcy avoid the problems they experienced as a result of not connecting with their customers.

higher or lower than planned, and (3) shipments of merchandise are delayed in transit. Understanding the consequences of each situation illustrates the interrelationship of merchandising activities with the merchandise budget. Such occurrences, though, serve to make retailing a challenging and exciting career choice.

LO 4 Inventory Planning

How does a retailer determine the makeup of its inventory?

The dollar-merchandise plan is only the starting point in merchandise management. Once the retailer has decided how many dollars can be invested in inventory, the dollar plan needs to be converted into an inventory plan. On the sales floor, items are sold, not dollars. The assortment of items that make up the merchandise mix must then be planned.

Optimal Merchandise Mix

Exhibit 9.2 shows the three dimensions of the optimal mix: variety, breadth, and depth. Each of these dimensions needs to be defined; however, to do so, it is necessary that we first define a merchandise line (or category). A **merchandise line** consists of a group of products that are closely related because they either are intended for the same end use (all televisions), are sold to the same customer group (junior miss clothing), or fall within a given price range (budget women's wear). Today, as was discussed in Chapter 5, more than 90 percent of grocery retailers use the term category management to refer to their management of categories as a strategic business unit. That is, a supermarket buyer using category management would no longer be concerned with GMROI for just the Tide or Cheer detergent. Instead, that buyer would be concerned with the GMROI for the entire detergent line or category. For that buyer, the line or category is his or her strategic business unit. If the buyer focused only on the items, problems could quickly arise. For instance, price promoting Tide might increase Tide sales, but how much of the sales increase would come from existing customers merely switching from other products not on sale? Similarly, the buyer in such a situation must also consider to what extent some customers will simply stockpile (buy extra now and less in the future)? Taking a category perspective, the retailer might choose to price promote an item that is above the average margin for the category. If done well, the increase in the discounted product could bring up the average margin, instead of lowering it. This isn't always possible, but it's one of several concepts that retail buyers think about when managing a category.

merchandise line
Is a group of products that are closely related because they are intended for the same end use (all televisions); are sold to the same customer group (junior miss clothing); or fall within a given price range (budget women's wear).

Variety

The **variety** of the merchandise mix refers to the number of different merchandise lines a retailer chooses to stock in its store. For example, department stores have a large variety of merchandise lines. Some have more than 100 departments carrying such lines as menswear, women's wear, children's clothing, infant's wear, toys, sporting goods, appliances, cosmetics, and household goods. Others, like PetSmart, carry only one basic merchandise line: pet supplies. In the middle of these two would be a retailer such as Sports Authority, selling a complete range of sporting apparel and equipment.

variety
Refers to the number of different merchandise lines that the retailer stocks in the store.

Breadth

Breadth, also called **assortment**, refers to the number of brands that are found in a single merchandise line. For example, a supermarket will have a wide breadth or

breadth (or assortment)
The number of merchandise brands that are found in a merchandise line.

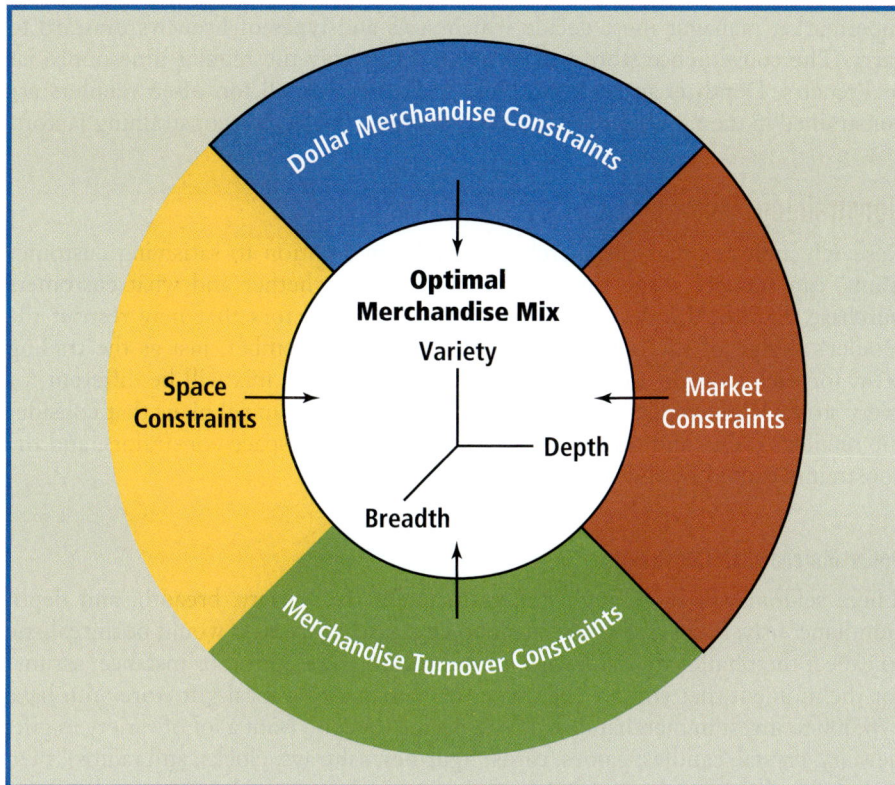

Exhibit 9.2
Dimensions of and Constraints on Optimal Merchandising Mix

assortment in the number of different brands of mustard it carries: six or seven national or regional brands, a private brand, and a generic brand. The 7-Eleven convenience stores, however, will offer very little breadth by generally carrying only one or two brands in any merchandise line. The breadth might change with time. For example, many clothing retailers now have as much as three times the selection in the misses department over the petites department (as customer sizes[6] and manufacturer product styles have changed).

Breadth is particularly a problem for retailers selling private-label brands. Retailers seek a proper balance between their own private labels and the national brands they carry. This is because private-label brands, as noted in Chapter 4, offer the retailer lower costs and higher gross margins; however, the retailer also needs national brands to draw customers into its store. Yet sometimes a powerful manufacturer may try to tie some of its merchandise lines together. In other words, if the retailer wishes to carry one product, the manufacturer stipulates that the retailer must also carry its entire product line. When retailers are faced with such a dilemma, a **battle of the brands** can occur in which the retailer, in determining the breath of its product assortment, has its own products competing with the manufacturer's products for shelf space and control over display location. One consequence of such a battle of the brands is that many retailers now stock one or both of the top brands in a product line or category as well as their own private brand. Consequently, many so-called third-tier brands have been left off store shelves.

Depth

Merchandise **depth** refers to the average number of stock-keeping units (SKUs) within each brand of the merchandise line. In the preceding example, the

battle of the brands
Occurs when retailers have their own products competing with the manufacturer's products for shelf space and control over display location.

depth
Is the average number of stock-keeping units within each brand of the merchandise line.

supermarket manager must decide which sizes and types of French's mustard to carry. The convenience store will probably carry only the regular nine-ounce jar of French's. Depth is an acute problem today because all too often retailers are constrained in the number of SKUs they can carry by specific constraining factors.

Constraining Factors

Research indicates that the merchandise mix, in addition to satisfying customer wants, can actually shape those wants and impact whether and what customers purchase.[7]Exhibit 9.2 details the four constraining factors that may restrict the retailer's design of the optimal merchandise mix. Remember, just as the trading areas for each store in a chain are different, the optimal mix will be different for every store. Merchandise mix decisions are a blend of financial plans that consider the retailer's dollar and turnover constraints, the store's space constraints, and the constraints caused by the actions of competitors.

Dollar-Merchandise Constraints

There seldom will be enough dollars to emphasize variety, breadth, and depth simultaneously. If the decision is made to emphasize variety, it would be unrealistic to expect the retailer to also have a lot of breadth and depth. For instance, assume for the moment that you are the owner or manager of a local gift store. You have $70,000 to invest in merchandise. If you decide that you want a lot of variety in gifts (jewelry, crystal, candles, games, cards, figurines, ashtrays, clocks, and radios), then you obviously cannot have much depth in any single item such as crystal glassware.

consignment (pay from scan)
Is when the vendor retains the ownership of the goods and usually establishes the selling price; it is paid only when goods are sold.

Some retailers try to overcome this dollar constraint by shifting the expense of carrying inventory back on the vendor. When a retailer buys a product on **consignment**, the vendor retains the ownership of the goods, usually establishes the selling price, and is paid only when the goods are sold. (This is different from the use of the word *consignment* to describe customers taking products to stores like Play It Again Sports to resell merchandise to other customers with the store taking a percentage of the profit). *Pay from scan* is a more recent term that some retailers are beginning to use when describing consignment. Pay from scan (or consignment) helps reduce risk for seasonal products such as greeting cards, books, magazines, or dated food products (e.g., chips or soda). The manufacturer usually sends a field representative to the retail store to pull the remaining product off the shelf when the sell-by date passes. One of the benefits of pay from scan is that a retailer can have a lot of holiday greeting cards or promotional displays and not worry about having to (1) put them in storage somewhere for a year or (2) spend precious markdown dollars on them. However, consignment doesn't come free. Manufacturers usually pass along a higher initial cost to the retailer to cover the returns. Still, retailers don't have to worry about magazines or chips expiring every month. It's a trade-off that retailers must make product by product or category by category: higher initial margin or less risk.

extra dating (EX)
Allows the retailer extra or interest-free days before the period of payment begins.

Another approach the retailer might try to get is **extra dating (EX)**, where the vendor allows the retailer some extra time before paying for the goods. For example, most textbook publishers either sell their books on consignment or give the bookstores an extra 60 days in which to pay. In this way your campus bookstore orders its books in early July for an early August delivery. The bookstore then sells the books in late August or early September. However, because the books were sold on consignment, or with extra dating, the bookstore does not have to pay the publisher until October.

Space Constraints

The retailer must also deal with space constraints. If depth or breadth is wanted, then space is needed. If variety is to be stressed, then it is also important to have enough *empty* space to separate the distinct merchandise lines. For example, consider a single counter containing cosmetics, candy, fishing tackle, women's stockings, and toys. This would obviously be an unsightly and unwise arrangement. As more variety is added, empty space becomes necessary to allow the consumer to clearly distinguish between distinct product lines.

Most retailers have operation guides that tell how much space should be between each fixture, rack, display, and so forth. They also have to decide how tall they want their fixtures to be. A retailer could have taller shelf sections (gondolas) that hold more products; however, at some point, it would start to feel like a warehouse. Conversely, the retailer could use shorter shelves that customers find more visually appealing, but this tactic provides less space for products. For example, Walmart is taking out many of its risers in its stores to be more visually appealing. While this impacts store atmospherics, it also reduces how much inventory the total store can hold. It either has to give up products (go narrower in breadth or depth), go leaner on inventory (risking out of stocks) and requiring more trucks on the road, or have more trailers behind the store (in which there is usually more theft, product and package damage, and outside temperature changes that can freeze or melt some products) where permitted.

Retailers, especially in the grocery business, have been able to turn this space constraint into an advantage by charging manufacturers slotting fees, which were discussed in both Chapters 6 and 8, to carry their products.

Merchandise-Turnover Constraints

As the depth of the merchandise is increased, the retailer will be stocking more and more variations of the product to serve smaller and smaller segments. Consequently, inventory turnover will deteriorate and the chances of being out of stock will increase. One does not have to minimize variety, breadth, and depth to maximize turnover, but one must know how various merchandise mixes will affect inventory turnover.

Market Constraints

Market constraints also affect decisions on variety, breadth, and depth. The three dimensions have a profound effect on how the consumer perceives the store and consequently on the customers that the store will attract. The consumer perceives a specialty store as one with limited variety and breadth of merchandise lines but considerable depth within the lines handled. An individual searching for depth in a limited set of merchandise lines such as formal menswear will thus be attracted to a menswear retailer specializing in formal wear. On the other hand, the consumer perceives a general merchandise retailer such as Target as a store with lots of variety and breadth in terms of merchandise lines but with a more constrained depth. Therefore, someone who needs to make several purchases across several merchandise lines and is willing to sacrifice depth of assortment would be more attracted to the general merchandise retailer.

The constraining factors make it almost impossible for a retailer to emphasize all three dimensions. However, retailers can take some comfort in the fact that greater product selection does not necessarily mean that the consumer will get more enjoyment from the shopping experience. Research has found that retailers can cut SKUs without lowering consumer perceptions of selection. In fact, Procter

& Gamble (P&G) claims that in the laundry category 40 percent of SKUs could be eliminated and 95 percent of consumer needs would still be met.[8] Some consumers may even be more satisfied with the smaller selection.[9] This is important for retailers using the category management system to remember. After all, category management, in its effort to increase profits, typically reduces the number of SKUs as it seeks to increase inventory turnover. Nevertheless, if you are going to lose customers, you should seek to lose the less-profitable ones by properly mixing your merchandise in terms of variety, breadth, and depth within the dollar, space, turnover, and market constraints.

Managing the Inventory

After deciding the relative emphasis to be placed on the three dimensions of the merchandise mix, you need to decide when to order and reorder the desired merchandise lines and items. Ideally, as shown in Exhibit 9.3, a retailer selling a basic stock item, one that should always to be in stock, would receive the reordered merchandise just as it is needed. However, a retailer selling a seasonal item, as shown in Exhibit 9.4, would want to be completely sold out at the planned out-of-stock date.

Both Exhibits 9.3 and 9.4 recognize the fact that it annually costs the retailer between 20 percent and 25 percent to carry inventory. Some of these costs are direct, such as interest on the money borrowed to pay for the inventory or insurance and warehousing expenses, and other costs may be indirect, such as what the retailer could have made elsewhere when it uses its own money to pay for the inventory.

The retailer tries to achieve the optimization of its inventory dollars by closely monitoring its inventory. One of the great difficulties many retailers face is that inventory figures, including "perpetual inventory" (real-time updating) are often wrong as much as 40 percent of the time.[10] One way to fix (or decrease) the problem is to use radio frequency identification (RFID) barcode data. An RFID tag consists of a tiny digital signal processor embedded in a product, package, or box. It allows retailers to account for merchandise without the use of hand counts, which often leads to missed items in the stockroom, on risers, on the wrong shelves, or in customer carts. They also allow for faster reorders (as the merchandise is being sold). However, with all their potential benefits, RIFDs still present some issues that are described in this chapter's case.

Managing inventory turnover is one of the most important things retailers do. It is not easy. Just when you think you have the forecasts correct, customers change their minds. For example, after nearly 50 years of being a top seller, Barbie's worldwide sales have hit the skids, dropping double digits over the last few years.[11] As a result of these sales decreases, Mattel is trying to reconnect Barbie, perhaps ironically, with *older* girls ("tweens")[12] and even trying to sell bridal Barbie wear to Japanese adult women, among other strategies. More information about how the vicious battle[13] between Barbie and Bratz affects retailers' inventory management is found in this chapter's "Retailing: The Inside Story."

Another problem can arise when retailers use the wrong baseline in making their forecast. For example, *Spiderman* was a huge success back in 2002, not only at the movie box office but also for several retail merchandise categories (e.g., toys, activities, electronics such as video games, music, movies).[14] The next year, retailers were excited to jump on board the *Hulk* movie bandwagon. This author and several other buyers sat in on meetings with the movie studio and licensing and manufacturing company managers. They planned for another *Spiderman*; however, as the

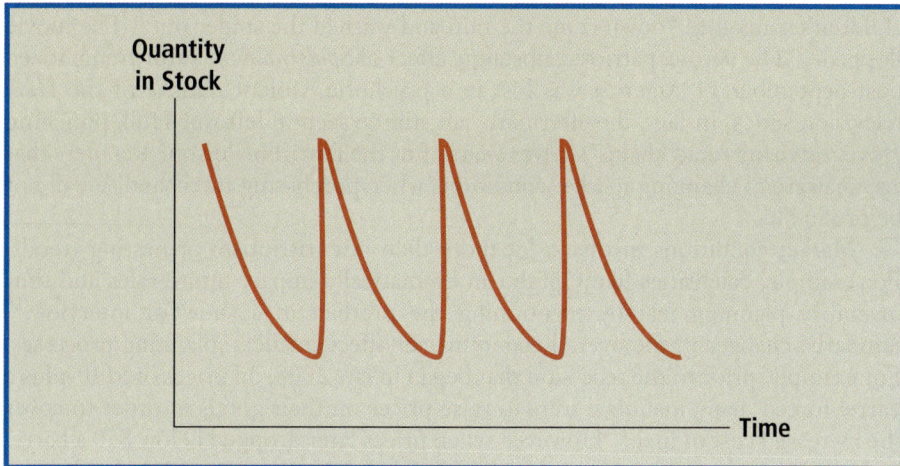

Exhibit 9.3
Inventory Management for a Retailer Selling a Basic Stock Item

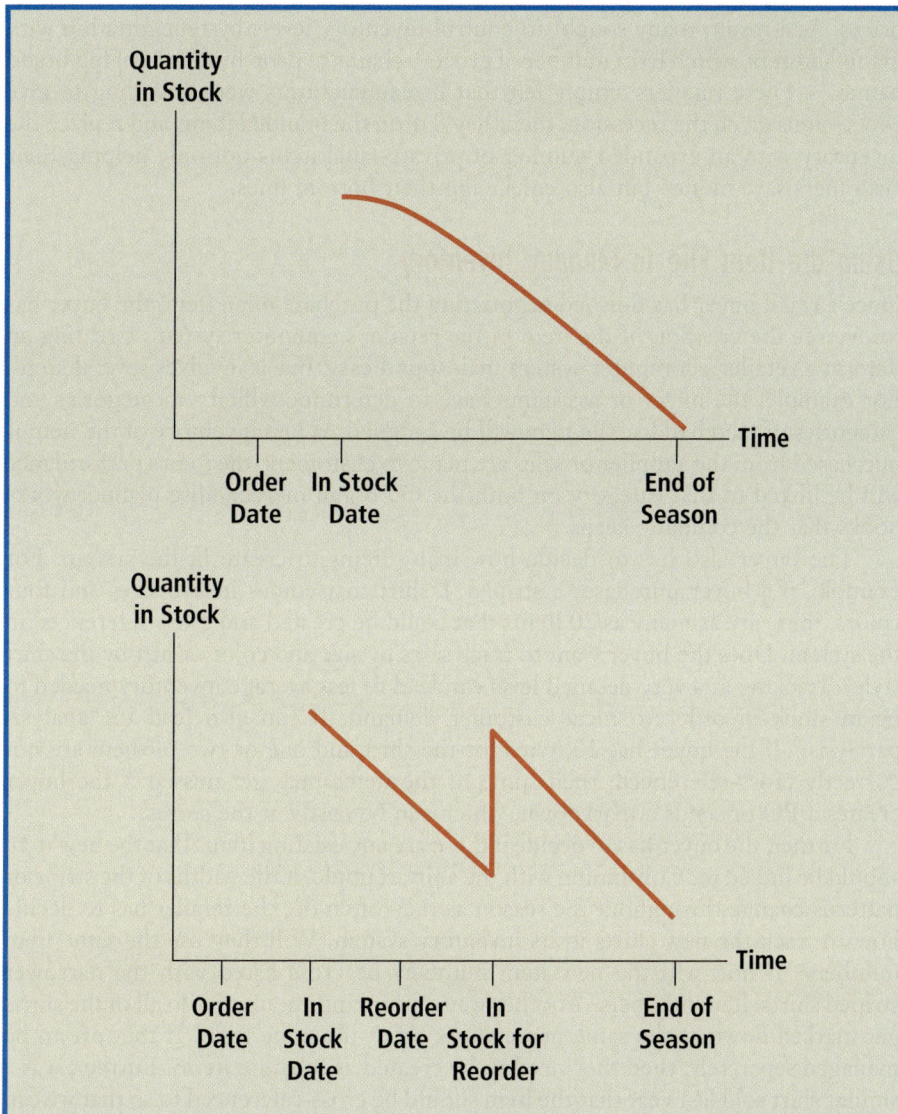

Exhibit 9.4
Inventory Management for a Retailer Selling a Seasonal Item

children's song goes "down came the rain and washed the spider out." The movie flopped.[15] The heroic, patriotic, nostalgic effect of *Spiderman* on a still-traumatized post-September 11 America was lost in a psychotic, violent remake of the *Hulk* television series. In fact, the aftermath can still be seen in leftover Hulk punching gloves on many retail chains' shelves years after the film. The lesson? Retailers that are unaware of changing market conditions when purchasing merchandise will not be profitable.

Market conditions involve a lot more than just patriotism or nesting trends. For example, celebrities like Oprah can dramatically impact future sales and thus inventory planning just by mentioning the product in a show or interview.[16] Similarly, changes in the overall economy can affect retailers' planning processes. For example, prior to the recession that began in late 2008, oil prices of $140-plus a barrel forced many manufacturers to raise prices on their goods in order to cover the increased cost of fuel.[17] However, when prices later dropped below $50 a barrel in early 2009, a majority of retailers neglected to see a corresponding drop in the price they paid for their merchandise. With a recession in full swing, many questioned whether their customers would or even could continue to pay the higher prices. As a result, many sought to control inventory levels by renegotiating with manufacturers, which led a number of grocery chains to drop hundreds of big brand names.[18] These retailers simply felt that if manufacturers were unwilling to give concessions given the recession, then they'd drop the branded items and replace the inventory with an expanded number of private-label items not only helping their customers save money but also enhancing their bottom lines.

Using the Item File to Manage Inventory

Once a retail buyer has finished negotiating the purchase of an item, the buyer has to oversee the creation of the item in the retailer's computer system. Creating an item in a retailer's computer system may sound easy, but it involves several steps. For example, the buyer or assistants have to determine which subcategories and categories of merchandise the item will be assigned. When inventory of the item is purchased from the supplier or sales are made to customers, the item's performance will be linked to that category on both the OTB and merchandise planner workbooks that the company keeps.

The buyer also has to decide how many items to create in the system. For example, if a buyer purchases a striped T-shirt that comes in five sizes and four colors, there are as many as 20 items that could be created and cross-referenced in the system. Does the buyer want to track sales by size and color or just by the shirt style? Tracking at a very detailed level can lead to less average inventory needed to be in stock in order to meet customer demand. It can also lead to "analysis paralysis." If the buyer has 20 items for the shirt and one or two of them are not correctly cross-referenced, then some of the items may get missed if the buyer creates a PO or sends a markdown, which can be costly at the stores.

Further, the buyer has to decide if there are any existing items that the new item should be linked to. Continuing with the shirt example, if the widths of the stripe or patterns change throughout the season as they often do, the retailer has to decide how to track the new shirts in its inventory system. Will they use the same item numbers? If not, will the new item numbers be cross listed with the narrower striped shirts' item numbers? Another way of thinking about it is, do all of the shirts get marked down at the same percentages off at the same time? If they are to be managed separately, then they need to be created as separate items. Further, was a similar shirt sold last year that the item should be cross-referenced to so that we can

Retailing: The Inside Story

Whose Brat Is It?

Barbie recently celebrated her 50th birthday. So how does a 50-year-old concept keep connecting with young girls? Like many beauty contests, competition can matter a lot.

Over the past decade Barbie, a leading and well-recognized Mattel branded product, has had a tough time staying connected with kids. However, at the same time a company named MGA has enjoyed considerable success targeting Barbie's market with its Bratz line of dolls. Bratz dolls have a bigger head to body ratio (with big eyes, mouths, etc) and trendier clothes, and they are supposed to be teenagers (versus the "adult" doll Barbie). Many people see their attitude—well, the name says it. Mattel tried to compete by launching its own hip-hop Flavas that looked a lot like Bratz but with tattoos and less clothing. A number of customers found them racially offensive or thought they encouraged a "bad girl" image to kids. In the end, Flavas didn't work and Mattel soon discontinued the line of dolls.

Interestingly, the creator of the Bratz line was a former Mattel doll designer. Knowing that the artist who started the Bratz line originally came up with the idea while employed by Mattel, Mattel took MGA to court, arguing that it owned the rights to Bratz. In late 2008, the court ruled that the Bratz toy line did, in fact, belong to Mattel, *even though the company had no interest in it several years ago* when the artist initially tried to pitch the concept prior to leaving and joining MGA. The judge ordered MGA to send all the unsold merchandise to Mattel, pay the company money based on the past several years of Bratz sales, and turn over all of the Bratz designs to Mattel in 2009. As of mid 2009, Mattel hadn't stated to retailers whether it will actually produce Bratz or simply let it die, and MGA was involved in final appeals of the decision.

So, in the meantime, who owns the right to produce and sell Bratz? It is an important question not just for MGA or Mattel, but for the many retailers who have been successfully selling the Bratz dolls. With the answer unknown, several retailers have stopped replenishing them until the future becomes clearer. In the interim, Barbie's kid sister, Skipper, is being reintroduced after disappearing in the 1990s, and

Getty Images

(continued)

Retailing: The Inside Story *(continued)*

Barbie has been redesigned to be "trendier" in an attempt to reconnect with tweens. Perhaps it is a sign that Mattel doesn't plan on using the Bratz product. These types of legal tug-of-wars over brands and copyrights are happening more and more between manufacturers. While less competition might help Barbie a little bit in her beauty competition, it doesn't help retailers who miss out on profits because they are sitting with empty shelves where Bratz once sat.

Based on the author's experiences working with Walmart: "Bratz Ruling Hands Mattel Big Choices," *Wall Street Journal*, December 5 2008: B1, B6, and "Toy Markets Reach into the Product Attic," *Wall Street Journal*, March 3, 2009: B1.

compare year-to-year performance? Maybe the prior year it was bought from a different supplier, so it needs to be created as a new item in the system (to reflect the different supplier and costs) but linked to the other item for comparison. It might sound easy to do this for one shirt, but the process has to be done for every item that's going to the stores. Some retailers may decide the information gained from this type of item-level tracking isn't worth the costs of doing so, and they simply place stickers with prices on the items. Most of the larger, national retailers use very advanced tracking software so they can reorder products for each store in a way that the stores stay in stock, but not overstocked. Some large-scale retailers have a corporate PO department solely to create and manage items and purchase orders in the retailer's computer system.

The other decision facing the buyer is, will the item be displayed everyday on permanent store fixtures (described in Chapter 13) or will the item be a "special buy"—a display item featured on a stack base in the aisle, at the front of the store, or on endcaps (displays at the end of aisles)? While both methods require inventory management, adding it to the shelf means another item has to be deleted and marked down to open up room for the new item. Making a shelf-space drawing (normally called a *planogram* or *modular*) takes several weeks of measuring product dimensions, uploading them, and adding the UPCs to the shelf-space software (i.e., programs like Prospace or Spaceman). Stores have to reset the shelves (which takes valuable store employee time and wages). To not overwhelm the store employees or customers, most retailers have an annual shelf-space review calendar. When possible, each department is assigned a different week or time of the year to physically reset the shelves in the stores.

Basic stock items then need to be replenished, which means setting up a forecast usually based on the history of a similar item. Buyers need to be careful in deciding which existing items to use for the new item's history. For example, say a retailer decided to carry a new line of fashion-print bedsheets. If the retailer used an existing white bedsheet item for the sales pattern, then it might be in trouble toward the end of the year. At many retailers white sheets have a sales bump toward the end of October that fashion sheets wouldn't have. Why? Because some customers buy the white sheets to use in homemade Halloween costumes. Using the white sheets as a history would result in an overstock of the fashion sheets in early November.

Sometimes special buys might also be replenished to avoid sending too much inventory at one time. Replenishment (buying and selling inventory) affects the merchandise budget and, in turn, the retailer's financial statements. Replenishment can be difficult because so many things can affect it—from weather to transportation problems (like dock strikes or backlogs in port inspections) to manufacturing problems. Manufacturing problems aren't just related to assembly lines. Competitors are always trying to find ways to gain an edge over the competition, and they

Tim Boyle/Getty Images

Adjustable shelves on store fixtures makes it easier for retailers to replenish products that sell at different rates and have different physical dimensions.

increasingly seem to be using the court system to impact competition. Remember, the story from the chapter's "Retailing: The Inside Story" box described how the actions of a supplier's competition can affect a retailer's replenishment of a successful item.

Conflicts in Stock Planning

Stock planning is an exercise in compromise and conflict. The conflict is multi-dimensional because not everything can be stocked. Some of the more common conflicts are described below.

1. Maintain a strong in-stock position on genuinely new items while trying to avoid the 90 percent of new products that fail in the introductory stage. The retailer wants to carry the new products that will satisfy customers. If the consumer is sold a poor product; it hurts the retailer as much as, if not more than, the manufacturer. The problem becomes one of screening out poor products before they reach the customer. Any screening device, however, has error; the retailer might end up stocking some losers and turning down winners. Thus, a basic conflict arises, but even the best of buyers will make some mistakes and be forced to use markdowns to unload slow-selling merchandise.

2. Maintain an adequate stock of the basic popular items while having sufficient inventory dollars to capitalize on unforeseen opportunities. Many times, if the retailer fills out the model stock with recommended quantities, there is little if any money left over for the super buy that is just around the corner. But if the retailer holds out that money and cuts back on basic stock, then customers may be lost and that super buy may never surface. For this reason, it is important that retailers realize that they should never be out of stock on staples and best-selling products.

3. Maintain high inventory-turnover goals while maintaining high gross-margin goals. This is perhaps the most glaring conflict. Usually, items that turn over more rapidly have thinner gross margins. Therefore, developing an inventory plan that will accomplish both objectives is surely challenging.

4. Maintain an adequate selection for customers while not confusing them. If customers are confronted with too many similar items, they will not be able to make up their minds and may leave the store empty-handed and frustrated. On the contrary, if the selection is inadequate, the customer will again leave empty-handed. Thus, a delicate balance needs to be struck between too little and too much selection.

5. Maintain space productivity and utilization while not congesting the store. Take advantage of buys that will utilize the available space but avoid buys that cause the merchandise to spill over into the aisles. Unfortunately, some of the best buys come along when space is already occupied.

Reviewing Inventory Performance

At the end of the selling season, the buyer reviews the entire merchandise performance in what many retailers call a *line review*. The process takes a few weeks. The buyer meets with all of the suppliers one on one (usually in one-hour meetings) where they use the supplier performance card and reports showing how each item supplied by the supplier did over the selling season (as compared to the category average and total). They might try to renegotiate the vendor contract or simply jump right into item negotiations, including which items are going to be discontinued and marked down (and who will fund the markdown[19]), which items will stay, and which new items might be added to either the planogram or as seasonal displays. Hundreds of reports are run by the buyer. Some buyers will run an *80-20 report*, showing which items do most of the business (20 percent of the items often do 80 percent of the business) and which items could be dropped. In dropping items, they need to consider the market basket—a given item may not be a top performer, but maybe it's the reason that people come to the store. Line reviews involve taking a lot of data and trying to summarize it in a digestible manner. They also involve understanding trends and fashion. Thus, to be successful, buyers need to have both creative and quantitative analysis capabilities. If they don't, they often are paired with assistants who can complement their strengths.

As should be readily evident at this point, inventory management is no easy task. Equally challenging is the selection of vendors from whom to purchase merchandise.

LO 5

How do retailers select proper merchandise sources?

Selection of Merchandising Sources

After deciding on the type and amount of inventory to be purchased, the next step is to determine where the retailer is to obtain its merchandise. All too often people have misconceptions about how retailers choose and negotiate with vendors. In reality, with proper planning and control, it can be a very rewarding experience, especially when customers react positively to merchandise selection. However, no matter how rewarding a buying experience is, it will also be grueling. Retail buyers must not only determine what merchandise lines to carry but also select the best possible vendor to supply them with these items while simultaneously negotiating the best deal possible with that vendor.

AP Photo/Jae C. Hong

Retail buyers and manufacturers meet at trade shows such as the International CES (Consumer Electronics Show) pictured here.

Unless the retailer owns a manufacturing or wholesale operation or both, the retailer must consider many criteria when selecting a merchandise source. These criteria depend on the retailer's type of store and merchandise sold. Generally, the following criteria, which may vary across merchandise lines, should always be considered: selling history, consumers' perception of the manufacturer's or wholesaler's reputation, reliability of delivery, trade terms, projected markup, quality of merchandise, after-sales service (such as helping manage the retailer's replenishment system or perform annual shelf-space reviews), transportation time, distribution-center processing time, inventory carrying cost, country of origin, fashionability, and net cost.

The retail buyer also has to consider the size of the vendor. Is the vendor large enough to provide product to all of the retailer's stores? If so, is it big enough to replenish the items so they stay in stock without having too much inventory on hand? Is the vendor big enough to staff any support functions for the retailer? Pepsi and Coke can both send field employees into retail stores to restock and rotate soda products. A unique, local mom-and-pop beverage manufacturer probably couldn't do that. Further, if the retailer decided to drop the item to pursue a different strategy, is the vendor big enough that dropping the item won't hurt the vendor? For example, in 2005, nearly 12 percent of General Mills net sales were to Walmart. In 2007, as a result of Walmart's growth in supercenters, this concentration had increased to 20 percent of global sales (or 27 percent of U.S. sales), and no other retailer accounts for even 10 percent or more of the manufacturer's sales. This situation is similar for Dial Corporation, Unilever, Procter & Gamble, Energizer, Kellogg, Gillette, and Kraft Foods. In fact, for some divisions of these large manufacturers, Walmart now accounts for more than a third of their business. Thus, there is truth to the story that "when Walmart sneezes, the manufacturers get pneumonia."[20] However, since these large vendors supply hundreds of items to Walmart and other retailers, if one item is discontinued by a large retailer, these manufacturers are not going to suffer major damage. However, if a larger-scale retailer started doing business with a small, entrepreneurial manufacturer who had

Global Retailing

Would You Like That ($50 Video Game) in Paper or Plastic?

There is currently a big push toward "sustainable packaging" as part of green-marketing campaigns by many retailers, and these campaigns are affecting both retailers and manufacturers around the globe. For example, Unilever worked with Walmart in the summer of 2008 to launch "sustainability kitchens" in Asda stores across the United Kingdom. Some people, though, are asking if retailers are going too far in their march to decrease the global footprint of packaging activities. On the Walmart blog (http://checkoutblog.com), the buyer for video games recently discussed switching to cardboard packaging for video games. He proposed that making the switch would save the equivalent in greenhouse gas emissions of 4,000 cars. Within one month, there were 50 comments posted to the blog. Most said they didn't want Walmart to switch to cardboard boxes for video games. Customers said the cardboard boxes are ugly (pointing out the problems with VHS cardboard cases), don't ship well (get broken), or protect their $50 investment, and they like to display the games—meaning they'd just have to go buy an empty case and throw away the cardboard (so greenhouse gases would actually go up).

Several of the other buyers on the blog talk about other ways for retailing and manufacturing to be globally greener.

For each suggestion, there is a laundry list provided in the comments about the incremental problems the changes would create. For example, one corporate executive suggested that Walmart might require all dairy milk providers to use cows that are not treated with rbST (an artificial growth hormone that makes cows produce more milk). The blogger listed several benefits to customers. However, the 250-plus comments all talked about how if the cows produce less milk, then (1) dairy farmers get less money per year (and they're already struggling) and (2) more cows have to produce milk to keep production up. Using more cows means more CO_2 emissions from the cows and more crop land needed to feed the additional cows—translating into higher prices on wheat and corn in a time when wheat crops are being globally destroyed by diseases. What looks like a simple global improvement can have a lot of unanticipated effects. What do you think—would you want your $50 video game in paper or plastic?

Source: Unilever's 2008 Annual Report; "Wal-Mart Tastemakers Write Unfiltered Blog," *New York Times*, March 3, 2008: C1, C3; and Walmart's blog http://www.checkoutregister.com, March 31, 2009.

---

a single blockbuster product, what would happen if the retailer needed to discontinue it? Would the vendor go out of business? Would the retailer be accused by the manufacturer, the media, or customers of *putting* the vendor out of business? Such an occurrence is covered in the chapter's "Global Retailing" box.

Country of origin is also becoming a more important issue every day as governments use trade agreements to limit the amount of merchandise that can be imported from various countries. In addition, consumers are becoming aware of sweatshops and the use of child labor in certain countries, and they are rebelling against the buying of products manufactured in these areas. While laws regulating country of origin have long applied to apparel, one of the many initiatives found in the Farm Security and Rural Investment Act requires country-of-origin labeling for beef, lamb, pork, fish, perishable agricultural commodities, and peanuts. This is increasingly important for buyers to consider given there were recently several situations in which dozens of manufacturers in China used melamine, a plastic derivative, in baby formula, chocolate, and pet food to make the products look like they had more protein in them. Many toys were also recalled over the last few years because several China-based manufacturers used lead paint beyond that permitted by law. (The lead-based paint is shinier and requires less primer.) The public outrage over the children and pets that became sick or died has resulted in a renewed and stronger call for labeling where products are made and testing what is in them.

Although consumers say they want to know where their food comes from and what is in it, most are unaware of the costs associated with tracking and testing these products, the amount of record keeping needed, and loss of sales resulting from the higher prices. The Grocery Manufacturers of America claim such laws are unworkable and will do little to maintain the safety and purity of the U.S. food supply. Is the cost worth it? Are you willing to pay the extra nickel or dime on every product to know where your food, clothing, and purchases of electronics were made? And how do such laws apply to retailers in the resale markets? For example, the U.S. federal government recently passed a law that took effect in February 2009 in which all products for children younger than 12 (regardless of when they were made) have to be tested for lead and certain other chemicals.[21] This means thrift stores, consignment shops, and online auctions and resellers (like eBay or Amazon) are going to encounter a lot of difficulty or need to shut down a big part of their business. However, some local manufacturers have used the situation to help their locally produced products. For example, they'll have "Made in the USA" stickers on them when selling in the United States.

Even something as seemingly minor as the number of units in a pack can also be a significant factor in choosing a vendor. Walmart, for example, once asked a vendor to ship some school supplies in packs of 10 instead of 80. Working with vendors in this way allowed the retail chain to increase inventories by only 4 percent while increasing sales by more than 12 percent. The $1.4 billion saved by such vendor negotiations was made available for other uses.[22] In 2006, Walmart went a step further and changed the way store employees ordered merchandise. It pruned the assortment of merchandise available in stores to emphasize the items that sell best in each category. Thus, many consumers were surprised that some of their favorite products were no longer carried in the new streamlined Walmart. The retailer's reasoning was that focused, "uncluttered" stores will produce more sales than those laden with merchandise. The resulting drop in inventory costs bolstered the retailer's margins. Walmart's decision has had a ripple effect across the industry.

Taking the assortment reduction a step further, several retailers are rediscovering smaller stores.[23] For example, Tesco has recently started putting in very small "Fresh & Easy" stores in the United States. Interestingly, Walmart, in response, is trying to compete with Tesco through its new Marketside stores (about 15,000 square feet), which are half the size of the existing, small Neighborhood Market stores. These smaller stores have considerably less selling space than a 208,000-square-foot Supercenter store. (In addition, these stores don't have any reference to Walmart in them as the giant retailer tries to position these units as a friendly neighborhood grocer.) With a lot less space, these retailers have to decide which few items from their long list of available items they will sell.

Like everything else, tailoring merchandise assortments to each individual store involves a trade-off that the retailer must consider. By creating a "store of the community," the retailer may successfully meet most local needs, but this tailoring of merchandise may increase the frustrations of tourists or other "outshoppers." For example, when customers visit a McDonald's, Kohl's, or Target store in any part of the country, often they expect to have the same products across the chain. Further, at some point, the scale advantage (of buying for hundreds or thousands of stores) could disappear as each store assortment is customized. Part of the lower costs that large-scale retailers enjoy is due to their large purchases of each item.

Likewise, in cases where a manufacturer offers to co-op some expenses—for example, advertising or display support—the amount of price reduction has been shown to have a significant effect on the purchase decision.[24] Some retailers also check to see whether the same merchandise will be made available to a nearby competitor; in such cases, it may be advantageous for the retailer to use a private label. Another advantage to the private label is that some manufacturers will not sell

vendor profitability analysis statement
Is a tool used to evaluate vendors and shows all purchases made the prior year, the discount granted, the transportation charges paid, the original markup, markdowns, and finally the season-ending gross margin on that vendor's merchandise.

confidential vendor analysis
Is identical to the vendor profitability analysis but also provides a three-year financial summary as well as the names, titles, and negotiating points of all the vendor's sales staff.

a product to certain retailers. For example, some discounters which try to offer lower prices by carrying only the "hottest" toys, claim that some vendors will not sell them the hot toys for fear of losing business to smaller chains and independents that sell toys year-round and not just at Christmas.

Recent research concludes that the use of private-label brands (1) increases as the perceived consequences of making a buying mistake decrease, (2) increases when the different brands in the category are perceived to have a wide variance in quality, and (3) decreases if the category benefits are deemed to require actual trial and experience rather than being accessible through a search of package label information.[25]

One of a retailer's greatest assets when dealing with a vendor is the retailer's past experiences with that vendor. Whether you are a small retailer doing all the buying yourself or a new buyer for a large chain, you should always approach vendors with two important pieces of information: the vendor-profitability analysis statement and the confidential vendor analysis. The **vendor-profitability analysis statement** (see Exhibit 9.5) provides a record of all the purchases you made last year, the discount granted you by the vendor, transportation charges paid, the original markup, markdowns, and the season-ending gross margin on that vendor's merchandise.

The **confidential vendor analysis** (see Exhibit 9.6) lists the same information as the profitability analysis statement but also provides a three-year financial summary as well as the names, titles, and negotiating points of the entire vendor's sales staff. This last piece of information is based on notes taken by the buyer during and after buying trips in previous seasons.

Based on the information obtained in the previous two reports, some retailers classify vendors into different categories (called class A, B, C, D, or E vendors) using both performance and brand-positioning information and the retailer's

Exhibit 9.5
Vendor-Profitability Analysis

Vendor Name	Purchases		Discount and Anticipation (%)	Freight (%)	Markup % Landed Loaded	Markdown		Gross Margin Percentage	Vendor No.
	Cost	Retail				$	%		
Anderson Sports	62,481	129,861	7.1	1.4	50.7	20,211	15.6	46.2	273359
Jack Frost, Inc.	26,921	53,962	8.0	1.3	49.4	3,233	6.0	50.5	818922
Sue's Fashions	25,572	51,930	8.1	1.8	49.9	6,667	12.8	47.1	206284
Jana Kantor Asso.	14,022	29,434	8.0	0.8	52.0	481	1.6	55.1	050187
Pierce Mills	12,761	25,438	9.5	1.7	49.8	7,858	30.9	33.1	132886
Ray, Inc.	2,196	4,416	8.0	1.8	49.4	754	17.1	43.8	148296
Dusty's Place	2,071	4,332	8.0	1.3	51.6			55.4	662411
Lady Carole	1,050	2,100	8.0	2.1	48.9			52.9	676841
Jill Petites	740	1,584	10.4	0.5	54.2	640	40.5	29.2	472977
Andrea's	198	410	8.0	0.8	51.1			55.0	527218

Cost: your cost
Retail: your original selling price
Discount and anticipation %: discount received for early payments
Freight %: your shipping expenses
Markup % Landed Loaded: [Retail selling price − (Cost + Freight)]/Retail selling price
Markdown: Amount original selling price is reduced
Gross Margin %: [Actual selling price − (Cost + Freight − Discount and Anticipation)]/Actual selling price

Trip Dates <u>Fall Market</u> **City** <u>Dallas</u> **Buyer's Name** <u>Cooper</u> **Dept. Name** <u>Women's Wear</u> **Dept. No.** <u>491</u>

Vendor/Address Phone No./Floor No.		Volume History 200X 200X 200X			Markup History 200X 200X 200X			Markdown History 200X 200X 200X			Vendor Executives & Titles	Remarks
West Texas Blouse	Spring	590.5	719.4	330.8	47.5	47.7	46.7	2.4	5.3	4.4	Larry Wilcox (VP)	Cash Discount
	Fall	1002.8	706.7		47.3	47.5		3.4	7.8		Julie Davin	Prone to co-op
	Year	1593.3	1426.1		47.4			3.1			Ted Rombach	ads
	Objectives:											
	Results As of 5/22:											
Flatland Fashions	Spring	224.5	230.2	210.8	47.7	50.0	47.2	6.5	8.5	3.8	Joe Hall (P)	
	Fall	175.8	230.5		47.3	47.6		17.0	9.0		Richard Reel	Will deal on
	Year	400.3	460.7		47.5	48.8		11.1	8.7			transportation
	Objectives:											
	Results As of 5/22:											
Southern	Spring	-0-	42.3	50.7		48.4	45.4	-0-	9.1	4.2	Jackie Poteet (SM)	
	Fall	37.0	69.2		47.1	42.3		7.7	7.8		Boonie Hanley	"Quantity"
	Year	37.0	112.5		47.1	44.7		7.7	8.2		Carol Little	
	Objectives:											
	Results As of 5/22:											
Gallo	Spring	21.7	195.0	55.6	46.9	50.0	48.3	1.3	0.2	1.2	Ruth Wilson (P)	
	Fall	-0-	13.9		-0-	46.7		-0-	2.0		John Murphy	Easier of the
	Year	21.7	33.4		46.9	48.6		1.3	0.9			two
	Objectives:											
	Results As of 5/22:											

Exhibit 9.6
Confidential Vendor Analysis

opinion on the vendor's other attributes. Regarding performance and positioning, if the supplier can produce very profitable items but doesn't have a brand the retailer needs, then the supplier could make private-label products for the retailer. If the supplier has an important brand but not the best prices, then it can still fill an important niche. When the supplier doesn't carry a needed national product *and* it doesn't have the best prices, the supplier is not very valuable unless it can provide information, trends, or something else that the retailer needs.

Currently, there is a big focus in many retailers on after-purchase service. In thinking about the service relationship, retail buyers usually think about both the vendor company and the vendor representatives. Retailers often have a certain level of trust toward the selling organization (S trust) and a separate level of trust toward the supplier's sales representative (SR trust). Retailers depend on the supplier to make and ship products. They depend on representatives to keep their promises, inform the retailers about the latest sales trends and what they see going on in competitors' stores (when walking through the stores, not divulging trade secrets), and occasionally help them manage the inventory and sales numbers.

Sometimes a retail buyer might trust a supplier but not the supplier's current representative (or vice versa). While working with several retailers, one of the authors has noted that in situations of high-supplier, low-representative trust, the retail buyer works with the supplier in using retail production-ordering systems (like Walmart's CPFR—see Chapter 4) to produce inventory just in time for the retailer. In some circumstances, retailers might let very trusted suppliers write themselves purchase orders in comanaged systems without ever needing a signature from the retailer.

In situations of lower-supplier, high-representative trust, a retail buyer seeks the sales rep's input, but either doesn't trust the supplier to comanage the retailer's inventory systems, or believes the supplier has a different business philosophy from the retailer (such as "we win, you lose"). In situations of high-supplier, high-representative trust, a retailer's buyers and manufacturer's sales reps may sit down and discuss how to create a new product related to an upcoming movie's release or special event, including what the shape of the product should look like, the wording (if any) on the product, the packaging, the advertising, and so on. However, when the retailer doesn't trust either the supplier or the supplier's representative, it is likely to engage in a "transaction" relationship. Here the retailer works with the supplier only because it is either unable to get a needed product from any other source or the supplier simply provides a price advantage that cannot be ignored.

LO 6 · Vendor Negotiations

What is involved in the vendor–buyer negotiation process and what terms of the contract can be negotiated?

Even buyers who choose not go to market and instead have their vendors come to them, evaluate their vendors. For years, many grocers felt that firms like Procter & Gamble treated retailers poorly. These grocers needed the many products that P&G manufactured, but they did not appreciate P&G's "We win, you lose" attitude, which forced retailers to purchase the complete line of P&G products in order to earn merchandising money. Over the last half-decade, however, P&G has developed a program in which it helps all its customers formalize their merchandising plans for the coming months and no longer requires grocers to purchase slow-moving products. This new attitude of "Let's both win" has seen many supermarket managers reclassify P&G as more of a collaboration relationship. With some retailers, P&G is even working together to design new products and advertising copy, building a co-creation relationship. P&G has obviously determined that it can only be as successful as its retailers let it be. Philips Electronics and many of its retailers are beginning to do similar activities.[26]

After selecting the vendors, the retailer still must make decisions on the specific merchandise to be bought. Some products, such as the basic items for a particular department, are easy to purchase; others, especially new items, require more careful planning and consideration. Retailers should concern themselves with several key questions prior to selecting a product for purchase:

1. Where does this product fit into the strategic position that I have staked out for my department?
2. Will I have an exclusive with this product, or will I be in competition with nearby retailers?
3. What is the estimated demand for this product in my target market?
4. What is my anticipated gross margin for this product?
5. Will I be able to obtain reliable, speedy stock replacement?
6. Can this product stand on its own or is it merely a "me-too" item?
7. What is my expected turnover rate with this product?
8. Does this product complement the rest of my inventory?

The climax of a successful buying plan is active **negotiation**, which involves finding mutually satisfying solutions for parties with conflicting objectives. The effectiveness of this buyer–vendor relationship depends on the negotiation skills of both parties and the economic power of the firms involved.

negotiation
Is the process of finding mutually satisfying solutions when the retail buyer and vendor have conflicting objectives.

The retail buyer must negotiate price, delivery dates, discounts, shipping terms, and return privileges. All of these factors are significant because they affect both firms' profitability and cash flow.

In recent years, both manufacturers and retailers have become increasingly aware of the cost of carrying excess inventory. Likewise, both parties have become more concerned with the time value of money and the resulting effect on each firm's cash flow. Since both parties involved in the negotiation process are aware of these costs and are trying to shift them to the other party, most negotiations produce some conflict. However, a successful negotiation is usually accomplished when both parties realize that the other should serve as its partner during the upcoming merchandising season. Both the buyer and the vendor are seeking to satisfy the retailer's customers better than the competition. Therefore, buyers and vendors must resolve their conflicts and differences of opinion, remembering that negotiation is a two-way street and that a long-term profitable relationship is the goal. After all, the vendor wants to develop a long-term relationship with the retailer as much as the retailer does with its customers.

What can be negotiated? There are many aspects to the terms of a sale (prices, freight, delivery dates, method of shipment and shipping costs, exclusivity, guaranteed sales, markdown money, promotional allowances, return privileges, and discounts), and life is simplest when there are no surprises. Therefore, the smart buyer leaves nothing to chance and discusses everything with the vendor prior to signing the purchase orders. The buyer and seller must together work out future plans using the buyer's merchandise budget and planned turnover. Therefore, the buyer and seller should seek to make negotiations a win–win situation or collaboration in which neither side feels like a loser. The essence of negotiation is to trade what is cheap to you but valuable to the other party for what is valuable to you but cheap to the other party.

The smart buyer puts all the upcoming areas of negotiations and previous agreements in letter form and distributes it before going to market. This helps to eliminate any misunderstandings afterward. Price, of course, is probably the first factor to be negotiated, but it is always smart to begin negotiating on factors where agreement can be reached the most easily. Negotiations that tend to focus too much on the "difficult" terms early tend to become more problematic and leave each party feeling as though it's in a battle rather than a partnership. Consequently, the new buyer would be smart to remember the old adage "First you get along, then you go along" when entering into negotiations.

As price is often a hot topic on many buyer's minds, they should attempt to purchase the desired merchandise at the lowest possible net cost, yet not expect unreasonable discounts or price concessions. Buyers must be familiar with the prices and discounts allowed by each vendor. This is why past records are so important. However, the buyer must remember that his or her bargaining power is a result of his or her planned purchases from the vendor. As a result, a large retailer may be able to purchase goods from a vendor at lower prices than a small mom-and-pop retailer. Five different types of discounts can be negotiated: trade, quantity, promotional, seasonal, and cash.

Trade Discount

trade discount

Is also referred to as a **functional discount** and is a form of compensation that the buyer may receive for performing certain wholesaling or retailing services for the manufacturer.

A **trade discount**, sometimes referred to as a **functional discount**, is a form of compensation that the buyer may receive for performing certain wholesaling or retailing services for the manufacturer. Because this discount is given for the performance of some service, the size of the discount will vary with the type of service performed. Thus, variations in trade discounts are legally justifiable on the basis of the different costs associated with doing business with various buyers.

Trade discounts are often expressed in a chain, or series, such as "list less 40-20-10." Each figure in the chain of discounts represents a percentage reduction from the list price of an item. Assume that the list price of an item is $1,000 and that the chain of discounts is 40-20-10. The buyer who receives all these discounts would actually pay $432 for this item. The computations would look like this:

List price	$1,000
Less 40%	− 400
	600
Less 20%	− 120
	480
Less 10%	− 48
Purchase price	$ 432

To see how the various chains of discount permit a vendor to compensate the members of the supply chain for their marketing activities, let's look at the preceding example. Assume that the manufacturer sells through a supply chain that includes manufacturer's agents, service wholesalers, and small retailers. The purchase price of $432 is accorded to the manufacturer's agent, who negotiates a sale between the manufacturer and the service wholesaler. The manufacturers' agent then charges the service wholesaler $480 for the item, thus realizing $48 for rendering a number of marketing activities. The service wholesaler, in turn, charges a retailer $600 for the item, thus making $120. The retailer then sells the item at the suggested list price of $1,000, thus making $400 in gross margin to cover expenses and make profit.

Trade discounts are legal where they correctly reflect the costs of the intermediaries' services. Sometimes, large retailers want to buy directly from the manufacturer and pay only $432 instead of $600. This action would enable the large retailer to undercut the competition and is illegal, unless one of the three defenses of the Robinson-Patman Act explained in Chapter 6 can be applied.

Quantity Discount

A **quantity discount** is a price reduction offered as an inducement to purchase large quantities of merchandise. Three types of quantity discounts are available:

1. A **noncumulative-quantity discount** is a discount based on a single purchase.
2. A **cumulative-quantity discount** is based on total amount purchased over a period of time.
3. **Free merchandise** is a discount whereby merchandise is offered in lieu of price concessions.

Noncumulative-quantity discounts can be legally justified by the manufacturer if costs are reduced because of the quantity involved or if the manufacturer is meeting a competitor's price in good faith. Cumulative discounts are more difficult to justify since many small orders may be involved, thereby reducing the manufacturer's savings.

For an example of how a quantity discount works, consider the following schedule:

Order Quantity	Discount from List Price (%)
1 to 999	0
1,000 to 9,999	5
10,000 to 24,999	8
25,000 to 49,999	10

If a retailer that had already purchased 500 units wanted another 800 units, it would have to pay list price if the vendor uses a noncumulative policy. However, the retailer would receive a 5-percent discount on all purchases if the vendor uses a cumulative pricing policy.

Quantity discounts might not always be in the seller's best interest and should always be viewed by the buyer as an invitation for further negotiations. Consider the following price schedule published by a computer manufacturer:[27]

Quantity	Unit Price ($)
1–19	795
20–49	749
50–149	699
150–249	659

Let's say that you, a buyer for a retail chain, want 19 of these computers, and your cost is $15,105 (19 × $795). But 20 would cost only $14,980 (20 × $749). What do you do?

You actually have four choices:

1. Tell the manufacturer to ship 20 computers for $14,980 and you keep the extra one.
2. Tell the manufacturer to ship you 19 computers at $14,980 and have it keep the other one.
3. Order 20 but tell the manufacturer to ship you only 19 and to credit you for the other computer at $749.
4. Negotiate a purchase price.

quantity discount
Is a price reduction offered as an inducement to purchase large quantities of merchandise.

noncumulative quantity discount
Is a discount based on a single purchase.

cumulative quantity discount
Is a discount based on the total amount purchased over a period of time.

free merchandise
Is a discount whereby merchandise is offered in lieu of price concessions.

This example is based on "Unauthorized Channels of Distribution: Gray Markets," by Roy Howell, et al, *Industrial Marketing Management* 15 (November 1986): 257-263. Used with permission of the authors.

Whenever quantity discounts are offered, buyers should always check to see if the total purchase price may be lower if they order more.

Many times, retailers can make a quick profit from utilizing quantity discounts by selling the extra merchandise to a diverter to sell in a gray market. The diverter, who is not an authorized member of the marketing supply chain but still functions as an intermediary, will be able to purchase these goods cheaper from the retailer than it can from the manufacturer and will then sell this excess merchandise to other retailers. Also, such discounts allow the manufacturer to have its products sold in discount stores without offending all of its authorized retailers. However, many authorized retailers are upset when diverters provide discounters with such merchandise. Some department stores have dropped cosmetic lines when discounters, most of whose cosmetics are diverted, started to carry the lines. Costco acknowledges that it will try to buy directly from manufacturers, but in instances where the manufacturers refuse, Costco will make a legal purchase through a third party. Little wonder that Costco has a vice president of "diverting" who purchases more than $200 million worth of merchandise from unauthorized vendors.[28]

Consider the previous retailer who needed only 19 computers and purchased 20. Here the retailer sold the extra computer to a diverter for $600. As a result, the retailer was better off by $725 (the $125 difference in price between ordering 20 versus 19 units plus the $600 from the diverter) than it would have been had it bought only 19 computers at $795 each. The diverter could now profit by selling the computer to another retailer for something more than $600.

Today, diverters are important members of the retailer's supply chain, especially in the grocery and computer fields. However, despite the problems discussed in Chapter 5 that some manufacturers have with diverters, not all manufacturers or retailers feel the same way about them. In fact, some manufacturers develop their pricing policies to enable diverters to function economically. By doing this, they can increase sales by reaching markets they can't enter under normal operating conditions.

Promotional Discount

promotional discount
Is a discount provided for the retailer performing an advertising or promotional service for the manufacturer.

A third type of discount is a **promotional discount**, which is given when the retailer performs an advertising or promotional service for the manufacturer. For example, a vendor might offer a retailer 50 extra jeans if (1) the retailer purchases 1,250 jeans during the season and (2) runs two newspaper advertisements featuring the jeans during the season. One of the main reasons manufacturers offer such discounts is that the rates newspapers charge local retailers are often lower than the rates charged to national manufacturers. These discounts are legal as long as they are available to all competing retailers on an equal basis.

Seasonal Discount

seasonal discount
Is a discount provided to retailers if they purchase and take delivery of merchandise in the off season.

Retailers can earn a **seasonal discount** if they purchase and take delivery of the merchandise in the off-season (e.g., buying swimwear in October). However, this does not mean that all seasonal discounts result in the purchase of merchandise out of season. Retailers in resort areas often take advantage of these discounts since swimwear is never out of season for them. As long as the same terms are available to all competing retailers, seasonal discounts are legal.

Cash Discount

cash discount
Is a discount offered to the retailer for the prompt payment of bills.

The final discount available to the buyer is a **cash discount** for prompt payment of bills. Cash discounts are usually stated as 2/10, net 30, which means that a 2-percent discount is given if payment is received within 10 days of the invoice date and the net amount is due within 30 days.

Although the cash discount is a common method for encouraging early payment, it can also be used as a negotiating tool by delaying the payment due date. This future-dating negotiation may take many forms. The following are several of the most common:

1. **End-of-month (EOM) dating** allows for a cash discount and the full payment period to begin on the first day of the following month instead of on the invoice date. End-of-month invoices dated after the 25th of the month are considered to be dated on the first of the following month.

2. **Middle-of-month (MOM) dating** is similar to EOM except the middle of the month is used as the starting date.

3. **Receipt of goods (ROG) dating** allows the starting date to be the date goods are received by the retailer.

4. Extra (EX) dating merely allows the retailer extra or free days before the period of payment begins.

5. A final discount form to be considered, but which is not widely used today, is anticipation. **Anticipation** allows a retailer to pay the invoice in advance of the expiration of the cash discount period and earn an extra discount. However, anticipation is usually figured at an annual rate of 7.0 percent, which is near the current cost of money.

Many vendors have eliminated the cash discount because retailers, especially department stores, have been taking 60 to 120 days to pay and still deduct the cash discount. In fact, many vendors require new accounts to pay up front until credit is established.

Delivery Terms

Delivery terms are another factor to be considered in negotiations. They are important because they specify where title to the merchandise passes to the retailer, whether the vendor or buyer will pay the freight charges, and who is obligated to file damage claims. Retailers will often be quoted a different cost or price from a vendor if the *free on board* (FOB) is the vendor's factory versus the retailer's factory versus the retailer's stores. Both the location of title transfer and who pays transportation can be negotiated together or separately. The three most common shipping terms are

1. **Free on board factory**. The buyer assumes title at the factory and pays all transportation costs from the vendor's factory.

2. **Free on board shipping point**. The vendor pays the transportation to a local shipping point, but the buyer assumes title at this point and pays all further transportation costs.

3. **Free on board destination**. The vendor pays all transportation costs, and the buyer takes title on delivery.

For consignment (pay-from-scan) merchandise, the FOB is at the retailer's cash register. Consignment is not usually discussed as an FOB point because there is no specified time of transfer (it could be purchased by a customer one day after arriving in the store or several months after sitting on the self). The other FOB points usually have explicit dates or windows of time printed on each purchase order. While delivery terms (including consignment) may not appear to be a big deal at

end-of-month (EOM) dating
Allows the retailer to take a cash discount and the full payment period to begin on the first day of the following month instead of on the invoice date.

middle-of-month (MOM) dating
Allows the retailer to take a cash discount and the full payment period to begin on the middle of the month.

receipt of goods (ROG) dating
Allows the retailer to take a cash discount and the full payment period to begin when the goods are received by the retailer.

anticipation
Allows the retailer to pay the invoice in advance of the end of the cash discount period and earn an extra discount.

free on board (FOB) factory
Is a method of charging for transportation where the buyer assumes title to the goods at the factory and pays all transportation costs from the vendor's factory.

free on board (FOB) shipping point
Is a method of charging for transportation in which the vendor pays for transportation to a local shipping point where the buyer assumes title and then pays all further transportation costs.

free on board (FOB) destination
Is a method of charging for transportation in which the vendor pays for all transportation costs and the buyer takes title on delivery.

times, the author saw 10-percent to 20-percent differences on vendors' price quotes to a major mass merchandise retailer across products in home furnishing, apparel, and household products. Most retailers don't take advantage of price differences in logistics because the buyers normally don't get rewarded for it on their annual performance evaluation (e.g., a buyer would be better off with a vendor warehouse FOB that has a higher gross margin but lower net margin than selecting a store FOB with a lower gross margin but a higher net margin).

Packaging

While not a discount, packaging is becoming a hot negotiation point, especially with many retailers asking for more PDQs (cardboard display boxes that often have to be painted by manufacturers to match store marketing guides) and for more sustainable (i.e., environmentally friendly) packaging materials. Whether the product is shrink wrapped or in a clam shell, a blister pack, or a solid paperboard box, each packaging display method changes the cost and is usually negotiated as part of the price.

LO 7

In-Store Merchandise Handling

What are the various methods of handling the merchandise once it is received in the store to control shrinkage, including vendor collusion, and theft?

The retailer must have some means of handling incoming merchandise. For some types of retailers (e.g., a grocery store), this need will be significant and frequent; for others (e.g., a jeweler), it will be relatively minor and infrequent. Frequent and large deliveries entail considerable planning of merchandise receiving and handling space. For instance, consider that a full-line grocery store must have receiving docks to which 40- to 60-foot semitrailers can be backed up. Similarly, space may be needed for a small forklift to drive between the truck and the merchandise receiving area to unload the merchandise. Subsequently, the merchandise will need to be moved from the receiving area, where it will be counted and marked, to a storage area, either on the selling floor or in a separate location.

The point at which incoming merchandise is received can be a high-theft location. The retail manager needs to design the receiving and handling area to minimize this problem. Some thefts involve the retail employees themselves; others involve outsiders. In 2007, the National Retail Security Survey found that the average shrinkage rate for the nation's largest retailers was 1.4 percent of their annual sales; the lowest percent in the 17-year history of the survey. This translates into an industry-wide net loss of $34.3 billion.[29] The survey claims that the decrease in shrinkage is due to retailer investment in deterrence technology. (**Shrinkage**, which is calculated "at retail," is the loss of merchandise due to theft, loss, damage, or bookkeeping errors.) One growing problem area appears to be in organized crime. In response, many retailers have formed their own special organized-crime-prevention units. Therefore, several types of shrinkage caused by theft will be mentioned in the following discussion. Most discussions of shrinkage attribute theft to one of three culprits—vendors, employees, and customers.

shrinkage
Represents merchandise that cannot be accounted for due to theft, loss, or damage.

Vendor collusion includes the types of losses that occur when merchandise is delivered. Typical losses involve the delivery of less merchandise than is charged for, removal of good merchandise disguised as old or stale merchandise, and the theft of other merchandise from the stockroom or off the selling floor while making delivery. This type of loss often involves both the delivery person and the retail employee who signs for delivery and the two splitting the profit from the collusive activity.

vendor collusion
Occurs when an employee of one of the retailer's vendors steals merchandise as it is delivered to the retailer.

Employee theft occurs when employees steal merchandise where they work. Although no one knows for sure how much is stolen annually from retailers (since all shrinkage statistics are based only on apprehensions), as many as 30 percent of American workers admit to stealing from their employers, even if they take only small items like a pen or pencil. Although some of the stolen goods come from the selling floor, a larger percentage is taken from the stockroom to the employee lounge and lockers, where it is kept until the employees leave with it at quitting time. Employee theft, which amounts to more than $800 per apprehension, is most prevalent in food stores, department stores, and discount stores. Considering that these types of stores are usually larger in size, sales volume, and number of employees, the lack of close supervision probably contributes to this problem. Exhibit 9.7 shows 50 ways that an employee can steal from a bar.

Customer theft is also a problem. In fact, more than a dozen shoppers are caught for every case of employee theft, although the average amount of merchandise recovered is less than $50. Stealing merchandise from the stockroom and receiving area may be easier than taking it from the selling floor for several reasons. First, much of the stockroom merchandise is not ticketed, so it is easier to get it through electronic antishoplifting devices. Second, once the thief enters the stock area, there is very little antitheft security. Most security guards watch the exits and fitting rooms (and even grandmothers stuffing clothing into a stroller do get caught—as witnessed by one of the authors). Third, there is usually an exit in the immediate area of the stockroom through which the thief can carry out the stolen goods. Some retailers have wired these exits to set off an alarm when opened without a key, helping to reduce thefts somewhat. Another innovative retailer, after determining that employees were hiding merchandise in the compressed and discarded boxes that were left out as trash, started using a special spiked baler that punched holes in boxes to damage any stolen merchandise.

The retailer must be aware that there are numerous opportunities for receiving, handling, and storage thefts. Therefore, steps should be taken to reduce these crimes. The retailer cannot watch the employees every minute to see whether or not they are honest, but some surveillance is helpful. However, the retailer must consider the employees' and customers' rights to privacy versus the retailer's right to security. Legislation is currently being considered by several states that would, if approved, allow the use of electronic monitoring by video and audio systems only when advance notice is given. In effect, workers and shoppers must be informed when they are being monitored. They also have to decide which theft is worth prosecuting. Walmart just revised its rules to allow prosecution of 16-year-olds (it was 18 or older before) and call police regardless of the child's age or theft amount if the store cannot reach the child's parent within 30 minutes or the parent doesn't show within 60 minutes after contact.[30] For example, a man in Florida was charged with shoplifting (valued at $2) and trespassing when an off-duty sheriff's deputy confronted him over 10 raspberry jellybeans he had sampled in the candy area.[31] The man said he just wanted to try them to see if he wanted to buy them. This customer had been shopping at the grocery for 30 years, and assuming he has another 20 or so years of shopping, the store probably lost his customer lifetime value over the $2 shoplifting and trespassing charge. Further, it probably got a lot of other people mad who read about it in the local papers. Retailers obviously have a right and a need to protect their investments. Sometimes, though, they need to think about the reasonableness of it—and the total impact on future sales.

The amount of storage space the retailer needs is related to the physical dimensions of the merchandise and the safety stock level needed to maintain the desired rate of stock turnover. For example, furniture is bulky and requires

employee theft
Occurs when employees of the retailer steal merchandise where they work.

customer theft
Is also known as shoplifting and occurs when customers or individuals disguised as customers steal merchandise from the retailer's store.

IT IS A DUMB BARTENDER WHO CAN'T BUY OUT THE BOSS IN 6 MONTHS.

1. The "Phantom Register" trick: Set up an extra register in bar for use only during busy times. The income from this register is not totaled on master tape and funds are skimmed by the bartender.
2. Serve and collect while register is being read between shift changes.
3. Claim a phony walkout and keep money received from customer.
4. Pick up customer's cash when he or she isn't paying attention.
5. Fake a robbery of the night deposit on way to bank. It is difficult for owners to prove this fake occurred.
6. Add phantom drinks to a customer's "running tab."
7. The "Phantom Bottle" ploy: Bring your own bottle of liquor onto shift and pocket cash from its sale.
8. The "Short Pour" trick: Just pour less than shot to cover "giveaway" liquor costs.
9. Don't ring up any sale and keep the cash.
10. The "Short-ring" trick: Under-ring the correct price of item and pocket the difference.
11. The "Free-Giveaway" trick: Give drinks to friends in anticipation of larger tips.
12. Mislead the owner regarding the number of draft beers that can be poured from a keg.
13. Undercharge for drinks with the anticipation of a larger tip.
14. Reuse register drink receipts.
15. Trade drinks to the cook for meals.
16. Add water to liquor bottle to maintain inventory.
17. Substitute lower-priced liquor when asked for call brands.
18. Collude with the delivery person, sell "stolen" products that he or she provides, and split the profit.
19. Ask for kickbacks from liquor distributor.
20. Dispense and register one shot on computerized dispenser system, while short-shotting the liquor into two glasses.
21. Short-change a customer when he or she is a "little under the weather" and claim it was an "honest" mistake if caught.
22. Claim a returned drink: Extra drink produced and can be sold by bartender.
23. Count missing bottles as "to go sale" when bar is selling both liquor to go and by the drink.
24. The "Owner Is a Jerk" ploy: You, the bartender, are the only person in charge of liquor pickup, check-in, and stocking.
25. Maids sell complimentary cocktail or wine coupons from hotel room to bar personnel, which you can place in register for cash.
26. Add two different customer drinks together and charge both customers, claiming misunderstanding in who was purchasing the round.
27. Ring food items on liquor key to cover high liquor cost percent.
28. Sell "after-shift drinks" to customers, not having them consumed by other employees.
29. Pour not enough liquor into blended fruit drinks to cover other shortages.
30. Have customer sign credit card voucher in advance and then overcharge the ticket.
31. Claim opening bank was short.
32. Total out register in midshift. Start new tape. You keep both new tapes and cash.
33. Incorrect "overring" or "void" of register.
34. Make sales during tape changes.
35. Mistotal the amount on the credit card or change the amount after customer leaves.
36. Take money from the game machines or jukeboxes.
37. Accumulate the guest checks to ring up after customer leaves so as to change the amount or leave out items.
38. Run credit card through twice.
39. Sell empty kegs and returnable bottles to an off-premise retailer.
40. Place the tip jars next to cash register—easy to place cash in tip jar and ring "no sale" for register activity.
41. Falsify cumulative register readings and "losing" tape.
42. Add extra hours to your time card and split it with the shift manager.
43. Help the shift manager claim a fictitious employee on payroll.
44. Take home food or liquor or fake a burglary.
45. Take funds from vending machines.
46. Ring up sales at happy hour prices, but charge regular bar prices to the customer when he or she is keeping receipts.
47. Servers charge for happy hour hors d'oeuvres and bar snacks.
48. Hold back bank deposits for a couple days and invest or borrow money or just don't deposit money (or lesser amount) and keep difference.
49. Handwrite bar tabs and ring up lesser amounts on the register.
50. Wrap booze into garbage can for later retrieval.

Exhibit 9.7
50 Tricks for Bartenders

considerable storage space; grocery items turn over frequently, so more merchandise is usually needed than can be displayed on the shelves. This excess inventory causes retailers to stack boxes and cartons on the floor of the stockroom. In most cases, however, this scenario is inefficient and costly given that the retailer is probably paying employees anywhere from $5 to $15 per hour to keep the storeroom in order. Thus, in most cases, some type of mechanized equipment will be used to increase productivity. For instance, rather than simply hand carry incoming merchandise, employees might use one of the numerous types of carts made for this purpose. Also, instead of stacking the cartons and boxes directly on the floor of the stockroom where they must remain packed and risk being damaged, the merchandise can be unpacked, checked, inventoried, ticketed, and then placed on shelves or in bins until needed. By doing this, one can increase the amount of merchandise stored per square foot by decreasing the amount of packing material. A tidy, well-ordered stock area is less tempting to dishonest employees.

Although much theft results from in-store merchandise handling, retailers must also be aware of how theft in transit may influence their ability to have the appropriate amount of merchandise on hand. Therefore, retailers must not only plan to have the appropriate amount of merchandise on hand for customers but also ensure that the merchandise purchased for the store shelves actually arrives. Whether a retailer outsources its logistics or employs its own transportation force, ensuring that the merchandise makes it from the warehouse to the retail floor is critical for success.

So what can happen to merchandise in transit? Hijacking. A significant amount of shipment hijacking does occur in the United States, but the global playing field can be truly fraught with peril. Consider, for instance, the case of a truck carrying a load of consumer electronics bound for Paraguay. Deep in the heart of the Brazilian jungle, the driver sees that the road ahead is blocked. As he comes to a stop, the driver realizes that his truck is about to be hijacked. Luckily, he has brought an off-duty Brazilian police officer with him to help protect the shipment. The police officer exits the cab of the truck, and the driver immediately senses the feeling of familiarity between his security officer and one of the bandits. It seems that the bandit is also a police officer. After a brief discussion, the truck is allowed to move on with its shipment. This may sound like fiction but it is a true story. And even though the shipment was consumer electronics, other high-value products such as apparel, perfume, cigarettes, and alcohol are also subject to hijacking. Whether on land, sea, or air, hijacking is a relatively common occurrence in the retail supply chain.

The probability of theft in transit varies considerably from region to region. Although relatively few shipments are hijacked in Canada, the United States, and Western Europe, regions such as Eastern Europe, Latin America, Russia, and Southeast Asia are the most dangerous. Deteriorating economic conditions in these regions have increased organized-crime activity, resulting in increased theft of cargo. For many people in these regions, hijacking one shipment of consumer electronics can generate more cash than the average person in the area makes in a lifetime.

Although statistics related to the theft of cargo is difficult to obtain because few companies want to publicize their security problems, losses due to hijacking and the resulting disruption to retail operations are a major concern. However, losses due to hijacking are avoidable to a degree. Here are some tips that retailers and their supply-chain partners can employ to minimize the threat of hijacking.

1. Eliminate the retailer's name from the side of containers carrying the cargo. For a consumer electronics company such as Best Buy, putting its name on the truck signals to all that a shipment of consumer electronics is inside. It's tantamount to saying, "Steal me."

2. Install electronic monitoring devices on all shipment vehicles. Whether shipping via land, sea, or air, being able to track the container in which the merchandise is shipped can help determine its location when hijacked.

3. Carefully screen all internal transportation personnel as well as third-party logistics personnel in each global market. Given the nature of their jobs, these personnel are under loose supervision, and higher security standards are therefore critical.

4. Hire security personnel for each shipment. It is much easier for a single person to collude with others than for multiple people to conspire.

As retailers continue to expand globally, the risks involved in international hijacking will continue to grow. As mentioned earlier, RFID also poses a problem here because anyone with an RFID scanner could sit on the side of a road or go through a shipping dock and immediately know exactly what is inside any truck or container. However, by implementing a few security measures, retailers can minimize disruption to their supply of merchandise, thus increasing the level of satisfaction to customers by minimizing out of stocks.

SUMMARY

Merchandise management is the analysis, planning, acquisition, and control of inventory investments and assortments in a retail enterprise. An understanding of the principles of merchandise management is essential to good retail management. A major part of merchandise management is planning. The retailer needs to plan (1) how many dollars to invest in inventory at different times of the season and (2) what to purchase with these dollars.

LO 1

What are the major steps in the merchandise buying and handling process?

The major steps include dollar-merchandise planning, dollar-merchandise control, inventory planning, selection of merchandise source, vendor negotiations, item creation and location (shelf or special display), replenishment and in-store handling, merchandise-line review, and markdowns.

LO 2

What is the difference between the four methods of dollar-merchandise planning used to determine the proper inventory stock levels needed to begin a merchandise selling period?

In the section on dollar-merchandise planning, we discussed how four types of inventory methods are used in retailing today: the basic stock (which is used when retailers believe that it is necessary to have a given level of inventory available at all times plus a variable amount of inventory that is tied to forecasted sales for the period), percentage variation (which assumes that the percentage fluctuations in monthly stock from average stock should be half as great as the percentage fluctuations in monthly sales from average sales), weeks' supply (where the beginning inventory level should be set equal to a predetermined number of weeks' supply), and stock-to-sales (where the retailer wants to maintain a specified ratio of inventory to planned sales).

LO 3

How does a retailer use dollar-merchandise control and open-to-buy in the retail buying process?

Once the buyer has planned the dollar merchandise to have on hand at the beginning of each month (or season), it is essential that the buyer does not make commitments for merchandise that would exceed the dollar plan. In short, the dollars planned for merchandise need to be controlled by a technique called *open-to-buy*. OTB represents the dollar amount that a buyer can currently spend on merchandise without exceeding the planned dollar stocks discussed previously.

The OTB figure should not be set in stone because it can be exceeded. Consumer needs are the dominant consideration. If sales exceed planned sales, then additional quantities should be ordered above those scheduled for purchase according to the merchandise budget. Usually this is done by decreasing future quantity for a different merchandise line that is not performing as well.

How does a retailer determine the makeup of its inventory?

LO 4

The dollar-merchandise plan is only the starting point in determining a merchandise line, which consists of a group of products that are closely related because they are intended for the same end use, are sold to the same customer group, or fall within a similar price range. Once the retailer has decided how many dollars can be invested in inventory, the dollar plan needs to be converted into inventory. However, there seldom will be enough dollars to emphasize all three inventory dimensions: variety, breadth, and depth. Therefore, retailers must select a merchandise mix that appeals to the greatest number of profitable market segments.

How do retailers select proper merchandise sources?

LO 5

In addition to deciding what and how much to purchase, successful merchandise management must also consider vendor selection and negotiations. In this section, we reviewed the major factors (selling history, consumers' perception of the manufacturer's reputation, reliability of delivery, trade terms, projected markup, quality of merchandise, after-sale service, transportation time, distribution-center processing time, inventory carrying cost, country of origin, fashionability, and net landed cost) that are important in the selection of a vendor and how a buyer prepares for a buying trip.

What is involved in the vendor–buyer negotiation process and what terms of the contract can be negotiated?

LO 6

The climax of a successful buying plan is the active negotiation, which involves finding mutually satisfying solutions for parties with conflicting objectives, with those vendors that the retailer has identified as suitable supply sources. The effectiveness of this buyer–vendor relationship depends on the negotiation skills of both parties and the economic power of the firms involved. The retail buyer must negotiate price, delivery dates, discounts (trade, quantity, promotional, seasonal, and cash), delivery term, and return privileges. All of these factors are significant because they affect both the firm's profitability and cash flow.

What are the various methods of handling the merchandise once it is received in the store to control shrinkage, including vendor collusion, and theft?

LO 7

The chapter has a discussion on in-store merchandise receiving, handling, and storage as a means to control losses by theft. Not only can theft occur from employees and customers but also vendor collusion is a major source of loss.

TERMS TO REMEMBER

merchandise management
gross margin return on inventory
   (GMROI)
basic stock method (BSM)

percentage-variation method (PVM)
weeks' supply method (WSM)
stock-to-sales method (SSM)
open-to-buy (OTB)

merchandise line	cumulative-quantity discount
category management	free merchandise
variety	promotional discount
breadth	seasonal discount
assorment	cash discount
battle of the brands	end-of-month (EOM) dating
depth	middle-of-month (MOM) dating
consignment	receipt of goods (ROG) dating
pay from scan	extra dating (Ex)
extra dating	anticipation
vendor-profitability analysis statement	free on board (FOB) factory
confidential vendor analysis	free on board (FOB) shipping point
negotiation	free on board (FOB) destination
trade discount	shrinkage
functional discount	vendor collusion
quantity discount	employee theft
noncumulative-quantity discount	customer theft

REVIEW AND DISCUSSION QUESTIONS

LO 1

What are the major steps of the merchandise buying and handling process?

1. How often do most retailers renegotiate vendor contracts?
2. What must happen after a buyer agrees to purchase a product yet before a purchase order can be created?
3. How do replenishment orders affect the merchandise dollar planner and open-to-buy calculation?

LO 2

What are the differences between the four methods of dollar-merchandise planning used to determine the proper inventory stock levels needed to begin a merchandise selling period?

4. If your annual inventory-turnover rate is four times, which inventory stock level method would you use and why?
5. The Corner Hardware Store is attempting to develop a merchandise budget for the next 12 months. To assist in this process, the following data have been developed. The target inventory turnover is 4.8, and forecast sales are

Month	Forecast Sales
1	$27,000
2	26,000
3	20,000
4	34,000
5	41,000
6	40,000
7	28,000
8	27,000
9	38,000
10	39,000
11	26,000
12	28,000

Develop a monthly merchandise budget using the basic stock and percentage variation methods.

How do retailer's use dollar-merchandise control? Describe how open-to-buy is used in the retail buying process.   `LO 3`

6. What problems can occur to buyers open-to-buy if they misjudge planned sales?
7. What does the term *open-to-buy* mean? How can it be used to control merchandise investments?
8. A buyer is going to market and needs to compute the open-to-buy. The relevant data are as follows: planned stock at end of March, $319,999 (at retail prices); planned March sales, $149,999; current stock on hand (March 1), $274,000; merchandise on order for delivery, $17,000; planned reductions, $11,000. What is the buyer's open-to-buy?

How does a retailer determine the makeup of its inventory?   `LO 4`

9. What are the major constraints in designing the optimal merchandise mix?
10. How can merchandise lines have too much breadth yet not enough depth?
11. To the extent that the merchandise mix can actually shape customers' wants and impact whether and what customers purchase, what level of ethical responsibility does the retailer have toward the customer?
12. Manufacturers of so-called third-tier brands argue that they are being squeezed out of many stores by the major brands. Do you agree with that statement? Why?
13. What does *item cross-reference* mean?
14. If a shirt came in five sizes, four colors, and three styles, what possible considerations must be given prior to determining how many item numbers should be created?
15. Who is involved a merchandise-line review?
16. What happens to items that are not going to be discontinued?
17. How long does a merchandise-line review normally take?

How does a retailer select proper merchandise sources?   `LO 5`

18. What do you think is the most important criterion in selecting a vendor? Why?
19. Why should a new buyer look over the previous buyer's confidential vendor analysis before going to market?

What is involved in the vendor–buyer negotiation process, and what terms of the contract can be negotiated?   `LO 6`

20. If a vendor ships you $1,000 worth of merchandise on April 27 with terms of 3/20, net 30 EOM, how much should you pay the vendor on June 8?
21. A retailer purchases goods that have a list price of $7,500. The manufacturer allows a trade discount of 40-25-10 and a cash discount of 2/10, net 30. If the retailer takes both discounts, how much is paid to the vendor?
22. How can cumulative-quantity discounts be considered to be anticompetitive?
23. How can manufacturers stop retailers from diverting their brand-name goods to discounters?

LO 7

What methods are available to the retailer for controlling loss through shrinkage, vendor collusion, and theft?

24. What is the worst type of shrinkage—employee theft or customer theft? What is your reasoning?
25. Should a retailer's right to security take precedent over an employee's and a customer's right to privacy when the retailer sets up an electronic monitoring system in its stores to curb losses from theft?
26. Where should retailers draw the line when it comes to prosecuting shoplifting? Should customers who eat grapes "to test them" be prosecuted?

SAMPLE TEST QUESTIONS

LO 1

Which of the following impact dollar-merchandise planners?
a. product purchases
b. markdowns
c. both of the above
d. none of the above

LO 2

Determine the buyer's BOM for August using the percentage variation method based on the following information: planned sales for August = $170,000; average monthly sales = $142,000; average stock for the season = $425,000.
a. $466,900
b. $390,000
c. $254,400
d. $425,000
e. $453,800

LO 3

The open-to-buy concept provides information about how much the buyer can order at:
a. the beginning of a merchandising period.
b. the middle of a merchandising period.
c. the end of a merchandising period.
d. anytime during the merchandising period.
e. anytime a vendor fails to ship merchandise on time

LO 4

Which of the following factors is not a constraint on the retailer's optimal merchandise mix?
a. space
b. merchandise turnover
c. legal issues
d. dollar merchandise
e. market

LO 5

A vendor-profitability analysis statement:
a. is a vendor's financial statement that is made available to all retailers.
b. is a retailer's analysis of the profitability of the different vendors and their lines from the prior year.
c. is a schedule maintained by the retailer that shows each vendor's initial data for new lines, shipment of orders, and gross margins.

    d. is a retailer's financial statement used by the vendor for determining credit limits.

    e. contains a list of who provided the retailer with discounts during the prior three years.

A cumulative-quantity discount is based on: `LO 6`

    a. a single purchase.

    b. the total amount of merchandise purchased over a period of time.

    c. the total amount of merchandise purchased since you began dealing with a vendor.

    d. the amount of free merchandise a vendor is offering.

    e. buyer purchases of more than 50,000 units.

Which two parties are usually involved in losses due to vendor collusion? `LO 7`

    a. delivery people and customers

    b. retail employee signing for the delivery and delivery person

    c. vendor sales representative and retail employee signing for the delivery

    d. customers and vendor sales representative

    e. vendor sales representative and retailer's accountant

WRITING AND SPEAKING EXERCISE

As the newly hired intern in the shoe department for a mid-sized apparel chain operating in six Northeastern states, you have been invited to attend your first buyer's meeting. Teresa, the new junior and misses buyer stood up during a weekly merchandise meeting at the retailer's corporate office to show off the newest trend in fashion junior clothing: sweatpants and shorts with words like "hottie," "angel," and "devil" printed in bold letters across the seat of the pants. At the time, a few other retail chains were just beginning to sell similar pants and shorts with writing across the seat of the pants. She showed the crowd of other retail buyers and operational heads several examples of the product. She highlighted the high margin and strong chance of market success. When she asked if there were any questions, another buyer raised his hand. He asked, "I wonder if we should be selling this to teenage girls? Do we have a moral responsibility to not sell a product like this that could increase promiscuity or simply decrease girls' self-worth or self-esteem?" An executive vice president of merchandise then stood up and responded, "Retailers don't have a moral responsibility. That's the media's role. We just sell the product."

Just then your boss asked you, "What do you think Theresa should do?" Explain your reasoning.

RETAIL PROJECT

Retailers are starting to experiment with corporate blogs open to the public. While blogs are not new, letting employees write them and say whatever they want to (about the retailer, manufacturers, stores, society, etc.) is a new and nervous thing for retailers. For example, Walmart has a blog (http://checkoutblog.com) where several buyers write about new products, ideas, and so on related to their merchandise categories. Sometimes they make positive statements, other times they criticize things, and sometimes they pose questions for customers.

Go to any corporate blog you choose, examine the posting and the comments, and think about what is actually being done about the topic. Do you think these blogs help or hurt the retailers? Should retailers let employees post whatever comments they want to say—or should they be approved first? Finally, *who* do you think is actually making comments on the blog? Is it really customers or manufacturers or retailers using pseudonyms? Is it 50 people or one person pretending to be 50 people? In short, how much (or when) do you think the retailer can trust the comment feedback?

PLANNING YOUR OWN RETAIL BUSINESS

Alexia White is in the process of developing the merchandise budget for the gift shop she is opening next year. She has decided to use the basic stock method of merchandise budgeting. Planned sales for the first half of next year are $200,000, and this is divided as follows: February = 9 percent, March = 10 percent, April = 15 percent, May = 21 percent, June = 22 percent, and July = 23 percent. Planned total retail reductions are 9 percent for February and March, 4 percent for April and May, and 12 percent for June and July. The planned initial markup percentage is 48 percent. Alexia desires the rate of inventory turnover for the season to be two times. Also, she wants to begin the second half of the year with $90,000 in inventory at retail prices.

Develop a six-month merchandise budget for Alexia.

Retail Pricing

OVERVIEW:

In this chapter, we examine the retailer's need to make pricing decisions. We begin with a discussion of the impact of a firm's objectives on its pricing policies and strategies. After reviewing several strategies, we look at why initial markups and maintained markups are seldom the same. We also discuss how a retailer establishes an initial markup. We conclude this chapter with a discussion of why and how a retailer takes markdowns during the normal course of business.

LEARNING OBJECTIVES:

After reading this chapter, you should be able to:

1. Discuss the factors a retailer should consider when establishing pricing objectives and policies.
2. Describe the differences between the various pricing strategies available to the retailer.
3. Describe how retailers calculate the various markups.
4. Discuss why markdown management is so important in retailing and describe some of the errors that cause markdowns.

Pricing Objectives and Policies

LO 1

What factors should a retailer consider when establishing pricing objectives and policies?

Although most retailers have grown savvy about cutting costs, few have figured out how much money they have passed up by using outdated pricing strategies and tactics. After all, pricing is an important contributor to profitability. The price of an item multiplied by the quantity sold is equal to the retailer's revenue, and Chapter 8 illustrated the correlation between revenue and profit. Nevertheless, retailers today tend to routinely overprice some products and underprice others.

When making pricing decisions, retailers must remember that they are never going to be right every time. However, such decisions are a great deal less difficult if the retailers have been performing their other activities correctly. Pricing, as we pointed out in our retail strategic planning and operations management model (Exhibit 2.6), is an interactive decision made in conjunction with the firm's mission statement, goals and objectives, strategy, operational management (i.e., merchandise planning, promotional mix, building and fixtures, and level of service), and administrative management. However, as pointed out in this chapter's "Retailing: The Inside Story" box, too many retailers believe that the only way to attract consumers is by running a sale.

Retailing: The Inside Story

Everybody Loses in a Price War

Years ago, retailers used to run only two heavily discounted sales a year, Washington's Birthday (February 22) and Founder's Day (which is funny because it seemed that every retailer was founded in late July.). These sales were designed to get rid of old seasonal merchandise and open up room for the upcoming season's new items priced with higher markups. Today, however, it seems that retailers have one, and sometimes two, sales per week. As a result, many retailers tell the authors that the average American considers something a bargain only when the discount exceeds 40 percent off the original selling price. One retailer even cited a study that found that 88 percent of Americans buy food items on sale versus 44 percent for toys, and 44 percent of Americans comparison shop for brand-name products.

Based on this information, it is easy to conclude that the current level of price cutting is actually shortsighted; it has taught consumers to purchase only when an item's on sale. This behavior was likely enhanced by the recent economic slowdown when retailers, experiencing a slowdown in sales, often reacted like used-car salesmen, offering shoppers two-for-one deals, "50 percent off" the entire stock, and direct-mail coupons.

Over the short run, price cutting may give retailers what they want, revenues, but at what cost? By one retail consultant's calculations, more than 80 percent of all department store items are currently being sold at discount prices compared with 40 percent a decade ago. In addition, the number of recent store closings has led some consumers to believe that a "big sale" isn't just to clear out seasonal inventory; it's the forerunner of liquidation. As a result, many choose to wait for even better prices.

Even as the economy improves, there is no sign that the sale epidemic will do anything but grow. To make matters worse, the long-term effects of such heavy discounting are expected to have a negative impact for future retailers. Deals and sales promotions may increase sales today, but for too many companies they've become an addiction. Too many retailers, especially grocery and department stores, rely on "promotional prices" to draw consumers into their stores without considering their impact on the income statement. Some experts blame Walmart's "everyday low prices" (EDLP) strategy — whereby a retailer charges the same low price every day throughout the year and seldom runs out of the product — for this overemphasis on price. After all, the chain's sophisticated buying process and its Retail Link system, which was described in Chapter 5's "What's New?" box, has allowed Walmart to undercut competitors and still hold profit margins. Other retailers, such as Lane Bryant, have controlled costs and lowered prices by selling just one size category of women's clothing.

These low prices have forced competitors to use heavy promotions to keep up. It is little wonder that today's consumers expect a deal on almost everything they buy. Discounting strategies are used so regularly that consumers avoid any product that isn't marked down at least 25 percent. In fact, many consumers have now gotten into the habit of waiting for the "70% off" sales before buying apparel. Yet small grocery store operators are probably the worst offenders in this "markdown war" as they lower prices to either hold or win back market share when supercenters enter their trade areas.

Retailers have forgotten one of the cardinal rules of retailing—compete on price only in the short term unless you are the low-cost operator. Small operators that have been successful in their battles with the supercenters, such as Food4Less in Missouri, have instituted the same buying processes as the big retail chains and have used their intimate size to more closely monitor their market. Losers, on the other hand, have been those that lower prices to the point where they lose money on each sale. These retailers have effectively taught their customers to value price while overlooking the retailers' possible advantages in product selection or great service.

Retailers should know how to solve the problem. To sell more at full price, retailers must differentiate themselves from rivals and convince shoppers to pay more for the added service or convenience they offer. Others should be creative by adopting similar techniques to those described in Chapter 1's "Service Retailing" box, which focused on Moore's Bike Shop. In addition, retailers should focus on brand building, a tactic many have all but abandoned. The reason? A store can typically move two to three times the normal volume of a product during a week when it's on sale. Advertising and marketing are much slower to take effect and harder to measure—but they're critical to ensuring long-term survival. However, that is *not* easy to do when your competitors continue to cut prices.

Today, when one retailer cuts prices, everyone seems to follow. A prime example of this "follow-the-leader" tactic occurred during the 2008 Christmas season when Saks Fifth Avenue chose to slash prices by 70 percent on its designer clothes prior to the holiday season even beginning. Almost at once, competitors and shoppers panicked—many retailers immediately matched Sak's prices and saw their gross margins vanish; shoppers, worried they might miss out on the sale, rushed out and purchased. Saks, after all, had started this price war because it didn't want to be stuck with inventory after Christmas; however, like all price wars, this one ended badly. Within a week, retailer after retailer dropped prices even further, resulting in the earliest shoppers having paid higher prices and all retailers suffering losses.[1]

For retailers selling services, pricing is even more difficult. This is because services are intangible, not easily stored, and cannot be returned to the vendor for credit. A movie theater, for example, running a hit movie during a blizzard has the same fixed costs of being open as it would any other night. The theater manager cannot resell the empty seats at a later date and he cannot increase attendance on the night of the blizzard by reducing ticket prices. Consequently, as discussed in Chapter 2's "Retailing: The Inside Story" box, service retailers, like airlines, hotels, golf courses, and even universities, are now using yield-management techniques when making pricing decisions.

Interactive Pricing Decisions

As shown in Exhibit 10.1, pricing decisions should be interactive. Specifically, the decision to price an item at a certain level should be related to the retailer's decisions on lines of merchandise carried, location, promotion, credit and check cashing, customer services, desired store image, and the legal constraints discussed in Chapter 6.

Remember that just as each retailer is different, each retailer's pricing decision must also be different.[2] After all, price is the easiest element of the retail mix for a

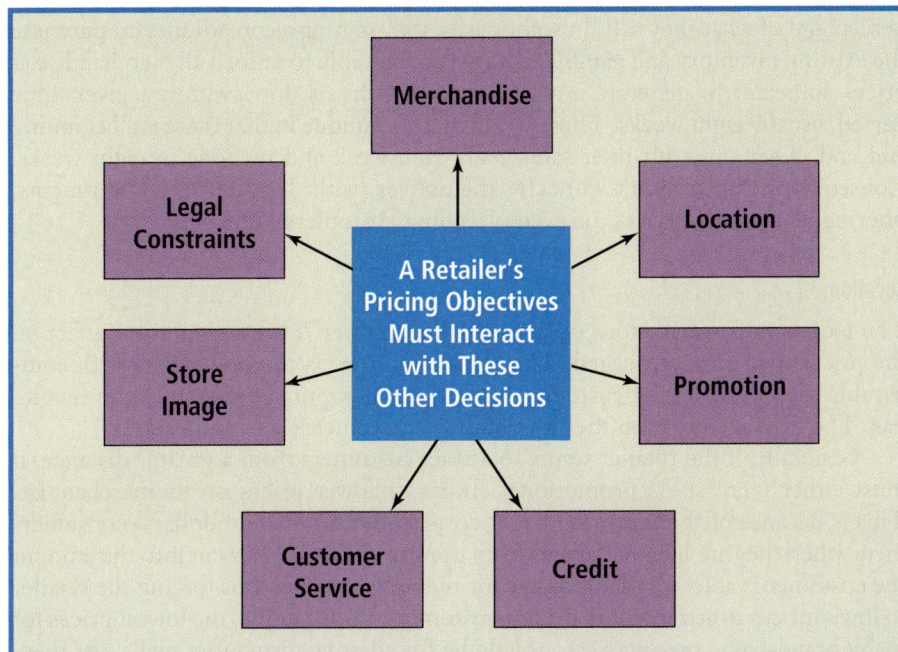

Exhibit 10.1
Interaction Between a Retailer's Pricing Objectives and Other Decisions

Merchandise

Legal Constraints

Location

A Retailer's Pricing Objectives Must Interact with These Other Decisions

Store Image

Promotion

Customer Service

Credit

competitor to copy. Consider for a moment the price of gas. When a gas station lowers its price, all the other stations in the immediate area soon match or beat that price. This is why a long-term, differential advantage based on price is difficult if not impossible to obtain.[3]

Merchandise

Retailers should not set prices without carefully analyzing the attributes of the merchandise being priced. Does the merchandise have attributes that differentiate it from comparable merchandise at competing retailers? What is the value of these attributes to the consumer? Consider, for example, Wright's Market in Opelika, Alabama, a small town near Auburn University. Jimmy Wright has made a success of a small grocery business (his store is only 22,000 square feet) by offering the highest quality meat available. Using the slogan "We have the best meat at the best price," more than 50 percent of his $160,000 weekly sales come from the meat department.

Merchandise selection presents the retailer with another decision: the range of prices to be made available to the consumer. Remember, the retailer's controllable element of price can be either the cost of goods sold or the gross margin that is added to the cost. The retailer, in deciding to buy an item to sell at a specific price, may either purchase lower-cost merchandise and have a high gross margin to offset the higher expenses needed to sell at that price or purchase more expensive goods and reduce the gross margin and expenses in order to sell at a given price. One drug store chain has gone so far as to use algorithms to determine prices. As a result, the chain raised the prices of some cough medicines. (After all, sick people don't shop around.) In addition, the per-pill price of the 50- and 100-pill bottles of certain pain relievers used to be lower than on the 24-pill bottle. Now it's higher because the kinds of people who buy jugs of pills are a bit less sensitive to a higher unit price.[4]

The one situation in which price interacts only with merchandise for sale and not with the other retail decision areas is in the case of liquidators. Liquidators purchase the entire inventory of a "dead" retailer only to run a *going-out-of-business* (GOB) sale. They generally assume responsibility for everything and agree to take a percentage of what they sell. In some cases, they may agree in advance to purchase the existing inventory and gamble that they will be able to unload all merchandise at prices sufficient to generate a solid profit. All this is done within a given time period, usually eight weeks. Thus, GOB sales are unique in that there is a beginning and end. They must hit their sales goals each week and be gone in eight weeks. Consequently, they don't concern themselves with long-term commitments, offering additional services, or even offending customers.[5]

Location

The location of a retail store, as discussed in Chapter 7, has a significant effect on the prices that can be charged. The closer the store is to competitors with comparable merchandise and customer service, the less pricing flexibility the retailer has. The distance between the store and the customer is also important.

Generally, if the retailer wants to attract customers from a greater distance, it must either increase its promotional efforts or lower prices on its merchandise. This is because of the increased travel costs (in both time and dollars) consumers incur when they are located farther from the store. Travel costs cut into the amount the customer is able or willing to pay for the merchandise, thus forcing the retailer to lower prices to attract more distant customers. For example, the lowest prices for many brand-name products can usually be found at factory outlet malls, yet these

The one situation where price interacts only with merchandise for sale and not with the other retail decision areas is in the case of liquidators.

locations usually have the highest travel costs. This is why for many consumers it is cheaper to purchase the merchandise at a nearby retailer. However, catalog and online retailers break down location barriers by providing a national and worldwide presence. Pricing for these retailers is balanced between charging higher prices for providing greater customer convenience and lower prices for products with higher volume and lower operating expenses.

Promotion

The next chapter illustrates how promotion can increase demand for the retailer's merchandise. However, this does not mean that pricing and promotion decisions are independent. Rather, retailers that promote heavily while remaining very price competitive may experience increases in demand greater than either a high-promotion or lower-price strategy would produce independently. Imagine, for example, a retailer establishing low prices but not promoting them in the marketplace. How would consumers know of the price cuts? Alternatively, imagine heavy promotion but no cut in prices. Obviously, each would generate demand, but the interactive and cumulative effects of both are likely to be much greater.

Credit and Check Cashing

For a given merchandise price level, retailers that offer either purchases on credit, even if only using bank cards, or check-cashing services will often experience greater demand than those that offer neither. In addition, retailers who provide both financial services may be able to charge slightly higher prices than those who do not while generating the same level of demand. This has become increasingly true for check-cashing services over the past decade as a large number of consumers don't have bank accounts. The offering of check cashing has been found to be an effective means to attract Hispanics, whose wealth is soaring, despite the fact that almost 60 percent of this market doesn't have a bank account.[6]

E-tailers targeting teens also have a special problem with regard to credit. Online purchases require a credit card, yet teenagers under 18 are not legally liable for their credit-card debts. However, nothing prohibits an e-tailer from issuing a credit card to a minor. In fact, consumer advocates charge that both banks and click-and-brick retailers are loosening their rules about who can get credit and are carefully looking the other way when minors apply. This is because credit-granting retailers are able to develop a strong loyalty with those teenagers. They also assume that the parents will bail out the teenager if he or she gets into credit trouble.

Customer Services

Retailers that offer many customer services (e.g., delivery, gift wrapping, alterations, more pleasant surroundings, sales assistance) tend to have higher prices. A decision to offer many customer services will automatically increase operating expenses and thus prompt management to increase retail prices to cover these additional expenses. However, such a policy may also result in higher profits. Consider the case of women's dresses. Customer service used to be common in department stores that took 50-percent to 60-percent initial markups, but pricing pressure by discounters has forced most department stores to respond by cutting markups and service. Women purchasing dresses began to feel neglected in department stores, especially when they had to start paying for alterations. Specialty stores have picked up on this; as a result, they offer the consumer greater assistance in selecting and trying on a dress, something unheard of in the low-price stores. Another example of a retailer justifying a higher price by offering outstanding service is No Kidding. This small toy store in an affluent suburb just west of Boston cannot compete with the retail megamarkets on either price or variety. Therefore, it does not carry the extremely popular items, such as Xboxes, which everybody else discounts; instead, it stocks items not available in the larger stores. What enables No Kidding to produce a profit at a time when most small toy shops fail is the makeup and behavior of its sales staff. This well-informed staff is primarily made up of moonlighting teachers who can discuss the finer points of play and inform the purchaser of what is developmentally correct for a child of a certain age. In addition, the store wraps gifts at no charge, accepts returns without a receipt, and donates part of its profits to local schools and public television.[7] In fact, many consumers are willing to pay more for extra service. Consequently, it is important to remember that customer service decisions interact strongly with pricing decisions.

It is also important to note that service standards vary greatly by country. For example, Japan has extremely high service standards in retail operations. In Japan, gift wrapping is customary, and retailers commonly accept merchandise for return even after the product has been well used. Alternatively, many countries throughout the world do not accept returns regardless of reason. In these retail operations, once the product is sold, it is no longer the retailer's concern. This is truly a situation of *caveat emptor*—let the buyer beware. Given differences in expected service levels, retailers must adapt pricing levels accordingly.

Store Image

One of the cues a customer uses in determining a retailer's image is the retailer's prices. If not offset by a poor location with poor service and merchandise selection, prices aid the customer in developing an image of the store, either consciously or unconsciously. If an exclusive, high-fashion store, such as Nordstrom, started to discount its merchandise heavily, it simply would not be the same store in the eyes of its customers. The merchandise, store decor, and personnel might remain unchanged,

When floor-covering retailers offer free installation, the cost of providing this service must be factored into the prices the retailer charges.

but the change in pricing strategy would significantly alter the overall store image. Thus, pricing policies and strategies interact with store image policies and strategies.

Legal Constraints

Pricing decisions must be made only after examining the impact of the legal environment. This is especially true for the retailer seeking to operate in more than one state, as laws often vary between states. As pointed out in Chapter 6, a retailer may not set a price in collusion with a competitor, may not offer different prices to different retail customers, may not sell below cost, and may not claim or imply in any ads that a price has been reduced unless it really has.

The other environmental factors we discussed in Part 2 (consumer behavior, competitor behavior, channel relationships, the socioeconomic environment, and the technological environment) should also be considered when the retailer is developing its overall pricing and market strategy. Still, pricing decisions are easy to make in the United States when compared to some other countries' retail environments. As pointed out in Chapter 6's "Global Retailing" box, for example, laws in France require that products be sold to all retailers—big and small alike—for the same price, thus making it tough for discounters to get any kind of pricing advantage. Furthermore, while reducing prices is quite common in the United States and hardly seems controversial, it can present major problems for an American firm entering Germany, as discussed in this chapter's "Global Retailing" box.

In the United States, there are laws against vertical monopolies and other restraints on trade to ensure fair competition. American consumers can buy from a full-price retailer or a discounter. American discounters depend on bulk-purchase discounts from manufacturers, rapid inventory turnover, inexpensive real estate, and price-conscious shoppers who are willing to perform some marketing-channel functions themselves.

Global Retailing

Loss-Leader Pricing Isn't Legal Everywhere

Walmart doesn't make too many mistakes when developing retail strategies. However, it made a major error in Germany when it failed to understand how German laws regulate pricing.

In 1997, Walmart bought Germany's 21-store Wertkauf chain. A year later, it added the 74-unit Interspar chain, giving the American retailer between 2 percent and 4 percent of the local market. Before the American retail giant arrived, domestic discounters dropped their prices, much like American retailers do when preparing for Walmart to enter their local markets. In an effort to gain market share, Walmart decided to lower its prices on some basic food items, such as milk and bread, below the prices charged by competitors Aldi and Lidl. Walmart admitted that in some cases the new prices were below its cost, effectively making the products loss leaders. These loss-leader promotions continued for more than three weeks with Aldi and Lidl lowering their prices as well, resulting in a price war. German consumers, however, were not that happy with the low prices. They felt that since Walmart failed to deliver the promised "excellent customer service," lowering prices was just a means to drive smaller competitors out of business, after which Walmart would raise prices. However, as was pointed out in Chapter 7's "Retailing: The Inside Story" box, this isn't the way Sam Walton wanted his stores to operate.

In September 2000, the German Federal Cartel Office concluded that Walmart, Aldi, and Lidl were each in violation of the Act Against Restraints of Competition. As a result, the three competitors were required to raise their prices and prohibited from ever again using a loss-leader pricing strategy in Germany.

Walmart's mistake was that it failed to realize that German law and customs are very different from United States and European Union (EU) laws. U.S. and EU laws are principally concerned with the protection of competition, not competitors, and thus generally view low prices, even below-cost prices, as procompetition, but the U.S. laws on pricing are intended to protect competition and competitors, which benefit customers but are not proconsumer per se. (It should be remembered that both U.S. and EU laws view loss-leader prices that are intended to harm competition as illegal.) As a result, pricing practices that are legal outside Germany could be illegal in Germany. Although German law does not act as an absolute bar to all below-cost pricing, it does create limitations on pricing strategies that are not present in major jurisdictions outside of Germany.

After pulling out of Germany in 2006, Walmart's senior management concluded that the retailer's biggest mistake was its failure to study the legal issues (it also violated many German employment laws) before attempting to apply the company's highly successful U.S. formula in an unmodified manner to the German market. As a result, Walmart's withdrawal from Germany turned out to be a $1 billion fiasco for a retailer not used to making mistakes.

In addition, while Walmart made some other bad cultural flubs in Germany, such as selling ride-on lawn mowers in a country that lacked American-style suburbs, it did introduce "singles shopping nights." Here German customers could look for love along with their groceries and were treated to sparkling wine and oysters at the store.

Source: Based on the authors' various experiences working with Walmart and on Andreas Knorr and Andreas Arndt, "Why Did Walmart Fail in Germany," Institute for World Economics and International Management, June 24, 2003.

Pricing Objectives

A retailer's pricing objectives should be in agreement with its mission statement and merchandising policies. Some objectives may be profit-oriented, some may be sales-oriented, and some may seek to leave things just as they are. However, by beginning with the proper pricing objectives, the retail manager can establish pricing policies that will complement the retailer's other decisions and help attract the desired target customers.

Profit-Oriented Objectives

Many retailers establish the objective of achieving either a certain rate of return or maximizing profits.

Target Return

A **target-return objective** sets a specific level of profit as an objective. This amount is often stated as a percentage of sales or of the retailer's capital investment. A target return for a supermarket might be 2-percent net profit on sales.

Profit Maximization

The objective of **profit maximization** seeks to obtain as much profit as possible. Some people claim that this pricing policy "charges all the traffic will bear." Retailers know that if they follow such a policy, they are inviting competitors to enter the market. Thus, in general, a retailer should seek to set prices, not to get as much as possible from each customer, but at a level conducive to build customer loyalty and withstand the competition. However, in some cases, a retailer may have a temporary monopoly and want to take advantage of it. The first fast-food outlets in a university's student center, knowing that others would follow shortly, often charged high prices, only to lower them when competition finally entered the market. This is known as **skimming** or trying to sell at the highest price possible before settling on a more competitive level.[8] Other retailers may take the opposite approach and use **penetration**, which seeks to establish a loyal customer base by entering the market with a low price. For example, many locally owned retailers such as coffee shops often charge low prices, hoping to make stopping at their store a habit for their customers before a large chain operator such as Starbucks enters their trade area.

Sales-Oriented Objectives

Sales-oriented objectives seek some level of unit sales, dollar sales, or market share but do not mention profit. Two of the objectives most commonly used in retailing are growth in market share and growth in dollar sales. Although both of these objectives are used by many retailers today, especially smaller retailers, the achievement of either does not necessarily mean that profits will also increase. After all, if a retailer lowers prices, gross margin will go down and sales may improve, but the retailer will not necessarily make more money.

Status Quo Objectives

Retailers who are happy with their market share and level of profits sometimes adopt status quo objectives or "don't rock the boat" pricing policies. Many supermarkets gave up on the extra profits and increases in market share that "double coupons" might have brought because they were afraid of what competitive actions would result. It should be noted that pricing actions such as double couponing are not always effective and profitable. Many times, especially when other retailers match the promotion, coupons are only used by the retailer's regular customers, which simply reduces the retailer's profit.

Also, some retailers prefer to compete on grounds other than price. Convenience stores, for example, seldom match the prices of nearby supermarkets. Still, retailers such as McDonald's and Burger King who want the consumer to focus on factors such as quality of food, service, and locational convenience instead of price are sometimes forced to drop prices by promoting "value meals" in the face of mounting competition just to maintain status quo market share.

Pricing Policies

Pricing policies are rules of action, or guidelines, that ensure uniformity of pricing decisions within a retail operation. A large retailer has many buyers who are involved in pricing decisions. By establishing the store's overall pricing policies, top

---

target return objective
Is a pricing objective that states a specific level of profit, such as percentage of sales or return on capital invested, as an objective.

profit maximization
Is a pricing objective that seeks to obtain as much profit as possible.

skimming
Is a pricing objective in which price is initially set high on merchandise to skim the cream of demand before selling at more competitive prices.

penetration
Is a pricing objective in which price is set at a low level in order to penetrate the market and establish a loyal customer base.

merchandising executives provide these buyers with a framework for adopting specific pricing strategies for the entire organization.

A retail store's pricing policies should reflect the expectations of its target market. Very few retailers can appeal to all segments of the market. Low- and middle-income consumers are usually attracted to low-priced, discount stores. The middle-class market often shops at moderately priced general merchandise chains. Affluent consumers are frequently drawn to high-priced specialty stores that provide extra services. Only supermarkets are able to cross the various income lines, and even then there is some basis for segmentation. Successful retailers carefully position themselves in a market and then direct their specific pricing strategies toward satisfying their target market. Many times the proper pricing policies influence consumers to patronize one store over another.

In establishing a pricing policy, retailers must decide whether they should price below, at, or above market levels.

Pricing Below the Market

below-market pricing policy
Is a policy that regularly discounts merchandise from the established market price in order to build store traffic and generate high sales and gross margin dollars per square foot of selling space.

Because of the recent economic slowdown, a large segment of any trade area now buys primarily on the basis of price. A **below-market pricing policy** is also attractive to many retailers such as discounters and warehouse clubs. Such a policy doesn't mean that the retailer sells every item in its store at a price lower than can be found elsewhere in its trading area. Rather, the retailer is more intent on how its prices are perceived versus those of the competition. Remember that not even Walmart will have the lowest price on every item a consumer will typically purchase during a given week. Instead, the chain endeavors to have the lowest total cost for all items purchased.

Below-market retailers must buy wisely, which may include closeouts and seconds; stock fast-selling merchandise; curtail customer services; and operate from modest facilities. Also, some of them choose to stock private-label brands extensively and enhance their low-price image by promoting the price differences between their private brands and comparable national brands. That some retailers are successful with such a policy is evident by the fact that many local retailers, especially restaurants, now use warehouse clubs and supercenters as their suppliers. Besides being known as a "tough, obnoxious, and insane" competitor, the retailer who uses this policy benefits by discouraging some competitors from entering a given trading area so as to avoid head-to-head battles.[9] However, for retailers to consistently price below the market and be profitable, they must concentrate on generating gross-margin dollars per square foot of space, not the gross-margin percentage. After all, profitability is not directly related to the gross-margin percentage of the product sold but the amount of gross margin per unit sold times the number of units sold. Consequently, below-market retailers must always try to increase the sales per square foot of store space since they have already reduced their markups.

A growing number of retailers today are becoming increasingly concerned that the growth of the Internet will forever change the way retailers set prices. Because of eBay's introduction of the cyberauction for overstocked, vintage, or used items; Priceline.com's "name-your-own-price" policy for travel; and Amazon.com's continued introduction of more general merchandise items to offer on the Internet, many people have come to believe that all retailers will soon be forced to sell below market. (Never mind that it is impossible for all retailers to sell below the average selling price for all items.) Nowhere is this more evident than in the chapter's "What's New?" box illustration, which shows that even the smallest of buyers and sellers can use cyberspace to learn what the "market price" is.

Pricing at Market Levels

Most merchants want to be competitive with one another. Retailers' use of comparison shoppers—that is, having employees visit competitors' retail outlets in order to compare prices—stems from this basic premise. Competitive pricing involves a **price zone**, a range of prices for a particular merchandise line that appeals to customers in a certain demographic group, such as Target selling women's tops from $14.99 to $29.99. However, it is important to remember that zones may vary across groups. Dillard's does not necessarily need to match the prices of Target, yet Dillard's should maintain prices similar to those of Macy's, particularly when they compete in the same mall. Alternatively, Target should be competitively priced with Walmart. Pricing at market levels is extremely important for e-tailers given the ease with which consumers can compare prices across different Internet retailers.

price zone
Is a range of prices for a particular merchandise line that appeals to customers in a certain market segment.

The size of a retail store affects its ability to compete on price. Small retailers usually pay more for their merchandise and have higher expenses as a proportion of sales than larger retailers. Although many small retailers have joined voluntary cooperative chains to reduce their expenses through quantity discounts, they

What's New?

The Internet Has Come to Garage Sales

A decade ago, when one of the authors' in-laws passed away, the family had a garage sale to clear out some of the items that had accumulated in the house for more than 50 years. During this sale, the author noticed that many of the early arrivals—some even before the sale was to open—were professional antique dealers. One dealer purchased six old Coca-Cola serving trays for 50 cents each. The family was happy to get the $3 for the set until one family member happened to walk by the dealer's storefront and see the trays selling for $45 each. (The author told his family that this is to be expected when professionals visit garage sales.)

However, more recently, that same author, while walking through his neighborhood, happened on a garage sale. While looking over two full bookshelves, he noticed a set of books, in very good condition, that he enjoyed reading while visiting his aunt and uncle's house in the 1950s. The books were about a fictional hero named Baseball Joe, who was modeled somewhat after Babe Ruth. While deciding whether to pay $5 for each of the five books, a young man, who appeared to be a college student, put away his BlackBerry and picked up the books. Later that night, the author went on Google and found out that Baseball Joe books were selling for between $20 and $50, depending on their condition.

About a month later, the author attended the city's Friends of the Library's annual used book sale. He was surprised that among the early attendees were four book wholesalers armed with handheld UPC scanners, similar to the RFID scanners

mentioned in Chapter 9, and push carts. They were searching for used textbooks and general reading books with values substantially higher than the couple of bucks the library was charging.

Next, following a hunch, the author searched Google for "buying at garage sales." In less than a second, 75 million sites were listed. The first site was titled *eBay Guide—Buying at a Garage Sale for eBay Resale*. A couple other titles listed on that first page were *How to Find Garage Sale Gold—Get Rich Slowly* and *The Pocket Idiot's Guide to Garage and Yard Sales*.[10]

Thus, what was once a casual family or neighborhood activity of cleaning out the closets and garage and putting every unneeded item on the lawn has been transformed by the free-market economy. Today, every shopper is a professional, at least in waiting. Wired small-scale e-tailers now rely on global-positioning services to quickly travel from sale to sale. Using special scanners, these individuals quickly check the price of items such as used books and CDs that have bar codes printed on them. For older items that lack bar codes, these buyers simply access the web using their cell phones and check eBay for a current price quote.

The lesson to learn for garage-sale organizers, even civic groups such as the Friends of the Library, is this: eBay is a great guide to use when pricing one's stuff so as to increase one's revenue. However, the question remains: Has the Internet taken the fun out of the garage sale?

Service Retailing

For Auto Dealers, Profit Isn't Always in the Showroom

A half-century ago, many Americans were "shade tree mechanics," performing many minor repairs and services on their own cars. Even a decade ago, many continued to use a neighborhood mechanic to work on their cars. Not anymore. Today's automobile has more than 100 microprocessors (computers on a chip), all to ensure that the car runs smoothly. This is great as long as the microprocessors work; however, when they fail, today's car must be hooked to more monitors than you'd typically see in an operating room on the set of *ER* or *House*. These repairs are expensive, too. Consider, for example, when the computer chip that drives an electronic fan blade fails—it can cost upward of $500 to replace. Similarly, a computer-assisted six-speed transmission could run into the thousands of dollars in repair costs. As a result, dealers now know that servicing has become the most profitable part of their business; the other two sources of profit are new and used vehicle sales.

New vehicle sales aren't as profitable as they used to be because price competition is near perfect. After all, anyone can now go online and access the dealer's cost. In addition, the customer can not only negotiate with local dealers but also shop over the Internet with dealers hundreds, if not thousands, of miles away. For example, one of the authors had a close friend who was able to purchase a 2009 Chevrolet Corvette, listed at $58,000, for $47,750 from a dealer on the East Coast, some 2,000 miles away. Even with the delivery charge to his home, the price was still thousands less than the best offer from his local Chevrolet dealer. Perhaps this is why, after paying the salesperson's commission, a typical dealer's profit on a new vehicle sale is only a small amount. Used car sales, on the other hand, offer a better opportunity for profit. After all, every used vehicle is different in terms of condition, even if it is the same model year, which makes price negotiation more difficult. Therefore, gross margins on the sales of used vehicles are more profitable than those on new vehicles—often between 15 percent and 20 percent. However, the real profit opportunity for dealers isn't selling cars, but servicing them. After all, the sale of parts and services has gross profit margins of more than 50 percent. Thus, successful new car dealers today realize that their profits depend not only on selling new units but also on developing repeat business from their customers. This is especially true today given that Americans are now keeping their cars for an average of eight to eleven years.

There are several strategies to gain this repeat business. First, the dealer can convince new car purchasers that it is less risky to prepay for costly auto repairs by purchasing an extended warranty, which is a form of insurance. This allows the dealer to actually make money on the expected service problems, regardless of where the repairs are performed. The extended warranty on a $40,000 automobile can cost anywhere from $1,500 to $3,000, depending on the length and components covered. Incidentally, the dealer and the insurance carrier usually split the revenue, thereby adding an extra $750 to $1,500 profit to the sale. Some dealers have even found they can increase the sale of such packages by adding it to the monthly payment so that the monthly fee on a 60-month finance contract is only $30 to $60 more (or roughly a dollar or two a day). Of course, the person selling the warranty is careful to mention that a single component could cost that amount if it failed.

Another option that a number of dealers are now pursuing is providing lifetime oil, lube, and tire-rotation services every 5,000 miles for free. You might ask, "How can someone make money giving away a product and service for free?" In this case, the approximate $15 cost for the labor, oil, and filter is an opportunity for service mechanics to check whether alignment issues are present, test the shocks or struts for excessive wear, examine the brakes, and determine whether the tires need replacing. In addition, the service technician can identify items in need of repair that are under warranty and bill these costs to the auto manufacturer. Further, the oil and lube service provides the service representative an opportunity to sell fuel filters, fan belts, and transmission or radiator flushes.

All in all, the sale of warranties or the provision of free oil and lube services represents a great profit opportunity for dealers. These services not only entice the owner to repeatedly visit the dealer throughout the life of the automobile but also lure him or her into the showroom to look at new vehicles because these types of services can usually be done in 60 minutes. Yes, people still buy autos on impulse and do fall in love with new models. By providing such services, the dealer is performing retailing's first task—get customers into your store several times a year. Besides, this activity is often cheaper than advertising. After all, the cost of a full-page advertisement in the local newspaper of a large city on the weekend or a few 60-second spots during a local television show could cost $5,000 to $10,000. If this ad brought in 200 potential customers, it would cost the dealer about $50 per showroom visitor generated (significantly more than the cost of an oil change).

continue to experience a cost disadvantage. For these reasons, small retailers such as mom-and-pop grocery stores and convenience stores often stress convenience and service rather than price in their retailing mix. However, even in these cases, it is important that one's prices not be too far out of line.

Sometimes, as this chapter's "Service Retailing" box illustrates, circumstances force retailers to price at the market but at a price so low that it generates a very low profit. This is what is happening today with new car dealers as a result of the recent recession.

Pricing Above the Market

Some retailers, either by design or circumstance, follow an **above-market pricing policy**. Certain market sectors are receptive to high prices because nonprice factors are more important to them than price. Some retailers such as Nordstrom offer such outstanding service that they have minimal price competition. Other retailers, such as small neighborhood drugstores and hardware stores, are forced to price above the market because of their high cost structure and low sales volume. Some other factors that permit retailers to price above market levels include the following.

- **Merchandise Offerings**. Some consumers will pay higher-than-average prices for specialty items, an exclusive line, or unusual merchandise. Prestige retailers such as Gucci and Neiman Marcus carry high-priced specialty items.
- **Services Provided**. Many communities have service-oriented merchants with a loyal group of customers who are willing to pay higher prices to obtain an array of services ranging from wardrobe counseling to delivery. Nordstrom's clerks, for example, have a habit of doing such special things as dropping off

above-market pricing policy
Is a policy where retailers establish high prices because nonprice factors are more important to their target market than price.

Beth A. Keiser/AP Photo

Retailers that use above-market pricing often offer exclusive merchandise lines coupled with high levels of customer service.

purchases at a customer's home, sending thank-you notes to customers, and even ironing a newly purchased shirt so the customer can wear it that day.

- **Convenient Locations**. The convenient location of gift shops in hotels, airline terminals, and even downtown office buildings allows them to charge higher prices. Knowing that consumers value time, fast-food retailers select sites adjacent to residential areas.

- **Extended Hours of Operation**. By remaining open while other stores are closed, some merchants are able to charge higher-than-average prices. Service plazas on interstate highways justify their higher prices by never closing.

LO 2

What are the various pricing strategies available to the retailer?

Specific Pricing Strategies

Various pricing strategies are adopted by the traditional bricks-and-mortar retailers in an effort to achieve certain pricing objectives. The pricing strategies should be in accord with the other components of the store's retail mix: location, promotion, display, service level, and merchandise assortment.

Customary Pricing

customary pricing
Is a policy in which the retailer sets prices for goods and services and seeks to maintain those prices over an extended period of time.

Customary pricing occurs when a retailer sets prices for goods and services and seeks to maintain those prices over an extended period of time. Movies and vending-machine products are common examples of items that use customary pricing. Here retailers, such as movie theaters with their $8 ticket prices, seek to establish prices that customers can take for granted over long periods of time.

Variable Pricing

variable pricing
Is a policy that recognizes that differences in demand and cost necessitate that the retailer change prices in a fairly predictable manner.

Variable pricing is used when differences in demand and cost force the retailer to change prices in a fairly predictable manner. Flowers, for example, tend to be priced higher when demand is greatest around Mother's Day and Valentine's Day. It is a common practice for most resorts to increase their rates on premium rooms in June, a busy wedding time. Limo rentals are usually priced higher in the spring because of weddings, proms, and graduations. Tuesday and Wednesday nights tend to have lower demand for movies and dining out, so many theaters and restaurants offer specials on those nights. Fresh fruits tend to sell for less during their growing seasons when the retailer's costs are down. In addition, many restaurants offer the same meal at lunch as for dinner but with a discounted lunch price (often 10 percent to 20 percent lower) to increase demand.

Flexible Pricing

flexible pricing
Is a policy that encourages offering the same products and quantities to different customers at different prices.

Flexible pricing means offering the same products and quantities to different customers at different prices. Retailers generally use flexible pricing in situations calling for personal selling. The advantage of using flexible pricing is that the salesperson can make price adjustments based on the customer's interest, a competitor's price, a past relationship with the customer, or the customer's bargaining ability. Most jewelry stores and automobile dealerships use this pricing policy, although not all customers like it.[11] For example, your college probably uses some form of flexible pricing for athletic events. Tickets on the 50-yard line are more expensive than those in the end zone. Also, student tickets are probably cheaper. This illustration highlights the key problem with flexible pricing—you don't want those with the lower-priced tickets (students) being able to resell their tickets to the higher-priced market (the general public).

Many types of retailers use flexible pricing by varying their prices and giving discounts to special consumer groups such as loyalty club members, senior citizens, and the clergy. Interestingly enough, some analysts predict that since a baby-boomer now reaches age 60 every eight seconds, senior-citizen discounts can be expected to disappear over the next decade. Today, some employee groups, credit unions, and housing or neighborhood groups have negotiated price discounts with selected retailers. In fact, the recent downturn in the economy has increased the importance of flexible price as more shoppers are engaging in old-fashioned haggling. This has forced retailers eager to make sales to become flexible. While most major chains don't want to go on record saying they will engage in price negotiation, these retailers do say that the increased level of autonomy at the store level seems to be good for creating the impression that these are neighborhood stores, not just uncaring national chains.

However, Americans are nowhere near what some Chinese consumers do to negotiate lower flexible prices. In China, to the dismay of many retailers, some of the country's 1.3 billion consumers have started shopping in teams to haggle for bigger discounts. This team purchasing practice begins in Internet chat rooms (such as 51tuangou.com—the Chinese word *tuangou* means "I want to team buy"), where they hatch plans to buy appliances, furnishings, food, and even cars in bulk. Next, they show up en masse at stores to demand discounts.[12]

Flexible pricing, although popular because it seeks to match levels of supply and demand, does have its disadvantages. Costs can dramatically increase, and revenues decrease, as customers begin to bargain for everything. Similarly, customers may get mad at the retailer and take their business elsewhere when they find that they paid more than a friend did for the same product. This is why the one-price policy is so popular in the United States.

One-Price Policy

Under a **one-price policy**, the retailer charges all customers the same price for an item. A one-price policy may be used in conjunction with customary or variable pricing. For example, all people buying a Big Mac at the same McDonald's will pay an identical price. Roland Hussey Macy, the founder of Macy's Department Store, is often credited with the one-price policy, but recently the authors found evidence that a Sacramento retailer, Weinstock & Lubin, was using this policy in 1875, nearly four decades before Macy's.[13] This policy allowed for efficiency and fairness in handling customer transactions in a large store, where the selling activity is delegated to salespersons that have varying degrees of loyalty to the retailer. If salespersons are permitted to bargain over price, then customers who are shrewd and assertive could conceivably negotiate terms that are unprofitable to the retailer.

A one-price policy, therefore, speeds up transactions and reduces the need for highly skilled salespeople. Most catalog operators adopt a one-price policy since they are forced to retain their prices until the expiration date of the catalog, which can be six months from its issuance. Many manufacturers encourage retailers to follow a one-price policy to maintain the image of their products. They do so by advertising the suggested retail price on the packaging and using personal selling techniques to persuade retailers to maintain that price. However, such a pricing policy will work only if the vast majority of retailers voluntarily agree to stick to the plan. Otherwise, a flexible price retailer will know the price it has to beat.

one-price policy
Is a policy that establishes that the retailer will charge all customers the same price for an item.

Price Lining

price lining
Is a pricing policy that is established to help customers make merchandise comparisons and involves establishing a specified number of price points for each merchandise classification.

To simplify pricing procedures and help consumers make merchandise comparisons, some retailers establish a specified number of price lines or price points for each merchandise category. Once the price lines are determined, these retailers purchase goods that fit into each line. This is called **price lining**. For example, in men's slacks, the price lines could be limited to $29.95, $49.95, and $69.95. The monetary difference between the price lines should be large enough to reflect a value difference to consumers. This makes it easier for the salesperson to either trade up or trade down a customer. **Trading up** occurs when a salesperson moves a customer from a lower-priced line to a higher one. **Trading down**, which gained in popularity during the recent slowdown, occurs when a customer is initially exposed to higher-priced lines but expresses the desire to purchase a lower-priced line.

trading up
Occurs when a retailer uses price lining and a salesperson moves a customer from a lower-priced line to a higher one.

Retailers select price lines that have the strongest consumer demand. By limiting the number of price lines, a retailer achieves broader assortments, which leads to increased sales and fewer markdowns. For example, a retailer who stocks 150 units of an item and has six price lines would likely have an assortment of only 25 units in each line. On the other hand, if the 150 units were divided among only three price lines, there would likely be 50 units in each line.

When retailers are limited to certain price lines, they become specialists in those lines. This permits them to concentrate all their merchandising and promotional efforts on those lines, thus defining their store image more clearly. In addition, they direct their purchases to vendors who handle those lines. The vendors, in turn, provide favored treatment to their large-volume retailing customers. Other advantages of price lining include buying more efficiently, simplifying inventory control, and accelerating inventory turnover. From the shopper's perspective, it is easy to shop when price lining is used because differences are perceived among the various price points.

trading down
Occurs when a retailer uses price lining, and a customer initially exposed to higher-priced lines expresses the desire to purchase a lower-priced line.

An analysis of a store's best-selling price lines is essential prior to making any decision to alter them. Generally, middle-priced lines should account for the majority of one's sales. When the bulk of sales occur at the extremes of the price lines, the retailer should take corrective actions. These include altering the assortments in the current price lines, changing the price lines, redirecting the salespersons' efforts, developing more effective promotions, or adjusting the total marketing mix to a new target market.

Odd Pricing

odd pricing
Is the practice of setting retail prices that end in the digits 5, 8, 9—such as $29.95, $49.98, or $9.99.

The practice of setting retail prices that end in the digits 5, 8, or 9—such as $29.95, $49.98, or $9.99—is called **odd pricing**. A quick look at retail advertisements in the newspaper will reveal that many retailers use an odd-pricing policy. Retailers feel that this policy produces significantly higher sales, and recent evidence suggests they might be correct.[14] Presumably, consumers tend to focus most of their attention on the digits left of the decimal and overlook the cents.[15] Another theory suggests that the use of an odd price connotes "value" or a discounted price, thus encouraging the customer to purchase more units.[16]

While recent evidence suggests retailers may benefit from the way consumers perceive—or, more accurately, misperceive—odd prices, a more plausible explanation for its initial adoption back in the early part of the 20th century was the lack of a sales tax. In those days, merchandise was priced in even dollars, thus making it easy for salespersons to pocket the occasional one-, five-, or ten-dollar bill or gold piece since they did not have to make change for the customer. When Marshall Field caught on to this, he devised the first odd-numbered pricing system to stop the practice. Field ruled that, "We'll charge 99 cents instead of even dollars. This will force the clerks to ring up the sales, open the cash register, put the money in and give the customer a receipt and change."

Because odd prices are associated with low prices, they are typically used by retailers who sell either at prices below the market or at the market. Retailers selling above the market, such as Neiman Marcus and Nordstrom, usually end their prices with even numbers, which have come to denote quality. These retailers would likely sell an item for $90.00 rather than $89.99. Prestige-conscious retailers are not seeking bargain hunters as customers.

Multiple-Unit Pricing

With **multiple-unit pricing** the price of each unit in a multiple-unit package is less than the price of each unit if it were sold individually. Grocery retailers use multiple-unit pricing extensively in their sales of cigarettes, lightbulbs, candy bars, and beverages. Apparel retailers often sell multiple units of underwear, hosiery, and shirts.

Retailers use multiple-unit pricing to encourage additional sales and to increase profits. The gross margin that is sacrificed in a multiple-unit sale is more than offset by the savings that occur from reduced selling and handling expenses. Generally, multiple-unit pricing can be effectively employed for items that are either consumed rapidly or used together.

multiple-unit pricing
Occurs when the price of each unit in a multiple-unit package is less than the price of each unit if it were sold individually.

Bundle Pricing

Bundling generally involves selling distinct multiple items offered together at a special price. Here the perceived savings in cost or time for the bundle justifies the purchase. At the same time, bundling can increase the retailer's revenue since the customer may actually purchase more items than originally planned. For example, while airlines have been actively unbundling their prices, many travel agencies are now bundling their vacation packages. Here they package airfare, hotel, transfers, and meals together as a means of reducing price comparisons and increasing the number of options sold.

Today, a small number of retailers are testing nontraditional forms of bundling to encourage customers to patronize their establishments by providing nonrelated services gratis or for a small fee. For example, some movie theaters have found that the main obstacle encountered by parents when coming to the movies is finding child care. As a result, some theaters now offer either "Monday Night Is Baby's Night" for very young babies, or child-care centers for children aged 2 to 8. This latter bundling program seems to be going over well with parents who previously could only consider attending PG movies.

Grocery stores and physical fitness centers are also testing the addition of child-care facilities. Such action shows that retailers are becoming more oriented toward their customers' needs, especially when child and adult activities significantly diverge. Some parents, especially single parents, believe that certain errands and tasks, such as trips to the grocery store, can be sharing activities; however, these parents are also aware that most of the time their youngsters get bored sitting in a shopping cart.

The economic conditions of recent years have also caused some retailers, especially those selling services, to drop the idea of bundling their merchandise and instead unbundle them. These retailers hope that by unbundling their offerings they'll increase revenues without offending their customers. For example, apartments near universities now charge for parking spaces rather than provide them for free. Nevertheless, while airlines now charge for ticketing, snacks, and carry-on luggage, they have backed away from charging for use of the toilet, something European discounter Ryanair proposed in 2009.

Leader Pricing

leader pricing
Is when a high-demand item is priced low and is heavily advertised in order to attract customers into the store.

When **leader pricing** is used, a high-demand item is priced low and advertised heavily in an effort to attract consumers into a store. The items selected for leader pricing should be widely known and purchased frequently. In addition, information should be available that will permit consumers to make price comparisons. National brands of convenience goods such as Crest toothpaste, Mitchum anti-perspirant, Maxwell House coffee, and Coca-Cola are often designated as leader items.[17]

Leader pricing is usually part of a promotional program designed to increase store traffic. A successful program will produce additional sales for all areas of a store. In many instances, the price of the leader item is reduced only for a specific promotion. Some retailers, such as supermarkets, however, regularly feature leader items.[18] Today, many convenience stores use gasoline as a leader. These retailers reduce their gas prices by a penny or two to get customers into their store. Once in the store, customers are exposed to fast-food sandwiches, groceries, fresh produce, beverages, and even fresh flowers. In such stores, the inside merchandise contributes more than 70 percent to the store's gross-margin dollars and subsidizes its gasoline business. For those customers who just want gas, these stores have pay-at-the-pump facilities.

A retailer using leader pricing should carefully evaluate its usefulness. If consumers are limiting their purchases to only those leader items, then the policy is ineffective. Because leader items may be sold at or near a retailer's cost, higher-markup items must also be sold to generate a profit for the retailer. However, recent research has found that in the supermarket industry "cherry pickers," shoppers who buy only items on sale, aren't as numerous or as profit-draining as the industry once feared.[19]

loss leader
Is an extreme form of leader pricing where an item is sold below a retailer's cost.

An item that is sold below a retailer's cost is known as a **loss leader**. For example, every St. Patrick's Day, many supermarkets sell corned beef at a loss in hopes of attracting consumers to their stores and making a profit on the rest of their purchases. This chapter's "Global Retailing" box shows the costly error made by Walmart when it tried to use loss-leader pricing upon entering the German market.

The pricing actions of discounters using below-market pricing have forced manufacturers to change their pricing strategies, thus endangering another group of retailers—those using leader pricing. Retailers using everyday low prices want vendors to offer them constant prices throughout the year by phasing out virtually all deep discounts and offering them the same low price every day. For example, instead of selling retailers a case of peanut butter for $20 one week and offering it on sale the next week for $15, they want it priced at $18 every week. This would limit the ability of leader pricers such as supermarkets to continue their use of high–low pricing. **High–low pricing** involves the use of high everyday prices and low leader specials on featured items for their weekly ads. An example of a nonfood retailer that uses high–low pricing is JCPenney, which has regularly scheduled sales every week.

high–low pricing
Involves the use of high every day prices and low leader "specials" on items typically featured in weekly ads.

Bait-and-Switch Pricing

bait-and-switch pricing
Advertising or promoting a product at an unrealistically low price to serve as "bait" and then trying to "switch" the customer to a higher-priced product.

The practice of advertising a low-priced model of a shopping good such as a television or a computer merely to lure shoppers into a store is called **bait-and-switch pricing**. Once the shoppers are in the store, a salesperson tries to persuade them to purchase a higher-priced model. Bait-and-switch pricing, which was discussed in Chapter 6, is considered by the Federal Trade Commission to be an illegal practice when the low-priced model used as bait is unavailable to shoppers. Some in the industry describe the *bait* merchandise as being "nailed to the floor."

Private-Label Brand Pricing

A private-label brand can often be purchased by a retailer at a cheaper price, have a higher markup percentage, and still be priced lower than a comparable national brand. Private labels also permit the retailer a large degree of pricing freedom because consumers find it difficult to make exact comparisons between the private and national brands. Many retailers, like Marks & Spencer, Sears, and Walmart, price their private brands below the market. Canada's Zellers, a division of The Hudson Bay Co., has relied on private labels to respond to Walmart's invasion of its Canadian market. Backed by its motto "The Lowest Price Is the Law," Zellers uses private labels to give it exclusivity and quality, especially in apparel, where 80 percent of its line is private.[20]

Other retailers seeking to differentiate themselves from competitors are now using an above-market pricing approach for their private labels. Department stores that have been battered on price by discounters and specialty stores are now using private labels to improve their own image. Macy's, for example, uses its own "Hotel Collection by Charter Club" label to sell Italian-made $1,350 duvets and $275 pillowcases.[21]

Another variation of private labeling is not to use different brand names. This is common for retailers selling products where customers have limited knowledge, such as those selling mattresses. These operators want the national brand's appeal, but instead require different model numbers. This degree of consumer "blindness" allows the retailers to avoid having to match a competitor's price.

Using Markups

LO 3

How does a retailer calculate the various markups?

A retail buyer should be able to calculate rapidly whether a proposed purchase will provide an adequate markup or gross margin. The markup can be expressed in dollars or as a percentage of either the selling price or the cost of the good. There are times, however, when a retail buyer needs to compute the markdown, which is a reduction in the selling price of the goods. Markdowns are made in order to move certain merchandise, especially when the color or size assortments are no longer complete.

Calculating Markup

To calculate the selling price (or *retail price*), the retailer should begin with the following basic markup equation:

$$SP = C + M$$

where C is the dollar cost of merchandise per unit, M is the dollar markup per unit, and SP is the selling price per unit.

Thus, if the retailer has a cost per unit of $16 on a T-shirt and a dollar markup of $14, then the selling price per unit is $30. In other words, **markup** is simply the difference between the cost of the merchandise and the selling price, which is the same as gross margin.

markup
Is the selling price of the merchandise less its cost, which is equivalent to gross margin.

This markup is intended to cover all of the operating expenses (wages, rent, utilities, promotion, credit, etc.) incurred in the sale of the product and still provide the retailer with a profit. Occasionally, a retailer will sell a product without a markup high enough to cover the cost of the merchandise in order to generate traffic or build sales volume. For instance, many e-tailers originally expected high turnover to allow them to be profitable. However, low margins coupled with low traffic caused many to close before volume could make up for their low margins. This chapter, however, will only be concerned with using markup to produce a profit on the sale of each item.

Markup Methods

Markup may be expressed either as a dollar amount or as a percentage of either the selling price or cost. It is most useful when expressed as a percentage of the selling price because it can then be used in comparison with other financial data such as last year's sales results, reductions in selling price, and even the firm's competition. The equation for expressing markup as percentage of selling price is

$$\text{Percentage of markup on selling price} = (SP - C)/SP = M/SP$$

Although some businesses, usually manufacturers or small retailers, express markup as a percentage of cost, this method is not widely used in retailing because most of the financial data the retailer uses are expressed as a percentage of selling price. Nevertheless, when expressing markup as a percentage of cost, the equation is

$$\text{Percentage of markup on cost} = (SP - C)/C = M/C$$

Several problems occur when we attempt to equate markup as a percentage of selling price with markup as a percentage of cost. Since the two methods use different bases, we really are not comparing similar data. However, there is an equation to find markup on selling price when we know markup on cost:

$$\text{Percentage of markup on selling price} = \text{Percentage of markup on cost}/$$
$$(100\% + \text{Percentage of markup on cost})$$

Likewise, when we know markup on selling price, we can easily find markup on cost:

$$\text{Percentage of markup on cost} = \text{Percentage of markup on selling price}/$$
$$(100\% - \text{Percentage of markup on selling price})$$

The preceding equations convert percentage markup on cost to percentage markup on selling price and vice versa. Exhibit 10.2 shows a conversion table for markup on cost and markup on selling price. Let's go back to our original example of the T-shirt and see how easy it is to determine markup on selling price when we know the markup on cost and vice versa.

The retailer purchased the T-shirt for $16 and later sold it for $30. The difference between the selling price and the cost is $14. This $14 as a percentage of selling price (markup on selling price) is 46.7 percent ($14/$30). This same $14, however, represents 87.5 percent ($14/$16) of the cost (markup). In this example, if all we knew was that the T-shirt had an 87.5-percent markup on cost, we could determine that this was the same as a 46.7-percent markup on selling price:

$$\text{Percentage of markup on selling price} = \text{Percentage of markup on cost}/$$
$$(100\% + \text{Percentage of markup on cost}) = 87.5\%/(100\% + 87.5\%) = 46.7\%$$

Markup Percentage on Selling Price	Markup Percentage on Cost	Markup Percentage on Selling Price	Markup Percentage on Cost
4.8	5.0	32.0	47.1
5.0	5.3	33.3	50.0
8.0	8.7	34.0	51.5
10.0	11.1	35.0	53.9
15.0	17.7	36.0	56.3
16.7	20.0	37.0	58.8
20.0	25.0	40.0	66.7
25.0	33.3	41.0	70.0
26.0	35.0	42.8	75.0
27.3	37.5	44.4	80.0
28.0	39.0	47.5	90.0
28.5	40.0	50.0	100.0
30.0	42.9	66.7	200.0

Exhibit 10.2
Markup Conversion Table

Likewise, if we knew we had a 46.7-percent markup on selling, we could easily determine markup on cost:

Percentage of markup on cost = Percentage of markup on selling price/(100% – Percentage of markup on selling price) = 46.7%/(100% – 46.7%) = 87.5%

Exhibit 10.3 gives you the total picture of the relationships between markup on cost and markup on selling price. In Exhibit 10.3, you can see that dollar markup does not change as the percentage changes on cost or selling price. Dollar markup is presented as a percentage of cost or selling price.

Exhibit 10.4 reviews the basic markup equations.

Using Markup Formulas When Purchasing Merchandise

Although quite simple in concept, the basic markup formulas will enable you to determine more than the percentage of markup on a particular item. Let us work with the markup on selling price formula to illustrate how an interesting and common question might be answered. If you know that a particular type of item could be sold for $8 per unit and that you need a 40-percent markup on selling price to meet your profit objective, then how much would you be willing to pay for the item? Using our equation for markup on selling price, we have

$$\text{Percentage of markup on selling price} = (SP - C)/SP$$
$$40 = (\$8 - C)/\$8$$
$$C = \$4.80$$

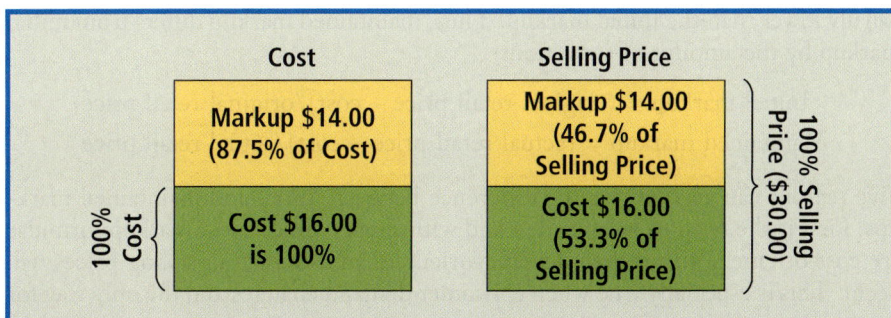

Exhibit 10.3
Relationship of Markups Expressed on Selling Price and Cost

Exhibit 10.4
Basic Markup Formulas

$$\% \text{ Markup on Selling Price} = \frac{\text{Selling Price} - \text{Cost}}{\text{Selling Price}} = \frac{\text{Markup}}{\text{Selling Price}}$$

$$\% \text{ Markup on Cost} = \frac{\text{Selling Price} - \text{Cost}}{\text{Cost}} = \frac{\text{Markup}}{\text{Cost}}$$

Finding % Markup on Cost When % Markup on Selling Price Is Known:

$$\% \text{ Markup on Cost} = \frac{\% \text{ Markup on Selling Price}}{100\% - \% \text{ Markup on Selling}}$$

Finding % Markup on Selling Price When % Markup on Cost Is Known:

$$\% \text{ Markup on Selling Price} = \frac{\% \text{ Markup on Cost}}{100\% + \% \text{ Markup on Cost}}$$

Finding Selling Price When Cost and % Markup on Cost Are Known:

$$\text{Selling Price} = \text{Cost} + \% \text{ Markup on Cost (Cost)}$$

Finding Selling Price When Cost and % Markup on Selling Price Are Known:

$$\text{Selling Price} = \frac{\text{Cost}}{(1 - \% \text{ Markup on Selling Price})}$$

Therefore, you would be willing to pay $4.80 for the item. If the item cannot be found at $4.80 or less, then it is probably not worth stocking.

Likewise, if a retailer purchases an item for $12 and wants a 40-percent markup on selling price, how would the retailer determine the selling price? Returning to our original equation (SP = C + M), we know that SP = C + 0.40P since markup is 40 percent of selling price. If markup is 40 percent of selling price, then cost must be 60 percent since cost and markup are the complements of each other and must total 100 percent. Thus, if

$$60\% \text{ SP} = \$12$$

then divide both sides by 60 percent:

$$\text{SP} = \$20$$

Initial Versus Maintained Markup

Up to this point, we have assumed that retailers have been able to sell the product at the price initially set when the product arrived at the store. We have assumed that the initial markup (the markup placed on the merchandise when the store receives it) is equal to the maintained markup or achieved markup (the actual selling price less the cost). Since in many cases the actual selling price for some of the firm's merchandise is lower than the original selling price, the firm's maintained markup is usually lower than the initial markup. Thus, maintained markup differs from initial markup by the amount of reductions:

Initial markup = (original retail price − cost)/original retail price
Maintained markup = (actual retail price − cost)/actual retail price

Five reasons can account for the difference between initial and maintained markups. First is the need to balance demand with supply. Since most markup formulas are cost-oriented, rather than demand-oriented, adjustments in selling prices will occur. This is especially true when consumer demand changes and the only way for retailers to reduce their inventory and make their merchandise salable is by taking a markdown or reduction in selling price. A second reason is stock shortages. Shortages can occur from theft by employees or customers and by mismarking the price when merchandise is received or sold. In either case, the selling price received for the goods will be less than the price carried in the inventory records. In fact, clerical error probably accounts for more stock shortages than theft. Third, there are employee and customer discounts. Employees are usually given some discount privileges after they have worked for the firm for a specified period of time. Also, certain customer groups (e.g., religious and senior-citizen groups) may be given special discount privileges.

The fourth reason is the cost of alterations. Some fashion-apparel items require alterations before the product is acceptable to the customer. While men's clothing is often altered free of charge, there is usually a small charge for altering women's wear. Nevertheless, this charge usually does not cover all alteration costs, so alterations are actually a part of the cost of the merchandise.

A fifth and final reason that initial markup may be different from maintained markup is cash discounts, which are offered to retailers by manufacturers or suppliers to encourage prompt payment of bills. Any cash discounts taken reduce the cost of merchandise and therefore make the maintained markup higher than the initial markup. This is just the opposite of the first four factors.

Some large retailers ignore cash discounts in calculating initial markup because the buyer may have little control over whether or not the discount is taken. The reason for this is that achieving discounts through prompt payment is thought to be the result of financial operations rather than merchandising decisions, and therefore the buyer should not be penalized if the discounts are not taken.

Planning Initial Markups

As the previous discussion illustrates, retailers do not casually arrive at an initial markup percentage. The initial markup percentage must be a carefully planned process. Markups must be large enough to cover all of the operating expenses and still provide a reasonable profit to the firm. In addition, markups must provide for markdowns, shortages, employee discounts, and alteration expenses (all of these together are referred to as *total reductions*), which reduce net revenue. Likewise, cash discounts taken, which increase net revenue, must be included.

Initial Markup Equation

To determine the initial markup, use the following formula:

Initial markup percentage = (operating expenses + net profit + markdowns
+ stock shortages + employee and customer discounts
+ alterations costs − cash discounts)/(net sales
+ markdowns + stock shortages
+ employee and customer discounts)

We can simplify this equation if we remember that markdowns, stock shortages, and employee and customer discounts are all retail reductions from stock levels. Likewise, gross margin is the sum of operating expenses and net profit. This produces a simpler formula:

Initial markup percentage = (gross margin + alterations costs − cash discounts
+ reductions)/(net sales + reductions)

Because some retailers record cash discounts as other income and not as a cost reduction in determining initial markup, the formula can be simplified one more time:

Initial markup percentage = (gross margin + alterations costs
+ reductions)/(net sales + reductions)

Regardless of which of the three formulas is used, the retailer must always remember the effect of each of the following items when planning initial markup: operating expenses, net profits, markdowns, stock shortages, employee and customer discounts, alterations costs, cash discounts taken, and net sales.

At this point, a numerical example might be helpful. Assume that a retailer plans to achieve net sales of $1 million and expects operating expenses to be $270,000. The net profit goal is $60,000. Planned reductions include $80,000 for markdowns, $20,000 for merchandise shortages, and $10,000 for employee and customer discounts. Alteration costs are expected to be $20,000, and cash discounts from suppliers are expected to be $10,000. What is the initial markup percentage that should be planned? What is the cost of merchandise to be sold?

The initial markup percentage can be obtained by using the original equation:

Initial markup percentage = ($270,000 + $60,000 + $80,000 + $20,000
+ $10,000 + $20,000 − $10,000)/($1,000,000
+ $80,000 + $20,000 + $10,000) = 40.54%

The cost of merchandise sold can also be found. We know that the gross margin is operating expenses plus net profit ($330,000). This gross profit is equivalent to net sales less cost of merchandise sold, where cost of merchandise sold includes alteration costs and where cash discounts are subtracted. Thus, in the problem at hand, we know that $1 million less cost of merchandise sold (including alterations costs and subtracting cash discounts) is equal to $670,000. Since the alterations costs are planned at $20,000 and cash discounts at $10,000, the cost of merchandise is equal to $660,000 ($670,000 − $20,000 + $10,000).

We can verify our result by returning to the basic initial markup formula: asking price minus cost divided by asking price. The asking price is the planned net sales of $1 million plus planned reductions of $110,000 ($80,000 for markdowns, $20,000 for shortages, and $10,000 for employee and customer discounts). The cost is the cost of merchandise before the alteration costs and prior to cash discounts, or $660,000. Using the basic initial markup formula, we obtain ($1,110,000 − $660,000)/$1,110,000, or 40.54 percent. This is the same result we achieved earlier.

The preceding computations resulted in a markup percentage on retail selling price for merchandise lines storewide. Obviously, not all lines or items within lines should be priced by mechanically applying this markup percentage, since the actions of competitors will affect the prices for each merchandise line. Thus, the retailer will want to price the mix of merchandise lines in such a fashion that a storewide markup percentage is obtained. To achieve this, some lines may be priced with considerably higher markups and others with substantially lower markups than the storewide average that was planned using the initial markup planning equation. It will be helpful to explore some of the common reasons for varying the markup percentage on different lines or items within lines.

Markup Determinants

In planning initial markups, it is useful to know some of the general rules of markup determination. These are summarized as follows:

1. As goods are sold through more retail outlets, the markup percentage decreases. On the other hand, selling through few retail outlets means a greater markup percentage.
2. The higher the handling and storage costs of the goods, the higher the markup.
3. The greater the risk of a price reduction due to the seasonality of the goods, the greater the magnitude of the markup percentage early in the season.
4. The higher the demand inelasticity of price for the goods, the greater the markup percentage.

Although these rules are common to all retail lines, other rules are unique to each line of trade and are learned only through experience in the respective lines—for example, how much to mark up produce in a supermarket during different seasons.

Markdown Management

LO 4

Why is markdown management so important in retailing?

Although retailers would prefer to have their initial markup (the one placed on the merchandise when the store receives it) equal to the maintained markup (the actual selling price less the cost), this seldom happens. **Markdowns**, which are reductions in the price of an item taken in order to stimulate sales, result in a firm receiving a lower price for its merchandise than originally asked. The markdown percentage is the amount of the reduction divided by the original selling price:

Markdown percentage = Amount of reduction/original selling price

markdown
Is any reduction in the price of an item from its initially established price.

Thus, maintained markup (sometimes referred to as *gross margin* or just plain *gross*) is the key to profitability because it is the difference between the actual selling price and the cost of that merchandise.

For effective retail price management, markdowns should be planned. This is true in principle because pricing is not a science with high degrees of precision but an art form with considerable room for error. If retailers knew everything they needed to know about demand and supply factors, they could use the science of economics to establish a price that would maximize profits and ensure the sale of all the merchandise. Unfortunately, retailers do not possess perfect information about supply and demand factors. As a result, the entire merchandising process is subject to error, which makes pricing difficult. Four basic errors can occur: (1) buying errors, (2) pricing errors, (3) merchandising errors, and (4) promotion errors.

Buying Errors

Errors in buying occur on the supply side of the pricing question. They result when the retailer buys the wrong merchandise or buys the right merchandise in too large a quantity. The merchandise purchased could have been in the wrong styles, sizes, colors, patterns, or price range. Too large a quantity could have been purchased because demand was overestimated or a recession was not foreseen. Whatever the cause of the buying error, the net result is a need to cut the price to move the merchandise. Often the resulting prices are below the actual cost of the merchandise to the retailer. Thus, buying errors can be quite costly. As a consequence, you might expect that the retail manager would wish to minimize buying errors. However, this is not the case. The retailer could minimize buying errors by being extremely conservative. It would buy only what it knew the customer wanted and what it could be certain of selling. Buying errors would be minimized, but at the expense of lost profit opportunities on some riskier types of purchase decisions. Recall that when we reviewed the determinants of markups, we mentioned that the greater the risk of potential price reductions, the higher the markup percentage. This is simply another way of recognizing that taking a gamble on some purchases that may be buying errors, can be profitable if initial markups are high. You may want to review the most common buying errors discussed in Chapter 9.

Chapter 3 explained that the demographics for baby boomers are different from those of Gen X or Gen Y consumers. These groups are not only different in age, but also in their buying behavior. However, many retailers employ buyers who are from the baby boomer generation. When boomers are buying for Gen X and Gen Y customers, it can be difficult for them to prevent buying errors unless they make an intentional effort to avoid such mistakes.

Pricing Errors

Errors in pricing merchandise can be another cause of markdowns. Errors occur when the price of the item is too high to move the product at the speed and in the quantity desired. The goods may have been bought in the right styles, at the right time, and in the right quantities, but the price on the item may simply be too high. This would create purchase resistance on the part of the typical customer.

An overly high price is often relative to the pricing behavior of competitors. Perhaps, in principle, the price would have been acceptable, but if competitors price the same item substantially lower, then the original retailer's price becomes too high.

Merchandising Errors

Although many new retailers believe that carrying over seasonal or fashion merchandise into the next merchandising season is the most common merchandise error, it really isn't. Failure by the buyer to inform the sales staff of how the new merchandise relates to the current stock, ties in with the store's image, and satisfies the needs of the store's target market is the most common merchandising error. Another mistake is the failure to keep the department manager and sales force informed about the new merchandise lines. Too many times, the new merchandise is left in the storeroom or the salespeople are not informed of the key features of the new item, and thus the customer will never be able to become excited about the new merchandise. Another merchandising error is improper handling of the merchandise by the sales staff or ineffective visual presentation of the merchandise. Mishandling errors include failure to stock the new merchandise behind old merchandise whenever possible or simply misplacing the merchandise. All too often a slow seller is a "lost" bundle of merchandise.

Promotion Errors

Finally, even when the right goods are purchased in the right quantities and are priced correctly, the merchandise often fails to move as planned. In this situation, the cause is most often a promotion error. The consumer has not been properly informed or prompted to purchase the merchandise. The advertising, personal selling, sales-promotion activities, or in-store displays were too weak or sporadic to elicit a strong response from potential customers.

Markdown Policy

Retailers will find it advantageous to develop a markdown timing policy. In almost all situations, retailers will find it necessary to take markdowns; the crucial decisions become when and how much of a markdown to take. In principle, there are two extremes to a markdown timing policy: early and late.

Early Markdown Policy

Most retailers who concentrate on high inventory turnover pursue an early markdown policy. Markdowns taken early speed the movement of merchandise and also generally enable the retailer to take less of a markdown per unit to dispose of the goods. One of the author's first bosses taught him early in his retailing career that "The first markdown is the cheapest to take. Therefore, once you take it, do not look back." In other words, when you as a buyer make a merchandising error, take your loss early and do not look back because taking that early markdown will allow the dollars obtained from selling the merchandise to be used to help finance more salable goods. At the same time, the customer seems to benefit, since markdowns are offered quickly on goods that some consumers still think of as fashionable, and the store has the appearance of having fresh merchandise. For example, the top 20 percent of women's apparel shoppers usually visit their favorite store three to four times a month. Thus, it is important for the retailer to always have the appearance of presenting fresh merchandise. Therefore, many fashion retailers use the following set of rules when taking early markdowns.

- After the third week, mark it down 25 percent from the original price.
- After the seventh week, mark it down 50 percent from the original price.
- After the 11th week, mark it down 75 percent from the original price.
- After the 16th week, sell it to an outlet store, give it to charity, or place it on an online auction.[22]

Another advantage of the early markdown policy is that it allows the retailer to replenish lower-priced lines from the higher ones that have been marked down. For instance, many women's wear retailers will regularly take slow-moving dresses from higher-priced lines and move them down to the moderate- or lower-priced lines.

Late-Markdown Policy

Allowing goods to have a long trial period before a markdown is taken is called a *late-markdown* policy. This policy avoids disrupting the sale of regular merchandise by too frequently marking goods down. As a consequence, customers will learn to look forward to a semiannual or annual clearance in which all or most merchandise is marked down. Thus, the bargain hunters or low-end customers will be attracted only at infrequent intervals.

Regardless of which timing policy a retailer follows, it must plan for these reductions. Markdowns are not always the result of buyer errors. They may simply be selling merchandise that is late in the season and before larger markdowns must be taken. Remember, when preparing a merchandise budget, the retailer must estimate reductions for that time period.

Amount of Markdown

An issue related to the timing of markdowns is their magnitude. If the retailer waits to use a markdown at the last moment, then the markdown should probably be large enough to move the remaining merchandise. As was mentioned earlier in this chapter's "Retailing: The Inside Story" box, the average American now considers 40 percent off the original price of an item to be a bargain. Thus, a late markdown should be at least this much. However, such a large amount is not necessary with an early markdown. An early markdown only needs to be large enough to provide a sales stimulant. Once sales are stimulated, the retailer can watch merchandise movement; when it slows, the retailer can provide another stimulant by again marking it down. Which strategy is more profitable depends on the situation. One rule of thumb for early markdowns is that prices should be marked down at least 20 percent in order for the consumer to notice. Recently, because they have lost their impact with the consumer, large chains have begun to move away from chainwide sales late in the selling season. They are now focusing on using early markdowns region by region based on supply and demand considerations.[23] Remember, however, that while some general rules regarding markdown percentage were presented, the actual markdown percentage should vary with the type of merchandise, time of season, and competition.

Often retailers are able to have their suppliers supplement their markdown losses with *markdown money* or some other type of price reductions.[24] Here's how it works: Let's say Acme Clothing Company delivers 100 sweaters to Judy's Dress Shop at the wholesale price of $40 each. Judy in turn plans to take her customary markup of 50 percent on the selling price in order to sell each sweater for $80, thus producing a gross margin of $4,000.

Some retailers regularly set their initial prices above manufacturer or market prices then quickly mark the merchandise down. Thus a sign such as 80% off, may not indicate an 80% markdown from the real selling price.

However, after three months, Judy still has 50 of the sweaters in stock, which she puts on sale for $50 each in order to move the merchandise. After selling the remaining sweaters, Judy's gross margin is only $2,500: (50 × $80) + (50 × $50) − (100 × $40).

The following month, Judy goes to market and visits the Acme showroom. Judy wants Acme to pay her the $1,500 she lost in taking the markdowns on their sweaters. Judy threatens Acme with a loss of future orders if it does not cover her losses. Does this sound fair to you?

Actually, this type of scenario happens quite frequently when buyers go to market. Buyers maintain that manufacturers should share in the responsibility when the merchandise does not sell as promised. Buyers claim that if the supplier cannot deliver the gross margin desired, then there is no reason to reorder from that supplier again. From the retailers' standpoint, when the manufacturer contributes markdown money, the manufacturers are really asking for a second chance to prove the salability of their lines. This markdown money could be in the form of cash payments or discounts on future purchases.

Now let's look at how the maintained markup percentage is determined. A retailer purchases the T-shirt used in an earlier example for $16 with the intent of selling it for $25 (an initial markup of 36 percent). However, the T-shirt did not sell at that price, and the retailer reduced it to $20 in order to sell it. This would result in a maintained markup of 20 percent:

$$\text{Maintained markup} = (\text{actual selling price} - \text{cost})/\text{actual selling price}$$
$$= \$4/\$20 = 20\%$$

The following formula can also be used to determine the maintained markup percentage:

$$\text{Maintained markup percentage} = \text{initial markup percentage}$$
$$- [(\text{reduction percentage})(100\%$$
$$- \text{initial markup percentage})]$$

where

$$\text{Reduction percentage} = \text{amount of reductions}/\text{net sales}$$

In the preceding example,

$$\text{Maintained markup percentage} = 36\% - [(\$5/\$20) \times (100\% - 36\%)]$$
$$= 36\% - 16\% = 20\%$$

SUMMARY

What factors should a retailer consider when establishing pricing objectives and policies?   LO 1

Pricing decisions are among the most frequent a retailer must make. They cannot be made independently because they interact with the merchandise, location, promotion, credit and check cashing, customer service, and store-image decisions the retailer has already made as well as with federal and state legal constraints.

The pricing objectives the retailer ultimately sets must also agree with the retailer's mission statement and merchandise policies. These objectives can be profit oriented, sales oriented, or seek to maintain the status quo.

STUDENT STUDY GUIDE

After establishing its pricing objectives, the retailer must next determine the pricing policies to achieve these goals. These policies must reflect the expectations of the target market.

LO 2

What are the various pricing strategies available to the retailer?

Among the strategies discussed were customary pricing, variable pricing, flexible pricing, one-price policies, price lining, odd pricing, multiple-unit pricing, bundle pricing, leader pricing, bait-and-switch pricing, and private-label brand pricing.

LO 3

How does a retailer calculate the various markups?

The basic markup equation states that, per unit, the retail selling price is equal to the dollar cost plus the dollar markup. Markups can be expressed as either a percentage of selling price or a percentage of cost to the retailer. Since the initial selling price that the retailer puts on a newly purchased item may not be attractive enough to sell all the inventory of that item, the price may need to be reduced. When we talk of actual selling prices versus initial selling prices, we mean the difference between an initial and a maintained markup.

Initial markups should be planned. Next, the initial storewide markup percentage can be determined by using operating expenses, net profit, alterations costs, cash discounts, markdowns, stock shortages, employee and customer discounts, and sales. The retailer must recognize that not all items can be priced by mechanically applying this markup percentage. Some lines will need to be priced to yield a considerably higher markup and others a substantially lower markup. The initial markup is seldom equal to the maintained markup because of three kinds of reductions: markdowns, shortages, and employee and customer discounts.

LO 4

Why is markdown management so important in retailing?

Because the retailer does not possess perfect information about supply and demand, markdowns are inevitable. Markdowns are usually due to errors in buying, pricing, merchandising, or promotion. Because markdowns are inevitable, the retailer needs to establish a markdown policy. Early markdowns speed the movement of merchandise and also allow the retailer to take less of a markdown per unit to dispose of the merchandise. Late markdowns avoid disrupting the sale of regular merchandise by too-frequent markdowns. The best policy from a profit perspective depends on the particular situation.

TERMS TO REMEMBER

target-return objective	price lining
profit maximization	trading up
skimming	trading down
penetration	odd pricing
below-market pricing policy	multiple-unit pricing
price zone	leader pricing
above-market pricing policy	loss leader
customary pricing	high–low pricing
variable pricing	bait-and-switch pricing
flexible pricing	markup
one-price policy	markdown

REVIEW AND DISCUSSION QUESTIONS

What factors should a retailer consider when establishing pricing objectives and policies?   **LO 1**

1. How does a store's location affect the price it can charge?
2. Is pricing really an interactive decision? Provide an example of how pricing should interact with the services offered by the retailer.
3. When should a retailer use the penetration pricing objective?
4. If a retailer wants to use an above-market pricing policy, how should that retailer's retailing mix be different from the competition?

What are the various pricing strategies available to the retailer?   **LO 2**

5. What is the difference between variable and flexible pricing? Does the demand for the item being sold affect either of these strategies?
6. Despite the lack of supportive research, odd-numbered pricing is still used in retailing today. Shouldn't gas stations drop those 0.9 cents from their posted prices and round them to the nearest penny?
7. Would you prefer to buy a car from a dealer using a flexible or a one-price policy? Why?
8. What type of retailer is most likely to use leader pricing?
9. In the United States, a loss leader is generally accepted as legal. Yet in other countries such a policy is illegal. What should it be?

How does a retailer calculate the various markups?   **LO 3**

10. Compute the markup on selling price for an item that retails for $49.95 and costs $31.20.
11. Complete the following:

	Dress Shirt	Sport Shirt	Belt
Selling price ($)	40.00	49.99	15.00
Cost ($)	23.00	25.35	6.50
Markup in dollars ($)			
Markup percentage on cost (%)			
Markup percentage on selling price (%)			

12. A buyer tells you that she realized a markup of $50 on an interview suit for a college senior. You know that her markup is 25 percent of retail. What did the suit cost her?
13. If the markup on cost is 76 percent, what is the markup on selling price?
14. Which is more important to a retailer—initial or maintained markup?
15. Can an initial markup ever be equal to the maintained markup? Explain.
16. Intimate Apparel wants to produce a 9-percent operating profit this year on sales of $1,200,000. Based on past experiences, the owner made the following estimates:

Net alteration expenses	$1,100	Employee discount	$5,400
Markdowns	61,000	Operating expenses	275,000
Stock shortages	12,200	Cash discounts earned	4,100

Given these estimates, what average initial markup should be asked for the upcoming year?

LO 4 Why is markdown management so important in retailing?

17. Why should a retailer plan on taking markdowns during a merchandising season?

18. Somebody once said, "Buyers only need to take a markdown when they make mistakes. Therefore, good buyers should never have to take markdowns." Do you agree with that statement? Explain your answer.

19. Which markdown policy would be best for sporting goods? Explain your reasoning. Would your answer be the same for a specialty apparel store?

20. The buyer for the women's sweater department has purchased wool sweaters for $35.69. She uses an odd pricing policy and wants to sell them at a 49-percent markup on selling price. At what price should each sweater be sold?

21. The buyer for men's shirts has a price point of $45 and requires a markup of 45 percent. What would be the highest price he should pay for a shirt to sell at this price point?

22. A buyer submits the following plans to his general merchandise manager: planned sales = $135,000; planned initial markup = 40 percent; planned reductions = $41,000. Based on these projections, what is the planned maintained markup percentage?

SAMPLE TEST QUESTIONS

LO 1 What word best describes the relationship between a retailer's pricing decisions and the merchandise, location, promotion, credit and check cashing, services, image, and legal decisions that retailers must make?

a. independent
b. separate
c. interactive
d. competitive
e. multifaceted

LO 2 If a retailer is offering the same products and quantities to different customers at different prices, the retailer has what kind of pricing policy?

a. two-price
b. customary
c. flexible
d. leader
e. variable

LO 3 If a retailer buys a product for $25 and sells it for $45, what is the markup percentage if the markup is based on the selling price?

a. 44.4 percent
b. 80 percent
c. 75 percent
d. 100 percent
e. 55.5 percent

An item was marked down to $19.99 from its original retail price of $29.99. What is the reduction percentage for this item?

a. 33.3 percent
b. 25 percent
c. 50 percent
d. 41.3 percent
e. 66.7 percent

WRITING AND SPEAKING EXERCISE

In March, you were hired by Jack Spengel to be his summer intern. Now it is late May and you have just reported for your first day on the job. Spengel's is a locally owned furniture store in a town of 12,000 in southwest Missouri, and Jack has operated the store for almost 40 years. The closest big-box furniture operation is Haverty's in Springfield, some 45 miles away.

Unfortunately, today is the worst possible day to start work. As you arrive about 10 minutes ahead of time, you see Jack and his daughter Sue arguing in the back office. An accountant who lives in Chicago, Sue has brought the grandkids home for the Memorial Day weekend. As you approach the office, you can hear Sue saying rather loudly "Dad, you got it all wrong. Saying we are the cheapest is dangerous. You can't position yourself by price, because all you are going to do is make your customers loyal to price. Besides, price is too easy to match or beat. And if you get your customers loyal to price, they will just drive over to Springfield."

Jack saw you and motioned you to come into the office. However, Sue continued. "Dad, you have to promote on the basis your location, outstanding service, your support of the local community, and just being price competitive. After all, the town folks won't drive to Springfield to save a couple of hundred dollars on a bedroom suite. When you purchased your automobile here, was Joe's [the local dealer] price as cheap as the dealers in Springfield? No, you bought it here because you wanted the convenience of having a local dealer servicing it. That's what I am telling you to do. Go back to your old slogan of 'Spengel's: Where Good Furniture Is Not Expensive.' Become more promotional. Dress up your store windows, rearrange your merchandise, set up a website, and shop the other stores in nearby towns to see what they are doing. Just get away from fighting a pricing battle that you can't win. Haverty's has too much buying power with the manufacturers."

With that, Sue left the office and never acknowledged you were there.

Upon turning his attention to you, Jack apologizes for involving you in the matter but states that he would like your input concerning who you feel is right. Therefore, prepare a presentation or memo telling Jack what he should do and explain the reasoning for each of your recommendations.

RETAIL PROJECT

On your next trip to a mall, visit all the anchor stores and leading apparel stores. Look around at displays and notice if they are having sales. Now, based on the amount of merchandise on sale and the amount of reductions, determine if each store is using an early or late markdown policy. Explain your reasoning for each store and especially explain the reasoning for differences between the stores. (*Note:* You can also do this project for different websites.)

APPLICATIONS

PLANNING YOUR OWN RETAIL BUSINESS

The online retail operation you recently opened is doing well, but you are uncertain of your pricing strategy. Currently, the typical customer purchases four items at an average price of $11.71 and for an average transaction size of $46.84. The cost of goods is 60 percent of sales, which yields a gross margin of 40 percent. You are considering lowering prices by 10 percent across the board so you can better compete with other music e-tailers. If you lower prices by 10 percent, you believe that the average number of items purchased per customer would rise by 25 percent. Assuming your assumptions are correct, should you lower prices by 10 percent across the board? If not, do you have an alternative pricing strategy to propose?

Advertising and Promotion

OVERVIEW:

Promotion is a major generator of demand in retailing. In this chapter, we focus on the role of advertising, sales promotion, and publicity in the operation of a retail business. Retail selling, another important element of promotion, will be discussed in Chapter 12. Our discussion here is directed at describing how retailers should manage their firms' promotional resources.

LEARNING OBJECTIVES:

After reading this chapter, you should be able to:

1. Name the four basic components of the retailer's promotional mix and discuss their relationship with other decisions.
2. Describe the differences between a retailer's long-term and short-term promotional objectives.
3. List the six steps involved in developing a retailer's advertising campaign.
4. Explain how retailers manage their sales promotion and publicity.

LO 1

The Retail Promotion Mix

What are the four basic components of the retailer's promotion mix, and how are they related to other retailer decisions?

promotion
Is a means that retailers use to bring traffic into their stores, and it includes advertising, sales promotion, publicity, and personal selling.

Retailers use **promotion** to generate sales by making their targeted customers aware of current offerings. This does not mean that sales cannot occur without using promotion. Some sales will always take place, even if the retailer spends no money on promotion. For example, households close to a retailer may shop there strictly for convenience, and a passerby might occasionally visit the store for an impulse purchase. Most retailers, however, use a combination of location, price levels, displays, merchandise assortments, customer service, and promotion as a means to generate store traffic and sales.

Retailers make trade-offs between the different elements of the retailing mix. Some retailers like Buckle, which handles medium- to high-priced casual apparel, footwear, and accessories for fashion-conscious young men and women and has almost 400 mall locations in 40 states, prefer to use prime, high-traffic mall locations. By paying a higher rent for the mall location, the retailer can participate in mall-sponsored promotions rather than develop its own promotions to generate customer interest. As a result, the Nebraska-based chain spends only 1 percent of its sales on promotions. Walmart is another retailer that spends only a small percentage (0.6%) of its sales on promotion.[1] Walmart believes that lower prices are more effective than location and heavy promotional expenditures in generating traffic. Thus, while direct promotional expenditures are not always a prerequisite for generating sales, they are a means of achieving sales above those that could be obtained merely by offering a lower price range, having a better location, or providing outstanding service. Many of today's successful retailers use promotion to not only bring traffic into their stores but also move the traffic to the various selling areas of the store and entice the traffic into purchasing merchandise.

Types of Promotion

Promotion has four basic components: advertising, sales promotion, publicity, and personal selling. Collectively, these components make up the retailer's promotional mix. Each component is defined as follows and will be discussed from a managerial perspective.[2]

1. **Advertising** is "paid, nonpersonal communication through various media by business firms, nonprofit organizations, and individuals who are in some way identified in the advertising message and who hope to inform [or] persuade members of a particular audience; includes communication of products, services, institutions, and ideas." Retail advertising's function is primarily to inform potential buyers of the availability and price of a retailer's offering with the objective of developing consumer preferences for a particular retailer. Retailers most commonly use the following advertising media: Internet, newspapers, radio, television, and printed circulars.

2. **Sales promotions** "involve the use of media and non-media marketing pressure applied for a predetermined, limited period of time at the level of the consumer, retailer or wholesaler in order to stimulate trial, increase consumer demand, or improve product availability." The most popular sales promotion tools in retailing are premiums, frequent-buyer programs, coupons, in-store displays, contests and sweepstakes, product demonstrations, and sampling.

3. **Publicity** is "non-paid-for communications of information about the company or product, generally in some media form." Popular examples are Macy's Thanksgiving Day parade and local retail support of various civic and educational groups.

4. **Personal selling** is "selling that involves a face-to-face interaction with the consumer." Personal selling is often used during the sale of shopping goods and is designed to assist the customer in gathering product information while simultaneously convincing the customer to purchase the retailer's particular products or services.

All four components of the retailer's promotional mix need to be managed from a total systems perspective. In other words, they need to be effectively blended together to achieve the retailer's promotional objectives and reinforce each other. If the advertising conveys quality and status, so must the sales personnel, publicity, and sales promotion; otherwise, the consumer will receive conflicting or inconsistent messages about the retailer, which will result in confusion and loss of patronage.

The management of promotional efforts in retailing must also fit into the retailer's overall strategy. Promotion decisions relate to and must be integrated with

advertising
Is paid, nonpersonal communication through various media by business firms, nonprofit organizations, and individuals who are in some way identified in the advertising message and who hope to inform or persuade members of a particular audience; includes communication of products, services, institutions, and ideas.

sales promotion
Involves the use of media and nonmedia marketing pressure applied for a predetermined, limited period of time at the level of consumer, retailer, or wholesaler in order to stimulate trial, increase consumer demand, or improve product availability.

publicity
Is non-paid-for communications of information about the company or product, generally in some media form.

personal selling
Involves a face-to-face interaction with the consumer with the goal of selling the consumer merchandise or services.

other management decisions such as location, merchandise, credit, cash flow, building and fixtures, price, and customer service. For example:

1. There is a maximum distance consumers will travel to visit a retail store. Thus a retailer's *location* will help determine the target for promotions. A retailer should direct its promotional dollars first toward households in its **primary trading area**, the area where the retailer can serve customers in terms of convenience and accessibility better than the competition, and then to **secondary trading areas**, areas where the retailer is still competitive, even if some competitors have a locational advantage. However, e-tailers who are global in presence must determine specific areas, whether they be countries or communities, in which to focus their promotional efforts.

2. Retailers need high levels of store traffic to keep their *merchandise* turning over rapidly. Promotion helps build traffic.

3. A retailer's *credit* customers are more store loyal and purchase in larger quantities. Thus, they are an excellent target for increased promotional efforts. Although the increased use of MasterCard, Visa, and Discover cards has impacted this retail advantage in recent years, many retailers have overcome this problem by developing their own cobranded cards or by using "No interest for 90 days" promotions.

4. A retailer confronted with a temporary *cash-flow* problem can use promotion to increase short-run cash flow.

5. A retailer's promotional strategy must be reinforced by its *building and fixtures* decisions. Promotional creativity and style should coincide with building and fixture creativity and style. If the ads are exciting and appeal to a particular target market, then so should the building and fixtures.

6. Promotion provides customers with more information. That information will help them make better purchase decisions because risk is reduced. Therefore, promotion can actually be viewed as a major component of *customer service*.

The retailer that systematically integrates its promotional programs with other retail decision areas will be better able to achieve high-performance results. One retailer developed a set of basic promotional guidelines that all retailers should follow:

- Try to utilize only promotions that are consistent with and will enhance your store image.

- Review the success or failure of each promotion to help in developing better future promotions.

- Wherever possible, test new promotions before making a major investment by using them on a broader scale.

- Use appeals that are of interest to your target market and that are realistic to obtain. For example, double couponing offers everybody a reward, but a sweepstakes has only one winner.

- Make sure your objectives are measurable.

- Make sure your objectives are obtainable.

- Develop total promotional campaigns, not just ads.

- The lower the rent, the higher the promotional expenses generally needed.

- New stores need higher promotional budgets than established stores.

- Stores in out-of-the-way locations require higher promotional budgets than stores with heavy traffic.[3]

Promotion in the Supply Chain

The retailer is not the only member of the marketing supply chain that uses promotion. Manufacturers also invest in promotion for many of the same reasons retailers do: to move merchandise more rapidly, speed up cash flow, and better retain customer loyalty. However, the promotional activities of the retailer's supply-chain partners may sometimes conflict with the retailer's promotions. There are three major differences in the way retailers and manufacturers use promotion:

1. **Product Image Versus Availability.** The manufacturer's primary goal is to create a positive image for the product itself and differentiate it from competing products. For example, when introducing a new product, a manufacturer will attempt to explain how the product works. Retailers, on the other hand, are primarily interested in announcing to their customers that they have the product available for purchase at a convenient location.

2. **Specific Product Benefits Versus Price**. Manufacturers generally do not care where customers make their purchases as long as they buy their product, which is why they promote the benefits of their products. Retailers, on the other hand, do not care which brand the customer purchases. (Remember, retailers carry products from many different manufacturers.) A retailer just wants the customer to make the purchase in its store. Thus, in addition to availability, retailers feature the product's price in their ads.

3. **Focused Image Versus Cluttered Ads**. In comparison to manufacturers, most retailers carry a larger variety and breath of products, while manufacturers produce a greater depth than most retailers carry. Thus, retail ads, which are usually geared toward short-term results, tend to be cluttered with many different products as opposed to the manufacturer's ad, which focuses on a single product theme.

Sometimes a lack of promotional harmony by supply-chain members results from other factors. Consider the case of the automobile channel. Assume that the country's rate of real economic growth has been negative for the past year; as a result, the country's auto sales are 20 percent lower than last year. The manufacturer believes that this economy is recovering and therefore does not want to get into a price war by offering major price rebates or other special promotions from the factory. However, the automobile dealers believe that the country is still in the midst of a recession. They feel that the manufacturer's advertising should be increased and that special allowances should be given for increased local advertising. They would also like to see the manufacturer tie in this increased advertising program with cash rebates paid for by the factory. Because the manufacturer and dealer have different beliefs about the economy's future, serious disagreements could occur between them.

A second possible source of problems is when the supply-chain members feel that the chain's promotional campaign is a mistake.

Many major supermarket chains, for example, print weekly circulars that allow their suppliers to advertise directly to their customers. In reality, the supermarket makes money on this promotion since together the suppliers, in total, pay more than the actual cost of the circulars. In addition, the suppliers must offer big discounts on the chain's purchases of the advertised items. As a result, many suppliers don't feel this is a good promotional investment. Nevertheless, most suppliers sign up for such a program to avoid angering the retailers that control so much of their business. Such different perceptions show why it is important for retailers to foster a cooperative relationship with their suppliers (discussed in

In the past circulars were generally distributed as free-standing-inserts in local newspapers. Today, with many consumers getting their news from the Internet, retailers now also make their circulars available as customers enter the store.

Chapter 5) so that the conflict can be resolved. A similar conflict occurred during the recent economic slowdown when retailers shifted some promotions, especially in-store types, toward their less-expensive private-label brands.[4]

LO 2 — Promotional Objectives

What are the differences between a retailer's long-term and short-term promotional objectives?

To efficiently manage the promotional mix, retail managers must first establish their promotional objectives. These promotional objectives should flow from the retailer's overall objectives that were discussed in Chapter 2. They should be the natural outgrowth of the retailer's operations management plans. As such, all promotional objectives should ultimately seek to improve the retailer's financial performance, since this is what strategic and administrative plans are intended to accomplish.

Exhibit 11.1 shows how promotional objectives should relate to financial performance objectives. As this exhibit shows, promotional objectives can be established to help improve both long- and short-term financial performance.

Long-Term Objectives

institutional advertising
Is a type of advertising in which the retailer attempts to gain long-term benefits by promoting and selling the store itself rather than the merchandise in the store.

Institutional advertising is an attempt by the retailer to gain long-term benefits by selling the store itself rather than the merchandise in it. By doing this, the retailer is creating a positive image for itself in the consumer's mind. Retailers using institutional ads generally seek to establish two long-term promotional objectives: creating a positive store image and public service.

Creating A Positive Store Image

The first long-term objective of a promotion is to establish or reinforce a positive store image, relative to its competitors, in its customers' minds. Here the retailer seeks to gain a differential advantage by establishing a favorable impression that is distinct from other retailers. By providing such an image, the retailer hopes to

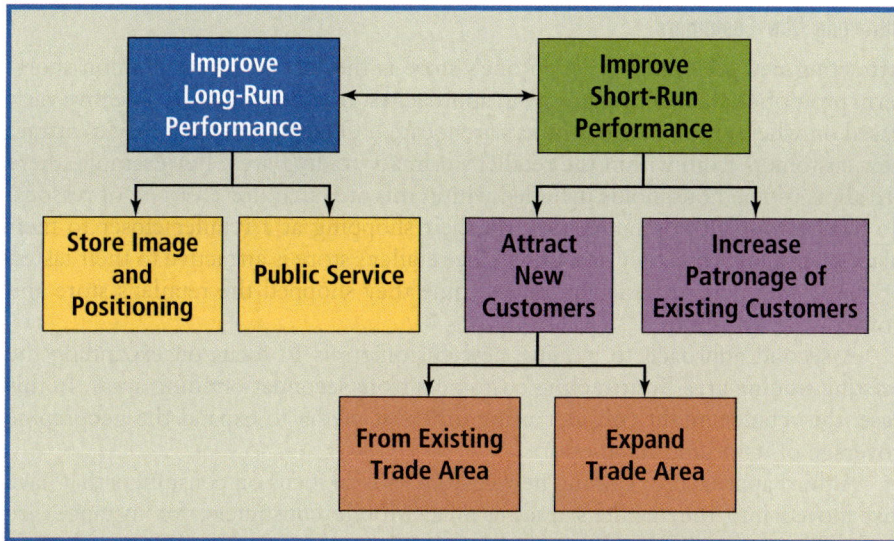

Exhibit 11.1
Possible Promotion
Objectives in Retailing

develop an ongoing relationship with the customer. Promotion that fulfills this objective will improve the retailer's long-term financial performance. Two of the most successful retailers in this area have been Neiman Marcus and Nordstrom. Today, when consumers think of these retailers, they perceive elegantly designed stores, top names in fashion, excellent customer service, and a helpful, knowledgeable sales staff. However, as you might expect, this type of promotion will also assist the retailer in the short run, such as when a consumer is seeking to purchase a gift for a special friend and the retailer's ad suggests that "perfect" gift. (A store's promotional efforts have been found to be a key predictor of store choice when gift shopping.)

Public-Service Promotion

The second long-term objective is directed at getting the consumer to perceive the retailer as a good citizen within the community. Retailers may sponsor public-service advertisements to honor local athletes and scholars as well as provide cash and merchandise to local charities. For example, some retailers offer meeting rooms for use by local civic organizations; some supermarkets have begun publishing consumer newsletters with health, cooking, safety, and beauty tips; still others sponsor programs on public-television stations.

Short-Term Objectives

Promotional advertising, on the other hand, attempts to bolster short-term performance by using product availability or price as a selling point. The two most common objectives of this type of promotion are increasing patronage from existing customers and attracting new customers.

Increasing Patronage From Existing Customers

Increased patronage is probably one of the most common promotional objectives found in retailing. Here the retailer seeks to encourage existing customers to make more of their purchases at the retailer's store.

Recently, one of the authors experienced such a promotion after buying a book on gardening at Amazon.com. Within a few days of making a purchase, he received a $50 coupon to purchase garden supplies from Amazon. Thus, Amazon.com's use of coupons to cross-sell is a clear attempt to increase patronage from its current customers.

promotional advertising
Is a type of advertising in which the retailer attempts to increase short-term performance by using product availability or price as a selling point.

Attracting New Customers

Attracting new customers to shop one's store is the second most common short-term promotional objective; however, approaches to achieve such an objective vary, based on where these new customers are located. One approach is to try to attract new customers from within the retailer's primary trading area. For example, there are always some households included within this area that, for a variety of reasons, do not patronize the retailer: they do their shopping at a retailer closer to their place of employment, they do not feel the retailer's store is attractive to their tastes, or they had a poor experience the last time they shopped the retailer's store and vowed never to return.

A second approach to gaining new customers is to focus on expanding the existing trading area by attracting customers from secondary trading areas. In this case, the retailer might consider using different media to expand the geographic coverage of its promotional efforts.

A third approach to gaining new customers is to focus on consumers that have just moved into the retailer's trading area. Mobile consumers, for instance, are generally more prone to use national retailers because of the familiarity with their product offerings, service levels, and prices. To overcome such issues, local retailers must rely on promotions that inform new customers of their offerings.

Interdependence

The two-way arrow in Exhibit 11.1 suggests that although promotional objectives are often established to improve either long- or short-term financial performance, each is also likely to benefit the other. For example, promotional efforts designed to build long-term financial performance are likely to have both immediate and cumulative effects. Similarly, efforts to promote short-term financial performance are likely to carry over, affecting the retailer's long-term future.

LO 3

Steps in Planning a Retail Advertising Campaign

What six steps are involved in developing a retail advertising campaign?

What is involved in planning a retail advertising campaign? As we discussed in Chapter 2, the elements of a retailer's advertising campaign are just one part of the company's overall strategy. A retailer's advertising campaign is a six-step process:

1. selecting advertising objectives,
2. budgeting for the campaign,
3. designing the message,
4. selecting the media to use,
5. scheduling of ads, and
6. evaluating the results.

Selecting Advertising Objectives

A retailer's advertising objectives should flow from its promotional objectives; however, they should be more specific because advertising itself is a specific element of the promotional mix. Objectives should only be chosen after the retailer considers several factors that are unique to itself: age of the store, its location, merchandise lines being sold, its competition, the size of its trading area, and what support is available from suppliers.

The specific objectives that advertising can accomplish are many and varied, and those chosen depend on the target market the retailer is seeking to reach. Examples of common objectives include the following:

- make consumers in your trading area aware that you offer the lowest prices (e.g., Walmart's "Save Money. Live Better.");
- make newcomers to your trading area aware of your existence (e.g., the Welcome Wagon coupons given to new residents of an area);
- make customers aware of your large stock selection (e.g., Nordstrom's promise of a free shirt if it is out of stock on the basic sizes);
- inform customers of your product offering (e.g., JCPenney's promotions as the exclusive retailer for Bisou Bisou clothing);
- increase store traffic at the beginning of an important holiday shopping season. (e.g., retailers offering the so-called Black Friday sales as described in the chapter's "Retailing: The Inside Story" box);
- increase traffic during slow sales periods (e.g., Subway sandwich shops' "Two for One Tuesdays");
- move old merchandise at the end of a selling season (e.g., the after-Christmas clearance sales that all retailers use);
- strengthen your store's image or reputation (e.g., Neiman Marcus's famous Christmas catalog, which generates news stories around the world when it is mailed to customers);
- make consumers think of you first when a need for your products occurs, especially if your products are not commonly purchased (e.g., St. Louis service retailer Frederick Roofing attempted to differentiate itself from its competitors with the creative but easy-to-remember jingle, "For a hole in your roof or a whole new roof—Frederick Roofing"); and
- retain your current customers (e.g., supermarket use of loyalty or frequent-shopper cards).

Many retailers use frequent shopper or loyalty cards. It is especially important that retailers scan the customer's loyalty card during a promotion since the resulting database that is created is used to help to evaluate the effectiveness of the sales promotion.

Neil Redmond/AP Photo

Retailing: The Inside Story

Black Friday Sales

Probably no retail promotion generates as much interest, traffic, or bad publicity as Black Friday. The name itself is something spooky in nature, and it isn't even a retailing term. Black Friday is a term originally coined by the cable news media to describe the big "sales" that occur the Friday after Thanksgiving. It is perceived as the kickoff to the holiday shopping season and is intended to get consumers into a retailer's store with the hope that they purchase additional full-margin items.

Black Friday is said to represent the day that retailers go "into the black"—that is, into profitability. However, think about the retail reporting calendar, which was discussed in Chapter 8. Black Friday normally falls at the end of the 10th month of a retailer's year. If a retailer isn't profitable by then, it is likely heading out of business. Further, while Black Friday is the busiest day of the Christmas shopping season in terms of traffic, the Saturday of the second last full weekend before Christmas is usually the biggest in terms of sales. (As a side note, the media also coined the term *Cyber Monday* for the first Monday following Thanksgiving. This term was derived from a time when shoppers chose to use their "faster" at-work computers for searches on the Internet, thus providing retail websites with their highest traffic and highest sales of the year. However, this term is now as outdated as the dial-up computers consumers used in their homes a decade ago. Today, most consumers have broadband and no longer need to wait and shop while at work. However, because of the past publicity generated by the term many retailers still continue to use Cyber Monday as a promotional event.)

All the media attention given to Black Friday has indeed turned it into a one-day, Super Bowl of shopping. In fact, one retail executive told the authors that she likens Black Friday to an endurance contest where shoppers start lining up for the 4 A.M. store openings shortly after midnight armed with their Internet postings of Black Friday sale items. However, it is the Internet postings that have most changed the nature of the day and the way people shop.

Roughly a decade ago, various websites began posting advanced copies of the Black Friday sale ads for more than 200 retailers. Today these websites (e.g., BFAds.net and gottadeal.com) are among the busiest sites on the Internet starting in mid-November. After all, they give consumers an advantage over traditional shoppers who will wait for the newspaper on Thanksgiving Day (e.g., they are able to perform price comparisons in advance and plan which stores to shop or when to visit each store).

Realizing the importance of having great deals on Black Friday, retailers are starting to develop plans for this day before spring arrives. However, the actions of some retailers can generate bad publicity for everyone. Some shady retailers try to sell a very cheap product with a very expensive warranty, others offer an item for a limited time period (e.g., between 5 A.M. and 7 A.M.), and others state in their ads "in-stock items only" while maintaining low inventories on hand. Still, while the above tactics may apply to only a few retailers, they do give retailing a bad image. However, the worst example of bad publicity resulting from a Black Friday sale occurred in 2008 when some 2,000 customers, in an attempt to be the first to enter a Long Island Walmart store, trampled an employee to death. Sadly, this probably proves what a "monster" retailers have created with their Black Friday sales.

Although the ultimate goal of every advertising campaign should be to generate additional sales, you should notice that "increase sales" is not listed as an advertising objective. This is because elements of the retail mix, beyond advertising, may negatively impact sales. For example, the retailer could select the wrong merchandise for its target customers, charge too high a price for its merchandise in comparison to the competition, or improperly display the merchandise in its store.

Regardless of the objective chosen, it must be aimed at a specific market segment and be measurable over a given time period. For example, Walmart recently sought to improve its image first by dropping the "roll-back" guy and then the smiley face. The object of the chain's new "Save Money. Live Better." campaign is directed at reminding consumers that during tough economic times, Walmart is the

Marc F. Henning/Alamy

Walmart's name itself is an example of the retailer's effort to reduce expenses. Sam Walton's original name choice was Walton's Market, but the sign maker suggested cutting costs by using Wal-Mart.

best way to save money.[5] Thus, a good description of this campaign's objective may be "to increase the level of awareness by 30 percent over the next six months among heads of middle-class and upper-middle-class households that [Walmart] has the merchandise they need, but at a lower price."

Budgeting for the Campaign

A well-designed retail advertising campaign requires money that could be spent on other areas (e.g., more merchandise or higher wages for employees). The retailer hopes that the dollars spent on advertising will generate sales that will in turn produce added profits, which can then be used to finance the retailer's other activities.

When developing a budget, the retailer should first determine who is going to pay for the campaign; that is, will the retailer be the sole sponsor or will it get co-op support from manufacturers or other retailers?

Retailer-Only Campaigns

If a retailer decides to do the campaign alone, it generally uses one of the following methods to determine the amount of money to be spent on the advertising campaign: the affordable method, the percentage-of-sales method, or the task-and-objective method.

The Affordable Method. Many small retailers use the **affordable method** by allocating all the money they can afford for advertising in any given budget period. This method should be employed when the amount spent on advertising will add substantially more value to the retailer than an alternate use of the funds such as increasing the sales force or adding more fixtures. Too much reliance on this method may lead to an inadequate advertising appropriation or to a budget that is not related to actual needs. A limitation of the affordable method is that the logic of

affordable method
Is a technique for budgeting advertising in which all the money a retailer can afford to spend on advertising in a given time period becomes the advertising budget.

this approach suggests that advertising does not stimulate sales or profits but rather is supported by sales and profits. However, some retailers have little choice but to use this approach. A small retailer cannot go to the bank and borrow $100,000 to spend on advertising. This is unfortunate because the small retailer might benefit more from advertising than from additional inventory or equipment. Thus, we can see that although the affordable method may not be ideal in terms of advertising theory, it is certainly defensible given the financial constraints that confront the small retailer.

percentage-of-sales method
Is a technique for budgeting in which the retailer targets a specific percentage of forecasted sales as the advertising budget.

Percentage-of-Sales Method. The **percentage-of-sales method** of budgeting for advertising is a type of *benchmarking* whereby the retailer uses the industry's best practices as a standard. Here the retailer targets a specific percentage of forecasted sales to be used for advertising based on the assumption that successful similar firms should be used as a guide.[6] Industry data, such as those shown in Exhibit 11.2, are often published by trade associations. These figures are averages, however, and do not reflect the unique circumstances and objectives of a particular retailer. A more suitable guide to the level of advertising expenditures is the retailer's past sales experience when the level of past expenditures has achieved management's objective. The average percentage of advertising expenditures to sales for the past several years can be applied to the current year.

Exhibit 11.2
Advertising as Percentage of Sales by Line of Trade

Line of Trade	NAICS	Ad Dollars as Percentage of Sales
Apparel and accessory stores	5600	5.2
Auto and home supply stores	5531	1.9
Bldg matl, hardwr, garden-retl	5200	2.1
Catalog, mail-order houses	5961	3.5
Cmp and cmp software stores	5734	0.3
Department stores	5311	5.1
Drug & proprietary stores	5912	0.7
Eating places	5812	2.9
Electronic parts, eq-whsl, nec	5065	0.5
Family clothing stores	5651	1.9
Furniture stores	5712	8.7
Grocery stores	5411	0.8
Hardwr, plumb, heat eq-whsl	5070	0.1
Hobby, toy, and game shops	5945	2.9
Home furniture & equip store	5700	6.4
Lumber & oth bldg matl-retl	5211	1.7
Misc shopping goods stores	5940	3.2
Miscellaneous retail	5900	0.6
Radio, tv, cons electr stores	5731	2.4
Record and tape stores	5735	2
Retail stores, nec	5990	4.1
Shoe stores	5661	2.3
Variety stores	5331	1.5
Women's clothing stores	5621	3.7

Source: From **Advertising Ratios & Budgets**, May 2008, published by Schonfeld & Associates. Used with written permission.

One weakness of the percentage-of-sales method is that the amount of sales becomes the factor that influences the advertising outlay. In a correct cause-and-effect relationship, the level of advertising should influence the amount of sales. In addition, this technique does not reflect the retailer's advertising goals. Rather than pinching pennies as consumers rein in spending, some retailers plow money into standing out from the crowd, hoping to grab market share and emerge from the economy's slump in better shape than their rivals. One of the author's early retail mentors, Louis Bing, always preached that "he never saw business so bad that he couldn't buy all of it he wanted." By that he meant that when business slowed and all his competitors reduced their ad budgets, he would then increase his ad expenditures. Without the clutter of competitors' ads, consumers became more aware of his ads and his sales increased, despite the general sales slowdown affecting the other local merchants. This strategy was built at least partly on the premise that shoppers typically are creatures of habit and that economic slowdowns offer an opportunity to change those habits as households try to economize. Besides, for publicly held companies, Wall Street tends to put less pressure on them to perform when the economy is weak, which can give these retailers room to finance strategic investments.

Another weakness of this method is that it gives more money to departments that are already successful and fails to give money to departments that could be successful with a little extra money. Percentage of sales does, however, provide a controlled, generally affordable amount to spend; if spent wisely, it may work out well in practice. Most retailers, especially the smaller ones, do not use ad agencies and lack the sophistication required to adequately implement the task-and-objective approach. A percentage-of-sales guideline allows the retailer to follow objectives in an affordable, controlled manner. If the dollars are carefully applied in appropriate amounts over the year in such a way that they relate to expected sales percentages in each month, the percentage-of-sales method can work well.

Task-and-Objective Method.   In the preceding budgeting methods, advertising seems to follow sales results. With the **task-and-objective method**, the logic is properly reversed; here retailers can see the relationship between promotions that change attitudes and behavior. Thus, advertising leads to some other measure of financial performance—hopefully, sales. Basically, the retailer prioritizes its advertising objectives and then determines the advertising tasks that need to be performed to achieve those objectives.[7] Associated with each task is an estimate of the cost of performing the task. When all of these costs are totaled, the retailer has its advertising budget. In short, this method begins with the retailer's advertising objectives and then determines what it will cost to achieve them.

More and more retailers, as well as malls, are moving toward this method as they realize that their shrinking funds can no longer be wasted on promotions that don't pay off.[8] Exhibit 11.3 gives an example of the task-and-objective method. Notice that the retailer has five major advertising objectives and a total of 11 tasks to perform to accomplish these objectives. The total cost of performing these tasks is $99,020. While the task-and-objective method of developing the advertising budget is the best of the three methods from a theoretical and managerial control perspective, not all retailers have adopted it because it is difficult to implement.

Many of the major retailers use a combination of the percentage-of-sales method, which they use to keep pace with competitors, and the task-and-objective method, which reflects the different tasks they must accomplish to reach their objectives. Thus, as shown in Exhibit 11.4, while the percentages for close competitors are similar, they differ somewhat because of the circumstances relating to

task-and-objective method

Is a technique for budgeting in which the retailer establishes its advertising objectives and then determines the advertising tasks that need to be performed to achieve those objectives.

	Objective and Task	Estimated Cost
Objective 1:	Increase traffic during dull periods.	
Task A:	15 full-page newspaper advertisements to be spread over these dates: February 2–16; June 8–23; October 4–18	$22,500
Task B:	Run 240 30-second radio spots split on two stations and spread over these dates: February 2–16; June 8–23; October 4–18	4,320
Objective 2:	Attract new customers from newcomers to the community.	
Task A:	2,000 direct-mail letters greeting new residents to the community	1,000
Task B:	2,000 direct-mail letters inviting new arrivals in the community to stop in to visit the store and fill out a credit application	1,000
Task C:	Yellow Pages advertising	1,900
Objective 3:	Build store's reputation.	
Task A:	Weekly 15-second institutional ads on the 10 P.M. television news every Saturday and Sunday	20,800
Task B:	One half-page newspaper ad per month in the home living section of the local newspaper	9,500
Objective 4:	Increase shopper traffic in shopping center.	
Task A:	Cooperate with other retailers in the shopping center in sponsoring transit advertising on buses and cabs	3,000
Task B:	Participate in "Midnight Madness Sale" with other retailers in the shopping center by taking out 2 full-page newspaper ads—one in mid-March and the other in mid-July	3,000
Objective 5:	Clear out end-of-month, slow-moving merchandise.	
Task A:	Run a full-page newspaper ad on the last Thursday of every month	18,000
Task B:	Run 3 30-second television spots on the last Thursday of every month	14,000
Total advertising budget		$99,020

Exhibit 11.3
Task-and-Objective Method of Advertising Budget Development

the other elements of their retail mixes. For example, Macy's department stores recently spent 4.9 percent of sales on advertising while some other department stores—Dillard's, Bon-Ton, and JCPenney's—spent 2.3 percent, 4.1 percent, and 6.6 percent, respectively. Target spent 1.9 percent while Walmart spent only 0.6 percent. Safeway spent 1.3 percent, while A&P spent 1.0 percent, Publix spent 0.8 percent, and Kroger spent only 0.7 percent.[9]

A retailer's promotional decisions can't always be determined solely by analytical or scientific methods. On the contrary, promotion offers the opportunity for highly creative thought. In fact, as noted throughout the text, creativity is probably the best way for retailers to differentiate themselves from competitors. Remember the example of IKEA in Chapter 2's "Global Retailing" box? This chapter's "Service Retailing" box discusses some of the creative methods used by retailers in one of the most competitive service industries—restaurants.

vertical cooperative advertising

Occurs when the retailer and other channel members (usually manufacturers) share the advertising budget. Usually the manufacturer subsidizes some of the retailer's advertising that features the manufacturer's brands.

Co-op Campaigns

Although most retail advertising is paid for solely by the retailer, sometimes manufacturers and other retailers may pay part or even all of the costs of a retailer's advertising campaign.

Vertical cooperative advertising allows the retailer and other supply-chain members to share the advertising burden. For example, a manufacturer may pay as much as 40 percent of the cost of a retailer's advertising that focuses on the manufacturer's products to a maximum of 4 percent of annual purchases by the retailer from the manufacturer. If the retailer spent $10,000 on advertising the

Line of Trade	Ad Dollars as Percentage of Sales	Line of Trade	Ad Dollars as Percentage of Sales
Building materials, hardware, & garden		Grocery stores	
Calloway's Nursery Inc	3.1	Whole Foods Market Inc	0.5
Fastenal Co	2.1	Winn-Dixie Stores Inc	1
Tractor Supply Co	2.1	Women's clothing stores	
Lumber & other building materials		Aeropostale Inc	0.5
Home Depot Inc	1.7	Ann Taylor Stores Corp	2.6
Lowe's Companies Inc	1.6	Cache Inc	2.9
Lumber Liquidators Inc	10.1	Cato Corp -Cl A	0.9
Department stores		Charming Shoppes Inc	3.8
Belk Inc	3.2	Chicos Fas Inc	5.4
Bon-Ton Stores Inc	4.1	Christopher & Banks Corp	1.3
Dillards Inc -Cl A	2.3	Dress Barn Inc	1.4
Gottschalks Inc	4.3	Limited Brands Inc	5.2
Kohl's Corp	5.4	Mothers Work Inc	1.5
Macy's Inc	4.9	New York & Company Inc	3
Penney (J C) Co	6.6	Talbots Inc	5.2
Variety stores		Wet Seal Inc	1
99 Cents Only Stores	0.5	Family clothing stores	
Big Lots Inc	2.2	Abercrombie & Fitch -Cl A	0.9
Dollar Tree Stores Inc	0.2	Amern Eagle Outfitters Inc	2.5
Family Dollar Stores	0.1	Buckle Inc	1
Freds Inc	1.6	Burlington Coat Factory Wrhs	2.2
Retail Ventures Inc	4.6	Casual Male Retail Grp Inc	8.7
Sears Holdings Corp	6	Citi Trends Inc	0.5
Target Corp	1.9	Gap Inc	3
Tuesday Morning Corp	4.3	Harolds Stores Inc	8.1
Wal-Mart Stores	0.6	Nordstrom Inc	0.9
Grocery stores		Pacific Sunwear Calif Inc	1.4
Great Atlantic & Pac Tea Co	1	Ross Stores Inc	0.8
Kroger Co	0.7	Stage Stores Inc	4.3
Pao De Acucar Brasil -Gdr	1.6	Stein Mart Inc	5.1
Publix Super Markets Inc	0.8	Syms Corp	2.9
Safeway Inc	1.3	Tjx Companies Inc	1.6
Supervalu Inc	0.4	Urban Outfitters Inc	2.8
Village Super Market -Cl A	0.8	Walking Co Holdings Inc	1.6
Weis Markets Inc	1.1		

Source: From **Advertising Ratios & Budgets**, May 2008, published by Schonfeld & Associates. Used with written permission.

Exhibit 11.4
Advertising Expenditures as Percentage of Sales for Some Leading Retailers

manufacturer's products, then it could be reimbursed 40 percent of this amount, or $4,000, as long as the retailer purchased at least $100,000 during the last year from the manufacturer.

There is a strong temptation among retailers to view vertical co-op advertising money as free. Retailers forget, however, that good advertising, like a good investment, should increase revenues from customers, not just from vendors. In

For years, restaurant owners have tried to determine the best way to promote a new restaurant. Many restaurant managers have felt the same as John Wanamaker, the merchant prince of Philadelphia department store fame, when he was asked about his advertising budget. He answered that he knew that half of his money was wasted, but he just didn't know which half. Consider the changing trends that have occurred over the last two decades as restaurants have entered the Dallas, Texas, market.

Two decades ago, for example, when Dallas-based sports bar and restaurant chain Dave & Busters first opened, most of its restaurants avoided advertising and relied on word of mouth. That strategy worked out just fine for Dave & Busters. Customers loved the games and good food and spread the word. Doing so, the restaurant used the money that might have been spent on advertising to ensure that every customer had a good experience. In fact, this strategy was so successful that it was widely copied and lost its effectiveness. As a result, Dave & Busters today advertises its new restaurants on local radio supported by direct mail and also conducts a nationwide campaign through drive-time radio and cable television outlets such as ESPN, TNT, TBS, the Comedy Channel, and Fox Sports.

Once word of mouth was no longer effective for promoting a new restaurant, Fox Sports Grill developed a new idea when it entered the restaurant scene in heavily populated North Dallas. (By the way, North Dallas is known as the burial ground for restaurants. Just recently, the famous Smith & Wollensky Steakhouse closed its restaurant in this area.) This sports bar, which features hardwood flooring, set up giant plasma TVs and projection flat screens that offered unobstructed views of all the latest sports action. At the same time, the bar provided sunken private areas complete with smaller televisions for individual viewing. Fox soon became the place to be seen for Dallas area sports figures, as one author can attest. In addition, the restaurant features a menu that includes superior cuisine ranging from pasta to chicken and shrimp to prime rib, as well as all kinds of burgers, sandwiches, and appetizers. All this and at affordable prices.

However, what was truly the creative genius behind the success of this sports bar was the fact that its advertisements featured one simple message: Fox was a sports bar *without smoking*.

Another Dallas-based restaurant, Del Frisco's Double Eagle Steakhouse, also realized that word of mouth was no longer effective, so its cofounder, Dee Lincoln, used publicity

Courtesy of De Frisco's Double Eagle Steak House.

Service Retailing (continued)

as an alternative to advertising when she opened a new restaurant in the Denver market. Lincoln paid a then-record $80,000 for a 1,309-pound Maine-Anjou crossbreed steer at Denver's National Western Stock Show. When her winning bid was accepted, an opposing bidder said, "Lady, you must either be really crazy or have too much money." Dee Lincoln got what she wanted—hundreds of thousands of dollars' worth of front-page newspaper coverage, not to mention radio and television publicity, for her high-quality steak-houses. It was no accident that all the media mentioned the newest restaurant in Denver. However, restaurant owners can't always be as lucky as Ms. Lincoln was to have a publicity-generating event available.

Thus, despite market changes over the last two decades, service retailers, such as restaurants, have come up with creative ideas for promoting their offerings. This is an especially difficult task for restaurants because a dining episode is essentially an experience, and the retailer's promotions must cut through the clutter of all its competitors' ads.

Source: Based on conversations with Dee Lincoln and the experience of the authors, all of whom have lived in Texas.

---

other words, even if the supplier is putting up 50 percent of the expense, the retailer must still pay the other 50 percent. In addition, since the supplier often exercises considerable control over the content of the advertising and its objectives may be different than the retailer's, the retailer may actually be paying 50 percent of the supplier's cost of advertising rather than vice versa. Also, suppliers know that it is a common media practice to offer local retailers a discount on rates relative to national advertisers. Thus, suppliers often use local retailers to get this discount on their ads.

Retailers must prioritize their objectives to determine whether they can get a better return on their money by using vertical co-op dollars or by assuming total sponsorship of advertising a message with high priority. Remember, in earlier chapters it was pointed out that retailers and their supply-chain partners often have different objectives. As a result, sometimes it can be more profitable for the retailer to pass up a co-op deal on one product line and spend the money on another line that is likely to have a higher sales impact.

To illustrate this line of reasoning, let's consider the following scenario. Assume that a retailer has $10,000 to spend on advertising and is considering the possibility of increasing advertising expenditures for either merchandise line A or line B. With line A, the vendor has offered a co-op deal, which roughly equates to the supplier paying 50 percent of the cost of the advertising. If the retailer selects this option, it would be able to purchase $20,000 of advertising for a $10,000 investment. No co-op deal is being offered by the supplier of line B because it is the retailer's private label, but line B is just now becoming very popular with the retailer's customers, and the retailer believes it could benefit substantially from $10,000 in advertising. What should the retailer do?

The answer to the preceding question will depend on two major factors. First, how much will the sales of line A increase as a result of $20,000 in advertising compared to the likely sales increase of line B that would result from a $10,000 increase in advertising? Second, what is the gross-margin percentage for each line? Let's assume these are the facts: Line A has 50-percent gross margin and line B has 60-percent gross margin. Currently, line A has sales of $160,000, and it is expected that a $20,000 advertising program would push sales up to $220,000. At the current time, line B has sales of $36,000, but it is expected that a $10,000 advertising program would increase the sales volume to $120,000.

Notice that line B, although its current sales are relatively low, is very responsive to advertising expenditures as compared to the responsiveness of merchandise line A. Here is the numerical analysis:

	LINE A		LINE B	
	Before	After	Before	After
Sales	$160,000	$220,000	$36,000	$120,000
Cost of goods sold	80,000	110,000	14,400	48,000
Gross margin	80,000	110,000	21,600	72,000
Advertising	0	10,000[a]	0	10,000
Contribution to profit	$80,000	$100,000	$21,600	$62,000

[a]Actually, $20,000 was spent, but the net cost to retailer was $10,000 since the supplier paid the other $10,000.

As you can see, the numerical analysis suggests that while the increase in line A's contribution to profit would be $20,000 ($100,000 versus $80,000), it would be $40,400 for line B ($62,000 versus $21,600). Therefore, it would be more profitable for the retailer to pass up the co-op deal on line A and spend the $10,000 on advertising line B, its private-label brand.

horizontal cooperative advertising

Occurs when two or more retailers band together to share the cost of advertising usually in the form of a joint promotion of an event or sale that would benefit both parties.

Horizontal cooperative advertising occurs when two or more retailers band together to share the cost of advertising. When used, this approach tends to give small retailers more bargaining power in purchasing advertising than they would otherwise have. Also, if properly conducted, it can create substantially more store traffic for all participants. For example, retailers in shopping malls will often jointly sponsor multiple-page spreads in newspapers promoting special events such as "Santa Land" or "Moonlight Madness" sales, while downtown merchants usually jointly sponsor "Sidewalk Days" or "Downtown Days" sales. The impact of these events on-store traffic is evident by the many malls that have recently turned a very slow shopping night (Halloween) into a very successful "Dead Night." By having a store-to-store program that provides a safe place for trick or treating, a mall can pull significantly more people into each retailer's store than each retailer could do individually for the same cost.

Another recent example of horizontal cooperative advertising occurred in 2008 and involved two retailers not normally associated with each other: Staples and Bed Bath & Beyond. In its first-ever tie-in with another national retailer, Staples formed a joint "Back to School" sweepstakes with a retailer it believed knew college students better than any other retailer and whose merchandise complemented Staples' own lines. By working together, the two retailers focused on making shopping for necessary products easier while reducing traveling in a period of high gas prices.

Designing the Message

The next step in developing an advertising campaign is to design a creative message and select the media that will enable the retailer to reach its objectives. In reality, these decisions are made simultaneously. Creative messages cannot be developed without knowing which media will be used to carry the message. This text, however, will cover media selection after discussing how retailers design their message.

Creative decisions are especially important for retailers because their advertising messages generally seek an immediate reaction from the consumer while having a short life span. The development of such messages is one of retailing's major challenges. If you have ever covered the retailer's name in a newspaper ad or tuned out the retailer's name in a broadcast ad, you know that all too often retailers lack originality in their ads. Here are a couple of examples of retailers who have demonstrated creativity when developing a promotional strategy.

T&M Appliance & TV of Clinton, Missouri, population 1,500, used a variation of the IKEA Christmas idea with decorating Halloween pumpkins. The five visits here involved picking up a free pumpkin with your parents, turning in the finished pumpkin, coming in to select the best pumpkin, stopping by after the citywide parade to see the store's decorations (including the pumpkins), and returning to select the best costume.

Another creative idea was developed by Orville's Home Appliances in Lancaster, New York. Realizing that consumers always like a "deal," the store's owner ran an ad offering the first 2,500 customers a chance to purchase an appliance and get a lifetime membership card in the store's "No Sales Tax for Life Club," which guaranteed that on all future purchases the member would not be charged sales tax. Sales more than doubled that first month of the promotion and even now about two or three sales per week involve the card. This promotion, which is really nothing more than a discount of less than 10 percent on merchandise with a large markup, has done what it was intended to do—draw customers into the store. (A follow-up note about this promotion: The New York State Division of Taxation required Orville to put a disclaimer on its ads stating it was a discount equal to the amount of the tax and that current sales taxes had to be paid.)

A fundamental principle of designing a message has always been to avoid drawing attention to your weaknesses. However, Winn-Dixie recently introduced a creative slogan—"Getting Better All the Time"—that acknowledged that the company had been bad. The supermarket chain had closed many nonproductive stores, and it used bankruptcy to end lots of unfavorable real-estate obligations. Today the company is much smaller, but as a result of its new campaign, it still has a good reputation in its trading areas. After all, how many retailers have been so honest as to say to their customers, "We know we've been bad. We're getting better. We're 'the beef people.' We've got good prices. Please come back and give us a chance"?[10]

Therefore, in view of the above, retail ads must accomplish these three goals:

1. attract attention and retain attention; that is, they must be able to break through the competitive clutter;
2. achieve the objective of the advertising strategy; and
3. avoid errors, especially legal ones.

Accomplishing these goals is, however, an extremely difficult task in today's marketplace, especially given the limited attention span of the time-pressed

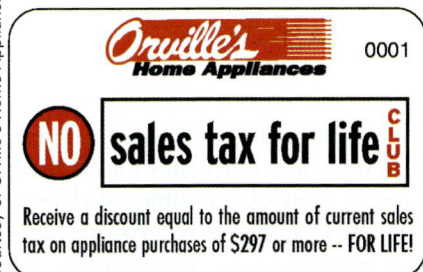

Orville's Home Appliances   0001

NO sales tax for life CLUB

Receive a discount equal to the amount of current sales tax on appliance purchases of $297 or more -- FOR LIFE!

Terms:
Card must be presented prior to making final product selection in order to receive discount.
Discount does not apply to delivery & installation charges.
Discount is valid for cardholder & immediate family only.
Clearance, scratch 'n dent, closeout, & display models excluded.
Builder Incentive & Corporate programs excluded.

Orville's "No Sales Tax for Life Club," promotion was a hit with everyone, except the state's Tax Department.

consumer. After all, newspapers and magazine readership is declining, and more and more consumers use their remote controls to skip or block television commercials. Consumers now spend their time twittering with friends, playing with their PlayStation3s, and surfing the Internet instead of using mass media for entertainment. Therefore, it is becoming imperative for retailers to find unique ways to break through the competitive clutter and then get and hold the consumer's attention. After all, if consumers have already seen or read the ad, why should they view it again? Some of the common approaches that retailers use to gain repeated viewing use the following genres.

Lifestyle:	Shows how the retailer's products fit in with the consumer's lifestyle.
Fantasy:	Creates a fantasy for the consumer that is built around the retailer's products.
Humorous:	Builds a campaign around humor that relates to using the retailer's products.
Slice of life:	Depicts the consumer in everyday settings using the retailer's products.
Mood or image:	Builds a mood around using the retailer's products.

Finally, before using the ad, the retailer should test it for mistakes. These mistakes could be either accidental or perhaps inserted by an unhappy employee. The authors have seen a promotion for an "early bird special" at a Texas mall drawing in which the customers could drop off their entries between 7 and 10 A.M.; unfortunately, the drawing was to be held at 9:30 A.M. In another case, a Sunday circular for a major East Coast retailer offered a special deal on Scrabble games. However, the adjoining picture had two young boys playing the game and one had just spelled the word RAPE. A Philadelphia clothing store's ad had this heading; "CLEARANCE SALE! SAVINGS LIKE THESE ONLY COME ONCE A YEAR," and a California florist once advertised a "PRE-GRAND OPENING CLEARANCE."

Just recently, KFC ran a new product introduction advertising campaign for grilled chicken that *Advertising Age* declared would go down in the "annals of marketing disasters." The ill-fated campaign began when KFC used Oprah Winfrey to offer two free pieces of grilled chicken, two sides, and a biscuit to anyone who downloaded a coupon within a two-day period. Within minutes, it was the number-one topic on Twitter. That night, blogs began reporting "riots" at New York City KFCs. The next day, local news crews across the country interviewed fuming customers getting turned away because some franchisees refused to honor the coupons since the company wouldn't reimburse their costs for the free meal. Consumers complained about rude service, and media complained about a PR team that seemed asleep at the wheel. On day three, the day after KFC pulled the promotion, NPR was calling KFC "the James Frey of fast food," referring to the author of a memoir praised by Ms. Winfrey that was later exposed as fiction. In the end, KFC made good on the coupons. However, in just a couple of days it strained relationships with KFC's three core constituents—consumers, media, and franchisees—not to mention the fact that it seemed to forget what the "F" in KFC stood for.[11]

Although the above errors are serious, they should not present legal problems. Retailers can accidentally violate some advertising laws, even if they are not trying to deceive the consumer. Chapter 6 discussed some of the various federal laws governing retail advertising. All too often, however, the retailer runs into trouble with state or local laws. Some states limit promotions involving games of chance, others regulate the use of ads with price comparisons among retail stores, and others restrict the use of certain words in the description of merchandise. For example, the Pennsylvania Human Relations Commission has issued guidelines against the use of the following words in real-estate ads because may tend to discriminate among consumer groups: *bachelor pad, couple, mature, older seniors, adults, traditional, newlyweds, exclusive, children,* and *established neighborhood.*

Internationally, individual countries—or, in some cases, groups of countries such as the European Union—set specific guidelines for advertising content that must be followed. For instance, in the European Union, advertising that is directed at a child or a young person is generally allowed; however, the ad must not directly encourage children or young people to buy a product and must not exploit their inexperience and credulity. In addition, the ad must not cause them any physical or mental harm. Ads that could conceivably cause minors physical or mental harm can only be broadcast between 11 P.M. and 6 A.M.

In addition, to the above, a smart retailer should prepare a message to be used in case of some type of emergency. For example, a Costco executive was recently quoted as saying as a result of an *E. coli* scare a decade ago that the retailer created a system that matched product purchases with a membership number. Thus, in 2009, when the peanut butter crisis occurred, the retailer was not only able to remove the involved products from its shelves but also immediately contract the 1.8 million members who purchased peanut butter at one of its warehouses.[12]

Media Alternatives

The retailer has many media alternatives from which to select. In the past, retailers generally categorized media as print (which included newspaper, magazines, and direct mail) and broadcast (which lumped radio and television together). Now, however, retailers are beginning to classify media using a managerial perspective that recognizes that newspapers and local television stations that use broadcast programming from the networks are mass-media alternatives aimed at a total market, while cable television, radio, magazines, direct mail, and the Internet can be more easily targeted toward specific markets. In addition, the recent recession has caused retailers to reevaluate the available media alternatives.

Newspaper Advertising

The most frequently used advertising medium in retailing is the newspaper. (Fashion magazines and newspapers are probably the only media that consumers will purchase specifically to see the advertising content.) Newspaper advertising is popular for retailers because of the following reasons.

1. Most newspapers are local. This is advantageous since most retailers appeal to a local trading area.

2. A low technical skill level is required to create advertisements for newspapers. This is helpful for small retailers.

3. Newspaper ads require only a short interval between the time copy is written and when the ad appears. Because some retailers do a poor job of planning and tend to use advertising to respond to crises (poor cash flow, slackening of sales, need to move old merchandise), the short lead time for placing newspaper ads is a significant advantage.

However, the recession has caused many families to discontinue their local newspaper subscriptions or at least cut back their subscriptions to Sundays only. As a result, many newspapers across the county have either gone out of business or have reduced the number of days published. In some cases, they have tried to convert to an Internet-only paper, but to date none have been successful. Another problem for retailers wanting to use this medium is that if the retailer has a specific target market, then much of its advertising money will be wasted using newspapers since their circulation is seldom able to match the retailer's target market. This criticism of newspaper advertising is particularly true for the under-25 segment. This group rarely reads newspapers and gets most of its news from the Internet. Also, retail newspaper advertising presents retailers with the following four disadvantages.

1. The fact that a consumer was exposed to an issue of a newspaper does not mean the consumer read or even saw the retailer's ad.

2. The life of any single issue of a newspaper is short—it's read and subsequently discarded.

3. The typical person spends relatively little time with each issue, and the time spent is spread over many items in the newspaper.

4. Newspapers have poor reproduction quality, which leads to ads with little visual appeal.

Still, despite these disadvantages, newspapers continue to be the number-one form of advertising for retailers. Many of the large bricks-and-mortar retailers, however, such as Kohl's and Target, primarily use newspapers to deliver their own centrally produced inserts.

A recent trend in newspaper advertising is the so-called adzine format. In the past, many consumers simply ignored supermarket ads because they were simply lists of items on sale and many of the items didn't pertain to their needs. However, since consumers enjoy reading magazines, grocers have evolved a new style of advertising. These lifestyle adzines, which are often published quarterly, present meal-time ideas that incorporate items on sale with recipes, pictures, and informational copy. Still, this concept depends on the newspaper's delivery system to reach all or a selected group of consumers, whether they are newspaper subscribers or not. After all, it is doubtful that Internet subscribers to a local paper will search out an ad for their local Dillard's or Macy's. Therefore, the recent demise of local newspapers is projected to have a negative impact on retailing in general.

Local and Cable Television Advertising

Over the past decade, some retailers such as Macy's have shifted away from newspapers and to television advertising as a means of reaching the elusive full-price shopper. After all, for a brand to be viewed as credible and top of the line, television is a more dynamic medium. Research suggests that, over time, the subtle and gradual effect from TV images on consumer memory is greater than the aural messages received from media such as radio. However, even though television advertising is a great image builder, it is expensive. A well-designed television ad may use up the total ad budget of a local retailer. Furthermore, for the small retailer or even an intermediate-sized retail chain, a television ad would reach well beyond its trading area. However, despite the expense of television advertising, the future of both local and cable is fuzzy.

Since the beginning of the recent recession, many local stations, with their viewership in decline and ad revenues on a downward spiral, have scaled back their original programming, reduced the number of weekend news shows, and trimmed staff. Some stations have even dropped news programs altogether or merged their news operations with other local stations. As a result, local stations have seen their market shares decline. Therefore, while local, regional, and national retailers such as car dealers spend about $20 billion on local TV-station ads, total local advertising revenue is down more than 30 percent from prerecession figures and is expected to decline further. It is unclear as to the eventual impact from this decrease, but it will change the way retailers advertise.[13]

Another disadvantage of using television advertising is that competition is high for the viewer's attention, especially with most consumers having access to more than 100 channels, as well as DVDs, not to mention TiVo. Thus, during commercials, the viewer may either use the remote control to surf other channels or, if the program was TiVoed, just skip the ads. Another complication for the retailer to consider is that the overall time spent watching television has decreased in recent years as many younger consumers have switched over to the Internet and PlayStation3.

However, in spite of the preceding drawbacks, television advertising can be a powerful tool for generating higher sales. The American public spends more time relaxing in front of the television than in any other recreational activity. Television has broad coverage; more than 98 percent of homes in the United States have at least one television set. These sets offer the retailer a vehicle in which both sight and sound can be used to create a significant perceptual and cognitive effect on the consumer. It should be noted that television penetration rates differ across the world, and therefore television's usefulness as a tool to reach consumers differs as well.

Also, the widespread development of cable television has made television attractive to small local retailers without expensively produced commercials. Local cable operators have been selling targeted advertising on cable channels ranging from the Food Network to the Home & Garden Network to ESPN and Fox Sports in hopes of matching a retailer's particular customer profiles.

Radio Advertising

Many retailers prefer to use radio because it can target messages to select groups. Most communities have five to 10 or more radio stations, each of which tends to appeal to a different demographic group. Through the use of proper variations in volume and types of sounds, retailers can use radio to develop distinctive and appealing messages and to introduce a store and its image to current and potential customers. In short, radio offers a lot of flexibility. Also, many radio audiences develop strong affection and trust for their favorite radio announcers. When these announcers endorse a retailer, the audience often listens. In fact one, of the authors recently began using ProFlowers.com (www.proflowers.com) and Goldline International (www.goldline.com) after repeatedly hearing his favorite morning talkshow host mention their products during his shows.

Radio advertising also has its drawbacks. Radio commercials, especially the uncreative ones, are not saved or referred to again like print media ads. In fact, some media experts claim that radio's lack of innovation is a major shortcoming. All too often, ad agencies and radio stations lack the creativity to help local retailers. The CBS radio network, claiming the last truly great radio campaign was Motel 6's "And we'll leave the light on for you," recently hired top creative people to stimulate better radio commercials at both the national and local levels.[14] In addition, radio is frequently listened to during work hours and during drive time (to and from work) and therefore tends, over time, to become part of the background environment. Since radio is nonvisual, it is impossible to effectively demonstrate or show the merchandise that is being advertised.

Magazine Advertising

Relatively few local retailers advertise in magazines unless the magazine has only a local circulation. Nationally based retailers such as JCPenney will allocate some of their advertising budget to magazines, but a majority of these ads tend to be institutional in nature.

Magazine advertising can be quite effective. In relation to newspapers, magazines perform well on several dimensions. They have a better reproduction quality and a longer life span per issue, and consumers spend more time with each issue of a magazine than a newspaper. For example, magazines have the unique quality of being shared among family and friends, thus extending the reach of the advertisement. An added benefit is that featured articles in a magazine can put people in the mood for a particular product class. For example, a feature article on home remodeling in *Better Homes and Gardens* can put people in a frame of mind to consider purchasing wallpaper, carpeting, tiling, draperies, paint, and other home-improvement items. The major disadvantage of using magazines is that the long lead time required prevents advertising with price appeals or any urgency in its messages.

Direct Mail

Direct marketing can be a powerful addition to the retailer's promotional strategy. With direct mail, the retailer can precisely target its message to a particular group as long as a good mailing list of the target population is available. Macy's, for example, uses a customer database to select targeted recipients for each of its roughly 300 annual catalog and promotional mailings. In addition, direct mail provides retailers a personal contact with individual consumers who share certain valued characteristics. Thus, while all of Macy's customers receive the Christmas catalog, only those who recently purchased a men's suit will receive a postcard promoting a sale on shirts and ties. Such messages can reach the consumer without being noticed by the competition. Finally, direct-mail results can generally be easily measured, thus providing the retailer with important feedback.

On the negative side, direct-mail advertising is relatively expensive per contact or message delivered. Also, the ability to reach the target market depends totally on the quality of the mailing list: If the list is not kept current, then advertising dollars will be wasted. For example, the University of Phoenix regularly sends the authors a direct-mail advertisement suggesting that they could further their career prospects if they had a bachelor's degree in business. Given that all three authors already have PhDs, is this an instance of wasted ad dollars? A related problem is the incidence of unopened or unexamined mail, especially when it is addressed to "Occupant" or is mailed using third-class postage.

Another negative of traditional direct mail is the increasing quantity of electronic direct mail, which is commonly known as *spam*. Although most Americans tolerate direct-mail solicitations, the infestation of unsolicited e-mail irritates nearly everyone. Currently, spammers and consumer groups are trying to settle this issue out of court without infringing on the spammers' right to free speech and their ability to conduct business. However, it appears that only the legal system will be able to settle this issue.

Internet

Clearly the Internet, with its various social networks ranging from MySpace to Facebook and LinkedIn to YouTube, is playing an important role as a way for consumers to establish their identities. While TV ratings and newspaper circulation have declined at an accelerating rate in recent years, Internet traffic is growing nearly 25 percent per year. Therefore, the Internet should now be an important promotional tool for retailers. Projections indicate that the current 160 million unique American users will grow to more than 200 million users in the next few years.

A key aspect of the Internet is in its ability to provide information on demand to customers. The communication elements of advertising, sales promotion, and public relations are all strategic options a firm can use when communicating with its various publics. For example, retailers may wish to provide online customers with samples of their advertising on their websites as Scottrade (www.scottrade.com) and The Gap (www.gap.com) have done. Another type of sales promotion occurs when retailers such as Victoria's Secret, Eddie Bauer, Kohl's, JCPenney, and Amazon offer online coupons on RetailMeNot.Com (www.retailmenot.com). A retailer can also use its website to share specific information on its good works through press releases and bylined articles. Other uses include advising investors of financial policies and explaining the firm's position on a social issue. Excellent examples of websites used in this manner are Walt Disney Company (www.disney.com) and Target (www.target.com). In essence, the Internet provides a platform for a retailer to employ a relatively low-cost, integrated marketing-communications mix, thus increasing shareholder value by enhancing the retailer's image by providing a variety of highly specialized information. Southwest Airlines' website (www.southwest.com) provides a good example of a fully integrated marketing-communications mix. Southwest offers online ticketing, investor information, and advertising as well as sales promotions and public-relations materials, thus effectively communicating with all of its relevant publics. Also, the Internet can pay off for smart shoppers. Ebates.com and yub.com, for example, offer visitors a cash-back refund when they register on the site and then make purchases at dozens of e-tailers.

Equally important for the e-tailer is the fact that various Internet providers offer so many tools to improve the effectiveness of their promotions. A search engine such as Yahoo not only can provide the e-tailer with extremely detailed demographic information about the people who click on its ads but also predict the probable response rate to the ads. It knows what time of day the ads are likely to be most effective, and, increasingly, by analyzing "click streams" on its network, a search engine can spot potential buyers at various stages of the consideration process. In other words, by looking at the billions of user clicks that flow through its servers every day, Yahoo is getting better and better at figuring out that a given pattern—say, a user who's looked up scuba diving on Yahoo Sports, checked out romance movies on Yahoo Entertainment, and compared Key West hotel prices on Yahoo Travel—is interested in taking a trip and is just beginning to think about a purchase. Such information is invaluable to a retailer such as Hyatt. Once Yahoo knows when and where a potential customer is in the trip-buying process, it can serve up the appropriate hotel or resort ad.[15]

Internet pop-up banners are a completely different story. They provide one of the few sources of revenue for most websites, especially news and magazine sites. Most consumers do not view them in a positive light but at the same time do not want to purchase subscriptions for every site they visit or provide masses of personal information that can be sold to marketing companies to provide an income stream for the website. Until these problems are solved, it is doubtful that Internet advertising will play a major role in the retailer's promotional mix.

coverage
Is the theoretical maximum number of consumers in the retailer's target market that can be reached by a medium and not the number actually reached.

reach
Is the actual total number of target customers who come into contact with an advertising message.

cumulative reach
Is the reach that is achieved over a period of time.

frequency
Is the average number of times each person who is reached is exposed to an advertisement during a given time period.

cost per thousand method (CPM)
Is a technique used to evaluate advertisements in different media based on cost. The cost per thousand is the cost of the advertisement divided by the number of people viewing it, which is then multiplied by 1,000.

cost per thousand— target market (CPM-TM)
Is a technique used to evaluate advertisements in different media based on cost. The cost per thousand per target market is the cost of the advertisement divided by the number of people in the target market viewing it, which is then multiplied by 1,000.

impact
Refers to how strong an impression an advertisement makes and how well it ultimately leads to a purchase.

Miscellaneous Media

The retailer can advertise using media other than those previously identified: Yellow Pages, outdoor advertising, transit advertising (on buses, cabs, and subways), electronic information terminals, specialty firms such as Welcome Wagons, and shopping guides (newspaper-like printed material that contain no news). Each of these is usually best used to reinforce other media and should not be relied on exclusively unless the retailer's advertising budget is minimal. Most retailers look on these media vehicles as geared mainly toward specific product advertising by manufacturers. However, that does not mean a retailer cannot make use of them because a new resident is still going to have to purchase food, clothing, and entertainment.

Media Selection

To select the best media, the retailer needs to remember the strengths and weaknesses of each medium and determine its coverage, reach, and frequency.

Coverage refers to the theoretical maximum number of consumers in the retailer's target market that can be reached by a medium—not the number actually reached. For example, if a newspaper is circulated to 35 percent of the 40,000 households in a retailer's trading area, then the theoretical coverage is 14,000 households.

Reach, on the other hand, refers to the actual total number of target customers who come into contact with the ad message. Another useful term is **cumulative reach**, which is the reach achieved over a period of time.

Frequency is the average number of times each person who is reached is exposed to an advertisement during a given time period.

Different media can be evaluated by combining knowledge of the ad cost for a medium and the medium's reach and cumulative reach. The most commonly used methods for doing this are the **cost per thousand method (CPM)** and **cost per thousand—target market (CPM-TM)**. The most appropriate way to compute the CPM is to divide the cost for an ad or series of ads in a medium by the total number of people viewing the ad. For example, if a newspaper ad costs $500 and is distributed to 38,200 households, then the CPM is $13.09 [($500/38,200) × 1,000)]. However, the ad may reach only 13,860 customers in the retailer's target market; the cost per thousand for the target market is $36.80 [($500/13,860) × 1,000]. As you can see, CPM-TM only measures members of the retailer's target market who are reached by the ad.

Comparing CPM and CPM-TM for different media vehicles can also provide information on their effectiveness. For example, let's compare billboard to cable-television advertising. Let's say that the billboard and cable both cost $1,000 a month and each reaches 1 million consumers. Here the CPM for both is $1.00. However, given the focused nature of cable, the retailer may hit 900,000 in its target market, thus having a $1.11 CPM-TM. The billboard, however, reaches only 500,000 of the retailer's targeted customers and as a result has a CPM-TM of $2.00. Comparing CPM-TMs, we can see that cable television (at $1.11) is more effective than the billboard (at $2.00) for the retail outlet. Thus, a medium such as television may cost more based on CPM, but if it has a significantly better CPM-TM, then it may be the better buy.

Lastly, **impact** refers to how strong an impression an advertisement makes and how well it ultimately leads to a purchase. As a result of the increase in media alternatives and the tendency of consumers to spend a stable amount of time on the various media, targeted ads have had a sixfold increase over the last decade.

Scheduling of Advertising

When should a retailer time its advertisements to be received by the consumer? What time of day, day of week, week of month, and month of year should the ads appear? No uniform answer to these questions is possible for all lines of retail trade. Rather, the following conventional wisdom should be considered.

1. Ads should appear on or right before the days when customers are most likely to purchase. If most people shop for groceries Thursday through Saturday, then grocery store ads might appear on Wednesday and Thursday.

2. Advertising should be concentrated around the times when people receive their payroll checks. If they get paid at the end of each month, then advertising should be concentrated at that point.

3. If the retailer has limited advertising funds, then it should concentrate its advertising during periods of highest demand. For example, a muffler-repair shop would be well advised to advertise during drive time on Thursday and Friday when the consumer is aware of his or her problem and has Saturday available for the repair work.

4. The retailer should time its ads to appear during the time of day or day of week when the best CPM-TM will be obtained. Many small retailers have discovered the advantages of late-night television.

5. The higher the degree of habitual purchasing of a product class, the more the advertising should precede the purchase time.

Many retailers use advertising to react to crises such as an unexpected buildup of inventory due to slow sales. Of course, in these cases the timing of ads is not planned in advance and is an ineffective method of scheduling retail advertising. The preceding rules are only suggestions based on conventional wisdom. Depending on the situation, a retailer may use a different scheduling plan to make the best use of its money. For example, earlier in the chapter it was mentioned that one of the author's retailing mentors suggested advertising when others were not and, to avoid getting lost in the crowd, cutting back on ads when competitors were advertising.

Evaluating the Results

Will the advertising produce results? It depends on how well the ads were designed and how well the advertising decisions were made. A consistent record of good retail-advertising decision making can be made only if the retailer effectively plans its advertising program.

Some retailers try systematically to assess the effectiveness and efficiency of their advertising. **Advertising effectiveness** refers to the extent to which the advertising has produced the desired result (i.e., helped to achieve the advertising objective). **Advertising efficiency** is concerned with whether the advertising result was achieved with the minimum effort (e.g., dollars).

The effectiveness or efficiency of advertising can be assessed on a subjective basis. Simply ask yourself, are you satisfied with the results produced? Do you believe you achieved those results at the least cost? Most, but not all, ineffective advertising is due to one of 10 errors:

1. The retailer bombarded the consumer with so many messages and sales that any single message or sale tended to be discounted. A retailer that has a major sale every week will tend to wear out its appeal.

advertising effectiveness
Is the extent to which the advertising has produced the result desired.

advertising efficiency
Is concerned with whether the advertising result was achieved with the minimum financial expenditure.

2. The advertising was not creative or appealing. It may be just more "me too" advertising in which the retailer does not effectively differentiate itself from the competition.

3. The advertisement didn't give customers all the information they needed. The store hours or address may be absent because the retailer assumes that everyone already knows this information. Or information may be lacking on sizes, styles, colors, and other product attributes.

4. Advertising dollars were spread too thinly over too many departments or merchandise lines.

5. There may have been poor internal communications among salesclerks, cashiers, stock clerks, and management. For example, customers may come to see the advertised item, but salesclerks may not know the item is on sale or where to find it, and cashiers may not know the sale price. Worst yet, for a variety of reasons, the advertised product may not be available when the consumer seeks to purchase it.

6. The advertisement was not directed at the proper target market.

7. The retailer did not consider all media options. A better buy was available, but the retailer did not take the time to find out about it.

8. The retailer made too many last-minute changes in the advertising copy, increasing both the cost of the ad and the chance for error.

9. The retailer took co-op dollars just because they were "free" and therefore presumably a good deal.

10. The retailer used a medium that reached too many people not in the target market. Thus, too much money was spent on advertising to people who were not potential customers.

LO 4 — Management of Sales Promotions and Publicity

How do retailers manage their sales promotion and publicity?

Retailers also use sales promotions, which provide some type of short-term incentive, and publicity to increase the effectiveness of their promotional efforts. The role of sales promotions and publicity in the retail organization should be consistent with and reinforce the retailer's overall promotional objectives.

Role of Sales Promotion

Sales promotion tools are excellent demand generators. Many can be used on relatively short notice and can help the retailer achieve its overall promotional goals. Furthermore, sales promotions can be significant in helping the retailer differentiate itself from competitors. Retailers have long known that consumers will change their shopping habits and brand preferences to take advantage of sales promotions, especially those that offer something special, different, or exciting.

Retailers must remember that, since all stores are able to shop the same vendors, merchandise alone does not make a store exciting. In-store happenings of sales promotion can generate excitement. Because of their poor record-keeping systems, many retailers fail to recognize that the role of sales promotion is quite large and may represent a larger expenditure than advertising. They know the cost of advertising because most of that is paid to parties outside the firm. However, the cost of sales promotions often includes many in-store expenses that the retailer does

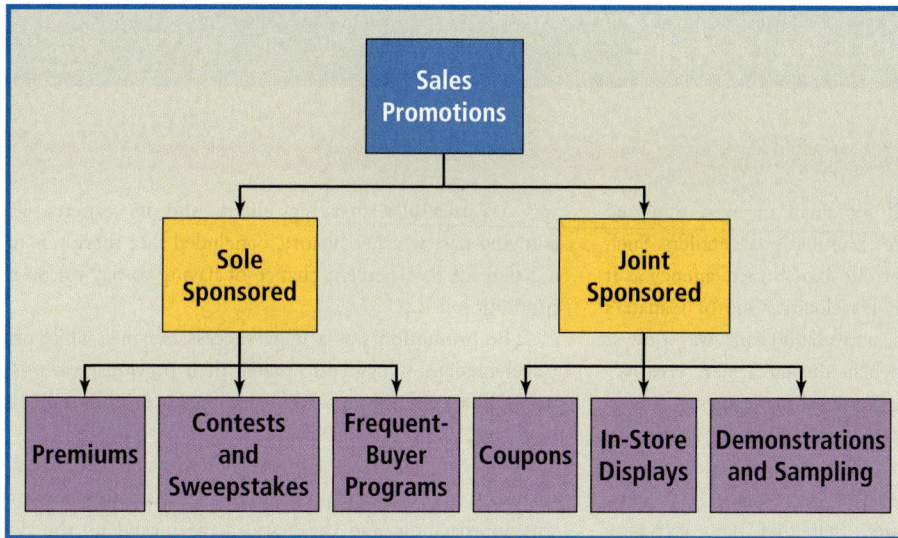

Exhibit 11.5
Types of Sales Promotion

not associate with promotion activities. If these costs were properly traced, then many retailers would discover that sales promotions represent a sizable expenditure. Therefore, promotions warrant more attention by retail decision makers than is typically given.

Types of Sales Promotion

As a rule, successful retailers break sales promotions into two categories: those where they are the sole sponsors and those involving a joint effort with other parties. These are shown in Exhibit 11.5.

Sole-Sponsored Sales Promotions

Just like advertising, sales promotions are an expense to the retailer that may or may not be shared with others. With sole-sponsored sales promotions, the retailer has complete control over the promotion but is also completely responsible for its costs. Although there may be some overlap in the sponsorship of these promotions, retailers generally consider the following sales promotions to be sole sponsored.

1. **Premiums** are extra items offered to the customer when purchasing a promoted product. Premiums are used to increase consumption among current consumers and persuade nonusers to try the promoted product. Generally, the retailer is solely responsible for such programs, although some exceptions may occur. An example of a successful premium is the free toy McDonald's gives away with the purchase of a Happy Meal.

2. **Contests and sweepstakes**, which face legal restrictions in some states, are designed to create an interest in the retailer's product and encourage both repeat purchases and brand switching. Although such programs usually produce only one grand prize winner, the selection of a prize that will appeal to a large segment of the market and the addition of smaller prizes make such promotions very popular with consumers. Many local restaurants use weekly drawings not only to generate business but also to track their customers. The chapter's "Global Retailing" box describes the success one Canadian travel agency had with a promotion surrounding snowfall on New Year's Day. This contest, which was an exception to the one-winner-only rule, not only had thousands of winners but also generated significant media coverage across Canada.

premiums
Are extra items offered to the customer when purchasing promoted products.

contests and sweepstakes
Are sales promotion techniques in which customers have a chance of winning a special prize based on entering a contest in which the entrant competes with others, or a sweepstakes in which all entrants have an equal chance of winning a prize.

Global Retailing

The Weather Outside Is Frightful. Isn't That So Delightful?

Sometimes it is very difficult for small or even midsized retailers to compete against large multinational retailers. Such was the case for a midsized Toronto-based travel agency as it went up against Expedia and Travelocity. One of Canada's largest online travel retailers, itravel2000.com was only a decade old in 2005. That's when, during a staff creative-planning session, it was first suggested that the agency should seek to differentiate itself with some type of a creative promotion. While it still isn't clear whose idea it was or whether the now highly successful New Year's Day Snow Promotion was even discussed that first day, it was a beginning. In fact, what did evolve over the next three years was a promotion that took Canada by storm—pun intended.

The "Let It Snow" promotion, which was introduced in late 2007, offered customers who booked their warm-weather vacation through itravel2000.com a chance to get back the cost of their entire warm-weather getaway, including flight and hotel (minus taxes and fees), if 12.7 centimeters (5 inches) of snow fell at one of four airports nearest them—specifically, Montreal, Toronto, Halifax, and Calgary—on New Year's Day 2008.

itravel2000.com protected itself from a catastrophic loss by taking out a large insurance policy with an online weather-risk-management firm, WeatherBill's. In fact, this promotion was WeatherBill's first big client, and its experts, after studying past weather history, concluded that there was only a 2 percent to 3 percent chance of having to pay off on this promotion.

The promotion was a huge success because, while other travel agencies struggled to match their previous year's sales, itravel2000.com saw a 25-percent increase in its fall 2007 bookings.

As New Year's Day approached, weather forecasters in eastern Canada started predicating that a strong snowstorm was approaching, and the news media picked up the story. After all, the holidays aren't normally big news days. This is the type of publicity money can't buy.

Sure enough, a big storm hit and by late evening most folks in Quebec knew they were going to be big winners, Toronto was going to be close. It had all the excitement of election night, and the media loved it.

In the end, Montreal's Pierre Elliott Trudeau International Airport was the only one that met the standard with 14.8 centimeters of snow falling during the 24-hour measuring period. Toronto just missed, and Calgary was clear and sunny. What made it even better for itravel2000.com was that it had just entered the Quebec market earlier that year. By the way,

Al Grillo/Canadian Press Images/AP Photo

the average rebate for the thousands of travelers in the contest was more than $2,000 in U.S. dollars.

Based on its success in 2008, the travel agency ran the same contest for New Year's Day 2009; this time, the people in Atlantic Canada won when the weather station in Halifax recorded 13.6 centimeters—so much for playing the percentages. Today, this contest is as much a part of Canada's winter as snowbirds heading south.

Many retailers across the world have similar contests, some based on Christmas Day's weather and other on

Groundhog Day's. However, the strangest contest occurred in 2008 when a Chicago furniture dealer promised a full rebate on all purchases made at its four stores April 1 and 15 if the Cubs became world champions that year. After all, despite being the preseason favorites in Las Vegas, they hadn't won a championship in a century. Sadly, both the Cubs and the furniture dealer folded that October.

Source: This box was prepared with the cooperation of Stuart Morris, Vice President of Marketing, itravel2000.com.

---

3. **Loyalty programs**, or frequent-shopper programs, are rapidly growing as retailers realize the importance of combining such promotions with their database systems to solidify their relationships with customers. Some retailers, such as those described in Chapter 2's "What's New?" box, credit loyalty programs for saving their customer base from attack by competitors. Other retailers think the benefits of using these programs are overrated. This chapter's "What's New?" box details the early development of loyalty programs.

loyalty programs
Are a form of sales promotion program in which buyers are rewarded with special rewards, which other shoppers are not offered, for purchasing often from the retailer.

Jointly Sponsored Sales Promotions

Jointly sponsored sales promotions offer retailers the advantage of using *other people's money* (OPM). Although in some cases such promotions require the retailer to partially relinquish control, the co-sponsor's monetary offering to the retailer often more than compensates. Retailers generally consider the following promotions to be jointly sponsored.

1. **Coupons** offer the retail customer a discount on the price of a specific item. Roughly 300 billion coupons are distributed annually in the United States, and there are more of them every year, although less than 2 percent of coupons are redeemed. Coupons represent a windfall for retailers worth more than $500 million since they receive, on average, a 10-cent coupon-redemption fee from the manufacturers.

    For manufacturers, a coupon is a form of advertising to entice a consumer to try a product, especially a new product. People may forget their coupon but buy the product anyway because they remember seeing the coupon ad. Coupons are also used to maintain a loyal base of customers for older brands such as Kellogg's Raisin Bran and Wisk as competitors attempt to get loyalists to switch brands by offering lower prices. However, given the recent downturn in the nation's economy, many retail experts see a shift in the way Americans approach spending money, so they expect "saving money" with the use of coupons to increase significantly over the foreseeable future.

2. **In-store displays** are promotional displays that seek to generate traffic, advertise, and encourage impulse buying. Displays such as **endcaps** (the

coupons
Are a sales promotion tool in which the shopper is offered a price discount on a specific item if the retailer is presented with the appropriate coupon at time of purchase.

in-store displays
Are promotional fixtures of displays that seek to generate traffic, highlight individual items, and encourage impulse buying.

endcaps
The display of products placed at the end of an aisle in a store.

What's New?

The History of Loyalty Programs

Many consumers are under the mistaken idea that loyalty programs began with the introduction of frequent-flyer programs by the airlines in the early 1980s. In reality, these programs have been around for almost 170 years. According to Clive Humby, the founder of dunnhumby, the first supermarket loyalty program can be traced back to England in 1844. It involved a co-op called the Rochdale Equitable Pioneers' Society and the dividend or "divi" it paid its members. (One early American effort to encourage customer loyalty was the S&H Green Stamps program, which began during the Great Depression.)

However, a major shortcoming of all these programs was that they were simply a type of discounting to customers based on the quantity of purchases. They really didn't add value to the retailer–customer dyad. In most cases, this problem was the result of the retailer not being able to match loyalty-card usage with customer data. Most retailers know that the top 20 percent of their customers account for about 80 percent of the sales and that the top 60 percent of their customers account for more than 90 percent of their sales. However, it has only been recently that retailers have begun to seek out ways of using the data from the loyalty programs to reward their regular customers. After all, don't these customers deserve their best deals, services, and privileges? In doing so, these retailers have discovered that there are three different loyalty strategies to use:

1. A *pure* strategy that strengthens the existing bond between a retailer and customers so that the retailer is able to discern what the customers really want and give them more of it. It could be as simple as having a larger deli selection, carrying the customers' shopping bags to the car, or having an easy-pay system at the gas pump. The pure strategy aims to establish a two-way dialog in order that the retailers can improve the offering.

2. A *pull* strategy means attracting customers by augmenting a retail offer so that customers will find that the purchase of one product means that they will get an offer on another linked product. This might even mean being able to get a discount or even a free product from a different provider. An example could be "Stay three nights and get a ticket to a major league game." This strategy is really an extension of "Buy one, get one free," or encouraging sales of an extra item.

3. A *push* strategy seeks to get customers to do something they haven't done before whether it's trying a new channel, a new form of payment, or buying a new product. It may be something as simple as encouraging the customer to use a debit card instead of a credit card, thereby lowing the retailer's bank fees.

Over the past decade, significant advances have been made in loyalty programs. In fact, one recent academic study concluded that an even higher customer-satisfaction level could be achieved by allowing different kinds of currencies to be used to obtain rewards. This sort of *combined currency* such as $39 plus 16,000 miles can be superior to a standard, single-currency price (where a person pays either $189 or 25,000 miles but not a combination of the two). Whichever currency is chosen, a good loyalty program will ensure that it will be market driven.

Finally, as of early 2009, the average U.S. household had signed up for 14.1 loyalty programs but only actively participated in 6.2 of them. The corresponding numbers in 2007 were 12 and 4.7.

Source: Based on Xavier Drèze and Joseph C. Nunes, "Using Combined-Currency Prices to Lower Consumers' Perceived Cost," *Journal of Marketing Research*, February 2004: 59–72; "Colloquy Releases 2009 Census," a white paper published by Colloquy (4445 Lake Forest Drive, Cincinnati, OH, 45242), April 10, 2009; *Scoring Points: How Tesco Continues to Win Customer Loyalty*, 2nd ed. (Kogan Press, Philadelphia: 2007); and material supplied by dunnhumbyUSA, Cincinnati, OH, and used with the written permission of dunnhumbyUSA.

---

register racks
The racks placed near the checkout to encourage impluse buying.

shelving at the end of an aisle) and **register racks** at checkout stands offer manufacturers a captive audience for their products in the retailer's store. (Remember, the retailer does not care which brand the customer purchases, just as long as the purchase is made in its store.) As a result, the manufacturer is willing to pay for the right to "rent" the space necessary for this display from the retailer.

Discussions with store managers and vendors indicate that there is a strong correlation between shoppers noticing an in-store promotion and a resulting impulse purchase. However, not all forms of in-store media are equal, nor is the effectiveness the same with different shopper segments. For instance, end-aisle displays and store flyers were the most noticed forms of in-store advertising overall, while shopping cart ads and in-store TV ads were largely ignored by today's on-the-go shoppers and are viewed by most vendors as a money grab by the retailer.[16] Chapter 13 will provide a greater discussion on in-store displays.

3. **Demonstrations and sampling** are in-store presentations or showings that are intended to reduce the consumer's perceived risk of purchasing a new product. These demonstrations, which accentuate ease, convenience, or product superiority, are paid for by the manufacturer at a price that is usually higher than the retailer's cost for providing that service.

   Joint demonstrations and sampling promotions can be undertaken with entities other than the retailer's suppliers or other retailers. Every spring, retailers, especially malls, invite landscapers and other lawn-care experts onto their grounds to promote their own merchandise and services because consumers are getting ready to prepare their own lawns for the summer and appreciate the convenience of visiting with all the lawn experts at one location. In addition to bringing merchandise for sale, many lawn professionals also bring samples of their work to place in the mall hallways or parking lot. This is truly a case of using OPM since the retailer and malls bear no expense for this promotion; the lawn-care folks are willing to do it as a form of self-promotion.

demonstrations and sampling
Are in-store presentations with the intent of reducing the consumer's perceived risk of purchasing a product.

Evaluating Sales Promotions

As Exhibit 11.6 indicates, sales promotions are intended to help generate short-term increases in performance. Therefore, they should be evaluated in terms of their sales and profit-generating capability. As with advertising, sales promotions can also be evaluated with sophisticated mathematical models; however, the development and use of such models is usually not cost effective. A simpler approach is to monitor weekly unit volume before the sales promotion and compare it to weekly unit volume during and after the promotion.

Tasks That Sales Promotions Can Accomplish
Get consumers to try a new product
Stimulate the sales of mature products
Neutralize competitive advertising and sales promotions
Encourage repeat usage by current users
Reinforce advertising

Tasks That Sales Promotions Cannot Achieve
Change the basic nonacceptance of an undesired product
Compensate for a poorly trained sales force
Give consumers a compelling reason to continue purchasing a product over the long run
Permanently stop an established product's declining sales trend

Exhibit 11.6
What Sales Promotion Can and Cannot Achieve

Publicity Management

Publicity was defined at the outset of this chapter as non-paid-for communications of information about the company or products, generally in some media form; however, this definition is actually misleading because in many instances publicity is a contracted service. An example of this may be the health reports on your local television news program. Sometimes these are, in fact, publicity, but at other times they may be part of the health provider's promotional contract with the station. Even when the retailer does not pay directly for publicity, it can be very expensive to have a good publicity department that plants commercially significant news in the appropriate places. It may be even more expensive to create news that is worth reporting. Consider Macy's Fourth of July fireworks display in New York, Lowe's and Home Depot's NASCAR sponsorship, McDonald's Ronald McDonald Houses, and Dee Lincoln's purchase of the crossbreed steer, described earlier in the chapter's "Service Retailing" box. All create favorable publicity, but all are expensive.

Recently, some experts suggested that publicity may be more important to a retailer than advertising. They claim that advertising can only maintain brands that have already been created by publicity. These experts cite examples such as the Cheese Cake Factory that have been built with virtually no advertising. Consider the case a few years back when Paris Hilton did an ad for Carl's Jr.'s Spicy BBQ Burger. The ad generated so much publicity across the country that many called the spicy ad nothing more than a naked publicity grab. Yet the media coverage generated was what the restaurant chain wanted. While it is doubtful that publicity is more important than advertising, as these experts claim, these examples do point out the importance of managing your firm's publicity.

Publicity (like other forms of promotion) has its strengths and weaknesses. When publicity is formally managed, it should be integrated with other elements of the promotion mix. In addition, all publicity should reinforce the store's image. Perhaps the major advantages of publicity are that it is objective and credible and appeals to a mass audience. Consider, for example the so-called Oprah effect that is generated when Oprah Winfrey mentions a book. The effect works for products as well. One of the author's favorite ice cream shops, Graeter's in Cincinnati, received

By sponsoring NASCAR, Home Depot has found a successful way to reach one of it core target markets.

five times its normal amount of orders via its toll-free phone number and website the day after Oprah called it the "best ice cream I've ever tasted" on her television show.

Today, however, the Internet has made it possible for angry consumers to rapidly spread false stories about any retailer. Unfortunately, only in rare circumstances do retailers ever find out who started the false rumors such as those stating that snakes were found in overcoats sold at a major retailer, a fast-food chain using worms in its hamburgers, a global furniture retailer selling a cactus filled with a nest of deadly spiders, and another fast-food retailer slaughtering chickens inhumanely. However, when the originators are located, it can be expensive for them. Recently, for example, Procter & Gamble Co. won a jury award of $19.25 million in a civil lawsuit filed against four former Amway distributors who were accused of spreading false rumors linking the giant manufacturer to satanism as a means to advance their own business. The distributors were found to have used a voicemail system to tell thousands of customers that part of Procter & Gamble profits went to satanic cults.[17] The most interesting thing about all these falsehoods is that the events related in the stories never actually happened to the people sending you the e-mail, but rather to some "friend of a friend."

For retailers to be able to handle these falsehoods, they must first be aware of them, so it is important for retailers to maintain a systematic program of monitoring the online rumor mill. For many retailers, simply checking general websites such as urbanlegends.com or urbanlegends.about.com may be effective. Remember back in Chapter 3 we pointed out the enormous number of websites with a retailer's name followed by the word *sucks*? These sites begin with the originator's complaints and soon generate both additional complaints and questionable events that, whether true or not, contribute to a negative public perception of the retailer. In other cases, individuals have created websites that work on misspellings of the retailer's name; examples include Untied Airlines: the Most Unfriendly Skies (untied.com) which is aimed at United Airlines and (unitedpackagesmashers.com) which targets United Parcel Service. Others use a play on the retailer's name such as againstthewal.com, which focuses on Walmart.

As a result, successful retailers who want to prevent such behavior have adopted a four-pronged plan:

1. Buy the URLs for their name followed by "sucks.com" or preceded by "ihate." In another example of creative planning, Neiman Marcus owns the "needless-markup" website, which takes customers to the regular Neiman Marcus home page.

2. Locate the website's creator and determine why he or she is angry. If possible, apologize and then fix the problem before it irritates others.

3. Tell your side of the story on your own website, as Starbucks has done.

4. When all else fails, take the hate-site creators to court. Many will back away from a costly court battle. The courts will find in favor of the retailer if libel or slander can be proven. There are a couple of legal precedents to keep in mind. First, the Sixth Circuit Court of Appeals has held that a domain name holder's use of another's trademark in a "fan" site did not run afoul of Section 1114 of the Lanham Act because of the presence of both a prominent disclaimer on the site disavowing any affiliation with the mark owner and a link to the plaintiff's official website. Second, the domain holder's use of the trademarks in conjunction with the word *sucks* in the domain names of noncommercial complaint sites did not violate Section 1114 of the Lanham Act because there was no likelihood of consumer confusion arising from that type of use, and because such speech is protected by the First Amendment of the U.S. Constitution.

One thing not to do, however, is to use a so-called search-engine-optimization tool, where you hire consultants or buy software that's supposed to make good information rise to the top of Google rankings. Even if it works—and it probably won't—it's just a temporary fix, says Daniel Solove, an associate professor at George Washington University Law School and the author of *The Future of Reputation: Gossip, Rumor, and Privacy on the Internet*.[18]

SUMMARY

LO 1

What are the four basic components of the retailer's promotion mix, and how are they related to other retailer decisions?

A retailer's promotion mix comprises advertising, sales promotions, publicity, and personal selling. All four components need to be managed from a total systems perspective and must be integrated not only with each other but also with the retailer's other managerial decision areas such as location, merchandise, credit, cash flow, building and fixtures, price, and customer service. In addition, the retailer must realize that its promotional activities may be in conflict with the way other supply-chain members use promotion.

LO 2

What are the differences between a retailer's long-term and short-term promotional objectives?

A retailer's promotional objectives should be established to help improve both long- and short-term financial performance. Long-term or institutional advertising is an attempt by the retailer to gain long-term benefits by selling the store itself rather than the merchandise in it. Retailers seeking long-term benefits generally have two long-term promotion objectives: creating a positive store image and promoting public service.

Short-term or promotional advertising attempts to bolster short-term performance by using product availability or price as a selling point. The two most common promotional objectives are (1) increasing the patronage of existing customers and (2) attracting new customers.

LO 3

What six steps are involved in developing a retail advertising campaign?

Developing a retail-advertising campaign is a six-step process: (1) selecting advertising objectives, (2) budgeting for the campaign, (3) designing the message, (4) selecting the media to use, (5) scheduling the ads, and (6) evaluating the results.

The advertising objectives should flow from the retailer's promotion objectives and should consider several factors that are unique to retailing such as the store's age and location, the merchandise sold, the competition, size of the market, and level of supplier support. The specific objectives that advertising can accomplish are many and varied, and the ones chosen depend on these factors.

When developing a budget, retailers must decide whether they can get a better return on their money with co-op dollars or by total sponsorship of advertising. In budgeting advertising funds, retailers tend to use the affordable method, the percentage-of-sales method, or the task-and-objective method. While most retail advertising is paid for solely by the retailer, sometimes manufacturers and other retailers may pay part or all of the costs for the retailer's advertising campaign. For example, vertical cooperative advertising allows the retailer and other supply-chain members to share the advertising burden while horizontal cooperative advertising enables two or more retailers to band together to share the cost of advertising.

Retailers must develop a creative retail ad that accomplishes three goals: attracts and retains attention, achieves its objective, and avoids errors. Some of the common approaches that retailers use to gain repeated viewing include showing how the retailer's products fit in with the consumer's lifestyle, creating a fantasy for the consumer that is built around the retailer's products, designing the campaign around humor that relates to the uses of the retailer's products, depicting the consumer in everyday settings using the retailer's products, and building a mood around using the retailer's products. Before publishing any ad, the retailer should test it with both consumer groups and legal experts for errors.

Once the budget is established, it should be allocated in such a way that it maximizes the retailer's overall profitability. In determining allocations, retailers can choose from a variety of media alternatives, primarily newspapers, television, radio, magazines, direct mail, and the Internet. Each medium has its own advantages and disadvantages. To choose among the media, the retailer should know their strengths and weaknesses, coverage and reach, and the cost of an ad.

After the retailer selects a medium, it must decide when the ad should appear. While there is no single "right" time to run an ad, conventional wisdom suggests that the ads should (1) appear on or slightly precede the days when customers are most likely to purchase, (2) be concentrated around the times when people receive their payroll checks, (3) be concentrated during periods of highest demand, (4) be timed to appear during the time of day or day of week when the best CPM (or CPM-TM) will be obtained, and (5) precede the purchase time, especially for habitual purchased products.

Advertising results can be assessed in terms of efficiency and effectiveness. Effectiveness is the extent to which advertising has produced the result desired. Efficiency is concerned with whether the result was achieved with minimum cost.

How do retailers manage their sales promotion and publicity?

LO 4

Retailers use sales promotions, which provide some type of short-term incentive, and publicity to increase the effectiveness of their promotional efforts. The role of sales promotions and publicity in the retail organization should be consistent with and reinforce the retailer's overall promotion objectives.

Sales-promotion tools are excellent demand generators. Many can be used on relatively short notice and can help the retailer achieve its overall promotion goals. Retailers usually break sales promotions into two categories: those where they are the sole sponsors (premiums, contests and sweepstakes, and loyalty programs) and those involving a joint effort with other parties (coupons, displays, and demonstrations and sampling).

Although retailers may not pay for publicity directly, the indirect cost can be quite significant. Most retailers do not have formal publicity departments or directors, but some of the larger and more progressive retailers do. The major advantages of publicity are that it is objective, credible, and appeals to a mass audience. The major disadvantage is that publicity is difficult to control and schedule.

TERMS TO REMEMBER

promotion	publicity
advertising	personal selling
sales promotions	primary trading area

secondary trading areas
institutional advertising
promotional advertising
affordable method
percentage-of-sales method
benchmarking
task-and-objective method
vertical cooperative advertising
horizontal cooperative advertising
coverage
reach
cumulative reach
frequency
cost per thousand method (CPM)

cost per thousand—target market
   (CPM-TM)
impact
advertising effectiveness
advertising efficiency
premiums
contests and sweepstakes
loyalty programs
coupons
in-store displays
endcaps
register racks
demonstrations and sampling

REVIEW AND DISCUSSION QUESTIONS

LO 1   **What are the four basic components of the retailer's promotion mix and how are they related to other retailer decisions?**

1.   What features should a retailer promote in its ads for national branded products? Are these the same features that should be promoted by the retailer for its private-label products?

2.   Why are the desired promotional outcomes for other members of a retailer's supply chain different from the retailer's promotional goals? Isn't the marketing supply chain supposed to be a partnership?

LO 2   **What are the differences between a retailer's long-term and short-term promotional objectives?**

3.   Explain how a long-term promotional objective can affect the firm over the short run.

4.   What do you think is the most important short-term objective for a retailer: increase patronage from existing customers or attracting new customers? Explain the reasoning behind your answer.

LO 3   **What six steps are involved in developing a retail advertising campaign?**

5.   Why don't retailers list "increasing sales" as their number-one advertising objective?

6.   Describe the three methods available to the retailer for determining the amount to spend on advertising. Which one is the best one to use? Which one is most commonly used by small retailers?

7.   Some retailers decline a vendor's offer of cooperative advertising; is this smart? After all, aren't they passing up "free" money?

8.   An old proverb claims, "Doing advertising without planning is like running a giant manure spreader; your advertising department throws words out the back faster than you can shovel money in the front." Do you agree or disagree with this statement? Explain your reasoning.

9.   From the creative standpoint, it is said that a retail ad should accomplish three goals. What are these goals, and is one of these more important than the others?

10.   How should a small-town retailer use the Internet?

How do retailers manage their sales promotion and publicity?   **LO 4**

11. What is sales promotion? How is it different from advertising?
12. What is publicity? Isn't this always free to the retailer? How does publicity fit into a retailer's promotional efforts?
13. What can retail managers do to prevent bad publicity about their stores from circulating on the Internet?

SAMPLE TEST QUESTIONS

Which of the following areas should not be taken into consideration by a retailer when formulating a promotional strategy?   **LO 1**

a. the retailer's credit customers.
b. the price level of the merchandise.
c. merchandise inventory levels.
d. the retailer's building and fixtures.
e. the retailer's net worth.

The two objectives of institutional advertising include: **LO 2**

a. creating a positive store image and public-service promotion.
b. increasing patronage from existing customers and attraction of new customers.
c. publicity and sales promotion.
d. advertising a sale and generating store traffic.
e. using other people's money and using co-op money.

Which of the following should not be part of The Campus Shoppe's advertising campaign's objectives. The Campus Shoppe desires   **LO 3**

a. to increase awareness of its two locations
b. among incoming freshmen
c. to 40 percent
d. over the next three months
e. All the above belong in the retailer's advertising objectives.

Consumer premiums are considered to be a form of: **LO 4**

a. joint-sponsored sales promotion.
b. publicity that utilizes OPM.
c. advertising.
d. personal selling.
e. sole-sponsored sales promotion.

WRITING AND SPEAKING EXERCISE

Most airline, hotel and motel, and even car-rental companies offer special discounts to large groups traveling together or going to the same location for a conference, meeting, or convention. These special discounts are made available by assigning a special code for the group members to use when making reservations. For example, in August 2012, if an individual were going to the shopping-center meeting in Las Vegas, American Airline's special 25-percent to 30-percent discount code is Star

#SZ9Z1K1, and the Delta code is File #ZX232. An individual attending the apparel market in Dallas during the same time period would be given different airline codes but be offered a similar discount. In addition, if some apparel buyers desired to rent a car, they could use code 79242, Group G3, at Hertz for an extra discount. These travel companies, however, don't want members of the general public to be able to use their codes to reduce travel costs.

Over the summer, you interned at a travel agency that obtained access to these codes and used them to generate a substantial sales increase by publishing an e-mail newsletter featuring an extensive list of locations and dates when these discounts were available. The customers could only take advantage of these discounts by purchasing their tickets and hotel and car reservations through your travel agency. Several airlines objected to this action, but since the recession had reduced their traffic, they let the travel agency continue to use the discounts. Besides, it was because of this additional business that the agency was able to hire you for the summer.

One night you were telling your mother about this setup and she asked if you were happy about doing it. How would you answer her?

RETAIL PROJECT

Find two current advertisements using the same medium (newspaper, television, radio, Internet, etc.) that you feel are effective in achieving their objectives and two that you do not feel are effective.

Explain what you feel each ad's objectives were and why you categorized them as you did.

In reviewing the ineffective ads, was something wrong with the creative design? Did they fail to hold the consumer's attention, or did they use the wrong medium to reach their intended market? How would you improve these ads?

PLANNING YOUR OWN RETAIL BUSINESS

Your Uncle Nick has agreed to sell you his supermarket where you have worked for seven years since graduating from college. Uncle Nick is 72 years old and is ready to step down from day-to-day management.

After operating the Crest Supermarket on your own for six months, you begin to analyze how you can increase store traffic and, consequently, annual sales and profitability. During a recent trip to the Food Marketing Institute convention, you ran across several successful grocers. Some of them competed largely on price, while others competed more on promotion and advertising.

You decide to pursue a heavy promotion-oriented strategy. Consequently, you budget to increase advertising by $20,000 monthly or $240,000 annually and to also have a weekly contest where you give away $100 in groceries to 25 families. This will cost you $130,000 (52 × $100 × 25) annually.

Currently, Crest Supermarket serves a trade area with a 2-mile radius and a household density of 171 per square mile. Seventy percent of these households shop at Crest an average of 45 times per year. Of those that visit Crest, 98 percent make a purchase that averages $24.45. Crest operates on a 25-percent gross margin.

You estimate that with your new promotion program, the radius of Crest's trade area will increase to 2.5 miles. Assuming that all other relevant factors remain constant (171 households per square mile, 70 percent of households shop Crest, 98-percent closure rate, $24.45 average transaction size, 25-percent gross margin percent), is the planned promotion program and investment of an additional $370,000 annually a profitable strategy?

(*Hint:* Assume the trade area is circular and thus its size in square miles can be computed as pi (3.142) times the radius of the circle squared. The total square miles of the trade area can be multiplied by the number of households per square mile to obtain total households in the trade area. This in turn can be multiplied by the percentage that shop at Crest, which in turn can be multiplied by the average number of trips annually to Crest, which will yield total traffic. This traffic statistic can be multiplied by the percent of visitors that make a purchase, which will yield total transactions. You should be able to figure out on your own the rest of the computations that are needed to determine if the promotional strategy is profitable.)

Customer Services and Retail Selling

OVERVIEW:

In this chapter, we demonstrate how customer services, including retail selling, generate additional demand for the retailer's merchandise. We also examine the determination of an optimal customer-service level. We conclude the chapter by looking at the unique managerial problems that retailers must address.

LEARNING OBJECTIVES:

After reading this chapter, you should be able to:

1. Explain why customer service is so important in retailing.
2. Describe the various customer services that a retailer can offer.
3. Explain how a retailer should determine which services to offer.
4. Describe the various management problems involved in retail selling, salesperson selection, and training and evaluation.
5. Describe the retail selling process.
6. Understand the importance of a customer service audit.

LO 1

Customer Service

Why is customer service so important in retailing?

The old rules about customer loyalty are obsolete. Today's customers are tired of making a series of wishes (see the shopper's wish list in Exhibit 12.1) before embarking on their planned purchases. Customers instead define loyalty on their terms, not those of the retailer. Little wonder, then, that the average retailer is expected to lose half of its customers every five years. Further, as Exhibit 12.2 illustrates, even those customers who continue to shop with a particular retailer—in this case, Walmart—are not always loyal. Without exception, it is a fact of life that all retailers must give consideration to the service level and services they offer their customers.

high-quality service
Is the type of service that meets or exceeds customers' expectations.

Delivering **high-quality service** means delivering service that meets or exceeds customers' expectations. Note that this definition mentions no absolute level of quality service. Instead, only service that meets and exceeds the expectations of customers is considered high quality. For example, suppose a consumer has lunch at a restaurant where he or she expects to have slow service but is served in 10 minutes. The next day at lunch, the same consumer eats at another restaurant where he or she expects to have fast service and again is served in 10 minutes. Even assuming that other factors such as cleanliness, friendliness, and food quality are equal, this consumer might report the service quality to be better in the first

Please ...	**Exhibit 12.1**
• Let me find a parking place near the store.	**A Shopper's Wish**
• Do not let me pay too much.	
• Have the sales staff pretend that they care.	
• Do not make me have to return anything.	
• Get me in and out as fast as possible.	
• Do not make me wait in line to make my purchase.	
• Let this experience be somewhat enjoyable.	
• Do not make me have to deal with other obnoxious shoppers.	

restaurant, because the 10-minute service was faster than expected, and report lower service quality in the second restaurant, because the 10-minute service was slower than expected. On an absolute basis, the service was the same in each case—good food in 10 minutes—but the customer's evaluation was different due to different expectations. Just the opposite may be expected at dinner. Here you will want to enjoy the time you are having with friends and family, and 10-minute service may be perceived as an unsatisfactory rush job because it prevents you from visiting with your friends. Another illustration of this concept occurs when customers have a problem with a purchase. When problems are handled swiftly and politely (above their expectations), customers will end up being more loyal to the retailer than those who never encountered a problem.

Remember back in the previous chapter when we quoted one of the author's mentors as saying that when business slowed and all his competitors reduced their ad budgets, he would then increase his ad expenditures? After all, without the clutter of competitors' ads, consumers became more aware of his ads and his sales increased, despite the general sales slowdown affecting the other local merchants. The same thing can be said about customer service. As the economy plunged into the recent recession, many retailers felt forced to trim costs, often cutting services so deeply that they drove away customers. However, as *BusinessWeek* noted in a cover story, successful firms such as Amazon.com, which was cited as the top-rated company, were those that safeguarded their service level. In fact, about half of them tried to avoid cuts to their customer-service budgets.[1]

One way in which retailers provide the high-quality service expected and reduce customer defections is through relationship retailing programs.[2] **Relationship retailing** includes all the activities designed to attract, retain, and enhance customer relationships. Retailing is no longer driven by the expansion of large, homogeneous, big-box chains offering only low prices. Profitable retailers of the future will be those who concentrate on building long-term relationships with customers by promising and consistently delivering high-quality products enhanced by high-quality service, shopping aids to ease the purchase process, and honest pricing to build and maintain a reputation for absolute trustworthiness. After all, loyal customers are less prone to shop other retailers selling the same merchandise mix and are less price conscious.[3] In addition, a U.S. Department of Commerce Office of Consumer Affairs study found that it costs a retailer five times as much money to attract a new customer as it does to convince a former customer to return.[4] As a result, today's retailers are not trying to maximize the profit on each transaction but are instead seeking to build a mutually beneficial relationship with their customers. Consider what retailers can learn from the hotel industry about relationship retailing. High-end hotels have long tracked customer information,

relationship retailing
Comprises all the activities designed to attract, retain, and enhance long-term relationships with customers.

	Shopped Monthly at Retailer								
	Kmart/Big Kmart	Target	Walmart	Small-Format Value Retailers	Drug Stores/ Pharmacies	JCPenney	Kohl's	Sears	Apparel Specialty Stores
Kmart/Big Kmart	100.00%	8.61%	7.93%	13.20%	9.85%	17.50%	11.93%	26.38%	12.02%
Target	34.18%	100.00%	22.93%	24.95%	32.70%	43.37%	52.26%	44.36%	48.89%
Walmart	65.97%	48.05%	100.00%	75.22%	57.42%	75.26%	67.02%	76.42%	62.28%
Small-Format Value Retailers	59.25%	28.20%	40.59%	100.00%	39.50%	50.22%	38.77%	59.17%	44.34%
Drug Stores/ Pharmacies	68.48%	57.30%	48.02%	61.21%	100.00%	66.46%	64.32%	72.62%	66.06%
JCPenney	20.40%	12.74%	10.55%	13.05%	11.14%	100.00%	21.91%	43.43%	21.38%
Kohl's	16.39%	18.10%	11.08%	11.87%	12.71%	25.82%	100.00%	27.96%	21.71%
Sears	12.20%	5.17%	4.25%	6.10%	4.83%	17.23%	9.41%	100.00%	9.74%
Apparel Specialty Stores	29.42%	30.14%	18.33%	24.18%	23.25%	44.86%	38.65%	51.54%	100.00%

Shopped Monthly at Retailer

Source: Retail Forward ShopperScape™, January 2008–December 2008

Exhibit 12.2
Monthly Cross-Shopping at Select Retailers and Channels, 2008

right down to pillow preferences or history of complaints and bad experiences. Today, airlines that follow this example are rolling out new technology that tells airport agents your ticket-buying and travel history, flagging key customers to flight attendants and instructing them to offer personalized apologies, and even having flight attendants deliver favorite drinks to elite-level customers when they are sitting in coach and thanking them by name for their business.[5] In another example of taking winning ideas from the hotels, some high-end retailers have started offering concierge services.[6] Other successful retailers are now copying Nordstrom,[7] Neiman Marcus, and online retailers by pitching products based on the customer's buying history as well as using powerful loyalty programs.[8]

The new operating maxim for all the retailers mentioned above is: "Proper management of relationships will produce a satisfied customer who will become a repeat customer. And repeat customers produce long-term profits." Leo Shapiro, a well-known retail consultant, claimed that the "dollars that walk out of a store every day to be spent at a competitor's store represent the most immediate, major source of potential sales and profit growth."[9] Robert Kahn, another retail consultant discussed earlier in the text, often argued that just reducing the amount of customer defections by as little as 10 percent can often double a retailer's profits. However, in what was probably the most powerful statement about the importance of customer relationship, one Walmart executive told the authors that the loss in future revenues to the chain from losing just one customer would exceed $200,000.[10] One sad note about customer service is that while modern retailing is spreading around the world, creating new retail stores may prove to be far easier than establishing good sales skills. Surliness, odd policies, and slow service appear to be common complaints in underdeveloped markets, especially from expatriates who are used to more customer-friendly policies.[11]

Profitable retailers can develop these relationships with their customers by offering two benefits: financial and social.

1. *Financial benefits* increase the customer's economic rewards. . Examples are the frequent-purchaser discounts or product upgrades already offered by some supermarkets, airlines, and hotels.

2. *Social benefits* increase the retailer's interaction with the customer. Chapter 13 will discuss how shopping can be a pleasant experience for the customer. Retailers must not forget that their stores must offer customers a combination of excitement and entertainment.

Exhibit 12.3 highlights the three basic tasks or activities that every retailer must perform. These tasks were first mentioned in Chapter 3: getting consumers from your trading area into your store, converting these consumers into loyal customers, and doing so in the most efficient manner possible. Chapter 7 described how retailers determine their trading area. The earlier chapters of Part 4, Chapters 8 through 11, discussed the first task: how retailers budget for and select their merchandise and then price and promote this merchandise. In addition, Chapter 8 covered the third task by describing the basic method for controlling inventory cost. The next two chapters will discuss the second and most important task: converting the consumer from your trading area who has decided to try your store into a loyal (and thus profitable) customer.

Due to significant cost cutting following the recent period of retailer consolidation and retrenchment caused by the recession, this second task is even more difficult. Retailers today are so standardized in either their physical layout or website design, with each one carrying the same merchandise styles and colors, that

Exhibit 12.3
Three Basic Tasks of
Retailing

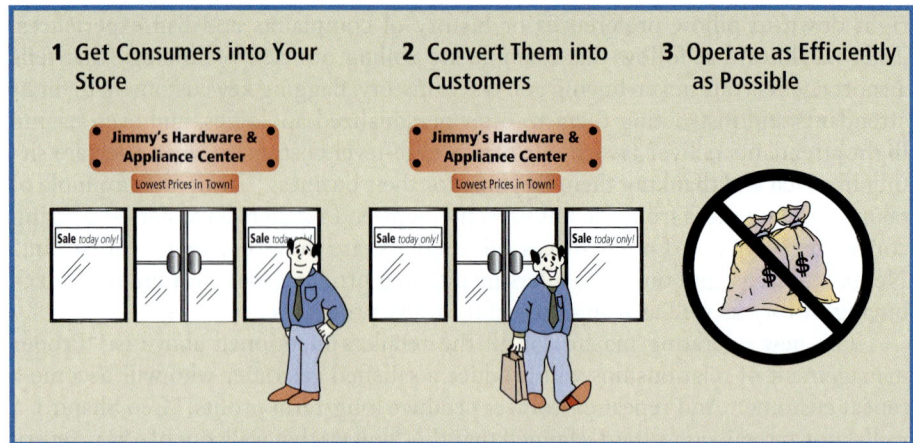

customers cannot tell them apart. More importantly, many current retailers have an indifferent and undertrained sales force. As a result, there is a complete breakdown of what is essential for a successful retailer: exciting merchandise backed up by outstanding service and personal selling that generates loyal customers. In recent years, intense competition from discounters caused many retailers to lower customer-service levels as a means of staying price competitive. These retailers felt that reduced service levels would lower their operating costs, thus allowing increased price competitiveness. For most customers, it is no wonder that shopping trips do not always meet their expectations and result in an unsatisfying experience.[12]

Retailers must differentiate themselves by meeting the needs of their customers better than the competition. Thus, successful retailers have again come to realize that customer service is a strength. Instead of frustrating the customer by not having the necessary stock on hand or the proper selling support on the sales floor, today's profitable retailers realize that customer service is a major demand generator. However, it is important that retailers also remember that when they encourage high customer expectations, the slightest disappointment in service can be a catastrophe. Even Nordstrom, the retailer most famous for its outstanding service, cannot please all its customers all the time. One blog recently quoted an unhappy customer as saying, "I ordered a jacket two weeks ago when it just went on sale. I called in and they said that there is one left in my size so I ordered it. The shipping came super fast, like in 3 days, however when I got my package it says it was a pair of men's pants. I was so confused as I did not order anything else from there but the jacket. I opened my package and it was a SKIRT!!!"[13] In this case, the Nordstrom salesperson probably made a mistake, causing the retailer to fail to live up to the very high expectations that it had trained its customers to expect. However, the retailer corrected the mistake, and most other bloggers praised the Seattle-based retailer not only for its great service but also for going the extra mile in solving their problems.

Customer service consists of all those activities performed by the retailer that influence (1) the ease with which a potential customer can shop or learn about the retailer's offering, (2) the ease with which a transaction can be completed once the customer attempts to make a purchase, and (3) the customer's satisfaction with the transaction. These three elements are the *pretransaction*, *transaction*, and *post-transaction* components of customer service. Some common services provided by retailers include alterations, fitting rooms, delivery, gift registries, check cashing, in-home shopping, extended shopping hours, gift wrapping, charge accounts,

customer service
Consists of all those activities performed by the retailer that influence (1) the ease with which a potential customer can shop or learn about the store's offering, (2) the ease with which a transaction can be completed once the customer attempts to make a purchase, and (3) the customer's satisfaction with the transaction.

parking, layaway, and merchandise-return privileges. It must be remembered that none of these services are altruistic offerings; they are all designed to entice the customers with whom the retailer is seeking to develop a relationship. After all, successful retailers don't try to satisfy customers just because customers deserve it. Rather, they do it because "firms that actually achieve high customer satisfaction also enjoy superior economic returns."[14]

Retailers should design their customer-service program around the pretransaction, transaction, and posttransaction elements of the sale in order to obtain a differential competitive advantage. After all, in today's world of mass distribution, most retailers have access to the same merchandise, so retailers can seldom differentiate themselves from others solely on the basis of merchandise stocked. The same can be said regarding location and store-design advantages. Retailers can, however, obtain a high degree of differentiation through their customer-service programs.

A retail shopping experience is more than negotiating your way through the retailer's store, website, or catalog; finding the merchandise you want; interacting (or not interacting) with the staff; and paying for the merchandise. It also involves your actions before and after the transaction. Therefore, serving the customer before, during, and after the transaction can help to create new customers and strengthen the loyalty of current customers. If customer service before the transaction is poor, then the probability of a transaction occurring will decline. If customer service is poor at the transaction stage, then the customer may back out of the transaction. And if customer service is poor after the transaction, then the probability of a repeat purchase at the same store will decline. The customer who visits a retailer and finds the service level below expectations or the product out of stock will become a **transient customer**. This transient or temporary customer will seek to find a different retailer with the level of customer service he or she feels is appropriate. At any given moment, for all lines of retail trade, there are a significant number of transient customers. The retailer with a superior customer-service program will have a significant advantage in turning these transients into loyal customers. Thus, customer service can play a significant role in building a retailer's sales volume.

Customer service cannot happen all by itself but must be integrated into all aspects of retailing. That is why the profitable retailers of the future will know that the demand for their merchandise is not simply price elastic, as economists would have us believe. It is also *service elastic*, which means that an increase in service levels of 1 percent will result in more than a 1-percent increase in sales.

transient customer
Is an individual who is dissatisfied with the level of customer service offered at a store or stores and is seeking an alternative store with the level of customer service that he or she thinks is appropriate.

Merchandise Management

Chapter 9 discussed the importance of merchandise management since one of the best ways a retailer can serve its customers is by having what they want in inventory. There are few things more disturbing to a customer than making a trip to a store for a specific item only to discover that the item is out of stock. This is why Nordstrom offers its customers a free dress shirt if it is ever out of stock on any of the basic sizes. This retailer wants its customers to be confident of locating any style, color, or size. Basically, the better the store is at allocating inventory in proportion to customer demand patterns, the better the customer will be served.

Building and Fixture Management

Retailers' decisions regarding building and fixtures can also have a significant effect on how well the customer is served. For example, consider how the following noncomprehensive list of building and fixture dimensions might influence customer service: heating and cooling levels; availability of parking space; ease of finding merchandise; layout and arrangement of fixtures; placement and cleanliness of restrooms and lounge areas; location of the check-cashing desk, complaint desk, and returns desks; level of lighting; and width and length of aisles.

Promotion Management

Promotion provides customers with information that can help them make purchase decisions. Therefore, retailers should be concerned with whether the promotion programs they develop, including those online, assist the consumer. The following questions can help the retailer assess whether its promotion is serving the customer:

1. Is the advertising informative and helpful?
2. Does the advertising provide all the information the customer needs?
3. Are the salespeople helpful and informative?
4. Are the salespeople friendly and courteous?
5. Are the salespeople easy to find when needed?
6. Are sufficient quantities available on sales-promotion items?
7. Do salespeople know about the ad, what's being promoted, and why?

This list is not comprehensive. It is intended only to show that customer-service issues need to be considered when designing promotional programs.

Price Management

Price management will also influence how well the customer is served. Are prices clearly marked and visible? Is pricing fair, honest, and straightforward? Are customers told the true price of credit? These questions suggest that the pricing decision should not be isolated from the retailer's customer-service program.

Credit Management

The management of credit, in-house or cobranded with a bank or large financial institution, should also be integrated into the customer-service program. After all, credit, along with the retailer's layaway plans, is a significant aid in both encouraging loyalty and helping consumers purchase merchandise. However, this facet of the retailer's business must be monitored closely. Target in 2007, for example, was one of the nation's top credit-card issuers. The Minneapolis-based retailer developed various promotional campaigns whereby users of the Target-branded financial products were given compelling reasons to shop at Target more often, as well as to spend more on each visit.[15] In addition, Target's financial products contributed more than 20 percent to the retailer's 2007 profits.[16] However, at the end of Target's 2007 fiscal year, the company had $8.62 billion in loans outstanding on it Visa cards, which could be used anywhere, and its private-label cards, which are for purchases at Target only. This amount was 29 percent greater than the total ($6.71 billion) at the end of 2006.[17] Thus, as the economy slowed during 2008 and the credit crisis grew, Target found out that it had offered too much credit to struggling borrowers who would soon be unable to pay off their debt. As a result, in early 2009 Target posted a 22-percent drop in yearly earnings as the discount chain struggled with a lower growth in sales and a major increase in bad-debt expenses.[18]

Retailers are able to generate additional profits by co-branding their name with financial institutions, such as VISA.

A Recap

Integration between the elements of the retail mix is important when retailers develop their customer-service programs. Much of what has already been discussed in this book relates, either directly or indirectly, to one of the three broad categories of customer service: pretransaction, transaction, and posttransaction. Successful retailers view customer service as a way to gain an advantage over the competition. As a result, even discounters are beginning to empower all their employees, not just management, to do whatever is reasonable to take care of the customer.

Common Customer Services

LO 2

What are the various customer services that a retailer can offer?

Much of the discussion in previous chapters on location, merchandise, pricing, and promotion had implications for serving the customer. However, many of the more popular types of customer service have not been mentioned or have received sparse coverage. Let us review some of them.

Pretransaction Services

The most common **pretransaction services**, which are provided to the customer prior to entering the store, are convenient hours and information aids. Each service makes it easier for the potential customer to shop or to learn of the retailer's offering.

The chapter's "Global Retailing" box shows examples of information aids that were *not* too beneficial to the customer because something was lost in translation from a retailer's native language into English.

pretransaction services
Are services provided to the customer prior to entering the store.

Convenient Hours

The more convenient the retailer's operating hours are to the customer, the easier it is for the customer to visit the retailer. Convenient operating hours are the most

Global Retailing

International Information Aids Mistakes

There are usually significant differences between domestic and foreign retail markets. However, nowhere have international retailers had more problems than when their employees try to write signs and instructions in a foreign language such as English and don't check these signs for errors. Frequently, poor knowledge of the customer's language results in unintentional but highly "interesting" signage. Consider the following errors by foreign retailers trying to translate into English:

Cocktail lounge in Norway:	LADIES ARE REQUESTED NOT TO HAVE CHILDREN IN THE BAR.
In a Nairobi restaurant:	CUSTOMERS WHO FIND OUR WAITRESSES RUDE OUGHT TO SEE THE MANAGER.
Hotel in Vienna:	IN CASE OF FIRE, DO YOUR UTMOST TO ALARM THE HOTEL PORTER.
Mexico City discount store:	AMERICAN WELL SPEAKING HERE.
Paris dress shop:	DRESSES FOR STREET WALKING.
Tokyo hotel's rules and regulations:	GUESTS ARE REQUESTED NOT TO SMOKE OR DO OTHER DISGUSTING BEHAVIORS IN BED.
Hong Kong dentist:	TEETH EXTRACTED BY LATEST METHODISTS.
Rome laundry:	LADIES, PLEASE LEAVE YOUR CLOTHES HERE AND SPEND THE AFTERNOON HAVING A GOOD TIME.
French hotel:	PLEASE LEAVE YOUR VALUES AT THE FRONT DESK.
Athens hotel:	WE EXPECT OUR VISITORS TO COMPLAIN DAILY AT THE OFFICE BETWEEN THE HOURS OF 9 AND 11 A.M.
Tokyo hotel:	THE FLATTENING OF UNDERWEAR IS THE JOB OF THE CHAMBERMAID - TO GET IT DONE, TURN HER ON.
Paris hotel:	SPLENDID VIEWS AND A FRENCH WIDOW IN EVERY ROOM.
Bangkok dry cleaner:	DROP YOUR TROUSERS HERE FOR BEST RESULTS.
Amsterdam hotel:	YOU ARE ENCOURAGED TO TAKE ADVANTAGE OF OUR CHAMBERMAIDS.
Hotel in Acapulco:	THE MANAGER HAS PERSONALLY PASSED ALL THE WATER SERVED HERE.
Swiss restaurant:	SPECIAL TODAY ... NO ICE CREAM.
Hong Kong tailor shop:	ORDER YOUR SUMMER SUIT NOW. BECAUSE OF BIG RUSH WE EXECUTE CUSTOMERS IN STRICT ROTATION.
Hotel room notice in Thailand:	PLEASE DO NOT BRING SOLICITORS INTO YOUR ROOM.
Hotel brochure in Italy:	THIS HOTEL IS RENOWNED FOR ITS PEACE AND SOLITUDE. IN FACT, CROWDS FROM ALL OVER THE WORLD FLOCK HERE TO ENJOY ITS SOLITUDE.
Hotel lobby in Bucharest:	THE LIFT IS BEING FIXED FOR THE NEXT DAY. DURING THAT TIME WE REGRET THAT YOU WILL BE UNBEARABLE.
Supermarket in Hong Kong:	FOR YOUR CONVENIENCE, WE RECOMMEND COURTEOUS, EFFICIENT SELF-SERVICE.
Hotel in Zurich:	BECAUSE OF THE IMPROPRIETY OF ENTERTAINING GUESTS OF THE OPPOSITE SEX IN THE BEDROOM, IT IS SUGGESTED THAT THE LOBBY BE USED FOR THIS PURPOSE.
Laundromat in Italy:	AUTOMATIC WASHERS: PLEASE REMOVE ALL YOUR CLOTHES WHEN RED LIGHT GOES ON.
Department store in London:	BARGAIN BASEMENT UPSTAIRS.

basic service that a retailer should provide to its customers. Retailers must ascertain what their customers want and weigh the cost of providing those wants against the additional revenues that would be generated. If a retailer's target customers want longer hours because of their work schedules, then the retailer should do so provided it is profitable. Some retail entrepreneurs are now serving their time-deprived customers with round-the-clock food service, auto-repair, and medical services. Some merchant groups have started banding together to start a concierge service at the local commuter train station that—for a fee paid by the merchants—will return video rentals, handle dry cleaning, pick up prescriptions, and do other shopping chores for the commuter.

A retailer's operating hours also depend on the competition. If a competitor is willing to stay open until 9 P.M. six nights per week to serve customers, it would probably not be wise to close every night at 6 P.M. unless a lease provision requires it. Several years ago, many bricks-and-mortar retailers transformed themselves into bricks-and-click retailers to compete with retailers who offer the most convenient hours: 24/7/365. However, in reaction to the economic downturn, many retailers, especially supermarkets, are now shutting down during the midnight to 6 A.M. shift. These decisions are only being made on a case-by-case basis after management determines the real value of these hours to their customers. In addition to reducing labor costs, most retailers closing during the early morning period often see a reduction in insurance fees. This is due to the fact that store robberies peak during that period.

The retailer must also remember that local and national laws, which were described in Chapter 6, may restrict the retailer's ability to set their hours of operations. For example, some states employ blue laws to restrict certain types of retailers from operating on Sundays. In Oklahoma and Texas, for example, new-car dealers must be closed one day each weekend.

Information Aids

As already mentioned, the retailer's promotional efforts help to inform the customer. Many retailers offer customers other information aids that help them enter into intelligent transactions. Today, for example, with the click of a mouse, consumers can not only search for products or services, but also determine what choices are available in local stores, the location of specific stores, and directions on how to get there. Consumers can also get information about return policies, credit policies, merchandise availability, and even merchandise prices on the websites of most major retailers. There are even websites where consumers experience first-hand a virtual walk through of the store. Other web retailers, such as The Gap, (www.gap.com) and Lands' End (www.landsend.com), let consumers move images of the latest fashions around on the screen to get a feel for how the different outfits will mix and match.

In addition, today's retailers realize that the store, be it a physical plant or an online location, is becoming more than merely a vehicle for transactions; it is now a place to encourage purchases even before the customers begin the transaction process. Consider what is currently happening with banks. Deregulation, mergers and acquisitions, and the proliferation of financial "products"—funds, trusts, and investment services—have, as will be discussed in greater detail in Chapter 13, caused banks to use their physical layouts to generate additional sales. In fact, after the collapse of Washington Mutual, the first thing J.P. Morgan did after taking over the Seattle-based bank was remodel its 900 branches. Renovations were made so as to free up room for J.P. Morgan to create locations within the building, complete with signage, to pitch credit cards, trust funds, investment services, mortgages, and other products to customers inherited from Washington Mutual.[19] This same concept should be used on the homepage of every retailer's website.

Transaction Services

In the past, retailers believed that transaction services meant employing salespeople who would personally take care of an individual customer. But for the profitable

Today, with the click of a mouse, consumers can not only search for the location of specific stores, but can also get information about return policies, credit policies, merchandise availability, and even merchandise prices for most major retailers.

transaction services
Are services provided to customers when they are in the store shopping and transacting business.

retailers of the future, the term **transaction services** will mean offering the conveniences customers need and then helping them get out of the store as fast as possible with their purchases. The most important transaction services are credit, layaway, gift wrapping and packaging, check cashing, gift cards, personal shopping, merchandise availability, personal selling, and the sales transaction itself. These services help to facilitate transactions once customers have made a purchase decision.

Credit

One of the most popular transaction-related services offered by retailers is consumer credit. Offering credit can be of great service to the customer because it enables shopping without the need to carry large sums of money. In addition, it allows the customer to buy now and pay later. Credit can be a benefit to the retailer also: It increases sales by increasing both impulse buying and purchases of expensive items. Of course, in-house credit can decrease profits if the credit policy is too lenient.

One final comment about the use of credit and debit cards: The percentage of customers using these payment instruments has grown to almost 60 percent of payments. As a result, more and more retailers have begun to fight with banks over the high fees charged to the retailer for using these financial products. In addition, because banks charge a lower fee to the retailer when customers use their PIN numbers rather than signing for the purchase, most retailers now steer their customers toward that form of payment.

Layaway

When a layaway service is offered, the customer can place a deposit (usually 20 percent) on an item, and in return the retailer will hold the item for the customer. The customer will make periodic payments on the item and can take it home when it's paid for in full. In a sense, a layaway sale is similar to an installment credit sale; however, the retailer retains physical possession of the item until the bill is completely paid. After years of seeing declines in the amount of layaway sales, retailers saw significant increases in their use during the 2008 Christmas season. This was probably the result of consumers having their credit-card limits reduced due to the recession.

A negative aspect of using layaways is that many items are never picked up by the customer. The retailer then has to return a "dated" item to regular inventory, where a markdown, which is usually larger than the first customer's initial payment, is required.

Gift Wrapping and Packaging

Customers are typically better served if their purchase is properly wrapped or packaged. The service may be as simple as putting the purchase into a paper bag or as complex as packaging crystal glassware in a special shatterproof box to prevent breakage.

The retailer must match its wrapping service to the type of merchandise it carries and its image. A discount grocer or hardware store does quite well by simply putting the merchandise into a paper sack. Specialty clothing stores often have dress and suit boxes that are easy to carry home. Some upscale retailers even put the purchased merchandise in decorated shopping bags or prewrapped gift boxes. This considerably reduces the number of packages that must be gift wrapped.

Many larger department stores and most gift shops offer a gift-wrapping service. Often there is a fee for gift wrapping unless the purchase price exceeds some limit, usually $10 or $25. Many other retailers also offer a courtesy wrap, which consists of a gift box and ribbon, or a store wrap that identifies the place of purchase. This type of wrap is not only a goodwill gesture but also a form of advertising.

Check Cashing

Most retailers offer some form of check-cashing service. The most basic type consists of allowing customers to cash a check for the amount of purchase. Most retailers now have online acceptance systems on their registers that make check cashing as easy as using a credit card. Other retailers provide their customers with an identification card that entitles them to pay for merchandise with a personal check. More generous check-cashing retailers allow qualified customers to cash checks for amounts above the purchase price, usually not for more than $20.

Check cashing has been found to be an effective means of attracting certain market segments and is based on the premise that consumers will spend more if they have cash in their pockets. This trend has resulted in some supermarket chains becoming the biggest check-cashing operators in some cities, often times bigger than the banks, especially in urban areas where many customers don't have checking accounts.

Gift Cards

Due the recent number of store failures, the popularity of retailers' gift cards, especially during holiday season, has probably peaked for the time being or until the economy improves. Nevertheless, many consumers continue to view gift cards as the perfect present because they are fun to receive, they make shopping easier, and consumers can use them to take advantage of after-Christmas sales. In fact, according to the National Retail Federation, one in every six dollars of future Christmas sales will be used for a gift card.

Still, gift cards are a year-round service being sold by retailers ranging from Macy's to Starbucks and from Amazon.com to Home Depot. One key reason for the popularity of today's plastic gift card is that it is a "stored value" card as opposed to an old-fashioned gift certificate. Thus, when a consumer spends $33 from a $100 plastic card, the card automatically updates the balance. This is more efficient and much less time consuming than making the retailer reissue a new gift certificate for the $67 balance.

The major impact of gift cards on retailers is the postponement of sales since retailers can't count a gift card as a sale at the time of purchase. Instead, they must wait until the gift card is redeemed for merchandise. As a result, most of the more than $25 billion spent on gift cards in November and December will not show up in holiday sales but instead as sales when the gift cards are actually redeemed.[20]

Personal Shopping

personal shopping
Occurs when an individual who is a professional shopper performs the shopping role for another; very upscale department and specialty stores offer personal shoppers to their clients.

Recent changes in family lifestyles have left many Americans, especially when both spouses are working professionals, without enough time to accomplish all they need and want to do. Other shoppers hate browsing in stores more than they hate doing household chores. Successful retailers have sought to aid these consumers by offering personal-shopping services. **Personal shopping** is the activity of assembling an assortment of goods for a customer. This can be as varied a service as picking out clothing, filling a nonstore order (many retailers now offer key customers an 800 phone number or a website address), assembling a supply of groceries and sending them to the customer's home, or selecting a wedding gift. Personal-shopping services are one of the best ways to build a relationship with the customer. A common misconception about personal shoppers is that they cater only to celebrities. However, because most retailers don't charge extra for the service, it is available to everybody.

The newest type of personal shopper is the health advocate. For professionals and other affluent consumers short of time, but with a serious illness, these advocates research new treatments, cut through medical bureaucracy, and frame medical decisions more objectively than stressed-out patients and their family members.

Merchandise Availability

Merchandise availability as a service simply relates to whether the customers can easily find the items they are looking for. A customer might be unable to find an item for one of three reasons: (1) The item is out of stock, (2) it is not located where the customer looks for it, or (3) the customer does not know what is really needed. The retailer can minimize out-of-stock conditions by good merchandise management although some out-of-stock situations are inevitable. The customer's ability to locate a needed item in the store can be increased by having proper in-store signage, displays, helpful and informative employees, and a well-designed layout. The problem of not knowing "what is really needed" is more difficult to overcome. Most major retailers have a bridal registry, both in-store and online, with easy-to-remember phone numbers to help solve one such problem. For example, at Chicago's old Marshall Field's (which has been renamed Macy's, after the merger between Federated and May), the number is 1-800-2-I DO I DO; at JCPenney it is 1-800-JCP-GIFT; and at Target it is 1-800-888-WEDD.

Merchandise availability is an element of customer service that many retailers take for granted, but they shouldn't. When customers do not find items they are looking for in a store—regardless of the cause—they will remember their bad experiences and will probably tell their friends.

Personal Selling

Another important transactional service that retailers can offer is a strong, customer-oriented retail sales staff. A good job of personal selling, resulting in a need-satisfying experience, or even skilled suggestive selling will greatly enhance customer satisfaction. One study found that in 73 percent of the cases where the customer had the "best ever shopping experience," there was sales-force involvement. The same study also pointed out the dangers of ineffective sales personnel—81 percent of the time when a customer had the "worst ever shopping experience," there was direct employee involvement.[21] Personal selling will be discussed in detail later in this chapter.

Sales Transaction

The final service to be discussed is the sales transaction itself or the interaction between the retailer, its employee, and the customer. Some discounters, seeking to invoke a positive, personal touch, made headway with a "greeter" to acknowledge customers when they enter the store. Probably the two most overlooked problems involving transaction services are having clean restrooms and minimizing dwell time, which is the amount of time a consumer must spend waiting to complete a purchase. The majority of all shopping experiences should be recreational and entertaining. This is especially true for retailers selling nonessential products such as books. Therefore, the retailer should never do anything that might drive the consumer away. Leonard Riggio, the feisty CEO of Barnes & Noble, recognized this truth and chose to provide customers Starbucks coffee, comfy chairs, a clubby atmosphere, and, yes, public restrooms.[22] Sam Walton believed that his restrooms should be the best in town so that a woman would never want to leave his stores to rush home for a bathroom visit. In fact, whenever Sam visited a store, he and his wife, Helen, always checked the restrooms.[23]

As noted above, all retailers face unique challenges in determining how to deal with customers in their stores. However, as the chapter's "Service Retailing" box illustrates, these decisions are far more complex for those retailers whose interaction with the customer is conducted in the customers' home.

Another issue facing the retailer is how to handle dwell time. As noted earlier, **dwell time** refers to the amount of time a consumer must spend waiting to complete a purchase. This time greatly influences the customer's expectations and evaluations of the retailer. Customers understand that certain waiting periods are required, especially for services, that cannot be produced ahead of demand. However, they must perceive that the line or waiting time is shortening. One successful supermarket has determined that more than half the time customers spend in its meat market is spent in waiting for their orders. Thus, the supermarket tries to give them meal ideas for their next shopping trip. It not only passes the time but also leads to future sales.

It may seem like a simple thing, but for any retailer serving hundreds of customers daily, the decision on how to line them up can have a major impact on customer satisfaction. This decision affects all retailers from the U.S. Postal Service to fast-food operations and hotels to banks. Currently, most retailers are moving away from multiple lines and opting for the single, serpentine line. This type of line, which was first made popular at amusement parks, got its name because of its long, snakelike shape. Multiple lines cause customer frustration because other lines inevitably move faster. In recent years, the frustration of waiting to complete the transaction—the dwell time—has become a threat to retailers. According to a study

dwell time
Refers to the amount of time a consumer must spend waiting to complete a purchase.

Service Retailing

Etiquette Guidelines for Service Retailers

Many service retailers don't work from their own location but must go to the customer. Some, such as lawn-care specialists, work outside the customer's home but others, such as home-improvement and repair contractors, must enter the customer's home to complete the assigned job. Anytime a service provider enters a private home, there is the possibility of being put in an awkward situation.

Most of the major service franchisors try to avoid these situations by having all franchisees follow a detailed operating-policy manual. This manual covers hiring and training procedures as well as providing operational and financial guidance. One common guideline is to require the franchisee to obtain a police background check on applicants before making the hiring decision. Many service franchisors now insist that all service technicians be bonded, that they wear uniforms with collared shirts and slacks, and that they wear plastic protective shoe coverings when entering a home. Despite these and other similar upgrades in professionalism, not every unfortunate contingency can be anticipated. How does a service retailer prepare its employees for that "once-in-a-million" situation?

One service provider who provides outstanding training in this sensitive area is Ted Tenenbaum, the owner of the Mr. Handyman franchise in Los Angeles. Mr. Tenenbaum's employees provide all types of home maintenance including electrical, plumbing, drywall repair, painting, and tiling. Like all Mr. Handyman franchisees across America, Tenenbaum's workers specialize in jobs that are too small for most general contractors. Because his employees spend the bulk of their time inside customers' homes, Tenenbaum's training sessions focus on teaching a "common sense" level of business etiquette that is specific to the nature of the work. Since every situation is different, these guidelines are not written in

stone and posted for every employee to memorize. Instead, Tenenbaum attempts to instill the idea that a combination of common sense and basic etiquette will forestall many of the problems that service retailers might encounter. Here is an overview of Ted Tenenbaum's unwritten rules:

Whatever You See, Pretend You Don't See It. Whether it is a pair of racy underwear in the middle of the floor or the homeowner walking around in flimsy clothing, the worker didn't see it.

Don't Stare Too Long at Anything. After all, if you followed the first guideline, you didn't see anything.

Never Get in the Middle of Any Domestic Argument and **Agree with Everyone and then Switch the Conversation to Something Else.** Feuding parties often like to involve a neutral third party. The third party can never win—so always try to avoid such situations.

Never Be Alone in a Room with a Child. What would happen if a child were to stumble and fall, start crying, and a parent walks in the room to see a service tech with an arm around the child trying to provide comfort? Or what if the child cuts himself on a tool or replacement part?

Be Sure to Compliment at Least One Item or Feature in the Customer's Home. You always want to get on the customer's good side.

Mr. Tenenbaum's final, and probably most important, guideline is

Call Me If You Are Ever Frightened.

With etiquette guidelines such as these, it is little wonder that Hollywood celebrities use his service. But don't ask Ted or his techs about these celebrities. They won't say anything out of school.

Source: Based on information provided by Ted Tenenbaum and used with his written permission.

---

conducted by one major retailer, 44 percent of its customers would rather clean their bathrooms, 20 percent would rather sit in traffic, and 18 percent would rather visit the dentist than stand in a checkout line. Another survey asked more than a thousand women what they found most stressful when shopping. Here 33 percent said the checkout lines.[24] Thus, dwell time is such an important issue that today big chains now monitor checkout times. One retailer explained to an author that it takes an extra minute and three seconds when a customer uses a check instead of a credit card. However, the most frustrating wait for most consumers is the time spent on the phone trying to bypass those annoying voice robots to reach a real, live customer-service agent. One consumer advocate offered four suggestions to the authors as a means to avoid this problem:

1. Mention the name of the company's competitor. Most systems have been set up to recognize these names and to serve you immediately.

2. Call the extension number for new service. If you're a prospective customer, a company will snap to answer your call.

3. Press every number as fast as you can. This makes the system think you're on a rotary phone—or that you're about to disconnect. Either way, you're next in line.

4. Ask for the collections department. In these economic times, the collections department tends to answer calls quickly, and you can jump to the head of the line for your desired department this way.

However, as the "Global Retailing" box in Chapter 14 illustrates getting to a real, live customer-service agent doesn't always solve the problem when that task has been outsourced to someone in a different country.

Posttransaction Services

The relationship between the retailer and the consumer has become more complex in today's service-oriented economy. Many products—such as computers, automobiles, travel, and financial services—require an extended relationship between the retailer and consumer. The longer this period of time can be extended by ensuring the customer's satisfaction with the product, the greater the chances that future sales will result. The most common **posttransaction services**, which are provided after the sale has been made, are complaint handling, merchandise returns, merchandise repair, servicing, delivery, and postsale follow-ups. Posttransaction services are especially important for online retailers since there usually isn't a face-to-face relationship involved; it is all done via the computer.

posttransaction services
Are services provided to customers after they have purchased merchandise or services.

Complaint Handling

Customer dissatisfaction occurs when the customer's experience with the retailer or product fails to live up to expectations. The proper handling of customer complaints can mean a big difference in retail performance. Dealing with customers is a sensitive issue because it involves employees who make human errors dealing with customers who make human errors. In essence, this doubles the chance of misunderstandings and mistakes between the two parties. Unfortunately, these mistakes and misunderstandings often lead to a poor image of the retailer, no matter whose fault they might be. Therefore, it is essential that retailers try to solve customer complaints effectively. However, if the retailer is going to be able to solve the problem, the consumer should follow a few simple rules when complaining. This chapter's "Retailing: The Inside Story" box looks at this issue from the retailer's point of view. After all, if retailers are able to solve the customer's problem the right way, then the customer will not only continue to shop with the retailer but also may influence others to shop there through the use of word of mouth.[25]

There are several ways of handling and solving customer complaints. Regardless of the method used, retailers should follow the six rules shown in Exhibit 12.4. For a large retailer, the central complaint department is most efficient. Here a staff that is specifically trained for this task handles all customer complaints. This method leaves the sales force free to do its job and allows the customer to deal

Retailing: The Inside Story

A PR Representative Tells You Her Side of the Story

We understand you are angry, upset, disappointed and no one can ever right the wrong that has been done to you. However, if you want any resolution to your complaint, consider us, the retailer's representatives, your advocate, not your adversary. Be polite. Help us understand and empathize with you. Share your emotion of the incident and how it made you feel, but don't be emotional. We will do whatever we can to help you, regain your trust, and exceed your expectations.

A family from England was disappointed upon arriving at Disneyland when the California theme park was closed on Monday and Tuesday during the off-season for maintenance. This family was shocked to find the park closed, just like the Griswold family's arrival at Walley World in the 1983 movie, *National Lampoon's Vacation.* (Remember that this movie was based on screenwriter John Hughes' experience on his own family's 1958 trip to Disneyland.) Understandably, the letter was full of emotion. The parents demanded the park reimburse them for their entire vacation, including airfare and all accommodations and expenses during their U.S. tour. And they pointed out numerous times that their children never saw Mickey Mouse. Unfortunately, their travel agent had not checked into the hours of operation prior to booking their trip, and, as sad as this incident was, Disneyland could not be held responsible for all the costs incurred. However, the family was offered free admission to the park on a future visit and autographed photos of Mickey were personalized and sent to each of the children. Be reasonable about your desired compensation or resolution.

Unless you have a valid legal claim for damages, please don't threaten to sue us, especially if you want a speedy resolution. Most employees handling complaints have the ability and resources to compensate you in some reasonable fashion. Once the threat of a lawsuit enters the picture, your complaint goes directly to the attorneys for their legal response and any type of resolution at that point is questionable and will be costly.

Make sure your complaint is valid. When teenagers wore obscene T-shirts to the park, they were told by security to turn their shirts inside out to be admitted. No, they were not compensated for any embarrassment they may have experienced or reimbursed the cost of a new shirt from the gift shop, if they chose that option. There are signs posted at the entrance regarding appropriate attire, and there is such a thing as common sense. Don't visit an amusement park on the 4th of July, Memorial Day weekend, Labor Day weekend, or any other major holiday and then complain about lines for rides or attractions. And it is not reasonable that costumed characters with large, clumsy furry gloves would have the ability or intention to touch a child inappropriately. Chip 'n' Dale just wouldn't do that.

Offer us your feedback. Remind us that you understand we want to hear from you so we can improve our services and products. By sharing your concerns with us, we are able to look into your complaint and fix the problem, and at the same time keep our relationship with you for many years to come.

At a new Albertson's grocery store in Florida, a neighbor complained that the parking lot lights were shining into the bedroom, causing a variety of problems for him and his wife. The letter expressed their concern and an interest in reaching a solution to their sleepless and unromantic nights. The solution was simple: The store replaced the flood lights with directional lights facing away from the neighbors. The couple was happy, the marriage saved, and loyalty earned. Request the action you desire to reasonably resolve your issue.

Give us the opportunity to share information with you and clarify our policies and procedures. When guests complained about food not allowed in the park, it was an opportunity to explain the policy and provide information about the picnic area we created just outside the entrance, including lockers and restrooms. When mothers complained about breast feeding not being allowed in public areas, we were able to share the concerns expressed by other parents who had objections to this practice and then told them about the baby station we provided, equipped with elderly nannies, rocking chairs, free baby food, and a quiet, private environment. Complaints like these are opportunities to not only recover but also build loyalty.

Thank us for helping you, before we help you.

Source: This box was written by Anne Alenskis, a public relations professional who has worked for a variety of firms, including retailers ranging from Albertson's to Walt Disney. In addition, she has taught public-relations classes at Boise State University.

1. Acknowledge the importance of the customer. Before the customer even begins to explain his or her problem, acknowledge that the customer is important by telling him or her that you are there to help. Try to ease the customer's frustration.

2. Understand the customer's problem. Ask all the questions needed to completely understand the situation. Determine the responsibilities of each party and what went wrong. Do not assign any fault at this stage.

3. Repeat the problem (as you understand it) to the customer. Without interrupting the customer, paraphrase the problem as you understand it.

4. Think of all possible solutions. Using your creative powers, think of all possible, even wild, solutions that could remedy the problem.

5. Agree on the solution. Determine the solution that is fair to both parties and then have both parties agree to it.

6. Above all, make sure the customer leaves feeling as you would want to feel if you were the customer. If you would not be satisfied with the solution if you were the customer, start over. Remember, it is better to lose a little now than to take a chance on losing a customer for life.

Exhibit 12.4
Six Rules to Follow When Handling a Customer's Complaint

with someone who has the authority to act on most complaints. Many large retailers have even established an 800 number so that they may properly handle complaints with minimal effort on the part of the customer. Although, as was discussed in the section on dwell time, the long wait to talk to a real live person may only increase the consumer's level of frustration.

Some retailers have the individual salesperson handle complaints. They believe that a friendly, sympathetic attitude exhibited by the salesperson will have a positive effect on future sales, especially if the complaint is about a product rather than the retailer or sales force. This method does, however, have several disadvantages. First, the individual salesperson often does not have the authority to settle problems and must call in someone else to handle the situation, forcing the customer to restate the problem. A second drawback of this system is the fact that a salesperson who is listening to a past customer complaint cannot serve current customers who, incidentally, are overhearing the complaints.

Some retailers are making an all-out effort to stop complaints before they occur. Ohio's Sun Television & Appliances has hired an outside marketing firm to do daily computerized price checks on all comparable merchandise. If somebody beats Sun's price within 30 days of any customer's purchase, the customer automatically gets a check in the mail for the difference.[26] Other retailers seek to stop complaints before they happen by using guarantees. Costco, for example, has what many consider the greatest guarantee in retailing. Its "diamond guarantee" promises to pay a member $100 if a gem it sells is appraised for less than double the Costco price.[27]

Regardless of the complaint-handling system, the retailer needs to remember three things when handling complaints: The customer deserves courteous treatment, a fair settlement, and prompt action. Remember, even if the sale is lost, the customer need not be lost. The proper handling of complaints has a substantial payback for the smart retailer. Sometimes, however, the customer makes it difficult for even the best retailer to handle a complaint and make the customer happy. Luckily for frontline employees, there are online support groups: www.customerssuck.com and www.retail-sucks.com. Through these websites, employees can share and vent their frustrations regarding unruly and sometimes just plain stupid customers.

All too often when consumers complain to a retailer about some problem, they start the letter by saying something like—"I am so mad I am never going to shop with you again." When they say that, what incentive could a retailer have to try to win back the customer? The chapter's "Retailing: The Inside Story" box, which was written by an individual who actually read and responded to such letters, provides some helpful hints for the consumer to use when writing a retailer to complain, as well as some things not to say. Hopefully, after reading this box, the reader will know what to say and write so that any problems can be easily solved.

Merchandise Returns

A return policy can range from "No returns, no exchanges" to "The customer is always right." The handling of merchandise returns is an important customer service, sometimes making the difference between turning a profit and losing money. As was pointed out earlier, successful retailers are well aware that it costs five times as much money to get a customer into your store as it does to make a sale to someone already there. Therefore, since *customer retention* is so important, why would a retailer ever seek to lose one due to the mishandling of a return? Retailers therefore need to decide if they want to use either of the extreme policies mentioned above or a more moderate one. Few services build customer goodwill as quickly as a fair return policy. It is important that the retailer's return policy be consistent with its image. A mistake that some retailers make is to follow the policies (such as "No receipt, no return," having a "30-day limit" on returns, or having a $20 to $30 restocking fee) established by the competition. Since a retailer is trying to differentiate itself from the competition, saying it has a similar return policy as competitors isn't the best strategy. Still, it must acknowledged that returns are an expense to the retailer.

While no one is sure of an exact figure for fraudulent returns and abuses, most retailers believe the number to be in excess of $20 billion per year. Some common examples of this fraud and abuse are:[28]

It is important that retailers remember that the proper management of merchandise returns will produce a satisfied customer who will become a repeat customer that will produce long-term profits for the retailer.

Brad Smith/Tyler Morning Telegraph/AP Photo

Renting, Not Buying. Some consumers buy merchandise such as a laptop computer to use for a semester with the intention of returning it when done. A customer-service representative of a hardware store told the authors that one of the most commonly returned items is a plunger: "It wouldn't be so bad, but usually they come back in a plastic bag just after they have been used." However, what is probably the most abused return policy is that of an electronic retailer getting back a large screen television set the Monday after the Super Bowl.

Fraudulent Employee Actions. Typically, employees return merchandise they stole for cash. This may also involve using falsified, stolen, or reused receipts to return the merchandise.

Shoplift Returns: Items are shoplifted with the intention of returning them for cash.

Price switching: Lower-priced tags are put on merchandise with the intention of returning them for full retail price—and the original price tag back on the items.

Research has also shown that approximately 75 percent of all shoppers never return purchases and that only 1 percent of consumers are responsible for fraudulent or abusive returns.[29] Even so, it is important that a retailer set a return policy that considers the effect on both sales and expenses. Thus, retailers must estimate the salvage value of returned merchandise that is probably out of its peak selling season, the probability of losing a customer, and the transaction costs of returning merchandise. There is also an opportunity cost—the foregone interest or return on investment dollars. This money is tied up in merchandise that is in the possession of the customer but will be returned.

One innovative approach to dealing with the 1 percent abusers is a new technology used by retailers such as Target and Walmart that tracks the buying and return activity of shoppers, especially those returns without a receipt. After shoppers reach the retailer's return limit within a given time period,[30] they are informed that they can't make more exchanges at any of the retailer's stores for as long as a year. Such actions allow retailers to offer the other 99 percent of consumers a more lenient and flexible return policy.

Servicing, Repair, and Warranties

Any new product with more than one moving mechanical part is a candidate for future service or repair. In fact, even items without moving parts such as clothing, coffee tables, and paintings are candidates for repair. Retailers who offer merchandise servicing and repair to their customers tend to generate a higher sales volume. And if the work they perform is good, they can also generate repeat business. For example, if the service department of a TV and appliance store has a reputation for doing good work at fair prices, then customers will not only purchase TVs at the store but also tend to purchase radios, stereos, and washing machines.

Repair servicing, especially repairs involving warranties, is perhaps one of the most difficult customer services to manage. While good repair service can stimulate additional sales, many customers will never be satisfied because it is difficult to schedule appointments. In today's urban environment, it is virtually impossible for retailers to schedule a repair call or delivery within even a three-hour time frame. Traffic, parking, and the inability to predict exactly how long each call will take make scheduling uncertain. These factors often make it difficult for today's two-wage-earner families to be home when the retailer's personnel arrive. In addition, in many cases, buyers are confused by warranties, especially since some involve free replacement parts but not labor. (The legal issues pertaining to

Marcio Jose Sanchez/AP Photo

Got problems with your new computer? Call the Geek Squad. They will immediately send a "geek" who will arrive in a "Geekmobile" (a black-and-white Volkswagen Beetle) wearing a white shirt, white socks, black tie and black pants. Don't let the looks fool you, these "geeks" are the experts that Best Buy customers can call any time of the day or night.

warranties were discussed in Chapter 6.) These disgruntled customers will tell their friends, relatives, and acquaintances of their experiences.

Delivery

Delivery of merchandise to the customer's home can be a very expensive service, especially because of the high cost of fuel. Retailers such as florists can offer free delivery (which is actually absorbed in slightly higher prices) or they can charge the customer a small fee to help offset the cost. Nonetheless, the extra business derived from providing delivery may be worth the expense if the merchandise and customer characteristics warrant it. For example, when consumers think of delivery, they usually think of Domino's Pizza. When Thomas Monaghan started the company, pizza already enjoyed widespread popularity. He soon realized that success could come by focusing on fast, free delivery, something no one else did.[31] However, with higher gasoline prices, the days of free pizza delivery for Americans may soon end. Despite the risk that extra charges will alienate customers, Pizza Hut, Domino's, and Papa John's have been testing the addition of a delivery fee in an attempt to bolster their bottom line.

The final step of the delivery process is installation. As products become more technically advanced, more people are looking for someone who can actually install it for them. Some retailers refer to these consumers, especially senior citizens, who did not grow with all the modern technology, as the "do-it-for-me" segment. Best Buy, for example, has taken this delivery and installation process to the next level with its Geek Squad.

Postsale Follow-Up

Retailing's job is not over when the cash register rings. It is only starting. Many retail salespeople spend a great deal of time and energy to get a customer to say yes, but most don't spend enough time trying to keep that purchaser a loyal customer. Earlier in the chapter it was pointed out that it costs a retailer five times as much to attract a first-time customer as it does to persuade a former customer to return, so it's important that the retailer care for its current customers. This may involve just a follow-up phone call to see how the product is working, to remind a customer about an upcoming sale, or suggest that it might be time to reorder. Southwest Airlines, for example, sends out special deals to its Rapid Rewards (loyalty club) members who haven't flown with the airlines over the past year. One final comment on postsale follow-up: The Internet is rife with sounding boards for disgruntled shoppers to vent, so it is wise to have someone check these blogs on a regular basis. One such blog is http://getsatisfaction.com. This website seeks to bring customers and company employees together to make things better for everyone. So far, it has helped: 14,748 companies, 15,299 employees, and 11 million customers have worked together to improve 21,733 products and services.[32]

Determining Customer-Service Levels

It is not easy to determine the optimal number and level of customer services to offer. Theoretically, however, one could argue that a retailer should add customer services until the additional revenue that is generated by higher service levels is equal to the additional cost of providing those services. In the short run, cutting back on costly customer services can usually increase profits, but such an action may present serious long-run problems as customers may shop elsewhere seeking better services.

Deciding what specific customer services to offer in order to increase sales volume is a difficult question for any retailer. Exhibit 12.5 lists six factors to be

LO 3

How should a retailer determine which services to offer?

Exhibit 12.5
Factors to Consider When Determining Customer Services to Offer

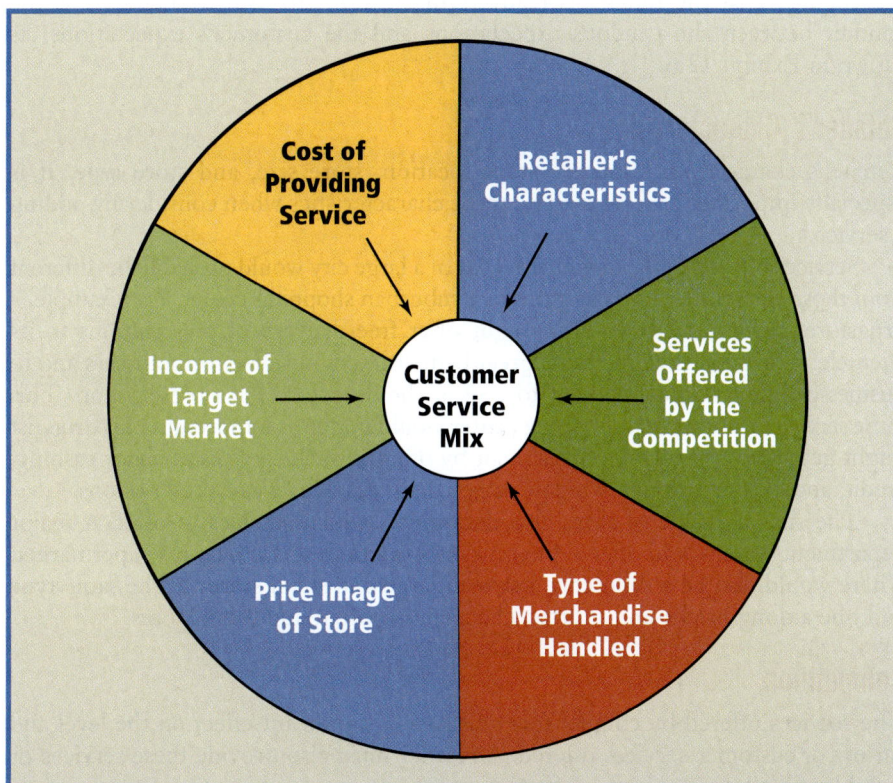

Cost of Providing Service

Retailer's Characteristics

Income of Target Market

Customer Service Mix

Services Offered by the Competition

Price Image of Store

Type of Merchandise Handled

Exhibit 12.6
How the Retailer's Sales
Force Meets the
Expectations of Both
Vendors and Customers

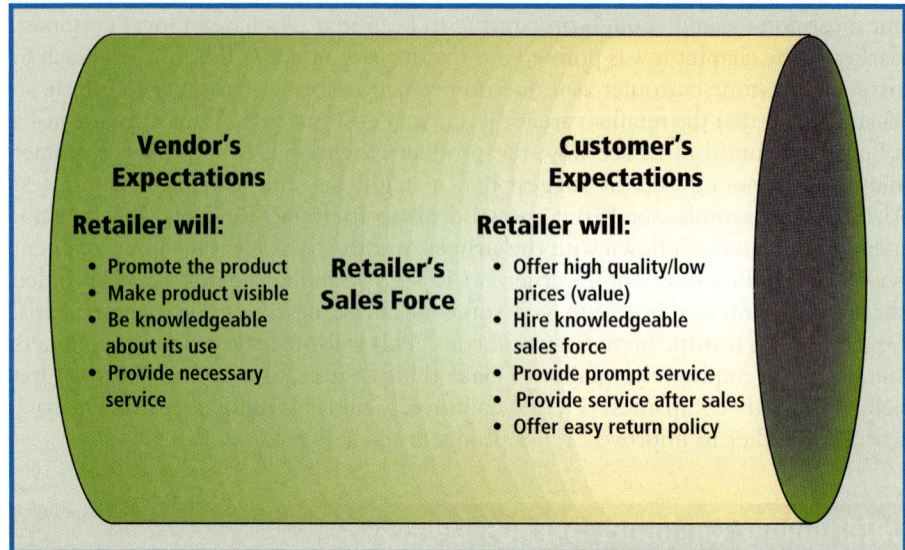

considered when determining the customer services to offer: (1) the retailer's characteristics, (2) the services offered by the competition, (3) the type of merchandise handled, (4) the price image of the retailer, (5) the income of the target market, and (6) the cost of providing the service. It is the retailer's job to study these six areas to arrive at the service mix that will increase long-run profits by retaining current customers, enticing new ones, and projecting the right image. Above all else, retailers must remember to be realistic and not expect to satisfy the wants and needs of all customers. No strategy could be less profitable than trying to satisfy everybody. What the retailer is really trying to do is to use its sales staff as the conduit between the vendor's expectations and the customer's expectations, as shown in Exhibit 12.6.

Retailer's Characteristics

Retailer's characteristics include store location, store size, and store type. It is especially important to look at these three characteristics when considering adding a service.

Services offered in the downtown area of a large city would probably be different from those offered by a similar store in a suburban shopping center. For example, a drugstore in the downtown area might offer free delivery of prescriptions to its clientele. This service would be of great benefit to city dwellers without cars and to businesspeople who do not want to wait at the drugstore for a prescription. This same service in a suburban shopping center would not be as important. This druggist might get a better return on investment by offering such services as check cashing, credit, and a drive-through window rather than free delivery of prescriptions.

The size and type of store also determines which services to offer. A major department store would offer a different assortment of services than a supermarket. There would also be a difference between large and small stores of the same type and one among bricks-and-mortar, clicks-and-mortar, and e-tail stores.

Competition

The services offered by competitors will have a significant effect on the level and variety of customer services offered. A retailer must also provide these services or suitable substitutes, or it may offer lower prices.

Suppose there are three clothing stores of the same general type, price range, and quality within a given area. Store A and store B offer free gift wrapping, standard alterations, bank-card credit, and a liberal return policy. Store C, on the other hand, offers only standard alterations and has an exchange-only return policy. Customers who are shopping for gifts will generally prefer stores A and B to store C because they feel confident that whatever they purchase will ultimately be just right. It can even be gift wrapped at the store. If the gift is not suitable, then the receiver can exchange it or get a cash refund. In this situation, store C can do two things to compete: add different services and decrease prices.

Type of Merchandise

The merchandise lines carried can be an indication of the types of services, especially personal selling, to offer. The principal reason is that certain merchandise lines benefit from knowledgeable sales personnel; for example, would you want a less-than-knowledgeable salesperson to assist you in purchasing an engagement ring for the woman of your dreams? Or worse, would you want your boyfriend buying your engagement ring at a self-service discounter, even it offers a "diamond guarantee" that it will appraise for double the selling price. In addition, other products benefit from coupling them with complimentary services: bicycles and free assembly, major appliances and delivery, and sewing machines and free sewing lessons.

Price Image

Customers usually expect more services from a retailer with a high-price image than from a discounter. When a customer perceives a retailer as having high prices, it also sees the retailer as possessing an air of luxury. Therefore, the services rendered by this retailer should reinforce the image of luxury or status. Some of the typical high-price-image services include personal shopping, a home-design studio, free gift wrapping, free delivery, free alterations, and sales personnel who are more professional in both appearance and manner.

On the other end of the scale, discounters need not offer luxury services because customers who shop there are seeking low prices, not pampering. A discounter or store with a low-price image might offer such basic services as free parking, layaway, bank-card credit, and convenient store hours.

Target-Market Income

The higher the income of the target market, the higher the price that consumers will pay. The higher the prices consumers will pay, the more services the retailer can profitably provide. Some customers may expect more services than retailers can afford, and retailers must avoid the strong temptation of providing costly services to such consumers. In the long run, the retailer will have to raise prices to pay for the services, and then it will most likely lose customers at the lower income boundary of its target market.

Cost of Services

It is important that retailers know the cost of providing a service so that they can estimate the additional sales needed to pay for the service. For example, a customer service expected to increase costs by $20,000 per year for a store operating on a gross margin of 25 percent would have to stimulate sales by at least $20,000/0.25, or $80,000. In this sense, customer services are evaluated in a manner similar to promotional expenditures. The key criterion becomes the financial effect of adding or deleting a customer service. As a result, some national retailers have started charging for their catalogs after decades of providing them free. Research determined that although nearly 20 percent fewer customers received the catalog; those who did felt that they had made an investment ($5). As a result, these customers increased their purchases by 25 percent.

Another way of expressing the cost of having poor service is to examine what the costs would be if a store did not offer good service. After all, retailers should be aware of the loss in revenue from losing a customer. Let's consider what happens to a small 25-store supermarket chain. If this chain alienated only one customer per week per store, the chain would lose almost $100,000 in annual revenue from just the customers lost during one year. (This is based on the assumption that grocery business is repeat business and that the real revenue loss is the $75 that the average customer spends weekly at that chain.) It is important for the retailer to compare the costs of taking care of those unhappy customers to the costs of replacing them. One online broker, for example, has determined that it costs $350 to acquire a new customer and that each customer generates more than $600 in profit.[33] Therefore, always remember that, on average, it costs five times as much money to replace that lost customer as it would have if the old one had been kept. That is why customer service is so important in today's economy.

LO 4 — Retail Sales Management

What are the various management problems involved in retail selling, salesperson selection, and training and evaluation?

Retail salespeople and the service they provide are a major factor in consumer purchase decisions. For example, if the retail salesperson is rude or unhelpful, customers often walk out of the store empty-handed. The salesperson is a major determinant of a retailer's image. When the salesperson is available, friendly, appropriately dressed, and helpful, customers are often influenced to enter into a transaction with the retailer. The management of the retail sales force plays a crucial role in the success or failure of retail operations.

Types of Retail Selling

In many retail settings, the employees are called *salespersons* or *order takers*. For example, consider the role of salespeople in a typical fast-food restaurant such as McDonald's, Burger King, or Wendy's. Most order takers simply ask the customers, "Can I take your order?" Little if anything related to the actual sale occurs. Similarly, in a discount department store such as Target, Kohl's, or Walmart, salespeople may show a customer where a specific product is or, if the product is not on the shelf, may go to the storeroom to attempt to locate the item. However, seldom do they attempt to sell merchandise or demonstrate its use. In fact, one discounter's policy is to provide next to no sales help. Some discounters do not want to get into the business of person-to-person selling. Retailers that employ order takers are appealing to those customers who want value instead of service. Nonetheless, one must recognize that these order takers can influence demand, especially in a negative manner. If you stand at the counter of a McDonald's and no one asks you for your order, you may get frustrated and leave the store without making a purchase.

Retail employees who are most appropriately labeled *salespersons* should be order getters rather than order takers. Order getters are involved in conversations with prospective purchasers for the purpose of making a sale. They will inform, guide, and persuade the customer to culminate a transaction either immediately or in the future. For example, in many restaurants whether or not customers choose to order dessert is related to the relationship they have established with their hosts or hostesses.

The degree of emphasis the retailer places on its employees being order getters depends on the line of retail trade and the retailer's strategy. Retailers that concentrate on the sale of shopping goods (e.g., automobile dealers, furniture retailers, computer retailers, and appliance retailers) want their salespeople to both get and take orders. In lines of retail trade where predominantly convenience goods are sold (gasoline service stations and grocery retailers), the role of the salesperson (or what many call the *retail clerk*) is that of an order taker. In terms of strategic orientation, it is generally true that retailers with high margins and high levels of customer service place more emphasis on order getting. Those with low margins and a low customer-service policy tend to emphasize order taking. Clearly, however, regardless of the line of retail trade and the retailer's strategic thrust, all retail enterprises must carefully evaluate the role of the salesperson in helping to generate demand.

Salesperson Selection

Selecting retail salespeople should involve more than casually accepting anyone who answers an ad or walks into the retailer seeking a job. In fact, the casualness with which many retailers have selected people to fill sales positions is one cause of poor productivity.

Criteria

To select salespeople properly, retailers must decide on their hiring criteria. What is expected from retail salespeople? Are retailers looking for a sales force that has low absenteeism and a willingness to work nights and weekends or the ability to generate a high volume of sales? Are they seeking other qualities or a combination of factors? Unless retailers know what they are looking for in salespeople, they will not acquire a sales force that possesses the proper qualities.

However, good results are dependent not only on the salesperson's characteristics but also on how satisfied the salesperson is with the job and how the sales job was designed. Retail-selling jobs should be designed to have high levels of variety (the opportunity to perform a wide range of activities), autonomy (the degree to which an employee determines the work procedures), task identity (the degree to which an employee is involved in the total sales process), and feedback from supervisors and customers.

Predictors

Once retailers determine the hiring criteria, they must then identify the potential predictors to meet the chosen criteria. The most commonly used predictors in selecting retail salespeople are demographics, personality, knowledge and intelligence, and prior work experience. We will discuss criteria for selecting managerial trainees later in the chapter.

Demographics. Depending on the specific line of retail trade, demographic variables can be important in identifying good retail salespeople. For example, a music store appealing to teens will probably benefit from having retail salespeople who are younger than 30 years of age. A high-fashion women's apparel store appealing to 30- to 50-year-old, career-oriented, and upwardly mobile females would probably not desire inexperienced salespeople just out of high school. Interestingly enough, a famous study by J.D. Power & Associates of more than 33,000 new-car buyers has shown that female salespersons scored higher or at least equal to men in 13 of the 15 categories evaluated. The two items where men scored best were knowledge of models and features and competitive vehicles. Women, however, scored substantiality higher in sincerity, honesty, and concern for the buyer's needs.[34] Obviously, there are exceptions to the preceding cases, but the essential point is that demographics play an important role in the retail sales process.

Personality. An applicant's personality can reflect on his or her potential as a retail salesperson. Most retailers prefer salespeople who are friendly, confident, consistent, and understanding of others. These personality traits can be identified either through a personal interview with the applicant or by personality-inventory tests. In most lines of retail trade, the personal interview is sufficient.

Knowledge and Intelligence. Many products that retailers sell are technically complex. Consider, for example, camcorders, plasma screens, TiVos, DVDs, and Xboxes. Salespeople with knowledge of these products will be better able to sell them. Similarly, to be able to respond competently to customer inquiries, retail employees need to possess a level of education and intelligence compatible with the job description.

Experience. One of the most reliable predictors of success as a salesperson is prior work experience, especially selling experience. If applicants have performed well in prior jobs, then there is a good chance that they will perform well in the future. However, many applicants for retail selling jobs are young and have no prior work experience of any magnitude. These applicants are better assessed on their personal character and apparent ambition, drive, and work ethic. This could be indicated by leadership positions in clubs or student organizations, timely graduation, and the display of ambition during the interview process.

Salesperson Training

After salespeople are selected, they will need some form of training. This is true even if they have selling experience. In their training programs, retailers can explain their own policies. Furthermore, retailers usually want inexperienced salespeople to become familiar with and knowledgeable about their merchandise, warranties and return policies, the different customer types they may have to deal with, and the selling strategies appropriate for these different customers. Even order takers need training in greeting a customer, thanking customers, and using a point-of-sale terminal. Best Buy does an extremely good job of training new sales employees. Relative to sales, Best Buy now spends more on employee training than any other retailer.

As illustrated in the chapter's "Service Retailing" box, probably the most important skill the retailer can teach the new sales staff is common customer etiquette and courtesy. Office Depot's employee training manual, for example, says that employees are to offer fanatical customer service by "doing, with truth and compassion, whatever it takes and then some, to win the customer's heart forever." A discount chain insists that its sales staff carry the following "crib sheet" about being customer friendly with them at all times they are on the sales floor.

Customer Friendly Means
Smiling
Greeting the customer

Being as helpful as you would want somebody to be to you
Using the customer's name (if possible)
Saying "Thank You"

The importance of being customer friendly can be shown in studies from the medical field. These studies found that the doctor's competence and prescribed method of treatment played a very small role in determining if a malpractice suit would be filed. Rather, it was the interpersonal skills that the doctor used with the patient that was the determining factor.[35]

Retailer's Policies

In most situations, the salesperson provides the interface between the customer and retailer. It is thus important for the salesperson to become familiar with the retailer's policies, especially those that may involve the customer directly. Some of these policies relate to merchandise returns and adjustments, shoplifting, credit terms, layaway, delivery, and price negotiation. In addition, the retail salesperson should be knowledgeable about work hours, rest periods, lunch and dinner breaks, commission and quota plans, nonselling duties, and standards of periodic job evaluation. Sales employees should also be informed about criteria used for promotion and advancement, as well as dismissal and termination, within the retail enterprise.

Merchandise

If the merchandise includes shopping goods, then the retailer will want to familiarize its salespeople with the strengths and weaknesses of the merchandise so they can advise customers on the best items to meet their needs. The retailer may also suggest that the salesperson become knowledgeable of the competitor's merchandise offerings and their strengths and weaknesses.

Increasingly, retail salespeople need to be familiar with the warranty terms and serviceability of merchandise the retailer handles. This implies that the salesperson know something about the reputation of each manufacturer the retailer represents.

Customer Types

Many retailers have recognized that an important way to increase customer satisfaction is by having their salespeople identify and respond to certain customer types.[36] Various customer types are described in Exhibit 12.7. By knowing how to handle each of these customers, the salesperson can generate additional sales. Too many times, retailers dwell on handling the technical details of the job rather than the feelings of a customer. One retail salesperson (who should go online at the customerssuck.com website mentioned earlier in the chapter) said this about her training program: "The computer training was real good. I know how to do all this technical stuff, but nobody prepared me for dealing with all these different types of people."

Customer Choice Criteria

The retail salesperson should also learn how to identify the customer's choice criteria and how to respond to them.[37] There are four choice criteria situations: (1) The customer has no active product choice criteria; (2) the customer has product choice criteria but they are inadequate or vague; (3) the customer has product choice criteria but they are in conflict; and (4) the customer has product choice

Characteristics	Basic Types	Recommendations
Don't trust any salesperson. Resist communication as they have a dislike of others. Generally uncooperative and will explode at slightest provocation.	**Defensive**	Avoid mistaking their silence for openness to your ideas. Stick to basic facts. Tactfully inject product's advantages and disadvantages.
Intense, impatient personality. Often interrupt salespersons and have a perpetually "strained" expression. Often driven and successful people who want results fast.	**Interrupter**	Don't waste time; move quickly and firmly from one sales point to another. Avoid overkill since they know what they want.
Confident in their ability to make decisions and stay with them. Open to new ideas but want brevity. Highly motivated by self-pride.	**Decisive**	No canned presentations. The key is to assist. Don't argue or point out errors in their judgment.
They worry about making the wrong decision and therefore tend to postpone all decisions. Want salesperson to make decision for them.	**Indecisive**	Avoid becoming frustrated yourself. Determine as early as possible the need and concentrate on that. Avoid presenting customer with too many alternatives. Start with making decisions on minor points.
Friendly, talkative types who are enjoyable to visit with. Many have excess time on their hands (e.g., retirees). They usually resist the close.	**Sociable**	You may have to wait out these customers. Listen for points in conversation where you can interject product's merits. Pressure close is out. Subtle friendly close needed.
Quick to make decision. Impatient, just as likely to walk out as they were to walk in.	**Impulsive**	Close as rapidly as possible. Avoid any useless interaction. Avoid any oversell. Highlight product's merits.

Exhibit 12.7
Various Customer Types

criteria that are explicit and well defined. For each situation there is an appropriate selling strategy that the salesperson should learn.

No Active Product Choice Criteria.　The best sales strategy when the customer does not have a prior criteria set is to educate the customer on the best choice criteria and how to weigh them. For example, a prospective customer enters an automobile dealership to purchase a used automobile but does not know what criteria to use in selecting the best car. The salesperson may present convincing arguments for considering four criteria in the following order of importance: warranty, fuel economy, price, and comfort. Once the salesperson and customer agree on this list, they can work together at finding the used car that best fits the criteria.

Inadequate or Vague Choice Criteria.　When the criteria are inadequate or vague, the range of products that will satisfy them is often wide. Perhaps the easiest thing for the salesperson to do is to show that a particular product fits a customer's choice criteria. Because the choice criteria are vague, this would not be difficult, and little actual selling may be involved. However, the customer may have trouble believing that the product the salesperson selected is the best one to meet his or her needs. The customer may therefore choose to shop around at other locations.

If the salesclerk is interested in building repeat business and customer goodwill and has a wide range of products to sell, then a preferable strategy would be to help the customer define his or her problem in order to refine the choice criteria. The customer and salesclerk can work together in defining the criteria of a good product and then select the product that best fits the criteria.

Choice Criteria in Conflict.　Prospective customers with choice criteria that are in conflict frequently have trouble making purchase decisions. There are two basic ways in which choice criteria can be in conflict. First, the customer may want a product to possess two or more attributes that are mutually exclusive. For example, a person purchasing a mountain bike may wish it to be of high quality and low price. This person will quickly find that these two attributes do not coexist. The best strategy in this situation is for the salesperson to play down one of the attributes and play up the other. A second way the choice criteria can be in conflict is when a single attribute possesses both positive and negative aspects. Consider a person thinking of purchasing a high-performance automobile. High-performance automobiles have both positive aspects (status, speed, and pleasure fulfillment) and negative aspects (high insurance rates and low mileage per gallon). For this type of conflict, the best selling strategy is to enhance the positive aspects and downplay the negative aspects.

Explicit Choice Criteria.　When the customer has a well-defined, explicit choice criteria, the best selling strategy is for the salesperson to illustrate how a specific product fits these criteria. "The salesclerk guides the customer into agreeing that each attribute of his product matches the attributes on the customer's specification. If, at the end of the sales talk, the customer does not agree to the salesclerk's proposition, he appears to be denying what he has previously admitted."[38]

Evaluation of Salespeople

Evaluation of salespeople seeks to determine each salesperson's value to the firm. That determination is important as a basis for salary adjustments, promotions, transfers, terminations, and sales reinforcement. The retailer should develop a systematic method for evaluating both individual salespeople and the total sales staff. Rather than subjectively evaluating performance, the manager should develop explicit performance standards.

Performance Standards

Several standards can be developed to measure a salesperson's performance. Some standards apply only to individual efforts, whereas others assess both individual and total sales-force effort.

conversion rate
Is the percentage of shoppers that enter the store that are converted into purchasers.

Conversion Rate.   The **conversion rate** is the percentage of all shoppers who make a purchase—that is, who are converted into customers. This is a measure of the sales force's performance, not the individual salesperson's.

A poor conversion rate can be caused by a variety of factors. Perhaps there were not enough clerks on hand when customers needed them. This could have resulted in numerous unassisted searches and long customer waits, causing many customers to exit the store without making a purchase. Or the number of salesclerks could have been adequate to handle the flow of customers, but the salespeople may not have done a good selling job. A poor selling job could have several causes, including giving inadequate product information, disagreeing or arguing too strongly with the customer, demonstrating the product poorly, having an unfriendly attitude, or giving up on the sale too early. However, all of these factors are really related to poor training, which is the underlying reason for poor sales. A low conversion rate might also have been due to factors beyond the salesperson's control, such as inadequate merchandise levels. The important point is that when a substandard conversion rate exists, the retailer should identify the causes and remedy the situation because even a small increase in the conversion rate can have a major impact on retail sales.

Marvin Rothenberg, a retired retail consultant, studied what happened in four chains operating a total of 68 department stores.[39] He found that 131,328,000 sales opportunities a year (that is, 2.4 million shoppers who averaged 1.9 shopping visits per month and 2.4 departments per trip) produced only 38 million sales transactions. Thus, 93 million departmental shopping visits resulted in "no sale."

In fact, 49 million of the departmental shoppers who made no purchase did not even have contact with a salesperson or a cashier. Another 44 million had contact with a salesperson but did not buy anything. And among these two segments of 93 million shoppers already in the departments, 28 million came into the department with the intent to make a specific purchase! In total, 71 percent of all the departmental shopping visits resulted in shoppers either having no contact with sales personnel or having the wrong kind of contact; as a result, they made no purchase. No wonder that, in another study, Rothenberg found that one-third of customers who entered a store with the expressed intent of making a specific purchase walked out without making any purchase. It is obvious that a small increase in converting these nonpurchasing consumers into customers could increase sales dramatically, even if the shopper is only in the store as a means to combat loneliness.

For example, if these retailers did nothing more than just contact half the 49 million customers who had no sales contact, and if the conversion rate among this group was only half of what it was among those who had sales contact, then the number of sales transactions, currently 38 million, would increase by 15 percent (half of 49 million who had no contact multiplied by half of the conversion rate for those who had contact equals 5.6 million more sales transactions). That's an opportunity to add 15 percent to sales by doing nothing more than what is already being achieved when customers contact a salesperson. Yet for many retailers this is a lost opportunity as they either do not want to (or do not know how to) train their sales staff in the proper methods of approaching and assisting customers and more generally providing customer service. Worse yet are those retailers who view their sales force as an operating expense and not as an investment. As such, they want to cut back on expenses and end up with too few salespeople on duty. Either way, the retailer is missing out on a great opportunity to increase sales.

Some online retailers, realizing the importance of converting as many lookers into buyers as possible, are chatting up customers to get them to stay on their site longer and hopefully buy something. Such strategies are especially beneficial to the small online retailers because it offers a relatively low-cost way to track consumer behavior and concerns and react accordingly. The strategy also allows small online companies, with their limited promotional and research budgets, to copy some of the personalized attention that bricks-and-mortar stores are able to use.

Sales per Hour. Perhaps the most common measure of sales-force performance is sales per hour. Sales per hour is computed by dividing total dollar sales over a particular time frame by total salesperson or sales-force hours. A retailer can compute this simple measure for each salesperson, any group of salespeople, or the entire sales force. It can also be computed for various days, weeks, or months.

When employing this measure, remember that standards should be specific to the group or person being evaluated for a particular time period. For example, in a department store, the sales per hour of selling effort cannot be expected to be the same for the toy department as for the jewelry department. Nor could one expect the same sales per hour during July and December because of the heavy Christmas demand for toys and jewelry. In some lines of retail trade, particularly those selling high-ticket items such as automobiles, the key performance measure is gross profit generated per salesperson.

Use of Time Standards can be developed for how salespeople should spend their time. A salesperson's time can be spent in four ways:

1. *Selling time* is any time spent assisting customers with their needs. This could be time spent talking, demonstrating a product, writing sales receipts, or assisting the customer in other potentially revenue-generating ways.

2. *Nonselling time* is any time spent on nonselling tasks such as marking or straightening up the merchandise.

3. *Idle time* is time the salesperson is on the sales floor but is not involved in any productive work.

4. *Absent time* occurs when the salespeople are not on the sales floor. They may be at lunch, in the employee lounge, in another part of the store, or in some inappropriate place.

The retailer may develop standards for each of these ways to spend time. For example, the standard time allocation may suggest that salespeople spend 60 percent of their time selling, 28 percent of their time on nonselling activities, 5 percent idle, and 7 percent absent. Any deviation from these standards should be investigated, and corrective measures should be taken if necessary.

Data Requirements

To establish proper standards of performance, the retailer needs data. What are good standards for the conversion rate? sales per hour? time allocation? Only data

What's New?

The Increasing Use of Mystery Shoppers

Recent economic conditions have increased the pressure for retailers to deliver high-quality customer service so as to not lose any customers to the competition. This in turn has created a lucrative new industry of so-called snoopers to help retailers monitor the implementation of their policies and the preparedness of their employees for the unexpected. These mystery shoppers, or as some prefer to call themselves—quality-assessment specialists—not only test the traditional bricks-and-mortar retailers selling general merchandise but also even visit such nontraditional places as churches. After all, with church attendance declining, no house of worship wants to lose members because of dull sermons, dirty pews, ineffective greeters, or stale donuts at the after-service social.

In a typical mystery-shopping experience, an anonymous trained researcher engages the retailer's staff in the store, over the telephone, or on the Internet and seeks to complete a required task such as purchasing a product or making a customer-service inquiry. The shopper then completes a detailed report on the various aspects of the shopping experience. This report covers such topics as:

- Are your customers greeted with a smile and offered assistance?

- Are your sales associates informing your customers of new items or innovative solutions to their needs?

- Do sales associates know when to offer additional items to complement a purchase?

- Are your customers pleased with the way they were treated?

- Do your customers feel loyal to your business?

- What occurs in your business when you are not there?

- How clean were the store's shelves?

The details provided in the report are as objective as possible and focus primarily on the facts of the experience. For example, mystery shoppers report the exact amount of time until they are greeted in the store, verbatim conversations with employees, the length of time they waited in line to purchase their products, and the physical appearance of displays in each aisle of the store. Therefore, a key skill of mystery shoppers is a keen memory because no notes can be taken during the retail shopping experience but can only be recorded once the mystery shopper is clear of the retailer's presence.

A clear advantage of mystery shoppers is that they provide an independent assessment of the customer-service operations rather than relying on employees for customer-service assessments. Thus, all retail sectors can benefit from the independent assessment of service quality that is provided through mystery-shopping programs. Whether one speaks of clothing retailers, hotels, restaurants, or financial services, mystery shopping can help retailers or their channel partners assess the experience of a retailer's customers. Such data provides valuable information on the retailer's particular strengths and weaknesses. For example, one well-regarded liquor manufacturer wanted to ensure the quality of training that its retailers maintained regarding the preparation of its product. To that end, the manufacturer hired a market research firm to send out mystery drinkers to ensure that the retailers used branded glasses, swizzle sticks, and ice buckets to guarantee the perfect gin and tonic.

While such shoppers were once used primarily by retailers to identify employees who were lax in their responsibilities, the general demeanor of mystery-shopping programs has changed considerably. Today, the most successful mystery shopping programs are aimed at identifying areas for retail improvement. Rather than focusing on any specific employee's shortcomings in the customer-service experience, retailers are using the data from mystery-shopping research to develop more effective training and employee-reward programs to heighten their level of service.

The demand for mystery shoppers by retailers throughout the world is evidenced by the fact that the practice has spawned a whole new segment of market research. In fact, the demand for mystery shoppers has grown so strong that almost every market research firm now offers this service to its clients. As one can imagine, the task of assessing service is a key area of strategic retail importance as customers continue to demand increasing levels of service quality.

One word of caution before considering going to work as a mystery shopper. Many scammers have recently figured out how to pose as legit employers. Therefore, check all offers with the Mystery Shopping Providers Association (www.mysteryshop.org) and your Better Business Bureau. Also, never send the employer money—that is a sure sign of a scammer.

Source: Based on "Private Eyes," *Shopping Centers Today*, April 2008: 19–20; "Get Paid to Shop," *AARP Magazine*, May/June, 2008; Adam Finn and Ujwal Kayande, "Unmasking a Phantom: A Psychometric Assessment of Mystery Shopping," *Journal of Retailing*, Summer 1999: 195–217; and the authors' experiences with mystery shoppers.

will help answer these questions. For bricks-and-mortar retailers, data can come from retail trade associations, consulting firms, or the retailer's own experience.

Once the retailer obtains the data on which to base standards, it must collect additional data continually or at least periodically on actual performance. For example, an increasing number of retailers today survey their customers and use other programs, such as mystery shoppers, to evaluate their salespeople. In fact, a whole service industry specializing in mystery shopping has developed, as detailed in the chapter's "What's New?" box. The results of mystery shopper surveys, along with the employee's actual conversion rate, sales per hour, and time allocation must be compared to their respective standards. If the actual data differ significantly from the standard, then an investigation of the cause is warranted. Both favorable and unfavorable variances should be investigated because a retailer may learn just as much from unusually good performance as from unusually poor performance.

The Retail Sales Process

LO 5

What steps are involved in the retail selling process?

Several basic steps occur during the retail selling process. The length of time that a salesperson spends in each one of these steps depends on the product type, the customer, and the selling situation. Exhibit 12.8 details the sales-process model.

Prospecting

Prospecting is the search process of finding those who have the ability and willingness to purchase your product. Prospecting is particularly important when the store is full of customers. A salesperson should be aware that good prospects generally display more interest in the product than poor prospects that are "just looking." Salespeople should take advantage of the behavioral cues shown in Exhibit 12.7.

prospecting
Is the process of locating or identifying potential customers who have the ability and willingness to purchase your product.

Approach

The salesperson may meet hundreds of customers a day, but the customer is only going to meet the salesperson once that day. Therefore, especially given the economic slowdown, it is extremely important to remember that the first 15 seconds sets the mood for the sale. The salesperson must use this time to begin enhancing the shopping experience of everyone who walks through the front door. Therefore, the sales presentation should never begin with "May I help you?" or any other question to which the customer may respond negatively. A simple "Good morning" (afternoon, evening) or any other greeting acknowledging the customer's presence should do. Nordstrom's trains its sales force to mention an item the customer is wearing as an approach if something better is not evident.

The key to a successful approach is discerning the customer's needs as soon as possible by asking the right questions and listening. What the salesperson hears about the customer's problem or need is more important than anything the salesperson can possibly contribute at this point. The salesperson should ask only a few well-chosen questions to find out more about the need or problem to be solved. The salesperson should also find out if the user of the product is a different individual than the customer. Remember the salesperson should ask only as many questions as needed, and let the customer do the talking. One well-known retail sales trainer was famous for telling her trainees that you can close more sales with your ears than with your mouth. Listening to the voice of the customer is *key*.

Step 1—Prospecting

Decide who can benefit from your product.

a. Find prospects.

b. Qualify prospects (determine whether a prospect has the ability, buying power, and willingness to make a purchase).

Step 2—Approach

The first 15 seconds are the key as they set the mood for the sale.

a. Never say, "May I help you?"

A single "Hello," "Good morning," or "What may I show you?" makes the customer realize that you are glad they are in your store.

b. Determine the customer's needs as early as possible.

Listen—*What you hear* is more important than anything you could possibly tell your customer. Ask a few well-chosen questions—What do I need to know?

1. Product needed or problem to be solved.

2. User of the product (tell me about so-and-so).

Step 3—The Sales Presentation

Get the customer to want to buy your product/service.

a. Pick the right price level.

If uncertain, ask, "Is there a price range you have in mind?" Remember, you can't pick out the *right product* for the uncertain customer if the price is wrong.

b. Pick the right product.

Match user and need with product. Show the customer at least two items.

c. Show the merchandise in an appealing manner.

1. Make the merchandise stand out.

2. Show the item so that its good points will be seen.

3. Let the customer handle the merchandise.

4. Stress the features of the product.

5. Explain the benefits of these features.

6. Appeal to the customer's emotions.

d. Help the customer decide.

1. Handle objections.

2. Replace unneeded items.

3. Watch for unconscious clues.

4. Stress features and benefits of "key" product.

Step 4—Closing the Sale

Reach an agreement.

a. What is going on in the customer's mind?

b. Four effective ways to close.

1. Make the decision for the customer.

2. Assume the decision has already been made.

3. Ask the customer to choose.

4. Turn an objection around.

Step 5—Suggestion Selling

Follow up leads to other sales.

Sales Presentation

Once the initial contact has been established and the salesperson has listened to the customer's problems and needs, the salesperson is in a position to present the merchandise and sales message correctly. How the salesperson presents the product or service depends on the customer and the situation. The key, however, is to get the customer to want to buy your product or service. The salesperson might begin by determining the right price range of products to show the customer. A price too high or too low will generally result in a lost sale. If uncertain, the salesperson should ask the customer about the price range desired.

Next, the salesperson should pick out what he or she believes will be the right product or service to satisfy the customer's needs. The salesperson should be careful not to show the customer too many products so as to avoid confusing him or her.

The salesperson should tell the customer about the merchandise in an appealing way, stressing the features that are the outstanding qualities or characteristics of the product, and have the customer handle the merchandise. The salesperson can then help the customer decide on the product or service that best fulfills the customer's needs. The salesperson should handle any objection that the customer might have, replace the unneeded items, and continue to stress the features and benefits of the product the customer seems most interested in.

Closing the Sale

Closing the sale is a natural conclusion to the selling process. However, for most salespeople, closing the sale is the most difficult part of the job. In fact, by some estimates, almost three-quarters of all "lost" sales occur during this stage of the selling process because the salesperson didn't "ask for the sale." The salesperson was either afraid of rejection or, worse, was unaware that the customer was ready to make the purchase. Remember, the salesperson is there to help the customer solve a problem, and so should not be afraid to ask for the sale. The key to closing the sale is to determine what is going on in the customer's mind. Exhibit 12.9 lists some of the things a salesperson should watch for at this stage of the selling process. If the salesperson waits too long or is too impatient in completing this step, then the customer will be gone before the salesperson realizes it. There are four effective ways to close a sale: (1) make the decision for the customer, (2) assume that the decision has been made and ask if the sale will be cash or charge, (3) ask the customer to select the product or service, and (4) turn an objection around by stressing a positive aspect of the product. For example, a salesperson might suggest that, although the initial cost of a product might be high, its longer life span will reduce total cost.

In Chapter 3's discussion of the consumer behavior model, postpurchase resentment was described. This can occur whether the consumer is buying a car, a blazer, or spring break get-a-way. Usually, the more expensive the purchase, the greater the doubt and the higher the risk of dissatisfaction. Over the years, good salespeople, selling expensive products, have found three easy steps to be effective when dealing with this problem:

1. Always congratulate the customer for making a wise decision. As soon as customers agree to a purchase, assure them that others have been happy with their decision to purchase the same item, and you know they will be equally satisfied.

2. Always send a thank-you note. Nordstrom's system has shown everyone the value of these notes by the positive customer responses and referrals.

closing the sale
Is the action the salesperson takes to bring a potential sale to its natural conclusion.

Exhibit 12.9
Some Closing Signals the Salespeople Should Watch For

The customer reexamines the product carefully.

The customer tries on the product (i.e., trying on a sport coat or strapping on a wristwatch).

The customer begins to read the warranty or brochure.

The customer makes statements similar to the following:

> I always wanted a compact disc player.
>
> I never realized that these were so inexpensive.
>
> I bet my wife would love this.

The customer asks questions like:

> Does this come in any other colors?
>
> Do you accept Discover cards?
>
> Can you deliver this tomorrow?
>
> Do you have a size 7 in this style?
>
> Do you accept trade-ins?
>
> Do you have any training sessions available?
>
> Do you have it in stock?
>
> What accessories are available?
>
> Where would I take it to get it serviced?
>
> Is it really that easy to operate?

3. Get the customer in possession of the product as quickly as possible. If the products can't be delivered immediately, then send updates on the progress of those orders, even if it is only a phone call or e-mail.

Suggestion Selling.   An effective salesperson continues to sell even after the sale has been completed. An additional sale is always possible. The salesperson should find out if the customer has any other needs or if the customer knows of anybody else with needs that can be solved with the salesperson's product line. Many retailers refer to suggestion selling as "filling the basket." A couple of examples would be selling a Valentine's gift to a college student for his girlfriend and then asking if he needs help with a gift for his mother or suggesting an extra ink cartridge to a customer that just purchased a printer (because most cartridges in printers are only half-full).

Many customers appreciate suggestion selling because it often eliminates a second shopping trip. However, it may also decrease a consumer's satisfaction with the retailer as some customers view suggestion selling as an annoyance.

LO 6

The Customer-Service and Sales-Enhancement Audit

What is involved in a customer-service audit?

Up to this point, we have discussed the level and type of sales personnel needed in a retail operation; the types of retail selling; the selection, training, and management of the sales force; the factors to consider when evaluating individual salespeople, and how to sell in a retail store. These are microapproaches to improving the productivity of an individual. How do we get macro answers for the performance of a whole department or a whole store? Remember the example earlier in this chapter of those retailers who had 49 million possible buyers walk out of their stores without any salesperson contact? One solution is an audit of the retailer's customer-services and sales-enhancement programs.[40]

Such an audit, which can easily be performed by the retailer's own staff or by a consultant, provides the direction that enables retailers to capture the unrealized potential of customers who walk out with no salesperson contact. It analyzes current levels of performance by selling area within each store, revealing how customers shop the store and the extent of the service they receive. It is *not* an attempt to learn what the customers want (e.g., friendly and competent salespeople, low prices, free assembly); instead, it concentrates on the facts of their shopping experience.

The audit is usually performed by having the retailer's staff, or hired researchers, intercept customers as they leave the store and asking about their experience in the store. The number of customers interviewed should reflect the size and shopping patterns of each store. The objectives of the audit are to:

- identify the service, salesmanship, and sales-enhancement methods that will produce more sales from the existing shopping traffic;
- target the methods by store and selling area that will produce the most significant improvements; and
- determine the added sales that can be generated by improving the accepted service level, salesmanship, and sales-enhancement programs.

Upon completion, the audit provides management with a detailed analysis of current sales activity by location and by selling area. It identifies how and where additional sales volume is available. It measures, analyzes, and reports on the specific factors.

BASIC SERVICE

1. *Customer contact.* In stores that purport to offer service, there can be no sale if the shopper has no contact with a salesperson or a cashier. Increasing the number of shoppers who are approached increases the number of shoppers who are likely to buy.

2. *Salesperson-initiated contact.* Motivated salespeople—those who do not wait for customers to approach them—can prevent walkouts and generate more sales from shoppers who otherwise might have to spend shopping time looking for a salesperson.

3. *Customer acknowledgment.* Greeting customers within a short time frame also prevents walkouts and provides more shopping time. It keeps the shopper in a favorable buying mood.

SALESMANSHIP

4. *Merchandise knowledge.* A salesperson with product knowledge can answer a shopper's questions, enhance the transaction, help to consummate the sales, prevent lost sales, and even add to the purchase.

5. *Needs clarification.* Asking the proper questions enables the salesperson to present and show the proper merchandise.

6. *Active selling.* Actively selling the merchandise and volunteering advice about the use and care of the goods, as well as stating the advantages of ownership, helps to consummate the sale.

7. *Suggestion selling.* Suggesting additional or complementary merchandise may increase the value of the sale. (The audit should also measure the number of times that suggestion selling resulted in an additional purchase.)

SALES ENHANCEMENT

8. *Impulse purchasing.* Proper selection of merchandise, packaging, location within a department, presentation, and then servicing the transaction will increase the productivity of shopping traffic.

9. *Walkouts.* Retaining sales that would otherwise be lost is one of the most direct and immediate routes to sales improvement. Offering the desired goods in easy-to-find locations is the most obvious method for reducing walkouts. However, customer contact and salesmanship can be a major deterrent of walkouts among those who come to buy.

These elements of service, salesmanship, and sales enhancement are measured and reported by selling area within each store, enabling management to apply targeted training programs. It is usually not necessary to spend the money to train or retrain all personnel in each store for each of the techniques. However, when applied, the method can add significantly to the value of each transaction. For example, for the four chains cited in our earlier example, the incremental sales transactions for the average salesperson after the audit were:

10 percent . . . when the salesperson initiated the contact with the shopper,

3 percent . . . when the salesperson acknowledged the customer's presence in a timely manner,

12 percent . . . when the salesperson was able to answer the customer's questions,

14 percent . . . when the salesperson asked questions to clarify the shopper's needs,

18 percent . . . when the salesperson actively "sold" the merchandise, and

48 percent . . . when the salesperson suggested additional or complementary merchandise and the suggestion was taken.

No incremental addition to the average salesperson can be calculated for increasing contacts with shoppers, for improving the rate of impulse buying, or for reducing walkouts. The reason is obvious: When these techniques are applied and are successful, an entirely new transaction is created!

To provide management with an action program, the customer service and sales-enhancement audit includes a series of exception reports that show specifically what improvement is necessary within each selling area at each company store. The dollar value also is listed so that management can know the added volume that is available by applying targeted retraining programs. The report should list the causes of walkouts for each selling area at each location. Management therefore receives an analysis of current performance by selling area at each company location and the specific action necessary to capture unrealized potential. The dollar opportunity is also calculated to highlight the value of each improvement. Exception reports make it easy to implement the program.

Every day, within all types of stores, there are "acres of diamonds in their own backyards." Shoppers are continuing to visit stores in large numbers, many of them willing, able, and anxious to be converted into buyers. Management's task is to identify where and how that can be accomplished. That is the function of the audit.

SUMMARY

Why is customer service so important in retailing? **LO 1**

This chapter emphasizes that customer service is a key revenue-generating variable for the retailer. To properly manage the customer-service decision area, the retailer needs to build a customer relationship by integrating customer service with merchandise, promotion, building and fixtures, price, and credit management. Only an integrated customer-service program will allow the retailer to achieve maximum profits.

What are the various customer services that a retailer can offer? **LO 2**

Customer services are classified into pretransaction, transaction, and posttransaction services. Pretransaction services make it easier for a potential customer to shop at a retailer's location or learn about the retailer's offering. Common examples are convenient hours and informational aids. Transaction-related services make it easier for the customer to complete a transaction. Popular transaction-related services are consumer credit, gift wrapping and packaging, check cashing, gift cards, personal shopping, merchandise availability, personal selling, and the transaction itself. Posttransaction services influence the customer's satisfaction with the merchandise after the transaction. The most frequently encountered services are handling complaints, merchandise returns, servicing, repairing and warranting, delivery, and postsale follow-up.

How should a retailer determine which services to offer? **LO 3**

Conventional wisdom suggests that the retailer should consider six factors when establishing the mix of customer services: retailer's characteristics, competition, type of merchandise, price image, target market income, and cost of the service.

What are the various management problems involved in retail selling, salesperson selection, and training and evaluation? **LO 4**

This chapter also illustrates the role of managing the retail salesperson. Regardless of whether salesclerks are primarily order getters or order takers, they play an important role in the demand for a retailer's products. However, the role played by the order getter is obviously more important in this regard.

Various criteria to be used in the selection of a selling staff and its training program were discussed. The section ended by reviewing performance evaluation of retail salespeople.

What steps are involved in the retail selling process? **LO 5**

The retail selling process consists of five steps—prospecting, approach, presentation, close, and suggestion selling. The length of time a salesperson spends on each step depends on the product type, customer, and selling situation.

What is involved in a customer-service audit? **LO 6**

An audit of the retailer's customer-services and sales-enhancement programs enables retailers to capture the unrealized potential of customers who walk out without being contacted by a salesperson. It analyzes current levels of performance by selling area within each company store, revealing how customers shop the store and the extent of the service they receive. It is *not* an attempt to learn what the customers want but concentrates on the facts of their shopping experience.

TERMS TO REMEMBER

high-quality service
relationship retailing
customer service
transient customer
pretransaction services
transaction services

personal shopping
dwell time
posttransaction services
conversion rate
prospecting
closing the sale

REVIEW AND DISCUSSION QUESTIONS

LO 1   **Why is customer service so important in retailing?**

1. Your store manager just told you that since profits have been falling over the past year, he has recommended to the owners that they could increase profits by cutting back further on customer services. After all, customers don't really expect service anymore. Agree or disagree with this statement and explain your reasoning.

2. Should the level of service offered by a retailer be directly proportional to the gross margin obtained from the sale of the merchandise? In other words, the more profitable the item, the greater the service level that should be extended. Explain the reasoning behind your answer.

3. Should online customers expect the same type of service that bricks-and-mortar customers get from retailers selling similar merchandise? Explain the reasoning behind your answer.

LO 2   **What are the various customer services that a retailer can offer?**

4. A major discounter was recently quoted as saying that he "no longer worries about dwell time. After all, low price is the only factor that drives sales." Do you agree or disagree with this statement? What is your reasoning?

5. Some discounters not only have a "no layaway" policy but also will only accept cash. They don't accept checks or credit and debit cards. Will this hinder these stores in the marketplace? Because of the slowing economy and the high fees banks charge on the cards, as well as bad checks, is the trend moving away from accepting these forms of payment? What would you suggest retailers do? Explain your reasoning.

LO 3   **How should a retailer determine which services to offer?**

6. How does the type of customer affect the level of customer service a retailer should offer?

7. Shouldn't all retailers seek to exceed their competition's level of customer service? Explain the reasoning behind your answer.

LO 4   **What are the various management problems involved in retail selling, salesperson selection, and training and evaluation?**

8. Develop a list of predictor variables you would use to screen applicants for a sales position in (a) a jewelry department in a high-prestige department store, (b) a used-car dealership, (c) a health club, and (d) an antique shop.

9. A men's clothing store chain has analyzed the annual sales per salesperson in 10 of its stores nationwide. The sales per salesperson range from a low of

$121,000 to a high of $248,000. Develop the list of factors that might help to explain this wide variation.

What is involved in the retail selling process?   **LO 5**

10. When you are shopping for yourself, do you appreciate it when the salesperson uses suggestion-selling techniques? Does the type of merchandise make a difference in your answer?
11. What should retail salespeople know about customer choice criteria?
12. Why is selling so much more important for retailers of services than it is for retailers selling physical products?

What is involved in a customer-service audit?   **LO 6**

13. Why is it so important that a retailer's sales personnel be taught that each customer must be contacted by a sales associate each time the customer enters the store? Don't some customers just want to be left alone to look around?

SAMPLE TEST QUESTIONS

A transient customer is a consumer who visits a retailer: **LO 1**

a. and finds the item desired in a matter of minutes.
b. only when his or her regular retailer is closed.
c. that does not meet his or her customer-service expectations.
d. while on vacation.
e. and then visits all the other retailers in the neighborhood.

Merchandise availability is an example of: **LO 2**

a. cost of sales.
b. a pretransaction service.
c. an operating cost.
d. a posttransaction service.
e. a transaction service.

Which of the following is not a factor in determining the service level to offer?   **LO 3**

a. income of target market
b. price image of the retailer
c. services offered by the competition
d. firm's management structure
e. retailer's characteristics

Which one of the following factors is not one of the elements that need to be considered when designing a sales job?   **LO 4**

a. feedback from supervisors
b. the number of complaints a salesperson should have to handle
c. the amount of variety involved
d. the appropriate degree of autonomy
e. the level of task identity present

LO 5 **What is the first step that a salesperson should take during the sales presentation?**

a. inform the customer about the merchandise in an appealing manner
b. select the right product or service that the salesperson believes will satisfy the customer's needs
c. greeting the customer
d. help the customer to decide on the product that best fulfills the customer's needs
e. determine the right price range of products

LO 6 **Which of the following is not an objective of a customer-service audit?**

a. It is an attempt to learn what are the most important considerations for customers when choosing a store—that is, low prices or ease of the transaction.
b. It identifies the service, salesmanship, and sales-enhancement methods that the retailer can use to produce more sales from the existing shopping traffic.
c. It targets which methods can be used to produce significant customer-service improvement.
d. It helps determine the added sales that can be generated by improving the current level of customer service.
e. All of the above are customer-service audit objectives.

WRITING AND SPEAKING EXERCISE

For the past eight years, six retired Dillard's employees have gotten together for lunch on the first Thursday of every month at a fancy downtown Continental restaurant called Café Pairee. These six women had worked together for more than 20 years and now looked forward to visiting with each other and hearing the latest news about each other's families at these local luncheons.

Since they were regulars at Café Pairee, the staff had gotten to know them and would often bring out five ice teas, two coffees, and one hot tea to the big table at the far end of the café as soon as the first one arrived. The staff would also get updates on the families and knew that the ladies would spend almost two hours enjoying each other's company. Besides, since they were a party of six, the Café's policy was to add a 20-percent gratuity to the bill. That usually meant a $25 tip for the college student waiting on them.

Sue Brewer, the day-shift manager, made it a habit to stop by the Dillard's table, as it was called, and greet everyone. In fact, last month she even brought out the café's new chef, Michael, to meet the group. Chef Michael had recently replaced Chef Robert, and Robert had become a favorite of the six women. During their initial visit with Chef Michael, he invited the women to visit his kitchen with any questions, and he encouraged them to make suggestions for the new menu he was developing.

This month, on Chef Michael's recommendation, Melinda O'Conner switched from ordering her usual chicken salad and chocolate cheesecake to substitute shrimp salad instead. When the salad arrived, Melinda was aghast to see that shrimp was not deveined. (To *devein* shrimp is to remove the black "vein" that runs along the back of the shrimp. This is actually its digestive tract. Even though these veins are edible, if eaten they can taste gritty and dirty, particularly with larger prawns or shrimp.) Melinda ate around the shrimp and simply said she wasn't hungry when the waiter asked if there was a problem.

When they got to the parking lot, Melinda announced in no uncertain terms that she would never come back to this place. "Chef Robert would never serve shrimp that way," she stated. "If Chef Michael was too lazy or too cheap to serve shrimp this way, I am afraid to see what else he is doing in the kitchen." Two others agreed with Melinda, and it was decided to switch locations for next month's lunch.

That night, Helen Sewell called Melinda and asked if Melinda thought it was a good idea to call Sue Brewer and explain the situation. After all, she told Melinda, when they were on the floor at Dillard's, they would want to know why they lost a customer. Melinda agreed that it was a good idea.

Prepare a message for Helen and Melinda to give to Sue.

RETAIL PROJECT

As you are approaching graduation, you decide that you need a new suit for interviewing. In considering your shopping alternatives, you decide to compare online clothing stores versus bricks-and-mortar stores.

Determine the difference in the amount of time involved in shopping between the two types of retailers, the time it would take for you to obtain the clothing from each, and prices. Which would you choose to use?

PLANNING YOUR OWN RETAIL BUSINESS

Donnelly's Jewelers, a family business your grandfather started in 1952, had annual sales last year of $900,560. Your parents, who purchased this business from your grandfather in 1981, have asked you to help them develop a strategy to improve sales. Since you plan to open a second Donnelly's Jewelers store on graduation with your family's support, you want to use this opportunity to impress your parents with your business and retail-marketing skills.

In reviewing the records of the store, you were surprised to find that a record had been kept of how many shoppers visited the store on a daily basis. For the most recent year, you computed that there were 15,000 visitors and that 2,803 of these made a purchase. You also have spent the last few weeks observing the salespeople (including your parents) make sales presentations. Your observation is that they do a good job on approaching shoppers and making a sales presentation, but they are quite weak and passive on closing a sale. You also have observed little effort is made to cross-sell merchandise.

Your recommendation is to have a local professor who teaches a course in personal selling conduct a sales-training workshop. This two-day workshop would cost $5,000. After consulting with the professor, you both believe the training should produce an increase in average transaction size of $30 and an increase in the conversion rate of 5 percent.

Based on the preceding information, show the impact on annual sales of the proposed training program.

Store Layout and Design

OVERVIEW:

In this chapter, we discuss the place where all retailing activities come together—the retail store. The store can be the most meaningful form of communication between the retailer and its customers. Most important, the store is where sales happen—or fail to happen. We will see that, despite its hundreds of elements, the store has two primary roles: creating the proper store image and increasing the productivity of the sales space. We identify the most critical elements in creating a successful retail store and describe the art and science of store planning, merchandise presentation, and design.

LEARNING OBJECTIVES:

After reading this chapter, you should be able to:

1. List the elements of a store's environment and define its two primary objectives.
2. Discuss the steps involved in planning the store.
3. Describe how various types of fixtures, merchandise-presentation methods and techniques, and the psychology of merchandise presentation are used to increase the productivity of the sales floor.
4. Describe why store design is so important to a store's success.
5. Explain the role of visual communications in a retail store.

LO 1

Introduction to Store Layout Management

What are the elements of a store's environment?

The previous chapter discussed how customer service and personal selling can be used to develop a relationship with the customer. This chapter examines another method retailers can use to initiate and continue this relationship—the retail store itself. Retailers must never forget the old axiom that "we all sell discretionary merchandise; therefore, we must package it with theater and excitement." They also must recognize that a retail store is different than an Internet site because "shopping is a contact sport" and how the store engages and interacts with the shopper is critical to its success. Today's finicky customers demand sizzle with their steak. *Setting* and *presentation* are now critical factors in serving the customer. All too often the retailer, realizing the importance of getting customers into a store, develops an excellent promotional campaign only to have the customer become turned off when entering the store. Successful retailers today use their stores as a means to excite their customers so that they will spend more time looking and viewing merchandise, which will subsequently enhance sales. The last thing a retailer needs is for customers to enter its store and then to walk out empty handed.

No other variable in the retailing mix influences the consumer's initial perception of a bricks-and-mortar retailer as much as the store itself. Unfortunately, many retailers do not realize how valuable the hundreds of thousands of dollars— and, for larger stores, millions of dollars—that need to be invested in a store design and atmosphere that can serve as a platform for an engaging and valuable shopping experience. Consequently, successful retailers today are spending a great deal of time and effort making sure the right things happen in their stores so that the right customers enter the stores, shop, and spend money. Simply put, for retailers the store is "where the action is," and this includes such seemingly minor details as the placement and display of merchandise. Consider, for example, petite sizes are for women who are 5 feet, 4 inches or shorter. For years, many department stores located their petite sizes either next to or between the misses and plus sizes. Department stores sold versions of the same products in the misses, women's, and petite departments, often with racks of similar styles in different sizes across the aisle from each other. The boundaries between departments were blurred, and department store petite lines were considered frumpy. Thus, the mixing of misses, plus sizes, and petites reduced the possibility of a sale. As a result of this ineffective merchandising, petite departments in some department stores have been eliminated or reduced in size.

There are many consultants available to help the retailer with store design. London-based Shopworks (shopworks.co.uk), for example, uses consumer research to guide design and is guided also by the concept that shopping is about money and cash flow for the retailer. Shopworks designs appealing and engaging stores; more importantly, these store designs enhance space productivity and thus retailer profitability. Unlike some other consulting firms, they also assist on implementation and execution of their designs. New York–based Envirosell (www.envirosell.com) is another research and consulting firm specializing in studying retail and service environments. Founded by Paco Underhill, one of the first researchers to study how people shop, Envirosell bases its recommendations after videotaping and tracking shoppers in the stores, often for weeks at a time. In fact over a year's time, the firm collects more than 50,000 hours of shopping behavior video. One of the benefits of such research is that Envirosell concluded that, as a result of the recent recession, consumers now make more decisions about what to buy when they are in the store, not before entering the store.[1]

Although this chapter is concerned with the physical store, the same factors may be used to develop an e-tailer's "virtual store." Just as with a bricks-and-mortar location, the first impression is most important. After all, most consumers spend less than five seconds at a website the first time they visit. Therefore, there is a limited window of opportunity to capture the attention of an online user. Although there is no strict list of do's and don'ts, given that the online "rules" are constantly changing, a few underlying fundamentals have been identified that can drive repeat visits and encourage purchasing:

- *Keep content current.* Online consumers browse frequently, so it is very important to continually update information on the site. Two aspects should be considered: merchandise presentation and merchandise description. In merchandise presentation, the web offers e-tailers a plethora of presentation options. Not limited by physical restraints, e-tailers can provide consumers with 3-D presentations that allow a 360-degree view of merchandise. In the merchandise description, write in "web-ese." Online consumers scan information as opposed to reading it.

- *Make the site easy and enjoyable to use.* Ease of use is a primary concern for online consumers. This means that users with little or no experience either online or with your product category should be able to move easily about the site and find the information they desire. Much like signage in a bricks-and-mortar world, e-tailers must clearly show the way for online consumers.

- *Structure an online community where consumers can interact with one another or contribute to the site's content.* The virtual world allows for new methods of integrating customers into a retailer's business. Offering potential consumers an opportunity to become involved in the site can build a loyal clientele. A breakthrough entrepreneurial e-tailer is Threadless, headquartered in Chicago (www.threadless.com/retail), which involves potential customers by engaging them in regular T-shirt contests. Potential customers design T-shirts, and then the Threadless customer community votes on the designs; the winning designs are produced for sale both online, as the firm began, and now offline in its retail stores.[2]

Although a store is composed of literally thousands of details, the two primary objectives around which all activities, functions, and goals revolve are store image and space productivity. However, before discussing these two objectives, it is important to identify the elements that compose the store environment (shown in Exhibit 13.1), each of which will be discussed in detail in this chapter.

Elements of the Store Environment

The first decision to make in planning a store is how to allocate the retailer's most scarce resource—space. Space is scarce because it is costly, and a retailer has limited capital it can invest in its store. Consider that annual leases can range from $15 per

Exhibit 13.1
Elements That Compose the Store Environment

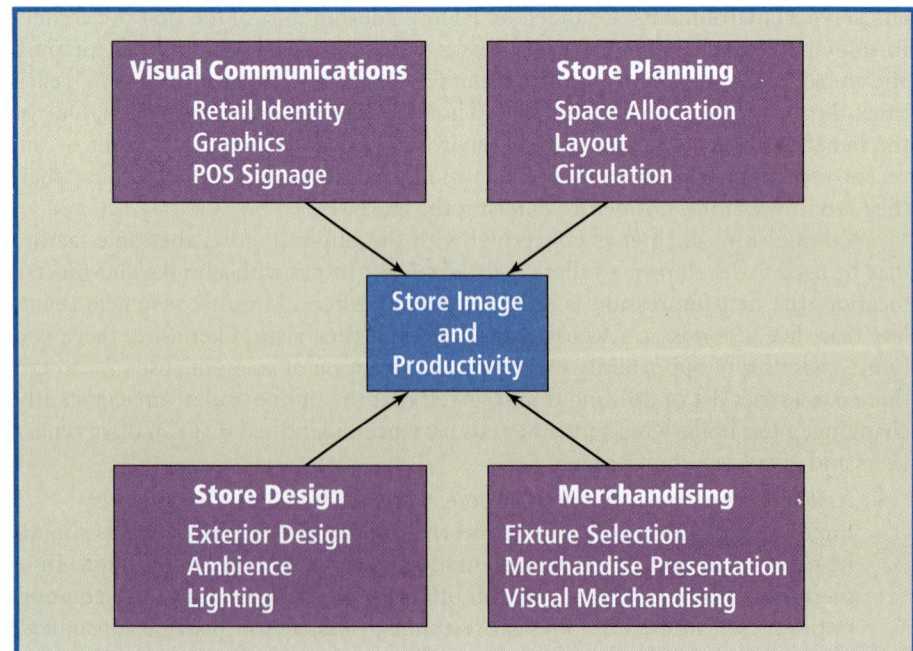

Visual Communications
- Retail Identity
- Graphics
- POS Signage

Store Planning
- Space Allocation
- Layout
- Circulation

Store Image and Productivity

Store Design
- Exterior Design
- Ambience
- Lighting

Merchandising
- Fixture Selection
- Merchandise Presentation
- Visual Merchandising

foot to more than $100, and new construction including land can exceed $300 per square foot. Making productive use of the store space through thoughtful space allocation thus becomes pivotal to enhancing image and space productivity.

The retailer creates a store layout that shows the location of all merchandise departments and the placement of circulation aisles to allow customers to move through the store. As discussed above, the merchandise presentation must be exciting so as to catch and hold customers' attention, be easy to understand, and encourage shoppers to browse, evaluate (especially if the decision is being made in the store), and buy. Therefore, the presentation of the merchandise is a critical factor in the selling power of a store and has a significant effect on the store image. Bookstores can display books either with the cover of the book facing out (called a *face-out*) so it is in full view or with only the spine of the book showing where the viewer can see the title and author but not the cover (called *spine-out*). A bookstore with a high percentage of face-outs, for example, can create the image of being a specialty book boutique that carries a limited selection of exclusive titles and is, therefore, a rather pricey place to shop. A bookstore with virtually all spine-outs is often perceived as cramming in a huge selection of titles sold at low prices. Thus, merchandise presentation is a critical factor in determining both store image and productivity.

Most shoppers are accustomed to noticing the layout and design of a store, which is composed of all the elements affecting the human senses of sight, hearing, smell, and touch. An effective store layout and design, including the storefront, creates a comfortable environment that enhances the merchandise and entices shoppers to browse and buy. Lighting is an important element that should not be overlooked. Both display and in-store lighting help create the proper image and also draw customers' eyes around the store and onto merchandise, and they ultimately encourage a customer to purchase the product.[3] Likewise, in-store graphics such as art, photography, and signs form an important visual communication

Michelle D. Bridwell/PhotoEdit

A bookstore with a high percentage of face-outs creates the image of being a specialty book boutique, while a bookstore with virtually all spine-outs is often perceived as cramming in a huge selection of titles sold at low prices.

link between the store and its customers by providing much-needed information on how to shop in the store. The chapter's "Retailing: The Inside Story" box gives a description of how supermarket managers have perfected the art of store design and layout. Importantly, geographical positioning systems (GPS) are now moving into the store where there are increasingly Wi-Fi networks. This allows retailers to no longer rely on some of the rules of thumb that are discussed in "The Inside Story" but to obtain accurate maps of how their customers navigate through their particular store.[4] Sometimes retailers tend to forget the lessons in the "The Inside Story" box. For example, many managers ignore their own 25-25-50 rule on endcaps. This rule states that 25 percent of all endcaps should be advertised sale merchandise that the customer will seek out and another 25 percent should be unadvertised sale items that will cause the customer to be alert when looking at an

Retailing: The Inside Story

Consumer Behavior: Supermarket Style

It's unknown how many supermarket managers took a consumer behavior class in college, but they sure know how to practice the art.

OBSERVE:

Not only are most consumers right-handed but also they think "right-headed."

- Since supermarkets make more money on their store's private-label brands, they stock the store brands to the right of the name brands so that the consumer has to reach across the store brand to grab the name brand.

- Since shoppers are more prone to look right, supermarkets display the higher gross-margin merchandise on the right side of an aisle, as gauged from the predominant direction of cart traffic. Also, displays should be set so that they are visible on the right side as shoppers travel the predominant path.

- Since 90 percent of all customers entering a store turn right, that area is the most valuable for the store. Thus it is no accident that the produce area, a deli, or a bakery is the first section that a customer will reach. That is because they can see, feel, and smell the merchandise. This in turn will get their mouths watering and make them hungry. Supermarket managers will tell you that their best customer is a hungry customer.

- When customers enter a store and begin to turn right, they tend to scan the entire store from left to right and then fix their eyes on an object (sign or merchandise) at a 45-degree angle from the point of entry.

- Grocers also use the most recognizable brand to lead off the product category as the consumer is walking toward it. In other words, they use Coca-Cola to lead off soft drinks, Fusion to lead off razors, and Secret to lead off deodorants.

Most consumers think "neatness" counts.

- Merchants sometimes try to make their point-of-purchase displays look like a mess. These so-called dump displays, which are affectionately known by some grocers as "organized chaos," are deliberately arranged in a haphazard fashion so the items inside look cheap and are, therefore, perceived as a great bargain. The same thought process works for merchants leaving out open cartons piled on top of another. Usually the items are not on sale, they merely look "hot" or such a "great deal" that the retailer cannot keep the merchandise in stock.

- For the same reason, handwritten (as long as they are legible) signs create the impression of recently lowered prices (i.e., there has not been time to get the printed signs). Thus, even though they do not always look great, handwritten signs move the merchandise faster than standard printed signs.

Most consumers are likely to focus on a large central display.

- The point-of-purchase displays at the end of each supermarket aisle (known in the trade as *endcaps*) are usually the focus of customers' attention as they wheel their carts through the store. Thus, a smart retailer knows to follow the 25-25-50 rule.

Consumers are creatures of habit, and when something is out of place they become more sensitive to their environment.

- Every supermarket will make regularly scheduled display changes for staple items such as cake mixes, salad dressings, and cereals. They do not want to move the items to new locations because that may upset time-pressed customers. However, by changing shelf displays of these staples, the grocer draws the attention of the customer, thereby increasing the chances of an impulse sale.

There is a little bit of greed in every one of us.

- Supermarket managers may put a limit on the purchase of a sale item, by advertising "Limit 4 to a Customer." Not only will consumers think that the limit restrictions mean it's a great deal but also they will often buy the limit, even if they don't need that many.

- Another version of the above is the special "10 for x" where x is a whole dollar amount, such as 10 for $9, or 10 for $6. Many of these promotions are mix and match deals in which the customer can choose among several different items. In many cases, the new "sale" price is slightly higher than the typical sale price. Retailers have found that selling an item on sale at $0.79 each usually results in one sale. However, at 10 for $8, or even $9, many consumers will stock up and buy more than one unit.

- Similarly, many customers will get so excited by finding a great price on a staple like peanut butter that they will fail to notice that the item's complementary products—in this case, jelly and bread—may have had their prices increased.

Source: Based on insights provided Jim Lukens, Paul Adams, Zack Adcock, and Paul Easter.

endcap. The remaining 50 percent should be regular-priced seasonal or impulse merchandise. Retailers tend to violate this rule when manufacturers offer money for the right to set up their own displays. While the managers will gain a short-term profit by renting out most of their endcap space, they often destroy the long-term profits that a well-defined endcap policy generates.

Objectives of the Store Environment

The two primary objectives of creating the desired store image and increasing space productivity amount to a simple description of the three basic tasks of retailing described in Exhibit 12.3 on page 438:

- get customers into the store (*market image*);
- once customers are inside the store, convert them into customers buying merchandise (*space productivity*); and
- do this in the most efficient manner possible.

Getting customers into the store and getting them to purchase and doing this with efficiency is illustrated by the recent experience of a couple of menswear retailers. If you were to visit Lost Boys in Washington, D.C., you might first think it may be a bar catering to young professionals. After all, customers can be seen sipping beers and watching television programming on a giant flat-screen television. Kesner, an upscale men's store in New York's West Village, has a similar atmosphere and has a full bar located by the fitting rooms.

In both of these stores, the liquor and beer is free of charge. You might wonder how serving free drinks can be cost efficient? However, men do not like to shop; when they do shop, they do so hastily. Thus, creating a relaxing shopping atmosphere and becoming more at ease after a drink and casual conversation, the men purchase more clothing. Most retailers who have adopted this approach have found that the free liquor is cheaper than investing money in traditional advertising to build store traffic. Seldom does traditional media advertising work for men; when it does, they rush into the store and rush out with either nothing or a small purchase. Thus, this technique enhances the store image, builds store traffic, and creates additional sales transactions in a cost-efficient way.[5]

The retailer must constantly balance the first two elements of the model because they are sometimes at odds. After all, some customers may be attracted because they expect a nice, clean, uncluttered shop with low prices. However, store management realizes that low prices result in high inventory turnover, and high turnover often means a congested shopping environment. Remember the example from Chapter 11's "Inside Story" box about the congestion that results when retailers have major sales on Black Friday and people start to line up hours beforehand. This problem, of course, is not as severe with low prices in general but it does present an interesting paradox. Increased store traffic is good because traffic leads to more sales and hence profitability, but if store traffic is too high the store becomes congested and the store image deteriorates.

David Young-Wolff/PhotoEdit

Since a face-out presentation takes up more space than a spine-out, discounters, and other retailers relying on high inventory turnover rates, find it is practical to use spine-outs on a high percentage of the total merchandise on the floor.

Developing a Store Image

The starting point in creating this image, of course, is the merchandise carried in the store, along with the retailer's promotional activities, customer service, cleanliness, and sales force. That the store image serves a critical role in the store selection process is best illustrated by the fact that in the supermarket industry overall cleanliness is the most important criterion in deciding where to shop. That is why many supermarkets today not only provide moist sanitary wipes for their customers but also run the shopping carts through a car-wash–type mist where a disinfecting peroxide solution is sprayed onto carts. This is to protect infants and young children from potential contamination due to contact with a shopping cart handle. The other important criteria for selecting a supermarket are low prices, accurate price scanning, pleasant clerks, clearly labeled prices, and well-stocked shelves.

To further illustrate the importance of store image, consider for a moment the words 7-*Eleven*. For most people, these words represent more than just two numbers. Together, they form the name of one of the most familiar retailers, the worldwide chain with more than 27,000 convenience stores.

The thoughts and emotions this logo evokes in customers constitute 7-Eleven's store image. Regardless of what its managers would like its market image to be, regardless of what image they have tried to create, the store's actual image exists only in the heads and hearts of consumers. Many factors influence that image.

First, the name itself has a great influence. If the stores were called "8-Twelve," we all might have a different image in our heads. The name was created in 1946 to stress the stores' operating hours, 7 A.M. to 11 P.M. every day, then unheard of in retailing.[6] The rhythm and rhyme of *seven* and *eleven* allow the name to roll easily off the tongue and be memorable, even if the customer does not shoot craps. (In craps, a 7 or an 11 on the shooter's first roll is a winner.) The orange and green colors of the logo suggest quality. The storefront, historically a large black mansard roof, conveys a heavy, masculine appearance, and the windows plastered with price savings signs suggest a promotional environment. When you walk in the store, a buzzer warns clerks of entering shoppers, suggesting a concern about safety and theft. The smell of cheese nachos and the sight of sausages and hot dogs rolling around on the hot dogger create a certain atmosphere. Even the uniforms worn by the store clerks leave an impression, which joins all other impressions to create 7-Eleven's store image in our minds. The consumer's image of a store, therefore, is a combination of out-of-store factors—location (Chapter 7), advertising and publicity (Chapter 11), and the various services offered (Chapter 12)—plus the dozens of in-store variables perceived by the consumer.

In fact, 7-Eleven has conducted experiments to change its store image to that of a high-quality food-service provider. Managers have altered not only the merchandise mix but also such store variables as colors, layout, light levels, and aisle widths to affect the consumer's perception of a 7-Eleven store. The company continues to innovate with store design and recently transformed a dozen stores into Kwik-E-Marts, the fictional convenience stores of *The Simpsons* fame. The transformation was temporary and was part of a campaign to promote the opening of *The Simpsons Movie*.[7] This is why planning the store environment is so important to a retailer. Although advertising and other promotional activities are important in establishing a desired store image, the store itself makes the most significant and lasting impression on our collective consciousness, and it is here that the retailer must focus great energy. Today, McDonald's, after 30 years without a major design overhaul, is tempting fate by testing a change in its appearance. The redesign (comfortable armchairs, cool hanging lights, funky graphics, photos on the walls, and Wi-Fi access) is risky and has many franchisees up in arms over the high costs of a makeover, which in some cases can exceed $1 million. A big part of the remodeling cost is the elimination of the bright red obtrusive roofline and an obtrusive set of highly vertical golden arches that, to virtually all customers and franchisees, make up the hallmark of a McDonald's restaurant. In its place is a new, gently curving golden arch feature over a flat roof. Critics argue customers will not be able to identify the restaurants and that they will look too much like Wendy's, Subway, and other fast-food restaurants. However, company officials believe the overhaul is needed to conform to its revamped menu of healthier items aimed at attracting a new breed of customer. After all, McDonald's seeks to be a "forever young" brand, and the new layout is another way of delivering on that promise.[8] Layout makeovers are complicated by the knowledge that consumers are extremely fickle, able to change their feelings about retailers at any time for little substantive reason, and the fact that today there are more stores than ever vying for limited consumer dollars. It is not surprising that image engineering—the ability to create and change a store's image—becomes more important every day for a retailer's survival.

Increasing Space Productivity

The store's image attracts customers. However, when customers are visiting the store or its website, the retailer must also convince them to make a purchase. Therefore, a store must increase its space productivity, a goal that is summarized in a simple but powerful truism in retailing: *The more merchandise customers are exposed to that is presented in an orderly manner, the more they tend to buy.* The typical shopper in a department store goes into only two or three shopping areas per trip. By carefully planning the store environment, the retailer can encourage customers to flow through the entire store—or at least through more shopping areas—and see a wider variety of merchandise. As a general rule of thumb, customers need to pass within four feet of the merchandise for it to capture their attention and cause them to slow down. Of course, with poor merchandise display even passing within four feet will not cause the customer to pause and look at the merchandise. The proper use of in-store advertising and displays will let the customer know what's happening in other departments and encourage a visit to those areas. Remember the discussion in the previous chapter of J.P. Morgan remodeling the 900 Washington Mutual branches? Morgan was attempting to expose customers to more bank products. Today, one of the major factors behind the success of Wells Fargo Bank is that it sells each customer an average of 5.6 products, twice as many as rival banks do.[9] Conversely, however, the retailer does not want to have merchandise pushed into every conceivable nook and cranny of the store so that customers cannot get to it. This is especially true today because retailers have noted the need to scale back on their merchandise assortments so that customers could more easily navigate the aisles. This is because today's shoppers now spend 20 percent more time going up and down an aisle as they did just a few years ago. Today, due to the economic slowdown, consumers want to read labels carefully and compare price versus need.[10] As a result, many retailers are now focusing more attention on in-store marketing. This is based on the theory that marketing dollars spent inside the store—in the form of store design, merchandise presentation, visual displays, and in-store promotions—should lead to significantly greater sales and profit increases than marketing dollars spent on advertising and other out-of-store vehicles such as public relations and promotions. After all, it is easier and more cost effective to get a consumer who is already in your store to buy more merchandise than planned than to persuade a new consumer to come into your store.

One factor that detracts from space productivity is shrinkage, or the loss of merchandise through theft, loss, and damage, which was discussed in Chapter 9. It is called **shrinkage** because retailers usually do not know what happened to the missing items, only that the inventory level in the store has somehow shrunk. Even stores that move customers through the entire space and effectively use in-store marketing techniques to maximize sales can fall victim to high shrinkage. Remember, when a store sells an item for $1.29, it earns only a small percentage of that sale, perhaps ranging from 15 cents to 60 cents. When that item is stolen, lost, or damaged, however, the store loses the cost of that $1.29 item—for example, 69 cents—and this loss is deducted from the store's overall profit. Shrinkage ranges from 1 percent to 4 percent of retail sales. Although this may seem like a small number, consider that after-tax profit for many retailers' is little more than 4 percent, so high shrinkage alone can make the difference between a profit and a loss. Also, because of the high cost of theft, retailers are employing a greater number of security guards and loss-control specialists. This adds to their costs and results in higher prices for legitimate customers. For this reason, all 50 states have passed special laws that they call "civil recovery" that enable retailers to seek more from the shoplifter than the return of the price of the item but also additional charges often up to three times the cost of the item or more to help recover the costs of theft protection.[11]

To enhance space productivity, retailers today must incorporate planning, merchandise presentation, and design strategies that minimize shrinkage by avoiding displaying merchandise in hidden areas of the store. They should also seek to reduce the number of times merchandise must be moved, during which time damage and loss can occur.

shrinkage
Represents merchandise that cannot be accounted for due to theft, loss, or damage.

LO 2 Store Planning

What is involved in store planning?

Planning an effective retail store resembles planning an effective piece of writing, and moving through a store as a customer is similar to reading an article or a chapter in a book. The merchandise, like text, is there for you to review, understand, and consume. But just as a book needs more than words to make sense, a store needs more than merchandise to be shopable.

The store's layout and design can be compared to the organization of chapters, sections, and subsections in this book. Grouping the words and thoughts into mental "chunks" makes the book easier to digest and understand. Unless a store specializes in only one product type—for example, candles—it would be impossible to shop if that store were not broken into departments and categories. The books would be mixed in with the shovels, the DVDs would be found among the garden plants, and you wouldn't know where to begin.

Signs and graphics are similar to the headings and punctuation, which give cues to understanding the organization of both a book and the merchandise in a store. Without headings and subheadings, this chapter would be a stream of words, very difficult and, worse, boring to read and understand. Similarly, without signs, a store would seem like an endless sea of racks and merchandise, annoying to understand and shop.

Finally, the photos, exhibits, charts, and boxes in this book are the retail equivalent of the visual displays and focal points, where merchandise is pulled off the shelf or racks and displayed in theatrical vignettes. Successful retailers use these settings to break up the store space, illustrate merchandise opportunities in the store, and visually demonstrate how certain merchandise goes together or can work in the consumer's life. Like photos and exhibits in a book, these visual displays elaborate on the text, or the bulk of merchandise on the racks, to make statements.

Most important, a retail store and a piece of writing are very similar in the way they affect the consumer. Many writing coaches teach aspiring writers that each time an uncommon word is used or a punctuation mark is missing, the reader hits a "speed bump" in the writing and must mentally pause to consider what is meant. After hitting three speed bumps, the reader may conclude that the writing is too difficult to understand and quit reading.

The same is true in a retail store. All cues must work subliminally to organize the merchandise and guide shoppers effortlessly through the store. Each time shoppers become a bit confused as to where they are, where they need to go, how much an item costs, or where certain merchandise is, they become frustrated. The first or second instance may not even be consciously noticed, but shoppers may quickly become frustrated and walk out, concluding that the store is too hard to shop. Exhibit 13.2 is a list of warning signs that managers should look for, because each warning sign indicates a speed bump waiting to drive customers away from a store.

Most shoppers cannot consciously identify the elements of a good store, but they certainly know when these elements are missing. We have all experienced the feeling that a store seems to "really have it together"—for example, the Apple Store, Niketown, IKEA, REI, and Bass Pro Shops Outdoor World. These exemplary stores are easy to shop, fun, and exciting; the merchandise is easy to understand; the associates seem friendly. You conclude that these stores are a great place to shop, and with any luck you are completely oblivious to the thousands of little details that have guided you through the shopping experience.

In retailing, the term **floor plan** indicates where merchandise and customer-service departments are located, how customers circulate through the store, and how much space is dedicated to each department. The floor plan, which is based around the predicted demands of the store's targeted customer, serves as the backbone of the store and is the fundamental structure around which every other element of the store environment takes shape. Successful retailers, such as Walmart with its Retail Link, which was covered in Chapter 5's "What's New?" box, analyze their sales along with the demographics of the store's trading area when developing a floor plan. These retailers then structure the merchandise to the needs of each store. Thus, it is not uncommon for two Target or Best Buy stores in the same city to be different in both merchandise carried and in its presentation. This is called

floor plan
Is a schematic that shows where merchandise and customer service departments are located, how customers circulate through the store, and how much space is dedicated to each department.

Exhibit 13.2
These Warning Signs May Indicate a Space Problem

- Open spaces on the selling floor, even if the product is on hand
- Cluttered and disorganized aisles, hallways, and stockrooms
- Excessive time required to put away new receipts
- Insufficient staging space for large shipments of advertised products
- Sales associates continually required to leave the sales floor to locate additional merchandise
- Poor utilization of vertical space and excessive time required to retrieve products stored on high shelves
- Sales lag expectations for specific locations where space or fixtures are a known issue
- Off-site storage or multiple stockrooms required for a single commodity

microretailing
Occurs when a chain store retailer operating over a wide geographic area, usually nationally, tailors its merchandise and services in each store to the needs of the immediate trading area.

microretailing, and it means that each store's offerings are tailored to the trading area being served. As we mentioned earlier, Wi-Fi combined with GPS is allowing retailers to better understand how to merchandise their stores based on actual store traffic within each store.

In addition, successful retailers place merchandise in key strategic locations. For example, H.E.B. Grocery Company places the jelly next to the peanut butter, facial tissues next to the cold medicines, and chocolate syrup next to the ice cream. (Next time you are in a supermarket, see if it locates such items together.) Other profitable retailers know that toys and movies are kid magnets and thus display snacks right next to them. Another simple rule to follow is to think of the age of the consumer. For example, a retailer should never put a child's toy on the top shelf where kids can't reach it or denture cream on the bottom shelf where seniors can't easily bend down and get it. Therefore, the store's layout and design, including merchandise location, must be carefully planned to meet the retailer's merchandising goals, make the store easy to understand and shop, and allow merchandise to be effectively presented. In the case of McDonald's new store concept, which was discussed earlier, the dining area is now separated into three sections with distinct personalities and objectives. In the "linger" zone are Wi-Fi connections, sofas, and armchairs that allow young adults to linger and socialize or hang out. In the "grab and go" zone are barstools and tall counters for customers to eat alone while they watch the news or weather or sports on plasma TV's. Finally, in the "flexible" zone, families have booths with flexible seating. Incidentally, each of the three zones has different music piped to it.[12]

Merchandise location, or what is often referred to as *adjacencies* in the retail trade, can be especially frustrating for certain customers because they don't fit neatly into predetermined merchandise categories. Consider, for example, the earlier discussion on petite clothing. The importance of merchandise adjacency can also be observed the next time you visit a supermarket. Notice, for instance, that some products are displayed by keeping all the brands from one manufacturer together (cereals, frozen pizzas, and salad dressings) while other products are grouped by category (canned vegetables and fruit, bars of soap, and baking aids such as flour and sugar).[13]

It is interesting to note that some retail innovations have actually broken established retail trade practices when it comes to merchandise adjacencies. One notable example of this is the warehouse club. Costco, for example, uses crazy product positioning as part of its selling formula. The retailer has found that putting toothpaste next to golf clubs and cereals next to computer tables not only increases impulse purchasing but provides customers with a "thrill-of-the-hunt" psychological lift when they find something.[14] Such positioning tends to make customers more alert as to what is available, and retailers know that 30 percent to 50 percent of all bricks-and-mortar purchases are impulse buys.[15] Perhaps a more notable example is Ethan Allen, which broke all of the rules in terms of the traditional merchandise adjacencies in furniture retailing. The established practice was to group all couches in one corner, all tables in another corner, all beds in another corner, and so on. Ethan Allen changed all of this by presenting complete rooms of furniture around a theme, which enabled shoppers to visualize how furniture would look in their own homes. Not only did the store image of the furniture store improve but also shoppers found themselves purchasing furniture items they had not planned because they could see how various pieces of furniture could be integrated into their homes.

stack-outs
Are pallets of merchandise set out on the floor in front of the main shelves.

Almost as important as merchandise adjacencies is the reduction of **stack-outs**, those pallets of merchandise set on the floor in front of the main shelves. Although stack-outs may improve the short-run sales of the featured product, their negative impact may offset these marginal sales. As Robert Kahn, the late editor of *Retailing Today* and highly regarded retail consultant, pointed out many times in his newsletter, when there is a stack-out and the customer does not have a specific need on that aisle, then the customer will skip that aisle. This phenomenon is known in retailing as the dreaded "butt-brush," which holds that the likelihood of a woman being converted from a browser to a buyer is inversely proportional to the likelihood of her being brushed on her backside while she is examining merchandise.[16] Thus, any item that requires extensive examination by a woman should never be placed in a narrow aisle. Also, since 30 percent to 50 percent of all purchases are impulse, the retailer may actually lose sales when shoppers ignore certain aisles, especially when the product being considered requires some type of examination or inspection. This is especially true of electronic products such as televisions and computers; retailers don't seem to realize that too many merchandise items stuffed onto shelves, display tables, and walls can create congestion and prevent customers from an engaging shopping experience, and thus sales will falter.

Allocating Space

The starting point for developing a floor plan is analyzing how the available store space, usually measured in square footage, should be allocated to various departments. This allocation can be based on mathematical calculation of the returns generated by different types of merchandise. However, before describing this process, we must understand the various types of space in the store.

Types of Space Needed

Shoppers are most familiar with the sales floor, but this is not the only element in a retail store with which the planner must contend. There are five basic types of space needs in a store: (1) back room; (2) office and other functional spaces; (3) aisles, service areas, and other nonselling areas of the main sales floor; (4) wall merchandise space; and (5) floor merchandise space. The retailer must balance the quest for greater density of merchandise presentation with the shopability and functionality of the store. Since space is the retailer's ultimate scarce resource, rarely can the retailer fully achieve all of its desired goals. Rather, most retailers find themselves compromising on one or more dimensions, carefully weighing priorities, strategies, and special constraints. In reviewing each of these space categories, keep in mind that the overall goal is to make the largest possible portion of the space available to hold merchandise and be shopable.

Back Room. To operate virtually any type of retail store, some space is required as back room, which includes the receiving area to process arriving merchandise and the stockroom to store surplus merchandise. The percentage of space dedicated to the back room varies greatly, depending on the type of retailer, but the amount of space is shrinking for all types. Historically, backroom percentages have ranged from nearly 50 percent in some department stores to as little as 10 percent in some small specialty and convenience stores. General merchandise stores have historically dedicated about 15 percent to 20 percent of their store space to the back room. The need to squeeze more sales out of expensive retail space, coupled with new distribution methods allowing smaller, more frequent merchandise deliveries from suppliers (called *quick response inventory* or *efficient consumer response*, depending on the industry involved), has allowed retailers to shrink their back rooms, with department stores cutting back to about 20 percent, and others reducing theirs to 5 percent or even less.

Some recent retail formats, such as warehouse clubs, have receiving areas but virtually no backroom stock capacity. In these stores, the store fixtures are usually large warehouse racks that carry shopable inventory at reachable heights (up to 84 inches) and large pallets or cartons of excess inventory at higher levels. These racks can be as tall as 15 feet.

By using this strategy, warehouse clubs are taking advantage not only of the width and depth of the store but also the height. In other words, while retailers pay expensive rents for their store space, as measured in *square* footage, the store and the merchandise can be stacked as high as possible at little additional cost, using the *cubic* footage of the store. The ability of shoppers to reach does limit the height at which *shopable* merchandise can be stacked, but it does not limit the use of this high space to carry excess inventory. The same inventory carried in the back room would require additional square footage, causing either higher rent or reducing the amount of shopable space. Essentially, the sales floor doubles as the back room. This stocking method visually creates a dramatic low-cost image in the store, which can be advantageous to value-oriented retailers but detrimental to fashion or high-end retailers. This can be observed in how new-car dealers merchandise their inventory in their showrooms and on their car lots. Whereas a Chevrolet, Ford, or Honda dealer may pack its showroom and car lot with hundreds of cars all very close together, a high-end dealer selling Jaguar, Porsche, or Ferrari will have only a sampling of cars in the showroom that are elegantly displayed as almost pieces of art or jewelry, with relatively few models on the car lot.

Offices and Other Functional Spaces.   Every store must contain a certain amount of office and other functional space. This often includes a break room for associates, a training room, offices for the store manager and assistant managers, a cash office, bathroom facilities for both customers and employees, and perhaps other areas. Though necessary, the location of such functional spaces receives a lower priority than the location of the sales floor and stockroom. Often they are located on mezzanines over the front of the store or over the back stockroom, or in side spaces too small to be stockrooms.

Aisles, Service Areas, and Other Nonselling Areas.   Even on the main sales floor, some space must be given up to nonselling functions, the most obvious of which is moving shoppers through the store. The retailer's first step, particularly in larger stores, is to create main aisles through which shoppers will flow on their way through the store and secondary aisles that draw customers back into the merchandise. These aisles must be large enough to accommodate peak crowds, and in bigger stores they may be as wide as 15 feet. The amount of space dedicated to aisles can be significant. For instance, a 15-foot aisle running around the perimeter of an 80,000 square-foot store (the size of a typical discount store) may consume 12,000 square feet, or 15 percent of the entire space! Retailers also need to pay particular attention to aisle width for disabled persons, and this is especially true in terms of checkout lanes where the width of accessible checkout aisles must be at least 36 inches wide for lengths greater than 24 inches long and at least 32 inches wide for lengths 24 inches or less. Also depending on the number of checkout aisles a store has, a certain number must be handicapped accessible.[17] In addition, counter height cannot exceed 36 inches. There are many other guidelines for store design for the handicapped or disabled, and some are unique to certain lines of retail such as restaurants and self-service gasoline stations.[18] You can also obtain detailed information on the various legal aspects of the American Disabilities Act at www.ada.gov.

In addition to aisles, space must be given to dressing rooms, layaway areas, service desks, and other customer-service facilities that cannot be merchandised. While the retailer always attempts to minimize the amount of nonmerchandisable space, customer service is an equally important part of a store and should not be shortchanged.

Wall Merchandise Space.   The walls are one of the most important elements of a retail store. They serve as fixtures holding tremendous amounts of merchandise as well as providing a visual backdrop for the merchandise on the floor. For example, many shoe stores are narrow at the entrance—sometimes less than 18 feet but usually 100 or 200 feet in depth. An effective wall display is to have the back wall lined from floor to ceiling with the particular type of shoe, such as athletic shoes, for which the store is known.

Floor Merchandise Space.   Finally, we come to the store space with which we as shoppers are most familiar—the floor merchandise space. Here many different types of fixtures are used to display a wide variety of merchandise. Generally speaking, retailers use bulk fixtures on the floor to carry large quantities of merchandise. But increasingly, retailers are realizing that the best goal is not to just cram the largest possible amount of merchandise on the floor but to attractively and effectively display the largest amount that customers can understand and shop. In many cases, less merchandise display is more dramatic and stimulates higher sales and thus more space productivity than more. Incidentally this also enables the inventory productivity as measured by gross margin return on inventory to be higher.

Space-Allocation Planning

To determine the most productive allocation of space, the retailer must first analyze the profitability and productivity of various categories of merchandise. According to one study, around 20 percent of the average retailer's inventory is either obsolete or not wanted by the retailer's target market.[19] Such a high percentage indicates the importance to retailers of analyzing the profitability and productivity of all merchandise.

There are several methods for measuring profitability and productivity. Regardless of the method used, the results must relate some type of output performance measure (e.g., net sales, net profit, or gross margin) to the amount of space used in the store in order to get a productivity figure to help determine the best allocation of the square footage. Two situations may cause a retailer to perform these tasks: revising the space allocation of an existing store and planning a new store.

Improving Space Productivity in Existing Stores.   A retailer that has been in business for some time can develop a sales history on which to evaluate merchandise performance, refine space allocations, and enhance space productivity. One easy measure to use is the **space productivity index**, which compares the percentage of the store's total gross margin dollars for a particular merchandise category to its percentage of space utilized. An index rating of 1.0 would be an ideal department size. If the index is greater than 1.0, then the product category is generating a larger percentage of the store's gross margin than the percentage of store space it is using, and the retailer should consider allocating additional space to this category. If the index falls below 1.0, then the product category is underperforming relative to other merchandise, and the retailer might consider reducing its space allocation. The merchandise-productivity analysis shown in Exhibit 13.3 indicates that in this

space productivity index
Is a ratio that compares the percentage of the store's total gross margin that a particular merchandise category generates to its percentage of total store selling space used.

Category	Total Sales	Sales as % of Total	Total Sq. Ft.	Sq. Ft. as % of Total	Sales per Sq. Ft.	Total G.M. $	G.M. $ as % of Total	Space Productivity Index
Softlines								
Juniors	259,645	3.9	1,602	2.9	162.08	211,497	4.57	1.58
Dresses	47,829	0.7	608	1.1	78.67	33,426	0.72	0.66
Misses	512,458	7.7	3,702	6.7	138.43	429,403	9.29	1.39
Womens	170,819	2.6	1,934	3.5	88.33	148,899	3.22	0.92
Boys	184,485	2.8	2,542	4.6	72.58	144,866	3.13	0.68
Mens	751,604	11.3	3,591	6.5	209.30	603,330	13.05	2.01
Infants	204,983	3.1	1,658	3.0	123.63	142,545	3.08	1.03
Toddlers	47,829	0.7	497	0.9	96.24	43,261	0.94	1.04
Girls	191,318	2.9	2,542	4.6	75.27	157,573	3.41	0.74
Lingerie	273,311	4.1	2,431	4.4	112.43	262,548	5.68	1.29
Accessories	245,980	3.7	1,602	2.9	153.55	238,735	5.16	1.78
Jewelry	129,823	1.9	829	1.5	156.60	123,484	2.67	1.78
Total Softlines	3,020,084	45.2	23,537	42.6	128.31	2,539,566	54.92	1.29
Hardlines								
Domestics	498,792	7.5	4,531	8.2	110.08	407,745	8.82	1.08
HBA	464,628	7.0	1,989	3.6	233.60	153,153	3.31	0.92
Housewares	457,795	6.8	3,591	6.5	127.48	254,979	5.51	0.85
Cosmetics	75,160	1.1	608	1.1	123.62	55,913	1.21	1.00
Tobacco	140,187	2.1	221	0.4	634.33	37,349	0.81	2.02
Candy	144,944	2.2	387	0.7	374.53	88,179	1.91	2.72
Sporting Goods	184,485	2.8	2,652	4.8	69.56	129,948	2.81	0.59
Stationery	307,475	4.6	2,763	5.0	111.28	254,150	5.50	1.10
Furniture	75,160	1.1	1,547	2.8	48.58	60,333	1.30	0.47
Home Entertainment	601,284	9.0	2,265	4.1	265.47	255,973	5.54	1.35
Toys	300,642	4.5	2,431	4.4	123.67	143,429	3.10	0.70
Seasonal	145,333	2.2	2,652	4.8	54.80	90,168	1.95	0.41
Hardware/Paint	163,986	2.5	2,100	3.8	78.09	111,274	2.41	0.63
Pet Supplies	13,666	0.2	55	0.1	248.47	13,094	0.28	2.83
Auto Accessories	81,993	1.2	1,271	2.3	64.51	29,227	0.63	0.27
Total Hardlines	3,655,480	54.8	29,061	52.6	125.79	2,084,914	45.08	0.86
Nonselling	—	—	2,652	4.8	—	—	—	—
Total Scores	6,675,564	100.0	55,250	100.0		4,624,480	100.00	1.00

Exhibit 13.3

Merchandise Productivity Analysis

store, softlines (apparel and apparel accessories) categories, with an index of 1.29, are performing very well and perhaps should be given more space. On the other hand, hardlines (nonapparel products), with an index of 0.86, are underperforming and should be considered for downsizing.

Of course, as with all financial analysis, the space-productivity index is simply a tool to help management make decisions, not a decision-making formula. Even though a certain category may have a low index, senior management may retain its full space because a new buyer has just been hired or because the category is an important image builder. A high-index category might not be given more space if management expects a hot fashion trend to cool off soon and believes the space-productivity index for that category will drop accordingly. Also, the space-productivity indexes can only be computed on merchandise the retailer has a history of selling. For this reason, it does not help to reveal that a hardware store may find it profitable to stock bottled water and soda or that a supermarket may find it profitable to devote space to a branch bank or beauty salon.

Space Allocations for a New Store.   When a retailer is creating a new store format, no productivity and profitability data are available on which to base the allocation of space. In these situations, the retailer bases space allocation on industry standards, previous experience with similar formats, or, more frequently, the space required to carry the number of items specified by the buyers. Kroger, for example, used information obtained from existing stores to revamp its beverage section at new locations. In its newer stores, one side of a 48-foot-long aisle was committed to bottled waters and new energy drinks—some 150 different types. At the same time, Kroger reduced the space normally allocated for traditional colas.

Once a detailed assortment plan has been created, typical stock levels are estimated based on minimum and maximum quantities. The retailer can then determine the amount of shelf space required to carry this merchandise. By determining the space for each item and then for each category and department, the retailer can develop the floor plan for the store. As you can imagine, optimizing a store's space is a grueling process.

Robert Kahn, who was also a member of Walmart's board of directors, once explained to Sam Walton that one of the problems with retailers was that they thought the best way to get higher sales per square foot (which they recognized was an important factor in store profitability, since higher sales would reduce operating expenses as a percentage of sales) was to run more ads and add more merchandise displays. Thus, retailers at the time reduced their aisle space and stacked the merchandise so high that many customers either could not reach the top or were afraid to touch the displays.[20]

Kahn, however, had his own ideas about customer behavior in the store and explained that there was a better formula for higher sales per square foot:

$$\text{Sales per square foot} = f\,[(\text{Number of customers}) \times (\text{Length of time they spend in the store})]$$

Therefore, according to Kahn's theory, retailers should concentrate on the time customers spend browsing and experiencing the store (this doesn't include the dwell time of waiting in line to check out), not on how much merchandise they are exposed to. Based on this concept, Kahn outlined four things that Walmart should do:

1. Ensure that in every aisle, a customer with a cart can comfortably pass another customer with a cart without having to ask that customer to move.

2. Make the restrooms the best in town so that a customer will never leave the store and rush home to use the bathroom.

3. Put at least one bench in each store, in the alcove at the front door. When Walmart opened the first American hypermarket, discussed in the chapter's "Global Retailing" box, Kahn went to the grand opening. Afterward, he kiddingly told Sam to put 10 to 12 benches inside each hypermarket and have a vendor sponsor (pay for) each bench. Sam Walton thought this was a dumb

idea because as he told Kahn "if they (the customers) are sitting, they ain't buying."

4. In all large stores, install a coffee stand catty-corner from the snack bar so that customers can recharge themselves in order to spend more time and money shopping.

All these ideas seemed to agree with Sam Walton's concept that a retailer was a failure if, after getting customers to come into the store, the retailer did not do everything possible to satisfy all their needs and overcome their desire to go elsewhere for merchandise.

Global Retailing

Hypermarkets: A Retailing Lesson

The hypermarket is a retailing format that first integrated a supermarket with a department store. At 250,000 square feet, it is one and a half times larger than the traditional 140,000- to 160,000-square-foot supercenter. These enormous retail outlets, which often carry more than 200,000 SKUs, are able to provide a seemingly endless array of products from apparel to electronics to fresh groceries in one stop. The first hypermarket, located near Paris, France, was opened in 1962 by Carrefour.

The original idea behind this format was to offer a wide variety of products in one location, thereby lowering operating costs and passing the savings along to consumers. Consumers would be offered the convenience of a one-stop, self-service shopping area with weather protection and adequate parking. In the beginning, European hypermarkets were typically located on the edge of town, near major access roads and residential areas so that customers could reach the facility without spending time commuting. In fact, the name *Carrefour* means crossroads, which is where the early Carrefour Hypermarkets are ideally located. Prior to hypermarkets, European consumers had to travel to larger metropolitan areas to have convenient, one-stop access to all their shopping needs.

Soon after their introduction, European lawmakers became skeptical of hypermarkets, especially their effect on small retail businesses. Therefore, in parts of Europe, legal statutes limiting their development were passed. Still, despite these regulations, today the number of hypermarkets continues to increase slightly (0.6% per year). Also impacting their growth in Western Europe is the demographic change toward smaller households. Thus, while hypermarkets continue to appeal to multiperson households, they don't offer the same attraction for single-person households, the most rapidly growing market segment.

Given the restrictive regulatory climate and the demographic changes in Western Europe, the hypermarket format sought new locales. Central and Southern European consumer markets provided great opportunities since these nations were relatively new to free-market economies and had little experience with modern retail formats. Former Communist-bloc countries such as the Czech Republic, Hungary, Poland, and Slovakia were particularly attractive to the hypermarket chains. The dynamically growing countries in Central and South America were also receptive to the hypermarket.

However, despite the success of the hypermarket in Europe and Central and South America, it didn't meet the same level of success in U.S. markets. In 1987, Walmart introduced its first Hypermart USA, with 220,000 square feet, in Garland, Texas, and soon expanded to six other locations. While the U.S. hypermarkets were similar to the European model, with restaurants, full-scale grocery sections, and general merchandise, they never achieved consumer acceptance. Whether the downfall of hypermarkets was caused by their sheer size (stockers wore roller skates to move around the store quickly) or the lack of excitement these warehouse-type stores provided is still open to debate. However, Walmart immediately recognized its mistake and scaled down the format into our present-day supercenters.

Hypermarkets illustrate the important lesson that not every form of retail presentation can be easily transferred from country to country. Rather, in order to be successful, retailers must adapt their marketing strategies to fit the specific consumer markets they enter. Despite the current endless discussion of "global villages," it is evident that a single, uniform marketing strategy cannot be successfully exported from one country to another.

Source: Prepared by Professor Deborah Whitten, University of Houston-Downtown.

As an experiment, Walmart built 10 new 85,000-square-foot stores and 10 new 115,000-square-foot versions. The stores had identical amounts of fixtures and merchandise. The larger stores used the extra 30,000 square feet for wider aisles and extra space at the increased number of checkouts (obviously, the time spent in the store was to reflect shopping or browsing time and *not* the dwell time spent waiting to check out) and to project an open, friendlier image. Also, the new restrooms, which were checked every two hours for cleanliness, had tile, not cement, floors; diaper-changing shelves in both the men's and women's restrooms; and easy-to-clean vinyl-covered walls. Eight to 10 benches were placed in the main aisles. However, Walmart dropped Kahn's coffee bar idea.

The first indication of the success of the larger store was that its parking lots were always full because shoppers were spending so much more time in the store. Sales figures showed that the larger stores not only had higher sales but also were also producing higher sales per square foot of store space than the smaller stores despite all that "wasted" aisle space. Walmart did not know exactly what the customers were doing in these larger stores, just that they were spending more time and money. As a result, Walmart went with the larger store model and increased the parking spaces from five to six per 1,000 square feet of store space. However, the benches were dropped because, as mentioned earlier, Sam felt that if the customers were sitting, they weren't buying.

Kahn used the experience as the basis in 1998 for his work as an expert witness supporting a suit by two disabled individuals under the Americans with Disabilities Act (ADA). The case involved R. H. Macy Company, which purchased an O'Connor, Moffat & Co. store in San Francisco during the 1940s. Despite three expansions, the store still had inadequately sized aisles. Macy's, along with the California Retailers Association and its own expert witnesses, claimed, "It's pretty basic in retail. Inventory per square foot drives sales per square foot, which drives profit." Kahn used the Walmart experience to show that a "reduction in nonaisle space permitted greater access to merchandise, which in turn leads to an increase in sales. If Macy's was correct, why didn't all retailers eliminate all aisles and stack merchandise to the ceiling to maximize profit?"[21] While this case was settled out of court, five years later a California court ruled that the now-bankrupt Mervyn's department store chain didn't have to expand its aisles to ease shopping for disabled customers because Mervyn's would lose $30 million a year in profits due to remodeling expenses, causing the company to shut down some of its 126 California operations.[22] Despite the rather general guidelines of the ADA, it is important that retailers do not lose sight of the fact that 21 percent of the U.S. population has some type of disability. To put this in perspective, this is higher than the percentage of Hispanics in the United States. The disabled represent more than $175 billion in annual discretionary spending, which makes them a larger buying group than tweens (8- to 14-year-olds). Clearly, the disabled customer is an important and valuable market segment. Today, profitable retailers need to understand the relationship between "the store needs and objectives and those of disabled customers."[23] This is especially important with the aging of the population since older customers have more physical disabilities. However, these older disabled individuals still want to eat out, travel, visit museums and other attractions, and shop for themselves and their grandchildren.

Planograms.   After retailers have allocated space for all of their departments, they then decide how and where retail products should be displayed on the store shelves. This is accomplished by using a planogram. A **planogram**, which was first introduced in Chapter 9, is graphic schematic which shows the precise location of every

planogram
Is a schematic that illustrates how and where a retailer's merchandise should be displayed on the shelf in order to increase customer purchases.

SKU on a shelf or other merchandise display. This schematic points out not only the location of the item but also the desired quantity, including the number of facings and the item's *adjacencies*, or what products it should be displayed alongside. A planogram is designed to allow the retailer to increase space productivity by taking into account inventory turnover, space and inventory investment requirements, and gross margins of the SKUs. Incidentally, one of the first assignments many college graduates have when they go to work for consumer packaged goods companies is to call on retailers and to persuade them to follow the manufacturer's suggested planogram. To create an effective planogram, the developer, which could be the retailer, the manufacturer, or both working together, needs not only to be creative but also to understand the financial aspects of merchandising performance, which was covered in Chapter 8, Chapter 9, and Chapter 10. The planogram developer should review sales history on a continual basis to see if pricing, promotion, or logistical changes need to be made. At the end of each season, both the retailer and vendor will conduct a formal planogram review to determine the performance of all stock items. Those that don't perform as planned may be discontinued or be marked down. Both decisions will impact the retailer's future merchandise budget. Also, if a product is dropped, space is then available for a new item.

Historically, planograms were developed by manufacturers to help persuade retailers where and how to display their products. Today, however, planogram software is the preferred method for space planning. Two of the most popular software programs are the Apollo space-management program, which is marketed by IRI; and Spaceman, which is marketed by ACNielsen. Both IRI and Nielsen specialize in collecting information on product movement at retail and thus are in an excellent position to be objective and scientific in the development of planograms for retailers.

Circulation

The circulation pattern not only ensures efficient movement of large numbers of shoppers through the store, exposing them to more merchandise, but also determines the character of the store. For instance, upon entering a Bass Pro Shops Outdoor World, the consumer views outdoor scenes through graphic and physical design elements. In addition, the store is usually connected to a lake or other natural feature. These scenes pull customers through the store and allow them to view more merchandise and often test the merchandise.[24] Similarly, Disney Stores are designed to communicate the fun and excitement of the theme parks and famous characters and to entice customers to walk to the back wall. After all, chances are good that when customers get to the back, they will return using a different route. This will expose them to more merchandise and increase the chance of a sale. Four basic types of layout are used today (free flow, grid, loop, and spine), each of which is described in the following discussion. Shoppers have been trained to associate certain circulation patterns with different types of stores, so in reading these descriptions, try to think of how they are used in the various stores you shop and the store image they evoke in your mind.

Free Flow

free-flow layout
Is a type of store layout in which fixtures and merchandise are grouped into free-flowing patterns on the sales floor.

The simplest type of store layout is a **free-flow layout** (Exhibit 13.4) in which fixtures and merchandise are grouped into free-flowing patterns on the sales floor. Customers are encouraged to flow freely through all the fixtures since there are usually no defined traffic patterns in the store. This type of layout works well in

The ability of disabled shoppers to navigate aisles and shop a store should be considered in all aspects of store design.

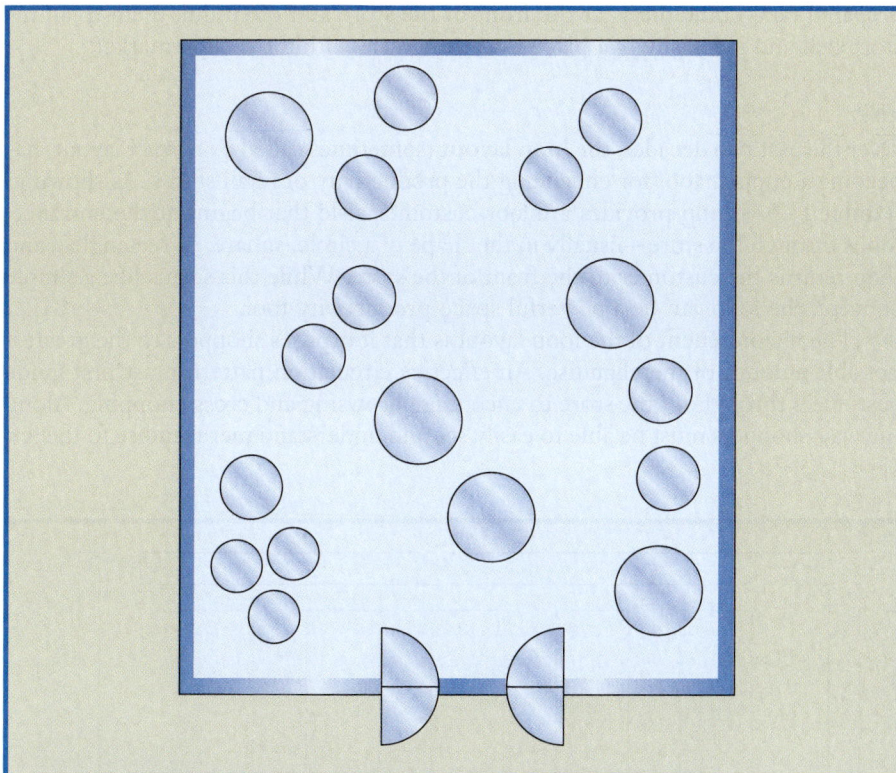

Exhibit 13.4
Free-Flow Layout

small stores, usually less than 5,000 square feet, in which customers wish to browse through all of the merchandise. Generally, the merchandise is of the same type, such as fashion apparel perhaps categorized only into tops and bottoms. If there is a greater variety of merchandise (for instance, men's and women's apparel, bedding, and health and beauty aids), a free-flow layout fails to provide cues as to where one department stops and another starts, confusing the shopper.

Grid

grid layout
Is a form of store layout in which the counters and fixtures are placed in long rows or "runs," usually at right angles, throughout the store.

Another traditional layout pattern is the **grid layout**, in which the counters and fixtures are placed in long rows or "runs," usually at right angles, throughout the store. In a grid layout (Exhibit 13.5), customers circulate up and down through the fixtures, and, in fact, the grid layout is often referred to as a *maze*. The most familiar examples of the grid layout are supermarkets and drugstores.

The grid is a both a historically and contemporarily popular shopping layout, best used in retail environments in which the majority of customers wish to shop the entire store. In supermarkets, for instance, many shoppers flow methodically up and down all the fixture runs, looking for everything they might need along the way. However, if the shopper wishes to find only several specific categories, the grid can be confusing and frustrating, because it is difficult to see over the fixtures to other merchandise (especially today because fixtures have become higher). For example, supermarkets move customers through the entire store by placing the meats, dairy goods, and other frequently purchased items at the rear of the store. However, retailers should employ this strategy carefully. Forcing customers in a hurry all the way to the back of a large store will frustrate many customers and lead some to go elsewhere for merchandise. For this reason, many supermarkets such as Albertson's, recognizing the high demand for home meal replacements, are placing these freshly prepared take-home meals at the front of the store and often link them to an in-store deli and increasingly a place to eat the meal within the supermarket.

Loop

loop layout
Is a type of store layout in which a major customer aisle begins at the entrance, loops through the store—usually in the shape of a circle, square, or rectangle—and then returns the customer to the front of the store.

Over the past two decades, the **loop layout** (sometimes called a *racetrack* layout) has become a popular tool for enhancing the productivity of retail stores. As shown in Exhibit 13.6, a loop provides a major customer aisle that begins at the entrance, loops through the store—usually in the shape of a circle, square, or rectangle—and then returns the customer to the front of the store. While this seems like a simple concept, the loop can be a powerful space-productivity tool.

The major benefit of the loop layout is that it exposes shoppers to the greatest possible amount of merchandise. An effective circulation pattern must first guide customers throughout the store to encourage browsing and cross-shopping. Along the way, shoppers must be able to easily see and understand merchandise to the left

Exhibit 13.5
Grid Layout

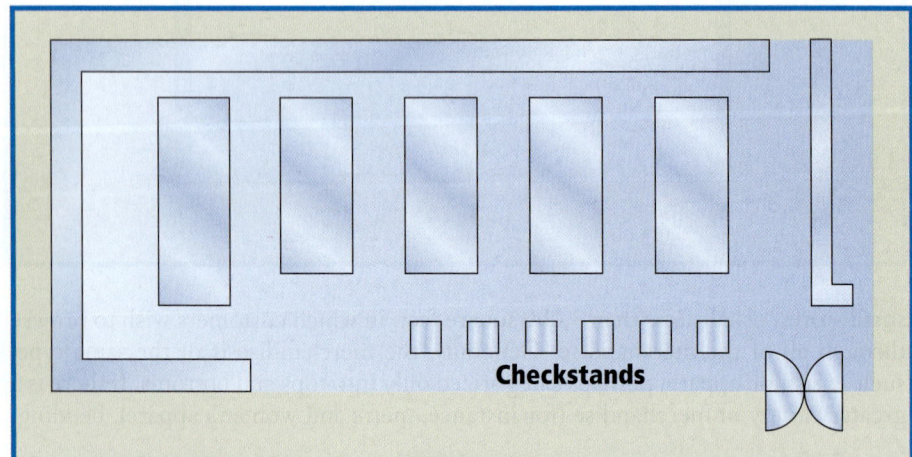

Checkstands

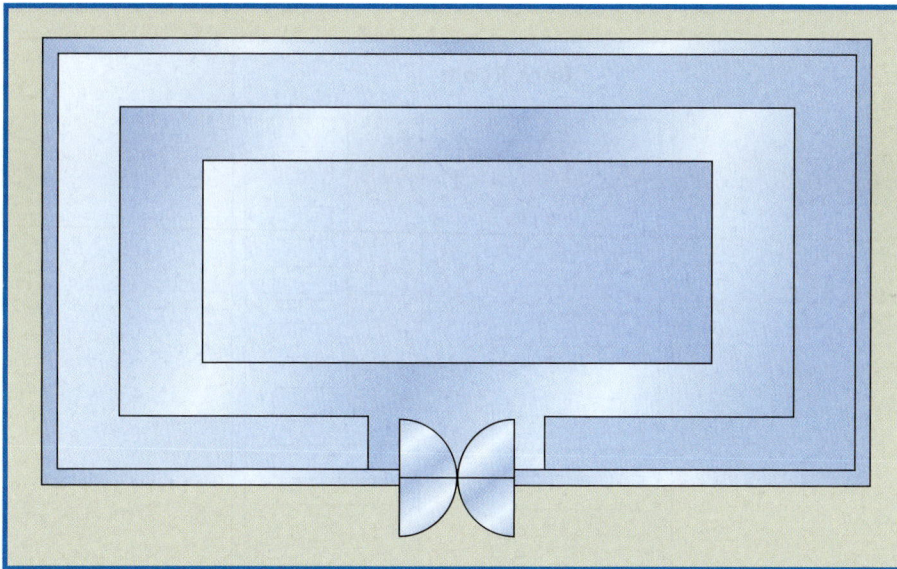

Exhibit 13.6
Loop Layout

and right, so ideally the main aisle should never stray more than 60 feet from any merchandise. The way to simultaneously accomplish these two goals is to create a main circulation loop that mirrors the configuration of the outside walls of the store and is never more than 60 feet from the outside wall. In larger stores, the interior island of the loop can itself be too large to easily see across, and internal walls may be created to shorten sightlines to merchandise. As traditional department stores such as JCPenney and Dillard's have gone to more self-service, they are increasingly employing the loop layout.

Spine

The **spine layout**, which is shown in Exhibit 13.7, is essentially a variation of the free-flow, grid, and loop layouts and combines the advantages of all three in certain circumstances. A spine layout is based on a single main aisle running from the front to the back of the store, transporting customers in both directions. On either side of this spine, each merchandise department branches off toward the back or side walls. Within these departments, either a free-flow or grid layout can be used, depending on the type of merchandise and fixtures in use. The spine is heavily used by medium-sized specialty stores, either hardlines or softlines, ranging in size from 2,000 to 10,000 square feet. Often, especially in fashion stores, the spine is subtly set off by a change in floor coloring or surface and is not perceived as an aisle, even though it functions as such.

Shrinkage Prevention

When planning a store's layout and design, the prevention of shrinkage due to theft, damage, and loss must be considered. This is especially important because $40 billion is lost annually by retailers to theft alone.[25] Some layouts will minimize vulnerability to shoplifters. One of the most important considerations when planning the layout is visibility of the merchandise. Most shoplifting takes place in fitting rooms, blind spots, aisles crowded with extra merchandise, or behind high displays. Fitting rooms, one of the most common scenes of the shoplifting crime, should be placed in visible areas that can be monitored by associates. Historically, display fixtures have been kept no higher than eye level to allow store associates to monitor customers in other aisles. Recently, mass merchandisers have found that increased

spine layout
Is a type of store layout in which a single main aisle runs from the front to the back of the store, transporting customers in both directions, and where on either side of this spine, merchandise departments using either a free-flow or grid pattern branch off toward the back side walls.

Exhibit 13.7
Spine Layout

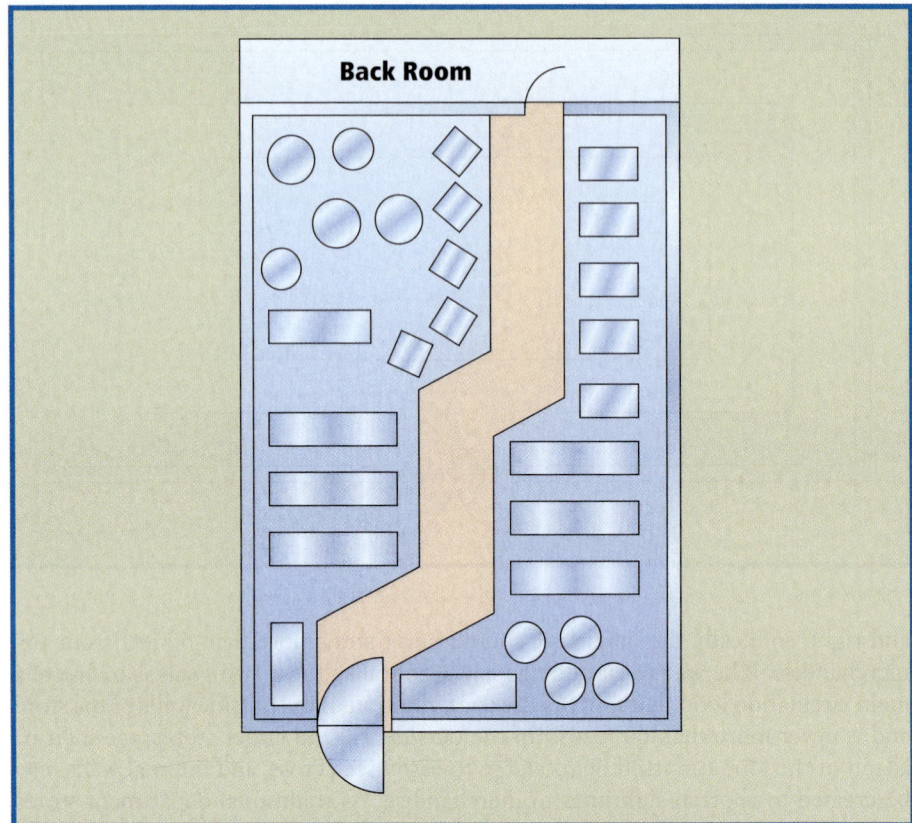

Exhibit 13.7
Spine Layout

sales from the greater merchandise intensity of higher fixtures outweigh the increase in shoplifting due to reduced visibility. This depends greatly on merchandise type, however. Expensive items that are easily placed into pockets and handbags, such as compact discs or drill bits in a hardware store, are high-theft items and are usually kept on low fixtures to discourage shoplifting. The manager's office and other security windows can be an excellent deterrent to shoplifting if they are placed in an obvious area above the sales floor level, where managers can easily see the entire store. Also large circular mirrors placed high and reflecting down an aisle allow employs to see customers in aisles—and shoplifters have learned to avoid these aisles. Electronic security systems, including sensor tags and video cameras, have become very popular and are usually in a highly visible location to serve as a deterrent.

LO 3

How are the various types of fixtures, merchandise-presentation methods and techniques, and the psychology of merchandise presentation used to increase the productivity of the sales floor?

Planning Fixtures and Merchandise Presentation

Retailing is theater, and in no area is that more true than in merchandise presentation. Recently, retailers have been increasing their emphasis on presentation as competition has grown and stores try to squeeze more sales out of existing square footage. There are two basic types of merchandise presentation: visual merchandising and on-shelf merchandising. In thinking of retailing as theater, visual merchandising is analogous to the stage props that set scenes and serve as backdrops.

In Chapter 3, the text discussed the behavioral differences between Gen Xers and baby boomers. Many retailers have begun to redesign their store layouts to reflect these differences. Probably nowhere is this more evident than in the way

Service Retailing

Stores and Hotels Have Identical Objectives and Fixturing Is a Key Success Factor

Three basic tasks of retailing that were described in Exhibit 12.3 and again on page 485 of this chapter are to:

- get customers into the store (market image);
- once they're inside the store, convert them into customers (space productivity); and
- do this in the most efficient manner possible.

For a hotel, the tasks are identical. Hoteliers need to get travelers or visitors to book rooms in their hotels. Once in their rooms, the task is to get them to dine in the hotel or their room and purchase from the gift shop and increasingly use other hotel services such as the hotel spa, yoga classes, or cooking classes.

New hotels face this challenge, but at least they can work with an architect, interior designers, and a host of other enterprises such as restaurant and spa consultants to design the ideal hotel for the intended target market. But what about the hotel that becomes dated and worn? This is actually a quite common problem because a hotel room that is used more than 60 percent of the available nights becomes quite worn, shabby, and generally unappealing after four or five years. Certainly, a modest remodeling with new paint, bedding, and carpet can remove these problems. In today's competitive hotel market, though, much more is needed. It is not unusual for a hotel to spend between $7,500 and $15,000 or more per room for a major hotel renovation. For a 1,000-room hotel, this is between $7.5 million and $15 million. Hoteliers have found that this type of expenditure is actually the most efficient way to increase a hotel's overall profit.

Even though hotels are in the service business, their fixtures or tangible evidence is very important. If, for example, you go to one of the online travel sites such as Expedia and look into booking a hotel, you will see that it will provide the ratings and remarks by 25 of the most recent visitors that stayed at the hotel and agreed to rate the hotel. A sampling of favorable comments include such statements as: "The room was spacious and nicely appointed"; "The room was spotless and comfortable"; "The room had one of the most comfortable beds I have slept in"; "The bathroom tub was large enough for me to relax in." These comments should not be surprising because Expedia rates hotels on four attributes: hotel service, hotel condition, room cleanliness, and room comfort. Thus, the tangible evidence or the hotel fixtures are 75 percent of the rating even though the hotel is in the service business. And you can be fairly assured that if a visitor is put in an unsanitary room where the bed was uncomfortable and the overall hotel looked to be in poor condition, the service of the personnel will be negatively affected. Recall also that the ratings are posted on Expedia's website on a 1 to 5 scale, with 5 reflecting higher performance. Thus, when a hotel has dated and worn fixtures, everyone knows about it and patronage declines.

Let's return to an examination of the space productivity of the hotel versus the retail store. As we have learned, the sales per square foot of retail space is a key metric of space productivity in retailing. For hotels, this equates to the annual revenue per hotel room or per bed. This measure can be broken down into two multiplicative components: the number of nights (days) per year the room is booked and the average price per night (day). Thus, if a hotel room is booked 60 percent of the time, it is booked 365 times 60 percent, or 219 nights annually. If we assume it is booked for an average price of $235 per night, then the total annual revenue is $29,565 ($219 \times 135). Consider now an investment of $10,000 per room to renovate the hotel. Where should the money be primarily spent (other than in the lobby and restaurants)? The same place you would spend it in your home. The bathroom is a high priority, as are new tile and granite countertops and perhaps a jetted tub. Then the bed, mattress, and linens would be a major expenditure to help ensure a comfortable and restful night. Of course, the room would get new window treatments, flooring, and mirrors and accent pieces. If the hotel can move the occupancy from 60 percent to 72 percent, and the average room night from $135 to $150, then the annual revenue per room rises to $39,420 (72 percent $\times 365 \times 150$), or approximately $10,000 more per year. Stated another way, the $10,000 investment per room pays off in 12 months, which is a very efficient way to increase the profitability of the hotel. In addition, the above illustration assumes there is no increase in dining in the hotel and use of other services. Therefore, even a slight improvement in those areas will accelerate the payback.

Just like with retail stores, the more upscale the image you desire, the more the investment in those special things that make a retail space or a hotel a special experience. For instance, Starwood is currently revamping Le Meridien, its European subsidiary, to be a European version of its W Hotels chain in the United States. Le Meridien had Le Labo design a unique fragrance for the hotel chain, and distinctive sounds fill the rooms, elevators, and lobbies with music composed by Henri Scars Struck. Le Meridien strives to be

(continued)

chic, cultured, and discovery oriented. Guests will be able to view art exhibits and attend lectures on a variety of topics such as coffee preparation. The aim is for guests to leave the hotel with a feeling that their lives have grown.

Another trend among the upscale hotels is the sale of their most popular fixtures to their guest through online stores. Westin became aware of this opportunity when it launched its Heavenly Bed in 1999. Quickly guests began to inquire if they could purchase the complete bed—box springs, mattress, sheets, pillow cases, and so on. Westin has now sold more

than 30,000 beds, 100,000 pillows, and 32,000 sheet sets. You might be interested in seeing the variety of fixtures that the leading upscale hotels sell. For Westin, see www.Westin-hotelsathome.com; for Ritz-Carlton, see www.ritzcarlton-shops.com; and for W hotels, see www.whotelsthestore.com.

Source: "Style Makeover at Hotel Aims to Dress Up the Guest Experience," *Advertising*, November 9, 2007: C5; "Hotels Want You to Take Stuff Home," *Los Angeles Times*, April 17, 2009; www.expedia.com; and authors' repeated travels and quests for hotels with superior service and amenities.

---

hotels have begun to repackage themselves to attract Gen-X travelers, as this chapter's "Service Retailing" box illustrates.

Merchandise presentation is a complex activity best learned on the retail floor. While this text will not attempt to teach the art and science of merchandise presentation, you should be familiar with a number of basic components of merchandise presentation and their potential impact on store image and sales, including fixture type and selection and certain techniques and methods of on-shelf merchandising.

on-shelf merchandising
Is the display of merchandise on counters, racks, shelves, and fixtures throughout the store.

On-shelf merchandising, which describes the merchandise that is displayed on and in counters, racks, shelves, and fixtures throughout the store, represents the stars on our theater stage. This is the merchandise that the shopper actually touches, tries on, examines, reads, understands, and, we hope, buys. Recall our earlier advice: "Shopping is a contact sport." Therefore, on-shelf merchandising must not only present the merchandise attractively but also display the merchandise so it is easy to understand and accessible. Further, it must be reasonably easy to maintain, with customers themselves able to replace merchandise so it is equally appealing to the next shopper. It must not be so overwhelming that the customer is afraid to touch the merchandise. After receiving more than 25,000 complaints a year regarding injuries from falling merchandise, Walmart has sought to reduce the height level of merchandise displays in every store. Despite the efforts of top management, many managers still falsely believe the best way to improve sales (and their year-end bonus) is to cram as much merchandise as possible into the store.

Fixture Types

Store fixtures fall into three basic categories: hardlines, softlines, and wall fixtures.

Hardlines Fixtures

The workhorse fixture in most hardlines departments is known as the *gondola*, so named because it is a long structure consisting of a large base and a vertical spine or wall sticking up as high as eight feet, fitted with sockets or notches into which a variety of shelves, peg hooks, bins, baskets, and other hardware can be inserted. The basic gondola can hold a wide variety of merchandise by means of hardware hung from the vertical spine. Think of your last trip to a discount store or supermarket. The long, heavy-duty fixtures fitted predominantly with shelves are gondolas. In addition to the gondola, a few other types of fixtures are in common use today:

tables, large bins, and simple flat-base decks. These fixtures are commonly used in promotional aisles to display advertised or other special-value merchandise.

Softlines Fixtures

The bulky gondola is inappropriate for fashion-oriented softlines merchandise. A large array of fixtures has been developed to accommodate the special needs of softlines, which are often hung on hangers. As shown in Exhibit 13.8, the four-way feature rack and the round rack are the two fixtures most heavily used today. These smaller, specialized fixtures have replaced the straight rack, a long pipe with legs on each end from which rows of apparel were hung, and which for generations was the most prevalent softlines fixture. Although it held a great quantity and was easy to maintain, the straight rack provided few opportunities to differentiate one style or color of garment from another, which merchants have found is the key to selling more. A straight rack is like the hanger rod in your closet, and what you see when you open your closet is nothing more than sleeves. You know your own clothes, so sleeves are enough to tip you off to what the rest of the garment looks like. When you are shopping, however, the more of the garment you are exposed to and the more varieties of size, silhouette (shape), and color, the more you are apt to buy. So merchants prefer *face-out* presentations over *sleeve-out* presentations. The face-out concept can apply not only to softlines such as apparel but also to hardlines. Often for hardlines the exposure of the full visual of the product can attract the customer to the item. For instance, a new-car dealer can stack its new vehicles in a grid format similar to a normal parking lot; however, all the potential car shopper will then view are hoods and trunks or the back ends of the vehicles. Displaying the autos face-out would create a dramatically different effect and pull the customer to the new vehicles. Of course, face-outs take up more space than sleeve-outs, so it is impractical to face out all or even a high percentage of the total merchandise on the floor.

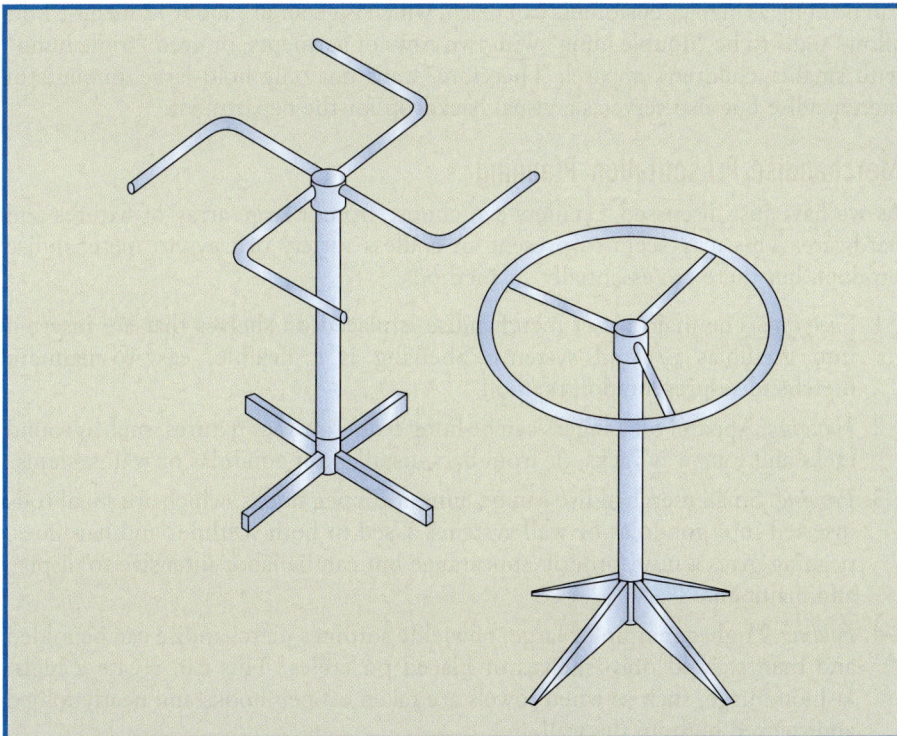

Exhibit 13.8
Four-Way Feature Rack and Round Rack

bulk or capacity fixture
Is a display fixture that is intended to hold the bulk of merchandise without looking as heavy as a long, straight rack of merchandise.

feature fixture
Is a display that draws special attention to selected features (e.g., color, shape, or style) of merchandise.

The round rack is known as a **bulk or capacity fixture** and is intended to hold the bulk of merchandise without looking as heavy as a long straight rack of merchandise. Although it is smaller than the straight rack, it too allows only sleeve-outs unless fitted with special hardware. The four-way rack, on the other hand, is considered a **feature fixture**; even though it holds fewer items, it presents merchandise in a manner that permits the shopper to glimpse at a garment's style and key characteristics (such as color or shape). The ingenious design also allows it to hold a large quantity of merchandise on the hanger arms behind the four face-outs. However, to be easily shopped, all the merchandise on one arm must be the same type of garment with variations only in color and size. In its recent effort to attract a more upscale consumer, Walmart is moving away from its old mantra of "Stack it high, watch it fly" and toward a greater use of these fixtures. However, the retailer should be warned that when the front garment does not match those behind it, the four-way is poorly merchandised and leaves the customer in the same quandary as the straight rack.

Wall Fixtures

The last type of fixture is designed to be hung on the wall. To make a store's plain wall merchandisable, it is usually covered with a skin that is fitted with vertical columns of notches similar to those on the gondola, into which a variety of hardware can be inserted. Shelves, peg hooks, bins, baskets, and even hanger bars can be fitted into wall systems. Hanger bars can be hung parallel to the wall, much like a closet bar, so that large quantities of garments can be sleeved-out, or they can protrude perpendicularly from the wall, either straight out (*straight-outs*) or angled down (*waterfalls*), to allow merchandise to be faced out. The primary quality to remember about wall systems is that walls can generally be merchandised much higher than floor fixtures. On the floor, round racks are kept to a maximum of 42 inches so that customers can easily see over them to other merchandise, but on the wall garments can be hung as high as customers can reach, which is generally about 72 inches. This allows walls to be "double hung" with two rows of garments, or even "triple hung" with smaller children's apparel. Therefore, walls not only hold large amounts of merchandise but also serve as a visual backdrop for the department.

Merchandise-Presentation Planning

As we have just discussed, retailers can choose from a large array of fixtures and hardware. This may seem to present an endless variety of ways to merchandise product, but there are essentially six methods:

1. *Shelving*. The majority of merchandise is placed on shelves that are inserted into gondolas or wall systems. Shelving is a flexible, easy-to-maintain merchandise-presentation method.

2. *Hanging*. Apparel on hangers can be hung from softlines fixtures, such as round racks and four-way racks, or from bars installed on gondolas or wall systems.

3. *Pegging*. Small merchandise can be hung from peg hooks, which are small rods inserted into gondolas or wall systems. Used in both softlines and hardlines, pegging gives a neat, orderly appearance but can be labor intensive to display and maintain.

4. *Folding*. Higher-margin or large, unwieldy softlines merchandise can be folded and then stacked onto shelves or placed on tables. This can create a high-fashion image, such as when towels are taken off peg hooks and neatly folded and stacked high up the wall.

5. *Stacking*. Large hardlines merchandise can be stacked on shelves, the base decks of gondolas, or *flats*, which are platforms placed directly on the floor. Stacking is easily maintained and gives an image of high volume and low price.

6. *Dumping*. Large quantities of small merchandise can be dumped in bins or baskets inserted into gondolas or wall systems. This highly effective promotional method can be used in softlines (socks, washcloths) or hardlines (batteries, grocery products, candy), and creates a high-volume, low-cost image.

The method of merchandise presentation can have a dramatic impact on image and space productivity. Different merchandise-presentation methods have been shown to strongly influence buying habits and stimulate consumers to purchase more. There is a certain "psychology of merchandise presentation" that must be carefully considered in developing merchandise-presentation schemes. Only between one-third and one-half of store shoppers make an impulse (unplanned) purchase, and these purchases are made by only 60 percent of the shoppers who actually enter the store with the intent of making a specific purchase. Thus, 40 percent of the shoppers who enter a store to make a purchase are "wasted" because the store failed to use merchandise presentation to generate additional purchases.[26] This is why department store design incorporates a gauntlet of goodies to stimulate impulse buys. For example, cosmetics, usually the store's most profitable department, is always near the main entrance. Typically, the department is leased to cosmetic companies that use their own salespeople to sell the perfume, lipstick, and eye shadow. Other high-impulse items (e.g., jewelry, handbags, and shoes) are usually nearby, while the "demand" products (e.g., furniture) are on upper floors. These stores would be unprofitable if they failed to induce a significant amount of impulse buying.

The following are three key psychological factors to consider when merchandising stores:

1. *Value and fashion image*. One of merchandise presentation's most important psychological effects is to foster an image in the customer's mind of how trendy, exclusive, pricey, or value oriented the merchandise is. For each of the merchandise-presentation methods mentioned previously, we discussed its effect on price image. By changing the merchandise-presentation method, we can change the perception of our towel display from common, high volume, and high value to an exclusive selection of high-fashion merchandise that is typically branded by a well-known designer such as Ralph Lauren, which presumably will be at higher prices. Note that this concept of using merchandise presentation to reinforce a value or fashion image can also be done with service retailers. Consider, for example, how Cost Cutters Family Hair Care displays hair-care products on a high series of shelves in the waiting area that is lighted with fluorescent light fixtures. And then contrast that with how a high-end beauty or barbershop perhaps coupled with a health spa would most likely display the merchandise on glass tables with flowers surrounding the hair-care products and spotlights on the merchandise.

2. *Angles and sight lines*. Research has shown that as customers move through a retail store, they view the store at approximately 45-degree angles from the path of travel, as shown in Exhibit 13.9, rather than perpendicular to their path. Incidentally, this 45-degreee angle approximates the extent to which the typical person can turn his or her head. Although this seems logical, most stores are set up at right angles because it is easier and consumes less space. Therefore,

Exhibit 13.9
45-Degree Customer Sightline

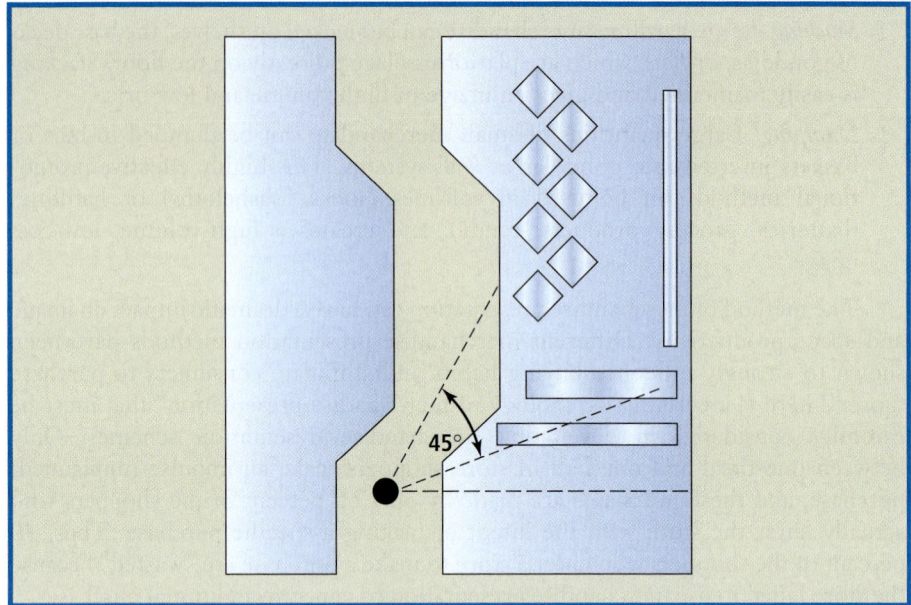

Exhibit 13.10
Vertical Color Blocking

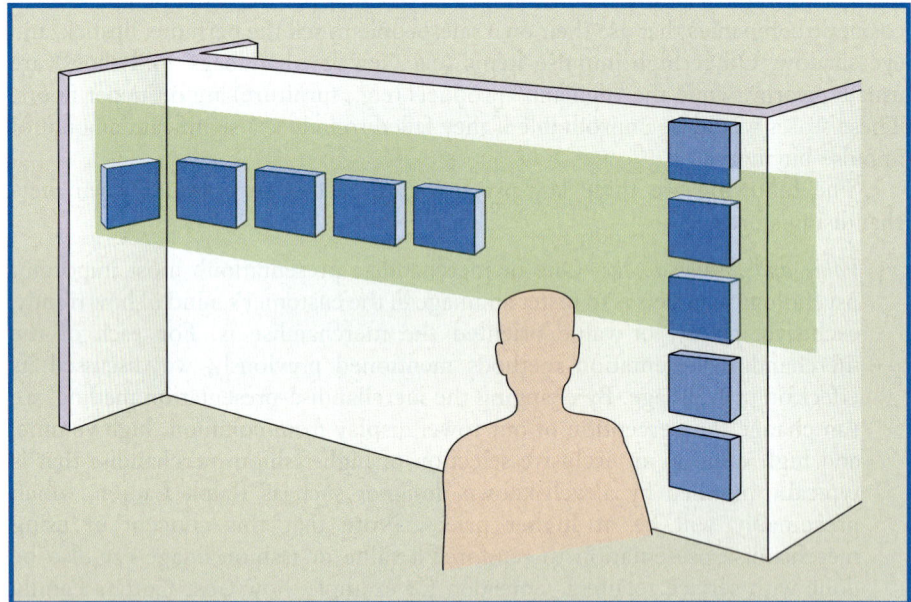

merchandise and signage often wind up being at a 90-degree angle to the main aisle. Exhibit 13.9 also shows how four-way feature racks can be more effectively merchandised by being turned to meet the shoppers' sight lines head-on.

3. *Vertical color blocking*. To be most effective, merchandise should be displayed in vertical bands of color wherever possible. As customers move through the store, their eyes naturally view a "swath" approximately two-feet high, parallel to the floor, at about eye level. This is shown in Exhibit 13.10. This visual swath of merchandise will be viewed as a rainbow of colors if each merchandise

item is displayed vertically by color (e.g., the vertical columns represent different colors, and within these colors could be different sizes). This method of merchandise presentation creates such a strong visual effect that shoppers are exposed to more merchandise, which in turn increases sales. In addition, when shopping for clothing, customers most often think first of color. Thus, they can easily find the column of color on display and locate their size. United Colors of Benetton, with more than 5,500 stores in 120 countries, is perhaps the leader in effectively using vertical color blocking as a signature element of its store designs.

Selecting Fixtures and Merchandise-Presentation Methods

Proper fixtures emphasize the key selling attributes of merchandise while not being overpowering. A good guideline for selecting fixtures—although it is not always possible to follow—is to *match the fixture to the merchandise, not the merchandise to the fixture*. This means you should only use fixtures that are sensitive to the nature of the merchandise. All too often, though, retailers are forced to put merchandise on the wrong fixture.[27]

Consider intimate apparel, for instance. This is a fast-selling, high-margin merchandise category that can enhance a retailer's image in fashion merchandising. Though retailers entering this business might be tempted to place intimate apparel on existing shelves of a gondola, they would be well served to consider special fixtures that enhance the delicate qualities of intimate apparel. A large, metal, bulky gondola will overpower a small, delicate intimate-apparel item, and therefore reduce sales potential. More delicate fixtures made of softer materials will enhance sales. Likewise, it would not be effective to bulk stack fragile merchandise because the weight of items might damage those lower in the stack. It would not make sense to peg hook large, bulky items because they take up too much room and might be too heavy for the peg hooks.

Visual Merchandising

The second type of merchandise presentation, **visual merchandising**, is the artistic display of merchandise and theatrical props used as scene-setting decoration in the store. While on-shelf merchandising must be tastefully displayed to encourage shopping, a store with just on-shelf merchandising would be dreary. Many low-price stores contain little visual merchandising, and they do appear more boring than their upscale cousins in fashion retailing, which concentrate heavily on visual merchandising displays, or *visuals*, as they are often called.

An effective visual merchandising display has several key characteristics. Visual displays are not typically associated with a shopable fixture but are located in a focal point, feature area, or other area remote from the on-shelf merchandising and perhaps even out of reach of the customer. Their goal is to create a feeling in the store conducive to buying merchandise.

Another characteristic of visual merchandising is its use of props and elements in addition to merchandise. In fact, visuals do not always include merchandise— they may just be interesting displays of items somehow related to the merchandise or to a mood the retailer wishes to create. A prop might be a wooden barrel, a miniature airplane, or a mock tree with autumn leaves. Visuals are like the illustrations and design elements in a book that make it interesting; they tell the customer whether this is an upscale, serious shopping experience; a frivolous, fun shopping experience; or a down and dirty, low-price shopping experience. Claire's stores, for example, makes shopping fun for tweens, teens, and young adults. In

visual merchandising
Is the artistic display of merchandise and theatrical props used as scene-setting decoration in the store.

addition, Claire's is mother friendly; moms are comfortable with their daughters in this store and this is important since mom is often the person paying the bill. The stores are clean, bright, and easy to shop with an inviting image set off by purple-and-pink carpeting, white ceiling tiles, and accent lighting that attracts attention even across a crowded mall corridor. The merchandise is easily accessible, so even the youngest girls can hold up an item to see how it looks.[28]

To be most effective, however, visuals should incorporate relevant merchandise. In apparel retailing, mannequins or figure forms are used to display merchandise as it might appear on a person rather than hanging limply on a hanger. This helps the shopper visualize how these garments will enhance her or his appearance. Good fashion visuals include more than just one garment to show how tops and bottoms go together and how belts, scarves, and other accessories can be combined to create an overall fashion look. This is called *accessorization*. When successful, visuals help the shopper translate the merchandise presentation from "garments on a rack" to "fashionable clothes that will look good on me." However, the importance of visuals is not restricted to fashion merchandise. Bass Pro Shops is a long-time user of visuals in its stores and has gone digital with an in-store media network that uses flat video screens to entertain and educate shoppers. In addition, these flat screens, with their vivid scenes of the outdoors, also provide targeted advertising at point of sale.[29] You should expect more and more retailers using video screens as visual merchandising props. H&M, a fashion retailer founded in 1947 in Sweden, is pushing the technology edge by teaming up with Electronic Arts to create *The Sims 2: H&M Fashion Stuff* digital computer game that includes digital garments, a fashion runway, and other digital material. The retailer should be careful in setting visuals to make sure that the displays do not create walls that make it difficult for shoppers to reach other areas of the store. In addition, the retailer should carefully consider the placement of signs. A popular fast-food restaurant increased sales when it changed the sign placement featuring its specials from being visible to patrons on their way to the restrooms. Now the signs are visible as the customers exit the restrooms and are more relaxed.[30]

LO 4 Store Design

Why is store design so important to a store's success?

Store design is the element most responsible for the first of our two goals in planning the store environment: creating a distinctive and memorable store image. Store design encompasses both the exterior and the interior of the store. On the exterior, we have the storefront, signage, and entrance, all of which are critical to attracting passing shoppers and enticing them to enter. On the inside, store design includes the architectural elements and finishes on all surfaces such as wall coverings, floor coverings, and ceilings. There are literally hundreds of details in a store's design, and all must work together to create the desired store **ambience**, which is the overall feeling or mood projected by a store through its aesthetic appeal to the human senses. For instance, Warren Buffett's Nebraska Furniture Mart uses noncomposite panels, which not only lower heating and cooling costs but also create an upscale look.[31] Another example of this concept is Marketside, a new Walmart prototype that helps the customer deal in an innovative way with the age-old question, "What's for dinner tonight?" Marketside is smaller than a conventional supermarket and offers a wide selection of fresh ingredients, prepared meals, and everyday favorites at very affordable prices. Customer service is also a high priority as store associates offer knowledgeable advice about healthy eating, natural and organic products, and other customer concerns.

ambience
Is the overall feeling or mood projected by a store through its aesthetic appeal to human senses.

The chapter's "What's New?" box illustrates how retailers today are designing both high-tech and high-touch experiences into shopping.

Storefront Design

If the retail store can be compared to a book, then the storefront, or store exterior, is like the book cover. It must be noticeable, easily identified by passing motorists or mall shoppers, and memorable. The storefront must clearly identify the name and general nature of the store and give some hint as to the merchandise inside. Generally, the storefront design includes all exterior signage and the architecture of the storefront itself.

In many cases, the storefront includes display windows, which serve as an advertising medium for the store. Store windows must arrest the attention of passing shoppers, enticing them inside the store. Therefore, windows should be maintained with exciting visual displays that are changed frequently, are fun and exciting, and reflect the merchandise and service offering inside. Always remember that in those few seconds that the customer is approaching the store—and especially the last 25 to 50 feet—he or she is already forming an opinion about the store and the merchandise and services in it.

Interior Design

Unless you have ever been responsible for redecorating a house or room, you may be unaware of the dozens of design elements that go into a physical space. We can break interior design into two types of elements: the finishes applied to surfaces and the architectural shapes. Think of all the elements from the floor to the ceiling. First, we have some type of floor covering placed over a concrete or wood floor. At the least, this finish is stain or paint, but vinyl, carpet, ceramic tile, and marble are more frequently used. Each of these different surfaces creates a different impression on the shopper. An unpainted concrete floor conveys a low-cost, no-frills environment. A color-stained floor can convey a rustic yet sophisticated look and feel. Vinyl floor covering makes another statement; depending on its quality, sheen, color, and design pattern, the image can vary from very downscale to very upscale. Carpet suggests a homelike atmosphere conducive to selling apparel. Ceramic tile, travertine, and especially porcelain or marble suggest an upscale, exclusive, and probably expensive shopping experience.

Retailers have even more options for covering the walls from paint and wallpaper to hundreds of types of paneling. The ceiling must also receive a design treatment, whether it is finished drywall (a very upscale image because it is an expensive process), a suspended ceiling (very common and economical, though not distinctive), or perhaps even an open ceiling with all the pipes and wires above painted black (which suggests a low-price warehouse approach but also could be successful in sports bars or other casual eating establishments). Then there are thousands of types of moldings that can be applied to the transitions from floor to wall to ceiling, and hundreds of architectural design elements that can be incorporated.

Lighting Design

Another important, though often overlooked, element in a successful store design is lighting. Retailers have come to understand how lighting can greatly enhance store sales. One of the early keys to success for Blockbuster Video was its move away from the 100-watt bulbs used by its competitors to brighter lights. Brighter lighting in a wine store also influences shoppers to examine and handle more merchandise.

What's New?

High Tech and High Touch Enhances the Shopping Experience

Store-based retailers must recognize that customers today who can easily shop for virtually anything on websites that are increasingly easy to navigate, highly interactive, and exciting, are not going to settle for a store design that is boring and out of date with contemporary needs. In addition, any customer 25-year-old and younger has grown up with cell phones, personal computers, video cameras, and other computer-based telecommunications that are highly interactive and enabling. In fact, those older than 25 and even those older than 50 have also increasingly become not only comfortable with these technologies but also demanding that retailers embrace computer-enabled telecommunications.

As a consequence of the trends in telecommunications technology, more and more retailers are using electronic media in their stores to include television displays of merchandise and Internet kiosks for merchandise and service searching. Pierce's Northside Market in Madison, Wisconsin, recently placed three large-screen plasma TVs in its 25,000-square-foot store. One was placed in the back of the store near the frozen foods so that shoppers who are buying frozen foods could see, for example, shish kabobs on the grill. Hopefully, this screen image will lead customers to the meat and produce departments to buy ingredients for their own shish kabobs. The plasma near the produce department features the orchards and farms that produced the grocer's fruits and vegetables. The sitting area adjacent to the deli has a fireplace, comfortable seats, and even some wireless PC desks. Over the fireplace is the third 60-inch plasma TV—with photos of farms surrounding Madison, local landmarks, and, of course, more "beauty" shots of items available in the store. The premise behind three televisions in a small grocery store is that people "eat with their eyes." How many times have you heard someone say that you shouldn't shop when you're hungry? With time-starved shoppers pushing shopping carts, why not show them some great prepared meal ideas and get them to visit the meat department to buy some T-bones?

Another innovator is Bloom (www.shopbloom.com), a new chain of grocery stores by Food Lion, which has developed personal scanners for its regular shoppers. This innovative technology provides a customer-friendly and highly engaging shopping experience. Using their Bloom Breeze Cards, shoppers obtain a personal scanner to carry about the store, which allows them to scan items and bag them in their carts as they shop. The scanners also enable the customer to have a running tally of how much they are spending and thus monitor their budget. Instant messages can also be sent to

Courtesy of Pierce's Northside Market

customers, alerting them when prescriptions have been filled or their deli orders are ready for pickup. Shoppers check out simply by going to any checkout lane and scanning an "end of trip" bar code; the order automatically downloads to a register. Hence, there is no need to unload and reload the cart, bringing the average checkout time down to 33 seconds. Based on nearly two years of consumer research and analysis, Bloom stores also feature customer-friendly aisle layouts and free-standing and wall-mounted kiosks for locating and then downloading recipe ideas or learning about wine selections, checking prices, or finding the right wine to go with a meal.

High-tech telecommunications, however, are not the only means a retailer can use in its store to provide an engaging experience. In fact, in the grocery business, Whole Foods prides itself in focusing on high-quality natural and organic products. The company has recently developed an in-store spa at its Preston Road store in Dallas. This approach is more of a high-touch approach, in contrast to the high-tech approach that Bloom uses, to developing an engaging shopping experience. The spa is located on the store's second floor and has seven treatment rooms, its own retail space (a

store within a spa within a store), and a private veranda balcony "for outdoor relaxation, spa meals and retreat." The spa applies the same natural standards as the Whole Food grocer downstairs by opting for fresh, plant-based, and naturally derived ingredients and only using products that haven't been tested on animals. Customers who are pressed for time are catered to by the offering of a menu of quick services such as a mini-manicure and a 25-minute Swedish massage, along with a wide range of more indulgent treatments. A concierge service provides personal shopping, which allows customers to multitask. A shopper merely hands over his or her shopping list and a Whole Foods employee navigates the store aisles to collect the groceries while the customer is pampered in the Whole Foods spa.

Source: "In a Shift, Marketers Beef Up Ad Spending Inside Stores," *Wall Street Journal*, September 21, 2005: A1–A8; information supplied by Jim Lukens, DW Green Company, and Jim Maurer, Pierce's Northside Market; and personal visits to Bloom (www.shopbloom.com) and Whole Foods (www.wholefoodsmarket.com).

Department stores, on the other hand, have found that raising lighting levels in fashion departments can actually discourage sales because bright lighting suggests a discount-store image.

Lighting design, however, is not limited to simple light levels. Contemporary lighting design requires an in-depth knowledge of electrical engineering and the effect of light on color and texture. Retailers have learned that different types and levels of lighting can have a significant impact on sales.[32] In addition, the types of light sources available have multiplied quickly. Today, there are literally hundreds of light fixtures and lamps (bulbs) from which to choose. Increasingly, retailers are also recognizing that lighting is a large contributor to energy cost and energy waste, and thus energy efficient lighting is a very high priority in both new buildings and store remodeling.

Many retailers are actually using too much outdoor lighting today, probably because of the increasing risk of accidents or lawsuits. Lighting is measured in foot-candles. One foot-candle is a unit of illuminant equal to one lumen per square foot. Research findings suggest that customers in urban areas feel safest in parking lots lighted to the level of five foot-candles, while those in suburban parking lots prefer three foot-candles. (By comparison, one foot-candle lights most roadways, and full moonlight is 1/100th of one foot-candle.) However, most businesses, especially gas stations, restaurants, and convenience stores, are now lighting at 100 to 150 foot-candle levels. This not only substantially increases costs but also causes "light pollution" for the neighborhood.[33]

Sounds and Smells: Total Sensory Marketing

Effective store design appeals to the human senses of sight, hearing, smell, and touch. Obviously, the majority of design activity in a retail store is focused on affecting sight. For example, have you ever gone into a Walmart store and had the greeter say "Hello" to you? Sam Walton's wife, Helen, suggested the idea of the greeter as a way to put customers in a better mood and to convey a feeling of warmth toward the retailer. However, Sam Walton soon came to realize another benefit of greeters—they slowed customers down as they entered the store. The first 20 feet inside a store is a decompression chamber for customers as they adjust to the different lighting and climate of the store. Customers are often unable to pick up visual cues until they adjust to their new environment. Thus, greeters allowed Walmart to not only convey a positive message but also forced customers to slow down to return the greeting and then become aware of the merchandise at the front of the store. Sam Walton actually added 30 feet to this effective selling area. Today, supermarkets and other retailers are using a similar tactic with the area between the parking lot and the front door to the store. For this critically important area, they are incorporating "plazas," thus allowing their customers to enter the store through an attractively designed area, as opposed to older stores that typically have shopping carts and soda machines at their front doors. Some of the more progressive retailers now have water fountains, plants, and seating areas directly in front of their stores. Others slow down the consumer with a community area near the front of the store, even incorporating small stage areas for local bands to play on the weekends. Thus, rather than a Coke or Pepsi machine parked in the front of the store, they have a BBQ grill with burgers and hot dogs, music, and happy and entertained customers entering the store.

Research has shown that senses other than sight can also be very important, and as a result many retailers are beginning to engineer the smells and sounds in their stores. Smell is believed to be the most closely linked of all the senses to memory and emotions. Bakeries, coffee shops, popcorn vendors in movie theaters, and specialty shops that sell coffee or tobacco often attract customers through the smells that emanate from their products. Retailers hope that using smells as an in-store marketing tool will put consumers "in the mood."[34] Victoria's Secret has deployed potpourri caches throughout its stores, and in fact now sells them to create the ambience of a lingerie closet. The Walt Disney Company uses the smell of freshly baked cookies on Main Street in the Magic Kingdom to relax customers and provide a feeling of warmth. Regardless of the smell used, it must be consistent with the store's image. For example, a natural foods store should employ natural scents such as potpourri or sandalwood rather than artificial scents that are typical of modern floor cleansers. A large department or grocery store should also create islands within the store with distinct smells. For example, shoppers may find it natural to move from fresh produce, to bakery, to coffee, and then to meats and to seafood. A store should also have neutral zones where shoppers can recover their olfactory senses. Some believe that a strong coffee scent actually serves as a powerful neutralizer. However, the type of aroma to use depends on the merchandise being sold and the target customer. You may want to use a floral aroma for men because it will remind them of their mothers and trigger a happy memory or feeling of security. For teenagers, some retailers have used smells that resemble airplane or automobile exhaust. Nike has discovered that putting customers in a room with the odor of old sneakers had a positive effect on their desire to buy new ones.[35]

Retailers have piped music such as Muzak into their stores for generations, believing that a musical backdrop will create a more relaxing environment and encourage customers to stay longer.[36] Increasingly, music is being seen as a valuable marketing tool because the right music can create an environment that is both soothing and reflective of the merchandise being offered. For example, a jeans retailer might play hip-hop near baggies and classic rock over by the Dockers. Researchers believe that while the tempo of music affects how long shoppers stay in a store, the type of music may be just as influential on how much they purchase. One study found that restaurant patrons spent an average of 10 percent more per meal when classical music was playing and more on after-dinner coffee. The classical music created an air of sophistication, reflected in the more sophisticated (higher-priced) entrées chosen by the diners.[37] Thus, while classical music is soothing and has been shown to encourage customers to linger and select more expensive merchandise,[38] it may be inconsistent with the desired ambience of a trendy fashion store catering to college-age women. Today, some retailers are experimenting with placing advertisements into the background music. Other retailers have found a different use for this canned music. A shopping mall in Australia plays Bing Crosby music to drive out the kids who want to hang out after school. In addition, the mall uses pink fluorescent lights, which supposedly highlight pimples. The New South Wales train service in Australia uses canned music at stops in high-crime areas to keep the undesirable element away.[39]

Retailers also must recognize that different seasons of the year and the holidays or cultural events that surround them can motivate shoppers to purchase and more generally have a memorable shopping experience. As they evolved, humans developed music to celebrate life-cycle events and annual celebrations. Music thus gave these events and times special meaning. Therefore, retailers need to understand the culture they operate in, as well as the role of music throughout the seasons. Christmas music with a heavy Christian meaning may be appropriate for some situations, but in other cases Christmas music that is more nondenominational may be better choice. In even other situations, Arabic, Jewish, or Hindu music may be more appropriate. Also music could be used to draw attention to "select" merchandise within the store. For example, playing French music to call attention to French wines can result in increased sales.[40]

Visual Communications

LO 5

What is the role of visual communications in a retail store?

The last chapter was devoted to the retail selling process. However, sales associates cannot always be available to assist customers, particularly in this era of increased competitive pressure and reduced gross margins, which have caused many retailers to cut costs by reducing their sales staffs. Even department stores, which staked their reputations on high levels of personal customer service, have had to reduce their service levels and learn to rely on alternative service strategies. How, then, can retailers provide good selling communications and high customer service while controlling labor costs?

The answer is visual communications in the form of in-store signage and graphics. The "What's New?" box discussed earlier describes how retailers can plan the store environment to incorporate signs, large photo panels, and other visual devices that serve as silent salespersons, providing shoppers with much-needed information and directions on how to shop the store, evaluate merchandise, and make purchases. Because these visual communications are inanimate objects that stay permanently in place, they require a one-time-only installation cost and low maintenance and can be relied on to perform their function, the same way, for every shopper. Unlike sales associates, visual communications are never late for work, are never in a bad mood, and never mistreat customers. Of course, neither are they as effective as a good sales associate who provides the personal touch that makes customers feel welcome and comfortable. But when carefully balanced with personal service, visual communications, with their reliability and low cost, can create an effective selling environment and are therefore becoming an important tool in the store designer's toolbox. Recognizing that retail service is sparse, some manufacturers are experimenting with in-store Internet kiosks where customers can go online and have a live chat with a customer-service representative to get their questions answered.

Earlier we likened a retail store to a well-written book. Visual communications are akin to the headlines, subheads, illustrations, and captions that give the reader direction and illustrate the written descriptions. These visual communications must address the questions of the shopper: What is it? Where is it? Why should I buy it? How much does it cost?[41] Without visual communications, a store would resemble a newspaper full of words but no headlines—a jumbled, incomprehensible mess of merchandise. An effective visual communications program includes a range of messages from large and bold directives used sparingly to provide cues to the gross organization of the space to the smaller, more specific, and plentiful messages that describe actual merchandise. A visual communications program includes the following important elements.

Name, Logo, and Retail Identity

The first and most visible element in a comprehensive visual communications program is the retailer's identity, which is composed of the store name, logo, and supporting visual elements. The name and logo are seen not only on the storefront and throughout the interior but also in advertising and all communications with consumers. Therefore, they must be catchy, memorable, and, most of all, reflective of the retailer's merchandising mission. Historically, many retail companies have taken the names of their founders, as is the case with most department stores. That practice has fallen out of vogue, however, as retailing has become a game of crafty store images and catchy retail identities. A founder's name rarely captures the merchandising spirit of a company as well as names such as Bath & Body Works, Office Depot, The Home Depot, and Toys "R" Us. Probably no name captured the essence of its business better than that of a store frequented by Bernie Madoff, the convicted stock swindler. Trillion was the super-high-end men's clothier in Palm Beach. Late-night television hosts joked that it was for people who wouldn't be caught dead at a store called "million" or even "billion."[42] Given the ever-increasing barrage of advertising messages and the waning effectiveness of each message, retailers have found it necessary to choose names that are highly distinctive as well as descriptive of their unique offerings. Today's hottest logos, reflecting "American values," include Nike, Apple, Starbucks, L. L. Bean, Cheesecake Factory, and Old Navy. Sometimes even the names of retailer failures have value. Recently, the sons of Merv Morris, the founder of Mervyns department stores, purchased the department store's name, intellectual property, and online properties with plans to revive the brand. In a similar move, some of the same liquidators that had led other failed stores through their dying days have expressed an interest in buying the brand names Circuit City, Sharper Image, Linens 'n Things, and Bombay. The liquidators say they see themselves as brand-licensing experts who will receive royalties for the products without the need to pay rent or a sales staff. And besides it will be cheaper to open a new operation with a familiar name than developing a new name.[43]

Once a name has been chosen, a logo is developed to visually portray the name in a creative and memorable manner. Again, the key is to keep the logo simple and easy to understand, while making it exciting enough to leave a lasting image in the customers' minds. The logo is often accompanied by taglines that provide more description of the store concept such as Walmart's "Save Money, Live Better." This simple yet compelling tagline communicates that Walmart customers will pay lower prices than if they shopped the competition; as a result, they will be able to use their savings to have a better life.

The logo's most prominent placement is on the outside of the store. This is critical to attracting customers and creating high store traffic. Another reason the store name and logo should be succinct and descriptive is that they often play to motorists passing by at 45 miles per hour.

Institutional Signage

Inside the store, the first level of visual communications is known as *institutional* signage, or signage that describes the merchandising mission, customer-service policies, and other messages on behalf of the retail institution. This signage is usually located at the store entrance to properly greet entering customers, as well as at service points such as the service desk, layaway window, and cash registers. In addition, some retailers place customer-service signage throughout the store to reinforce special policies several times during the shopping trip. This signage might include messages such as "Lowest Price Guaranteed" and "All Major Credit Cards Accepted."

Directional, Departmental, and Category Signage

Directional and departmental signage serves as the highest level of organization in an overall signage program. For instance, when you enter a Lowe's with its more than 25-foot ceilings and large metal warehouse racks organized into a grid shopping pattern and covering several acres of floor space, it would be very difficult to find merchandise without Lowe's use of large and bold signs showing the location of the paint department, plumbing department, electrical department, lumber department, and gardening department. These signs are usually large and placed fairly high, so they can be seen throughout the store. They help guide the shopper through the store and locate specific departments of interest. Not all stores use directional signage. It is not necessary in smaller stores, but in virtually all stores larger than 10,000 square feet, some type of departmental signage is used. Once a shopper locates and moves close to a particular department, category signage is used to call out and locate specific merchandise categories. Category signage is usually smaller since it is intended to be seen from a shorter distance and is located on or close to the fixture itself. For instance, the departmental sign might say "Sporting Goods," be two feet high and six feet wide, and hang from the ceiling. On the other hand, the category signage might be only six inches high and two feet wide, affixed to the top of the gondola, and read "Hunting," "Tennis," or "Fitness."

Point-of-Sale Signage

The next level of signage—even smaller and placed closer to the merchandise—is known as *point-of-sale* (POS) signage. Because POS signage is intended to give details about specific merchandise items, it usually contains more words and is affixed directly to fixtures. POS signage may range in size from 11 by 17 inches to a 3-by-5-inch card with very small type describing an item. Always, however, the most important function of POS signage is to clearly state the price of the merchandise being signed.

POS signage includes a set of sign holders used throughout the store, along with a variety of printed signs that can be inserted into the hardware. Store associates mix and match the signage and hardware as directed by management so that POS signage changes frequently. Special POS signs for sales, clearance, and "As Advertised" are often different colors than the normal price signage to highlight these special values.

Lifestyle Graphics

Visual communications encompass more than just words. Many stores incorporate large graphics panels showing so-called lifestyle images in important departments. These photo images portray either the merchandise, often as it is being used, or simply images of related items or models that convey an image conducive to buying the product. In a high-fashion department, lifestyle photography might show a scene of movie stars arriving at a nightclub in very trendy fashions, suggesting that similar fashions are available in that department. In sporting goods, a lifestyle image might show an isolated lake surrounded by autumn-colored trees, with mist rising off the water and the sun rising in the background.

Retailers must be careful when choosing lifestyle photography; as the saying goes, "Beauty is in the eye of the beholder." One person's lifestyle is not necessarily another's, so lifestyle photography must be kept very general to be attractive to the majority and offensive to none. Increasingly, photo panels and lifestyle imagery, which can be expensive to create, are being provided free of charge to retailers by merchandise vendors, who are looking to gain an advantage for their products on the retail floor.

SUMMARY

LO 1

What are the elements of a store's environment?

In this chapter, we focused on the retail store, a key factor influencing the consumer's initial perception of the retailer. It must effectively convey the store image desired by the retailer and provide a shopping environment that is conducive to high sales. The guiding principle in effective store planning, merchandise presentation, and design is that the more merchandise customers are exposed to, the more they tend to buy. This depends largely on planning the name, logo, and visual appearance of the store to convey a desired market-positioning image. Although retailers work diligently to influence their images, true store image is an amalgam of all messages consumers receive from advertising to stories they hear from friends and to the store itself.

LO 2

What is involved in store planning?

Store planning refers to developing a plan for the organization of the retail store. First, the retailer must decide how to allocate the available square footage among the various types of selling and nonselling space needed. This is usually accomplished by conducting a mathematical analysis of the productivity of various merchandise categories. By comparing the sales or gross margin produced by various categories with the space they use, the retailer can develop a plan for the optimal allocation of available space. Next the floor plan is created, showing the placement and circulation patterns of all merchandise departments. Finally, thought must be given as to how the floor plan can help reduce shrinkage.

How are the various types of fixtures, merchandise-presentation methods and techniques, and the psychology of merchandise presentation used to increase the productivity of the sales floor?   **LO 3**

Fixture selection and merchandise presentation are critical to exposing customers to the maximum amount of merchandise. There are many types of store fixtures, as well as specific methods of merchandise presentation, that have been shown to maximize merchandise exposure and lead to increased sales. Particularly, there is a psychology of merchandise presentation that utilizes customers' natural shopping behaviors and adopts merchandise presentation to match them. In addition to maximizing sales, fixture selection and merchandise presentation must conform to operational constraints and be easy to maintain.

Why is store design so important to a store's success?   **LO 4**

The most visible elements of the store are the design of its storefront and the interior decor. The storefront or exterior must be eye-catching, inviting, and reflective of the merchandise inside. The interior design must be comfortable, put the shopper in the proper buying mood, and provide a backdrop that enhances but does not overpower the merchandise. The store designer must always remember that shoppers are there to look at the merchandise, not the store design.

What is the role of visual communications in a retail store?   **LO 5**

A successful selling environment is based on effective visual communications with the customers. Since shoppers require information even when sales associates are not available, visual communications must be used throughout the store to provide direction, specific information, and prices. A visual communications program begins with the store name and logo and includes a range of interior signage that walks the customer through the buying experience.

Finally, there are literally hundreds of details in a successful retail store, and all must be carefully coordinated to create a cohesive, targeted store image that reflects the retailer's mission.

TERMS TO REMEMBER

shrinkage
floor plan
microretailing
stack-outs
space productivity index
planogram
free-flow layout
grid layout

loop layout
spine layout
on-shelf merchandising
bulk or capacity fixture
feature fixture
visual merchandising
ambience

REVIEW AND DISCUSSION QUESTIONS

What are the elements of a store's environment?   **LO 1**

1. Why is it important for retailers to use their stores as a means to excite their customers?
2. What is merchandise presentation, and how does it impact sales?
3. What is the simple but powerful truism in retailing that store planners can follow to increase the space productivity of a store environment? Does this truism also hold true for e-tailers? Why?

4. What is the 25-25-50 rule regarding endcaps? Why shouldn't endcaps be 100-percent sale items?

LO 2

What is involved in store planning?

5. Discuss the various types of space in a retail store, describing the role of each.
6. Identify the four main types of store layouts, discussing their differences and impact on customers.
7. What is a planogram? Why must the vendor be involved in helping the retailer develop the planogram?
8. Describe the space-allocation planning process. How is this process different for updating an existing store versus opening a new store?

LO 3

How are the various types of fixtures, merchandise-presentation methods and techniques, and the psychology of merchandise presentation used to increase the productivity of the sales floor?

9. Discuss the different uses of bulk or capacity futures and feature fixtures.
10. In what ways should new stores be designed differently from older stores so as to reflect the differences in Gen X and Gen Y customers?
11. If retail space is such a scarce resource, then what is wrong with the mantra of "Stack it high, watch it fly" so as to stock more merchandise in the limited available space?
12. What is the psychology of merchandise presentation, and how is it used? Can it be used by e-tailers?

LO 4

Why is store design so important to a store's success?

13. What are the goals of interior and exterior design?
14. Which is more important in achieving retail sales—a store's external or interior appearance?
15. Why is the background music so important to a store's performance?

LO 5

What is the role of visual communications in a retail store?

16. Why are so many people purchasing the brand names of failed retailers? After all, aren't they worthless?
17. Why is the retailer's logo so important? Why isn't the founder's name a good choice for the name of a retail store?

SAMPLE TEST QUESTIONS

LO 1

The two primary objectives of the store environment are:

a. effective sales management and creating a distinctive ambience.
b. creating the store image and increasing space productivity.
c. creative merchandise presentation and effective store traffic control.
d. maximizing impulse purchase opportunity and effective shelf space allocation.
e. maintaining market share and effective merchandise control.

LO 2

The goal of store layout and design in store planning should be to:

a. maximize customer access to high-profit items.
b. evenly divide floor space between the five functional areas of a retail store.
c. make the store easy to understand and shop and allow the merchandise to be effectively presented.

d. allow for the rapid restocking of valuable shelf space in low turnover merchandise categories.

e. design a that which maximizes backroom stock capacity.

The psychology of merchandise presentation refers to the fact that: **LO 3**

a. different merchandising methods can strongly influence the store's image and its sales.

b. psychologists should always be hired as merchandisers.

c. merchandise presentation teaches consumers how to shop effectively.

d. social factors strongly influence shopping behavior.

e. shoppers can be classified according to psychological tests.

Store design does all but which of the following?   **LO 4**

a. It is responsible for creating a distinctive and memorable store image.

b. It maximizes sales transactions per customer visit.

c. It includes the architectural elements and finishes on all surfaces.

d. It seeks to attract passing shoppers and entice them to enter the store.

e. It encompasses the store's exterior and interior.

Which of the following is not part of a visual communications program?   **LO 5**

a. store name and logo

b. institutional signage

c. directional and category signage

d. lifestyle graphics

e. television advertising

WRITING AND SPEAKING EXERCISE

You are the vice president of store operations for a small chain of women's apparel stores. The chain's flagship is a 15,000-square-foot store located in an upscale neighborhood shopping district in a growing section of Austin, Texas. Despite the recent national economic slowdown, sales have increased in eight of the chain's nine stores over the past three years. Nevertheless, the chain's president believes that sales should have increased even more, especially at the flagship store. Therefore, she has budgeted $500,000 for capital improvements, both external and internal, to capture these "missing" sales. The store facilities manager, however, believes that the half-million dollars could be better spent on new fixtures to increase the amount of merchandise available on the floor. His idea is to shrink the width of all the aisles, place more bulk fixtures on the floor, and double stack all the folded merchandise.

You believe that the merchandise is already crammed in too tightly and that there are too few feature presentations of fashions currently available. It is your idea to lease the empty 4,000-square-foot store next door. This space used to be occupied by a national gift store that was recently liquidated, despite being highly successful at the location next to you. By using the $500,000, you could acquire the lease and open the wall between the stores. The additional room would allow for increased merchandise presentation, increased aisle widths, and increased dressing-room space and backroom storage.

You already have a meeting scheduled with the president for next week, so prepare a memo evaluating all three proposals and make a recommendation as to what should be done.

RETAIL PROJECT

Let's look more closely at some of the attributes that often influence supermarket choice decisions. Nine frequently cited attributes are:

1. low prices,
2. choice of national versus private labels,
3. physical characteristics (including decor, layout, and floor space),
4. fast checkouts,
5. produce quality,
6. convenience (including hours, location, ease of entrance and parking, ease of finding items),
7. services (including credit, delivery, return policy, and guarantees),
8. store personnel (including helpfulness, friendliness, and courtesy), and
9. advertised "specials" in stock.

For your assignment, you are to rank these attributes in order of importance to you. After ranking them, take the most important attribute and assign it the value of 10, take the second most important attribute and assign it the value of 9. Continue to do this for your top five attributes, with your fifth attribute getting a value of 6.

Now visit two supermarkets or supercenters and assign a value (1 being very poor, 10 being very good) to the stores' performance on your five attributes. Multiply your rank value by their performance value for each attribute and sum the total. Is the store with the highest total points your favorite? If not, why is there a difference?

If you were planning to shop on the Internet for clothing, what "store" attributes would be the most important?

PLANNING YOUR OWN RETAIL BUSINESS

After graduation from college, you opened a swimwear store called the Zig Zag on South Padre Island. The building you located is 400 square feet and had been vacant for 18 months. Because of the limited amount of start-up capital you had to invest in the business, you moved into the building without remodeling either its exterior or its interior.

During the first year, the Zig Zag had 13,400 visitors, of whom 3,350 made a purchase. The average transaction size was $38. The Zig Zag operates on a gross margin of 55 percent and has annual fixed operating expenses of $30,000. Variable costs were 15 percent of sales. The two primary fixed expenses are rent of $1,100 a month and salaries of $1,200 a month. You keep all profits in the business to reinvest in inventory and other immediate business needs.

Because your first year was profitable, you are now considering remodeling the store. Your landlord will not help with these expenses. To paint the exterior would cost $1,400. For the interior, you are thinking of tiling the floor in a zigzag pattern, which will cost $1,600. In addition, new lighting and some new fixtures would cost $4,000.

You believe these changes will increase traffic by 10 percent and that your closure or conversion rate will increase to 30 percent. Will your proposed changes pay for themselves the first year?

Retail Administration

Chapter 14
Managing People

Managing People

OVERVIEW:

In this chapter, we examine the role that people—the human factor—play in retail firms. In retailing, the human factor is composed of employees and customers. Both are critical to carry out a successful retail strategy. Retailers, therefore, must recruit the right employees and customers and then manage these relationships if they are to achieve profitable results. Both outstanding employees and desirable customers have many options; thus, employees must be competitively compensated, and customers must be offered more compelling value than they can achieve from competing retailers.

LEARNING OBJECTIVES:

After reading this chapter, you should be able to:

1. Explain why intangible people resources can provide a more competitive advantage than tangible resources.
2. Describe how to recruit both the right employees and the right customers to be the store's partners.
3. Explain how to manage employees and customers to develop long-term profitable relationships.
4. Discuss how to compensate employees and offer customers a compelling value proposition.

LO 1

Intangible People Resources Make the Difference

Why are intangible people resources more important than tangible resources to a retailer's competitive advantage?

Starting with Chapter 3, we have attempted to illustrate how retailers have long divided consumers into various segments and created brand images for selected segments. Well, today's retailers have gone a step further by trying to create brand images of themselves as employers. They hope that if they can convey to the world why their workplace is appealing and unique, then they will have an easier time attracting the very best workers.[1] Thus, the dominant theme of this chapter is that a retailer's *people* resources are more important than its *tangible* (bricks and mortar) resources. *People*, as used in this chapter, refers to both customers and employees. The earlier chapters have already discussed the importance of customers. However, many retailers fail to give equal significance to employees.

The data suggest that the successful retailers of the future will be those that devote the maximum effort to hiring good employees and retaining them. Today, some 15 million people work in the U.S. retail industry, making it the nation's third largest private-sector employer. Also, labor is the retailer's greatest expense outside of the cost of merchandise because of the sheer number of employees involved. Incidentally, although the average pay for retail clerks isn't particularly lucrative, the retailer's total employee cost including fringe benefits is approximately 50 percent of its total store operating expenses (expenses excluding the cost of merchandise). Therefore, it is important that management work with the employees to improve their efficiency and effectiveness, which will enable their pay to rise and thus result in lower labor turnover. However, the sad truth is that as a result of the recent recession, many retailers began to look at their workers as costs to be reduced, not as revenue generators. Probably the best example of such miscalculations was that of Circuit City. Back in 2003, the now-defunct electronic retailer in one day laid off its 3,900 highest-paid commissioned salespeople, or 20 percent of its total sales force. Because of their selling capabilities and product experience, these individuals were able to gain additional sales. To replace the 3,900 laid-off sales staff, Circuit City then hired about 2,100 lower-paid hourly workers. This swapping of expensive labor with lower-paid workers also changed the routines of the remaining staff and in many cases left a store void of leadership.[2] Other retailers have already begun to use technologies as replacements for some employees. Hilton Hotels is using guest self-service kiosks at some of its wholly owned properties. Hilton believes that the kiosks will improve guest service by reducing time spent in lines, thereby increasing customer convenience, and reducing transaction costs (labor costs). Although the kiosks are built to be user friendly, hotel staff will be available to answer questions and assist guests. Your neighborhood supermarkets and discount stores may already be offering a similar concept with self-checkouts. Other examples of retailers using technology to replace people include the increased usage of radio frequency identifiers and the placement of in-store kiosks to allow customers to look up information themselves.

It is important, however, that retailers realize that all these investments in tangible assets (land, building, technology, equipment and fixtures, and merchandise) will not produce a profitable return unless the retailer is willing to invest in recruiting, motivating, and retaining the right people. These people are the retailer's employees and customers because a store without employees and customers cannot make any sales.

As noted above, too many retailers become shortsighted when bad times occur. As a result, they often fail to give the same care to their investments in intangible assets such as employees and customers that they do to their tangible investments. This is myopic because it is easy for a competitor to copy or replicate the tangible. Land, buildings, technology, equipment and fixtures, and merchandise are all easy to buy and sell in the marketplace, so retailers gain little relative advantage by their tangible presence in the end. An Office Depot store and a Staples store look very similar, as do competing Lowe's and Home Depot stores. However, a retailer with superior employee and customer resources will enjoy a differential advantage over the competition. To be successful, retailers must view labor costs, as well as the expenses of attracting and retaining customers, not as *costs* but as *investments* in obtaining a sustainable competitive advantage. Not to be overlooked is the fact that the retailer wants to have employees who love what they are doing. After all, interacting with an unhappy and disgruntled

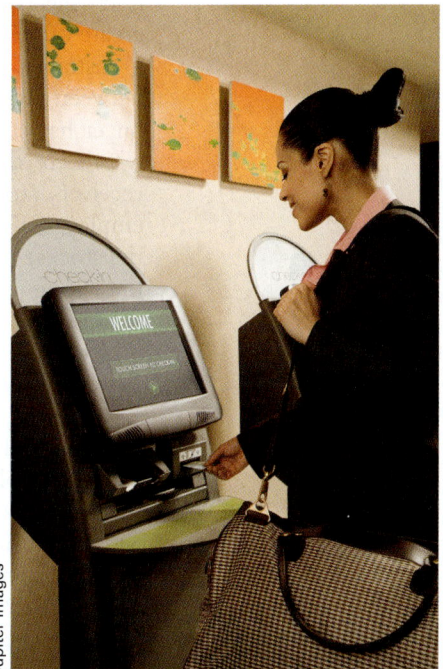

Jupiter Images

Successful retailers realize that investments in tangible assets, such as this kiosk, will not produce profits unless they also invest heavily in intangible assets—employees and customers.

employee often makes co-workers and customers unhappy.[3] By some estimates, those unhappy, disengaged workers—"those that have quit but forgot to tell you"—cost American firms in excess of $250 billion annually.[4]

Similarities Between Employees and Customers

While everyone can make the distinction between a retail employee and a retail customer, few choose to focus on their similarities. These similarities far outweigh the differences, and the inability to realize this can limit retail success. After all, whether an individual is an employee or a customer, that individual must perform some task in the economic-exchange process so as to create value. Lacking a complete knowledge of the retail process, many consumers fail to see themselves as performing a retailing task. Yet many retailers are being forced to follow the example of Hilton Hotels. Another service retailer group, the airlines, has also shifted two retailing tasks—ticketing and issuing boarding passes—to the customer. This is the result of staff cutbacks caused by the industry's multiple bankruptcies, as well as by the economic slowdown. Airlines are now at the point where they have more tasks to perform than employees to perform them, so they must pass them off to the customer, just as they have done with fees. (See the "Retailing: The Inside Story" box in Chapter 1.)

Just like employees, *customers need to be recruited, motivated, and compensated for their efforts*. In this sense, clearly the customer is similar to an employee, but what about the employee as a customer? Some forward-thinking retailers have begun to refer to employees as *internal customers*. Retailers must remember that all employees are part of the service delivery chain in which each performs some task in the economic-exchange process. With a division of labor, each employee performs microspecializations that are combined with the work of other microspecialists to create value along a service chain. Consider, for example, a JCPenney store. Before a customer purchases a pair of Arizona jeans, a number of microtransactions between the firm's associates have already occurred. As described in Chapter 5, a buyer has contracted with an apparel manufacturer in Asia to produce the jeans, which are then shipped to a distribution center. At the distribution center are receivers, stockers, and retrievers. Each of these individuals is a customer of another employee. For example, the retriever of merchandise is a customer of the stocker. If the stocker places the jeans in the wrong bin location, then the retriever may pick the wrong jeans. If the wrong jeans are picked, then they are likely to be sent to a store that does not need them, and thus the store manager or active wear merchandise manager is not served well. This service chain continues until the customer purchases an item from the store.

Actually, the division of labor and development of microspecialists within retailing is the cause of many customer-service problems. Have you ever experienced a problem with a salesclerk? The clerk may proclaim, "Well, I need to check with my boss." This person is another microspecialist who may then need to check with his or her boss (also a microspecialist), and the buck keeps being passed. For this reason, many retailers are trying to *empower* employees to better serve not only external customers but also internal customers, or other employees.

One successful retailer whose excellent service has already been discussed several times in this text is Nordstrom's. Nordstrom's employees, as well as the employees of other great retailers, are able to provide great service because they have been empowered by their employers to take care of the customer. **Empowerment** simply means giving the employee the "power to make things right for the customer." An empowered retail employee:

empowerment
Occurs when employees are given the power in their jobs to do the things necessary to satisfy and make things right for customers.

1. seeks to understand the customer's problem,
2. desires to develop a relationship with the customer,
3. understands the value of customer loyalty, and
4. is allowed or encouraged by management to solve the customer's problem.

The profit impact of empowering employees is dramatic. For many retailers, providing good customer service can make the difference between success and failure. Because retailers operate on a low net profit margin, even a small increase in sales-force productivity—whether measured in sales per employee hour or gross margin per employee hour—often translates directly into an improvement in profits. Consequently, retailers are now expanding their efforts to improve labor's productivity, especially that of the sales force, by training and empowering employees. Consider the following situation: A customer comes in to an appliance dealership to purchase a specific clothes dryer, and the only unit left is the display model on the sales floor. Unfortunately, this model has a scratch on the left side panel that will probably not be seen when placed in the customer's home. The dryer is priced at $600, so in order to not lose the sale; the salesperson offers a $50 reduction in price. The end result is higher self-esteem among employees because they have been trained and are permitted to "make things right" without having to seek the permission of a higher authority. In addition, the lower price has also increased the customer's satisfaction. Combined, these two factors will reduce employee turnover because happy situations don't cause conflicts. Another retailer who has done an excellent job of keeping customers and employees happy is Amazon.com, which *BusinessWeek* honored with its 2009 Customer Service Award. In fact, Amazon earned the award for strong service by letting customers get what they want without ever talking to an employee. After all, purchases are made with a few mouse clicks. Packages arrive on doorsteps quickly, and this happens with monotonous regularity. But when things go wrong at Amazon—and they occasionally do—the company's employees get involved. That may be where Amazon stands out most markedly from other companies.[5] It is also a great place to work. One ex-student told the authors that it is a place that rewards innovation and allows an individual to move from one functional area to a whole different area seamlessly. And the former student didn't even discuss the benefits of all the stock options granted the employees.

In summary, what customers and employees have in common is that they both perform retail tasks, and they both serve the other. It is important to remember that employees must not only serve customers but also other employees (internal customers). Recognizing that employees and customers must always serve each other is the beginning point of servant leadership. With **servant leadership**, employees recognize that their primary responsibility is to be of service to others. Many of the great retail leaders of the past century epitomized this attitude of servant leadership. For example, Jeff Bezos recently spent a week working in an Amazon distribution center in Lexington, Kentucky. He wanted to see what it's like to be a rank-and-file Amazon employee. Other famous servant leaders included James Cash Penney (founder of the JCPenney Company), Stanley Marcus (former chairman of Neiman Marcus), Sam Walton (founder of Walmart), Leslie Wexner (founder of The Limited), Mary Kay Ash (founder of Mary Kay Cosmetics), and Bernie Marcus and Arthur Blank (co-founders of Home Depot).

servant leadership
An employee's recognition that their primary responsibility is to be of service to others.

Employees and Customers are Profit Drivers

This chapter began by emphasizing that retailers must view their employees and customers as investments. Therefore, an important question becomes how much a retailer should be willing to invest in recruiting an employee or a customer. Unfortunately, there is no single correct answer for this question. The answer depends on how much value the retailer thinks an employee or customer can contribute to the firm's bottom line by directly or indirectly causing revenue to increase more than their cost. If a retailer takes an investment versus an expense, or cost, perspective then that retailer is addressing this issue from a long-term perspective.

Consider these two examples. The amount Amazon spends on direct-marketing efforts to a household should result in profit on sales that exceeds the cost of the marketing efforts. Similarly, when an employer decides to reduce labor costs by substituting less-effective workers for skilled workers, revenues can be lost. This is what happened to Circuit City. The chapter's "Global Retailing" box describes the experiences of people dealing with a retailer's overseas call centers. After all, the approximate cost of offering a live, American-based, customer-service agent averages somewhere around $7.50 per phone call, while outsourcing calls to live agents in another country brings the average cost down to about $2.35 per call.[6] Of course, these call-center problems are not just unique to overseas operators. In fact, as far back as 1882 the *New York Times* noted, "There is nothing that will so excite the irritability of a person, apparently, as the telephone."[7]

Global Retailing

Have You Ever Had an Unsatisfactory Experience with a Foreign Call Center?

Sometimes Americans forget that they can have difficulties understanding their fellow citizens from different parts of the United States. Nevertheless, it seems that everyone wants to share an unhappy experience with a foreign call center. However, the word *unhappy* may explain the real problem. After all, if they weren't already unhappy, they probably wouldn't be calling for help.

Here are some of the responses the authors got when they asked consumers about their experiences with foreign call centers.

I called my insurance company (yes, it is major firm listed on the NYSE) about a life insurance policy on their toll free line. My insurance agent retired several years ago. After telling the young man at the call center (which was in Central America) that my zip code was 79416, he told me my nearest agent was in Oklahoma City. Now OKC is 400 miles from West Texas.

So I asked if he was sure, he was. Then I asked him to check again, after checking and finding the same results, he then inquired "are there any other zip codes near your home?"

x x x

I spent quite a bit of time on a retailer's website trying to find a center in the U.S. I could speak to . . .

found one in Ohio (not for calling, but to e-mail inquiries). One e-mail later, they had realized the error and had removed the late fee and finance charge from the bill. I was so close to never stepping foot inside that retailer's store again. BTW, last year I put over $4,500 on the store's in-house account.

x x x

The company my "other" works for followed the lemmings overseas as a cost and efficiency move (or so management thought). After spending a ton of money on "diction" training and giving everyone "American names," management concluded that they made a major mistake. Most of our customers do not want to deal with people they cannot understand over the phone. Sharing and working spreadsheets is one thing. Speaking clearly over the phone is another.

x x x

Last night I had to keep saying "excuse me" because the female couldn't be understood. Finally I solved the problem by thanking her and going to retailer's website and used its "message center." It took 48 hours to get everything fixed, but at least the typed word doesn't have an accent.

x x x

I like to start my conversation by asking the person at the other end of the line, "How is the weather in Mumbai today?" Today, the person responded "I don't know. I am in the Philippines."

x x x

After my divorce I changed my last name back to my maiden name. When I called a credit card company to get my name changed on my account, a gentleman from somewhere overseas gave me a long lecture on the evils of divorce and refused to change my name.

x x x

I had such bad experiences with one retailer's call center routing me overseas that I ended up closing my account because they were harassing me for paying two days late!! I thought I had signed up for automatic payment, but I missed hitting one submit button. Even after going down to the store and talking with the local manager, they didn't update their info and kept calling. After that whole debacle, I really think stating where the call is going can be a competitive differentiator (if in the United States in this case).

x x x

I was a long-time customer of one airline, but I have gradually migrated to Southwest Airlines initially because of the baggage fees and the fact that virtually every time I tried to call the old airline, after the recorded push 3, push 4, push 1 routine, would be connected to someone overseas whom I had a difficult time understanding (especially when flying out of a city like Indianapolis. It seems that nobody over there can pronounce that city's name.) Now that they stopped outsourcing their calls overseas, I may go back, it's going to be awhile before I come back because Southwest is generally on-time, hassle-and-fee-free, and I'm guaranteed to get a full-sized 737 ... not a regional jet which I dislike. My old airline may have saved $25 million per year thru this call center outsourcing, but I'm guessing they lost a lot more than that every year with customer dissatisfaction. In fact, I may never have tried Southwest Air if they had a better call center.

The basic point of the examples in the "Global Retailing" box is clear: The gross profit generated by an employee or customer must exceed the cost of servicing these employees and customers. Employees and customers whose gross profit generated greatly exceeds their cost to the retailer will be the people who are most important to the retailer's success. In the case of customers, as a rule, retailers have found that 20 percent of the customers generate 80 percent of the sales. These are the frequent and heavy shoppers who make up the most loyal core of customers. The same 80–20 rule holds for retail salespeople. Furniture, jewelry, auto, and insurance salespeople all generally follow the 80–20 rule: 80 percent of retail sales come from 20 percent of the salespeople.

As previously mentioned, when some retailers think of people, they usually think of employees. However, this chapter also considers how customers can be managed with some of the same processes used in managing employees. The authors feel that retail managers must be encouraged to think of their customers as employees and that their employees be treated like customers. Retailing is an exchange relationship, and in exchange relationships people want to be "treated right." This means being treated honestly, fairly, and with respect. Only by treating people right will retailers be able to have enduring and profitable relationships with their employees and customers.

Good customer and employee relationships are more than just additive in their effect on a retailer's performance; the effect is synergistic. Think about it. Recall a time when you were treated rudely by a retail employee. Most likely this person did not have a good relationship with his or her employer; perhaps the employee was upset about working conditions or treatment by a supervisor. Or maybe it was that disengaged worker discussed earlier who quit but forgot to tell the boss. In return, because employees are only human, this person took out these bad feelings on other employees (internal customers) and on customers like you. This unfair treatment made you mad, and you in turn got mad at the employee and the store, which only increased the employee's unhappiness. Such behavior can be said to have a multiplying effect as the unhappy employee takes out his or her frustrations on the next customer.

LO 2 — Obtaining the Right People

What is the process for recruiting the right employees and customers?

Retailers must remember that human resources are acquired in a competitive marketplace. Even in poor economic times, good employees will seldom come knocking at a retailer's door. After all, when talented workers or managers are looking for employment, they seldom think of contacting retail firms because of the reputation, sometimes unwarranted, many retailers have for low starting wages. Therefore, retailers must aggressively seek out and recruit good employees; in so doing, they must compete with other industries for labor resources.

Perhaps even more competitive is the marketplace for customers. In any community in the United States with a population of more than 50,000, an individual consumer has many choices. And if the choices in the immediate community are limited, then the consumer can shop on the Internet, through the mail, or perhaps travel 20 to 40 miles to a larger city. These alternatives allow individuals to expand their shopping options immensely. To recruit the most profitable customers, a retailer must offer a compelling **value proposition** (the promised benefits a retailer offers in relation to the cost the consumer incurs) and build long-term relationships with these customers.

value proposition
Is the promised benefits a retailer offers in relation to the cost the consumer incurs

Customer Relationship Management

An increasingly popular technology for cultivating and maintaining the right customers is **customer relationship management (CRM)**.[8] CRM is composed of an integrated information system in which the fundamental unit of data collection is the customer, supplemented by other relevant information about the customer, including purchasing behavior. Customer data at the most microlevel is captured, including merchandise and services purchased, store location, time of purchase, demographic information, and satisfaction data such as customer complaints. For example, by using such a system, if an airline loses a customer's bag or cancels his or her flight because of a mechanical problem, then the next time that customer shows up at the airport, an agent will personally apologize and offer the traveler a free pass to an airport lounge because of the troubles.[9]

customer relationship management (CRM)
Is comprised of an integrated information system where the fundamental unit of data collection is the customer, supplemented by relevant information about the customer.

Historically, retailers have thought of their businesses in terms of merchandise. As a result, merchandise management became so fundamental that every unique item of merchandise had its own identifier, or stockkeeping unit (SKU). However, retailers develop relationships with customers, not SKUs. Customers—not merchandise—are the ultimate source of profitability. Despite knowing this, almost all retailers can tell you how many SKUs they have in their store, as well as the dollar value of their inventory, but few retailers know how many unique customers they have who patronize their store. Following are some fundamental questions that a CRM system can answer.

1. How many unique customers patronize the store over a given time frame (week, month, and year)?

2. What is the average transaction size in terms of dollars and units purchased by type of customer? For instance, do customers between the ages of 21 and 33 have a different transaction profile than those aged 34 to 54?

3. What is the profitability of groups of customers or the profitability of a particular customer?

4. Is the customer profile at a retailer's stores in one region or part of a city different from the profile in another area?

5. Was the recent direct-mail promotion cost effective? This analysis can be broken down to the level of the specific customer.

6. Which customers purchase the same items repeatedly versus trying new items? For predictable purchase items, the retailer can notify the customer when he or she may need to restock. The retailer can also notify a more opportunistic customer of new merchandise items.

Of course, CRM can help the retailer answer literally hundreds of other questions. After all, with each customer ID, the retailer has data on the time of day, location, price paid, and any other important information about every purchase. Those retailers who are on the leading edge of CRM are the ones that have integrated their CRM system with their suppliers, advertising agencies, and other members of the supply chain. This collaborative effort can enable the entire supply chain to be more customer focused. For example, Tesco's integration of a CRM program to its "Clubcard" has been cited as the main reason that it has been able to withstand Walmart's U.K. invasion.[10] However, this Tesco example (Chapter 2's "What's New?" box) also illustrates that the overall goal of CRM is not just to generate reports or data but also to provide the retailer with a tool to develop a long-term profitable relationship—target marketing—with a customer that is mutually beneficial. How can this be done? Here are a few examples.

1. A retailer could analyze transactional data by time of day and day of week, find the times of day when its most profitable customers shop, and schedule key associates to better serve these customers at these hours.

2. A retailer might find that sales or visits from a customer have been declining. In such cases, the retailer could target specific marketing programs toward that customer. These special programs could be direct mail, coupons, or a special call from the customer's most frequently used sales associate.

3. CRM can help the retailer identify the types of merchandise to stock during certain seasons based on customer preferences. If a customer has been purchasing toddler's clothing for a year or so, then the retailer may want to alert the customer about its children's clothing department. Based on past purchases and the family demographic information in the CRM system, the retailer can predict future purchases and that the next size up from toddlers' is children's.

4. A retailer's customer-service personnel can see a complete record of the customer's purchase history and prioritize the special treatment the customer may deserve based on his or her profitability to the retailer. In short, knowing the cost of losing a customer can be a strong motivator for doing everything in terms of customer service to retain that customer.

On the leading edge of CRM are those retailers that have integrated their CRM system with their suppliers, advertising agencies, and other members of the supply chain. This collaborative effort enables the entire supply chain to be more customer focused. This is especially important when a product in the food-distribution channel needs to be recalled (see the case at the end of Chapter 5) or products sourced in other countries where nonconforming ingredients (such as lead-based paint) may be used. With a contemporary CRM system, the retailer has knowledge of who purchased the product that needs to be recalled and can also trace backward in the channel to the source of supply.

Employee Sources

Where does a retailer obtain employees? The eight employee sources shown on the left side of Exhibit 14.1 are the most common: competitors, walk-ins (both in person at the store and online at the retailer's website), employment agencies (including online at websites such as monster.com), schools and colleges, former employees, advertisements, recommendations, and customer referrals. Given the economic environment, the source seeing the most expanded use in recent years is former employees. A recent survey by the American Association of Retired Persons (AARP) found that eight out of 10 of its members either want to continue to work or need to work past age 65. This means that college students must be extra prepared for their first postgraduation job search because employers will value the experience that older workers bring to the job.[11]

Customer Sources

The second column of Exhibit 14.1 lists sources of customers. These include competitors, walk-ins (again in the store or on the website) advertisements, employees, and referrals from other customers. Essentially these sources are not that different from the sources used for gathering employees. Many customers can be obtained from competitors that have stockout problems or other failures in customer service. In fact, retail patronage research has demonstrated that many customers do not go about selecting which stores to patronize, but which stores to avoid. After a customer has decided where *not* to shop, the remaining options become the ones that win the customer's patronage. As discussed in Chapter 7, traffic is also a major source of customers. High levels of consumer traffic passing by a store will result in more walk-ins. Finally, satisfied employees will promote the store to their family and friends. Employees who praise the store where they work are especially credible because they should know the store best. This is particularly true for service retailers. Many hospital workers tell negative stories about their environment and the level of patient care and service, and this can have a very negative effect on the health provider's ability to attract patients (if the patients have a choice). Conversely, of course, satisfied customers can become enthusiastic about the retailer resulting in referrals to friends and acquaintances. But even though an enthusiastic customer may demonstrate a strong commitment to the retailer, an unhappy customer is likely to tell more friends and potential customers than a satisfied customer will.[12]

Exhibit 14.1
Sources of Retail Employees and Customers

Employees	Customers
Competitors	Competitors
Walk-ins	Walk-ins
Employment agencies	Advertisements
Schools and colleges	Employees
Former employees	Customer referrals
Advertisements	Affinity programs
Recommendations	Customer agency
Customer referrals	

In addition to the preceding traditional sources of customers, retailers are recognizing the potential value of tying-in with other groups. For example, the American Automobile Association (AAA) provides members with discounts at many motels, hotels, restaurants, and other retailers that cater to the automobile traveler. And AARP offers member discounts on travel, financial services, lodging, prescription drugs, and many other products and services (see www.aarp.org/benefits). AARP currently offers discounts on rental cars (Avis, Hertz, and National Car Rental, among others), hotels (AmeriSuites, Best Western, Days Inn, Holiday Inn, and Sheraton), and many other products. It is interesting to note that this program doesn't just attract older consumers. Anyone, even students, as long as they list their correct date of birth on their AARP application, can obtain an associate AARP membership card and the good deals on travel.[13]

Another unusual source for capturing customers is the equivalent of an employment agency but is more akin to a customer agency, which is used for some products and services where the typical customer may not have the knowledge and information to make an informed decision. One such example is the selection of a college, especially for a first-generation student. There are more than a thousand choices in the United States for a four-year undergraduate education. Prices range from less than $7,000 per year to more than $45,000 per year. Consequently, many parents are retaining college consultants who provide a good match between the demands of colleges for students and the desires and needs of various students. (Perhaps some of you used such a service when you were selecting your college.) Another example relates to major household redecorating or renovation. It is not unusual for a couple who purchased a 2,500-square-foot house in 1979 for $65,000 to decide after the last child has gone off to college to redecorate and renovate the house. Many people prefer to renovate in order to stay in a well-liked neighborhood. However, a major redecorating and renovation of a house that cost $65,000 in 1979 may cost $100,000 or more now. For most such major projects, the house owner would retain an interior designer and a general contractor who would guide the couple in what to purchase and where. Consequently, the interior design consultant is a major gatekeeper and source of customers for many home-improvement retailers.

Fancy/Veer/Corbis

During the recent economic downturn, many interior designers found a large segment of their customers came from households that decided to remodel their houses rather than move to a larger home.

Screening and Selecting Employees

Hiring the wrong person is costly in terms of both time and money. Making a hiring mistake can lead to turnover of both employees (the mishired individual and maybe other good employees) and customers. Therefore, before beginning the discussion of human resource (HR) issues, it is important to point out that these issues are extremely complex—too much so for retailers without special training in that area. The authors strongly recommend working with HR professionals. However, retailers must still understand and implement basic procedures for selecting employees.[14] Regardless of the specific source, in today's environment all job applicants should be subjected to a formal screening process to sort potentially good from potentially bad employees. Nevertheless, as with any judgment process, some mistakes will happen. But fewer errors occur when *potential* employees are screened. Today, however, some retailers have attempted to reduce costs in the hiring process by using online personality tests early in the process. By testing earlier, the time required by the store managers in interviewing applicants is reduced.[15] Home Depot, for example, uses test kiosks in its store. This way Home Depot can obtain more information more cheaply. Also, because the responses are made to the computer directly rather than on paper or to an interviewer, respondents feel that the information is more readily subject to instant checking and verification with other databases. Thus, to avoid potential embarrassment, applicants are assumed to be more truthful. As a result, these tests have an excellent record of screening out low-integrity applicants, thereby avoiding the types of irresponsible and counterproductive behaviors that drive managers crazy: disciplinary problems, disruptiveness on the job, chronic tardiness, and excessive absenteeism. A big advantage of this system for Home Depot is that the retailer used to hire only one or two of 30 or more applicants who completed the application and interview process. Now the figure may be as high as 20 out of 30.[16]

Retailers tend to vary in the amount of additional screening they use. In addition, to the outside verification just discussed, there are four other types of screens: application forms, personal interview, testing, and references. The total applicant pool for a particular job is progressively reduced as the applicants are subjected to each screen.

Application Forms

As a matter of procedure, all applicants should be asked to fill out an application form. The application form should conveniently and compactly capture the individual's identity, training, and work history that relates to his or her performance of the job tasks. Title VII of the Civil Rights Act of 1964 prohibits employers from discrimination in employment on the basis of race, color, religion, sex, or national origin; the Age Discrimination in Employment Act of 1967 (ADEA) prohibits employers from discrimination in employment on the basis of age; and the Americans with Disabilities Act of 1990 (ADA) prohibits employers from discrimination in employment on the basis of handicap/disability. Thus, the employer is effectively prohibited from asking any questions whose answer could be used to discriminate between two different groups of applicants.[17] Many times a resume is substituted for an application form. The chapter's "What's New?" box provides some ideas on using a resume to differentiate yourself from other job applicants.

There are two more important things to remember when preparing that resume. Many large retailers now keep a huge database of job applicants so they can search for certain key words such as *supervised staff* if they want someone with management experience. As a result, any online application is funneled through such a system. Therefore, applicants must be clear and descriptive when listing their achievements on their resumes.[18] These scanners can also be used to pick up such "little white lies" as phony degrees, majors, and organizations. In addition, it is wise for applicants to avoid using a video resume. Retailers have been advised by their legal staffs to proceed with caution when receiving video applications. After all, by accepting them, they may be making themselves liable to charges of discrimination. By viewing the video, they are seeing a physical representation of the candidate—including race, national origin, and age. As a result, a rejected applicant might say, "The reason the retailer didn't [interview] me is because you can tell I'm a minority [or old or handicapped]." Therefore, most employers will tend to ignore video resumes.[19]

What's New?

Does Your Resume Sell You?

Your resume may be the most important document you will ever write. It will be an employers' first impression of you and, given the ease by which resumes may be sent electronically, it must make you stand out from the thousands of other resumes that an employer will see. Sound daunting? Not really.

Your resume is critical, but let's look at what its purpose is—to impress a potential employer with your background and qualifications so that the employer will want to invite you for an interview. Your resume does not get you a job, but it is a vital first step in your journey for that perfect job. In short, it must "sell" what you have to offer an employer.

Students often get confused and even hit a "dead end" by worrying about what their resume should "look" like; frankly, what it looks like is far less important than what it has to say. There are countless resume styles, but the style really isn't the most important thing. It must be arranged in some logical way (but not necessarily the same logical way that your roommate uses) and be easy to read, and it must highlight your accomplishments and be free of spelling and grammatical errors. College career centers will have sample resumes, but be careful not to make your information or sales message fit any one sample or template. It is a great idea to have a professional from the career center look at your resume, critique it and offer suggestions, and explain why and how those suggestions might help your resume sell you better. In addition, another person can often catch misspellings, which might seem very minor but can be the mistake that keeps your resume from being considered further.

For most students, one page is long enough; a few with considerable work experience, internships, or leadership positions, may need two pages. College students seeking their first professional position, however, should never have more than two pages. Arrange your resume into logical headings. "Education," "Work Experience," "Activities," and "Leadership" are common ones, but this is not an exhaustive list. Under "Education," list your college or university, degree, major, when you will receive that degree, and GPA (if you have done well academically). This brings up another point—what is a good GPA? There is no simple answer to that question, but remember that by omitting any reference to your academic performance you are allowing the employer to make his or her own assumptions—and often those assumptions will be far worse than the real story. Remember that there are several ways to word your GPA while being honest, accurate, and still selling yourself. For example, is your major GPA higher than your overall? Last 60 hours better than your first 60 hours?

If you have had an internship, then you may want to create a separate heading for that—describe what you accomplished and where and when you did it. Employers are always interested in what you've actually accomplished. They understand that most college students are young and haven't had the same opportunities that an older candidate might have. What they do want to see is what you have accomplished in the time you've been given. This can take many forms including volunteer work (which could become a separate heading), work experience, organizations in which you've held leadership positions, or honors and awards that make you stand out. Did you work while completing your degree? If so, tell the employer; employers are always impressed with candidates who can juggle work, school, and campus activities—and do all of them well. After all, that is what most workdays will be in your first job—doing multiple tasks, sometimes with little supervision but with high expectations. Things in your past that show you can do that will serve you well in your job search.

Source: Prepared by David Kraus, Director of University Career Services, Texas Tech University.

From the list of qualified applicants who filled out an application or submitted a resume, the retailer must select the best possible subset of candidates for each job.

Personal Interview

Those applicants who possess the basic characteristics needed to perform the job should be personally interviewed. This important step allows the retailer to assess how well qualified the applicants are for the job. By its very nature, an interview is subjective, but in a well-structured interview a retailer can obtain information or at least gain insight into the attitudes, personality, motives, and job aspirations of the interviewee.

While the interview allows the retailer to assess how well qualified the applicants are for the job, it also provides an opportunity for the interviewee to ask questions about the retailer.

Many interviewers overlook the fact that the interview should be a two-way communication process. Not only does the retailer want to gather information about the applicant but also the applicant may desire information about the retailer. Allowing time for the interviewee to ask questions is essential if the retailer is competing for the talents of highly desired applicants. In fact, the interviewer may actually use part of the interview time to try to sell the applicant on working for the retailer as well as honestly explain what the job entails and thus avoid job dissatisfaction or possible legal complications based on misunderstandings.

One retailer that has been recognized for doing an exception job during the interview process is Ladybug Organic Coffee Company, a Portland, Oregon, coffee shop that also serves pastries and other light fare. The retailer uses a five-page job application form that includes 10 essay questions intended to weed out all but the most devoted and cheerful baristas and bakers. The types of questions used on this application are the same as those that many interviewees can expect to be asked when they interview with any successful firm. For example,

- "What is the most important thing that you have ever learned, and how has it changed your life?"

- "What is something that you do on a regular basis to make the world a better place?"

After all, according to Ladybug's owner, Angel O'Brien, as the economy worsens and baristas' jobs are increasingly threatened, the applicants' personality and character traits are likely to become even more important.[20]

As pointed out in the chapter's "Service Retailing" box, many retailers are now using online placement companies to aid them in locating applicants. However, the same Internet may actually be used to gather information about the applicant either before or after the interview phase.

A final note about the interview is that while it may be explicitly illegal to discriminate against disabled workers, research by MIT economists has found such laws have actually reduced the number of handicapped applicants hired. Either employers don't want to make necessary accommodations, or they are afraid of what happens if a new hire doesn't work out.[21] Overlawyered.com has the 2004 tale of a grocer who was broad-minded enough to take on a clerk with Down syndrome, fired the worker when it didn't work out, and ended up in a lawsuit.[22]

Testing

The more traditional hiring process usually involves some type of formal tests to be administered to applicants after they have received favorable ratings in their

Service Retailing

Corporate Websites, Social Networking, and Your Job Search

Technology, specifically the tools available on the Internet, has created a new paradigm for job seekers. What once was available almost exclusively through help wanted ads in newspapers is now available at your fingertips and in the comfort of your home or using your phone, 24/7. A simple Google search under "careers" yields 278 million potential websites; "jobs" yields 969 million—a long way from the local or even national newspaper ads of just a few years ago.

While the Internet has certainly made your search easier, at least in terms of potential sources of job and career information, it has also created a new set of issues and concerns for job seekers and employers. Students should understand that the resources available on the Internet are tools for them to use—convenient, accessible, fast, and portable, but still only tools to be effectively utilized. Corporate websites have much valuable information that can help students learn more about a particular potential employer—what they do, where they do it, their corporate philosophy, customers, and structure. And virtually every corporate site will have a link to employment or career opportunities. One click and you have a listing of available positions and, in most cases, can even apply online. Sounds simple, doesn't it? In some ways it is, but care must be taken when applying. As stated in the text, employers want to know what you have accomplished and how that applies to the particular position for which you are applying. Your resume must be tailored for each position and, if the site allows, a cover letter explaining your background and interest in each position. Remember—if it really is that simple, then thousands of your fellow students and other job seekers are doing the same thing you are. What makes you stand out? Unique? Who is the one they will want to interview from among the huge numbers of resumes they see each day?

An effective job search will take time and the use of all your resources. Your college career center is a great place to start. It can help you develop a plan; figure out what careers may be more in line with your interests, aptitudes, and strengths; develop a resume that can help sell your strengths; help with mock interviews to prepare for the real thing; identify specific websites that you might find helpful; provide numerous opportunities for you to interact with employers through companies that interview on your campus, and through job fairs, job postings, and seminars and events that bring in employers as presenters. Career centers will also have job postings on their websites, and these can be an extremely effective source for you—after all, these are employers who have contacted your school wanting to post a position that you and students from your school will see. Perhaps the employer

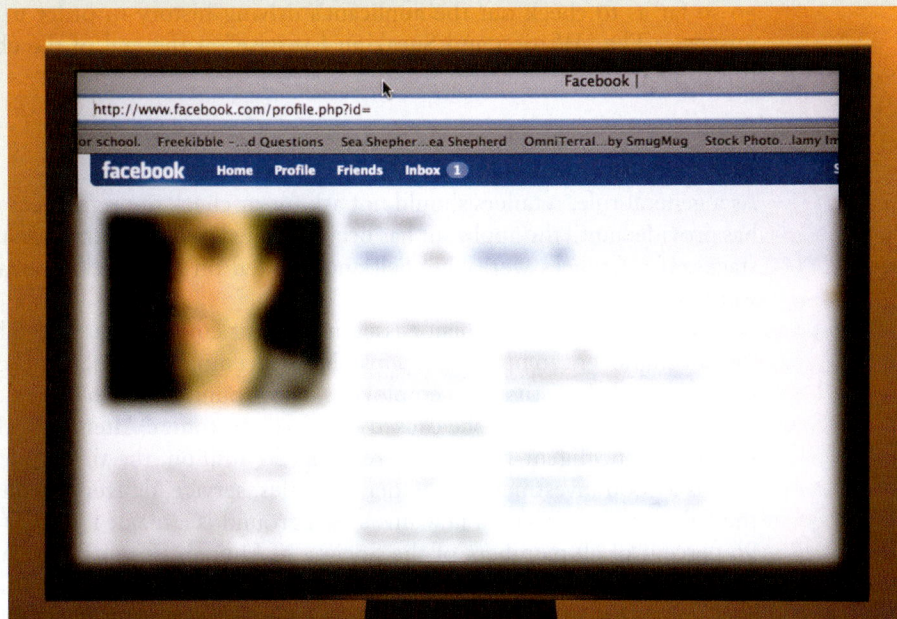

Eric Carr/Alamy

(continued)

Service Retailing (*continued*)

is an alum of your school or has hired graduates from there in the past with great success and wants more like them.

College students love their social-networking sites—Facebook, MySpace, and so on—and these provide a quick, easy way to keep in touch with friends. However, just as these sites have revolutionized the way in which students communicate, they have also provided potential pitfalls when it comes to job seeking. Who else can see the information about you that is on your Facebook site? Probably a lot more people than you might think, including potential employers. Surveys indicate that more and more employers are searching social-networking sites to learn more about a job candidate. Be very careful with pictures, posts that will be inappropriate for employers to see, the "Wall," and even comments and pictures that your friends may post. Be sure to get those photos of you acting "goofy" at that "wild party" from last year off your page. These can often cast you in an unfavorable light.

While the Internet has afforded student job seekers many options, keep in mind that employers are also given more avenues to post their available positions. They may choose to list their positions on a national website such as Monster or Career Builder, but students using only those resources are selling their potential opportunities short. Employers may choose to post positions on various college career centers, but these also will not encompass all opportunities. Employers may elect to simply post jobs on their own corporate website, making them easy to find but, with literally thousands of retailers, making a lengthy process for applicants. Focus on specific companies that interest you, do your research on those companies, get on their websites regularly, and pursue every opportunity for which you think you have the skills and background. Students who practice these techniques will be successful.

Source: Prepared by David Kraus, Director of University Career Services, Texas Tech University.

---

personal interviews. These tests, like the ones described earlier, look for certain characteristics such as honesty, intelligence, work ethic, leadership potential, particular interests, and personality traits. Other assessments used by retailers include credit checks with local credit bureaus. Most applicants are unaware that their chances of getting that job can be destroyed by a bad credit score. These credit checks include not only your payment history but also unpaid parking fines, library fines, unpaid speeding tickets, and any other bill more than 30 days old.[23] Today, the majority of retailers check out an applicant's credit history. Also, some retailers go so far as to check out the applicant's driving history in order to avoid hiring mistakes. The "Writing and Speaking Exercise" at the end of the chapter covers this topic in greater detail.

References

As a general rule, retailers should not ask for or check the references the applicant has provided until the applicant has been screened or filtered through the preceding stages. If references were obtained and verified on all initial applicants, the cost would be excessive.

Negligent hiring is a major issue in current employment law. The premise is that an employer can be held responsible for an employee's unlawful actions if it did not reasonably investigate an employee's background and then placed the employee in a position where he or she caused harm to a customer. After all, with the average verdict in a negligent-hiring case reaching $2 million, the time and money spent here is a good investment. Whether it is sales, service, delivery, or administration, the failure to investigate a new hire's background is a major mistake.[24] As a result, 96 percent of all members of the Society of Human Resource managers say that their firms now check references, credentials, or both.[25] As an additional precaution, some retailers even use a screening service that provides biweekly updates on current employees to protect themselves from future legal problems.[26]

When references and credentials are obtained and checked, the retailer should try to assess the honesty and reliability of the applicant. The reason for leaving the prior place or places of employment should also be investigated. The retailer should be interested in finding out what type of person will vouch for the prospective employee. Although most references provided by the applicant can be expected to give a neutral or favorable recommendation (if they give one at all), the reference check does give the retailer a means to verify the accuracy and completeness of the application. This is especially important since one study found that almost 50 percent of all resumes had at least one inaccuracy.[27] Many retailers have found greater success using telephone interviews instead of asking for written recommendations. This method enables retailers to gather more complete and honest evaluations than do letters, even if it is only in what the reference does *not* say about the applicant. After all, many reference sources, due to an anxiety of litigation, may fear putting any negative comments in writing.

One final comment on checking references: The retailer must tread carefully to avoid breaking federal and state laws. The personnel manager is well advised to visit the firm's legal staff yearly to determine the firm's and the applicant's legal rights. New laws are regularly being enacted by Congress and state legislatures and interpreted daily in courts cases throughout the country.

Screening and Selecting Customers

Retailers compete aggressively for customers, and you might believe it is unusual for a retailer to not want to do business with a customer. In a general sense, this is true. Retailers that are successful are both market and customer oriented and are always recruiting and welcoming new customers. However, the screening and selection of customers is more common than you might think. Bars and gambling establishments must screen for underage customers. A Porsche mechanic may not take customers with non-Porsche autos. Perhaps most predominant are universities that screen out and select the most desirable students.

When retailers screen or select customers, they must be sure not to violate any equal opportunity or discrimination laws. However, there are very legitimate reasons for screening and selecting customers. The most common include the following:

1. the inability to adequately service certain customers—for example, not accepting older children for a preschool;
2. the deterioration of a retailer's atmosphere if customers of a certain type are admitted, such as allowing individuals in bathing suits or T-shirts to enter a fine-dining establishment; and
3. the inability to profitably service customers—for example, Sam's Club and Costco charge a minimum annual fee to discourage customers who purchase only small quantities.

However, one must never use these screening criteria to illegally discriminate against certain groups. For instance the ADA requires that all businesses have access for handicapped individuals. A retailer cannot simply conclude that it is unprofitable to admit customers who are in a wheelchair or are blind and therefore choose not to serve them. However, it is perfectly legitimate for a retailer to decide, with the aid of its CRM system, that certain customers do not meet their standards. For instance, some restaurants set a minimum order. Each table is a valuable revenue-generating tool; if two people sit and converse for two hours and spend only $12, then considerable revenue may be foregone. In another case, an independent bicycle dealer fired an overbearing, demanding, and irritating customer whose behavior made it impossible for the retailer to ever obtain a profitable transaction.[28]

LO 3 | Managing People

How do retailers manage employees and customers?

Just hiring the right employees and attracting the best customers is not enough in today's environment. After all, both groups must be trained, developed, and motivated. Referring back to Chapter 8, employees and customers are not an expense; they are assets, and the retailer needs to invest in improving them. Therefore, employees and customers need to be managed. Many retailers have policies for managing their employees but seldom think of managing their customers. While customer management is not something to be ignored, this section begins with a discussion of managing employees.

The retailer must prepare programs for training employees to meet current or future job requirements, evaluating employees, and motivating them. After all, in an economy with a low unemployment rate, if an employee does not like something about the job, its training, or even his or her co-workers, then that employee can easily go elsewhere. In fact, even in the case of high unemployment it behooves the retailer to have low employee turnover because new employees are costly to train and risky to hire because they may not perform as expected. Therefore, the most critical job for retailers today is retaining current employees. A study of the supermarket industry by the Coca-Cola Retailing Research Council, for example, found that the median retention rate of hourly supermarket employees was 97 days—that is, one-half of all new supermarket hires terminate their employment within 97 days of starting work.[29] The study further found that the cost (including both direct and opportunity cost, which are described in Exhibit 14.2) of replacing this hourly employee was $4,291 for a union store and $3,372 for a nonunion store.[30] In all, employee turnover costs the average supermarket almost $190,000 annually in direct and opportunity costs.[31] Turnover is thought to be an even more serious problem in specialty stores since they typically hire part-timers at entry-level positions.

Exhibit 14.2
Various Types of Employee Turnover Costs

Direct: These costs are reflected on the retailer's financial statements.

- Cost of recruiting applicants
- Cost of evaluating applicants (including interviews, reference checks, and any testing)
- Cost of training classes (including management's time)
- Pay (including benefits) during period when new employee is taking training course
- Part of supervisor's pay (including benefits) to cover time spent helping new employee during first few weeks of job

Indirect: These activities cause a reduction in the firm's revenue. Thus, while they are not shown on the retailer's financial statements, they are still a cost.

- Loss of customers who were "loyal" to former employee
- Lost sales resulting from the employee's initial lack of product knowledge
- Lost sales and potential profits missed from alienated customers resulting from inexperience in retail selling
- Decrease in employee morale caused by the departure of an employee
- Effect of the employees' lower morale on customers

Turnover is a problem and a major cost in the realm of retail employees; a similar problem exists regarding customers. In Chapter 3, it was noted that, on average, it costs a retailer five times as much to recruit a new customer as it does to retain an existing customer. However, most retailers fail to recognize this obvious fact. One of the authors was consulting with an auto dealer on retail advertising and promotion. The dealership was selling more than 1,200 new cars and more than 300 used cars a year and had a very successful service and body shop. The dealership spent more than $1 million annually on advertising. Research revealed that the dealership received approximately one complaint letter a week about warranty claims or about the service and body shop. The typical complaint protested a charge that ranged from less than $200 to $1,500, with the average being $425. In short, the total complaints for a year were around $22,000. One of the recommendations was to allow the service manager to waive charges at his discretion and charge these to the general marketing expense of the dealership (as much as $30,000 per year). This meant that the waiver of the fees would not influence the profitability of the service and body shop. The following year, the dealership won a regional award from Ford Motor Company for outstanding customer service in the auto service and body shop area of the business. However, the more interesting thing was that the general manager was now receiving about one letter a month from customers praising the service area. And you can bet these customers told their friends. If the dealership had taken the equivalent amount of money and spent it on advertising to attract new customers, it would not have yielded these results.

Training and Developing Employees

Retailers wanting the best return on their human resource investment should provide training and development for both new and existing employees. Training and development are consistent with the concept of human resource planning. After all, there is no such thing as a "natural" salesperson or manager. Like any other talent, this ability must be carefully taught and monitored with a training program.

Training is not a one-time event. It must be ongoing because employees will not enjoy their jobs without the necessary knowledge to perform their assigned tasks. When employees aren't happy at work, they switch jobs. Therefore, retailers today must view training as a process of continuing education. For example, many of the country's most successful retailers, such as Target and McDonald's, invest a great deal of money in order to maintain their competitive position. Thus, as an individual's responsibilities increase, so do the training and development. Employees are taught not just technical skills but also administrative and people skills such as functioning as a team. Each phase of development is built on the training that preceded it and includes training in merchandising, operations management, motivation, decision making, problem analysis, and time management.

In addition to developing a pool of future managers and assisting employees with current duties, training and development programs enable the employees to know their status within the firm; that is, where they stand and how they are doing. Generation Yers, in particular, provide a wealth of potential to employers because of their vigor, enthusiasm, talent, early experience, and high expectations.[32] Retail managers must remember that a career in their field is different from careers in other business fields. In the beginning, retailing is like an hour-glass. Starting at the base of the hourglass, the typical new college employee is broadly educated and once joining the retail enterprise becomes increasingly specialized in working toward the goal of being a buyer—the ultimate specialist. At the midpoint of the hourglass we see a narrow focus, but afterward the objective is to increase breadth, not specialty, with the goal of becoming a regional store or division manager. Stated alternatively, the new college graduate starts broadly by becoming an expert such as a lead buyer in a category and then if he or she is to progress further, becomes broader to handle more complex retail management roles.

Today there is a new type of training tool available to retailers. Online training is one of the fastest-growing ways of training employees at small retailers who cannot afford to have a complete training staff. For example, many of these smaller retailers use services such as www.videomedia.net to train their employees in sexual harassment issues and thus minimize their liability. In the event of any future claims, these retailers can prove that their employees were required to participate in this training and that the retailers made an effort to eliminate such harassment from the workplace. Unless other circumstances prevail, the retailer would probably not be liable.

The best training and development program devised is useless unless management adopts a philosophy of complete support. In the past, many retail executives got so tied up in merchandising concerns that they forgot about human resources—a big mistake.

Training and Developing Customers

Once again, the typical mindset of retailers or general businesspeople is that they train employees but not customers. Such thinking is myopic. Three retailers that have made training and educating customers a core part of their value proposition are Home Depot, Best Buy, and PetSmart. These three retailers provide short courses that instruct customers on how to use their products or engage in do-it-yourself projects. Two other examples from the current economy are Harley-Davidson, which

As higher gasoline prices cause some consumers to trade-in their cars for bikes, Harley-Davidson provides driving schools for these new bikers.

provides driving schools, especially for boomers as they return to the bikes of their past in order to reduce travel expenses; and local supermarkets that offer cooking classes as consumers seek to reduce the number of times they eat out.

Evaluating Employees

Performance appraisal and review is the formal, systematic assessment of how well employees are performing their jobs in relation to established standards, as well as the communication of that assessment to employees. Employees place a great deal of importance on appraisals, and the way the appraisal system operates affects morale and organizational climate in significant ways. Moreover, the appraisal system also has an impact on other human resource processes such as training and development, compensation, and promotion.

Informal appraisals tend to take place on an ongoing basis within the retail firm as supervisors evaluate their subordinates' work on a daily basis and as subordinates appraise each other as well as their supervisors. However, the formal, systematic appraisal of an individual is likely to occur at certain intervals throughout the year or when the employee is being considered for a wage increase, a promotion, a transfer, or an opportunity to improve job skills.

Retailers of all sizes should try to use objective criteria for the appraisal and review process whenever possible. Criteria for the objective review and appraisal of salespeople are shown in Exhibit 14.3. However, not every item that the retailer

performance appraisal and review Is the formal, systematic assessment of how well employees are performing their jobs in relation to established standards and the communication of that assessment to employees.

Exhibit 14.3
Criteria Used in the Appraisal and Review Process

Merchandise Procedures:	Is accurate in counting and inventorying merchandise.
	Prevents merchandise shrinkage due to mishandling of merchandise.
	Keeps merchandise in a neat and orderly manner on sales floor.
	Knows the design and specification of warranties and guarantees of the merchandise groups.
	Gets merchandise on sales floor quickly after merchandise arrival.
Customer Service Ability:	Provides courteous service to customers.
	Handles customer complaints and/or service problems as indicated by store procedure.
	Follows proper procedure concerning merchandise returns and layaways when conducted through credit transactions.
	Suggests add-on or complementary merchandise to customers.
Sales Ability:	Has strong ability to close the sale.
	Promotes sale of merchandise items having profit margins.
	Acts as a resource to other departments or other salespeople needing assistance.
	Works well with fellow workers in primary merchandise department.
Product/ Merchandise Knowledge:	Knowledgeable of design, style, and construction of merchandise group.
	Knowledgeable of special promotions and/or advertised sale items.
	Knowledgeable of material (fabrics), color coordination, and complementary accessories.
Store Policy:	Provides accurate and complete paperwork related to returned merchandise.
	Provides accurate and complete paperwork related to work schedules.
	Provides accurate and complete paperwork for cash and credit transactions.
	Shows up on time for work, sales meetings, and training sessions.
	Accurately follows day-to-day instructions of immediate supervisor.
	Employee's overall job-related attitude.

Source: Robert P. Bush, Alan J. Bush, David J. Ortinau, and Joseph F. Hair, Jr., "Developing a Behavior-Based Scale to Assess Retail Salesperson Performance," *Journal of Retailing,* Spring 1990: 119–136.

might want to evaluate can be quantified. Home Depot, for example, in its review of store managers considers only how three goals—cleaner warehouses, stocked shelves, and top customer service—were achieved.[33] In larger retail operations and for middle to senior management positions, the retailer may use a committee, frequently consisting of the vice president or assistant vice president of human resources or personnel and one or two other executives, to evaluate each middle to senior management employee. The store managers of large chains are reviewed in a similar manner by middle or regional management. Some retailers, especially smaller ones, sometimes forgo the formal evaluation process and judge a salesperson on the basis of dollar sales, number of transactions, errors, on-time performance, ratio of returned merchandise, and customer complaints.

It is important to recognize several key factors in conducting performance appraisals. First, evaluation should be an ongoing process, not just a periodic review. Regularly scheduled review times should not keep supervisors from appraising or coaching their subordinates whenever necessary. Second, employees seek feedback, or information about how well they are doing their jobs, and this feedback should be provided on a timely and relevant basis. Third, the person doing the review should know what the job being reviewed entails and what the performance standards are. Employees can justifiably become upset with the review process when the reviewer is not aware of the problems and limitations of the job under review. Fourth, different supervisors are likely to rate personnel with different degrees of leniency or severity. Therefore, not only should the person conducting the review understand the performance standards, but at least two people should contribute to the evaluation. Finally, research has shown that the particular method of reviewing the employee does not matter. Retailers have found success with various types of measures, including the rating scale, checklist, freeform essay, and rankings.

Evaluating Customers

It is important for employers not only to evaluate employees on their performance but also to evaluate customers for their contributions to the retailer's financial objectives. A variety of retailers, including Neiman Marcus, Safeway, American Airlines, and Fidelity Investments, have detailed profiles on their most profitable customers. However, increasingly CRM is allowing the retailer to evaluate the profitability of each of its customers.

Retailers doing this have discovered some interesting information about their *top shoppers*, or that 10 percent to 20 percent of customers account for nearly 80 percent of their sales. For example, these shoppers are very loyal; many have been the retailer's customers for more than two decades. They tend not to read the competitors' ads but instead look for good deals among the various products in the retailer's store. For them, price shopping is a decision made in the store about what brand to buy and not a decision about where to shop. They really wish the retailer would use its CRM-developed loyalty program to make them feel special. And they focus on people, relating to store employees far more than other shoppers do.[34] Therefore, the critical building blocks for CRM include some type of customer-identification process coupled to product or service identification codes. Consider how grocery stores can do it. Here virtually 100 percent of the merchandise has a uniform product code (bar code) that is scanned at the time of checkout. If this data can be coupled with customer data when the customers use their loyalty cards, then the grocer can compute sales and profit for each customer and do this by any time period (weekly, monthly, annually) desired. Remember the point above that 10 percent to 20 percent of a retailer's customers account for 80 percent of its sales. However, now the retailer can know the precise sales and profits of all loyalty card shoppers and can use this data to decide which customers should be offered special services or special prices. Delta Airlines, for example, offers its frequent fliers who travel more than 25,000 miles annually preferred boarding, free upgrades to better seating, and a special phone line for customer service. Recently, a sister of one of the authors was trying get back home after a busy trip. Her flight was canceled, and she was told that she would have to take a connecting flight home. Worse yet, she was also informed that she would have to settle for a center seat in coach on a flight with two stopovers. Because she travels two to three round trips a week, she had averaged more than 100 round trips a year on that airline over the past couple of years. The author's sister asked the gate agent to check her CRM file. After looking at it, the agent asked, "Would you like a window or aisle in first class?" The agent realized that this customer had her choice of airlines, and the agent wasn't going to be responsible for her switching carriers.

Motivating Employees

Human resource management goes beyond selecting, training, and compensating employees. It also involves motivating them to improve current performance. A successful retailer today must constantly motivate all employees to strive for higher sales figures, decrease expenses, communicate company policies to the public, and solve problems as they arise.

Motivation is what drives a person to excel at the activities he or she undertakes such as a job. In 2009, both *FORTUNE Magazine* and *Fast Company* magazine spotlighted one e-tailer for its efforts to motivate employees so that both employees and customers stayed happy.[35] The retailer is Zappos, an online shoe seller that not only gives free shipping on all purchases—both ways—but also offers a 365-day return policy. In addition, new employees are actually offered a $2,000 bonus to quit after a four-week paid training program. It's one final effort to weed out the half-hearted (only three people accepted in 2008). As an added benefit to motivate employees, the e-tailer offers free lunch in the cafeteria. Okay, it's—cold cuts—but still. The company doesn't require attendance but still offers regular happy hours, a nap room, profit sharing, and pays for everyone's health insurance in full. It even provides a full-time life coach. People come in to bitch, to look for confidential advice on how to move up—or out—or just to talk. The only rule is that they sit on a red velvet throne. One other motivating factor is the fact that any employee can give any other employee a $50 bonus for a job well done. After all, all these motivating tools may not directly translate to profits, but Zappos considers them essential. Of the life coach, Alfred Lin, Zappos's chairman, chief operating officer, and chief financial officer, says, "You can't provide great service if you're upset about something in your life. He, the life coach, easily pays for himself." The retailer's CEO, Tony Hsieh, polls managers after they've taken teams to dinner or on a hike, and they invariably talk about improved communication, greater trust, and budding friendships. "Then we ask, 'How much more efficient do you think your team is now?'" Hsieh says. "The range is anywhere from 20 percent to 100 percent."[36]

Little wonder then that 75 percent of the company's sales are from repeat customers.[37] Zappos is built around the idea that it is the retail manager's job to

motivation
Is the drive that a person has to excel at activities, such as a job, that he or she undertakes.

motivate all employees in a manner that yields job satisfaction, low turnover, low absenteeism, and profitable results.

It is critical to recognize that when motivating employees that economic incentives are only part of the solution. There are a variety of noneconomic motivators of employees that, as you will soon see, can either motivate or demotivate employees.

What is known as *esprit de corps* occurs when a group of workers feel a common mission and a passion for that mission and a pride in being a part of the group. *Motivating example:* A new employee at Southwest Airline, which is known for its esprit de corps, immediately identifies with his or her team workers and thus obtains great enjoyment from working for Southwest Airline. *Demotivating example:* A new employee joins a retail firm that has been family owned and operated for 75 years. All of the middle- to senior-level employees are family members (sons, daughters, grandchildren, cousins, etc.) of the founding family. The new employee feels she is not part of the inner group and thus does not identify and develop an esprit de corps the family members have for the organization.

Voice is the extent to which employees can express their ideas, suggestions, and views with their superiors. *Motivating example:* At Target stores, employees are encouraged to be open in their communication and suggest ways for improving the firm and service to customers. *Demotivating example:* At too many retail stores, employees need to follow strict guidelines on how to act in their jobs (this is often true at fast-food restaurants). These employees are cogs in a machine and are not expected to be creative, and thus their voices are ignored.

Scheduling reflects the hours and days an employee is required to work. *Motivating example:* A large national retailer develops a policy to allow workers, especially single parents with young children, to have flexible work hours. *Demotivating example:* A retailer is very rigid, and all employees need to work a strict work week and take vacations when assigned and not when requested.

Feedback reflects the extent to which superiors provide regular appraisals and coaching of employees. *Motivating example:* A retailer assigns each new employee a mentor who helps to coach the employee and develop his or her potential in the organization. *Demotivating example:* A retailer practices the old sink-or-swim method of developing employees. After six months, an employee who is not performing is terminated, and the successful employees are advanced in the organization. There is little feedback prior to termination.

Job enrichment will be discussed on page 555. *Motivating example:* A leading home-improvement retailer provides college graduates who start as management trainees in the store with tasks and activities that provide a lot of skill variety and autonomy. *Demotivating example:* A large supermarket chain hires college graduates as management trainees but does not allow these employees to feel empowered and in control of their destiny. Tasks and activities are codified in an employee job manual in which these tasks and activities are broken down into more than 100 things that need to be performed weekly on a precise time schedule. Control is achieved by superiors reviewing the task and activity checkoff list and reprimanding employees who step outside their area of responsibility.

Motivating Customers

Retailers use a variety of demand stimulation tools to motivate customers to purchase or purchase in greater quantities. Most of these programs are based on the assumption that customers are motivated primarily by such economic incentives as price, free merchandise, and so on. However, innovative retailers are recognizing that other factors can motivate customers. For instance, Sewell Auto in Texas and Click in Arizona and California, with its state-of-the-art CRM, is able to stay in contact with its customers and send them birthday cards, special notes, coupons, and other marketing materials to motivate continued patronage.

Customers cite many of the things that a retailer controls as the motivator for their purchases. However, major life changes, such as a new baby, new job, or a new home would also be examples of factors (outside of the retailer's influence) that would motivate a purchase. Nevertheless, it is surprising how much motivation can be stimulated or triggered by the retailer. Here is a list of the key nonprice elements that can either motivate customers to make a purchase or deter them from using a retailer.

1. Merchandise (including quality, style and fashion, assortment, national versus private labels). *Motivating example*: A Safeway customer is positively motivated by the high-quality assortment of fresh vegetables and fruit. *Demotivating example*: A customer shopping at a local women's apparel store is demotivated by the large number of out-of-season dresses and outdated (last year's) color selection.

2. Physical characteristics (including decor, layout, and floor space). *Motivating example:* A family on its first trip to Disney World is highly motivated to purchase gift items due to the high-impact decor and layout of the on-site gift shops. *Demotivating example*: A shopper visits a newly opened hardware store and is turned off by the very narrow and poorly lit aisles. The shopper is actually driven to get out of the store as quickly as possible rather than linger, explore, and potentially purchase more products. Compare this store's image to one of an open and well-lit Lowe's home-improvement store.

3. Sales promotions. *Motivating example:* A customer is relaxing on a Friday afternoon and notices a special sales promotion at the local mall that starts at 8 A.M. on Saturday morning. The first 100 shoppers will receive a free $25 gift certificate. The customer awakens early and is in line by 7:15 A.M. and is happily one of the first 100; by 7:45 A.M., there are 300 people lined up to shop at the mall. *Demotivating example*: A department store customer who lives 50 miles from the store is attracted to visit because of a special sales promotion. The customer arrives the first day of the "sale" only to find that the sale merchandise has already been sold. This is a disincentive to travel for future purchases at this store.

4. Advertising. *Motivating example:* A customer shopping for an auto develops a positive image of the dealership and is motivated to patronize the dealership due to the professional way it advertises autos and showcases compelling features of the autos as well as its high level of customer service. *Demotivating example*: A customer shopping for a new car is afraid to enter a new dealership whose slick, fast-talking TV salesperson promises the best deal in town if you will only visit the dealership.

5. Convenience (including hours, location, ease of entrance and parking, ease of finding items). *Motivating example:* A family stops along the interstate to refuel and finds that the service station has a new food court with a McDonald's and a Dunkin' Donuts shop. In a 15-minute stop, four stomachs are refueled as well. *Demotivating example*: A once-popular family-style restaurant no longer seems safe to clientele because the neighborhood around the restaurant has deteriorated into a high-crime area. Many of the restaurant's old customers are now forced to drive several miles out of the neighborhood to other restaurants.

6. Services (including credit, delivery, return policy, and guarantees). *Motivating example:* Knowing that most people have trouble envisioning how new furniture will look in their home, a furniture store has a liberal return policy. Customers can return furniture within 72 hours if they don't like the way it fits their décor. Even if a small return fee is charged, most customers find it very reasonable. *Demotivating example*: A retailer's signage throughout the store repels customers because it boldly proclaims that all sales are final and there are no returns.

7. Store personnel (including helpfulness, friendliness, and courtesy). *Motivating example:* Nordstrom's sales associates go out of their way to help a visiting customer from out of town. The customer is very uncertain on how to dress for a special event, and the salesperson coaches the young man through the entire purchasing process. The customer ends up with a new business suit, shoes, accessories, and a level of satisfaction seldom achieved in retailing today. *Demotivating example*: An elderly lady new to the community walks into what appears to be a very upscale women's apparel store but is ignored by the store personnel, who are busy helping younger, more fashionably dressed customers. The sales associates do not even acknowledge the elderly lady's presence. The lady walks out, determined to never return.

LO 4 — Compensation

What methods can retailers use in compensating their employees and customers?

As all businesspeople know, human resources are not free goods. They are expensive; in retailing, employee costs (including benefits) typically represent 50 percent of operating expenses. However, as we illustrated at the beginning of this chapter, customers can also perform work activities. The key point to keep in mind is that the more work you ask the customer to perform, the lower the price they will be willing to pay. In short, their price savings become a way of compensating them for their work. Very simply that is why self-service retailers can sell at lower prices.

Employee Compensation

Compensation is one of the major variables in attracting, retaining, and motivating human resources. The quality of employees that can be attracted, whether as salesclerks or executives, is directly proportional to the compensation package offered. Naturally, other things besides compensation are important to employees. According to a report by Deloitte & Touche's Human Resource Strategies Group, "more flexible, portable benefits systems with fewer links to age and service" are desired by today's retail associates. In addition, these benefits should be compatible with the employee's lifestyle choices.[38]

Here the term **compensation** includes direct-dollar payments (wages, commissions, and bonuses) and indirect payments (insurance, vacation time, retirement plans). Compensation plans in retailing can have as many as three basic components: a fixed component, a variable component, and a fringe-benefit component. The **fixed component** typically is composed of some base wage per hour, week, month, or year. The **variable component** is often composed of some bonus that is received if performance warrants. Salesclerks may be paid a bonus, usually from 5 percent to 10 percent of sales above some established minimum; department managers may receive a bonus based on the profit performance of their department.

compensation
Includes direct dollar payments (wages, commission, bonuses) and indirect payments (insurance, vacation time, retirement plans).

fixed component
Typically is composed of some base wage per hour, week, month, or year.

variable component
Is often composed of some bonus that is received if performance warrants.

Workers in restaurants often receive tips, a variable component that the retailer does not control. Finally, a **fringe-benefit package** may include such things as health insurance, disability benefits, life insurance, retirement plans, the use of automobiles, and financial counseling.

Each of the three components helps the retailer achieve a different human resource goal. The fixed component helps ensure that employees have a source of income to meet their most basic financial obligations. This helps fulfill the employees' physiological needs. The variable component allows the retailer to offer employees an incentive for higher levels of effort and commitment, which helps fulfill a belongingness and social need among employees for special recognition in return for high performance. The fringe-benefit component allows the retailer to offer employees safety and security. Retail employees have a need to be protected and cared for when they are faced with difficult times or when they become too old to provide for themselves. Also, certain employees (especially executives) have a need for prestige and status.

The best combination of fixed, variable, and fringe-benefit compensation components depends on the person, the job, and the retail organization. There is no set formula. Some top retail executives prefer mostly salary, others thrive on bonuses, and still others would rather have more pension benefits. The same holds for salesclerks. Therefore, the compensation package needs to be tailored to the individual. We now focus our attention on compensation of the sales force, but the same principles will apply to managers.

Retail sales clerks that are paid a commission often spend time studying their past sales performance and sales goals for the upcoming season because the achievement of these goals can significantly increase their compensation.

fringe-benefit package
Is a part of the total compensation package offered to many retail employees and may include health insurance, disability benefits, life insurance, retirement plans, child care, use of an auto, and financial counseling.

Common Types of Compensation Programs for a Sales Force

Retail sales-force compensation programs can be conveniently broken into three major types: (1) straight salary, (2) salary plus commission, and (3) straight commission. Each method has its advantages and disadvantages.

Straight Salary

In the straight salary program, the salesperson receives a fixed salary per time period (usually per week) regardless of the level of sales generated or orders taken. However, over time, if the salesperson does not help generate sales or take enough orders, he or she will likely be fired for not performing adequately. Similarly, over time, if the salesperson helps to generate more than a proportionate share of sales or fills more than a proportionate number of orders, then the retailer will be unable to retain the employee without a raise.

Many small retailers use this compensation method because they typically assign tasks such as stock rearranging, merchandise display, and other nonselling duties to their salespeople. Therefore, if the employees were paid on a commission basis, they would spend little, if any, time on their nonselling duties, and the retail organization would suffer. Many promotional and price-oriented chain stores whose salespeople are merely order takers will use the straight salary method because the salesperson is not much of a factor in generating sales. Also, most clerks and cashiers, as well as other lower-level retail personnel are almost always paid straight salaries.

The salesperson may view this plan as attractive because it offers income security or as unappealing because it gives little incentive for extraordinary effort and performance. Thus, for this method (the easiest plan for the employee to understand) to be effective, it must be combined with a periodic evaluation so that superior salespeople can be identified and singled out for higher salaries.

Salary Plus Commission

Sometimes the salesperson is paid a fixed salary per time period plus a percentage commission on all sales or on all sales over an established quota. Because merchandise lines and items can vary in terms of gross margins, some retailers pay commissions on gross margin dollars generated. The fixed salary is lower than that of the salesperson working on a straight salary plan, but the commission structure gives one the potential to earn more than the person on the straight salary plan. In fact, most salespeople on the salary plus commission program earn more than their counterparts on a straight salary program.

This plan gives the employees a stable base income—and thus incentive to perform nonselling tasks—but it also encourages and rewards superior effort. Therefore, it represents a good compromise between the straight salary and the straight commission programs. In many cases, top management generally receives a salary and a bonus based on overall store or department performance.

Straight Commission

Income of some salespeople is limited to a percentage commission on each sale they generate. The commission could be the same percentage on all merchandise or it could vary depending on the profitability of the item.

The straight commission plan provides substantial incentive for retail salespeople to generate sales. However, when the general business climate is poor, retail salespeople may not be able to generate enough volume to meet their fixed-payment obligations (mortgage payment, auto payment, food expenses). Because of that problem, most retailers slightly modify the straight commission plan to allow the salesperson to draw wages against future commissions up to some specified amount per week.

A major problem with the straight commission plan is that it may provide the retail salesperson with too much incentive to sell. As a result of the income insecurity features of this plan, the employee may begin to use pressure tactics to close sales, hurting the retailer's image and long-run sales performance. Similarly, the employee may not be willing to perform other duties such as helping customers with returned merchandise or helping to set up displays. After all, compensation is paid to sell, not to handle customer complaints or displays. Generally, sales personnel for high-price merchandise or high-ticket items (such as automobiles, real estates, jewelry, and furniture, as well as those items requiring the sales personnel to prospect or seek out potential customers—that is, insurance and door-to-door selling) are paid this way.

An Ernst & Young survey reported that 51 percent of the retailers polled used a salary plus commission plan, and 38 percent used straight commission.[39] Exhibit 14.4 summarizes the attributes of each of these plans. During the late 1990s, some retailers began to reduce the commission portion of employee-compensation plans and increase the salary portion. This was an attempt to reduce consumer distaste for what was perceived to be "high-pressure selling." However, as retailers have

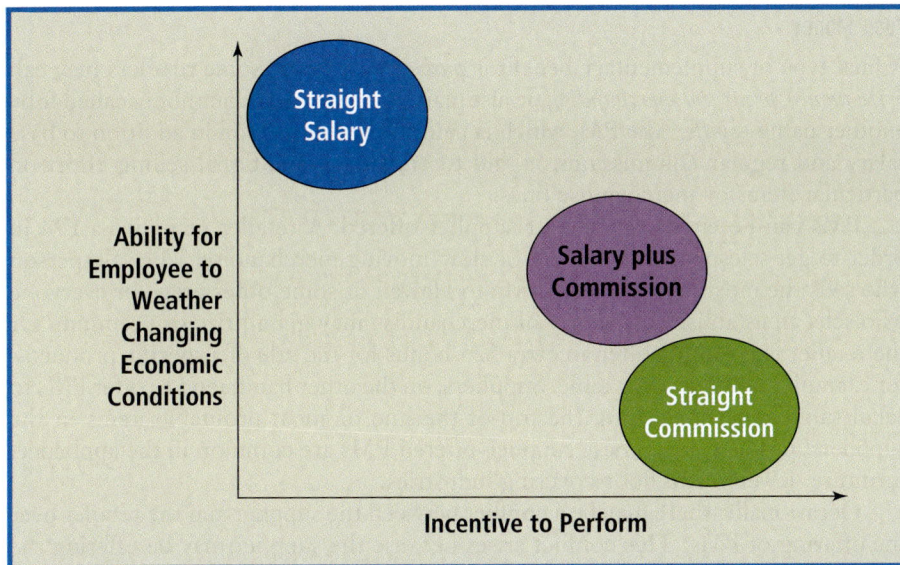

Exhibit 14.4
Attributes Of Compensation Plans

Straight Salary

Salary plus Commission

Straight Commission

Ability for Employee to Weather Changing Economic Conditions

Incentive to Perform

faced a tight labor market and the need to increase productivity in recent years, the trend has begun to reverse.

Supplemental Benefits

In addition to regular wages (salary, commission, or both), retail salespeople also can receive four types of supplementary benefits: employee discounts, insurance and retirement benefits, child care, and push money (or *spiffs*).

Employee Discounts

Almost all retailers offer their employees discounts on merchandise or services they purchase for themselves or their immediate family. About the only line of trade where these discounts are not offered is grocery retailing, because grocery retailers operate on relatively thin gross margins.

Insurance and Retirement Benefits

Historically, retail personnel were not provided any insurance or retirement benefits. However, with recent changes in the federal employment laws, this is no longer the case. In addition, many retailers are providing their part-time employees with either free or low-cost group health and life insurance. Still others are making profit sharing, stock ownership, and retirement programs available to salespeople and all other employees.

Child Care

In an effort to attract employees from single-parent and two-wage-earner families, some U.S. businesses have begun to provide child care for employees' children during working hours. Retailers have just started providing child care, a program that experts agree will be a necessity in upcoming years. However, with health-care costs rapidly increasing, some retailers have delayed plans to add child care due to the added expenses.

Push Money

A final type of supplementary benefit is *push money*, which some retailers may call *prize money*, *premium merchandise*, or just plain *PM*. Retailers commonly called it by another name—*spiffs*. The PM, which is paid to the salesperson in addition to base salary and regular commissions, is said to encourage additional selling effort on particular items or merchandise lines.

PMs can be either retailer- or supplier-offered. A retailer may give a PM in order to get salespeople to sell old or slow-moving merchandise. The salesperson who sells the most may win a free trip to Hawaii or some other prize, or everyone who sells an established quantity of merchandise may get a prize or premium. Or the retailer may simply offer an extra $25 bonus for the sale of a specific product— for example, a dining room table. Suppliers, on the other hand, tend to offer PMs to retail salespeople for selling the top-of-the line or most profitable items in the suppliers' product mix. These supplier-offered PMs are common in the appliance, furniture, jewelry, and floor-covering industries.

Occasionally, there may be a conflict between the supplier and the retailer over the offering of PMs. This conflict arises because the supplier may be offering the retailer's salespeople an incentive to push an item or merchandise line that may not be the most profitable line for the retailer or the best for the customer, although it may be highly profitable to the supplier. Some retailers prefer to keep all PMs for themselves because they believe they are already paying a fair wage to their salespeople.

Compensation Plan Requirements

Regardless of what method a retailer ultimately determines to use in compensating its employees, the method should meet the following requirements.

1. *Fairness*: The plan does not favor one group or division over any other group or division or enable such a group to gather disproportionate reward to contribution. It must also keep compensation costs under control so that they do not put the store at a competitive disadvantage.

2. *Adequacy*: The level of compensation should enable the employee to maintain a standard of living commensurate with job position and to maintain job satisfaction.

3. *Prompt and regular payments*: Payments should be made on time and in accordance with the agreement between employer and employee. In incentive plans, greater stimulation is provided when reward closely follows the accomplishment.

4. *Customer interest*: The plan should not reward any actions by an employee that could result in customer ill will.

5. *Simplicity*: The plan must be easy to understand so as to prevent any misunderstandings with the resultant ill will. This should also enable management to minimize the worker hours needed to determine compensation levels.

6. *Balance*: Pay, supplemental benefits, and other rewards must provide a reasonable total reward package.

7. *Security*: The plan must fulfill the employee's security needs.

8. *Cost effective*: The plan must not result in excessive payments, given the retailer's financial condition.

While none of the three plans discussed above satisfies all of these requirements to the maximum level, awareness of these requirements will aid in the selection of the best plan given the individual circumstances. In fact, it is not uncommon for the same retailer to use more than one plan in the same store as different divisions or departments have different needs.

Job Enrichment

A planned program for enhancing job characteristics is typically called *job enrichment*. **Job enrichment** is the process of enhancing the core job characteristics for the purpose of increasing worker motivation, productivity, and satisfaction. There are five core job characteristics that should be increased:

1. *skill variety*, or the degree to which an employee can use different skills and talents;

2. *task identity*, or the degree to which a job requires the completion of a whole assignment that has a visible outcome;

3. *task significance*, or the degree to which the job impacts other employees;

4. *autonomy*, or the degree to which the employee has freedom, independence, and discretion in achieving the outcome; and

5. *job feedback*, or the degree to which the employee receives information about the effectiveness of his or her performance.[40]

job enrichment
Is the process of enhancing the core job characteristics to improve the motivation, productivity, and job satisfaction of employees.

Job-enrichment programs have their base in motivation theory, which suggests that job factors themselves—job challenge, independence, and responsibility—are powerful motivators.

Retail management has long recognized that paying attention to job characteristics and descriptions, work scheduling, job sharing, and employee-input programs will have a positive effect on employee productivity and satisfaction. Retailers using the job-enrichment program must be careful in presenting it to the employees; otherwise the employees may feel that they are being asked to do too many tasks without being compensated for the extra workload.

Customer Compensation

The best way to think of customer compensation is in terms of the concept of value proposition. (Remember that earlier in the chapter a value proposition was defined as the promised benefits a retailer offers in relation to the cost the consumer incurs.) Each of the eight attributes mentioned above for motivating customers—price, merchandise, physical characteristics, sales promotions, advertising, convenience, services, and store personnel—is part of the value proposition. These attributes represent benefits and costs. The better the value equation (benefits versus costs), the more compelling the retailer's value proposition. Stated alternatively, if the consumer is expected to do more work (e.g., search for merchandise in the store, travel a large distance to an inconvenient store, and assume the risk of a no-return policy), then that customer will want to be compensated with a lower price. When retailers ask customers to perform more work, they must adjust their value proposition by lowering prices.

The value proposition notion, however, also illustrates that a firm does not have to use low prices to compensate customers. Alternatively, it can offer more benefits. In fact, if the retailer wants more pricing power (the ability to maintain or raise prices), it can only do this by offering the customer more benefits—such as what Starbucks offers its customers.

Retailing: The Inside Story

A Week in the Life of Terry J. Lundgren, Chairman, President, and CEO of Macy's, Inc.

When you're the CEO of a dynamic, fast-moving, and innovative company like Macy's, no day or week is "typical." That's what makes my job challenging, but also fun, interesting, and exhilarating. The days tend to be long—usually starting before 7 A.M. and often running through dinner events that can go to 10 P.M. or later. Weekends are devoted to a mix of business, family, and friends. To keep up this pace, you have to absolutely love your work. And I certainly do.

Just about everything I do falls into one of three categories—listening, decision making, and communicating.

Listening

Running a company with nearly 850 stores, 170,000 employees, and $25 billion in revenues means there is a lot I need to know. Good listening skills are critical, and so is a high level of curiosity that leads me to seek information and data that helps me understand the business. I spend at least part of every week in our stores across the country, walking the sales floor, talking to our associates, and observing our customers. I learn more from this than just about anything else I do because store visits help me stay in touch with what customers are thinking and buying. I visit between one and five stores every week, and most of the time I show up unannounced. That way there is no artificial preparation, and I see exactly what our customers see when they shop at our stores.

I also spend part of each week—typically on Mondays—with my Executive Committee in discussions about what is going on in the business and what we can do better. I also spend plenty of time (probably too much) reading financial reports, strategic briefings, and e-mails from customers, executives, store associates, vendors, other business leaders, and community officials. And then there's a steady stream of letters that arrive by snail mail. Although it can be overwhelming, I try to be disciplined in absorbing as much information as possible on a wide variety of subjects.

But no matter how busy I am, I reserve at least 30 minutes each week to meet face to face with rising young talent in our organization. This includes my Breakfast Club, a group of Macy's young professionals who generally are a few years out of college and work in various disciplines in the company. They provide me with a particularly fresh perspective on what Macy's is doing well and not so well, with a focus on innovation and creativity in the way we run the business and

serve customers. They also tell me that they appreciate the fact that the CEO makes time to listen to what they have to say and answer their questions.

Decision Making

While we have an outstanding team at all levels of the company and my executives run their specific areas of the business, many key corporate decisions rest with me. Some require the approval of the Macy's, Inc. Board of Directors, which I chair.

By listening intently and applying the experience I have accumulated over the years, I must decide on major strategic actions after seeking the advice and counsel of the outstanding team that surrounds me. A good example is the decision to create and (after a successful pilot) roll out a comprehensive nationwide localization initiative we call My Macy's. I also make the final decision on major merchandising moves, such as positioning Macy's as the exclusive retailer of brands such as the Martha Stewart Collection and Tommy Hilfiger. I approve all new store openings and store closings, major organizational changes, executive hiring, and significant capital expenditures. I'm called on every day to make dozens of decisions—some small and routine, some large and profound. To do this effectively, I must be fully informed, seek alternative points of view, and weigh all of the options in terms of potential risks and benefits.

Communicating

Moving Macy's continuously forward requires that everyone in our organization understand and buy into our vision for the future of the business. I believe in aggressively communicating personally to our people at all levels of the company. This is how I work to make our very large company feel smaller and more intimate. I communicate via small-group management meetings; in live webcasts each month, which connect 1,500 executives at a time in videos that stream over our computer and satellite networks that reach approximately 50,000 employees; in internal audio blogs that allow me to share my thoughts on a specific subject; and as I walk the aisles in our stores and the halls of our offices and facilities across America.

The same is true outside of the company. I meet regularly with large investors in Macy's, Inc., as well as with government officials, financial institutions, community leaders,

Retailing: The Inside Story (continued)

merchandise vendors, and others who need to understand what our company is doing. I visit college campuses as often as I can (especially the University of Arizona, my alma mater) to meet and coach emerging talent, as well as to tell the Macy's story. I serve on the boards of a number of nonprofit and business organizations ranging from Carnegie Hall to the National Minority Supplier Development Council. These are opportunities to both listen and communicate.

Given that Macy's is often in the news, I do regular interviews with national and trade media so they can accurately report on the progress our company is making. When I am able, I speak to large business and professional groups about Macy's strategies for growing as "America's department store."

All of this makes for a very full day, but I wouldn't trade it for anything in the world.

[The following is the actual schedule of Mr. Lundgren on the day the authors asked him for this information.]

5:45–6:45	At the Gym
7:30 A.M.	Breakfast with the CEO of Martha Stewart
9:00 A.M.	Meeting with CEO of Giorgio Armani and our teams about both the Bloomingdale's and Macy's opportunities. Very uplifting.
10:45 A.M.	Meet Victoria Beckham at Macy's Herald Square entrance.
11:00 A.M.	Introduce Victoria Beckham to customers, photographers, media for launch of Emporio Armani underwear.
11:30 A.M.	Interviews with NY Times, Entertainment Tonight, Women's Wear Daily, etc.

12:15–1:00	Respond to 40–50 e-mails, phone calls during lunch at desk
1:00 P.M.	Phone interview with Deborah Norville regarding her book on respect, "The Power of Respect."
1:30–3:00	Fall Marketing Budget (I approved a request for additional advertising funds to boost sales).
3:00–3:15	Meet with Finance Team and challenged them to find new expense reductions (not in marketing or customer facing areas).
3:15–3:30	Phone Calls
3:30–4:30	Touch base meeting with Chief Stores Officer—Fall season goals and objectives.
4:30–5:30	Touch base with Chief Merchandising Planning Officer—Fall season goals and objectives.
5:30–6:30	Touch base meeting with V.P. of Internal Communication—Fall season goals and objectives.
6:30–7:00	Respond to another 35 e-mails.
7:00–7:15	Change into black tie in office.
7:15 P.M.	Depart office for Parsons School of Design Black Tie Dinner
7:30 P.M.	Arrive at event. Photo Shoot with honoree—CEO of Calvin Klein, Lead Designer for Calvin Klein.
8:15 P.M.	My introduction speech and award presentation to CEO of Calvin Klein
10:00 P.M.	Heading home, reviewing tomorrow's agenda. Different subjects but similar schedule.

Source: Used with the written permission of Terry J. Lundgren, Chairman, President and CEO of Macy's, Inc.

Epiologue

Now that you have completed this class on retailing, the authors wanted to share with you what it takes as well as what is involved when you reach the top of the ladder in a retailing career. After all, many of the examples used in this text have dealt with decisions and actions taken by retailing's lower- to middle-level management. That was because this is where you will be in the next couple of years if you decide to begin a retailing career. However, for this chapter's "Retailing: The Inside Story" box, the authors wanted to show what is involved when you are in top management. We asked Terry J. Lundgren, chairman, president, and chief executive officer of Macy's, Inc., to describe his activities during a typical week and then provide us with his schedule for an average day. As you will see, he works an 18-hour day. However, it is an exciting day, and given his love of retailing, we doubt he would ever tire of it. As an aside, the authors knew Sam Walton, and while his day may not have had as many glamour activities, he was just as busy, and he also loved every minute of it.

SUMMARY

LO 1

Why are intangible people resources more important than tangible resources to a retailer's competitive advantage?

It is relatively easy for competing retailers to duplicate the tangible resources of each other. They can all purchase the same merchandise, equipment, and fixtures. People, however, are more difficult to replicate and thus become a source of differential competitive advantage. Employees can be even more valuable if they are empowered to make things right for the customer. Because intangible people resources are central to competitive advantage, the retailer should view employee costs and the cost of attracting and retaining customers as an investment. This investment can pay high dividends because the best employees and customers are profit drivers; often 20 percent of the customers or employees generate 80 percent of the retailer's profit.

LO 2

What is the process for recruiting the right employees and customers?

To recruit the best employees and customers requires considerable effort; however, the payoff can be enormous. Consequently, retailers are more systematically recruiting employees and customers. A popular technology to cultivate and maintain the right customers is customer relationship management. A retailer must screen and select employees as well as customers. Just as some potential employees should be avoided, it is also true that some customers are not appropriate for the retailer.

LO 3

How do retailers manage employees and customers?

Once an employee is hired or a customer obtained, the retailer must still be concerned about continuing to train and develop the employee, evaluating the employee, and motivating the employee.

Expenditures on training and development are an attempt by the retailer to increase the productivity of human resources. Employees can be trained to increase their productivity, and customers can be trained and developed to help establish long-term relationships.

The employee's performance should be subjected to an ongoing, formal, and systematic review process. This process will enable the employer to make better decisions concerning wage increases, promotions, transfers, and improvement in job skills. At the same time, the customer should be evaluated. CRM helps the retailer evaluate the profitability of single customers and groups of customers. This evaluation is critical to determining where to allocate future resources.

Employee motivation is also a topic of great importance, and we discussed some of the things successful retailers are currently using. We also showed how seven key offerings of the retailer (merchandise, physical characteristics of the store, sales promotions, advertising, convenience, services, and store personnel) can serve as motivators of positive patronage behavior but also can demotivate the customer if not appropriately managed.

LO 4

What methods can retailers use in compensating their employees and customers?

Compensation is crucial to attracting, retaining, and motivating retail employees. A good compensation program includes a fixed component to provide income, a variable component to motivate employees, and a fringe-benefit component to provide security and prestige. Special attention was paid to the advantages and disadvantages of the three types of compensation plans: straight salary, straight commission, and a combination of both.

Job enrichment is the process of increasing the skill variety, task identity, task significance, autonomy, and feedback from the job in an effort to improve worker motivation, productivity, and satisfaction and thereby reduce turnover.

A retailer's value proposition is the most important way to compensate customers. The retailer must offer benefits that exceed the costs (price and nonprice) that the customer incurs. If the value proposition is not sufficiently high, then customers will patronize other retailers where they can get a better overall deal (value).

TERMS TO REMEMBER

empowerment
servant leadership
value proposition
customer relationship management
   (CRM)
performance appraisal and review

motivation
compensation
fixed component
variable component
fringe-benefit package
job enrichment

REVIEW AND DISCUSSION QUESTIONS

Why do intangible people resources provide more competitive advantage than tangible resources?   **LO 1**

1. Explain why a retailer's investment in having the inventory desired by its target market is not sufficient by itself to offer a sustainable competitive advantage over the competition.

2. Should a retailer view its employees as a "cost" or as an "investment?" Support your reasoning.

3. In retailing, customers and employees are distinct groups and have little in common. Agree or disagree and explain your answer.

4. What does it mean to "empower" a retail employee? Give examples from your personal experience of situations where you felt a retail employee was not properly empowered.

What is the process involved in hiring the right employees and recruiting the right customers?   **LO 2**

5. What are the sources that a department store could use to recruit employees? Would the same sources be effective for use by a cell phone retailer such as a Sprint store?

6. Develop a list of predictor variables you would use to screen applicants for a sales position in (a) a jewelry department in a high-prestige department store, (b) a used-car dealership, (c) a health club, and (d) a fast-food chain.

7. Do a search on Google using your name and school (or hometown). Did you find anything that might embarrass you? What can you do about it? Now do the same on myspace.com.

8. Why might each of the following retailers—movie theater, hospital, amusement, theme park, and health club—desire to screen out certain customers? Employees?

LO 3   How do retailers manage employees and customers for long-term profitability?

9. Explain why turnover is costly in retailing regardless of whether it is employee turnover or customer turnover.
10. Why must training be an ongoing operation?
11. How can a retailer expect consumers to buy its products when its own employees shop elsewhere? As a result of this question, some clothing retailers have considered requiring that their employees only wear stores brands when working. Disregarding any possible legal issues, what would this do to employee motivation? How would you handle this problem?
12. What is customer relationship management, and how can it be used to develop more profitable customer relationships?

LO 4   What are the methods retailers can use in compensating their employees and offering customers a compelling value proposition?

13. If you were to go to work for a retailer today, what would be the most important supplemental benefit the retailer could offer you? Would this benefit change as your lifestyle changed?
14. What factors in the retailer's control have a positive effect on employee productivity?
15. What is a *value proposition*? How does a retailer's value proposition relate to customer retention and building profitable long-term relationships?

SAMPLE TEST QUESTIONS

LO 1   When retailers grant their employees empowerment, they are giving them:

a. the power to set their own hours.
b. the power to kick improperly dressed customers out of the store.
c. the power to determine what products should be featured in the retailer's weekly ad.
d. the power to make things right with the customer.
e. all of the above powers.

LO 2   Which of the following questions may a women's apparel store ask on an employment application?

a. What is your marital status?
b. What is your age?
c. Have you ever been arrested?
d. Are you handicapped?
e. The retailer is not allowed to ask any of the above questions since each of them can be used to discriminate against a minority or group of minorities.

LO 3   Training and development programs should:

a. only be concerned with new employees.
b. get rid of the least productive employees within the first two years.
c. be an ongoing process.
d. rely heavily on senior management's teaching skills.
e. only focus on operational skills.

For an individual who does not care about security but only wants to maximize his or her current earnings, the _____ compensation plan would be best.

   a. straight commission
   b. straight salary
   c. salary plus commission
   d. fringe-plus salary
   e. teamwork salary

LO 4

WRITING AND SPEAKING EXERCISE

The exercise for this chapter is different. The only writing you may have to do is to clear up some error such as on a credit report. However, before beginning any job search, please consider these 10 suggestions. They may make the difference in you getting the job of your dreams or missing out.

- Register with your college's career planning center and begin the process.
- Be aware that many employers require a drug test.
- Since one out of every four college students get mentioned in a police report sometime while they are a student, check with your campus police for any police reports on file for you. Ask if you should check with the municipal police if you had off-campus offenses. Most campus police departments will work with you in clearing your record of minor problems.
- Google yourself.
- Check your Facebook or MySpace accounts for any comments or pictures that could harm you.
- Order a free credit report from Equifax, Experian, or TransUnion. The three nationwide consumer-reporting companies have set up one central website, toll-free telephone number, and mailing address through which you can order your free annual report. To order, go to www.annualcreditre-port.com, call 877-322-8228, or complete the annual credit report request form and mail to Annual Credit Report Request Service, P.O. Box 105281, Atlanta, GA 30348-5281. Do not contact the three nationwide consumer-reporting companies individually.
- Be aware that Internet information is cached and can be found even after you have removed it.
- Check your outgoing messages on your answering machine and cell phone.
- Use your campus e-mail with your name, not some nickname, for professional correspondence.
- Have your resume critiqued by a counselor at your college's career planning center.

RETAIL PROJECT

Since retailers often lack legal expertise when making human resource decisions, it is a good idea to review the current laws before doing anything in this area. For your assignment, go to the federal Equal Employment Opportunity Commission's website (www.eeoc.gov). List five circumstances where sexual harassment may occur. Also, explain how may an individual waive his or her rights under the Age Discrimination in Employment Act?

PLANNING YOUR OWN RETAIL BUSINESS

During the planning process for starting a gift shop in a local resort town, you began to question and consider different compensation plans for the retail clerks. It was fairly standard in the area to pay retail clerks $6.25 an hour. However, as you visited gift shops that were paying these rather low wages you noticed that the clerks simply took orders and did not sell or try to answer any questions for customers. In a visit to a gift shop in Ft. Lauderdale last spring, you struck up a conversation with the owner. She was more than willing to share her experiences about retail clerks. In fact, after a lot of trial and error she decided to pay upper-quartile compensation. This consisted of a base wage of $9.50 an hour and a 3-percent commission on all sales. She mentioned that when she went to this type of system her average transaction size increased by 20 percent and that closure went from 28 percent to 40 percent. More importantly, she found that her bottom-line profit rose by 32 percent. In short, by paying more for retail clerks she increased employee productivity and the profits of her store.

For the gift shop you are planning, you initially estimated that traffic would be 30,000 visitors annually and that closure would be 24 percent. You estimated your average transaction size at $32. Your gross-margin percentage would be 60 percent, and fixed operating expenses would be $60,000 annually. Variable operating expenses would be 20 percent of sales. Under this plan, you would pay two full-time clerks $6.25 an hour, and you would fill in when things got busy.

Your new plan, which you want to evaluate, calls for paying the clerks $9 per hour plus 4 percent commission on all sales. Thus, your fixed operating expenses would go up by $3,000, and variable operating expenses would rise to 24 percent of sales. You believe that closure would rise to 32 percent and average transaction size would rise to $36. Which compensation strategy should you pursue?

Chapter 1

The Changing Role of Funeral Homes[1]

Mike Fallon had looked forward to going home for Christmas. He was about to graduate from a large state university with a degree in accounting and a minor in information Technology. Since he wanted to work in a CPA firm's tax division, he had even taken a retailing class. After all, he would be dealing with retail customers with his tax work. Still, the last thing he wanted to do at Christmas was discuss school subjects. However, that is just what happened when the family got together for Christmas dinner at his uncle's home.

Mike's mother's youngest brother was a church deacon, and somehow he changed the subject to the fact that so many nonparishioners wanted to use his church for weddings. Most of these requests were declined because of the demand by his current members. Somebody mentioned that with the number of people without church affiliation increasing across the county, she had seen a number of wedding chapels being built in middle- to larger-sized cities. That's when Uncle Bob took you back to your school work, especially that retailing class.

Uncle Bob was the family's funeral director. He and his two sons owned and operated the only locally owned mortuary in a city of 75,000. Over the past decade, he pointed out, his business had been radically changed. No longer do folks want a traditional funeral, complete with casket and burial at the local cemetery. Now, a third of all funerals involved a no-frills cremation and maybe a social "event" instead of a religious service. Since he is planning to remodel, he wants to know what you think about his "scrambled merchandising" idea.

Bob then explains that he is thinking of eliminating the chapel with its stained glass and pews and using the space for a multipurpose "family center" complete with a catering kitchen in the back where the flower room used to be and adding a 12-foot screen for multimedia memorial presentations. In addition, he wants to partner with a law firm to assist families with estate planning and making wills. Finally, he questions whether he should just remodel the chapel with its current drab entranceway into something brighter and cheerful, complete with an entryway removed from the funeral home. By doing so, he could use the chapel for weddings for the couples who were unable to locate a church.

Questions

1. Do you think couples would mind being married in a chapel located near a funeral home, even if it had a separate entrance and was beautifully decorated?

2. What would happen to those families who want a traditional funeral in a chapel? Would your uncle lose their business?

3. What other creative ideas would you suggest to your uncle?

4. What other data would you suggest that your uncle consider before making any decision?

5. What should your uncle do?

Chapter 2

The Missed Opportunity: The Sears Takeover of Lands' End[2]

When Sears bought Lands' End in 2002, many retail observers hailed the purchase. Sears, the troubled department store, had a loyal, more affluent customer for its hard goods lines, but had difficulty sparking interest in its soft goods. In contrast, Lands' End was the #1 specialty apparel catalog. Lands' End's traditional, casually styled merchandise matched Sears' all-American, good-value image, and would attract a more upmarket customer to Sears' apparel. Further, Sears could tap Lands' End's expertise in direct marketing, and its loyal customer database. Lands' End could broaden its customer audience through wider distribution through Sears with its 2,300+ stores.

The results fell short of expectations. By 2005, Lands' End was a relatively small presence in 370 Sears stores. Further, Sears seemed more interested in (or distracted by) its new owner, Kmart; in other private label brand names such as Lucy Pereda; and in developing new store concepts such as Sears Grand, The Great Indoors, and Orchard Supply Hardware.

Most conclude that the Lands' End brand did not live up to its potential in stores, largely due to mismanagement of a well-respected brand. At first, Sears s-l-o-w-l-y rolled out Lands' End merchandise into selected stores. Loyal Lands' End customers who heard about the acquisition ran to their local Sears store for the first time in years, but were often disappointed when the brand was not yet in stock. When Lands' End finally arrived in local Sears stores, it was poorly publicized. Often, no mention was made in local newspapers except in tiny print at the bottom of a Sears ad. Sears credit card customers received few promotional announcements, even in their bills. In-store Lands' End signage and displays could easily be overlooked. Even today, Lands' End merchandise is buried within the Sears online Web page rather than promoted as a flagship brand.

Sears seems to have underestimated the potential for Lands' End to drive new customers to its stores. Loyal Lands' End customers who decided to revisit Sears in search of their favored brand were often disappointed with the limited selection. Rather than driving differentiation between the brands, Lands' End merchandise often looked mundane and very similar to Sears's basics. Infighting between Sears and Lands' End resulted in many missed opportunities, leading observers to think that fear of cannibalization of Sears's existing brands was a driving issue. Sears claimed that the best-selling Lands' End golf jackets were priced too high for the "typical" Sears customer—forgetting that Sears wanted to attract more than the "typical" Sears clothing customer! In addition, many of the Sears stores did not stock Lands' End sweater sets so popular at holiday time, but stuck with cotton turtlenecks, khakis, and jeans, i.e., what every other mall retailer sold, usually more stylish.

Sears and Lands' End also seemed at odds in their pricing strategies, and ignored the differences in behavior among catalog shoppers and instore customers. While the Lands' End catalog places only limited amounts of merchandise on sale at any given time, bricks & mortar stores have to observe local conditions and sales seasons more carefully. For example, Sears stores in Sunbelt states maintained the full price on Lands' End winter coats through March—when temperatures easily hit the 70s and 80s. One executive stated that "Lands' End should not go on sale right now." This was fine for the upper Midwest, but not the Southern stores!

Recently when Sears executives examined the tepid sales of Lands' End merchandise in many stores, they concluded that an upscale customer was not ready to shop at Sears, and that Lands' End merchandise in stores should be scaled back.

Unfortunately, this action will lead to further disappointment for the Lands' End customer base.

Questions

1. Based on your knowledge of the two retailers, prepare a SWOT analysis for each of them prior to the Sears takeover. Based on your SWOT analysis, what are the pros and cons of the takeover?

2. What is the best strategy for Sears to use with Lands' End?

3. Can a retailer seek to satisfy two different target markets, as Sears tried to do with Lands' End?

4. Should Sears sell off Lands' End?

Chapter 3

The Mall's New Marketing Manager

As she had done for the past 11 years, Pat Snyder, the manager of South Park Mall's largest anchor store, attended the mall's monthly meeting of store managers. She was especially eager to attend this morning's meeting because Pam Donnelly, the mall's new marketing manager, was going to be introduced. Despite the fact that Snyder's 220,000 square foot department store had annual sales over $50 million, she was not involved in the selection process. Thus, this would be the first meeting between two of the mall's most prominent individuals.

Like other malls nationwide, the stores in South Park Mall had been experiencing a constant rate of sales over the last three years, not a steady increase of 2 percent to 5 percent annually as the stores had been accustomed to. Some store managers blamed these weaker sales on the economy, while others claimed it was the result of a failure to replace the department store that had served as the mall's other major anchor and which had gone bankrupt two years earlier. Instead, Snyder believed the lack of sales growth resulted from the previous marketing manger's failure to aggressively promote the mall. He was near retirement and didn't want to change the way things had always been done.

On entering the meeting, Pam Donnelly went directly to the point. She had spent the past two weeks, before anyone knew who she was, roaming throughout the mall and asking questions. Now she was proposing answers. Her major task was to generate an increase in the traffic of buyers, not just visitors who used the mall for social gatherings. To achieve this, she proposed the following:

1. Remove half of the benches in the mall's common area so that the mall could rent this space to various seasonal vendors, such as costume jewelry over Halloween. After all, during her tours of the mall she noticed that only the elderly appeared to be using the benches, and she felt their prime purchasing days where likely behind them. Besides, the vendors would not only attract additional customers but also provide the mall with incremental revenue to fund various new promotions.

2. Since it was doubtful that another large department store would move into the current vacant space, she proposed subdividing half that space into smaller stores that would feature products that would appeal to minority groups, such as the trade area's large Latino population. The remaining space would be used for some type of amusement area or park where mothers could leave their children while they shopped.

3. Starting the next month, Ms. Donnelly said that she wanted all shoppers younger than 17 to have adult supervision on Friday and Saturday nights. She claimed the policy was an attempt to create a family-oriented atmosphere. Donnelly said other malls, including the Mall of America, had already adopted this idea, and it was the result of feedback from shoppers, retailers, and community leaders. She added that she planned to beef up security to enforce this policy.

4. Finally, since she felt the mall should be attracting a younger customer, she was going to discontinue the policy of opening the common area at 6 A.M. each morning for "senior walks." She pointed out that this in no way communicated that seniors were not welcome at the mall but that it would reinforce the mall's image of having a family-oriented atmosphere.

Questions

1. Based on Chapter 's discussion of both the creative and analytical approach, are Pam Donnelly's ideas sufficiently creative to attract new business (sales), and what analyses should she have undertaken before making these recommendations?

2. What do you think of each of Pam Donnelly's ideas? What population and social or economic trends support your conclusion(s)? Why?

3. Because she is the manager of the mall's largest store, not only will other managers look to Pat Snyder for advice but also she carries considerable influence with Ms. Donnelly. What should Pat Snyder do? Why?

Chapter 4

Madison's Bike Wars[3]

Madison, Wisconsin, is home of the University of Wisconsin, where many of the more than 30,000 students and thousands of faculty and staff members find bicycling an easy way to get around the crowded campus, which borders Lake Mendota. Less than a mile up State Street from the university campus is the state capital, where even state employees often bike to work. Except for perhaps the coldest days of the year, you will always see cyclists in this university and state capital community.

Perhaps it not surprising therefore that Madison has been designated a gold-level Bicycle Friendly Community by the League of American Bicyclists; as such, it is also one of the best specialty bicycle retail markets in the country. Around the campus and capital and outward to the suburbs and outlying farms are hundreds of miles of paved bicycle pathways. This very proactive and bicycle friendly community is the home for Waterloo, Wisconsin–based Trek Bicycles' two company-owned stores, with the one located on the east side of the city being identified as the company's flagship store.

Erik's Bike Shop is a successful multistore retailer headquartered in Minneapolis–St. Paul market; it carries Specialized as its marquee brand. A few years ago, Erik's opened a store in Madison. Recently, Specialized announced to its dealers in Madison that Erik's planned to open a second store, reportedly within a block or so from the Trek flagship store on the city's east side. By the way, about a mile away from both the Trek flagship and the new Erik's, which will carry Specialized, is an established bicycle dealer that has carried both the Trek and Specialized brands for many years. To make matters worse, thousands of students each spring put up for sale their used bicycles as they graduate. Many of these bikes are high-performance Trek and Specialized brands. It seems like everyone is competing with everyone to sell bicycles in Madison.

To further complicate this situation, the Trek flagship and new Erik's store are located almost within sight of a large new Dick's Sporting Goods and a Target store. It is expected that these four retailers will beat on each other and will seek to become more efficient in order to survive. As a result, prices in Madison will be kept suppressed. In fact, consumers, particularly adult enthusiast cyclists, will be the clear beneficiaries of this most competitive of markets.

Questions

1. What market structure best describes the current market conditions for these four retailers—Trek, Erik's, Dick, and Target? Given the market structure you have chosen, in what manner do the current retailers compete?

2. What could happen to change the current market structure?

3. What about the current independent bicycle retailer that has been in the market the longest? Is the retailer in a dangerous place?

4. Can the independent retailer breakaway from the other four retailers? How?

5. If you were the independent retailer, what would you do? Why?

Chapter 5

Vending-Machine Operator Suffers the Cost of a Product Recall

While going to college, you have been working for a local vending-machine company. Your job, which entails about 20 hours a week, requires you replenish the snacks and cigarettes in 213 machines at 86 locations each week. These locations range from beauty and barbershops to small offices. The money was good because you were paid a commission; on average, you earned more than $200 a week.

Last Monday morning, just before you left for class, you received a phone call from your boss. You had to go to every one of your machines carrying crackers and snacks that used a peanut paste because they might have a potential salmonella contamination (68 of your 86 locations) and remove them. It seems that over the past two weeks, more than 600 possible cases of salmonella were reported in 44 states across the country, resulting in eight deaths. The Centers for Disease Control and Prevention associated the illnesses with a peanut paste made at a peanut-processing plant in Georgia. The paste was used in more than 1,900 different products, including some famous brand names such as Keebler, Little Debbie, and Austin Quality Food. However, no problems were reported in your trading area. Your company had been distributing some of the suspected products during the past month, and your boss knew that several route people, such as yourself, had distributed the infected items.

You know the consequences of selling a product that can cause salmonella, an organism that can cause serious and sometimes fatal infections in young children, frail or elderly people, and others with weakened immune systems. You also know that even healthy individuals infected with salmonella can get quite ill. Thus, you skipped class on Monday and stopped by all your accounts and removed the snacks. While doing this, you made some quick calculations and assumed that since no one locally had been reported as sick, the infected snacks must still be in the machines or, if a peanut-based item had been sold, a healthy person ate it and wasn't seriously affected.

Later that week, the wholesaler came by to pick up the recalled products. Your boss handed him a bill to cover the cost of the recall. After all, the route employees hadn't been able to handle any of the other tasks on Monday. They just took out the cracker and snack packages before anyone got sick. The wholesaler apologized but said that this was a cost of doing business as a distributor or retailer and his company couldn't pay. Besides, if they reimbursed you, every wholesaler would have to pay every retailer for every recall. After all, the costs of the nationwide recall were probably well beyond the manufacturer's ability to pay. Your boss became upset and claimed that he was totally justified in recovering the costs associated with this recall. Pulling product from the machines, isolating it in the warehouse, and exchanging it costs time and money. And this didn't count the missed sales that resulted from the time and attention the route paid to handling a recall and not refilling other fast-selling products.

In the end, the wholesaler agreed to pay for the cost of the products themselves but not for any others costs associated with the recall.

Questions

1. Is the wholesaler responsible if the manufacturer is unable to pay for all the costs of a recall?

2. If the manufacturer or wholesaler must pay for the legitimate costs of a recall, then who would determine the legitimacy of each cost and see that it was not creating an opportunity for middlemen to make an extra profit?

3. Would the results achieved in this case have been different if there was a real vendor–retailer partnership? How and why?

4. If the manufacturer must pay for the recall, would this cause some manufacturers to be more careful so as to avoid recalls? Or would it cause them to hesitate longer before deciding that a recall is necessary?

Source: This case is based on "Food Sellers Feel Effects of Peanut Recall," *Lubbock Avalanche-Journal*, January 29, 2009: A1, A5; and discussions with several vending-machine operators.

Chapter 6

The Changing Face of Tobacco Retailers[4]

Over the last half-century, Americans have become accustomed to the idea of being able to buy cigarettes at a variety of retail outlets ranging from vending machines in bars to restaurants, airports, supermarkets, convenience stores, gas stations, and discount stores. However, federal legislation may soon change the way tobacco is sold in the United States.

Walmart was one the first major retailers to address the tobacco issue. In 1990, Sam Walton admitted in a letter to a consultant that he was "still in a quandry [*sic*] on our direction for this very important issue."[5] The next year, the retailer announced the banning of smoking on all Walmart property, including the stores, as well as the removal of any cigarette vending machines. At the time, Walton was not aware of any vending machines, but as a precaution, he issued the "ban" order. Later, when Walmart expanded into Canada by purchasing 127 Woolco stores, Walton met with the pharmacists from the newly acquired stores. At their request, Walmart dropped the sale of tobacco in its Canadian stores. Members of the chain's executive committee decided to continue with the sale of cigarettes after Mr. Walton's death.

At the same time, various state and local agencies began to enforce age restrictions on the sale of cigarettes and other products such as firearms, spray paint (which was used for painting gang slogans), and even glue. Walmart even introduced a program into its scanners that froze the cash register when the SKU for one of these products was recorded until the clerk ascertained the age of the purchaser. As a result of the increased enforcement, some retailers, especially supermarkets and drug stores, began to drop tobacco. How would this affect the sale of these legal products, which account for more than $60 billion in sales per year?

If such a change were to occur, what retailers would benefit? Some experts think that if cigarettes are dropped by the mass sellers, one of the best prepared retailers is John Roscoe's family-owned Cigarettes Cheaper chain. This is a 400-store operation already doing $500 million in sales each year.

Cigarettes Cheaper, which sells only cigarettes in 1,200-square-foot outlets located primarily in strip malls, is second only to Walmart in total cigarette sales; it is a spin-off of Roscoe's Customer Company convenience store chain. The name Customer Company was a reflection of Roscoe's appreciation for his consumers. As a result, he offered the lowest possible prices on everything in the store. His tobacco stores follow the same philosophy by charging 20 percent less than nearby competitors for the average pack or carton of cigarettes.

The chain is able to charge such prices by taking advantage of every manufacturer discount available and realizing that its customers are not apt to buy just a pack or even a carton but will more likely purchase 10 to 12 cartons at a time. But low prices are not the only attraction. Roscoe's store (and similar operations) has a broader range of brands and packaging than other retailers, a regular diet of promotions, and a welcoming attitude toward smokers that is not always the case elsewhere.

These facts about Roscoe's operation are most impressive:

- No member of John Roscoe's family smokes, nor do any of them encourage anyone else to smoke.

- The stores put in a great deal of effort into controlling underage customers. All stores have a large sign stating "No Minors Allowed Inside," and a manager could lose his or her job for violating this rule.

Many retail experts think this might be the way all cigarettes are sold in the future. What do you think?

Roscoe says his stores are just there to serve the market. Do you agree with his right to do this? Do you agree with his decision to do this?

Chapter 7

Eminent Domain: Fair or Foul?

Prior to 2005, state and local governments had primarily used eminent domain to confiscate private land to build roads, schools, hospitals, and other public facilities. However, a 5-4 ruling by the U.S. Supremem Court (*Kelo v. City of New London, 125 S. Ct. 2005*) in June 2005, permitted eminent domain powers to be extended to confiscate waterfront homes in order to build an office complex and condominiums. As a result, some local and state governments are now using eminent domain to foreclose on private property so that real estate developers can build shopping malls that will pay more in property taxes to the community than the homes and small businesses they replaced.

These cities favor this expanded use of eminent domain to replace "blighted or deteriorating" private properties for "public use" by explaining that such action will benefit the general public by creating jobs and adding needed tax revenue to the area.

Many responsible city leaders acknowledge that eminent domain is not a power to be used lightly. Cities must be sensitive to those who will be displaced. However, as part of a legislative process, with citizen input and discussion, the use of eminent domain is one of the most powerful tools city officials have to cure neighborhood ills and rejuvenate city budgets.

While government officials admit to feeling sympathy for the existing property owners, they have a legal obligation to consider all of their citizens who will benefit from the job creation these projects bring. In addition, they point out that economic development is really cutthroat competition between neighboring communities. If one city or town doesn't offer incentives, its neighbors will.

Existing property owners oppose such action by claiming that the use of eminent domain to wipe out good, clean neighborhoods merely to increase tax revenues is a blow to the rights of all property owners. Theoretically, no property is now safe if some government body concludes that a developer can make better use of it. What is to become of the small business owner who has been at her current location for years and has built a loyal customer following? Others claim that once a city threatens the use of eminent domain, honest negotiations between the parties are over.

After hearing both sides of the argument, some state and local governments today are considering limits on the power of local governments to condemn private property and transfer it to real estate developers merely to improve a community's economic welfare. How can a community be better off if some of its citizens are made to suffer? Among the actions being considered are:

1. *Defining economic benefit.* This involves setting up a procedure to show that the economic benefits gained by the use of eminent domain far out-weigh the negative consequences to the existing property owners. This alternative would make it harder for governmental units to declare a neighborhood "blighted or deteriorating" strictly for economic development.

2. *Total ban.* This entails a complete ban on the use of eminent domain for economic development. This can be accomplished by specifically banning economic development as a reason for permitting eminent domain or by listing what end results can be sought by the use of eminent domain.

3. *Over compensation.* In an attempt to make eminent domain less desirable, local and state governments would have to pay 25 percent to 100 percent above

"fair" market value when they confiscate private property for economic development.

4. *Do nothing*. Don't establish separate rules for economic development. Government leaders must consider the benefits to society as whole and not just a few individuals. They must not enact one law for building highways and schools, a second law to eliminate "blight and/or deterioration," and a third law for economic development. After all, aren't all three situations the same?

Questions

1. Should local and state governments be allowed to use eminent domain for any reason? Explain your reasoning.

2. Should local and state governments be allowed to use eminent domain for economic development? Explain your reasoning.

3. When weighing the benefits of economic development, how can you measure the pain and suffering of the displaced property owners?

4. Of the four possible legislative solutions, which one do you favor? Why?

Chapter 8

Dolly's Place

After years of teaching retailing and marketing at the University of Southern Mississippi, Dolly Loyd decided to retire and return to her first love – running an apparel store on the Gulf Coast. Because she used to run such a department for a major retail chain before teaching, she kept up with the current trends in the industry. Dolly gained the support of an ex-high school classmate who, after making millions with an Internet startup, financed her new endeavor.

Today Dolly is beginning to make plans for the upcoming three-month spring season. Dolly anticipates planned sales of $250,000 for the season based on a planned initial markup of 45 percent. Within the season, planned monthly sales are projected to be as follows: 33 percent in February, 40 percent in April (Easter is April 12th), and 27 percent in May. To ensure a profitable season, trade association records were consulted. The records indicated: (1) The stock-to-sales ratios need to be 3. for February, 5.0 for March, and 6.0 for April; (2) reductions can be planned at 5 percent for February, 10 percent for March, and in an attempt to clear the store of old merchandise before her tourist season apparel arrives, a 20 percent reduction is planned for April; and (3) with the tourist season approaching, an inventory of $400,000 will be necessary to begin the summer season. Complete a three-month merchandise budget for Dolly.

Dolly's Place
Three-Month Merchandise Budget

Date: January 7, 2009
Season: Spring 2009

Spring	February	March	April	Seasonal Total
1. Planned BOM Stock				
2. Planned Sales				
3. Planned Retail Reductions				
4. Planned EOM Stock				
5. Planned Purchases @ Retail				
6. Planned Purchases @ Cost				
7. Planned Initial Markup				
8. Planned Gross Margin				
9. Planned BOM Stock/Sales Ratio	$3.0 \times$	$5.0 \times$	$6.0 \times$	
10. Planned Sales Percentage	33%	40%	27%	100%
11. Planned Retail Reduction	5%	10%	20%	11.05%

Planned Total sales for the period $250,000

Planned Total Retail Reduction Percentage For the Period 11.05%

Planned Initial Markup Percentage For the Period 45%

Planned BOM Stock for May $400,000

Chapter 9

The Sizing Problem[6]

Pam Lewis, the owner of the up-scale Pam's Place in the Chicago suburb of Lincoln-shire, had just entered what was to be the last vendor's showroom on her first day of this year's Dallas Apparel Market. She was excited about what she had seen that day and was already looking forward to a relaxing dinner with her former college room-mate and the next two days of buying. This last vendor was new to Pam, but she had heard other buyers saying wonderful things about it at the food court earlier that afternoon. Since it was near one of her Class A vendors, she decided to stop by.

Upon entering the showroom, Pam uttered her usual "What's new" to the man-ufacturer's sales rep.

"Depends on how important it is to you to make your customers very happy," was the quick reply. The salesperson then ushered Pam over to a display carrying slacks which featured a new fit technology. The key was the realization that a size 10 45 to 55 year-old women doesn't have the same shape as a size 10 25-year-old. Based on this fact, a new sizing system, called Fitlogic, is being used by the manufacturer. It is based on three body shapes that represent the most common female figures: straight sil-houette, curvy, and pearlike. These shapes are labeled 1, 2, and 3. Thus the vendor show Pam three different size 12 slacks, (12.1, 12.2, 12.3), one for each body shape.

The salesperson went on to explain that for women in the over 35 crowd, 40 percent are a 1 shape, 20 percent are 3s, and only 20 percent are a 2 shape, the silhouette currently used as the standard for sizing.

Pam remembered recently seeing the developer of this system on television dis-cussing why she thought it would revolutionize the way baby boomer women would purchase clothing. She even recalled an article in a trade journal about how a tele-vision shopping network, QVC, had great success with this concept. Still, she realized that the variety which would make the concept so appealing to her customers — multiple versions of the same size, each tailored to their body shape — would make it so unappealing to her as a buyer. After all, if she adopted the system for this line, she would have three times the number of items. They would require more display space and create a greater risk of future markdowns. It was a breadth versus depth issue to Pam because carrying the extra sizes would mean she would have to drop some other merchandise. Thus Pam, despite liking the fashions she saw in the showroom, was undecided as she left to meet her ex-roommate, Pat Marion, for dinner.

That night over dinner Pam described her day, especially this new fit technology. Then it hit her that there might be something to the system when Pat started telling her about her troubles in taking back some clothes that didn't fit her correctly. They were either too tight or too loose. Pam remembered something said on that television show about as women age, they not only change sizes but shapes. Twenty-five years ago, while in college, Pam and Pat were both a size 8 and often exchanged clothes. Now they were both size 12 but their shapes entirely different. Maybe if she was able to offer a better fitting line of clothing, not only would sales increase but customer returns would decrease. Pam decided that she would revisit the showroom first thing the next morning and get more information about this sizing system.

Questions

1. What do you believe is most important to the average customer; fit, price, style, or quality of workmanship? Which one do you believe is the greatest cause of customer returns?

2. Is this really a breadth versus depth issue?

3. Should Pam adopt this new sizing system? Explain your reasoning.

Chapter 10

Some Buying Issues

PART A   The buyer for the women's sweater department has purchased wool sweaters for $47.69. She uses an odd pricing policy and wants to sell them at a 47 percent markup on selling price. At what price should each sweater be sold? [answer: $89.98 or $89.99]

PART B   The buyer for men's shirts has a price point of $45 and requires a markup of 40 percent. What would be the highest price he should pay for a shirt to sell at this price point? [answer: $27]

PART C   The Men's Department buyer hopes to achieve net sales of $1,500,000 for the upcoming season. Operating expenses are expected to be $560,000 and retail reductions are $180,000. Management has set a profit goal of $110,000. What should the initial markup percentage be? [answer 50.6%]

PART D   A buyer submits the following plans to his general merchandise manager: Planned sales = $85,000; planned initial markup = 40%; planned reductions = $31,000. Based on these projections, what is the planned maintained markup percentage?

Chapter 11

Fallon's Department Store

Over the last decade sales at Fallon's Department Store have grown about 3 percent above the annual inflation rate. However, there has never been a complete review of the store's advertising expenditures. An advertising committee created by the chain's president, Mark Fallon, has maintained a budget of about 4 percent of sales, which he felt was similar to his competitors' budgets. In some years the budget was not completely used because of the difficulty in obtaining adequate newspaper space around Christmas. In other years a little extra was spent to meet particular activities of competitors. Management never considered that the initial budget was "set in stone" and always tried to adapt to the competitive environment as necessary. Fallon kept a close eye on the store's volume figures, and if a merchandise area needed additional advertising, he gave it more money. In addition, if a merchandise area developed individual "hot" items, extra advertising dollars were allocated to that area.

Recently Fallon called a meeting of key executives to discuss the advertising budget and how funds should be allocated between merchandise areas and advertising media. All the executives agreed that the store should spend at least 2 percent of sales on advertising. They reasoned that customers must be convinced that Fallon's offers value in its merchandise. No one could say why the minimum was 2 percent rather than 3 or 4 percent; it just seemed like a reasonable figure. The question was, "How much above this figure should Fallon's go?"

Shelby Wilcox, the controller, suggested that the answer is easy: Each advertisement has to pay for itself. After all, Fallon's advertising over the years has been merchandise advertising. Each department should be held to a contribution to overhead. If the decision maker is held to this goal, he or she should be allowed to make his or her own advertising decision. If the decisions are bad, the individual should be fired and replaced by someone who can make effective decisions. It is the merchandise area heads, Wilcox continued, who should add up the requests of the individual merchandise areas. The advertising budget will then be more or less a summation of these requests. Each buyer should determine: "Does the advertising for my area of concern pay or not?" If the summation of the various areas is less than 1 percent, then some method of allocating advertising up to 1 percent should be devised. But he expects that the requests of the areas will in fact add up to about 4 percent of sales.

Barbara Bowman, the general merchandise manager, held a slightly different view. She suggested that buyers and merchandise managers should be responsible not just for net profits or contribution to overhead, but also for the growth of the store and its image. The store uses sales of the merchandise areas as an indication of how the future growth criteria of the department store are being met. The initial and maintained markups are carefully monitored to make sure that the volume is not obtained at the cost of the store's image. The promotion of goods at low markup is thought to damage this image, particularly if the merchandise promoted is not a famous brand. Therefore, one cannot develop a budget or allocate that budget according to just one criterion – a criterion that few observers would accept, namely, short-term contribution or profits. While everyone wants to make the advertising budget scientific and relate to just one goal, perpetual hankering after this deal is futile. Bowman argued that three goals – 1) sales growth, 2) high markup, and 3) short-term profit – must be kept in mind at all times. One simply has to do the best that one can; advertising is an art, not a science.

Bowman concluded that the last year's budget should be used as a base. This base could be adjusted, if necessary, for exceptional performance the year before. The managers of each area should use the money the best way they know how, recognizing that these three goals apply to most of the areas.

Mark Fallon is more confused than ever after the meeting. He expected more agreement among people who have been in retailing so long.

Questions

1. How would you suggest that Mark Fallon set the firm's advertising budget?

2. How should he allocate the budget among the various merchandise areas?

3. If sales are growing faster than the rate of inflation, why should Fallon's even consider changing what they are doing?

Chapter 12

The Internship

Back in February, Kim Wake interviewed with JoBeth Brenholtz for a summer internship with Reed's. Ms Brenholtz's family has owned Reed's, a locally owned women's apparel store located in a neighborhood center near the campus, for more than a half-century. Kim explained to Ms. Brenholtz that she really wasn't sure if a career in retailing was what she wanted to do with her college education. JoBeth told her not to worry, that this was what the internship was for—to learn about and experience what was actually involved in a retailing career.

The Reed's internship would last 12 weeks, and during that time Kim would spend five weeks working on the sales floor, two weeks in the buying office, and a week apiece in display, receiving, and advertising promotion. The final two weeks would entail a special project.

Now it was late July, and Ms. Brenholtz's secretary called Kim while she was on the sales floor and asked if she could stop by JoBeth's office before the store opened the next morning. Kim guessed it would be about the special project.

Just before the store's 10 a.m. opening, Kim was ushered into the executive office suite. Kim was here once before, on her first day on the job. In fact, while she had seen Ms. Brenholtz occasionally walking the store over the past eight weeks, she really hadn't talked to her since that earlier visit. Kim had noticed that Ms. Brenholtz seldom did anything more than exchange pleasantries with the store's lower-level employees as she walked through the store.

After visiting with Kim about her internship experiences thus far, Ms. Brenholtz explained that she wanted Kim's special project to be a review of the store's operation. She realized that Kim was only going to be a college senior and had rather "limited" retailing experience. However, Kim's lack of long-held beliefs was appealing. The store needed a fresh analysis because sales had declined slightly the past three years after years of steady growth. The meeting ended with Kim asking if she could wait until the end of August to complete the report.

That night Kim started thinking about what she should say in her report. She remembered from her retailing class that the first two tasks of any retailer were to get consumers into the store and then convert them into customers. Despite her rather abbreviated retailing career, Kim had already become aware that the common retail excuse for poor sales was "lack of traffic." Still Kim wasn't sure what was the real problem. So she started a list based on her observations over the past two months at Reed's:

- In conversations with employees, no one had mentioned that store traffic had been declining over the past few years.

- She estimated that the store's conversion rate was around 20 percent.

- In reviewing her own training, she really didn't think that Reed's spent more than an hour covering store policies and procedures. When she went on the sales floor, the area manager spent time explaining the scanner and cash register, but nobody taught her about selling. She assumed that his was the way it was with all new salespeople.

- Kim has heard that the store had experienced a high amount of employee turnover over the past few years. While she wasn't sure of the actual number, she had observed that a significant number of sales positions were filled by part-timers.

- Over the past two months, she felt that the employees were doing a good job on what they were told to do. In fact, after her third week on the floor, the assistant store manager congratulated her for not having any errors cashing out of the register at the end of her shifts.

Questions

1. Should JoBeth Brenholtz spend more time on the sales floor? Why?

2. If Reed's were willing to spend more money to increase sales, should the retailer spend it on promotions to increase traffic or on training to increase the conversion rate?

3. Is it a mistake to have too many part-time employees? Does this situation impact customer service? How?

4. Do you agree or disagree with the statement that "Reed's seems to be a typical example of a retailer that doesn't evaluate employees on their ability to serve the customer but on their ability to cash out correctly." What should be done about this?

5. What should be the key point for Kim to address in this memo?

Chapter 13

The Unique Shop

You are the facilities manager for a chain of six women's apparel stores called the Unique Shop. The chain, which targets younger women, has its flagship store in the strip center near a college campus in a city of 120,000. The 15,000-square-foot store, which was last remodeled twelve years ago, has experienced consistent sales increases in recent years. However, the company president believes the store is missing even more sales since many competitors have left the campus area for one of two malls on the outskirts of the city.

Hoping to take advantage of this lack of competition, the president has budgeted about $400,000 for expansion next year. She plans on leasing the 5,000-square-foot empty storefront next door and increasing the aisle widths and number of dressing rooms while maintaining the same level of inventory. The merchandise manager, however, recommends that the $400,000 be used to buy new fixtures to increase the merchandise capacity of the existing store. His idea is to shrink the width of all aisles, fit more bulk fixtures on the floor, and double-stack all merchandise. After all, without these new racks and shelves, customers won't be able to see the merchandise. And if customers can't see the merchandise, they can't buy it.

When walking the store last week, you noticed that the merchandise is already crammed in too tightly and that customers were having trouble putting unwanted merchandise back on the racks and shelves. You also felt that there were too few feature presentations to support your fashion apparel. Finally, it bothered you that there was not a clear distinction between the various departments within the store.

Further, the president, and the marketing and merchandising personnel must understand their target customer groups to make the expansion plans most effective. If the store adds more merchandise, what type of merchandise should be added, targeting which types of customers? Even if little new inventory is added, what types of departments should be made distinctive?

Questions

1. What do you feel is more important for customers: increasing store space, which will take longer, and be more difficult, or adding more racks to the present store? Why?

2. If increasing total sales is the goal, which plan would you recommend? Explain your reasoning.

3. Describe some of the market segments that can be found in the customer category "young women"? How do their lifestyles influence different clothing needs? How could you use your customer base to help you decide which new merchandise categories to carry?

4. Could the president consider subleasing parts of a larger store to a compatible merchant? For example, should the store consider a coffee bar or a vintage clothing shop? What are some of the considerations in this decision?

Source: This case was prepared by Jan Owens, Carthage College, Kenosha, WI and used with her written permission.

Chapter 14

The Cliff Problem

Over the past twenty years, Carrie Taylor had taken a passing interest in her parents' furniture and appliance store. She had worked there part-time as an interior designer. However, she had no interest in the day-to-day operations of the store. After all, her college major was design and not business.

However, all that suddenly changed nine months ago when a drunk driver killed her father and seriously injured her mother. Carrie was now in charge of the family business. She soon became somewhat comfortable handling the daily management tasks but was unsure of what to do with one of her employees. Thus, as she prepared to leave for the High Point Furniture Market, she was determined to seek the advice of other independent retailers about how to handle the situation.

One of the first things that Carrie did on taking over was to establish a Saturday morning meeting whereby she could discuss the store's operations with all the employees. At her first meeting, she explained to everyone that they were a team and that she needed their help and support to carry out her parent's legacy. She asked what she could do to improve things. After listening to everyone and trying to solve all the issues, Carrie decided to bring in an outside speaker once a month to motivate the staff. One of the first speakers was a sales consultant who offered selling tips. Another early session involved a local high school instructor who was seeking to place an intern with the store. This morning, the speaker was from the local Chamber of Commerce. He spoke on the Chamber's plans and promotions to draw customers to the downtown business district over the next year.

However, ever since the first meeting, Carrie's superstar salesperson, Cliff Cochran, had not come to a meeting. Besides being a long-time employee of the store, Cliff had been a close friend of her father. In addition to missing the meeting, Cliff was often late coming to work.

Carrie began to worry that Cliff's behavior was going to affect the morale of the other five members of the selling team. However, he was the store's top producer, accounting for more than a third of the store's sales.

On her first night at the High Point Market, Carrie attended a reception. While seated at a table with three other independent owners and a sales rep for a major furniture line, she asked them for advice on her Cliff problem.

One of the owners asked Carrie about the feedback from others about the meetings. Were they beneficial enough to justify coming to work a half-hour early on Saturday? He wanted to know if many of the housekeeping announcements at the meeting could have been replaced with e-mails or posting on the employee bulletin board.

The sales rep said maybe it was a good, not a bad, thing. After all, if the others realized that if they increased production, they could miss the meeting also. Besides what was Cliff like once he got to work? Was he a leader by example? Did he take care to neatly arrange the merchandise displays and follow up on sales leads with phone calls or e-mail?

Another owner asked if Carrie tried to involve Cliff in the Saturday meetings. She felt that Cliff needed special "atta-boy" treatment. She suggested that Carrie feed his ego by asking him to develop a training session on closing the sale or some other topic. Everyone knows he is at the top of the sales ladder, so use his skills.

The sales rep also wondered if maybe Cliff was merely rebelling against the person who replaced his long-time friend. Maybe Carrie should go out of her way to help Cliff through this difficult period.

Questions

1. What criteria should be used to judge the importance and necessity of having a weekly Saturday morning training meeting? Do they really motivate a sales force?

2. If Cliff's problem is really one of motivation, then what would you recommend that Carrie should do? Why?

3. Should Carrie ever think about firing Cliff? After all, his behavior in recent months had become a major concern. Support your reasoning.

Source: This case is based on an idea from the "Strategy Zone," *NARDA Independent Retailer*, December 2005: 14, 26; and an author's experiences with a real-life Cliff.

A p p e n d i x

ANSWERS TO SAMPLE TEST QUESTIONS

Chapter 1

1. Answer c is correct. Answer a is wrong because retailing includes credit card purchases. Answer b is wrong because retailing is different in each country. Answer d is wrong because retailing involves selling to the final consumer, not the wholesaler. Answer e is wrong because retailing is a valued sector of the economy, and it does increase economic growth.
2. Answer e is correct as the other four answers were among the five ways of categorizing retailers listed in the chapter. The fifth way, which wasn't listed as a possible answer, was the Census Bureau's NAICS codes. The manager's gender should have no impact on a store's performance; besides, federal sex-discrimination laws would make this an illegal means for categorizing retailers.
3. Answer b is correct. However, we would hope that a retailer possesses the other four possible characteristics as well as being a leader.
4. Answer c is correct as the manager investigated both sources of supply and competition before making her decision.

Chapter 2

1. Answer b is the correct answer since market performance objectives seek to establish the retailer's dominance against the competition. Answers a and c are wrong because they are made-up terms. Answer d is wrong because societal performance is concerned with the broader issues of the world, and answer e is wrong because financial objectives are internally number oriented and dealing with profit or productivity.
2. Answer c is the correct answer. Answers a and b are wrong because price is the poorest way to differentiate yourself. Answer d is wrong because this action would restrict you from selling many of the top brands. Answer e is

wrong because the customers really don't see planning, only the results of planning.

Chapter 3

1. Statement b is the correct answer. Americans do move about a dozen times in their lifetime. Answer a is wrong because some baby boomers are already in their 50s. Answer c is wrong because small markets still represent great opportunities for retailers if they satisfy the consumers' wants and needs. Answer d is wrong because the U.S. growth rate is expected to be about 1 percent, and e is wrong because the growth rate has been declining in recent years.
2. Item c is the correct answer: The boomerang effect is a relatively new phenomenon that describes something many of today's students will face that previous generations did not have to face—returning home to live with their parents. Statements a, b, and d are at least true statements, but they have nothing to do with the boomerang effect. Item e could be true or not at the time you are reading this, but it also has nothing to do with the question asked.
3. Item d is correct since discretionary income is disposable income (which is all personal income minus personal taxes) minus the money needed for necessities. Statement e is wrong because, as we just noted, it is the definition of disposable income. The other three possible choices are just made-up definitions.
4. Item d is the correct answer. Answer a is incorrect because such resentment may have a long-term negative impact on the retailer's ability to regain that consumer as a customer. Item b is wrong because if the retailer is proactive with its customer-satisfaction program and responds quickly to the problem, the resentment can be overcome. Statement c is incorrect because most unhappy consumers don't make the retailer aware of their dissatisfaction. Therefore, it is up to the retailer to be vigilant, and monitor customer

satisfaction. Item e is not correct either. Retailers must measure customer satisfaction on an ongoing basis and compare customer-service ratings against preestablished benchmarks.

Chapter 4

1. Answer b is correct. Item e is true in rare cases, but the question asked for what structure *most* retailers are involved in. Answer d, while it is a type of market structure, is wrong because retailers don't operate in environments with horizontal demand curves. Items a and c, while sounding good, are made-up terms.

2. Item d is the correct answer because this involves different types of retailers competing with each other with similar products. Answer b is wrong because *intratype* refers to cases in which the same types of retailers compete with each other, and Walmart is a general merchandise store and not a grocer. Item c (scrambled merchandising) can be used to describe what Walmart is doing, but this term does not refer to a type of competition. Answer e refers to a situation in which a retailer dominates a single line of merchandise, not many lines as Walmart is doing with its supercenters. Answer a is wrong because it is a made-up, nonsense term.

3. Answer d is correct. Some might say that the retail accordion theory could be used by saying that the small original hamburger stand expanded to the large McDonald's and Burger King franchises of today and will get smaller as customers rebel. However, this isn't entirely accurate. Nevertheless, we didn't include the accordion theory as a possible answer. Item b is wrong because it describes a stage of growth that institutions pass through and not why they change formats. The other three possible answers are made-up terms.

4. Item d is the correct answer. Answer a is wrong because retailing is more diverse around the world, and b is wrong because success in one country doesn't guarantee success in other countries—witness the hypermarkets in the United States or the fact that Kmart, Sears, and JCPenney have abandoned their foreign expansion plans. Item c is wrong because the size of the average retailer is diverse. e is wrong because other countries have also developed successful new retailing formats—witness IKEA.

Chapter 5

1. Answer e is correct since facilitating institutions aid the supply chain by performing tasks that they are more capable of doing than the current supply chain members. Item a is wrong since some facilitating institutions may take possession of the merchandise but none of them take title. Item b is wrong since facilitating institutions do not take title to the goods, and answer c is wrong since they do not manage the supply chain and besides the goal of a supply chain is to minimize suboptimization since they cannot operate at 100-percent efficiency. Answer d is wrong since they cannot do all eight functions without taking title; besides, the text mentions that no one firm would want, or be able, to perform all eight functions.

2. Item e is the correct answer. Answers a and c are wrong since conventional channels, due to their loose alignment, are by their very nature not efficient. Item b is wrong because contractual channels are not loosely aligned since the contract directs each member's duties and responsibilities. Answer d is wrong since there is no feeling of partnership and cooperation in a conventional channel.

3. Answer b is correct. Item a is wrong even though it may be true that each member wants all the power, a supply-chain member is still dependent on the other members. Item c is wrong because no member can perform all eight functions. Answer d is wrong because a partnership should be committed to the life of the supply chain, and e is wrong because, if everybody wants to work independently of each other, there would not be a supply chain in the first place.

4. Answer a is correct because, to be successful, all the channel members must work as a team. Item b is wrong because, in some cases, especially those involving a small retailer and a larger manufacturer, it doesn't make sense to have a retailer direct the channel. Answer e is wrong for the same basic reason; a small manufacturer would never tell Walmart how to act. Answer c is incorrect because at times coercion is necessary to make some members realize that their actions hurt other members. Item d is not the correct answer because it doesn't work to set an arbitrary profit level. Profit should be based on the tasks performed.

Chapter 6

1. Answer e is correct since the major price discrimination law, the Robinson-Patman Act, is meant to protect competition by making sure that retailers are treated fairly by suppliers. The possible other answers pertain to laws covering other situations.

2. Answer e is correct since it involved a deceitful action (using another firm's trademark) that caused damage to the other firm. Item a is wrong because it did not cause damage to the competitor. Item b is wrong because it was not deceitful—the retailer told the truth. Answer c is wrong because it involves deceptive pricing. Answer d is perfectly legal since you did not do anything wrong.

3. Item a is the correct answer since an implied warranty of fitness for a particular purpose arises when the customer relies on the retailer to assist or make the selection of goods to serve a particular purpose. Answer b is wrong because an implied warranty of merchantability means that the retailer implies that the merchandise is fit for the ordinary purpose for which the product is usually purchased. Answer c is wrong because it is a made-up answer. Answers d and e are wrong because no verbal or written guarantee was mentioned in the question.

4. Answer b is correct since the purchase of the cat food was tied to the purchase of the unpopular product—litter. The other answers have nothing to do with the question.

5. Item b is the correct answer. While there are federal laws governing franchise operations, the most stringent laws are usually state laws since the state government wants to protect its citizens and locally owned franchise businesses, as well as voters, from the unfair practices of out-of-state franchisors.

6. Answer a is correct since it is a merchandising decision regarding the success or failure of merchandise. The other four answers pertain to the ethical decisions discussed in the chapter.

Chapter 7

1. Answer c is correct. It is not essential that a market segment create high sales, but it should be profitable. Answers a, b, d, and e are all criteria used to successfully reach a target market and thus are incorrect answers.

2. Item a is the correct answer. Since freestanding retailers are not part of a shopping center or CBD, they do not have direct competition. Answer b is not correct since it is an advantage of retailers in shopping centers. Item c is incorrect since freestanding retailers have more difficulty in attracting customers for the initial visit. Answer d is incorrect because freestanding retailers are not able to share advertising costs with other retailers as in a shopping center. Answer e is incorrect because freestanding stores can be either leased or purchased.

3. Item e is the correct answer. Answers a, b, c, and d are all purposes of geographical information systems, thus any one of these answers is not the single best choice.

4. Answer b is correct. The three steps presented are exactly as discussed in the textbook. Item a is wrong because the first step is incorrect, c is wrong because the second step is incorrect, d is wrong because all three steps are incorrect, and e is wrong because the third step is incorrect.

5. Answer e is correct. Items a and b by themselves are not the best answer because both are needed to do a site analysis. Answers c and d are incorrect because they are irrelevant to site analysis.

6. Item c is correct because alternative investments available to the retailer should not be a consideration in the selection of a site. Answers a, b, d, and e are incorrect because they are all important considerations in selecting the best site.

Chapter 8

1. Answer b is correct since current liabilities are listed on the balance sheet but are not included in the merchandise budget. The other answers are all included in the merchandise budget.

2. Answer d is correct since the income statement is a summary of the sales and expenses for a given time period. Item a is wrong because an expense report, while not mentioned in the chapter, only would cover expenses. Item b is wrong because even though the inventory valuation will affect the retailer's expenses, it also does not include sales. Answer c is wrong because the cash flow statement only deals with the inflow and outflow of cash, and e is wrong because gross margin only considers sales and cost of goods sold and does not include operating expenses.

3. Answer c is correct since the cost ($120,000) divided by sales ($200,000) is 0.6.

Chapter 9

1. Answer c is correct. Both product purchases and markdowns impact dollar-merchandise planners.
2. Item a is the correct answer since $425,000 \times 1/2[1 + ($170,000/$142,000)] = $466,901$. Answer e would be correct if the question asked for the basic stock method, not the PVM. Item d is the average stock for the season but not the correct answer. The other two answers are made-up numbers.
3. Since the key feature of OTB is that it can be determined at anytime during the merchandise period, item d is the correct answer. The other answers are wrong because they are time-specific.
4. Answer c is correct; the other four answers are the constraints listed in the text.
5. Answer b is correct since it best describes what is involved in a vendor-profitability analysis statement, which was defined in the text as a "record of all purchases you made last year, the discounts granted you by the vendor, transportation charges paid, the original markup, markdowns, and the season-ending gross margin on that vendor's merchandise." Answer a is wrong because it is about the vendor's financial statements, which are seldom provided to retailers. Answer c is wrong because it deals with new lines of merchandise, and answer d is wrong because it deals with the retailer's line of credit granted by the vendor. Answer e is wrong because it covers only one factor (discounts) covered by the vendor-profitability analysis statement.
6. Item b is the correct answer. Answer a is wrong because it describes a noncumulative-quantity discount, and c is wrong because it assumes the discount period starts with the beginning of the year, something that is not always true. Item d is wrong because it describes a different type of discount. Answer e is wrong because it is based on a specific quantity that may be too high or too low given the circumstances of the sale.
7. Answer b is correct since it is the combination of vendor and retail employees that is most often involved in collusion. Answers a and d are wrong because customers are not involved in vendor collusion. Items c and e are wrong because even though the sales representative or accountant may be involved, the people involved with delivery person must also be included.

Chapter 10

1. Answer c is correct since the retailer's pricing objectives must be interactive with all the other decision areas of the firm. Item a is incorrect since pricing cannot be independent of these other decision areas, and b is incorrect since pricing cannot be separate from these other areas. Answer d is wrong because the retailer's pricing objectives should not be in competition with these other areas. Answer e is incorrect since multifaceted has nothing to do with the question.
2. Item c is the correct answer since in this case the retailer offered the same merchandise to different customers at different prices. Answer e is incorrect because variable pricing means that the prices for all customers may change as differences in either demand or costs occur. Nevertheless, all customers will pay the same price unless the retailer also uses a flexible policy. Answer a is wrong because there is no such policy as "two-price." Answer b is incorrect because, with customary pricing, the retailer seeks to maintain the same price for an item over an extended period of time. Item d is incorrect because leader pricing involves taking a popular item and offering it for sale to everybody as a means of drawing these consumers into a store.
3. Answer a is correct since markup on selling price is SP – C/SP [($45 – 25)/$45 = 44.4%]. Answer b is incorrect since the question asked for markup on selling price, and 80 percent is the markup on cost. The other answers are merely made-up numbers.
4. This question was chosen because many students get confused about reduction percentage. Answer c is correct since reduction percentage is the amount of the reduction ($29.99 – $19.99 = $10) divided by net sales ($19.99). Answer a is the markdown percentage, which is the amount of the reduction divided by the original selling price ($10/$29.99). The other answers are made-up numbers, although e is the result of dividing the new selling price by the original selling price.

Chapter 11

1. Answer e is the correct answer. Even though the retailer may have a low net worth, this should not be taken into consideration when developing a promotional strategy. After all, the objectives will still be the same. The other four alternatives (credit customers, price level, merchandise, and building and fixtures) are managerial decisions that must be integrated into the retailer's overall plan.

2. The correct answer is a. Institutional, or long-term, advertising tries to create a positive store image and provide public service. Answer b lists the objectives for short-term, or promotional, advertising. Answer c lists the two other types of promotion, and d lists how a retailer might seek to obtain short-term results. Item e lists two other topics covered in this chapter that have nothing to do with the question.

3. Answer e is correct as all four of the alternatives belong as part of an ad's objectives.

4. Answer e is correct. Premiums are the extra items offered to customers when they purchased the promoted product. In a limited number of cases, when premiums could be joint-sponsored sales promotions (answer a), such promotions would not be beneficial to the retailer since the consumer could purchase the product from another retailer. The other three answers (b, c, and d) are other forms of promotion.

Chapter 12

1. Answer c is correct since the text explained that a transient customer is an individual who visits a retailer and finds the service level below expectations or the product out of stock. This transient or temporary customer will seek to find a retailer with the level of customer service he or she feels is appropriate. Answer a is wrong because, even though the dictionary defines *transient* as short-lived or not long-lasting, the term does not refer to length of time spent shopping. The other choices are wrong because they have nothing to do with a transient customer.

2. Answer e is correct since merchandise availability is a transaction service that helps build the relationship with the customer, thus making answers b and d wrong. Answers a and c are wrong because personal shopping is a

service, not a cost, despite the fact that there might be some additional cost involved.

3. Item d is wrong because, as shown in Exhibit 12.5, the other alternatives are factors that must be considered when determining the service levels to offer.

4. Answer b is correct since good results are dependent not only on the salesperson's characteristics but also on how satisfied the salesperson is with the job and how the sales job was designed. Retail selling jobs should be designed to have high levels of variety (c), autonomy (d), task identity (e), and feedback from supervisors and customers (a).

5. Item e is the correct answer since once the approach has been completed, the salesperson is in a position to present the merchandise and sales message correctly. The key to the presentation, however, is to get the customer to want to buy your product or service. Therefore, you must have the right price range of products to show the customer. Answer a is wrong because, if the price too high or too low, the sale will be already lost. Answer b is wrong because you cannot select the right product unless you know the right price. Answer c is wrong because the greeting occurs in the approach stage, and d is wrong because helping the customer decide is the last step of the presentation.

6. Answer a is correct. The audit isn't an attempt to learn what the customers want, rather it concentrates on the facts of their shopping experience. Answers b, c, and d concern that shopping experience.

Chapter 13

1. Answer b is the correct answer since the two primary objectives around which all activities, functions, and goals in the store revolve are store image and space productivity. Alternatives c and d have two worthwhile activities (merchandise presentation and traffic control; opportunities for impulse buying and shelf management) but by themselves they will not produce high-performance results. Answers a and e are wrong because, while its activities are also good traits, sales management (a) and maintaining market share (e) are not objectives of the store environment.

2. Answer c is correct since the store's layout and design must allow the store to be shopable and

the merchandise to be effectively presented. Answer a is wrong because even though the retailer would like all the customers to see every high-profit items, this is not always possible, and nothing was said about presentation of the merchandise. Item b is obviously wrong since it would be foolish to give offices, the back room, wall, and aisles as much space as the selling floor since this is not where sales are generated. Answer d is wrong because why would a retailer care to have rapid replacement in a low-turnover area? Answer e is wrong because retailers today want to minimize the space given to back rooms.

3. Answer a is the correct answer since the method of merchandise presentation has an impact on the store's image and space productivity. Answer b is obviously wrong since it would be foolish to hire a psychologist to do the store's displays. Item c is wrong because, by shopping effectively, the customer might not make any impulse purchases. Answer d is wrong because even though social factors may influence our behavior, this alternative has nothing to do with the question. Answer e is another obviously wrong choice because it would be foolish for this to be done.

4. Answer b is correct since store design is most responsible for developing a store image, which the other four alternatives are concerned with doing. Answer b, however, would not increase the productivity of the store.

5. Answer e is correct since visual communications is concerned with the message within the store, which is covered by the other four possible answers, and not those external to the store.

Chapter 14

1. Answer d is correct because empowerment gives the employee the power to make decisions so that the customer is taken care of. Answer a is wrong because it is the concept of teamwork, not empowerment, that lets the employees adjust their hours. Item b is wrong because empowerment is concerned with satisfying customers' problems, not enforcing dress codes. Item c is wrong because, while the employees may make suggestions for featuring products in the weekly ads, this decision is made by the buyer and department manager.

2. Answer e is correct. As noted in the text, none of these would be a valid reason for not hiring an applicant.

3. Answer c is correct since training and development must be viewed as a process of continuing education. Item a is wrong because existing employees must also undergo training to remind them of how things are done and to teach and inform them of new items. Answer b is wrong because even though employee turnover is expensive, it is better to get rid of unproductive employees as soon as possible. Answer d is wrong because senior management should be involved in the training process; their time will be more efficiently spent doing the things they are an expert in such as store management, buying, and finance. Answer e is wrong because training should cover all retail activities.

4. Item a is the correct answer because straight commission offers the greatest potential for instant income. Answer b is wrong because straight salary cannot be influenced in the short run by an individual's performance, and c is wrong because the commission in a salary-plus-commission plan will be lower than the straight commission to compensate for the employer taking some of the risk. Item d is wrong since it is not a compensation plan. Answer e is wrong since a teamwork salary is based on the entire team's performance, not just that of an individual.

Glossary

A

above-market pricing policy A policy appropriate to certain market sectors that are receptive to high prices because nonprice factors are more important to them than price.

accounts payable Amounts owed to vendors for goods and services.

accounts receivable Amounts that customers owe a retailer for goods and services; also called *notes receivable*.

active information gathering When a consumer proactively gathers information.

administered vertical marketing channel Similar to a conventional marketing channels except one member takes the initiative to lead the channel by applying the principles of effective interorganizational management.

advertising Paid communication through various media to inform or persuade a particular audience; its function is primarily to inform potential buyers of the availability and price of a retailer's offering with the objective of developing consumer preferences for a particular retailer.

advertising effectiveness The extent to which advertising has produced a retailer's desired result.

advertising efficiency Whether the retailer's advertising result was achieved with minimum effort (e.g., dollars).

affordable method When a small retailer allocates all the money it can afford for advertising in any given budget period.

ambience The overall feeling or mood projected by a store through its aesthetic appeal to the human senses.

anchor store A dominant large-scale store that is expected to draw customers to a shopping center.

anticipation Payment system that allows a retailer to pay the invoice in advance of the expiration of the cash discount period and earn an extra discount.

asset Anything of value owned by a retail firm.

asset turnover Retailer's annual net sales divided by total assets; ratio tells the retail analyst how productively the firm's assets are being used.

assortment The number of brands that are found in a single merchandise line; also called *breadth*.

auction house An establishment that buys and sells goods or services by offering them for bid, taking bids, and then selling merchandise to the highest bidder.

B

bait-and-switch advertising Deceptive advertising in which one product is promoted at an unrealistically low price to entice a customer before the customer is switched to a higher-priced product; also called *bait-and-switch pricing*.

basic stock method (BSM) Method used when a retailer believes it must have a given level of inventory available at all times; requires that the retailer always have a base level of inventory investment regardless of the predicted sales volume.

battle of the brands When a retailer has its own products competing with a manufacturer's products for shelf space and control over display location.

below-market pricing policy How a retailer's prices are perceived versus those of the competition; the goal is to have the lowest total cost for *all* items purchased and not necessarily the lowest price for individual items.

benchmarking When a retailer uses the industry's best practices as a standard for its advertising budget.

boomerang effect A contemporary phenomenon of the changing American household in which adult children leave but return later to live with their parents.

breadth The number of brands that are found in a single merchandise line; also called *assortment*.

breakeven point The point where total revenues equal total expenses.

bricks-and-mortar retailers Retailers operating in physical buildings.

bulk or capacity fixture A round rack that holds the bulk of merchandise without looking as heavy as a long straight rack of merchandise.

buying Career path that requires the use of quantitative tools such as merchandise budgets to develop appropriate buying plans for their merchandise lines; responsible for selecting merchandise and vendors and negotiating terms with them; and must coordinate with store managers to ensure they are meeting customers' needs.

buying power index (BPI) A single weighted measure that combines effective buying income, retail sales, and population size into an overall indicator of a market's potential.

C

cash discount Discount for prompt payment of bills; usually stated as 2/10, net 30, which means that a 2-percent discount is given if payment is received within 10 days of the invoice date and the net amount is due within 30 days.

category killer A retailer who carries a large amount of merchandise in a single category at such low prices that customers almost always purchase what they need, thus "killing" the competition.

category management The simultaneous management of price, shelf-space merchandising strategy, promotional efforts, and other elements of the retail mix within the merchandise category based on the firm's goals, the changing environment, and consumer behavior.

central business district (CBD) Usually an unplanned shopping area around the geographic point where all public transportation systems converge.

channel A set of institutions that moves goods from the point of production to the point of consumption; also called *supply chain*.

channel advisor (channel captain) A supply-chain member—wholesaler, broker, or manufacturer—who performs functions they might not otherwise perform such as making direct-to-store deliveries, increasing promotional allowances, extending payment terms, or producing special package sizes, any of which will help the retailer operate more efficiently.

clicks-and-mortar retailer Retailer that sells both online and in physical stores; examples include Coach and Tiffany's.

closing the sale The natural conclusion to the selling process; when the salesperson converts the potential customer into an actual purchaser.

coercive power Power based on B's belief that A has the capacity to punish or harm B if B does not do what A wants.

compensation Includes direct-dollar payments (wages, commissions, and bonuses) and indirect payments (insurance, vacation time, retirement plans).

comp shopping When an employee of one retailer goes into another retailer and checks prices on a select few items to see how competitive they are on a local basis.

confidential vendor analysis Lists the same information as the profitability analysis statement but also provides a three-year financial summary as well as the names, titles, and negotiating points of the vendor's sales staff.

consignment When a vendor retains ownership of goods in a retail establishment, usually establishes the selling price, and is paid only when the goods are sold; see also *pay from scan*.

consignment shop A secondhand store that offers used goods at lower cost than new products, with the seller only paying the store a portion of the sale proceeds when the item actually sells.

contests and sweepstakes Programs designed to create interest in a retailer's product and encourage both repeat purchases and brand switching.

contractual vertical marketing channel A supply chain that uses a contract to govern the working relationship between the members; includes wholesaler-sponsored voluntary groups, retailer-owned cooperatives, and franchised retail programs.

conventional marketing channel A supply chain in which each member is loosely aligned with the others and takes a short-term orientation.

conversion rate The percentage of all shoppers who make a purchase—that is, those who are converted into customers.

corporate vertical marketing channel Typically either a manufacturer that has integrated vertically forward to reach the consumer or a retailer that has integrated vertically backward to create a self-supply network.

cost method Method of inventory valuation that provides a book valuation of inventory based solely on a retailer's cost, including freight.

cost of goods sold Cost of merchandise that has been sold during a specified period.

cost per thousand method (CPM) Evaluating an advertising medium's reach and cumulative reach by dividing the cost for an ad or series of ads in a medium by the total number of people who view the ad.

cost per thousand—target market (CPM-TM) Evaluating an advertising medium's actual reach by dividing the cost for an ad or series of ads in a medium by the total number of actual customers who view the ad.

coupon An offer by a retailer that discounts the price of a specific item when used by a customer.

coverage The theoretical maximum number of consumers in the retailer's target market that can be reached by a medium—not the number actually reached.

cue Any object or phenomenon in the environment that is capable of eliciting a response.

culture The buffer that humankind has created between itself and the raw physical environment, including population characteristics and human-made objects; anything that humans can put onto a physical space, which then becomes an attribute of the physical space.

cumulative-quantity discount Discount based on total amount purchased over a period of time.

cumulative reach The reach of advertising achieved over a period of time.

current assets Include cash and all other items that the retailer can easily convert into cash within a relatively short period of time (generally, a year).

current liabilities Short-term debts that are payable within a year.

current ratio Current assets divided by current liabilities.

customary pricing When a retailer sets prices for goods and services and seeks to maintain those prices over an extended period of time.

customer relationship management (CRM) An integrated information system in which the fundamental unit of data collection is the customer, supplemented by other relevant information about the customer, including purchasing behavior.

customer satisfaction A measure of whether or not a customer's total shopping experience has met or exceeded his or her expectations.

customer services Activities performed by a retailer that influence (1) the ease with which a potential customer can shop or learn about a store's offering, (2) the ease with which a transaction can be completed once the customer attempts to make a purchase, and (3) the customer's satisfaction with the product or service after purchase.

customer theft Theft of merchandise by customers, also called "shoplifting".

D

deceptive advertising When a retailer makes false or misleading advertising claims about a product's physical makeup or its use or the benefits from its use.

deceptive pricing An unfair method of competition in which an item is advertised at an artificially low price and then hidden charges are added at checkout.

demand density The extent to which potential demand for a retailer's goods and services is concentrated in certain census tracts, ZIP-code areas, or parts of a community.

demonstrations and sampling In-store presentations or showings that are intended to reduce the consumer's perceived risk of purchasing a new product.

depth Average number of SKUs within each brand of a merchandise line.

direct supply chain When a manufacturer sells its goods directly to a final consumer or end user.

discretionary income Disposable income minus money needed for necessities to sustain life, such as minimal housing, minimal food, and minimal clothing.

disposable income All personal income minus personal taxes.

diverter Unauthorized member of a channel that buys and sells excess merchandise to and from authorized channel members.

divertive competition When retailers intercept or divert customers from competing retailers.

domain disagreements When there is disagreement about which members of marketing channel should make decisions.

drive Motivating force that directs behavior.

dual distribution When a manufacturer sells to independent retailers while simultaneously selling directly to the final consumer through its own retail outlets or through an Internet site.

dwell time The amount of time a consumer must spend waiting to complete a purchase.

E

ease of access The consumer's ability to easily and quickly find a website in cyberspace.

eBay An online auction and shopping website in which people and businesses buy and sell a broad variety of goods and services worldwide.

EDLP Everyday low price.

efficient consumer response (ECR) systems A system that is designed to obtain real-time information on consumers' actions by capturing SKU data at point-of-purchase terminals and then transmitting that information through the entire supply chain; also called a *quick response (QR) system*.

eminent domain law The inherent power of government to seize private property without the owner's consent in order to benefit the community.

employee theft When employees steal merchandise where they work.

empowerment In retailing, giving an employee the "power to make things right for the customer."

endcaps Product display at the end of a retailer's merchandise aisle.

end-of-month (EOM) dating Payment system that allows for a cash discount and the full payment period to begin on the first day of the following month instead of on the invoice date; EOM invoices dated after the 25th of the month are considered to be dated on the first of the following month.

ethics A set of rules or standards of moral responsibility for moral human behavior; often take the form of dos and don'ts.

exclusive distribution When only one retailer is used to reach the target market.

expertise power Power based on B's perception that A has some special knowledge or superior ability.

explicit code of ethics A written policy that states what constitutes ethical and unethical behavior.

expressed warranties Warranties that result from interactions between retailers and customers; may be written into the contract or orally stated.

extended problem solving When a consumer recognizes that a problem exists but does not have a strong preference for either a brand or a store.

extra dating (Ex) Payment system that merely allows a retailer extra or free days before the period of payment begins.

F

facilitating marketing institutions Supply-chain members that do not actually take title but assist in the marketing process by specializing in the performance of certain functions.

feature fixture A softlines merchandise display such as the four-way rack that holds fewer items but presents merchandise in a manner that permits shoppers to glimpse at a product's style and key characteristics such as color and shape.

FIFO Method that assumes the oldest merchandise is sold before more recently purchased merchandise is sold (first in, first out).

financial leverage Total assets divided by net worth or owners' equity; ratio shows the extent to which a retailer is using debt in its total capital structure.

first in, first out. *See* FIFO.

fixed component Part of compensation that is typically composed of some base wage per hour, week, month, or year.

flea market A type of market—indoors or outdoors—where inexpensive or secondhand goods are sold or bartered.

flexible pricing Offering the same products and quantities to different customers at different prices.

floor plan Indicates where merchandise and customer-service departments are located, how customers circulate through the store, and how much space is dedicated to each department; based around the predicted demands of the store's targeted customer.

franchise Form of licensing by which the owner of a trademark, service mark, trade name, advertising symbol, or method (the franchisor) obtains distribution through affiliated dealers (franchisees); each franchisee is authorized to sell franchisor's goods or services in either a retail space or a designated geographical area, with the franchise governing the method of business between the two parties.

free-flow layout The simplest type of store layout in which fixtures and merchandise are grouped into free-flowing patterns on the sales floor.

free merchandise Discount whereby merchandise is offered in lieu of price concessions.

free on board (FOB) destination Payment system in which a vendor pays all transportation costs, and the buyer takes title on delivery.

free on board (FOB) factory Payment system in which a buyer assumes title of goods at the vendor's factory and pays all transportation costs.

free on board (FOB) shipping point Payment system in which a vendor pays the transportation to a local shipping point, but the buyer assumes title at this point and pays all further transportation costs.

free riding When a consumer seeks product information and usage instructions about a product from a full-service specialty store but then purchases the product from a limited-service discounter or over the Internet.

freestanding retailer A retailer that generally locates along major traffic arteries without any adjacent retailers selling competing products to share traffic.

frequency The average number of times each person who is reached is exposed to an advertisement during a given time period.

fringe-benefit package May include such things as health insurance, disability benefits, life insurance, retirement plans, the use of automobiles, and financial counseling.

functional discount A form of compensation a buyer may receive for performing certain wholesaling or retailing services for a manufacturer; also called *trade discount*.

G

geographic information system (GIS) A computerized system that combines physical geography with cultural geography.

goal incompatibility When achieving the goals of either the supplier or the retailer would hamper the performance of the other.

goodwill An intangible asset, usually based on customer loyalty, that reflects the portion of the book value of a business entity not directly attributable to its assets and liabilities.

gray marketing When genuinely branded merchandise flows through unauthorized channels that cross national boundaries.

gross margin Difference between sales and cost of goods sold.

gross-margin percentage How much gross margin a retailer makes as a percentage of sales; also referred to as *gross-margin return on sales*.

gross margin return on inventory (GMROI) A single measure that incorporates profit and how quickly inventory sells; computed as (gross margin/net sales) × (net sales/average inventory at cost) = (gross margin/average inventory at cost)

gross sales A retailer's total sales, including sales for cash or for credit.

H

habitual problem solving When a consumer relies on past experience and converts the problem into a situation that requires less thought.

high–low pricing The use of high everyday prices and low leader specials on featured items for their weekly ads.

high-margin, high-turnover retailer Highly profitable strategy used by convenience food stores such as 7-Eleven, Circle K, and Quick Mart and concessions and sports apparel businesses at major athletic events. No examples of successful e-tailers using this strategy.

high-margin, low-turnover retailer Typically a bricks-and-mortar retailer; quite common in the United States—for example, furniture stores, high-end women's specialty stores and furriers, jewelry stores, gift shops, funeral homes, and most mom-and-pop stores.

high-performance retailer A retailer that produces financial results substantially superior to the industry average.

high-quality service Delivering service that meets or exceeds customers' expectations.

home page The first page of an e-tailer's website; essentially the e-tailer's storefront.

horizontal cooperative advertising When two or more retailers band together to share the cost of advertising.

horizontal price fixing When a group of competing retailers establishes a fixed price at which to sell certain brands of products.

I

impact How strongly an impression an advertisement makes and how well it ultimately leads to a purchase.

implicit code of ethics An unwritten but well understood set of rules or standards of moral responsibility.

implied warranty of fitness When a customer relies on a retailer to assist in or select goods to serve a particular purpose.

implied warranty of merchantability When a retailer implies that goods are fit for the ordinary purpose for which such goods are typically used; applies to both new and used merchandise.

income statement A summary of the sales and expenses for a given time period, usually monthly, quarterly, seasonally, or annually.

index of retail saturation (IRS) The ratio of demand for a product or service divided by available supply; measured as IRS = (H × RE)/RF.

informational power Power based on A's ability to provide B with factual data.

institutional advertising Attempt by a retailer to gain long-term benefits by selling its store rather than the merchandise in it.

in-store displays Promotional displays that seek to generate traffic, advertise, and encourage impulse buying.

intensive distribution When all possible retailers are used to reach the target market.

intertype competition The market state when different types of retail outlets (as defined by NAICS codes) sell the same lines of merchandise and compete for the same limited number of consumer dollars.

intratype competition When two or more retailers of the same type (as defined by NAISC codes in the Census of Retail Trade) compete directly with each other for the same household dollars.

inventory turnover Average number of times per year that a retailer sells its inventory.

J

job enrichment The process of enhancing core job characteristics for the purpose of increasing worker motivation, productivity, and satisfaction.

L

last in, first out. *See* LIFO.

leader pricing When a high-demand item is priced low and advertised heavily in an effort to attract consumers into a store.

legitimate power Power based on A's right to influence B or on B's belief that B should accept A's influence.

liability Any legitimate financial claim against a retailer's assets; classified as either current or long-term.

LIFO Method designed to cushion the effects of inflation by matching current costs against current revenues; costs of goods sold are based on the costs of the most recently purchased inventory, while the older inventory is regarded as the unsold inventory (last in, first out).

limited problem solving When a consumer has a strong preference for either a brand or a store but not both.

location Space in which business is transacted: a traditional store in a physical space, a person's home in relation to a print catalog or television shopping, or a virtual store in cyberspace.

long-term liabilities Notes payable and mortgages that are not due within the year.

loop layout A major customer aisle that begins at the store entrance, loops through the store—usually in the shape of a circle, square, or rectangle—and then returns the customer to the front of the store; a powerful space-productivity tool; sometimes called a *racetrack* layout.

loss leader An item that is sold below a retailer's cost in hopes of attracting consumers to its stores and making a profit on the rest of their purchases.

low-margin, high-turnover retailer Retail form that developed after World War II with the advent of the discount store. Makes less per unit sold but sells large numbers of units. Amazon.com is probably the best-known example of a low-margin, high-turnover e-tailer.

low-margin, low-turnover retailer A retailer that will not be able to generate sufficient profits to remain competitive and survive.

loyalty programs Reward programs offered by retailers to solidify their relationships with customers; also called *frequent-shopper programs*.

M

markdown money Funds that retailers arbitrarily deduct from vendors' payments when merchandise doesn't sell briskly enough.

markdowns Reductions in the price of an item taken in order to stimulate sales and leading to a firm receiving a lower price for its merchandise than originally asked.

market segmentation Method retailers use to segment, or break down, heterogeneous consumer populations into smaller, more homogeneous groups based on certain characteristics; helps retailers understand who their customers are, how they think, and what they do.

market share A retailer's total sales divided by total market sales or the proportion of total sales in a particular geographic or product market that the retailer has been able to capture; sales as a percentage of total market sales for the merchandise line or service category under consideration.

markup The difference between the cost of the merchandise and the selling price; the same as *gross margin*.

merchandise budget A plan of projected sales for an upcoming season, when and how much merchandise is to be purchased, and what markups and reductions are likely to occur.

merchandise line Group of products that are closely related because they either are intended for the same end use, are sold to the same customer group, or fall within a given price range.

merchandise management The analysis, planning, acquisition, handling, and control of the merchandise investments in a retail operation.

merchandising The planning and control involved in the buying and selling of goods and services to help a retailer realize its objectives.

metropolitan statistical area (MSA) Metropolitan area with a population greater than 50,000.

micromarketing Tailoring merchandise in a store to match the preferences of the neighborhood.

microretailing When a specific retail store's offerings are tailored to the trading area being served.

middle-of-month (MOM) dating Similar to *end-of-month dating* except the middle of the month is used as the starting date.

mission statement Basic description of a firm's fundamental nature, rationale, and direction.

monopolistic competition A market situation that develops when either retailers sell different (heterogeneous) products that consumers consider substitutes for each other or sellers may be the only ones selling a particular brand but face competition from other retailers selling similar goods and services.

motivation What drives a person to excel at the activities he or she undertakes such as a job.

multiple-unit pricing When the price of each unit in a multiple-unit package is less than the price of each unit if it were sold individually.

mutual trust When two parties such as a retailer and supplier trust each other.

N

negotiation Finding mutually satisfying solutions for parties with conflicting objectives.

neighborhood business district (NBD) A shopping area that evolves to satisfy the convenience-oriented shopping needs of a neighborhood.

net profit Operating profit plus or minus other income or expenses.

net profit margin Ratio of net profit (profit after taxes) to net sales.

net sales Gross sales less returns and allowances.

net worth Difference between a firm's total assets and total liabilities; also called *owner's equity* because it represents an owner's equity in the business.

noncumulative-quantity discount A discount based on a single purchase.

noncurrent assets Assets that cannot be converted into cash in a short period of time (usually, 12 months) in the normal course of business.

nonstore-based retailer A retailer that reaches customers at home, at work, or at places other than a store where they might be open to purchasing.

notes receivable Amounts that customers owe a retailer for goods and services; also called *accounts receivable*.

O

odd pricing The practice of setting retail prices that end in the digits 5, 8, or 9; this policy may produce significantly higher sales.

off-price retailers Retailers that carry only brands that they are able to get on special deals from manufacturers or close-out wholesalers.

oligopolistic competition A market situation that occurs the following conditions exist: essentially homogeneous products are sold (e.g., gasoline), there are relatively few sellers or many small firms who always follow the lead of the few large firms, and there is an expectation that any action by one party will be noticed and reacted to by the other parties in the market.

100-percent location Retail location where there is no better use for the site than the store being planned.

one-price policy When a retailer charges all customers the same price for an item; may be used in conjunction with customary or variable pricing.

one-way exclusive-dealing arrangement When a supplier gives a retailer the exclusive right to sell a product in a particular trade area but without the retailer agreeing to do anything in particular for the supplier.

on-shelf merchandising The merchandise that is displayed on and in counters, racks, shelves, and fixtures throughout the store; the merchandise that shoppers actually touch, try on, examine, read, understand, and buy.

operating expenses Expenses incurred by a retailer in running a business other than the cost of the merchandise—for example, rent, wages, utilities, depreciation, and insurance.

operating profit Difference between gross margin and operating expenses.

operations management Concerned with maximizing a retailer's use of resources and how the retailer converts these resources into sales and profits.

optional stock list approach A retail chain's list that gives each store the flexibility to adjust its merchandise mix to local tastes and demands.

other income or expenses Income or expense items that the firm incurs outside the course of its normal retail operations.

outshopping When residents travel to larger communities to shop because their own communities have merchandise that is priced too high, have poor selection, or have poor service.

overstored When a market has too many stores to yield a fair return on investment; when the number of stores per thousand households gets too large.

owner's equity Difference between a firm's total assets and total liabilities; also called *net worth*.

P

palming off When a retailer represents merchandise as being made by someone other than the true manufacturer.

passive information gathering Receiving and processing information about merchandise, services, stores, shopping convenience, parking, advertising, and any other factor that a consumer might consider in making a decision of where to shop and what to purchase.

pawn shop Retailer that offers monetary loans in exchange for an item of value; the pawner may purchase it back for the amount of the loan plus interest within a contracted period of time.

pay from scan More recent term that some retailers use to describe consignment.

penetration Seeking to establish a loyal customer base by entering the market with a low price.

percentage-of-sales method When a retailer targets a specific percentage of forecasted sales for advertising based on the assumption that successful similar firms should be used as a guide.

percentage-variation method (PVM) Method used when the retailer has a high annual inventory-turnover rate—six or more times a year.

perceptual incongruity When two parties such as a retailer and a supplier have different perceptions of reality.

performance appraisal and review The formal, systematic assessment of how well employees are performing their jobs in relation to established standards, as well as the communication of that assessment to employees.

personal objectives Relate to personal goals of employees, managers, or owners of a retail establishment; generally, three types of personal objectives: self-gratification, status and respect, and power and authority.

personal selling Selling that uses one-on-one communication with consumers.

personal shopping Assembling an assortment of goods for a customer; one of the best ways to build a relationship with a customer.

planogram A graphic schematic that shows the precise location of every piece of merchandise on a shelf or other merchandise display in a retail store.

point of indifference In Reilly's law of retail gravitation, the breaking point at which customers would be indifferent to shopping at either of two cities.

population variables Data used by retailers that classify consumers by such factors as population growth trends, age distributions, ethnic makeup, and geographic trends.

post-purchase resentment When a consumer's dissatisfaction with a product or service leads to feelings of resentment toward the retailer.

posttransaction services Services provided after a sale has been made, including complaint handling, merchandise returns, merchandise repair, servicing, delivery, and postsale follow-ups.

power The ability of one member to influence the behavior of other supply-chain members; the more dependent the supplier is on the retailer, the more power the retailer has over the supplier and vice versa.

predatory pricing When a retailer charges different prices in selected geographic areas in order to eliminate competition in those areas.

premiums Extra items offered to customers when they purchase a promoted product; used to increase consumption among current consumers and persuade nonusers to try the promoted product.

prepaid expenses Items such as trash collection or insurance for which the retailer has already paid but the service has not been completed.

pretransaction services Services provided to customers before they entering the retail store such as convenient hours and information aids.

price discrimination When two retailers buy identical amounts of "like grade and quality" merchandise from the same supplier but pay different prices.

price lining When a retailer establishes a specified number of price lines or price points for each merchandise category and then purchases goods that fit into each line.

price zone A range of prices for a particular merchandise line that appeals to customers in a certain demographic group.

primary marketing institutions Supply-chain members that take title to goods that move through the chain.

primary trading area The area in which a retailer can serve customers in terms of convenience and accessibility better than competitors.

private-label branding May be done as *store branding* in which a retailer develops its own brand name and contracts with a manufacturer to produce the product with the retailer's brand—or as a *designer line*, in which a known designer develops a line exclusively for the retailer.

problem recognition When a consumer's desired state of affairs departs sufficiently from his or her actual state of affairs.

productivity index An index that compares the percentage of the store's total gross margin dollars for a particular merchandise category to its percentage of space utilized.

productivity objectives Objectives that state how much output the retailer desires for each unit of resource input.

product liability laws Laws that invoke the "foreseeability" doctrine—a seller of a product must attempt to foresee how a product may be misused and warn the consumer against the hazards of misuse.

profit-based objectives Monetary goals that a retailer desires from its business; most common way to define profit is the aggregate total of net profit after taxes: the bottom line of the income statement.

profit maximization The goal of obtaining as much profit as possible.

promotion Generate sales by making a retailer's targeted customers aware of current offerings.

promotional advertising An attempt to bolster short-term performance by using product availability or price as a selling point.

promotional discount Discount given when a retailer performs an advertising or promotional service for a manufacturer.

prospecting The search process of finding those customers who have the ability and willingness to purchase a product.

publicity Free information about a company or product, generally in some media form.

public warehouse A facility that stores goods for safekeeping in return for a fee.

pure competition The condition that occurs when a market has homogeneous (similar) products; many buyers and sellers, all having perfect knowledge of the market; and ease of entry for both buyers and sellers.

pure monopoly When a seller is the only one selling a particular product and sets its selling price accordingly.

Q

quantity discount A price reduction offered as an inducement to purchase large quantities of merchandise.

quick response (QR) system A system that is designed to obtain real-time information on consumers' actions by capturing SKU data at point-of-purchase terminals and then transmitting that information through the entire supply chain; also called an *efficient consumer response (ECR) system*.

R

reach The actual total number of target customers who come into contact with an ad message.

receipt of goods (ROG) dating Payment system that allows the starting date to be the date goods are received by the retailer.

recycled merchandise retailer Retailer that offers low prices on reused merchandise.

referent power Power based on B's desire to be identified or associated with A.

register racks Racks at checkout stands that offer manufacturers a captive audience for their products in the retailer's store.

Reilly's law of retail gravitation Named for William Reilly, law that states that two cities attract trade from an intermediate location approximately in direct proportion to the population of the two cities and in inverse proportion to the square of the distance from these two cities to the intermediate place.

relationship retailing All of the activities designed to attract, retain, and enhance customer relationships.

retail accordion The contraction and expansion of merchandise assortment over time in a retail store as a store moves back and forth between being a narrow line and broad line retailer.

retail clusters Groups of stores closely located that share similar characteristics such as product category, store format, or customer demographics.

retailer-owned cooperative Wholesale operation that is organized and owned by retailers; most common in hardware retailing.

retail gravity theory Underlying consistencies in shopping behavior that allow for mathematical analysis and prediction based on the notion or concept of gravity.

retailing Final activities and steps needed either to place a product in the hands of the consumer or to provide a service to the consumer.

retail inventories Merchandise that the retailer has in the store or in storage and is available for sale.

retail life cycle An identifiable cycle in which a retailer starts, grows, matures, and then declines.

retail mix Combination of goals and tactics used by a retailer to appeal to its target market and thereby meet its financial objectives; includes merchandise, price, advertising and promotion, location, customer services and selling, and store layout and design.

retail price The selling price of an object.

retail store saturation Condition under which existing store facilities are utilized efficiently and meet existing customer needs.

return on assets (ROA) Annual net profit divided by total assets; depicts net profit return the retailer achieved on all assets invested regardless of whether the assets were financed by creditors or by the firm's owners.

return on net worth (RONW) Net profit divided by net worth or owner's equity; usually used to measure owner's performance.

returns and allowances Reductions from gross sales in which the retailer makes a financial adjustment for customers who became dissatisfied with their purchases and returned the merchandise to the retailer.

revenue per available seat mile (RASM) Strategy used by airlines to maximize revenue; usually effected by overbooking.

reward power Power based on the ability of A to provide rewards to B.

S

sales promotions The use of media and nonmedia for a period of time directed at the consumer, retailer, or wholesaler to stimulate or increase consumer demand or improve product availability.

same-store sales An individual store's sales compared to its sales for the same month in the previous year.

sandwich generational family Arrangement in which all three generations of a family—parents, grandparents, and children—live under the same roof. Also called *trigenerational family*.

scrambled merchandising A retailer's marketing of many different unrelated nondrug items such as food products, apparel goods, photo supplies, greeting cards, and seasonal items such as school supplies, gardening supplies and Christmas decorations, and even clothing.

seasonal discount Discount earned if a retailer purchases and take delivery of merchandise in the off-season.

secondary business district (SBD) A shopping area that is smaller than the CBD, revolves around at least one department or variety store, and is located at a major street intersection.

secondary trading area The area in which a retailer is still competitive, even if some competitors have better locations.

selective distribution When a smaller number of retailers are used to reach the target market.

servant leadership When employees act out of the recognition that their primary responsibility is to be of service to others.

set of attributes Characteristics of the store and its products and services; include such things as price, product quality, store hours, knowledgeable sales help, convenient parking, and after-sales service.

shopping center A centrally owned or managed shopping district that is planned, has balanced tenancy (the stores complement each other in merchandise offerings), and is surrounded by parking facilities.

shrinkage The loss of merchandise due to theft, loss, damage, or bookkeeping errors.

site analysis An evaluation of the density of demand and supply within each market; usually augmented by an identification of the most attractive sites that are currently available within each market.

skimming Trying to sell at the highest price possible before settling on a more competitive level.

slotting allowances Fees paid by a vendor for space (a slot) on a retailer's shelves as well as having a slot in the retailer's computer system for its UPC number; also called *slotting fees*.

slotting fees Fees paid by a vendor for space (a slot) on a retailer's shelves as well as having a slot in the retailer's computer system for its UPC number; also called a *slotting allowance*.

societal objectives A retailer's concern with broader issues in our society; five most frequently cited are employment objectives, payment of taxes, consumer choice, equity, and being a benefactor.

solidarity When a high value is placed on the relationship between a supplier and a retailer; an attitude and thus hard to explicitly create.

spine layout A store layout is based on a single main aisle running from the front to the back of the store, transporting customers in both directions; on either side of the spine, merchandise departments branch off toward the back or side walls; a variation of the free-flow, grid, and loop layouts that combines the advantages of all three in certain circumstances.

stack-outs Pallets of merchandise set on the floor in front of the main shelves.

standard stock list A list used by all stores in a retail chain so they can stock the same merchandise.

stimulus A cue (external to the individual) or drive (internal to the individual) that causes the individual to take some form of action.

stockout Situation in which products are not available for customers when they want them.

stock-keeping units (SKU) Are the lowest level of identification of merchandise.

stock-to-sales method (SSM) Ratio that tells the retailer how much inventory is needed at the beginning of the month to support that month's estimated sales.

stock-to-sales ratio The amount of stock to be on hand at the beginning of each month to support the forecasted sales for that month.

store-based retailer A retailer that operates from a fixed store location that requires customers to travel to the store to view and purchase merchandise and or services.

store compatibility When two compatible or very similar businesses locate near each other, they will show an increase in sales volume greater than what they would have achieved if they were located separately.

store management Career path that requires good people skills but gives an employee many chances to make decisions that affect a store's profitability.

store positioning Process by which a retailer distinguishes itself from competitors in specific ways in order to be the preferred provider for certain market segments.

strategic planning Adapting the resources of a firm to the opportunities and threats of an ever-changing retail environment.

strategy Carefully designed plan that shows how a retailer will achieve its goals and objectives.

supercenter A combination of supermarket and discount department store that carries more than 80,000 to 100,000 SKUs ranging from televisions to peanut butter and DVDs.

supply chain A set of institutions that moves goods from the point of production to the point of consumption; also called *channel*.

T

target market Group or groups of customers that the retailer seeks to serve; the segment of the market that the retailer decides to pursue through its marketing efforts.

target-return objective Sets a specific level of profit as an objective to meet.

task-and-objective method When a retailer prioritizes its advertising objectives and then determines the advertising tasks that need to be performed to achieve those objectives.

territorial restrictions Attempts by a supplier, usually a manufacturer, to limit the geographic area in which a retailer may resell its merchandise.

thematic maps Area maps that use visual techniques such as colors, shading, lines, and so on to display cultural characteristics of the physical space.

thrift shop A retail establishment operated by a charitable organization for fund-raising purposes; usually prices are extremely low.

total assets Current assets plus noncurrent assets plus goodwill.

total liabilities Current liabilities plus long-term liabilities.

trade discount A form of compensation a buyer may receive for performing certain wholesaling or retailing services for a manufacturer; also called *functional discount*.

trading area Geographic area from which a retailer, group of retailers, or community draws its customers.

trading down When a customer is initially exposed to higher-priced lines but expresses the desire to purchase a lower-priced line.

trading up When a salesperson moves a customer from a lower-priced line to a higher one.

transaction services Services such as credit, layaway, gift wrapping and packaging, check cashing, gift cards, personal shopping, merchandise availability, personal selling, and the sales transaction itself that facilitate transactions once customers have made a purchase decision.

transient customer A customer who will seek to find a different retailer with the level of customer service he or she feels is appropriate.

trigenerational family Arrangement in which all three generations of a family—parents, grandparents, and children—live under the same roof. Also called *sandwich generational family*.

two-way communication When two parties openly communicate their ideas, concerns, and plans.

two-way exclusive-dealing agreement When a supplier offers a retailer the exclusive distribution of a merchandise line or product if the retailer agrees to do something for the manufacturer in return.

tying agreement When a seller with a strong product or service forces a buyer (the retailer) to purchase a weak product or service as a condition for buying the stronger one.

U

understored When a market has too few stores to satisfactorily meet the needs of customers; when the number of stores per thousand households is small in comparison to other markets.

V

value proposition A clear statement of the tangible and intangible results a customer receives from using a retailer's products or services; the promised benefits a retailer offers in relation to the cost the consumer incurs.

variable component Part of compensation that is often composed of some bonus that is received if performance warrants.

variable pricing A pricing scheme used when differences in demand and cost force the retailer to change prices in a fairly predictable manner—for example, flowers are priced higher when demand is greatest around Mother's Day and Valentine's Day.

variety The number of different merchandise lines a retailer chooses to stock in its store.

vendor collusion The types of losses that occur when merchandise is delivered; losses involve the delivery of less merchandise than is charged for, removal of good merchandise disguised as old or stale merchandise, and the theft of other merchandise from the stockroom or off the selling floor while making delivery; often involves both the delivery person and the retail employee who signs for the delivery.

vendor-profitability analysis statement A record of all purchases made in a year, the discount granted by the vendor, transportation charges paid, and the original markup, markdowns, and season-ending gross margin on that vendor's merchandise.

vertical cooperative advertising When a retailer and other supply-chain members share the advertising burden.

vertical marketing channel A capital-intensive network of several levels that is professionally managed and relies on centrally programmed systems to realize the technological, managerial, and promotional economies of long-term relationships.

vertical price fixing When a retailer collaborates with a manufacturer or wholesaler to resell an item at an agreed-upon price; also referred to as *resale price maintenance* or *fair trade*.

virtual store The total collection of all the pages of information on a retailer's website.

visual merchandising The artistic display of merchandise and theatrical props used as scene-setting decoration in the store.

W

weeks' supply method (WSM) Formula used by retailers whose inventories are planned on a weekly, not monthly, basis and where sales do not fluctuate substantially; the inventory level should be set equal to a predetermined number of weeks' supply.

wheel of retailing theory Theory that holds that new types of retailers enter the market as low-status, low-margin, and low-price operators before they enter a trading-up phase and acquire more sophisticated and elaborate facilities, often becoming less efficient; these retailers eventually enter the vulnerability phase and must raise prices and margins to cover rising costs—becoming vulnerable to new types of low-margin retail competitors who progress through the same pattern.

wholesaler-sponsored voluntary group A group created by a wholesaler that brings together independently owned retailers and offers them a coordinated merchandising program

Y

yield management Understanding, anticipating, and reacting to changing customer needs in order to maximize the revenue from a fixed capacity of available services.

Chapter 1

1. "Freedom Is Still the Winning Formula," *Wall Street Journal*, January 13, 2009: A17.

2. This list is based in part on information from the MorningNewBeat.com, February 2008.

3. "Walmart Sets Seminar to Assess Economic Impact," *Wall Street Journal*, November 4, 2005: B2.

4. "One Nation Under Walmart," *Fortune*, March 3, 2003: 64–76.

5. "Walmart's Emergency-Relief Team Girds for Hurricane Gustav," *Wall Street Journal*, August 30, 2008: A3

6. "Walmart Goes Greener," *Shopping Centers Today*, March 2007: 9; "Turning Green into Gold," *Shopping Centers Today*, March 2006: 59–60.

7. "America's Most Admired Companies," *Fortune*, March 17, 2008: 111–116.

8. "The Unending Woes of Lee Scott," *Fortune*, January 22, 2007: 118–122.

9. "Walmart to Settle 63 Lawsuits over Wages," *Wall Street Journal*, December 24, 2008: B1.

10. "Green-Light Specials, Now at Walmart," *New York Times*, January 25, 2009: U1, U5; and "Green Gold," *Fortune*, September 15, 2008: 107–112.

11. "The World's Most Admired Companies 2009," *Fortune*, March 16, 2009: 76.

12. Andrea M. Dean and Russell S. Sobel, "Has Walmart Buried Mom and Pop? *Regulation*, Spring 2008: 38–45.

13. "Retail Relief," *Shopping Centers Today*, September 2008: 133–136.

14. "Not This Time," *Forbes*, October 13, 2008: 46.

15. "Like It or Not, Fliers Are Free to Roam about the Internet," *New York Times*, February 7, 2009: A1 & B5.

16. "Walmart with Wings," *BusinessWeek*, November 27, 2006: 44–45.

17. "Airfare Quotes that Lay Bare Hidden Fees," *Wall Street Journal*, March 10, 2009: D1, D4.

18. U.S. Bureau of Census, *Statistical Abstract of the United States: 2009*, Tables 1008, 1009, and 1011.

19. U.S. Bureau of Census, *Statistical Abstract of the United States: 2009*, Tables 1008 and 1009; and author calculations.

20. M. Miller. *YouTube for Business: Online Video Marketing for Any Business*. Toronto: Pearson Education-Que Publishing, 2008.

21. From a list compiled by the late Robert Kahn.

22. "Fuel Prices Drive Customers to Gas Up at Super-centers, Clubs," *Shopping Centers Today*, August 2008: 9.

23. "Costco's Artful Discounts," *BusinessWeek*, October 20, 2008: 58–60.

24. "Drugstores, Too, Feel Recession Pain," *New York Times*, January 3, 2009: B3

25. "Root Canal? Try Aisle Five." *BusinessWeek*, October 13, 2008: 16.

26. "Fewer Shopping Trips," *Shopping Centers Today*, September 2008: 15.

27. "Saving Sears Doesn't Look Easy Anymore," *New York Times*, January 27, 2008: 1, 8–9.

28. "Toy Story III: The Toys 'R' Us Story." Presentation by Rebecca Caruso at the Establishing a Distinctive Identity in a Changing Global Marketplace Conference at Notre Dame University, September 7, 2001.

29. "Toys 'R' Us Unwraps Plans for Expansion," *Wall Street Journal*, May 22, 2008: B1.

30. Used with the permission of Mike Kehoe, President, Perrocartón Advertising Agency, Santiago, Chile.

31. U.S. Bureau of Census, *Statistical Abstract of the United States: 2009*, Table 1008.

32. "How Strong Is the U.S. Consumer?" *BusinessWeek*, July 14, 2008: 28.

33. The Census Bureau no longer compiles data on chain store sales as a percentage of total retail sales. This information is based on estimates from various industry experts and older government data.

34. "Walmart Gives Makeover to Its Private-Label Line," *Wall Street Journal*, March 17, 2009: B2.

35. "Branching Out," *Shopping Centers Today*, March 2008: 33–34.

36. "First-Class Shopping, Food for Flyers," *Shopping Centers Today*, December 2008: 9; "On the Fly," *Shopping Centers Today*, November 2008: 59–61; "U.S. Airport Shops Go High-End," *Wall Street Journal*, December 20, 2005: D1, D3; and "High-Flying Retail: JFK's The Shops Raises Bar for Airport Retail with Posh Purveyors," *Shopping Centers Today*, May 2005: 213–214.

37. "Costco's Artful Discounts," op. cit.

38. "Americans Can't Get No Satisfaction," *Fortune*, December 11, 1995: 194.

39. "Costco's Artful Discounts," op. cit.

40. Roger Dickinson, "Creativity in Retailing," *Journal of Retailing* (Winter 1969–1970): 4.

41. Ibid.

Chapter 2

1. "Bigger and Bigger," *Fortune*, September 5, 2005: 104–107.
2. "Changing Course," Shopping Centers Today, April 2008: 63–64.
3. This information was provided to the authors by Robert Kahn.
4. Taken from Starbuck's website (www.starbucks.com/mission/default.asp), December 8, 2008.
5. Based on information provided by James Moore.
6. Taken from Borders' website (http://www.borders.com/online/store) on November 13, 2005 and January 8, 2009.
7. "What New Economy?" *Forbes*, April 17, 2000: 478.
8. "Borders Gets a New CEO as It Battles for Survival," *Wall Street Journal*, January 6, 2009: B1, B5.
9. "Starbucks Addresses the Price Issue and Breakfast," *New York Times*, March 3, 2009: B4.
10. "Starbucks Shifts Focus to Value, Cost Cutting," *Wall Street Journal*, December 5, 2008: B1; and "At Starbucks, a Tall Order for New Cuts, Store Closures," *Wall Street Journal*, January 29, 2009: B1, B4.
11. "A&P's Supermarket Shuffle," *Shopping Centers Today*, September 2008: 55–57.
12. Sidney Schoeffler, "Nine Basic Findings on Business Strategy," *PIMS Letter*, No. 1. Cambridge, MA: The Strategic Planning Institute, 1977.
13. For a detailed discussion of this material with examples, see "The Profit Wedge: How Five Measure Up," *Chain Store Age*, May 1998: 60–68.
14. "In Memoriam: Anita Roddick," *BusinessWeek*, September 24, 2007: 31.
15. Based on information provided by Robert Leffel of the Ethisphere Institute, December 10, 2008.
16. "Small Kresge Foundation Teaches Big Lessons in Investment Strategy," *Wall Street Journal*, August 30, 2008: B1, B7.
17. "Cautiously, Starbucks Puts Lobbying on Corporate Menu," *Wall Street Journal, April 12, 2005*: A1, A10.
18. "Winning Back Lost Customers," *Retail Issues Letter*, March 2001.
19. Based on information provided by Dan Butler, vice president of retail operations, National Retail Federation.
20. "For Fast Food's Gourmets: Off-the-Menu Spécialités," *Wall Street Journal*, May 18,2007: B6
21. Jay Fitzsimmons, senior vice president and treasurer of Walmart, quoted in MorningNewsBeat.com, March 24, 2003.
22. "Staying on Target," *Wall Street Journal*, May 7, 2007: B1, B2.
23. "Not Copying Walmart Pays Off for Grocers," *Wall Street Journal*, June 6, 2007: B1, B5.
24. "Too Good for Lowe's and Home Depot?" *Wall Street Journal*, July 6, 2006: B1.
25. "At Best Buy, Marketing Goes Micro," *BusinessWeek*, May 26, 2008: 52–54.
26. "How Jim Skinner Flipped McDonald's," *Wall Street Journal*, January 5, 2007: B1, B2.

Chapter 3

1. "Commentary by Professor Claes Fornell," *ACSI Report*, February 21, 2006. Used with the author's permission.
2. If you want to see the most recent data on ACSI data for the nation's leading retailers, go to www.theacsi.org/index.php?option=com_content&task=view&id=190&Itemid=199. The index for retailers is updated every February.
3. "Commentary by Professor Claes Fornell," *ACSI Report*, February 17, 2009. Used with the author's permission.
4. "It's Not Only about Price at Walmart, *New York Times*, March 2, 2007: C1, C2.
5. Based on information supplied by friends of the author; "The Raja of Rooms," *Forbes*, January 12, 2009: 92–93; and "Cheaper Sleeper," *Forbes*, October 13, 2008: 101.
6. "Costco's Artful Discounts," *BusinessWeek*, October 20, 2008: 58–60.
7. Unless otherwise noted, the statistical data used in this chapter will be the most recently posted information on the Census Bureau's website: http://factfinder.census.gov.
8. U.S. Bureau of Census, "Projections of the Population and Components of Change for the United States: 2010 to 2050" (www.census.gov/population/www/projections/files/nation/summary/np2008-t1.xls).
9. U.S. Bureau of Census, *Statistical Abstract of the United States: 2009*, Tables 11, 41.
10. "Five Things You Don't Know About Baby Boomers," *Stores*, June 2008.
11. "Boomer Bust: How Will the Economy Rebound without Post-War Babies Financing Their Harleys?" *Wall Street Journal*, October 21, 2008: A13.
12. "The Unretired," *BusinessWeek*, December 15, 2008: 46–49.
13. "Wealth Management Comes to Financial Services Firms," *St. Louis Post-Dispatch*, October 7, 2007: D1, D3.
14. "The Rich Are Duller," *Wall Street Journal*, July 13, 2007: W1–W2.
15. HaeJung Kim, Dee K. Knight, and Christy Crutsinger, "Generation Y Employees' Work Experience in the Retail Industry: The Impact on Job Performance, Job Satisfaction and Career Intention." Paper presented at the ACRA 2006 Spring Conference, Springdale, Arkansas, April 7, 2006.

16. "Five Things . . . ," op. cit.

17. "Older Consumers Don't Believe You," *Advertising Age*, August 14, 1995: 14.

18. "Reaching Gen Y on Both Sides of the Cash Register," *Texas A&M's Retailing Issues Letter*, 18(2), 2007.

19. "User-Friendly Finance for Generation Y," *BusinessWeek*, December 8, 2008: 66.

20. "Generation P: Yearning for a Cashless Society?" *Belleville News Democrat*, May 27, 2007: B5.

21. "Study: Generation Gap with Net Shopping," *Lubbock Avalanche-Journal*, February 15, 2008: B9.

22. "Teens Turn to Thrift as Jobs Vanish and Prices Rise," *Lubbock Avalanche-Journal*, April 20, 2008: D3.

23. Hispanicity, which is independent of race, is the only *ethnic* category, as opposed to *racial* category, which is officially collated by the U.S. Census Bureau. The distinction made by government agencies for those within the population of any official race category, including "white American," is between those with Hispanic ethnic backgrounds and all others of non-Hispanic ethnic backgrounds. In the case of white Americans, these two groups are respectively termed *white Hispanics* and *non-Hispanic whites*, the former having at least one ancestor from the people of Spain or Spanish-speaking Latin America, and the latter consisting of an ethnically diverse collection of all others who are classified as white American who are of non-Hispanic ethnic backgrounds.

24. The authors wish to acknowledge the assistance of Retail Forward for providing much of the data in the following section.

25. "Macy's Has High Hopes for Company's New Approach," *Cincinnati Enquirer*, February 7, 2009: C1, C3.

26. U.S. Bureau of Census, *Statistical Abstract of the United States: 2009*, Table 28.

27. U.S. Bureau of Census, *Statistical Abstract of the United States: 2009*, Tables 29 and 31, and authors' calculations.

28. "A Bigger Family Stays Closer to the Nest," *Wall Street Journal*, April 1, 1994: B1.

29. U.S. Bureau of Census, *Statistical Abstract of the United States: 2009*, Table 221.

30. Ibid.

31. U.S. Bureau of Census, *Statistical Abstract of the United States: 2009*, Table 222.

32. "U.S. Consumer—Like No Other on the Planet," *Advertising Age*, January 2, 2006: 3–5.

33. "My Daughter, the PhD," *BusinessWeek*, March 27, 2000: 30.

34. U.S. Bureau of Census, *Statistical Abstract of the United States: 2009*, Table 223; and author calculations.

35. U.S. Bureau of Census, *Statistical Abstract of the United States: 2009*, Table 56.

36. Ibid.

37. For a complete discussion of the consumer's behavior, especially differences between male and female shoppers, see Paco Underhill, *Why We Buy* (New York: Simon & Schuster, 1999).

38. U.S. Bureau of Census, *Statistical Abstract of the United States: 2009*, Table 58.

39. U.S. Bureau of Census, *Statistical Abstract of the United States: 2009*, Table 60; and author calculations.

40. U.S. Bureau of Census, *Statistical Abstract of the United States: 2009*, Table 62.

41. "They're Baaa-aack," *St. Louis Post-Dispatch*, May 3, 2008: 23.

42. "The College Credit-Card Hustle," *BusinessWeek*," July 28, 2008: 38–42; and "Students Suffocate Under Tens of Thousands in Loans," *USA Today*, February 23, 2006: B1, B2.

43. "Japan's 'Lost Generation,'" *BusinessWeek*, May 28, 2007: 40–41.

44. U.S. Bureau of Census, *Statistical Abstract of the United States: 2009*, Tables 585 and 586; and author calculations.

45. U.S. Bureau of Census, *Statistical Abstract of the United States: 2009*, Table 589.

46. U.S. Bureau of Census, *Statistical Abstract of the United States: 2009*, Table 591.

47. "Turnover Costs Sack Retailers," *Chain Store Age*, March 2000: 100–102.

48. U.S. Bureau of Census, *Statistical Abstract of the United States: 2009*, Table 674; and author calculations.

49. "Americans See 18% of Wealth Vanish," *Street Journal*, March 13, 2009: A1, A8.

50. "People Pulling Up to Pawnshops Today Are Driving Cadillacs and BMWs," *Wall Street Journal*, December 30, 2008: A1, A6.

51. U.S. Bureau of Census, *Statistical Abstract of the United States: 2009*, Table 656.

52. "'Wealth Effect' May Be Near Payback Time," *Wall Street Journal*, June 5, 2008: C1.

53. "Age before Beauty. No, Really," *BusinessWeek*, April 26, 2004: 14.

54. U.S. Bureau of Census, *Statistical Abstract of the United States: 2009*, Table 569.

55. U.S. Bureau of Census, *Statistical Abstract of the United States: 2009*, Table 578.

56. U.S. Bureau of Census, *Statistical Abstract of the United States: 2009*, Table 587.

57. U.S. Bureau of Census, *Statistical Abstract of the United States: 2009*, Table 677; and author calculations.

58. "Not Tonight, Honey: The Plight of the Dual-Income, No-Sex Couples," *Wall Street Journal*. April 3, 2003: D1.

59. "Crushed by . . . Savings," *Fortune*, March 6, 2006: 60.

60. U.S. Bureau of Census, *Statistical Abstract of the United States: 2009*, Table 1149.

61. U.S. Bureau of Census, *Statistical Abstract of the United States: 2009*, Table 1149.

62. "Hamburger Joints Call Them 'Heavy Users'—But Not to Their Face," *Wall Street Journal*, January 12, 2000: A1, A10.

63. Based on a Google search, January 5, 2009.

64. "Love the Customers Who Hate You," *BusinessWeek*, March 3, 2008: 58.

Chapter 4

1. Based on information provided in a speech by Best Buy CEO Brad Anderson at Texas Tech University, November 8, 2005.

2. "Supermarkets," *Shopping Centers Today*, May 2005: 16–35.

3. Fred Crawford and Ryan Mathews, *The Myth of Excellence: Why Great Companies Never Try to Be the Best at Everything* (New York: Crown Business, 2001): 21–39.

4. "Cigarette Tax Burnout," *Wall Street Journal*, August 11, 2008. A14

5. "High Fuel Costs Helping Small-Town Businesses, Pinching Distant Malls," *Lubbock Avalanche-Journal*, July 13, 2008: D4.

6. However, real-life retailers are not confronted by such a curve because they face a three-dimensional demand function. The three dimensions are (1) quantity demanded per household, (2) price at the retail store, and (3) distance from the individual's residence or place of work to the store. The quantity demanded by a household is inversely related to the price charged and distance to the store. This discussion is, however, beyond the scope of this text.

7. Anthony J. Capraro, Susan Broniarczyk, and Rajendra K. Srivastava, "Factors Influencing the Likelihood of Customer Defection: The Role of Consumer Knowledge. *Journal of the Academy of Marketing Science*, Spring 2003: 164–175.

8. "Retailers Demanding New Products Carry Category," KPMG Consumer Markets Insiders Focus (www.kpmginsiders.com), May 28, 2003.

9. "Web Can Pay Off for Traditional Retailers," *Wall Street Journal*, December 23, 2006: A7.

10. "In Tough Times, Spas Stress Stress," *New York Times*, February 8, 2009: TR 3.

11. "Drugstores Wage a Pricey Online Battle," *Advertising Age*, August 30, 1999: 26.

12. "Supermarkets, Warehouse Clubs Gas Up," *Shopping Center Today*, November 2005: 9.

13. "Anxiety Grows Around Starbucks Closings," *Wall Street Journal*, July 9, 2008: B1; "Fewer Starbucks," *BusinessWeek*, July 14, 2008: 8; and "Why Did Starbucks Cross the Road?" *Wall Street Journal*, April 3, 2007: B1, B2.

14. "Car Dealer Butch Suntrup Adds Insurance to His Business," *St. Louis Post-Dispatch*, August 13, 2008: C9.

15. "Retailers' Panty Raid On Victoria's Secret," *Wall Street Journal*, June 20, 2007: B1, B12.

16. Malcolm P. McNair, "Significant Trends and Developments in the Postwar Period." In A. B. Smith (ed.), *Competitive Distribution in a Free High-Level Economy and Its Implications for the University* (Pittsburgh: University of Pittsburgh Press, 1958).

17. Michael Levy, Dhruv, Robert Peterson, and Bob Connolly, "The Concept of the 'The Big Middle,'" *Journal of Retailing*, 81(2) (2005): 83–88.

18. Stanley C. Hollander, "Notes on the Retail Accordion," *Journal of Retailing*, Summer 1966: 29–40, 54.

19. "The Skinny on Handbag-Rental Services," *Wall Street Journal*, July 24, 2008; D2.

20. For a complete discussion of this theory see Shelby D. Hunt, *A General Theory of Competition* (Sage, CA: Thousand Oaks, 2000).

21. Shelby D. Hunt and Robert M. Morgan, "The Resource-Advantage Theory of Competition: Dynamics, Path Dependencies, and Evolutionary Dimensions," *Journal of Marketing*, October 1996: 107–114.

22. "IKEA Prefers Stores," *Shopping Centers Today*, February 2004: 9.

23. Market cap is the value of a company—that is, the market value of its outstanding shares. This figure is determined by multiplying a firm's current stock price by the total number of shares outstanding.

24. "Used Games Score Big for Gamestop," *Wall Street Journal*, January 21, 2009: B1; and "Thrift Shops on Easy Street," *BusinessWeek*, October 20, 2008: 60.

25. "People Pulling Up to Pawnshops Today Are Driving Cadillacs and BMWs," *Wall Street Journal*, December 30, 2008: A1, A6.

26. Based on information found at www.narts.org/press/stats.htm, January 15, 2008.

27. "New Threat to Retailers: Liquidations," *Wall Street Journal*, December 12, 2008: B1, B2; "Selling Out the Bare Walls," *BusinessWeek*, March 16, 2009; and "With Lots of Liquidation Sales Winding Down, Bargain Hunters Need to Remain Vigilant," *St. Louis Post-Dispatch*, March 7, 2009: A5.

28. "Flush Times for Liquidators," *Wall Street Journal*, January 20, 2009: B1.

29. "Hertz Takes Aim at Zipcar With Car-Sharing Service, *Wall Street Journal*, December 3, 2008: D2.

30. "The Skinny on Handbag-Rental Services," *Wall Street Journal*, July 24,2008; D2.

31. "Students Get a Break by Renting, Rather than Buying, Textbooks," *Kansas City Star*, February 24,2008: C3.

32. "Future of School Textbooks Written in Cyberspace," *Kansas City Star*, January 11, 2009: C1.

33. Walmart, 2008 Annual Report: 51

34. "Carrefour Braces for More Global Weakness," *Wall Street Journal*, January 16, 2009: B1; and "With Profits Elusive, Walmart to Exit Germany," *Wall Street Journal*, July 29, 2006: A1, A6.

35. "Dollar Store Chic," *Shopping Centers Today*, August 2008: 27.

36. "Best Buy Tales a Safe Route," *Wall Street Journal*, May 9, 2008: C3.

37. Michael J. O'Connor, "Global Marketing: A Retail Perspective," *International Trends in Retailing*, December 1998: 19–35.

38. "Apparel Retailers from Overseas Are Hitting the Malls in the U.S." *Wall Street Journal*, July 28, 2008: B1, B2.

39. Ibid.

40. "Aldi Looks to U.S. for Growth" *Wall Street Journal*, January 13, 2009: B1.

41. "Name Brands Are OK, but We Want Style," *Shopping Centers Today*, May 2005: 13.

42. "Target's New Eco-Apparel Line to Debut at Barneys New York." *Wall Street Journal*, May 1, 2008: D6.

Chapter 5

1. U.S. Bureau of Census, *Statistical Abstract of the United States: 2009*, Tables 1004 and 1007.

2. U.S. Bureau of Census, *Statistical Abstract of the United States: 2009*, Tables 1008, and 1017.

3. For a more complete discussion of this subject, see the special report "Managing the Trading-Partner Link Is the Key to Success," *Chain Store Age*, June 2003: 1A–12A.

4. For a more complete discussion on this subject, the reader should consult Robert Buzzell and Gwen Ortmeyer, "Channel Partnerships Streamline Distribution," *Sloan Management Review*, Spring 1995: 85–96.

5. F. Robert Dwyer and Sejo Oh, "A Transaction Cost Perspective on Vertical Contractual Structure and Interchannel Competitive Strategies," *Journal of Marketing*, April 1988: 21–34.

6. "Service Chains Are Best-Performing Franchisers," *Shopping Centers Today*, April 2008: 11.

7. Another good website to check for current information about franchising is www.entrepreneur.com/franchiseopportunities/index.html

8. "Credit Crunch Squeezes Franchisees," *Wall Street Journal*, September 29, 2008: B1.

9. "On Franchising," *Wall Street Journal*, November 25, 2008: B4.

10. Bert C. McCammon, Jr., "Perspectives for Distribution Programming." In Louis P. Bucklin (ed.), *Vertical Marketing Systems* (Glenview, IL: Scott, Foresman, 1970): 45.

11. "Walmart Era Wanes Amid Big Shifts in Retail," *Wall Street Journal*, October 3, 2007: A1, A17.

12. "Walmart Sneezes, China Catches Cold," *Wall Street Journal*, May 29, 2007: B1.

13. "TJX: Dressed to Kill for the Downturn," *BusinessWeek*, October 27, 2008: 60.

14. "101 Brand Names, 1 Manufacturer," *Wall Street Journal*, May 9, 2007: B1, B2.

15. "Why Deere Is Weeding Out Dealers Even as Farms Boom," *Wall Street Journal*, August 14, 2007: A1, A10.

16. "In a Clash of the Sneaker Titans, Nike Gets Leg Up on Foot Locker," *Wall Street Journal*, May 13, 2003: A1, A10.

17. "Manufacturers Find Ways to Navigate Web Retailing," *New York Times*, August 13, 2007: C4.

18. "A Deal with Target Put Lid on Revival at Tupperware," *Wall Street Journal*, February 18, 2004: A1, A9.

19. "Target Sneaks into Upscale Beauty Biz," *Shopping Centers Today*, May 2008: 36.

20. Robert Morgan and Shelby Hunt, "The Commitment-Trust Theory of Relationship Marketing," *Journal of Marketing*, July 1994: 20–38.

21. "Green Gold?" *Fortune*, September 15, 2008: 107–112.

22. Jan B. Heide and George John, "Do Norms Matter in Marketing Relationships?" *Journal of Marketing*, April 1992: 32–44; and James C. Anderson and James A. Narus, "A Model of Distributor Firm and Manufacturer Firm Working Partnerships," *Journal of Marketing*, January 1990: 42–58.

23. "P&G's Gillette Edge: The Playbook It Honed at Walmart," *Wall Street Journal*, January 31, 2005: A1, A12.

24. "Borders to Drop 'Sell or Return' Policy," *Lubbock Avalanche-Journal*, December 17, 2008: B9.

25. The authors want to acknowledge the contributions of many of their ex-students in this section. These students are now buyers, suppliers, vendors, and category managers. In addition, we want to give special credit to Wally Switzer, president of the 4 R's of Retailing, Inc., and Kevin Blackwell, General Manager of Sales & Marketing–Analytic Solutions, Bristol Technology Inc., for their suggestions in this section.

Chapter 6

1. Sherman Act, 26 Stat, 209 (1890) as amended, 15 U.S.C. articles 1–7.

2. "Supreme Court Ruling Won't Hurt Retail Competition," *St. Louis Post-Dispatch*, July 15, 2007: E1, E7.

3. For a more detail discussion of these laws, the reader should consult L. Louise Luchsinger and Patrick M.

Dunne, "Fair Trade Laws–How Fair?" *Journal of Marketing*, January 1978: 50–53.

4. "Bare Minimum," *Shopping Centers Today*, November 2008: 17–18.

5. "Price Fixing Makes Comeback After Supreme Court Ruling," *Wall Street Journal*, August 18, 2008; A1, A12.

6. "Minimum-Price Foes to Use eBay in Effort, *Wall Street Journal*, December 5, 2008: B7.

7. "Free Becomes Fighting Word," *Advertising Age*, January 24, 2005: 14.

8. "Effort to Quantify Sales of Pirated Goods Lead to Fuzzy Numbers," *Wall Street Journal*, October 10, 2007: B1; and "Fighting Fakes," *Forbes*, August 11, 2008: 44–47.

9. "For North Korea, Illegal Activities Are Vital," *Wall Street Journal*, July 13, 2007: B6.

10. "Faking Out the Fakers," *BusinessWeek*, June 4, 2007: 76–80.

11. "Landlords Face Real Fines for Fake Goods," *Shopping Centers Today*, April 2008: 11.

12. "eBay Fined over Selling Counterfeits," *Wall Street Journal*, July 1, 2008: B1

13. "eBay Wins in Fight Over Tiffany Counterfeits," *Wall Street Journal*, July 15, 2008: B1.

14. "Shop Wins Round In Victoria's Secret Case," *USA Today*, April 5, 2003: 5B.

15. Fred W. Morgan and Allen B. Saviers, "Retailer Responsibility For Deceptive Advertising And Promotional Methods." Paper presented at the Retail Patronage Conference, Lake Placid, NY, May 1993.

16. 227 F.3d 489, 497 (5th Cir). Section 43(a) of the Lanham Act states in part: "Any person who … in commercial advertising or promotion, misrepresents the nature, characteristics, quality, or geographic origin of his or another person's goods, services, or commercial activities, shall be liable in a civil action by any person who believes that he or she is likely to be damaged by such act."

17. Morgan and Saviers, op. cit.

18. Based on information supplied by Susan Busch, Director, Public Relations–Corporate for Best Buy, January 23, 2006.

19. *N. C. Freed Co., Inc. v. Board of Governors of Federal Reserve System* (CA2 NY) 473 F.2d 1210.

20. United States Public Law 92-573, Consumer Product Safety Act (1972).

21. Based on a news report from CNN Money issued July 16, 2008.

22. "Plaintiffs' Paradise," *Forbes*, May 21, 2007: 52–56.

23. "China Executes Former Chief of Food and Drug Administration," *Wall Street Journal*, July 11, 2007: A4.

24. "How to Right Retailing Wrongs," *Consumer Reports*, May 2006: 5.

25. Magnuson-Moss Warranty Federal Trade Commission Act, Public Law 93-637, 93rd Congress (1975).

26. *Burger King v. Weaver*, United States Court of Appeals, 11th Circuit, 96-5438, 1999.

27. *Eastman Kodak Company v. Image Technical Services* (1992), 112 S. Ct. 2072.

28. For a detailed analysis of the changes taking place in this area of government regulation, the reader should consult: "Antitrust Enforcers Drop the Ideology, Focus on Economics," *Wall Street Journal*, February 27, 1997: A1, A8.

29. "Oklahoma Death Grip," *Wall Street Journal*, March 18, 2005: W15.

30. "Court: No Mall Can Protest the Protests," *Shopping Centers Today*, February 2008: 7.

31. "Wine Lovers See Red over State Laws that Restrict Home Delivery of Bottles," *Wall Street Journal*, September 24, 2008: D1, D7.

32. "Taxing the Rich—Foods, That Is," *BusinessWeek*, February 23, 2009: 62.

33. "Exiling the Happy Meal," *Wall Street Journal*, July 22, 2008: A14; and "Push for Calories on Menus Gains," *Wall Street Journal*, June 11, 2008: A2.

34. "Will a Twist on an Old Vow Deliver for Domino's Pizza?" *Wall Street Journal*, December 17, 2007: B1, B2

35. "Supermarkets, Warehouse Clubs Gas Up," *Shopping Centers Today*, November 25, 2005: 9.

36. "Best Buy Increases Third-Quarter Net Earnings to $138 Million," a press release issued by Best Buy, December 13, 2005; and "Form 10-Q," a quarterly report issued by Home Depot on June 2, 2005.

37. "Gap Offers Unusual Look at Factory Conditions," *Wall Street Journal*, May 12, 2004: A1, A12.

38. K. Sudhir and Vithala Roa, "Do Slotting Allowances Enhance Efficiency or Hinder Competition," *MSI Reports*, 2005; working paper series, issue 4.

39. "Home Depot Fires Employees Amid Probe of Kickbacks," *Wall Street Journal*, August 2, 2007: A2

40. "Uninhibited, Uncut, Unrated DVDs Fly Off Shelves," *Advertising Age*, October 31, 2005: 9.

41. Information supplied by Bob Kahn to the authors.

42. This information was found at www.universitip.com/term-papers/Ethical-Aspects-of-Walmart's-Operation-207218424.html on February 15, 2009.

43. "Companies that Serve You Best, *Fortune*, May 31, 1993: 74–88.

44. "Best Buy's Giant Gamble," *Fortune*, April 3, 2006: 68–75.

Chapter 7

1. Albertson's, *Annual Report* (1998): 5.

2. Antichain legislation actually dates back to the early 1920s; by the middle of the Great Depression, these laws had been passed in 28 states. In fact, fair trade

laws were used as a form of antichain laws during this time period.

3. "Anti-Chain Ordinances Choke Some Neighborhoods," *Shopping Centers Today*, May 2008: 32; and "In San Francisco, It's Work to Find Toys," *New York Times*, December 25, 2007: C4.

4. Information taken from www.sprawl-busters.com, March 19, 2009.

5. The opinion page from *The Otago Daily Times*, November 26–27, 2005.

6. "Anti-Chain Ordinances Choke …" op. cit.

7. "Walmart to Push Into Urban Chicago," *Wall Street Journal*, February 11, 2009: B1.

8. "J.C. Penney Scales Back Plans for New Stores in '09," *Wall Street Journal*, June 26, 2008: B7; "Target to Open Designer-Focused Stores in New York," *New York Times*, September 2, 2008: C3; and conversations with executives from several of these firms during February 2009.

9. "Lease Land Mines," *Shopping Centers Today*, September 2005: 1, 11.

10. The share of a center's total square footage that is attributable to its anchors;

11. The area from which 60-80% of the center's sales originate.

12. "Mall Glut to Clog Market for Years," *Wall Street Journal*, September 10, 2008: B1.

13. "At Kennedy, Shopping and Dining, Followed by a Takeoff," *New York Times*, July 30, 2008: C4.

14. "Retailers Give It the Old College Try," *Wall Street Journal*, August 28, 2008: B8.

15. "Hot Kiosks and Carts," *Shopping Centers Today*, February 2003: 14–16.

16. "Sears Tries New Take on Online Shopping," *Chicago Tribune*, January 16, 2009: 29.

17. "Big Boxes Dig for Their Own Data," *Shopping Centers Today*, December 2005: 9.

18. "Entertainment Wizard," *Shopping Centers Today*, May 2008: 65–66; and "Malls Race to Stay Relevant in Downturn," *Wall Street Journal*, February 26, 2009: B1, B4.

19. William J. Reilly, *Methods for the Study of Retail Relationships* (research monograph no.4) (Austin: Bureau of Business Research, University of Texas, 1929).

20. P. D. Converse, "New Laws of Retail Gravitation," *Journal of Marketing*, January 1949: 379–384.

21. "In This Town, Even a Mall Rat Can Get Rattled," *New York Times*, December 20, 2006: A1, C19.

22. Bernard LaLonde, "The Logistics of Retail Location." In William D. Stevens (ed.), *American Marketing Proceedings* (Chicago: American Marketing Association, 1961): 572.

23. "Home Depot," *BusinessWeek*, February 13, 1995: 65.

24. "Why Did Starbucks Cross the Road?" *Wall Street Journal*, April 3, 2007: B1, B2.

25. Ibid.

26. Mobility can be viewed as both a household characteristic and a community characteristic. We chose to treat it as a community characteristic because the design of the community, the availability of public transportation, and the cost of operating an auto in any given area are determinants of mobility and are themselves characteristics of the community.

27. Walter Christaller, *Central Places in Southern Germany* (Carlisle W. Baskin, trans.) (Prentice Hall, NJ: Englewood Cliffs, 1966). This is an English translation of Christaller's 1935 book.

28. The essence of Applebaum's work, plus contributions from several of his students, can be found in William Applebaum and others, *Guide to Store Location Research with Emphasis on Supermarkets* (Curt Korhblau, ed., sponsored by the Supermarket Institute) (Reading, MA: Addison-Wesley, 1968).

29. This information is used with the written permission of Pitney Bowes Software Inc., 4200 Parliament Place, Suite 600, Lanham, MD 20706 (www.pbbusinessinsight.com).

30. "Cincinnati Center Never Says Die," *Shopping Centers Today*, April 2009: 5.

31. Richard L. Nelson, *The Selection of Retail Locations*, (New York: F.W. Dodge, 1958): 66.

32. "Big-Box Bedfellows," *Shopping Centers Today*, December 2005: 9.

33. Ibid.

Chapter 8

1. The 4-5-4 Calendar, which is widely used by retailers today, was derived in the 1930s to replace the straight comparison of calendar months to report monthly sales. This old method became problematic as Saturdays and Sundays became an increasingly large percentage of sales and the number of weekends in a month varied year to year. However, the layout of the 4-5-4 Calendar (52 weeks × 7 days = 364 days) results in one remaining day each year and, with the occurrence of a leap year, a 53rd week is sometimes added to the end of the calendar for sales reporting purposes only. Many retailers will choose to do this at the end of 2012. However, this text will ignore the 53rd week.

2. Based information contained in a letter from Sam Walton to Robert Kahn, November 30, 1989.

3. IRS Revenue Procedure 97-37.

4. Based on information supplied by the late Robert Kahn, a retail consultant and editor of *Retailing Today*.

Chapter 9

1. This chapter was written by Professor Jared Hansen, University of North Carolina at Charlotte.

2. "Fashion Takes a Beating," *Business Today*, March 8, 2009: 20; "Copy Protection for Fall Fashion: Designers' New Formal Looks Are Tougher to Knock Off; A Messy Mutton-Leg Sleeve," *Wall Street Journal*, October 27, 2007: W1, W4.

3. For a more detailed discussion of the effect of any retail holiday on retail sales, visit the National Retailing Federation website at nrf.com.

4. "The Best Investor of His Generation. So What Is He Doing with Sears?" *Fortune*, February 20, 2006: 90–104.

5. Sears 2009 annual letter to shareholders.

6. "Sears Customer is Left High and Dry: Washer Set Hasn't Arrived 4 Months after Sales," *St. Louis Post-Dispatch*, April 1, 2009: A1.

7. "Dressing Women of a Certain Size," *Wall Street Journal*, August 21, 2008: D1, D8.

8. Itamar Simonson, "The Effect of Product Assortment on Buyer Preferences," *Journal of Retailing*, Fall 1999: 347–370.

9. "P&G Slams Inefficient Marketing," *Marketing Week*, November 8, 1996: 26–27.

10. Susan Broniarczyk, Wayne Hoyer, and Leigh McAlister, "Consumers' Perceptions of Assortment Offered in a Grocery Category: The Impact of Item Reduction," *Journal of Marketing Research*, May 1998: 166–176; S. Iyengar and M. Lepper, "When Choice Is Demotivating: Can One Desire Too Much of a Good Thing?" *Journal of Personality and Social Psychology*, 6, 2000: 995–1006.

11. Tom Gruen, "Inventory Inaccuracy and Retail Shelf Out-of-Stocks: Understanding the Extent, Impact, and Traditional Measurement," *American Marketing Association Winter Educators Conference*, February 21, 2009; A Raman, N DeHoratius, and Z Ton, "Execution: The Missing Link in Retail Operations," *California Management Review*, 3(2001): 136–152.

12. "Profit at Mattel is Reduced by Half," *New York Times*, February 3, 2009: 3; "Weak Barbie Sales Hurt Mattel Net," *Wall Street Journal*, October 18, 2005: B2.

13. "Building an Edgier Barbie to Revive Franchise Sales," *Wall Street Journal*, December 24, 2008: B1, B8.

14. "Bratz Ruling Hands Mattel Big Choices," *Wall Street Journal*, December 5, 2008: B1, B6; "Judge Denies MGA's Request on Bratz Dolls," *New York Times*, January 1, 2009: 2.

15. "Spider Wares—Fans of the Marvel Comics Icon are Taking Advantage of the Wide Variety in Merchandise," *San Antonio Express*, May 3, 2002: F1; "Take That, Anakin—Spiderman Is a Retail Force to be Reckoned With," *Lexington Herald-Leader*, May 23, 2002: E2.

16. "What's Big and Green, and Desperate to Be a Hit All Over?" *New York Times*, April 10, 2008: E1.

17. "Better Scratch That Kindle Off Your List: Amazon's E-Book Gadgets Sell Out After Oprah's Plug; Calculating the Whim Factor," *Wall Street Journal*, December 4, 2008: D1, D8.

18. "The Middle Seat: Oil Is Cheaper, but Airline Fees Are Here to Stay; Carriers Have Long Wanted to Impose a la Carte Pricing; Paying for What You Use," *Wall Street Journal*, September 16, 2008: D1.

19. "Big Grocer Pulls Unilever Items over Pricing," *Wall Street Journal*, February 11, 2009: B1, B5. "Stores, Food Makers Compete on Retail Prices," *Idaho Press Tribune*, March 14, 2009: Business 7.

20. "Saks Settles Vendor Lawsuits: Retailer Was Accused of Forcing Suppliers to Share in Markdowns," *Wall Street Journal*, November 23, 2007: B4.

21. Based on information contained in Walmart annual reports for 2005 to 2009 and conversations with vendors.

22. "New Lead Test Law Causing Second-Hand Woes," *Times Leader*, January 8, 2009: A1; "Agency Rethinks Its Rules on Testing Products for Lead; Exemptions for Some Items Get a Tentative OK after Thrift Stores and Others Complain," *Los Angeles Times*, January 7, 2009: C3.

23. "Managing for Results," Walmart's 1998 *Annual Report*: 14.

24. "Fresh, but Far From Easy," *The Economist*, June 23, 2007: 77–79; "Marketside Dishes Convenience," *Retailing Today*, December 8, 2008: 13–16; Steve Martinez and Phil Kaufman, "Twenty Years of Competition Reshape the U.S. Food Marketing System," *USDA Amber Waves*, April 2008: 28–35.

25. Rockney G. Walters, "An Empirical Investigation into Retailer Response to Manufacturer Trade Promotion," *Journal of Retailing*, Summer 1989: 253–272.

26. Rajeev Batra and Indrajit Sinha, "Consumer-Level Factors Moderating the Success of Private Label Brands," *Journal of Retailing*, Summer 2000: 175–191.

27. From information in Phillip Electronics 2008 annual report and discussions with management.

28. This example is based on "Unauthorized Channels of Distribution: Gray Markets," by Roy Howell, Robert Britney, Paul Kuzdrall, and James Wilcox, *Industrial Marketing Management* 15 (November 1986): 257–263. Used with the permission of the authors.

29. "The Only Company Walmart Fears," *Fortune*, November 24, 2003: 158–166; and "Inside the Cult of Costco," *Fortune*, September 6, 1999: 185–190.

30. Richard C. Hollinger and Lynn Langton,*2007 National Retail Security Survey* (Gainesville: University of Florida, Department of Criminology, Law, and Society, 2008).

31. "Walmart to Crack Down on Young Shoplifters," *Wall Street Journal*, July 11, 2007: B4.

32. "The Price of Sampling, for the Cost of a Few Jelly Beans," MorningNewsBeat.com, October 29, 2007.

Chapter 10

1. "Saks Upends Luxury Market with Strategy to Slash Prices," *Wall Street Journal*, February 9, 2009: A1, A16.

2. For more details on how consumers process price information, see Sangkil Moon, Gary J. Russell, and Sri Devi Duvvuri, "Profiling The Reference Price Consumer," *Journal of Retailing*, 82(1) (2006): 1–11.

3. Roger Dickinson, "Pricing at Retail," *Pricing Strategy & Practice*, 1(1) (1993): 24–35.

4. "What the Traffic Will Bear," *Forbes*, July 3, 2006: 69–70.

5. "Selling Out the Bare Walls," *BusinessWeek*, March 16, 2009; and "With Lots of Liquidation Sales Winding Down, Bargain Hunters Need to Remain Vigilant," *St. Louis Post-Dispatch*, March 7, 2009: A5.

6. "Tapping A Market That Is Hot, Hot, Hot," *BusinessWeek*, January 17, 2005: 36.

7. "A Small Toy Store Manages to Level the Playing Field," *Wall Street Journal*, December 20, 1996: A1, A8.

8. It should be noted some academics consider skimming and even the use of couponing to be a form of price discrimination because it allows different groups of customers to pay different prices depending on what they are willing to pay. Remember, as was pointed out in Chapter 6, price discrimination is not always illegal.

9. Dickinson, op. cit.

10. Based on a March 17, 2009, Google search.

11. "No-Haggle Pricing Climbs Higher, Finds Fans among Affluent, Educated," *Advertising Age*, August 1, 2005: 23.

12. "Chinese Consumers Overwhelm Retailers with Team Tactics," *Wall Street Journal*, February 28, 2006: A1, A14.

13. Based on material found in the Robert Kahn Collection, University of Oklahoma.

14. Robert M. Schindler and Thomas M. Kibarian, "Increased Consumer Sales Response through Use of 99-Ending Prices," *Journal of Retailing*, 72(2) (1996): 187–199.

15. Manoj Thomas and Vicki G. Morwitz, "Penny Wise and Pound Foolish: The Left-Digit Effect in Price Cognition," *Journal of Consumer Research*, June 2005, 54–65.

16. Sandy Jap "Do Consumers Underestimate 9-Ending Prices?" *Stores*, 77 (1995): 1, 160; and Sandra Naipaul and H.G. Parsa, "Menu Price Endings that Communicate Value and Quality," *Cornell Hotel and Restaurant Administration Quarterly*, 42(1) (2001): 26–37.

17. For a more complete discussion of a store manager's ability to use this strategy, see Joel E. Urbany, Peter R. Dickson, and Alan Sawyer, "Insights Into Cross- and Within-Store Price Search: Retailer Estimates vs. Consumer Self-Reports," *Journal of Retailing* 76(2) (2000): 243–258.

18. For a more complete discussion of grocery pricing, see James Binkley and John Connor, "Grocery Market Pricing and the New Competitive Environment, *Journal of Retailing*, Summer 1998: 273–294.

19. Dinesh K. Gauri, K. Sudhir, and Debabrata Talukdar, "The Temporal and Spatial Dimensions of Price Search: Insights from Matching Household Survey and Purchase Data," *Journal of Marketing Research*, April 2008: 226–240.

20. "Zellers Fights Back, *Discount Merchandiser*, January 1996: 24–30.

21. "Going Private (Label)," *Wall Street Journal*, June 12, 2003: B1, B3.

22. Charles M. Wood, Bruce L. Alford, Ralph W. Jackson, and Otis W. Gilley, "Can Retailers Get Higher Prices For 'End-of-Life' Inventory Through Online Auctions?" *Journal of Retailing*, 81(3) (2005): 181–190.

23. "Sales May Go Out Like Last Year's Winter Coat," *Advertising Age*, April 25, 2005: 16.

24. "Marked Down," *Fortune*, August 22, 2005: 103–108.

Chapter 11

1. *Advertising Ratios & Budgets, published by* (Libertyville, IL: Schonfeld & Associates, May 2008).

2. The definitions of the four types of promotion are from *Dictionary of Marketing Terms* (Chicago: American Marketing Association, 1988) and reprinted with permission of the American Marketing Association.

3. This list was developed by the late Louis Bing, Bing Furniture Company, Cleveland, Ohio.

4. "Store Brands Squeeze Big Food Firms," *Wall Street Journal*, March 27, 2009: B1, B7.

5. For the background on how this ad campaign was developed, see "Walmart Enters the Ad Age," *Fortune*, August 18, 2008: 30.

6. Myron Gable, Ann Fairhurst, Roger Dickinson, and Lynn Harris, "Improving Students' Understanding of the Retail Advertising Budgeting Process," *Journal of Marketing Education*, 22(2) (2000): 120–128.

7. Ibid.

8. "Winds of Change," *Shopping Centers Today*, October 2005: 43–48.

9. This information was provided by Schonfeld & Associates, Inc., and is used with the firm's written permission.

10. "Second Chance," *Shopping Centers Today*, March 2008: 21–22.

11. "Grilled Chicken a Kentucky Fried Fiasco," *Advertising Age*, May 11, 2009: 1.

12. "How Do I Keep My Company's Reputation Intact When Our Industry Has Been Tainted by Bad News?" *Fortune*, March 16, 2009: 30.

13. "Local TV Stations Face a Fuzzy Future," *Wall Street Journal*, February 10, 2009: A1, A14; and "Local Media Are Getting Slaughtered," *BusinessWeek*, April 27, 2009: 72.

14. "King of All Radio," *Fortune*, April 14, 1997: 110–114.

15. Based on an illustration in "Yahoo's Brilliant Solution," *Fortune*, August 8, 2005: 42–52.

16. Based on information gathered between December 2008 and April 2009.

17. "P&G Wins Rumor Lawsuit," *Cincinnati Enquirer*, March 20, 2007: A7.

18. Statement by Daniel Solove, author of *The Future of Reputation: Gossip, Rumor, and Privacy on the Internet* (New Haven, CT: Yale University Press, 2007), as quoted in "How Can a Company Protect Its Reputation on Web Sites?" *Wall Street Journal*, February 26, 2008: B4.

19. While the names of the individuals and the mall have been changed, everything else is as it occurred.

Chapter 12

1. "Customer Service in a Shrinking Economy," *BusinessWeek*, March 2, 2009: 26–40.

2. For a detailed discussion of this topic, see Pratibha Dabholkar, David Shepherd, and Dayle Thorpe, "A Comprehensive Framework for Service Quality: An Investigation of Critical Conceptual and Measurement Issues Through a Longitudinal Study," *Journal of Retailing*, Summer 2000: 139–173.

3. Christian Homburg, Nicole Koschate, and Wayne D. Hoyer, "Do Satisfied Customers Really Pay More? A Study of the Relationship Between Customer Satisfaction and Willingness to Pay," *Journal of Marketing*, April 2005: 84–96.

4. "After All You've Done For Your Customers, Why Are They Still Not Happy?" *Fortune*, December 11, 1995: 178–182.

5. "Your Airline Wants to Get to Know You," *Wall Street Journal*, March 24, 2009: D1, D6.

6. "Latest Luxury: The Store Concierge," *Wall Street Journal*, December 20, 2007: B1, B2.

7. Stories about Nordstrom's customer service are legendary. There is even story that the retailer once took back a tire, something that Nordstrom's never sold. Check out this Snopes.com website (www.snopes.com/business/consumer/nordstrom.asp) to get the facts.

8. "Posh Retailers Pile on Perks for Top Customers," *Wall Street Journal*, April 26, 2007: D1, D2.

9. Leo J. Shapiro, "How to Increase Sales by 20 Percent Without Attracting Any New Customers," *International Trends in Retailing*, December 1998: 37–49.

10. Based on information presented at the Spring American Collegiate Retailing Association Conference, Springdale, AR, April 6–8, 2006.

11. "Customer Service Often Lags Retail in Newer Markets," *Shopping Centers Today*, May 2006: 172.

12. If you want to see the most recent data on ACSI data for the nation's leading retailers, go to www.theacsi.org/index.php?option=com_content&task=view&id=190&Itemid=199. This survey, which is updated quarterly, was discussed in Chapter 3.

13. Quoted from http://forum.purseblog.com/general-discussion/i-hate-nordstrom-242951.html on April 15, 2009.

14. Eugene W. Anderson, Claes Fornell, and Donald R. Lehmann, "Customer Satisfaction, Market Share, and Profitability: Findings from Sweden," *Journal of Marketing*, 58(3) (July 1994): 53–66.

15. *Target's 2007 Annual Report*: 13.

16. Ibid.: 16.

17. Ibid.: 25.

18. *Target's 2008 Annual Report*: 26, 33–34.

19. "WaMu's Branches Lose the Smiles," *Wall Street Journal*, April 7, 2009: C1, C3; and "Branching Out," *Shopping Centers Today*, March 2008: 33–34.

20. "Gift Cards Sales to Drop 5 Percent This Holiday, Survey Says," *Shopping Centers Today*, November 2008: 7.

21. SIRS presentation at National Retail Federation (NRF) Annual Convention 2000, January 18, 2000.

22. "Speaking Volumes," *Dallas Morning News*, April 16, 2000: 1H, 5H.

23. Based on a letter from Sam Walton to Robert Kahn, June 5, 1991.

24. *North American Retail Dealers Association Newsletter*, June 22, 2007: 1.

25. James G. Maxham III and Richard G. Netemeyer, "Modeling Customer Perceptions of Complaint Handling Over Time: The Effects of Perceived Justice on Satisfaction and Intent," *Journal of Retailing*, Fall 2002: 239–252.

26. "The Latest Weapon in the Price Wars," *Fortune*, July 7, 1997: 200.

27. "Inside the Cult of Costco," *Fortune*, September 6, 1999: 185–190.

28. *Second Annual Customer Returns in the Retail Industry*, a study conducted by King Rogers International, September 2004.

29. "Return Fraud and Abuse: How to Protect Profits," *Texas A&M Retailing Issues Letter*, 17(1) (2005).

30. The actual number of returns and the time period involved is confidential and varies by retailer.

31. Domino's press release, September 25, 1998.

32. As of April 15, 2009.

33. "In Search of Easy Money," *Forbes*, January 12, 2009: 36.

34. "Customers Like Buying Cars from Women, Survey Finds," *USA Today*, November 8, 1994: B1.

35. W. Levinson et al., "Physician-Patient Communication. The Relationship with Malpractice Claims Among Primary Care Physicians and Surgeons," *JAMA*, February 19, 1997: 553–559; Gerald B Hickson et al, "Obstetricians' Prior Malpractice Experience and Patients' Satisfaction with Care," *JAMA*, November 23/30, 1994: 1583–1587; Stephen S. Entman et al., "The Relationship Between Malpractice Claims History and Subsequent Obstetric Care," *JAMA*, November 23/30, 1994: 1588–1591.

36. For a more complete discussion of this subject, see Anne W. Magi, "Share of Wallet in Retailing: The Effects of Customer Satisfaction, Loyalty Cards, and Shopper Characteristics," *Journal of Retailing*, Spring 2003: 97–106; and Arun Sharma and Michael Levy, "Categorization of Customers by Retail Salespeople," *Journal of Retailing*, Spring 1995: 71–82.

37. Much of the following is based on John O'Shaughnessy, "Selling as an Interpersonal Influence Process," *Journal of Retailing*, Winter 1971–72: 32–46.

38. Ibid.: 41.

39. The following information was provided the authors by Marvin J. Rothenberg and is used with his written permission.

40. Ibid.

Chapter 13

1. "Getting the Most Out of Every Shopper," *BusinessWeek*, February 9, 2009: 45–46.

2. "Threadless: From Clicks to Bricks," *BusinessWeek*, November 26, 2007: 84.

3. Haim Mano, "The Influence of Pre-Existing Negative Affect on Store Purchase Intentions," *Journal of Retailing*, Summer 1999: 149–172.

4. "WiFi and GPS Move Outdoor Audience Measurement Indoors," *Business Wire*, April 10, 2008.

5. "Belly Up to the Bar and Buy Some Jeans," *Wall Street Journal*, April 2, 2009: D1, D6.

6. Alan Liles, *Oh Thank Heaven! The Story of the Southland Corporation* (Dallas: Southland Corporation, 1977).

7. "Who Needs the Kwik-E-Mart? 7-Eleven Does," *Lubbock Avalanche-Journal*, July 2 and 4, 2007: C5.

8. "Mickey D's McMakeover," *BusinessWeek*, May 15, 2006: 42–43.

9. "The Big Gamble," *Forbes*, October 27, 2008: 48–50.

10. "Getting the Most Out of Every Shopper," op cit.

11. "Big Retail Chains Dun Mere Suspects in Theft Demands for Money Can Leave Targets with Little Defense," *Wall Street Journal*, February 20, 2008: A1, A2.

12. "Mickey D's McMakeover," op cit.

13. This information was provided to the authors by Paul Adams, a supermarket consultant, April 15, 2009.

14. "Costco's Artful Discounts," *BusinessWeek*, October 20, 2008: 58–60.

15. Angela Hausman, "A Multi-method Investigation of Consumer Motivations in Impulse Buyer Behavior," *Journal of Consumer Behavior*, 17(5) (2000): 403–419.

16. "The Science of Shopping," *The New Yorker*, November 4, 1996: 66–75.

17. "Unhandicapped Access," *Shopping Centers Today*, September 2008: 97–100.

18. William D. Goren, *Understanding the Americans with Disabilities Act*, 2nd ed. (Washington, DC: American Bar Association, 2007).

19. John Rutherford, director of Kmart's vendor relations, in a speech titled "The Evolution of Profitability" given at the University of Arizona Southwest Retail Center's 4th Annual Global Retail Symposium, March 5, 1999.

20. Based on a November 30, 1989, letter from Sam Walton to Robert Kahn and numerous conversations on the subject with Robert Kahn.

21. Based on conversations with Robert Kahn.

22. "Mervyn's Doesn't Have to Widen Aisles," *Lubbock Avalanche-Journal*, November 6, 2003: D12.

23. Carol Kaufman-Scarborough, "Reasonable Access for Mobility-Disabled Persons Is More than Widening the Door," *Journal of Retailing*, Winter 1999: 479–508.

24. "Store Design Makes Waves for Bass Pro Shops" *Retailing Today*, September 10, 2007: 23.

25. Correspondence via e-mail with Dan Butler, National Retail Federation. April 20, 2009.

26. The preceding material was provided for the authors' use by Marvin J. Rothenberg.

27. For a more detailed discussion of this topic, the reader should consult the latest edition of Martin M. Pegler's *Stores of the Year* (New York: Retail Reporting Corporation).

28. "Girls Just Wanna Have Fun," *Shopping Centers Today*, September 2004: 21–22.

29. "Bass Pro Shops Goes Digital," *Chain Store Age*, May 2006: 180.

30. For more information on this subject, see Paco Underhill 2009 update of *Why We Buy: The Science of Shopping*.

31. "Form and Function," *Chain Store Age*, June 2003: 76.

32. "Blinded by the Light," *Progressive Grocer*, August 2000: 57–58.

33. Ibid.

34. "Something in the Air," *Shopping Centers Today*, July 2008: 35–37; and "Scents and Sensibility," *Time*, October 16, 2006: 66–67.

35. D. Douglas Graham, "Sell More with Store Design," *NARDA Independent Retailer*, February 2004: 6–10.

36. Charles Areni and David Kim, "The Influence of Background Music on Shopping Behavior: Classical Versus Top-Forty Music in a Wine Store," *Advances in Consumer Research*, 1993: 336–340.

37. Adrian C. North and Amber Shilcock, "The Effect of Musical Style on Restaurant Customers' Spending," *Environment and Behavior*, 35(5) (2003): 712–718.

38. Areni and Kim, op. cit.

39. Based on information supplied by Charles Areni, University of Sydney.

40. "Holiday Music Is Inescapable," *Wall Street Journal*, December 13, 2008: W1, W2.

41. Randahl Ramos, "Enhancing Your Customer's Shopping and Learning Experience," *NARDA Independent Retailer*, February 2005: 24.

42. "Shopping Spree Last for Madoff?" *Wall Street Journal*, January 10, 2009: B3.

43. "Brand Names Live After Stores Close," *New York Times*, April 14, 2009: B1, B7.

Chapter 14

1. "Employer Branding," *Wall Street Journal*, March 23, 2009: D7, D8.

2. z"Can Circuit City Survive Boss's Cure?" *Wall Street Journal*, February 11, 2008: B1, B3; and "New Recipe for Cost Savings: Replace Highly Paid Workers," *Wall Street Journal*, June 11, 2003: A1, A12.

3. "Why Aren't You Hiring People Who Love What They Do?" *Retailing Issues Letter*, 19(2) (2008).

4. Terri Kabachnick, "I Quit but I Forgot to Tell You," *Retailing Issues Letter*, 16(2) (2004).

5. "How Amazon Aims to Keep You Clicking," *BusinessWeek*, March 2, 2009: 34–40.

6. For a more complete discussion of all the issues dealing with call centers and other telephone problems, see Emily Yellin, *Your Call Is (Not That) Important to Us* (New York: The Free Press, 2009).

7. Ibid.

8. There is a disagreement among retail consultants over the terminology used in this section. Some argue that retailers should not use the term *CRM* but instead use CEM. After all, they claim, the focus of CRM is the optimization of transactions and business processes. The idea behind CRM was to manage a relationship with the customer, but the emphasis was on the management rather than on the customer. With CEM, the retailer must focus on the customers because they are the focal point. Here the emphasis is on all the contacts during the end-to-end experience, not just on transactions. In airlines, the end-to-end experience might be 24 hours. In food service, it might be less than two hours. The authors feel that both terms, CRM and CEM, really describe the same behavior and are interchangeable.

9. "Your Airline Wants to Get to Know You," *Wall Street Journal*, March 24, 2009: D1, D6.

10. "No. 1 Retailer In Britain Uses 'Clubcard' to Thwart WalMart," *Wall Street Journal*, June 6, 2006: A1, A12.

11. "Databank USA," *AARP Bulletin*, April 2009: 28.

12. David M. Szymanski, "Forget about Satisfied Customers, You Need Enthusiastic Customers," *Retailing Issues Letter*, Summer 2003: 1–6.

13. "AARP Skews Younger," *Fortune*, May 15, 2006: 36–40.

14. For a more complete discussion of this topic, the reader may want to consult a textbook on the subject. The authors recommend David Walsh, *Employment Law for Human Resource Practice* (Cincinnati: Thomson-West,2007). It is suggested that the reader pay particular attention to Chapter 4.

15. "Test for Dwindling Retail Jobs Spawns a Culture of Cheating," *Wall Street Journal*, January 7, 2009: A1, A10

16. "Retailers Using Computers to Screen Applications," *Shopping Centers Today*, October 1999: 50.

17. Section 703(e) of Title VII.

18. "How to Get a Job," *Fortune*, April 13, 2009: 48–56.

19. "Beware of That Video Resume," *BusinessWeek*, June 11, 2007: 12.

20. "An Application for Baristas That's More than Milk and Beans," *New York Times*, December 27, 2008: A17

21. Daron Acemogl and Joshua D. Angrist, "Consequences of Employment Protection? The Case of the Americans with Disabilities Act." NBER Working Paper Series, Vol. w6670, 1998.

22. "We're from the Government, and We're Here to Help You," *Forbes*, February 16, 2009: 12.

23. "A New Threat to Your Credit Rating," *Wall Street Journal*, January 3, 2006: D1, D2.

24. Robert Goldberg, "Pre-Employment Background Screening," *NARDA Independent Retailer*, December 2005: 12, 30.

25. "Eagle-Eyed Employers Scour Resumes for Little White Lies," *Wall Street Journal*, March 21, 2006: B7.

26. "Background Checks That Never End," *BusinessWeek*, March 20, 2006: 40.

27. Ibid.

28. "You're Fired," *Outspoken*, May 2009: 11.

29. Blake Frank, *New Ideas for Retaining Store-Level Employees*. A study for the Coca-Cola Retailing Research Council (Dallas: University of Dallas, 2000): 10.

30. Ibid., 6.

31. Ibid., 5.

32. "What's Different About the Y's," *BusinessWeek*, September 24, 2007: 56; and Hae Jung Kim, Dee K. Knight, and Christy Crutsinger, "Generation Y Employees' Work Experience in the Retail Industry: The Impact on Job Performance, Job Satisfaction and Career Intention." Paper presented at the ACRA 2006 Spring Conference, Springdale, Arkansas, April 7, 2006.

33. "Putting Home Depot's House in Order," *BusinessWeek*, May 18, 2009: 54.

34. "Understanding Your Top Shoppers: The Fuel That Drives Your Business!" Presentation by Glenn Hausfater at the 2006 FMI Show, Chicago, May 9, 2006.

35. "Zappos Knows How to Kick It," *Fortune*, February 2, 2009: 55–60; and "Zappos," *Fast Company*, March 2009: 75–76.

36. "Zappos Knows How to Kick It," 58.

37. Ibid.

38. "Hot Tamale," *Wall Street Journal*, January 28, 2006: B2.

39. *People in Retail. Ernst & Young Survey*, September 1990: 11.

40. J. Richard Hackman and Greg R. Oldham, *Work Redesign* (Reading, MA: Addison-Wesley, 1980): 77–80.

Case Section

1. This case was based on "Four Weddings and a Funeral," *BusinessWeek*, May 14, 2007: 18; and the author's experiences growing up in a family that ran a funeral home.

2. This case was prepared by Jan Owens, Carthage College, Kenosha, Wisconsin, and used with her written permission.

3. This case was based on "The Curse of Perfect Competition and How to Survive It," by Jay Townley and used with his written permission.

4. This case is based on information supplied by William Davidson and the late Robert Kahn, the two individuals to whom the third edition of this textbook was dedicated.

5. Letter from Sam Walton to Robert Kahn dated July 6, 1990.

6. This case is based on information supplied by Cricket Lee, CEO of Fit Technologies, Inc. (www.fitlogic.net) and used with her permission. Some readers may want to visit this website to determine what size would work best for them.

Subject Index

Company Name	Ticker Symbol	Website
7-Eleven	Tokyo(3382)	http://www.7-eleven.com
A&P	NYSE: GAP	http://www.aptea.com
AAMCO Transmission	NASDAQ(GS): ACAS	http://www.aamco.com
Abercrombie & Fitch	NYSE: ANF	http://www.abercrombie.com
Ace Hardware	Cooperative	http://www.acehardware.com
Aeropostale, Inc.	NYSE: ARO	http://www.aeropostale.com
Albertson's		http://www.albertsons.com
Aldi		http://www.aldi.com
Amazon.com	NASDAQ(GS): AMZN	http://www.amazon.com
American Airlines	NYSE: AMR	http://www.aa.com
American Association of Retired Persons	Association	http://www.aarp.org
American Automobile Association	Not-for-Profit	http://www.aaa.com
American Disabilities Act		http://www.ada.gov/
American Eagle Outfitters	NASDAQ(GS): AEOS	http://www.ae.com
Amway		http://www.amway.com
Ann Taylor	NYSE: ANN	http://www.anntaylor.com
AnnualCreditReport.com		https://int.annualcreditreport.com/
ASDA	Subsidiary (NYSE:WMT)	http://www.asda.co.uk
Australian Retailers Association (ARA)		http://www.retail.org.au/
Autobytel.com	NASDAQ(GM): ABTL	http://www.autobytel.com
Avis (Avis Group Holdings, Inc.)	Subsidiary (NYSE: CD)	http://www.avis.com
Avon	NYSE: AVP	http://www.avoncompany.com
Babyage.com		http://www.babyage.com/
Banana Republic	Subsidiary (NYSE: GPS)	http://www.bananarepublic.com or gap.com
Barnes & Noble	NYSE: BKS	http://www.barnesandnobleinc.com
Bass Pro Shops		http://www.basspro.com
Bed Bath & Beyond	NASDAQ(GS): BBBY	http://www.bedbathandbeyond.com
Benetton	NYSE: BNG[ADR]; Italian: BEN	http://www.benetton.com
Best Buy	NYSE: BBY	http://www.bestbuy.com
Best Western	Association	http://www.bestwestern.com
Big Lots	NYSE: BLI	http://www.biglots.com
BJ's	NYSE: BJ	http://www.bjs.com
Blockbuster Video	NYSE: BBI	http://www.blockbuster.com
Black Friday		http://bfads.net/
Bloom		http://www.shopbloom.com/
Bloomingdale's	Subsidiary (NYSE: FD)	http://www.bloomingdales.com
BookRenter.com, Inc.		http://www.bookrenter.com/
Borders	NYSE: BGP	http://www.bordersgroupinc.com
Brooks Brothers		http://www.brooksbrothers.com
Buckle	NYSE: BKE	http://www.buckle.com
Burger King	NYSE: BKC	http://www.burgerking.com
Burlington Coat Factory Warehouse Corp.		http://www.coat.com
CallawayGolf Company	NYSE: ELY	www.callawaygolf.com
CampusBookRentals, LLC.		http://www.campusbookrentals.com/
Canyon Ranch		http://www.canyonranch.com
CareerBuliders.com		http://caraerbuilder.com/
Carl's Jr.	NYSE: CKR	http://www.ckr.com
Carrefour	Euronext Paris: CA	http://www.carrefour.com
Century 21	NYSE: H	http://www.century21.com

Company Name	Ticker Symbol	Website
Graeter's		http://www.graeters.com
Great Indoors	Subsidiary, NASDAQ (GS): SHLD	http://www.sears.com
Gucci	Subsid., Euronext Paris: PP	http://www.guccigroup.com
H.E.B. Grocery		http://www.heb.com
Hallmark		http://www.hallmark.com
Handy Hardware	Cooperative	http://www.handyhardware.com
Harley-Davidson	NYSE: HOG	http://www.harley-davidson.com
Harrod's		http://www.harrods.com
Harry & David	NYSE: HND Proposed	http://www.bco.com
Hertz	NYSE: HTZ Propsed	http://www.hertz.com
Hilton Hotels	NYSE: HLT	http://www.hiltonworldwide.com
Holiday Inn	Subsid., AMEX: LGN	http://www.lodgian.com
Home Depot	NYSE: HD	http://www.homedepot.com
Hong Kong Retail Management Association		http://www.hkrma.org/en/index.html
Hudson Bay Co.		http://www.hbc.com
Hyatt		http://www.hyatt.com
iHate.com		http://whois.domaintools.com/ihate.com
IKEA		http://www.ikea.com/
International Franchise Association		http://www.franchise.org/
iThenticate		http://www.ithenticate.com/
itravel2000.com		http://www.itravel2000.com/ HomePage.aspx
J.C. Penney	NYSE: JCP	http://www.jcpenney.com
Japan Retailers Association		http://www.japan-retail.or.jp/ english/index.htm
Jewel/Osco	Bus. Seg., NYSE: SVU	http://www.jewelosco.com
KFC	Subsid., NYSE: YUM	http://www.kfc.com
Kmart	Subsid., NASDAQ(GS): SHLD	http://www.kmartcorp.com
Kohl's	NYSE: KSS	http://www.kohls.com
Kroger	NYSE: KR	http://www.kroger.com
L.L. Bean		http://www.llbean.com
Lands' End		http://www.landsend.com/
Lane Bryant	Subsid., NASDAQ(GS): CHRS	http://lanebryant.charmingshoppes.com
Laura Ashley	London: ALY	http://www.lauraashley.com
Liz Claiborne	NYSE: LIZ	http://www.lizclaiborne.com
Loblaw	Toronto: L	http://www.loblaw.com
Locatecell.com		http://locatecell.com/
Lowe's	NYSE: LOW	http://www.lowes.com
Macy's	NYSE: M	http://www.macys.com
Marks & Spencer	PinkSheets: MAKSY.PK[ADR]	http://www.marksandspencer.com
Mary Kay		http://www.marykay.com
McDonald's	MYSE: MCD	http://www.mcdonalds.com
McLane's (Berkshire Hathaway)	NYSE: BRK	http://www.berkshirehathaway.com
Meijer's		http://www.meijer.com
Merry Maids	Subsid., NYSE: SVM	http://www.servicemaster.com
Metro AG	German: MEO	http://www.metro.com
Midas Mufflers	NYSE: MDS	http://www.midasinc.com
Miraval		http://www.miravalresort.com/
Monster.com	NASDAQ(GS): MNST	http://www.monsterworldwide.com
Motel 6	Bus.Seg., EuronextParis: AC	http://www.motel6.com
Mr. Handyman		http://www.mrhandyman.com

Company Name	Ticker Symbol	Website
Sports Authority		http://www.sportsauthority.com
Sprawl-busters.com		http://www.sprawl-busters.com/
Staples	NASDAQ(GS): SPLS	http://www.staples.com
Starbucks	NASDAQ(GS): SBUX	http://www.starbucks.com
Starwood	NYSE: HOT	http://www.starwoodhotels.com
Stein Mart	NASDAQ(GS): SMRT	http://www.steinmart.com
Sterling Optical	OTC: ISEE	http://www.emergingvision.com
Stop & Shop	Subsid., NYSE: AHO[ADR]	http://www.stopandshop.com
Subway		http://www.subway.com
Sucks.com		http://www.sucks.com/
Supercuts	Bus.Seg., NYSE: RGS	http://www.supercuts.com
Sylvan Learning	NASDAQ(GS): EEEE	http://www.educate-inc.com
Sysco	NYSE: SYY	http://www.sysco.com
T.J. Maxx	Subsid., NYSE: TJX	http://www.tjx.com
Taco Bell	Bus.Seg., NYSE: YUM	http://www.tacobell.com
Talbot's	NYSE: TLP	http://www.talbots.com
Target	NYSE: TGT	http://www.target.com
Tesco	OTC: TSCDY.PK[ADR]	http://www.tesco.com
The Body Shop	OTC: LORLY[ADR]	http://www.the-body-shop.com
The Church		http://www.thechurch.ie/
The Container Store		http://www.containerstore.com
The Gap	NYSE : GPS	http://www.gap.com
The Limited	NYSE: LTD	http://www.limitedbrands.com
The New Zealand Retailers Association		http://www.retail.org.nz/
The Ritz-Carlton Company, L.L.C.		http://www.ritzcarltonshops.com/
The W store Hotels		http://www.whotelsthestore.com/
Threadless		http://www.threadless.com/retail
Tiffany & Company	NYSE: TIF	http://www.tiffany.com
Tommy Hilfiger		http://www.tommy.com
Toys 'R' Us		http://www.toysrus.com
Tractor Supply	NASDAQ(GS): TSCO	http://www.tractorsupplyco.com
Trader Joe's		http://www.traderjoes.com
Transparency International		http://www.transparency.org/
Travelocity	Subsid., NYSE: TSG	http://www.travelocity.com
Tribe		http://www.tribe.net/welcome
Tripadvisor		http://www.tripadvisor.in/
Tru Serv	Cooperative	http://www.truevaluecompany.com
Tupperware	NYSE: TUP	http://www.tupperware.com
turnitin		http://turnitin.com/static/index.html
United Airlines	NASDAQ(GS): UAUA	http://www.united.com
University of Phoenix	NASDAQ(GS): APOL	http://www.apollogroup.com
UPS	NYSE: UPS	http://www.ups.com
Urban Legends		http://urbanlegends.about.com/
US Census Bureau		www.census.gov
US Department of Labor		www.dol.gov
Vayama.com		http://www.vayama.com/
Victoria's Secret	Subsid., NYSE: LTD	http://www.limitedbreands.com
Video Media		http://www.videomedia.net/
Vons	Bus.Seg., NYSE: SWY	http://www.vons.com
Walgreens	NYSE: WAG	http://www.walgreens.com
WalMart	NYSE: WMT	http://www.walmartstores.com
Weather Trends International		http://www.wxtrends.com/
Wegmans Supermarkets		http://www.wegmans.com/
Wells Fargo	NYSE: WFC	http://www.wellsfargo.com
Wendy's	NYSE: WEN	http://www.wendys.com

Company Name	Ticker Symbol	Website
Westin		http://www.westin-hotelsathome.com/
Wet Seal	NASDAQ(GM): WTSLA	http://www.wetsealinc.com
Whole Foods	NASDAQ(GS): WFMI	http://www.wholefoodsmarket.com
Will it Blend		http://www.willitblend.com/
Williams-Sonoma	NYSE: WSM	http://www.williams-sonomainc.com
Yahoo	NASDAQ(GS): YHOO	http://www.yahoo.com
Zara	Subsid., Spanish ITX	http://www.inditex.com
Zellers	Subsid.	http://www.hbc.com/zellers